Public Budgeting Systems

Seventh Edition

Robert D. Lee, Jr.
The Pennsylvania State University
University Park, Pennsylvania

Ronald W. Johnson
Research Triangle Institute
Research Triangle Park, North Carolina

Philip G. Joyce
The George Washington University
Washington, District of Columbia

JONES AND BARTLETT PUBLISHERS
Sudbury, Massachusetts
BOSTON   TORONTO   LONDON   SINGAPORE

World Headquarters

Jones and Bartlett Publishers
40 Tall Pine Drive
Sudbury, MA 01776
978-443-5000
info@jbpub.com
www.jbpub.com

Jones and Bartlett Publishers
Canada
6339 Ormindale Way
Mississauga, ON L5V 1J2
CANADA

Jones and Bartlett Publishers
International
Barb House, Barb Mews
London W6 7PA
UK*

Jones and Bartlett's books and products are available through most bookstores and online book-sellers. To contact Jones and Bartlett Publishers directly, call 800-832-0034, fax 978-443-8000, or visit our website at www.jbpub.com.

Substantial discounts on bulk quantities of Jones and Bartlett's publications are available to corporations, professional associations, and other qualified organizations. For details and specific discount information, contact the special sales department at Jones and Bartlett via the above contact information or send an email to specialsales@jbpub.com.

ISBN-13: 978-0-7637-3129-8
ISBN-10: 0-7637-3129-3

Library of Congress Cataloging-in-Publication Data
Lee, Robert D.
    Public budgeting systems / Robert D. Lee, Jr., Ronald W. Johnson, Philip G. Joyce.—7th ed.
        p. cm.
    Includes bibliographical references and index.
    ISBN 0-7637-3129-3
        1. Budget—United States. 2. Budget process—United States. 3. Program
budgeting—United States. I. Johnson, Ronald Wayne, 1942- II. Joyce, Philip G., 1956- III.
Title.

HJ2051.L4 2003
352.4'973—dc21
6048   2003047434

Executive Editor: Jack Bruggeman
Production Manager: Amy Rose
Associate Production Editor: Renée Sekerak
Associate Editor: Chambers Moore
Associate Marketing Manager: Ed McKenna

Manufacturing Buyer: Therese Connell
Composition: AnnMarie Lemoine
Cover Design: Philip Regan
Printing and Binding: Malloy Incorporated
Cover Printing: Malloy Incorporated

Printed in the United States of America
10 09 08 07 06   10 9 8 7 6 5 4

Dedicated to
Robert, Craig, Cameron, and Leslie
and to
Carroll G. Johnson and Alline F. Johnson
and to
Rita, Christopher, Mariah, and Samuel

CONTENTS

Preface

This is a general book on public budgeting. Its purpose is to survey the current state of the art among all levels of government in the United States. Where their inclusion would be illustrative, we also use examples from other countries and from some nongovernmental organizations. In addition, we emphasize methods by which financial decisions are reached within a system and ways in which different types of information are used in budgetary decision making. We stress the use of program information, since budget reforms for decades have sought to introduce greater program considerations into financial decisions.

Budgeting is considered within the context of a system containing numerous components and relationships. One problem of such an approach is that, because all things within a system are related, it is difficult to find an appropriate place to begin. Although we have divided the text into chapters, the reader should recognize that no single chapter can stand alone. Virtually every chapter mentions some topics and issues that are treated elsewhere in the book.

A discussion of budgeting may be organized in various ways. Historical or chronological sequence is one possible method of organization, although this approach would require discussing every relevant topic for each time period. Another strategy is to arrange topics by level of government, with separate sections for local, state, and federal budgeting. Such an approach again would involve extensive rehashing of arguments and information. Yet another approach is to focus on phases of the budget cycle, from preparation of the budget through auditing of past activities and expenditures. Rigid adherence to this approach would be inappropriate, because the budget cycle is not precisely defined and many issues cut across several phases of the cycle. Another approach would be to organize the discussion around the contrast between the technical and political problems of budgetary decision making.

The organization of this book is a combination of these approaches. *Chapter 1, Introduction*, provides a general discussion of the nature of budgetary decision making, including distinctions between private and public budgeting, the concepts of responsibility and accountability in budgeting, the possibility of rationality in decision making, and the nature of budgeting and budget systems. *Chapter 2, The Public Sector in Perspective*, reviews the scope of the public sector, the magnitude of government, the sources of revenues, and the purposes of government expenditures. Budget cycles are the topic of Chapter 3, which summarizes the basic steps in budgeting — preparation and submission, approval, execution, and auditing. Together these chapters provide a basic framework for the remainder of the book.

The next three chapters focus on the budget preparation process. Their purpose is to provide the reader with an understanding of the types of deliberations involved in developing a proposed budget. *Chapter 4, Budget Preparation: The Revenue Side*, considers the different sources from which governments obtain their funds, the special concerns associated with limitations on taxing and spending, and estimating revenue for the next budget year. *Chapter 5, Budget Preparation: The Expenditure Side*, discusses early budget reform efforts and contemporary approaches to developing proposals for funding government programs. *Chapter 6, Budget Preparation: The Decision Process*, examines the process of putting together a budget proposal that includes recommended revenue and expenditure levels and then reviews the types of budget documents that are used in government.

Chapter 7, Policy and Program Analysis, is a transitional chapter that discusses the role of analysis in both budget preparation and approval. It covers techniques of analysis as well as their usage in the executive and legislative branches.

Chapters 8 and 9 deal with the budget approval process. *Chapter 8, Budget Approval: The Role of the Legislature*, provides a general account of the processes used by legislative bodies. *Chapter 9, Budget Approval: The U.S. Congress*, treats separately the special factors and problems associated with congressional budgeting.

The next three chapters concentrate on the execution phase of budgeting. *Chapter 10, Budget Execution*, considers the roles played by the chief executive, the budget office, and the line agencies; it treats separately the topics of tax administration, cash management, procurement, and risk management. *Chapter 11, Financial Management: Accounting, Auditing, and Information Systems*, presents the basic features of accounting systems and processes, explains the types of audits that are conducted, and discusses the nature of information systems used in budgeting and finance. *Chapter 12, Financial Management: Capital Budgeting and Debt*, examines capital budgeting as a decision process and the financing of long-term capital investments through debt instruments.

The final three chapters deal with special topics in government budgeting. *Chapter 13, Government Personnel and Pensions*, reviews the effects of personnel expenditures on budgets, paying particular attention to public pension systems. *Chapter 14, Intergovernmental Relations*, examines the financial interactions among governments, the types of fiscal assistance in use, and possible means of restructuring intergovernmental relationships. *Chapter 15, Government, the Economy, and Economic Development,* surveys the federal government's role in managing the economy and notes the ways that economic conditions affect state and local governments.

The book closes with some brief concluding remarks on themes that can be expected to receive considerable attention from budgeting practitioners and scholars in the next several years. The bibliographic note provides guidance on keeping informed about changes in the field of budgeting.

Overall, this edition retains the structure of the sixth edition but gives increased attention to some topics, such as program information and government's role in the economy. It also reflects the impact on budgeting of the tragic events that occurred on September 11, 2001, in New York City, Washington, D.C., and a field in rural Pennsylvania. Text, tables, and exhibits have been completely updated.

Drs. Lee and Johnson began the first edition as faculty members in the Institute of Public Administration at The Pennsylvania State University. Six editions later, Dr. Lee is Professor of Public Administration and Professor of Hotel, Restaurant, and Recreation Management and Associate Director of the School of Hotel, Restaurant, and Recreation Management at Penn State. Dr. Johnson is Senior Vice President for International Development at the Research Triangle Institute. With this new edition, we welcome Dr. Joyce, who is Associate Professor of Public Administration at The George Washington University. Dr. Joyce has a wealth of professional budgeting experience at both the federal and state levels of government.

Our hope is that this new edition will be useful to readers from many backgrounds and with widely diverse purposes.

Acknowledgments

Having gone through six previous editions, this book is necessarily the product of numerous individuals, not just its three authors. We are indebted to colleagues at The Pennsylvania State University, the Research Triangle Institute, and The George Washington University. Colleagues at other institutions, including a variety of colleges and universities, have provided valuable advice, as have students at many schools. In preparing the book, we received considerable advice from expert practitioners in the executive and legislative branches of federal, state, and local governments and from their counterparts in nonprofit organizations. The responsibility for the final product, of course, belongs to us alone.

Chapter 1

INTRODUCTION

In what many characterize as the *information age*,[1] it is to be expected that any book dealing with large organizations operating in the world economy would focus extensively on information. This book is about governmental institutions that operate in a world economy and society, and it is no exception in its extensive focus on information. This book is about budgets, budgeting systems, and budgeting processes, the nature of the decisions that are made, and the processes by which those decisions are made. As we will discuss throughout the book, budgeting has always been about information, and budget systems are about gathering the best information available, whether that information be primarily of a technical nature or primarily of a political nature, and bringing that information to bear on decisions about allocating resources to purposes.

Public budgeting involves the selection of ends and the selection of means to reach those ends. It involves the division of society's economic and financial resources between the public sector and the private sector and the allocation of such resources among competing public sector needs. Public budgeting systems are systems for making choices of ends and means. These choices are guided by theory, by hunch, by partisan politics, by narrow self-interest, by altruism, and by many other sources of value judgment.

Public budgeting systems work by channeling various types of information about societal conditions and about the private and public values that guide resource allocation decision making. Complex channels for information exchange exist. Through these channels, people process information on what is desired, make assessments of what is or is not being achieved, and analyze what might or might not be achieved. Integral to budgeting systems are intricate processes that link both political and economic values. In making decisions that ultimately determine how resources are allocated, the political process uses sometimes bewildering and often conflicting information about values, about actual conditions, and about possible condition changes. This book is an analysis of procedures and methods — past, present, and prospective — used in the resource allocation process.

This chapter examines some basic features of decision-making and budgeting systems. First, some major characteristics of public budgeting are explained through comparison and contrast with private forms of budgeting. Second, the development of budgeting as a means of holding government accountable for its use of society's resources is reviewed. Next, budgets and budgeting systems are defined. Finally, the role of information in budgetary decision making is considered.

Distinctions Regarding Public Budgeting

Budgeting is a common phenomenon. To some extent, everybody does it. People budget time, dollars, food — almost everything. The corner grocer budgets, General Electric budgets, and so do governments. Moreover, important similarities exist in the budgeting done by large public and private bureaucracies.[2]

Budgeting is intended as a mechanism for setting goals and objectives, for measuring progress toward objectives, for identifying weaknesses or inadequacies in organizations, and for controlling and integrating the diverse activities carried out by numerous subunits within large bureaucracies, both public and private. Budgeting is the manifestation of an organization's strategies, whether those strategies are the result of thoughtful strategic planning processes, of the inertia of long years of doing approximately the same thing, or of the competing political forces within the organization bargaining for shares of resources. Once resources are allocated through the budgetary process, the organization's strategies become apparent even if they have not been articulated as strategies. Budgeting means examining how the organization's resources have been used in the past, analyzing what has been accomplished and at what cost, and charting a course for the future by allocating resources for the coming budget period. Whether this process is done haphazardly or after exhaustive analyses prepared by staff, whether it is carried out by order of the chief executive officer or requires the extensive input of citizens and the development of a consensus among many individuals, it is still budgeting.

Budgeting is also about assigning responsibility for accomplishing the results intended by the executive and legislative branch actors that ultimately set the public budget. Budgets are executed by individuals within (mostly) large bureaucracies; budget allocations identify not only the amounts to be spent and the intended purposes of those expenditures, but also the unit within the bureaucracy, and by implication the individuals managing that unit, responsible for achieving the results intended in the budget decisions. In the contemporary age in which much of the value in any process — whether producing a commercial good or producing a public service — is in the information or knowledge applied, responsibility for budget decisions and budget implementation is vastly more decentralized than in the era when financial accounting systems produced mainly information about funds spent. This inevitably more decentralized environment has even led to the use of such terms as *responsibility budgeting*, though we will not use that term in this book to characterize a budgeting theory or system.[3]

Public and Private Sector Differences in Objectives

Resource Availability. Important differences exist between the private and public spheres. In the first place, the amount of resources available for allocation varies greatly. Both family and corporate budgeting are constrained by a relatively fixed set of available resources. Income is comparatively fixed, at least in the short run, and therefore outgo must be equal to or less than income. Of course, income can be expanded by increasing the level of production and work or temporarily by borrowing, but the opportunities for increasing income are limited.

Government, on the other hand, is bound by much higher limits, and in the United States at least, government does not use nearly all of the possible resources available to it. Only in times of major crises, such as World War II, has government in the United States begun to approach the limits of its resources. Then the federal government borrowed an amount that eventually came close to equaling the total production of the economy in a year. Rationing, price controls, and other measures were imposed so as to limit severely private sector consumption and instead allocate most of society's resources to the government. During other times, much is left to the private sector, with government using only a fraction of society's work force, goods, and services. In 2001, combined federal, state, and local government receipts amounted to more than 28 percent of total *gross domestic product* (GDP), with about two-thirds of that being the federal government; the 1990s into the new century saw a gradual increase in the size of government as a portion of the total economy.[4] Government has the power to determine how much of the society's total resources will be taken for public purposes; private parties operate within the limits of their ability to acquire resources through their market activities — selling their labor, selling goods, and so forth.

Profit Motive. Another major distinction between private and public budgeting is the motivation behind budget decisions. The private sector is characterized by the profit motive, whereas government undertakes many things that are financially unprofitable. In the private sector, profit serves as a ready standard for evaluating previous decisions; successful decisions are those that produce profits (as measured in dollars).

The concept of profit, however, can lead to gross oversimplifications about corporate decision making. Not every budget decision in a private firm is determined by the criterion of making an immediate profit. Sometimes corporations forgo profits in the short run. In the case of price wars, they attempt to increase their share of a given market even if it means selling temporarily at a loss. At other times, they incur large debts and take other apparently unprofitable actions to combat a hostile takeover — an attempt by an outsider to purchase enough stock to exercise control over a corporation's assets. Sometimes their major objectives are to produce a good product and to build public confidence. They have enough confidence in their pursuit of customer service that the result will be sustained long-run profits. At other times they undertake actions for mainly social motives, wishing to make a contribution to the society that sustains their corporate existence.

Large firms budget significant resources for research and development (R & D) activities, only a few of which eventually will lead to a product that generates large sales and profits. An R & D division can be evaluated over the long term by how many of its developments contribute to profits, but this kind of evaluation is difficult. Often, the results of R & D are subtle improvements in existing products, and measuring the amount of investment relative to the incremental profit gain is impossible. In this regard, private budgeting for R & D is no less difficult than the federal government's support of R & D.

Despite the inability to tie specific expenditures to the results of R & D, firms and governments continue to budget resources for R & D to create future productive capacity. A Congressional Budget Office review of studies estimating the value generated by R & D expenditures noted that although precise achievements are difficult to estimate, R & D spending does yield positive returns.[5] A National Academy of Sciences panel studied five federal agencies' implementation of the Government Performance and Results Act of 1993 to measure the results of their research and development activities. The study noted that the benefits of research are difficult to assess, concluding that "the most effective technique for evaluating research programs is review by panels of experts using the criteria of quality, relevance, and, when appropriate, leadership."[6]

Regardless of the role profit plays in the private sector, government decision making in general lacks even this standard for measuring activities. Exceptions to this generalization are government activities that yield revenues. State control and sale of alcoholic beverages, whether undertaken for profit or for regulation of public morals, can be evaluated, like any other business, in terms of profit and loss. Similarly, the operation of a water system, a public transit authority, or a public swimming pool can be evaluated in business profit-and-loss terms. This does not mean that each of these should turn a profit. After all, operating a public swimming pool may be the result of a decision to provide subsidized recreation to a low-income neighborhood whose residents cannot afford other private recreational alternatives. The budgeting process, however, can be used to assess the operation as a business to clarify the subsidy level and to aid decision makers in comparing costs with those for other public services provided free of direct charge (see Chapter 7).

Nevertheless, the majority of private sector budget decisions pertains to at least long-term profits, and most public sector budget decisions do not. Governments undertake some functions deliberately instead of leaving them to the private sector. Public budgetary decisions, for example, frequently involve allocation of resources among competing programs that are not readily susceptible to measurement in dollar costs and dollar returns. There are no easy means of measuring the costs and benefits of a life saved through cancer research, for example, although the value of future earnings sometimes is used as a surrogate measure of the value of life. Nor is there a ready means of clearly separating private incentives from public incentives. For example, although the National Cancer Institute spends millions of public dollars annually on cancer research, the amount is minuscule compared with the amount spent by private companies on research for cancer prevention and treatment.

Just because most public sector activities are not intended to be profitable, it does not mean that business-like measurement of results in relation to costs are rendered useless. Although not susceptible to bottom-line or profit-and-loss measurement, many government programs are able to measure their results in terms of output (efficiency) and outcome (effectiveness). Legislation passed in 1993 mandated the use of performance measures to improve the federal government's accountability for the results of its expenditures.[7]

Public and Private Sector Differences in Services Provided

Public Goods. Some government services yield public or collective benefits that are of value to society as a whole, whereas corporate products are almost always consumed by individuals and specific organizations. When Ford Motor Company produces automobiles, persons buying the automobiles use them to meet their own personal needs. When the Department of Defense produces a network for detecting a possible launching of intercontinental missiles against the United States, that network benefits the public in general. Economists call these kinds of products and services *public goods*; they have the property of nonexcludability. Once the detection network is in place, no one can be excluded from its benefits.[8]

Nor are there any alternatives; citizens may not shop around among different producers for the service of national defense. There are no rivals. Of course, few public products and services qualify as pure public goods, and many goods and services produced by governments are also produced by the private sector.

Externalities. Another class of government services consists of those from which individuals can be excluded but for which the benefits, or costs, extend beyond those involved in the immediate service provision. When Ford Motor Company sells a car, its stockholders enjoy the benefits of the profits, but those profits do not spill over to society at large. However, when a child is educated through a school system, not only does the child benefit, but society's productive capacity is also enhanced. Many private schools educate children for a profit, and the owners of the school enjoy the benefits of the profits along with the child and society. However, it seems unlikely that these same for-profit schools would willingly provide equivalent education to all children who cannot make tuition payments. Economists label the benefits that spill over to the rest of society *externalities.*[9] Governments provide at least some services that produce significant externalities because the private sector would provide these only to the extent that profit could be made. For example, education, if left entirely to the private sector, presumably would be available only to those who could pay, or would be provided in insufficient quantity and quality for the needs of society.

Pricing Public Services. Defining just what is clearly public in nature and determining what the private sector presumably cannot or will not provide is controversial. During the 1980s and 1990s, the federal government cut back on transfers to state and local governments, which also faced more stringent tax and spending limitations inspired by their voters (see Chapter 4). As a consequence, many services once thought to be exclusively public were converted into private services or to public services provided by private firms on a contract basis. That trend continued when state and local budgets shrank dramatically with the recession that started in 2001–2002. This trend advanced throughout many developing countries with public sectors even larger than in the United States. The Margaret Thatcher government of the United Kingdom, in privatizing many formerly public services, such as the water utilities throughout the United Kingdom, served as a model for the early 1980s movement in the United States. Although this type of conversion is not a new idea, one of the lessons learned throughout the world seems to have been that government may grow larger than most feel is beneficial and may be difficult to cut back when unconstrained by any kind of pricing mechanism, such as the private sector ultimately always faces.[10] One consequence of that lesson is that much more extensive user charges and various other fees now force those who benefit directly from a government service to pay for its cost (see Chapter 4). For example, in the 1990s the U.S. Coast Guard stopped providing towing services to disabled boats unless a genuine emergency exists; it instead notifies private operators, who charge the cost to the disabled boat captain. That practice has cut back significantly on calls for towing in general, with prices providing a rationing mechanism.

Other Public and Private Sector Differences. Whatever objectives other than profit private corporations may have, to stay in business they must seek economic efficiency and obtain the greatest possible dollar return on investments. In contrast, governments may be intentionally inefficient in resource allocations, undertaking services that the private sector would be reluctant to provide at all. For example, government-financed medical care for the elderly may be inefficient in the sense that, whereas other government programs might provide greater economic returns to society, it has been agreed that at least some support should be provided to the elderly. Governments are also charged with other unique responsibilities, such as intervention in the economy (see Chapter 15).

Another difference between private and public organizations lies in the clientele and the owners of the means of production. In theory, at least, both corporations and governments are answerable to their stockholders and clients. In the private sector, these individuals can disassociate themselves from firms. Their counterparts in the public sector are denied this choice, except through the extreme act of emigration. Private stockholders expect dollar returns on their investments, but because government costs and returns are not easily evaluated, the electorate has no simple measure for assessing the returns on the taxes they pay. Even so, many state and local governments provide annual reports to citizens that are similar in purpose to stockholder reports. These reports emphasize the investments government is making and the benefits citizens are receiving in lieu of profits.

Corporate budgetary decision making is usually more centralized than government decision making. Corporations can stop production of economically unprofitable goods such as Oldsmobiles. Given the nature of the public decision-making process, however, governments encounter more difficulty in making decisions both to inaugurate programs and to eliminate them. For example, despite apparent consensus of a majority of the population that the Medicare program, which assists the elderly in financing health care, should include some form of prescription drug coverage, different administrations and both political parties for years experienced major difficulty in producing a drug coverage component.

Responsible Government and Budgeting

The emergence and reform of formal government budgeting can be traced to a concern for holding public officials accountable for their actions.[11] The "reinventing government" movement represented the most recent manifestation of a rather ancient concern that public officials be held accountable for their actions, though some critics have held that the precepts of reinvention are not new, and not necessarily internally consistent.[12] In either case, the George W. Bush administration allowed at least the terminology associated with reinvention to die quietly. In a democracy, budgeting is a device for limiting the powers of government. Two issues recur in the evolution of modern public budgeting as an instrument of accountability — responsibility to whom and for what purposes.

Responsible to Whom?

Responsibility to Constituency. Basically, responsibility in a democratic society entails holding elected officials answerable to their constituents. Elected executives and legislative representatives at all levels of government are, at least in theory, held accountable through the electoral process for their decisions on programs and budgets. In actuality, budget documents are not the main source of information for decisions by the electorate. Obviously, most voters do not diligently study the U.S. budget before casting their votes in presidential and congressional elections. However, as the government's share of the total economy grows, it is increasingly clear that voters *do* hold elected representatives responsible for the overall budget, the budget deficit, and the general performance of the economy. That the electorate holds presidents responsible for the economy was evidenced in 1992 by President Bush's defeat in his bid for re-election. Eight years later, the 2000 election showed that even in the midst of a booming economy, many voters were more concerned about apparent ethical and moral lapses in the White House than their happiness with the economy.

State and local governments have specific creditors — the purchasers of bonds issued to finance long-term capital improvements. The interest rates that state and local governments have to pay on their bonds are affected by their ability to provide creditors with convincing evidence of their creditworthiness (see Chapter 12). Hence, financial institutions that purchase bonds and ratings institutions that rate state and local bonds are important constituents to whom these governments are accountable.

Because the public in a large society cannot be fully informed about the operations of government, the United States has used the concepts of *separation of powers* and *checks and balances* as means of providing for responsible government.

Power is divided among the executive, legislative, and judicial branches, and each provides some checks on the others. Thus, although the president is held responsible to Congress for preparation and submission of an executive budget, only Congress can pass the budget. In most states and many localities, the chief executive has a similar responsibility to recommend a plan for taxes and expenditures. The legislative body passes judgment on these recommendations and subsequently holds the executive branch responsible for carrying out the decisions.

Development of the Executive Budget System. The development of an executive budget system for holding government accountable was a long process that can be traced as far back as the Magna Charta (1215). The main issue that resulted in this landmark document was the Crown's taxing powers. The Magna Charta did not produce a complete budget but concentrated only upon holding the Crown accountable to the nobility for its revenue actions.[13] At the time, the magnitude of public expenditures and the use of these funds for public services were of less concern than the power to levy and collect taxes. It was not until the English Consolidated Fund Act of 1787 that the rudiments of a complete system were established, and a complete account of revenues and expenditures was presented to Parliament for the first time in 1822.[14]

The same concern in eighteenth-century England for executive accountability was exhibited in other countries. It was carried over to the American experience even prior to the ratification of the Constitution (1789). Fear of a strong executive branch was evidenced by the failure to provide for such a branch in the Articles of Confederation (1781). Fear of "taxation without representation" probably explains why the Constitution is more explicit about taxing powers than the procedures to be followed in government spending.

The first decade under the Constitution saw important developments that could have resulted in an executive budget system, but the trend was reversed in subsequent years. The Treasury Act of 1789, establishing the Treasury Department, granted to the secretary the power "to digest and prepare plans for the improvement of the revenue . . . [and] to prepare and report estimates of the public revenue and expenditures."[15] Alexander Hamilton, secretary of the treasury, in interpreting his mandate broadly, asserted strong leadership in financial affairs. Although the act did not grant the secretary power to prepare a budget by recommending which programs should and should not be funded, such a development might have subsequently occurred.

Instead, Hamilton's apparent lack of deference to Congress strengthened that body's support for greater legislative control over financial matters. To curtail the discretion of the executive branch, Congress resorted to the use of increasing numbers of line items, specifying in narrow detail for what purposes money could be spent.[16] The pattern emerged that each executive department would deal directly with Congress, thereby curtailing the responsibilities of the secretary of the treasury. The budgetary function of the Treasury Department became primarily ministerial. The Book of Estimates, prepared by the secretary and delivered to Congress, could have become the instrument for a coordinated set of budgetary recommendations; instead, it was simply a compilation of departmental requests for funds. A. E. Buck wrote, "Thus budget making became an exclusively legislative function in the national government, and as such it continued for more than a century."[17]

Modern Executive Budgeting. By the beginning of the twentieth century, changing economic conditions stimulated the demand for more centralized and controlled forms of budgeting. E. E. Naylor has written that before this time there was little "enthusiasm for action . . . since federal taxes were usually indirect and not severely felt by any particular individual or group."[18] By 1900, however, existing revenue sources no longer consistently produced sufficient sums to cover the costs of government. At the federal level, the tariff could not be expected to produce a surplus of funds, as had been the case. Causes of this growing deficit were the expanded scope of government programs and, to a lesser extent, waste and corruption in government finance. The latter is often credited as a major political factor stimulating reform.

Local government led the way in the establishment of formal budget procedures. Municipal budget reform was closely associated with general reform of local government, especially the creation of the city manager form of government. In 1899, a model municipal corporation act, released by the National Municipal League, featured a model charter that provided for a budget system whose preparation phase was under the control of the mayor. In 1907, the New York Bureau of Municipal Research issued a study, "Making a Municipal Budget," that became the basis for establishing a budgetary system for New York City.[19] By the mid-1920s, most major U.S. cities had some form of budget system.

Substantial reform of state budgeting occurred between 1910 and 1920. This reform was closely associated with the overall drive to hold executives accountable by first giving them authority over the executive branch. The movement for the short ballot, aimed at eliminating many independently elected administrative officers, resulted in governors being granted greater control over their bureaucracies. Ohio, in 1910, was the first state to enact a law empowering the governor to prepare and submit a budget. A. E. Buck, in assessing the effort at the state level, suggested that 1913 marked "the beginning of practical action in the states."[20] By 1920, some budget reform had occurred in 44 states, and all states had a central budget office by 1929.[21]

Simultaneous action occurred at the federal level, and much of what took place there contributed to the reforms at the local and state levels. Frederick A. Cleveland, who was director of the New York Bureau of Municipal Research and who played a key role in national reform, asserted that "it was the uncontrolled and uncontrollable increase in the cost of government that finally jostled the public into an attitude of hostility."[22] In response to this public concern, President Taft requested and received from Congress in 1909 an appropriation of $100,000 for a special Commission on Economy and Efficiency. Known as the Taft Commission, the group was headed by Cleveland and submitted its final report in 1912, recommending the establishment of a budgetary process under the direction of the president. This report was to spur activity at the state and local levels.

The Budget and Accounting Act, which established the new federal system, was not passed until 1921.[23] In the interim, deficits were recorded every year between 1912 and 1919 except 1916. The largest deficit occurred in 1919, when expenditures were three times greater than revenues ($18.5 billion in expenditures as compared with $5.1 billion in revenues). During this period, vigorous debate centered on the issue of whether budget reform would in effect establish a superordinate executive over the legislative branch. In 1920, President Wilson vetoed legislation that would have created a Bureau of the Budget and a General Accounting Office on the grounds that the latter, as an arm of Congress, would violate the president's authority over the executive branch. The following year, President Harding signed virtually identical legislation into law.

Thus, an executive budget system was established, despite a historical fear of a powerful chief executive. In 1939, the Bureau of the Budget was removed from the Treasury Department and placed in the newly formed Executive Office of the President. This shift reflected the growing importance of the bureau in assisting the president in managing the government. Ten years later, the budgetary task force of the First Hoover Commission on the Organization of the Executive Branch recommended that the Bureau of the Budget be reinstated in the Treasury Department, but the commission as a whole opposed the recommendation.[24] The Budget and Accounting Procedures Act of 1950 reinforced the trend of presidential control by explicitly granting the president control over the "form and detail" of the budget document.[25] The Second Hoover Commission in 1955 endorsed strengthening the president's power in budgeting as a means of restoring the "full control of the national purse to the Congress."[26] A president who had full control of the bureaucracy, then, could be held accountable by Congress for action taken by the bureaucracy.

One of the stated goals of the reform movement was to bring the sound financial practices of business to the presumably disorganized public sector — a goal often expressed by current reformers. Available evidence, however, indicates that business practices were not particularly exemplary at the turn of the century, suggesting that the reforms were largely invented within the public sector rather than being transferred into government from the outside.[27] It remains popular to advocate bringing good business practices to government, but the corporate accounting scandals that revealed allegedly false revenue claims in such giants as Enron suggest that private practices are not always exemplary.

Responsible for What?

Revenue Responsibility. The earliest concern for financial responsibility centered on taxes. As indicated above, the Magna Charta imposed limitations not on the nature of the Crown's expenditures but on the procedures for raising revenue. The same concern for the revenue side of budgeting was characteristic of the early history of budgeting in this country. The Constitution is more explicit about the tax power of the government than about the nature or purposes of government expenditures.

Expenditure Control, Management, and Planning. The larger the budget has become, the more the concern has shifted to expenditures. Increasing emphasis has been placed on the accountability of government for what it spends and for how well it manages its overall finances. Expenditure accountability may take several different forms. By the 1960s, expenditure accountability had gone through three stages.[28]

The first stage was characterized by legislative concern for tight control over executive expenditures. The most prevalent means of exerting this type of expenditure control is to appropriate by line item and object of expenditure. Financial audits are then used to ensure that money is, in fact, spent for the items authorized for purchase. This information focuses budgetary decision making on the things government buys, such as personnel, travel, and supplies — the objects of expenditure — rather than on the accomplishments of government activities. In other words, responsibility is achieved by controlling the resources or input side.

The second stage was a management orientation, with emphasis on the efficiency of ongoing activities. Historically, this orientation is associated with the New Deal through the First Hoover Commission (1949). The emphasis was on holding administrators accountable for the efficiency of their activities through methods such as work performance measurement.

The third stage of budget reform is identified with post-Hoover Commission concern regarding the planning function served by budgets. The traditional goal of controlling resource inputs may be accommodated in the short time frame of the coming budget year. Managerial control over efficiency, although aided by a longer time perspective, also may be accommodated in a traditional budget-year

Expenditures drive budget!

presentation. When the emphasis is shifted to accomplishing objectives, however, a longer time frame is necessary. Many objectives of government programs cannot be accomplished in one budget year. A multiyear presentation of the budget is thus necessary to indicate the long-range implications of current budget decisions. The advent of program budgeting in the 1960s and the focus on the ultimate results or outcomes of government programs (see Chapter 7) were the culmination of the planning focus on outcomes that must be measured outside the government itself. Control-oriented information such as objects of expenditure and managerial-oriented information such as the outputs produced by government activities (and the costs to achieve those outputs) do not really require measurement outside the orbit of governmental agencies.

Financial Management, Financial Condition, and Program Planning Revisited. Since those three stages were characterized in the 1960s, additional reform efforts have focused on other kinds of information needed for responsible government budgeting. Some have suggested that these emphases constitute additional or new stages of budget reform. One author has offered up prioritization, characterized by budget cutbacks in both federal and state government budgeting in the 1980s, as a fourth stage and accountability, emphasizing performance measurement, as a fifth stage.[29] Another has suggested a similar fourth stage, labeling it *limitation*, emphasizing the 1980s attempts to shrink the federal budget and state taxing and expenditure limitations (see Chapter 4).[30]

While it is clear that budgeting at the federal, state, and local levels continues to change in terms of emphasis and of focus, the labeling of additional *stages* is somewhat in the eye of the beholder. It is difficult to discern a major difference between *limitation* and *control*, for example. One criterion for applying the term *new stage* is whether new or substantially refined tools are deployed to focus more attention on new kinds of information relevant to budgetary decisions. The control, management, and planning reforms each included great emphasis on new or strengthened budgetary tools to aid decision making.

It is clear that some additional budgetary analysis and planning tools have become important in public budgeting systems, and it is useful to keep track by using the *stages* label. One new focal point is greater attention to the financial soundness of public sector institutions. Another focal point is renewed interest on program planning and performance measurement.

Financial Management and Performance Management. Publicly traded corporations have always had to answer to their stockholders for the financial condition of the corporation, and privately held companies at a minimum have to demonstrate sound financial condition to secure debt financing from lenders. But the application of financial management concepts to focus on the financial condition of government agencies was new in the late 1980s. Financial management can mean many things. It encompasses the desire for appropriate control over public funds. It certainly includes the desire for efficient public sector management. Financial management also entails the cost-effective accomplishment of the objectives of government programs, which has already been labeled a planning focus. But the last 20 years of the 1900s saw emphasis on new tools for measuring the financial condition of government, adapted from private financial and managerial accounting practices, and new mechanisms for ensuring that the government remains in a sound financial position. Such mechanisms encompass not only budgetary concerns regarding resource allocation but also the development of sound financing plans for meeting both short- and long-term resource requirements. Through the last decade of the 1900s into the new century, financial management has meant a renewed emphasis on performance measurement and performance improvement.[31]

One of the motivations behind the concern to hold government accountable for its long-run financial position was the New York City budget crisis of the mid-1970s. Following on the heels of that near-bankruptcy, both financial institutions that purchased municipal bonds and citizens who wondered about their own cities sought to improve the reporting of the long-term financial position of governments.[32] At the time, the general operating budget and related accounting reports often did not reveal the overall financial position of the government entity. All state governments, most local governments, and, of course, the federal government have some type of indebtedness. All three types of government also have various assets against which to compare that level of indebtedness. However, the long-run planning for debt retirement and the general strategies for managing existing assets do not receive much attention in budgeting systems. Concern at the federal level has led to a much greater emphasis on fixed asset management and increased attention in the annual budget to investments in long-lasting assets. The Governmental Accounting Standards Board Statement 34 (GASB 34) requires state and local governments and other public entities to report on their fixed assets (see Chapters 11 and 12). Whether one decides ultimately to label trends as new stages as we do here, it is clear that a strong, renewed emphasis on program and performance measurement has emerged, with significant efforts occurring at all levels of government. The "reinventing government" movement and the National Performance Review of the Clinton administration were just two examples of this trend.[33] Emphasis is placed on setting objectives and then motivating managers to be entrepreneurial in their pursuit of those objectives.[34] Other countries have also given the same emphases to results-oriented or value-driven budgeting as a primary tool in increasing the efficiency and reducing the size of the public sector.[35]

The notion of stages in budgeting can be overemphasized. Budget reform efforts for many decades have attempted to improve the capacity for decision-making systems to concentrate on accomplishing desired ends. Identifying three, four, or even five stages helps focus attention on what government is expected to be accountable for and where the locus of that accountability lies. The first stage would place the responsibility on the legislative branch as the principal authority for determining how resources should be allocated. The administrators' job, then, becomes perfunctory. The second stage may be seen as the beginning of a shift toward broader executive duties but limited to a concern for efficient management. The third stage is typified by program budgeting and management by objectives; it reflects the development of executive responsibility for formulating programs to achieve desired ends. The fourth stage, emphasizing overall financial planning, provides for executive responsibility in tying budgeting for current operations, capital facilities planning, asset management, and long-range debt financing into an integrated financial and management plan. The fifth stage renews the emphasis on performance measurement and evaluation within the context of budgetary allocation of resources and reinforces the notion of holding officials accountable through the budgetary decision-making process. Noteworthy in the most recent stage is the legislative branch taking an active and leading role in defining the emphasis through the passage of the federal Government Performance and Results Act of 1993.

Investment Versus Consumption. Another concern for budgeting systems that sometimes has been overlooked at the federal level is the role of government in aggregating capital for investment. Some government expenditures are really investments in future economic productivity; others primarily consume resources with little hope of any future payoff. Investment means creating additional productive capacity, such as improving transportation networks that reduce the cost of private sector economic activity through more efficient means of transportation and upgrading education systems that enhance the long-term ability to develop new products and new processes. All governments budget for these activities, but not all government budgeting systems make explicit the consumption versus investment tradeoffs in budget decisions. The argument can be made that some funds should be diverted away from social welfare programs that fail to produce new capability and toward investment opportunities that stimulate regional and national economic development. While most state and local governments employ formal capital budgeting techniques, federal agencies typically do not, although in specific types of investments such as information technology, formalized capital investment planning and analysis now is required (see Chapter 12).[36]

Most of the emphasis in this book is on the budget as an instrument for financial and program decision making at all levels of government — federal, state, and local. The one responsibility that most sharply differentiates federal budget decisions from state and local decisions is the federal government's responsibility for the overall state of the economy. The federal budget not only allocates resources among competing programs but it is also an instrument for achieving economic stability and growth (see Chapter 15). The responsibility to use it as an instrument of economic policy has been a part of the federal budgetary process since the Employment Act of 1946.[37]

Budgeting, then, is an important process by which accountability or responsibility can be provided in a political system. As has been discussed, responsibility varies both in terms of the people to whom the system is accountable and in terms of its purposes. Given the various forms of accountability and the types of choices that decision makers have available to them, different meanings can be attached to the terms *budget* and *budgeting system*. Depending on the purposes of a budget, decision makers will need different kinds and amounts of information to aid them in making choices. The following sections and subsequent chapters focus on the kinds of information required for different budgetary choices and the kinds of procedures for generating the necessary information.

Budgets and Budgeting Systems

What Is a Budget?

Budget Documents. In its simplest form, a budget is a document or a collection of documents that refers to the financial condition and future plans of an organization (family, corporation, government), including information on revenues, expenditures, activities, and purposes or goals. In contrast to an accounting operating statement, which is retrospective in nature, referring to past conditions, a budget is prospective, referring to anticipated future revenues, expenditures, and accomplishments. Historically, the word *budget* referred to a leather pouch, wallet, bag, or purse. More particularly, "In Britain the term was used to describe the leather bag in which the Chancellor of the Exchequer carried to Parliament the statement of the Government's needs and resources."[38]

The status of budget documents is not consistent across political jurisdictions. In the federal government, the budget has limited legal status. It is the official recommendation of the president to Congress, but it is not the official document under which the government operates. As will be seen later, the official operating budget of the United States consists of several documents — namely, appropriation acts (see Chapters 8, 9, and 11). In contrast, local budgets proposed by mayors may become official working budgets adopted in their entirety by the city councils.[39]

In still other instances, there may be a series of budget documents instead of one budget for any given government. These may include (1) an operating budget, which handles the bulk of ongoing operations; (2) a capital budget, which covers major new construction projects; and (3) a series of special fund budgets that cover programs funded by specific revenue sources (see Chapter 11). Special fund budgets commonly include those for highway programs, which are financed through gasoline and tire sales taxes. In such cases, revenue from these sources is earmarked for highway construction, improvement, and maintenance. As another example, fishing and hunting license fees may constitute the revenue for a special fund devoted to the stocking of streams and the provision of ample hunting opportunities.

The format of budget documents also varies. On the whole, budget documents tend to provide greater information on expenditures than on revenues, which are usually treated in a brief section. On the expenditure side, budgets are multipurpose, in that no single document and no single definition can exhaust the functions budgets serve or the ways they are used. At the most general level, however, budgets can be conceived of as (1) descriptions, (2) explanations or causal assertions, and (3) statements of preferences or values.

Budgets as Descriptions. Budgets are first descriptions of the status of an organization, whether it is an agency, a ministry, or an entire government. The budget document may describe what the organization purchases, what it does, and what it accomplishes. Descriptions of organizational activity are also common in budget documents; expenditures may be classified according to the activities they support. For example, a revenue department may be concerned with initial tax collection, taxpayer assistance, and audit/enforcement. Another type of description, organizational accomplishments, states the consequences of resource consumption and work activities for those outside the organization. For example, successful job placements for individuals finishing a vocational rehabilitation program constitute one type of outcome or consequence of a public expenditure. These statements require external verification of the effects of the organization on its environment.

As descriptions, budgets provide a discrete picture of an organization at a point or points in time — in terms of resources consumed, work performed, and external effects. The dollar revenues and expenditures, according to these types of descriptions, may be the only quantitative information supplied. Alternatively, information may be supplied about the number and types of personnel; the quantity and kinds of equipment purchased; measures of performance, such as the number of buildings inspected or the number of acres treated; and measures of impact, such as the number of accidents prevented, the amount of crop yield increases, and so forth. Generally, the more descriptive material supplied, the more the organization can be held accountable for the funds spent, the activities supported by those expenditures, and the external accomplishments produced by those activities. Much of the history of budget reform reflects attempts to increase the quantity and quality of descriptive material available both to decision makers and to the public.

Budgets as Explanations. When they describe organizations in terms of purchases, activities, and accomplishments, budgets also at least implicitly serve a second major function — explanation of causal relationships. The expenditure of a specific amount for the purchase of labor and materials that will be combined in particular work activities implies the existence of a causal sequence that will produce certain results. Regardless of how explicit or how vague the budget document or the statements of organization officials may be, budgetary decisions always imply a causal process in which work activities consume resources to achieve goals. Some organizations may have little accurate information about accomplishments, especially public organizations whose accomplishments are not measured in terms of profit and loss. Governments may choose not to be explicit about particular results because they are difficult to measure, politically sensitive, or both. Regardless of the availability of information or the willingness of an organization to collect and use it, the budget is an expression of a set of causal relationships.

Budgets as Preferences. Budgets are statements of preferences. Whether intended or not, the allocation of resources among different agencies, among different activities, or among different accomplishments reveals the preferences of those making the allocations. These may be the actual preferences of a few decision makers, but more often they are best thought of as the collective preferences of many decision makers arrived at through complex bargaining. A preference schedule reflects, if not any one individual's values, an aggregate of choices that become the collective value judgment for the local government, state, or nation.

What Is a Budgeting System?

Systems. Budgeting can best be understood as a kind of system — a "set of units with relationships among them."[40] Budgetary decision making consists of the actions of executive officials (both in a central organization such as the governor's office or the mayor's staff and in executive line agencies), legislative officials, organized interest groups, and perhaps unorganized interests that may be manifested in a generally felt public concern about public needs and taxes. All these

actions are related, and understanding budgeting means understanding the relationships. Such understanding is best achieved by thinking in terms of complex
systems.

A complex social system is composed of organizations, individuals, the values held by these individuals, the norms they act upon, and the relationships
among these elements. A system may be thought of as a network typically consisting of many different parts, with messages flowing among the parts. The elements of systems interact with each other to produce system results, or consequences, and the network of interactions may produce the same set of results
through several different paths, or the same path may from time to time produce
different outcomes.[41] Budgeting systems involve political actors, economic and
social theories, numerous institutional structures, and competing norms and values, all of which produce outputs in patterns not immediately evident from
studying only budget documents.

Budget System Outputs. In a budgetary system, the outputs flowing from the network of interactions are budget decisions, and these vary greatly in their overall
significance. Not every unit of the system will have equal decisional authority or
power. A manager of a field office for a state health department is likely to have
less power to make major budgetary decisions than the administrative head of
the department, the governor, or the members of the legislative appropriations
committees. Yet each participant does contribute some input to the system. The
field manager may alert others in the system to the emergence of a new health
problem and in doing so may contribute greatly to the eventual establishment of
a new health program to combat that problem. Furthermore, modern information
technology and the greater emphasis on responsibility at all levels of the organization for achieving results means the lower-level staff in an agency are much
more influential than they might have been in the past regarding how outcomes
of public programs are achieved or not achieved.[42]

Like the outputs of any other system or network, budget decisions are seldom
final and more commonly are sequential. Decisions are tentative, in that each
decision made is forwarded for action to another participant in the process. This
does not mean that all decisions are reversible. Major breakthroughs, such as passage of the Elementary and Secondary Education Act of 1965, which provided
substantial federal aid to education, are abandoned only in response to powerful
political pressure.[43] Subsequent budget decisions, therefore, are in large part
bounded by previous decisions. The subsequent decisions tend to center on the
question of changing the level of commitment — allocating more resources, fewer
resources, or different kinds of resources to achieve desired levels of impact or
different types of impact. The George W. Bush administration's *No Child Left
Behind Act*, which reauthorized major elements of federal assistance to elementary

and secondary education, continued most of the key elements of the original 1965 legislation, although giving great emphasis to testing student achievement as a means of ensuring accountability at the classroom level.[44]

System Interconnectedness. Another feature of a system is that a change in any part of it will alter other parts. Because all units are related, any change in the role or functioning of one unit necessarily affects other units. In some instances, changes may be of such a modest nature that their ramifications for other parts of the system are difficult to discern. However, when major budgetary reforms are instituted, they assuredly affect most participants. For example, if one unit in the system is granted greater authority, individuals and organizations having access to that unit have their decisional involvement enhanced, whereas those groups associated with other units have diminished roles.[45] Thus, each individual and institution evaluates budget reforms in terms of how political strengths will be realigned under the reforms.

Information and Decision Making

Types of Information

To serve the multiple functions described in the preceding section, budgeting systems must produce and process a variety of information. Most of the major reforms, whether attempted or proposed, in public budget systems have been intended to reorganize existing information and to provide participants with different types and greater quantities of information. Basically, two types of information exist: program information and resource information. The latter type is more traditional. People are accustomed to thinking of budgets in terms of resources such as monetary units and personnel. A budget would not be a budget if it did not contain dollar, ruble, or other monetary figures. Similarly, budgets commonly contain data on employees or personnel.

Conventional accounting systems provide much of the information that public organizations use for budgetary decisions. This type of information, however, is limited to the internal aspects of organizations — the location of organizational responsibility for expenditures and the resources purchased by those expenditures. When the decision-making system incorporates information about the results or implications of programs, however, one must leave the boundaries of the organization to examine consequences for those outside it. This step requires more extensive and more explicit clarification of governmental goals and objectives (see Chapter 5) and increases the importance of analysis (see Chapter 7).[46] This feature of budget reforms such as program budgeting, management by objectives, and zero-base budgeting, with their emphasis on program information and priority setting, has generated the most heat among critics of budget reform.[47]

Decision Making

Much of the criticism of reform has involved the argument that reform of decision-making systems must take into account the limitations on human capabilities to use all the information that might be collected and analyzed. Although sometimes subtle differences distinguish theories of decision making, the various theories can generally be classified into three basic approaches: pure rationality, muddling through or incrementalism, and limited rationality.[48] An early application of these notions to public sector decision making was Graham Allison's study of the Cuban Missile Crisis, *The Essence of Decision*, in which he characterized three models as rational, organizational, and governmental/political.[49] These are descriptive theories as well as prescriptions for how decisions ought to be made.

Rational Decision Making. Decision making according to the pure rationality approach consists of a series of ordered, logical steps. First, all of an organization's or a society's goals are ranked according to priority. Second, all possible alternatives are identified. The costs of each alternative are compared with anticipated benefits. Judgments are made as to which alternative comes closest to satisfying the relevant needs or desires. The alternative with the highest payoff and/or least cost is chosen. Pure rationality theories assume that complete and perfect information about all alternatives is both available and manageable. Decision making, therefore, is choosing among alternatives to maximize some objective function. The rational choice model is built on microeconomics and the notion of the individual actor making an optimal choice to maximize the decision maker's utility.

The applicability of the rationality model is limited, and few argue that it is a description of how ordinary human beings make decisions. It is most consistent with notions of technical or economic rationality, where objectives can be stated with some precision and the range of feasible alternatives is finite.[50] Also, the model can be of use where accurate predictions of behavior are possible, such as in the private market, where assumptions regarding rational behavior can be used to predict future economic trends.[51] As a description of how government budgeting works, however, the pure rationality model is obviously misleading. Meeting the complete requirements of even one of the steps is impossible. It has been argued that the costs of information are so high as to make it rational to be ignorant — that is, to make decisions on the basis of a limited search and limited information. Some attempts at budget reform have been criticized as attempts to impose an unworkable model, pure rationality, on government financial decision-making. The use of program information has been a particular target for criticism.[52] However, this criticism is somewhat misdirected in that it is not so much the information search cost that is limiting, but rather the individual decision-maker's perspective. Public budgeting decisions are made in a larger organizational context with numerous actors involved, a more complicated situation than the clear-sighted approach toward an agreed-upon objective that is the essence of the rational choice model.

Incrementalism. The second approach to decision making, muddling through (incrementalism), has been advocated by critics of pure rationality, such as Charles E. Lindblom, Aaron Wildavsky, and others.[53] According to this view, decision making involves a conflict of interests and a corresponding clash of information which result in the accommodation of diverse partisan interests through bargaining. "Real" decision making is presumed to begin as issues are raised by significant interest groups that request or demand changes from the existing state.[54] Decision making is not some conscious form of pure rationality, but is a process of incrementally adjusting existing practices to establish or reestablish consensus among participants. Alternatives to the status quo are normally not considered unless partisan interests bring them to the attention of the participants in the decision-making process. There is only a marginal amount of planned search for alternatives to achieve desired ends. The decisional process is structured so that partisan interests have the opportunity to press their desires at some point in the deliberations. Decisions represent a consensus on policy reached through a political, power-oriented bargaining process.

The most important characteristic of the muddling through or incrementalist approach as applied to budgeting is its emphasis on the proposition that budgetary decisions are necessarily political. Its descriptive appeal is that it more accurately depicts a process in which numerous actors, each with a different point of view, negotiate and bargain for a consensus. The larger the issue, the more difficult it is to achieve consensus for radical change, which results most often in incremental adjustments to the status quo.[55] Whereas a purely rational approach might suggest that budgetary decisions are attempts to allocate resources according to economic criteria, the incrementalist view stresses the extent to which political considerations outweigh calculations of optimality. The strongest critics of many budget reforms have tended to equate those reforms with seeking to establish the pure rationality model or a solely economic model, a description rarely accepted by those proposing budget reforms. As will be seen throughout this book, any "real" budget reform is forced to accommodate the political nature of decision making.

Limited Rationality. The third approach to decision making, a compromise between the other two approaches, is called limited rationality. This model recognizes the inadequacies in the assumptions behind the pure rationality description of decision making as applied to complex problems. While acknowledging the inherent constraints of human cognitive processes, limited rationality does not suggest that a deliberate search for alternative approaches to goal achievement is of no avail. Searching for alternatives is used to find solutions that are satisfactory but not necessarily optimal.

Substantial evidence, cited by some of the giants in budgeting (Wildavsky) and decision making (Lindblom), indicates that many decisions are indeed incremental, and clearly each budget decision does not require a thorough review of all options and careful calculations of the possible outcomes of each option. Yet major decisions that depart dramatically from the past are made in the budgetary process. Non-incremental change, such as the total reformation of a state Medicaid system, do occur.[56] And, of course, major events such as terrorist threats and creating a new agency such as the Department of Homeland Security cause non-incremental change. Furthermore, decision makers often do attempt to achieve public values and are motivated more by the social and economic problems their agencies must address than by bureaucratic budget maximizing and interest-group pressures.[57]

Limited rationality suggests that large forces are marshalled at times for major change, and incremental adjustments are made at other times for issues that do not generate demand for substantial departure from the status quo. Decision theories do differ in how they view the values that decision making serves and the capacities of decision makers to serve those values. One model assumes virtually no limits on human capacities for processing information, another suggests that decision making should be sensitive only to partisan political interests, and the third attempts to strike a balance between the other models. The history of budgeting and budget reform, we argue, reflects the tensions among these approaches to decision making.

◼ Summary

Public budgeting involves choices among ends and means. Public budgeting shares many characteristics with budgeting in the private sector, but it often requires the application of criteria different from those used by private organizations. Chief among these differences is that few public sector decisions can be assessed in terms of profit and loss. Private sector decisions, on the other hand, ultimately must consider the long-run profit or loss condition of the firm.

Budgeting systems involve the organization of information for making choices and the structure of decision-making processes. Public budgeting systems have evolved as one means of holding government accountable for its actions. Budgetary procedures are developed to hold the government in general accountable to the public, the executive branch accountable to the legislature, and subordinates accountable to their managers. Budgetary procedures also are developed to specify what the executive is accountable for. Concern for the financial solvency of some city governments and the size of the federal budget deficit and total debt have led to reform proposals to use budgeting as a device for holding governments accountable for their long-term financial position. Renewed interest is evident in holding governments accountable for achieving those programmatic results that citizens want and demand.

Budgetary systems work through information flows. However, each participant in the budgetary process pays selective attention to information. The various theories of decision making advanced differ in terms of how much information decision makers are willing and able to consider. The decision-making approach that seems best to characterize budgetary systems is the limited rationality approach. This approach underlies the discussions throughout this book.

Notes

1. P.F. Drucker, *Managing in the Next Society* (New York: St. Martins, 2002), 1–90.

2. A. Downs, *Inside Bureaucracy* (Boston: Little, Brown, 1967).

3. L.R. Jones and F. Thompson, Responsibility Budgeting and Accounting, *International Public Management Journal* 3 (2000): 205–227.

4. Office of Management and Budget, *Budget of the United States Government: FY 2003, Historical Tables* (Washington, DC: U.S. Government Printing Office, 2002), 295.

5. Congressional Budget Office, *CBO Staff Memorandum: A Review of Edwin Mansfield's Estimate of the Rate of Return from Academic Research and Its Relevance to the Federal Budget Process* (Washington, DC: U.S. Government Printing Office, 1993).

6. National Academy of Sciences, *Implementing the Government Performance and Results Act for Research* (Washington, DC: National Academy Press, 2001), 36.

7. U.S. General Accounting Office, *Managing for Results: Emerging Benefits from Selected Agencies' Use of Performance Agreement* (Washington, DC: U.S. Government Printing Office, 2000).

8. N. Bruce, *Public Finance and the American Economy*, 2nd ed. (New York: Addison-Wesley, 2000).

9. R.W. Tresch, *Public Finance: A Normative Theory*, 2nd ed. (New York: Academic Press, 2002).

10. L.R. Geri, Federal User Fees and Entrepreneurial Budgeting, *Public Budgeting and Financial Management* 9 (1997): 127–142.

11. M.J. White credits W.F. Willoughby's *The Problem of a National Budget* with an early (1919) statement of budgeting as a process for holding government accountable. M.J. White, Budget Policy: Where Does It Begin and End? *Governmental Finance* 7 (August 1978): 2–9.

12. D. Osborne and P. Plastrik, *Banishing Bureaucracy: The Five Strategies for Reinventing Government* (Reading, MA: Addison-Wesley, 1997). For the critics' view, see D.W. Williams, Reinventing the Proverbs of Government, *Public Administration Review* 60 (2000): 522–534.

13. C. Webber and A. Wildavsky, *A History of Taxation and Expenditure in the Western World* (New York: Simon & Schuster, 1986).

14. J. Burkhead, *Government Budgeting* (New York: Wiley, 1956), 2–4.

15. Treasury Act, Ch. 12, 1 Stat. 65 (1789).

16. A. Smithies, *The Budgetary Process in the United States* (New York: McGraw-Hill, 1955), 50.

17. A.E. Buck, *Public Budgeting* (New York: Harper and Brothers, 1919), 17.

18. E.E. Naylor, *The Federal Budget System in Operation* (Washington, DC: printed privately, 1941), 22–23.

19. Burkhead, *Government Budgeting*, 12–13.

20. Buck, *Public Budgeting*, 14.

21. Burkhead, *Government Budgeting*, 23; Y. Willbern, Personnel and Money, in *The 50 States and Their Local Governments*, J.W. Fesler, ed., (New York: Knopf, 1967), 391.

22. F.A. Cleveland, Evolution of the Budget Idea in the United States, *Annals* 62 (November 1915): 22.

23. Budget and Accounting Act, Ch. 18, 42 Stat. 20 (1921).

24. U.S. Commission on Organization of the Executive Branch of the Government, *General Management of the Executive Branch* (Washington, DC: U.S. Government Printing Office, 1949).

25. Budget and Accounting Procedures Act, Ch. 946, Title I, part I, 64 Stat. 832 (1950).

26. U.S. Commission on Organization of the Executive Branch of the Government, *Budget and Accounting* (Washington, DC: U.S. Government Printing Office, 1955), ix.

27. I.S. Rubin, Who Invented Budgeting in the United States? *Public Administration Review* 53 (1993): 438–444.

28. A. Schick, The Road to PPB: The Stages of Budget Reform, *Public Administration Review* 26 (1966): 243–258.

29. C. Tyer and J. Willand, Public Budgeting in America: A Twentieth Century Retrospective, *Journal of Public Budgeting, Accounting & Financial Management* 9 (1997): 189–219.

30. J.R. Bartle, Budgeting, Policy, and Administration: Patterns and Dynamics in the United States, *International Journal of Public Administration* 24 (2001): 21–30.

31. H.G. Frederickson, Measuring Performance in Theory and Practice, *PA Times* 23 (August, 2000): 8–10.

32. R.W. Johnson and A.Y. Lewin, Management and Accountability Models of Public Sector Performance, in *Public Sector Performance: A Conceptual Turning Point*, ed. T.C. Miller (Baltimore: Johns Hopkins University Press, 1984), 224–250.

33. National Performance Review, *Mission Driven, Results-Oriented Budgeting* (Washington, DC: U.S. Government Printing Office, 1993); J.R. Thompson, Reinvention as Reform: Assessing the National Performance Review, *Public Administration Review* 60 (2000): 508–521.

34. L.L. Martin, Outcome Budgeting: A New Entrepreneurial Approach to Budgeting, *Public Budgeting & Financial Management* 9 (Spring 1997): 108–126.

35. R. Allen and D. Tommassi, eds., *Managing Public Expenditure* (Paris: Organization for Economic Cooperation and Development, 2001).

36. Office of Management and Budget, OMB Releases New Business Reference Model to Improve Agency Management, press release (Executive Office of the President: Office of Management and Budget, July 24, 2002): *http://www.feapmo.gov*; accessed August 2002.

37. Employment Act, Ch. 33, 60 Stat. 23 (1946).

38. Burkhead, *Government Budgeting*, 2.

39. J.C. Powdar, *The Operating Budget: A Guide for Smaller Governments* (Chicago: Government Finance Officers Association, 1996); R.L. Bland and I.S. Rubin, *Budgeting: A Guide for Local Governments* (Washington, DC: International City/County Management Association, 1997).

40. G. Miller, Living Systems: Basic Concepts, *Behavioral Science* 10 (1965): 200.

41. K.E. Kendall and J.E. Kendall, *Systems Analysis and Design*, 5th ed. (New York: Prentice-Hall, 2001).

42. T.D. Lynch and C.E. Lynch, The Road to Entrepreneurial Budgeting, *Journal of Budgeting, Accounting & Financial Management*, 9 (1997): 161–180.

43. Elementary and Secondary Education Act, P.L. 89–10 (1965).

44. No Child Left Behind Act, P.L. 107–110 (2001).

45. L.R. Jones and J. McCaffery, Budgeting According to Aaron Wildavsky: A Bibliographic Essay, *Public Budgeting & Finance* 14 (Spring 1994): 16–43.

46. Stuart Nagel, ed., *Handbook of Public Policy Evaluation* (Thousand Oaks, CA: Sage, 2001).

47. A. Wildavsky and N. Caiden, *The New Politics of the Budgetary Process*, 4th ed. (New York: Longman Press, 2000); A. Schick, From the Old Politics of Budgeting to the New, *Public Budgeting & Finance* 14 (Spring 1994): 135–144.

48. G.D. Brewer and P. de Leon, *The Foundations of Policy Analysis* (Chicago: Dorsey, 1983).

49. N.A. Giannatasio, Budget Decision Making at the Grass–Roots Level, *Journal of Public Budgeting, Accounting & Financial Management*, 13 (2002): 48–82, evaluates Allison's decision-making model's applicability to public budgeting at the local level. G.T. Allison, *The Essence of Decision: Explaining the Cuban Missile Crisis* (New York: Harper, 1971).

50. The terms *technical* and *economic rationality* are the names of two of five basic types of rationality identified by P. Diesing, *Reason and Society* (Urbana: University of Illinois Press, 1962).

51. See M. Friedman, *Essays in Positive Economics* (Chicago: University of Chicago Press, 1953).

52. A. Wildavsky, *Speaking Truth to Power: The Art and Craft of Policy Analysis* (Boston: Little, Brown, 1979).

53. C.E. Lindblom, The Science of "Muddling Through," *Public Administration Review* 19 (1959): 79–88; L.R. Jones, Changing How We Budget: Aaron Wildavsky's Perspective, *Journal of Public Budgeting, Accounting & Financial Management* 9 (1997): 46–71.

54. J. White, (Almost) Nothing New under the Sun: Why the Work of Budgeting Remains Incremental, *Public Budgeting & Finance* 14 (Spring 1994): 113–134.

55. T.R. Oliver, The Dilemmas of Incrementalism: Logical and Political Constraints in the Design of Health Insurance Reforms, *Journal of Policy Analysis and Management* 18 (1999): 652–683.

56. C.S. Weissert and M.L. Goggin, Nonincremental Policy Change: Lessons from Michigan's Medicaid Managed Care Initiative, *Public Administration Review* 62 (2002): 206–216.

57. S. Cope, Assessing Rational-Choice Models of Budgeting — From Budget-Maximising to Bureau-Shaping: A Case Study of British Local Government, *Journal of Public Budgeting, Accounting & Financial Management* 12 (2000): 598–624.

Chapter 2

THE PUBLIC SECTOR IN PERSPECTIVE

One danger of generalizing about the size of the public sector of society is that any single generalization necessarily ignores important information. Although the statement "government is vast" may be valid, it fails to recognize the difficulties in determining what is and is not government or the fact that government is also small in some respects. This chapter describes the size and extent of the public sector, discusses the relative and absolute growth rates of government, and considers the general level of taxes and other revenue sources and the societal functions that these revenues support.

The chapter explores three main topics. The first is the relative sizes of the private and public sectors of society and the reasons for the growth of government. The second is the magnitude of government and the historical growth of local, state, and federal finances. In the third section, we contrast the purposes of government expenditures with the sources of revenue used by the three main levels of government in the United States.

Relative Sizes of the Private and Public Sectors

Basic to all matters of public budgeting is the issue of the appropriate size of the public sector. This issue is inherently political, not only in the partisan sense but also in the sense that it involves fundamental policy questions about what government should and should not do, and what it can and cannot do. At stake are congeries of competing public and private wants and needs and competing philosophies of the role of the public sector in society. A guiding principle for many of the framers of the Constitution was to keep the central government small to protect individual liberty. Other early leaders, such as Alexander Hamilton, sought a more activist role for the new government.[1]

Reasons for Growth

Value Questions. The issue of size relates to the values of freedom and social welfare. Keeping government small has been advocated as a means of protecting individuals from tyranny and stimulating individual independence and initiative.[2] On the other hand, faith in the private sector is sometimes criticized as causing the underfinancing of public programs and the failure to confront major social problems.[3] Some people argue that the wave of corporate scandals that occurred in 2002 (Enron and WorldCom, for example) was in part caused by placing too much faith in an unfettered — or more precisely, deregulated — private sector. Debates over the rise of the welfare and warfare states have been especially acrimonious.

The U.S. political system, of course, is not structured in such a way that any overriding decision is made as to the size of this sector. The multiplicity of governments makes it virtually impossible to reach any single decision about the appropriate size of this sector. Decisions relevant to size are made in a political context within and between the executive and legislative branches and among the three major levels of government — local, state, and federal. Each set of decisions contributes to an ultimate resolution of the question, but one must await the tally of all the decisions before one can perceive what has been deemed the appropriate size.

Government Responses. Why government expands has been the subject of extended debate.[4] One of the two main reasons is that government is "responsive" to the demands of society. Wagner's law, originally proposed in the 1880s, holds that economic development creates opportunities for new activities that government alone can perform.[5] The second reason is that government has a supposed propensity to be excessive.[6] In this case, government is seen to grow as a result of empire building by government bureaucrats, supported by political leaders.[7]

Among the numerous factors suggested as stimulating responses from government are the following:[8]

- *The need for collective goods.* Because defense, flood control, and some other programs benefit all citizens and cannot be handled readily by the private sector, government becomes involved. When wars occur, governments grow in size; after the conflict, they tend to remain larger than during the prewar period.

- *Demographic changes.* Increases in total population, newborns, and the elderly stimulate the creation and expansion of government programs.

- *Changes in living patterns.* As the population moves from rural to urban areas, and then from cities to suburbia, demands for government services follow them. More schools, roads, public utilities, and public safety need to be provided.
- *Externalities.* Air and water pollution produced by industrial firms, which are concerned mainly with making a profit, is a social cost and a condition that government is expected to control. Education also has important externalities: Uneducated people impose costs on others through the need for welfare and other social services, while educated people tend to be more productive and increase the total wealth of the society.
- *Economic hardships.* Depressions and other negative economic situations stimulate the growth of government.
- *High-risk situations.* When risks are high, the private sector is unlikely to invest large quantities of resources, so government is called upon to support programs. Examples include the development of nuclear energy as a source of electrical power and the space program. Once the risks of certain aspects of space activity became manageable as a result of government intervention, commercial interests engaged in space research and moved into the launching of private vehicles and satellites.
- *Technological change.* With the advent of new technology, government has been called upon to provide support, as in the case of roads and airports, to accommodate improved transportation modes and information highways such as the Internet, or to regulate new industries, as in the case of railroads, radio, and television.

While these reasons are helpful in explaining why government enters into the private sector, they do not sufficiently reflect the political considerations at stake when proposals are made for expanding or contracting the scope of the public sector. Any proposal for the expansion of services that results in an increase in taxes is likely to have some unfavorable political repercussions. Therefore, the size issue always relates to both government expenditures and revenues (taxes). Decision makers, no matter how crude or approximate their methods of calculating, attempt to weigh the merits of coping with the current situation with the available resources against the merits of recommending new programs that may alleviate problems but at the same time raise the ire of taxpayers. Taxpayer revolts — common events since the 1970s — may have had a significant influence in curtailing the growth of government at the state and local levels, although some research suggests that they have just shifted sources of funding to revenue sources that are not covered by tax and expenditure limitations.[9]

Private and Public Sector Boundaries

Major problems are encountered when attempts are made to gauge the sizes of the public and private sectors and to distinguish between one government and another. Government has become so deeply involved in the society that one may frequently have difficulty discerning what is not at least quasi-public. Moreover, governments have extensive relationships with each other, to the point where a discussion of any single government becomes meaningless without a discussion of its relationships with other governments.

Statistical data on government revenues and expenditures fail to reflect adequately the size of government. For instance, the entire political campaign process is clearly governmental in that funds are expended to elect people to political offices, yet most of these monies are not recorded as government expenditures.[10] Also, in cases where government activities require relatively little money and personnel but have a substantial impact on the private sector or other governments, the size of government tends to be understated. This is especially true with respect to regulatory activities, such as the control of interstate commerce, occupational safety, and environmental health by the federal government.

Nonexhaustive Expenditures. Complete reliance on revenue and expenditure data for measuring size is unwarranted for another reason. Sometimes the assumption is made that all government expenditures represent a drain on the private economy. In fact, government expenditures can be nonexhaustive as well as exhaustive. Exhaustive expenditures occur when government consumes resources such as facilities and manpower that might otherwise have been used by the private sector. Nonexhaustive expenditures occur when government redistributes or transfers resources to components of the society instead of consuming them. Interest payments on the national debt, unemployment compensation, aid to the indigent, and old-age and retirement benefits are major examples of nonexhaustive government expenditures.

Another form of nonexhaustive expenditures is investment for the future, whether for capital facilities or for services, as in education for children. Government aid to small businesses, support of research and development, and similar activities are forms of investment in future economic development. As a result of these kinds of expenditures, the cost of government is actually less than the total dollar figures reported in budgets, in the sense that what is spent will generate future revenue for both society and its governments.

Effects on the Private Sector. Government expenditures have specific effects on industries, occupations, geographic regions, and subpopulations. These effects are especially evident in the field of defense. During the Cold War, clusters of firms and their employees became highly dependent upon defense outlays, resulting in what President Eisenhower in 1961 decried as the military-industrial complex. The case could be made that a dangerous symbiotic relationship developed between the military, with its penchant for new weaponry, and corporations eager to supply such weaponry. Periodic scandals in defense contracting offer seeming confirmation of the fears expressed by President Eisenhower.

The effects of defense are particularly pronounced in regard to employment, despite the downsizing that has occurred since the end of the Cold War. In 2000, defense accounted for 0.5 percent of the private sector labor force and about one-fourth of the federal government's civilian labor force. In addition, the federal government hired 1.4 million people for armed forces duty based in the United States. Total military and civilian employment constituted 1.5 percent of total U.S. employment.[11]

The effects of defense expenditures upon the private economy also have been substantial. Defense expenditures account for a significant percentage of jobs in various industries, such as shipbuilding and aeronautics. The creation of defense-related jobs entices people into educational programs that develop the requisite skills. As a result, people are attracted into technical career fields that are dependent upon continued defense spending. These people suffer or flourish based on which policies prevail.

Geographic and Industry Effects. Military research, development, and procurement are of such great magnitude that many specific industries and corporations become quasi-public institutions. In 1999, the Department of Defense spent $135.2 billion in total contracts. Of this amount, $112.2 billion went to business firms in the United States. The remainder was provided to nonprofit or education institutions in the United States, intergovernmental contracts, or work done outside the United States.[12] Although cutbacks in defense in the mid-1990s most likely reduced these numbers, defense expenditures still greatly influence the private sector — in firms that engage in shipbuilding, aircraft construction, and communications, to name just three examples. Besides providers of military equipment, such as Boeing, General Dynamics, General Electric, and General Motors, numerous consulting and research and development firms are dependent on military expenditures. Nondefense contracting firms are similarly dependent, with 60 to 80 percent of their revenues coming from government contracts.

Employees of these varied private sector firms, judging from their length of service on government projects, are, in effect, career civil servants. One difference is that the pay of managerial staff in these firms is often higher than that of similarly trained government employees. (Professional salaries, such as for engineers and scientists, tend to be relatively equal, because government must meet private sector salaries to recruit and retain professionals.) Another difference is that private sector employees do not constitute a permanent expense to the government.

These workers are not protected by civil service laws and are ineligible for government pension benefits. Furthermore, when these workers' services are not needed, government has no obligation to them as it would to its own employees.

The geographic effects of defense expenditures are equally important because they are not uniformly distributed throughout the nation. In 2001, the Department of Defense spent $255 billion. Five states — California, Virginia, Texas, Florida, and Georgia — accounted for $104 billion, or more than 40 percent of that total.[13] The Department of Defense spent $149 billion for procurement contracts in the same year, with the same five states ranking as the top five recipients, and again accounting for 40 percent of all contracts.[14]

Defense, while the most striking example of private dependence upon public outlays, is not the sole example. Highway construction also involves large sums of public money. The employees of construction firms specializing in bridge and highway construction are, in effect, government employees. The same is true for suppliers of road-building equipment. In addition, the 1990s and early 2000s have seen a continued emphasis on contracting out as a means of producing public services. During the late 1990s, for example, when the number of federal civilian employees decreased by approximately 300,000, the number of individuals working for the federal government under contract increased substantially.[15] In some cases, the impact of government on an industry is greater as a result of what government does *not* do than what it *does* do. The federal government's failure to tax interest paid on home mortgages, for example, has a far greater effect on the housing industry than all federal expenditures for public housing and redevelopment.

The lack of clear-cut distinctions between the public and private sectors and between one government and another is evident in education. Elementary and secondary education is a function of local school districts, but about half the funds used by these districts come from state governments, with additional funds coming from the federal government. Public higher education is funded by the states, with important federal support, especially in the form of student aid and research financing. Governments also selectively subsidize private colleges and universities. Private corporations make important contributions to both public and private schools. In 2002, the U.S. Supreme Court ruled that it is constitutional for governments to use public funds to provide vouchers to parents whose children attend private or parochial schools.[16] This will undoubtedly become another area in which public funds have a substantial effect on private educational activity.

Subpopulation Effects. Taxes and expenditures affect different subpopulations in different ways. In the example given earlier of the federal government allowing income tax deductions for interest paid on home mortgages, the middle class and upper class benefit far more than lower-income groups, who typically are renters rather than homeowners. This tax expenditure — namely, the government's not taxing something that could be taxed — has a redistributional effect in favor of the middle and upper classes (see Chapter 4).

Government actions have important effects on generations, including those who will be born in years to come. Taxing and spending policies can help or harm children through health and education programs, the working-age population through transportation programs, and the elderly through government-sponsored nursing care and the like. Future generations benefit from government programs that encourage investment in economic development but may be harmed by excessive debts that governments may accumulate, especially the federal government.

The Magnitude and Growth of Government

There are many ways to measure the magnitude of government, but dollars and people are generally the easiest measures to apply. By focusing on revenues, expenditures, and numbers of employees, we can use comparable standards in contrasting governments with each other and with private organizations. These measures, then, are the main ones used in this section.

Some words of caution are warranted. Statistical data used in this and the following section are drawn from several sources, some of which are not in agreement. Therefore, some of the data reported here must be considered approximate. Another item to note is that the U.S. Census Bureau, primarily due to budgetary limitations, has scaled back the data it reports, the frequency of reporting, and the timeliness of the data.

Revenues

One approach to measuring organizations is to consider their revenues or receipts, which allows comparisons among private and public organizations.[17] **Table 2–1** ranks the 25 largest governments and industrial corporations in the world, as measured by revenues. Significantly, 14 of the 25 are governments, with the U.S. federal government ranked first. Until the Soviet Union disintegrated, it was unquestionably the second largest organization in the world, but Russia does not even appear in the top 25 (it is twenty-ninth). Four U.S. bureaucracies are included in the list of 25 — the federal government and the states of California, New York, and Texas. The listing is replete with intriguing contrasts; for example, Canada's government budget is smaller than the budget of New York State or Ford Motor Company.

Table 2–1 Twenty-Five Largest Governments and Industrial Corporations in the World by Revenues, 1997 (in Billions of Dollars)

Rank	Governments	Revenues	Industrial Corporations
1.	U.S. Federal Government	1676.8	
2.	Japan	767.3	
3.	Germany	647.6	
4.	France	573.3	
5.	Italy	499.7	
6.	United Kingdom	475.7	
7.	California	209.6	
8.	Netherlands	181.2	
9.		178.2	General Motors
10.	New York State	160.0	
11.	Spain	155.7	
12.		153.7	Ford Motor
13.		142.7	Mitsui
14.	Canada	132.0	
15.		128.9	Mitsubishi
16.		128.1	Royal Dutch/Shell Group
17.		126.6	Itochu
18.		122.4	Exxon
19.		119.3	Wal-Mart Stores
20.		111.1	Marubeni
21.	Texas	103.9	
22.		102.3	Sumitomo
23.		95.1	Toyota Motor
24.	Sweden	94.3	
25.		90.8	General Electric

Source: Data from Compendium of Government Finances, 1997 Census of Governments (Washington, DC: U.S. Government Printing Office, 2002), 22; The World's Largest Corporations, Forbes, 1998, F-1; and Government Finance Statistical Yearbook, (Washington, DC: International Monetary Fund, 2002). Data for Japan are from 1993, which is the most recent year available.

In a list of the top 50 organizations in the United States, 17 state governments are included (see **Table 2–2**). These states, in order of appearance, are California, New York, Texas, Florida, Pennsylvania, Illinois, Ohio, Michigan, New Jersey, Georgia, Washington, North Carolina, Massachusetts, Virginia, Wisconsin, Minnesota, and Maryland. Ranking ahead of eight of these states is New York City.

Table 2-2	Fifty Largest U.S. Organizations by Revenues, 1997 (in Billions of Dollars)

Rank	Organization	Revenue
1.	**U.S. Federal Government**	**1676.8**
2.	**California**	**209.6**
3.	General Motors	178.2
4.	**New York State**	**160.0**
5.	Ford Motor	153.7
6.	Exxon	122.4
7.	Wal-Mart Stores	119.3
8.	**Texas**	**103.9**
9.	General Electric	90.8
10.	International Business Machines	78.5
11.	**Florida**	**76.2**
12.	**Pennsylvania**	**72.3**
13.	**Illinois**	**66.7**
14.	**Ohio**	**66.0**
15.	**Michigan**	**61.8**
16.	Chrysler	61.1
17.	Mobil	60.0
18.	U.S. Postal Service	58.2
19.	Philip Morris	56.1
20.	**New Jersey**	**53.5**
21.	AT&T	53.3
22.	**New York City**	**52.8**
23.	Boeing	45.8
24.	Texaco	45.2
25.	State Farm Insurance	44.0
26.	Hewlett Packard	43.0
27.	E.I. DuPont	41.3
28.	Sears Roebuck	41.3
29.	**Georgia**	**40.0**
30.	**Washington**	**40.0**
31.	**North Carolina**	**39.0**
32.	**Massachusetts**	**38.2**
33.	Travelers Group	37.6
34.	Prudential Insurance	37.1
35.	**Virginia**	**36.7**
36.	Chevron	36.4
37.	Procter and Gamble	35.8

continues

Rank	Organization	Revenue
38.	Citicorp	34.7
39.	**Wisconsin**	**33.6**
40.	**Minnesota**	**33.3**
41.	Amoco	32.8
42.	Kmart	32.2
43.	Merrill Lynch	31.7
44.	**Maryland**	**30.9**
45.	J.C. Penney	30.6
46.	American International Group	30.5
47.	Chase Manhattan Corp.	30.4
48.	Bell Atlantic	30.2
49.	Motorola	29.8
50.	TIAA-Cref	29.3

Note: Governments appear in boldface.

Source: Data from *Compendium of Government Finances*, 1997 Census of Governments (Washington, DC: U.S. Government Printing Office, 2002), 22; and The World's Largest Corporations, *Forbes*, 1998, F-1.

These statistics dramatically underscore the need for caution in generalizing about governments or private corporations. It is necessary to recognize the important differences in the functions of government and industry and the methods by which these organizations make decisions. Differences also abound within each of these two types of organizations. The services provided and methods of decision making are not identical in the governments of Japan, Germany, and the United Kingdom, nor are they the same in such private corporations as General Motors, IBM, and Mitsubishi.

On the other hand, using the standard of size may provide more insights into the operations of organizations than simply classifying organizations as public or private, national or local, and so forth. Not all industrial firms are like General Motors, nor are all state governments like California's, but perhaps all organizations of any given size, regardless of their private or public character, exhibit some common traits.

Although total revenues or expenditures are useful as approximate guides in measuring the size of government, these data need to be assessed in light of the varied capabilities of societies to support government. Unfortunately, reliable international data are often unavailable. As a consequence, drawing useful comparisons among international organizations is difficult.

Even given these limitations, it is obvious that the U.S. economy is one of the most prosperous in the world. The high per capita gross domestic product (GDP) in the United States, $34,950 in 2000, has allowed for both big government and a large private sector. The nation has been able to afford government expenditures equal to about 28 percent of GDP ($9,815 per capita expenditures for the total of all governments in the United States in 2000).[18] This figure, however, is misleading as regards the size of the public sector in that as we noted above only about half of per capita expenditures goes toward the purchase of goods and services — the other half is used for transfer payments and interest payments on debt.

Expenditures

Because early records on state and local finance are spotty, reliance must be placed upon federal expenditure data to obtain some overall perspective of the growth of government since the eighteenth century. **Table 2–3** shows federal spending from 1789 through 2004 (estimated). During this period, expenditures rose from only $4.3 million in the first few years to more than $2 trillion annually (bear in mind that an important contributor to this difference is inflation).

The twentieth century has seen important differences in the expenditure patterns of the federal government and those of state and local governments. Federal

Table 2-3 Federal Government Expenditures, Selected Years, 1789–2004 (in Millions of Dollars)

Year	Expenditures	Year	Expenditures	Year	Expenditures
1789-91	4	1870	310	1945	92,712
1800	11	1875	275	1950	42,562
1805	11	1880	268	1955	68,444
1810	8	1885	260	1960	92,191
1815	33	1890	318	1965	118,228
1820	18	1895	356	1970	195,649
1825	16	1900	529	1975	332,332
1830	15	1905	567	1980	590,947
1835	18	1910	694	1985	946,423
1840	24	1915	746	1990	1,253,198
1845	23	1920	6,358	1995	1,515,837
1850	40	1925	2,924	2000	1,788,826
1855	60	1930	3,320	2002	2,052,320*
1860	63	1935	6,412	2003	2,128,230*
1865	1,298	1940	9,468	2004	2,189,095*

*Estimated.

Source: Data from *Historical Statistics of the United States, Colonial Times–1957* (Washington, DC: U.S. Bureau of the Census, 1960); and Office of Management and Budget, *Budget of the United States Government: Fiscal Year 2003* (Washington, DC: U.S. Government Printing Office, 2002).

expenditures have fluctuated most, primarily because of war-related activities. The first year in which federal expenditures exceeded $1 billion was 1865, the peak year of the Civil War. Later, in response to World War I, federal expenditures jumped from $0.7 billion in 1916 to $18.5 billion in 1919, then dropped to $6.4 billion the following year. They also increased from $13.3 billion in 1941, the year the United States entered into World War II, to $92.7 billion in 1945, then declined to $33.1 billion in 1948. During the Korean War, expenditures rose from $42.6 billion in 1950 to $74.3 billion in 1953, then dropped to $68.4 billion in 1955, after the war. In general, federal expenditures have risen during wartime and then declined, but not to prewar levels, resulting in a cumulative increase over time. The Vietnam War era departed from this pattern: Federal expenditures rose during and after the war. State and local expenditures, on the other hand, have fluctuated less. They have increased annually, except for a period of slight decline during World War II.

Important shifts have occurred in the extent to which the nation relies on different levels of government. At the turn of the century, local governments were by far the biggest spenders, followed by the federal government and then the states. During the Great Depression, federal spending spurted above local expenditures, and the gap has since been widening. As of 1998, federal expenditures stood at $1,652.6 billion compared with $930 billion for states and $885 billion for local governments. Caution should be exercised in interpreting these numbers, in that each includes intergovernmental transfers — namely, grants from one government to another. Total spending for all governments was $3,467.6 billion in 1998.[19]

Just as total expenditures have increased, so have per capita expenditures. In 1902, the total of all government expenditures in the United States was only $20 per capita; in 2000, the comparable figure was $9,815 per capita, an increase of more than 49,000 percent. These data, however, overstate the rising cost of government by not deflating for general price increases.

One means of controlling for price changes over time is to consider government expenditures as a percentage of GDP (**Figure 2–1**). From 1929 to 1996, the cost of government rose from 10 percent to 32 percent of GDP. Increases occurred in the 1930s due to the Great Depression, and then World War II brought expenditures to an all-time high, at about half of GDP. A sharp cutback followed in the postwar years, and expenditures dropped to a low of 19 percent. Since then the percentage has risen gradually, plateaued in the first half of the 1990s, and then fell in the latter half of the 1990s.

Public Employment

The rise of big bureaucracy in the federal government can be measured in terms of numbers of public employees. In 1816, there were fewer than 5,000 full- and part-time civilian employees in the federal service. Following the Civil War, however, greater growth was recorded. In 1871, there were more than 50,000 federal employees, and this number had doubled to 100,000 by 1881. The period of fastest growth was from the Great Depression through World War II. In 1931, there were still only 610,000 employees, but by 1945, the peak of the wartime economy, the federal civilian work force had climbed to nearly 4 million. Within a year, it was reduced to fewer than 3 million employees. Since then, only once, in 1950, has the federal work force dropped below 2 million. Federal civilian personnel averaged approximately 3 million between 1970 and 1995, but decreased to only about 2.8 million by 1999.[20]

Although the size of the federal bureaucracy is extraordinarily large, government personnel are geographically dispersed. In 2000, California had 265,000 federal civilian employees, a figure equal to more than half of Wyoming's population. If these employees were all located in one area, they alone, not counting their families, would form a metropolitan area somewhat larger than Baton Rouge, Louisiana, or Reno, Nevada. Federal employees are also numerous in other states, including Texas, with 175,000; Virginia, with 147,000; and New York, with 139,000.[21] In the 1990s, states such as these became painfully aware of their

Figure 2–1 | **All Government Expenditures as a Percentage of Gross Domestic Product, 1929–2001**

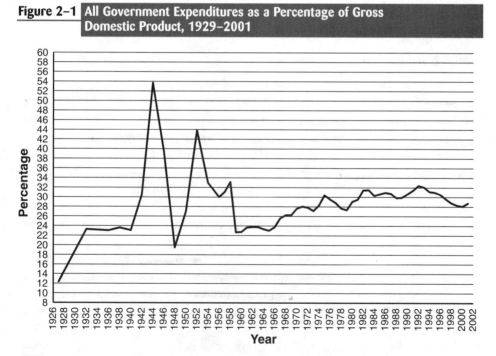

Source: Data from U.S. Bureau of the Census, *Historical Statistics on Governmental Finances and Employment*, 1967 Census of Government, Vol. 6, No. 5 (Washington, DC: U.S. Government Printing Office, 1969), 1, 36–47; and Council of Economic Advisors, *Economic Report of the President*, 2002 (Washington, DC: U.S. Government Printing Office, 2002), 320, 418.

dependence on federal employment as the government began to downsize the military, since about one of every three federal civilian jobs is in defense.

At the state and local levels, the number of employees has also increased. State employment grew from 3.8 million in 1980 to 4.8 million in 1999. In the same period, local employment increased from 9.6 million to 12.7 million.[22] Significantly, the growth at the local level has been accompanied by a decline in the number of local governments. In 2002, there were almost 88,000 local governments, 30,000 fewer than five decades earlier.[23] This decline is largely attributable to school district consolidation. Since 1972, the number of local governments has been increasing gradually, due mainly to increases in the number of special districts — that is, governments that typically provide a single service, such as water provision or recreation services.

Sources of Revenue and Purposes of Government Expenditures

Government does not simply get money and spend it in general. Rather, revenue is obtained from specific sources and spent for specific public goods and services. The following discussion considers the relationships between income and outgo, between the ways in which revenue is generated and the purposes of government expenditures.

Federal Revenues and Expenditures

The federal government obtains revenues from several different sources. By far, the major source of revenue for the federal government is the individual income tax. In fiscal year 2001, 50 percent of all federal revenues came from this source. Social insurance taxes (payroll taxes for Social Security and Medicare) accounted for another 35 percent of the total. Adding in the almost 8 percent contributed by corporate income taxes, these three sources accounted for 93 percent of all federal revenues. This distribution represents a substantial shift from the early 1900s, when customs duties and excise taxes were the major revenue sources. These sources now account for less than 5 percent of total federal revenues. **Table 2–4** shows a summary of federal revenues and expenditures.

There are two types of federal spending: discretionary spending, which is provided for through the annual appropriations process, and mandatory spending, which is provided for through "permanent" law. Discretionary appropriations provide for most of the core functions of government, including the operations of major federal departments. This category accounted for about 35 percent of all federal spending in 2001; about half of this amount went for defense. This represents a substantial decline in the relative importance of discretionary spending over the

Table 2–4 **Federal Revenues and Expenditures, 2001 (in Billions of Dollars)**

Source	Dollars	Percent	Source	Dollars	Percent
Total Receipts	1,991.0	100.0	Total Outlays	1,863.9	100.0
Taxes	1,933.9	97.1	Discretionary	649.3	34.8
Individual Income	994.3	49.9	Defense	306.1	16.4
Corporate Income	151.1	7.6	International	22.5	1.2
Social Insurance	694.0	34.9	Domestic	320.8	17.2
Excise Taxes	66.1	3.3	Mandatory	1,095.2	58.8
Estate and Gift	28.4	1.4	Medicaid	129.4	6.9
Custom and Duties	19.4	1.0	Social Security	429.4	23.0
Miscellaneous	37.8	1.9	Medicare	237.9	12.8
			Unemployment	27.9	1.5
			Other	270.6	14.5
			Net Interest	206.2	11.1
			Offsetting Receipts	-86.8	-4.7

Source: Congressional Budget Office, *The Budget and Economic Outlook: Fiscal Years 2003–2012* (Washington, DC: U.S. Government Printing Office, 2002).

past 40 years. In 1973, 50 percent of expenditures were discretionary, and the figure was 65 percent as recently as 1967.[24]

Mandatory spending (chiefly entitlements) accounted for about 60 percent of federal spending in 2001. The major entitlement (almost 40 percent of the total) is Social Security. The health entitlements (Medicare and Medicaid) make up one-third of all mandatory spending. The expansion of mandatory spending since the mid-1960s (fueled by President Johnson's "Great Society" programs) has increased the proportion of the federal budget devoted to mandatory spending. In 1990, mandatory spending was less than 50 percent of all federal spending. In 1970, the equivalent figure was 35 percent.

The other major category of federal spending is net interest. The federal government's spending on interest has increased and decreased, depending on the federal government's reliance on deficit-financing. In 2001, it was 11 percent of the budget; in 1995, that figure was 15 percent.

State and Local Revenues and Expenditures

Table 2–5 summarizes state and local revenues and expenditures. The first thing to note about state revenues is that more than one-fifth comes from other governments, mostly from the federal government. Of the remainder, sales and gross receipts taxes are the largest revenue sources, providing 21 percent of all state funds. Another 15 percent is obtained from individual income taxes. Not every state taps into each of the varied revenue sources that the states use. Some states have both a sales tax and an individual income tax. Others have only one or the other, with two states (Alaska and New Hampshire) having neither.

Local governments obtain one-third of their money from other governments and the rest mainly through the property tax and other sources. Of all local revenue, 24 percent comes from the property tax. A little less than 30 percent is obtained from charges, miscellaneous general revenue, and utility fees. While some local governments have income and sales taxes, these sources contribute only about 7 percent of all local revenues in aggregate.

State and local expenditures follow different patterns. Some expenditures that are important for the federal government are nonexistent in states and localities. For example, neither the states nor the governments are responsible for

Table 2–5 State and Local Revenues and Expenditures, 1998 (in Millions of Dollars)

Source	State and Local	State		Local	
	Dollars	Dollars	Percent	Dollars	Percent
Revenue	**1,720,889**	**1,103,239**	**100.0**	**909,661**	**100.0**
General Revenue	1,365,762	863,522	78.3	794,250	87.3
Taxes	773,963	473,051	42.9	300,912	33.1
Sales and Gross	274,883	226,643	20.5	48,240	5.3
Motor Vehicle Licenses	16,143	14,919	1.4	1,223	0.1
Individual Income	175,630	160,115	14.5	15,515	1.7
Corporate Income	34,412	31,089	2.8	3,323	0.4
Property	230,150	10,659	1.0	219,492	24.1
Other	42,745	29,626	2.7	13,119	1.4
Charges and Miscellaneous	336,751	149,682	13.6	187,068	20.6
Intergovernmental Revenue	255,048	240,789	21.8	306,270	33.7
Federal	255,048	224,444	20.3	30,604	3.4
State				275,666	30.3
Local		16,345	1.5		
Utility and Liquor Store	81,127	7,687	0.7	73,439	8.1
Insurance Trust	274,001	232,029	21.0	41,972	4.6

continues

Expenditures	1,529,308	929,952	100.0	884,759	100.0
Intergovernmental	3,536	278,853	30.0	10,095	1.1
Direct	1,525,762	651,098	70.0	874,664	98.9
General Expenditures	**1,314,496**	**548,800**	**59.0**	**765,698**	**86.5**
Education	450,365	118,563	12.7	331,802	37.5
Public Welfare	204,640	172,119	18.5	32,521	3.7
Health	44,391	23,130	2.5	21,261	2.4
Hospitals	69,633	28,486	3.1	41,148	4.7
Highways	87,214	51,971	5.6	35,243	4.0
Police Protection	50,475	7,165	0.8	43,310	4.9
Fire Protection	20,269			20,269	2.3
Corrections	42,479	28,679	3.1	13,800	1.6
Parks and Recreation	22,365	3,893	0.4	18,472	2.1
Natural Resources	17,492	12,883	1.4	4,609	0.5
Housing and Community Dev.	24,697	2,414	0.3	22,284	2.5
Sewerage	25,647	1,132	0.1	24,515	2.8
Solid Waste Management	16,118	1,988	0.2	14,130	1.6
Government Administration	70,727	29,692	3.3	41,035	4.6
Interest on Debt	64,554	26,776	2.9	37,778	4.3
Other	103,430	39,909	4.3	63,521	7.2
Utility	99,519	8,365	0.9	91,154	10.3
Liquor Store	3,346	2,820	0.3	526	0.1
Insurance Trust	108,400	91,113	9.8	17,287	2.0

Source: U.S. Bureau of the Census, *Statistical Abstract of the United States*, 2001 (Washington, DC: U.S. Government Printing Office, 2001) Tables 425,428, 436, and 439.

defense, postal service, or space exploration. When looking at direct expenditures (that is, expenditures that are actually made directly by the government, as opposed to assistance provided to some other level), public welfare is the largest expense for states, with education spending (primarily for higher education) ranked second. Other significant areas of state expenditure include social insurance, highways, and corrections.

Education spending is by far the largest category of local expenditures. The 37.5 percent spent on education is more than three times the percentage that is devoted to the second-ranked category, utility expenditure. Other significant areas of expenditure include public safety (police and fire) and hospitals.

Issues of relative contribution are clarified in **Table 2–6**, which displays federal, state, and local expenditures as percentage contributions to functional areas. This table shows that while one level of government is dominant in some functional areas (for example, the federal government spends all of the money for

national defense and space exploration, and most of the money for income security and Medicare), in other cases substantial sharing of responsibilities among
levels takes place. Transportation spending is substantially shared among the
three levels, whereas education spending is predominantly a state and local
responsibility.

Table 2-6 | **Direct Expenditures by Level of Government for Selected Functional Areas, 1998**

	Total	Federal	State	Local
	(Billions of Dollars)	Percent of Total Program		
National Defense and International Affairs	281.6	100		
General Science, Space, Technology, and Energy	19.5	100		
Natural Resources, Environment, and Agriculture	74.3	46	23	31
Transportation	127.5	32	41	28
Housing and Community Development	35.5	30	7	63
Education and Training	505.4	11	23	66
Health	245.4	54	21	25
Income, Social Security, and Medicare	1,009.8	80	17	3
Justice	136.1	17	26	57
General Government	86.4	18	34	47
Interest on Debt	305.8	79	9	12
Utility	99.5		8	92
Liquor Stores	3.3		85	15

Source: U.S. Bureau of the Census, *Statistical Abstract of the United States, 2001* (Washington, DC: U.S. Government Printing Office, 2001) Tables 425,439, 440, and 463.

 Summary

Government is indeed large. The growth pattern of the public sector has been an
upward one, and today drawing a definitive line between the public and private
sectors is virtually impossible. If present trends continue, government can be
expected to become even larger, albeit at a slower rate, providing more services
directly or ensuring the provision of services by regulating the private sector.

Governments in the United States differ in the types of revenue sources used
and the functions for which revenues are expended. The federal government
relies primarily on personal and corporate income taxes and social insurance

deductions; expenditures are concentrated in defense, international relations, and social insurance. States obtain one-fifth of their revenue from the federal government and the remainder largely from sales and individual income taxes; state expenditures are concentrated in education, social services, and welfare. Local governments receive one-third of their funds from other governments and one-fourth from property taxes; the most expensive function of local government is education.

Notes

1. S.H. Beer, *To Make a Nation: The Rediscovery of American Federalism* (Cambridge, MA: Belknap Press, 1993); L.D. White, *The Federalists: A Study in Administrative History, 1789–1801* (New York: Free Press, 1948).

2. M. Friedman and R. Friedman, *Freedom to Choose* (New York: Harcourt Brace Jovanovich, 1980); F.A. Hayek, *The Road to Serfdom* (Chicago: University of Chicago Press, 1945); P. Drucker and H. Finer, *The Road to Reaction* (Boston: Little, Brown, 1945).

3. J.K. Galbraith, *Economics and the Public Purpose* (Boston: Houghton Mifflin, 1973).

4. R.A. Musgrave and P.B. Musgrave, *Public Finance in Theory and Practice*, 5th ed. (New York: McGraw–Hill, 1989); D.N. Hyman, *Public Finance: A Contemporary Application of Theory to Policy*, 5th ed. (Orlando, FL: Dryden Press, 1996).

5. S. Abizadeli and A. Basilevsky, Measuring the Size of Government, *Public Finance* 45 (1990): 359–377.

6. W.D. Berry and D. Lowery, Explaining the Size of the Public Sector, *Journal of Politics* 49 (1987): 401–440; P.D. Larkey et al., Theorizing About the Growth of Government, *Journal of Public Policy* 1 (1981): 157–220.

7. R. Bird, Wagner's Law of Expanding State Activity, *Public Finance* 26 (1971): 1–26; J.M. Buchanan and G. Tullock, The Expanding Public Sector: Wagner Squared, *Public Choice* 31 (Fall 1977): 147–150.

8. M. Beck, *Government Spending: Trends and Issues* (New York: Praeger, 1981); M.S. Lewis–Beck and T.W. Rice, Government Growth in the United States, *Journal of Politics* 47 (1985): 2–30.

9. D.R. Mullins and P.G. Joyce, Tax and Expenditure Limitations and State and Local Fiscal Structure: An Empirical Assessment, *Public Budgeting & Finance* 16 (Spring 1996), 75–101.

10. N.W. Polsby, *Presidential Elections*, 10th ed. (New York: Chatham House, 2000).

11. U.S. Bureau of the Census, *Statistical Abstract of the United States: 2001* (Washington, DC: U.S. Government Printing Office, 2001), 319, 332, 367.

12. U.S. Bureau of the Census, *Statistical Abstract of the United States: 2001*, 326.

13. U.S. Bureau of the Census, *Consolidated Federal Funds Report* (Washington, DC: U.S. Government Printing Office, 2002), 23.

14. U.S. Bureau of the Census, *Consolidated Federal Funds Report*, 8.

15. For an articulation of this argument, see P. C. Light, *The True Size of Government* (Washington, DC: Brookings Insitution, 1999).

16. *Zelman v. Simmons–Harris*, 122 S.Ct. 2460 (2002).

17. The idea of comparing private and public organizations was suggested by Robert J. Mowitz, then Director, Institute of Public Administration, Pennsylvania State University.

18. Council of Economic Advisers, *Economic Report of the President* (Washington, DC: U.S. Government Printing Office, 2002), 320, 357, 410.

19. U.S. Bureau of the Census, *Statistical Abstract of the United States: 2001*, 268, 307.

20. U.S. Bureau of the Census, *Statistical Abstract of the United States: 2001*, 320.

21. U.S. Bureau of the Census, *Statistical Abstract of the United States: 2001*, 321.

22. U.S. Bureau of the Census, *Statistical Abstract of the United States: 2001*, 294.

23. U.S. Bureau of the Census, *Census of Governments: 2002, http://www.census/gov/govs/2002COGprelim_report.pdg*; U.S. Bureau of the Census, *Statistical Abstract of the United States*, 2001, 258.

24. Congressional Budget Office, *The Budget and Economic Outlook: Fiscal Years 2003–2012* (Washington, DC: U.S. Government Printing Office, 2002), 162.

Chapter 3

BUDGET CYCLES

Public budgeting systems, which are devices for selecting societal ends and means, consist of numerous participants and various processes that bring the participants into interaction. As described in preceding chapters, the purpose of budgeting is to allocate scarce resources among competing public demands so as to attain societal goals and objectives. Those societal ends are expressed not by philosopher kings but by mortals who must operate within the context of some prescribed allocation process — namely, the budgetary system.

This chapter provides an overview of the participants and processes involved in budgetary decision making. First, the phases of the budget cycle are reviewed. Any system has some structure or form, and budgetary systems are no exception. As will be seen, the decision-making process has several steps; detailed discussions of these steps are presented in subsequent chapters. The second topic is the extent to which budget cycles are intermingled within government and among governments.

The Budget Cycle

To provide for responsible government, budgeting is geared to a cycle. The cycle allows the system to absorb and respond to new information and, therefore, allows government to be held accountable for its actions. Although existing budget systems may be less than perfect in guaranteeing adherence to this principle of responsibility, the argument stands that periodicity contributes to achieving and maintaining limited government. The budget cycle consists of four phases: (1) preparation and submission, (2) approval, (3) execution, and (4) audit and evaluation.

Preparation and Submission

The preparation and submission phase is the most difficult to describe because it has been subjected to the most reform efforts. Experiments in reformulating the preparation process abound. Although institutional units may exist over time, both procedures and substantive content vary from year to year.

Chief Executive Responsibilities. The responsibility for budget preparation varies greatly among jurisdictions. Budget reform efforts in the United States have pressed for executive budgeting, in which the chief executive has exclusive responsibility for preparing a proposed budget and submitting it to the legislative body. At the federal level, the president has such exclusive responsibility, although many factors curtail the extent to which the president can make major changes in the budget. Preparation authority, however, is not always available to governors and local chief executives. While a majority of governors have responsibility for preparation and submission, some share budget-making authority with other elected administrative officers, civil service appointees, legislative leaders, or some combination of these parties. In parliamentary systems, the prime minister (chief executive) typically has responsibility for budget preparation and submits what is usually called the "government budget" to the parliament.

At the municipal level, the mayor may or may not have budget preparation powers. In cities where the mayor is strong — has administrative control over the executive branch — the mayor normally does have budget-making power. This is not necessarily the case in weak-mayor systems and in cities operating under the commission plan, where each councilor or commissioner administers a given department. Usually, city managers in council-manager systems have responsibility for budget preparation, although their ability to make budgetary recommendations may be tempered by their lack of independence. Managers are appointed by councils and commonly lack tenure. Even in a city in which the mayor or chief executive does not have budget preparation responsibility, this duty is still likely to be in the hands of an executive official such as a city finance director. Thus, a majority of cities follow the principle of executive budget preparation.[1]

Location of Budget Office. Budget preparation at the federal level is primarily a function of a budget office that was established by the Budget and Accounting Act of 1921.[2] That legislation established the Bureau of the Budget (BOB), which became a unit of the Treasury Department. With the passage of time, the role of the BOB increased in importance. In 1939, it became part of the newly formed Executive Office of the President. Given that the BOB was thought to be the "right arm of the president" — a common phrase in early budget literature — the move out of the Treasury, a line department, into the Executive Office of the President placed the BOB under direct presidential supervision. In 1970, President Nixon reorganized the BOB, giving it a new title, the Office of Management and Budget (OMB). The intent of the reorganization was to bring "real business management into Government at the very highest level."[3]

Steps in the Preparation Stage. In the federal government, budget preparation starts in the spring, or even earlier for large agencies. Agencies begin by assessing their programs and considering which programs require revision and whether new programs should be recommended. At approximately the same time, the president's staff makes estimates of anticipated economic trends to determine available revenue under existing tax legislation. The next step is for the president to issue general budget and fiscal policy guidelines, which agencies use to develop their individual budgets. These budgets are then submitted in late summer to the OMB. Throughout the fall and into the later months of the year, OMB staff members review agency requests and hold hearings with agency spokespersons. Not until shortly before the budget is to be released, usually in November and December and into January, does the president become deeply involved in the process. It culminates in February with the submission of a proposed budget to Congress.

At the state and local levels, a similar process is used where executive budgeting systems prevail. The central budget office issues budget request instructions, reviews the submitted requests, and makes recommendations to the chief executive, who decides which items to recommend to the legislative body. In jurisdictions not using executive budgeting, the chief executive and the budget office play minor roles; in this type of system, the line agencies direct their budget requests to the legislative body.

Political Factors. The preparation phase, as well as the other three phases in the budget cycle, is replete with political considerations, both bureaucratic and partisan, in addition to policy considerations. Each organizational unit is concerned with its own survival and advancement. Line agencies and their subunits attempt to protect against budget cuts and may strive for increased resources. Budget offices often play negative roles, attempting to limit agency growth or imposing agency budget cuts. Budget offices always are fully conscious of the fact that whatever they propose can be overruled by the chief executive. All members of the executive branch are concerned with their relationships with the legislative branch and the general citizenry. The chief executive is especially concerned about partisan calculations: Which alternatives will be advantageous to his or her political party? Of course, there is concern for developing programs for the common good, but this concern plays out in a complicated game of political maneuvering.[4]

Fragmentation. One complaint about the preparation phase is that it tends to be highly fragmented. Organizational units within line agencies tend to be concerned primarily with their own programs and frequently fail to take a broad perspective. Even the budget office may be myopic, although it will be forced into considering the budget as a whole. Only the chief executive is unquestionably committed to viewing the budget in its entirety in the preparation phase.

Approval

Revenue and Appropriation Bills. The budget is approved by a legislative body, whether Congress, a state legislature, a county board of supervisors, a city council, or a school board. The legislature reviews the executive's budget recommendations and often has access to the original agency budget requests, which enables it to make comparisons. Congress is normally not privy to original budget requests, although ways are often found to obtain this information, such as questions being put to agency representatives in committee hearings. The fragmented approach to budgeting in the preparation phase is not characteristic of the approval phase at the local level. A city council may have a separate finance committee, but normally the council as a whole participates actively in the approval process. Local legislative bodies may take several preliminary votes on pieces of the budget but then adopt the budget as a whole by a single vote.

States, in contrast, separate tax and other revenue measures from appropriations or spending bills. Some states place most or all of their spending provisions in a single appropriation bill, whereas others create hundreds of appropriation bills. Most state legislatures are free to augment or reduce the governor's budget, but some are restricted in their ability to increase the budget. Likewise, many parliamentary systems allow the parliament to modify — but not increase — the government's budget proposal.

At the federal level, the revenue and appropriation processes have been markedly fragmented and involve numerous committees and subcommittees. Not only have revenue raising and spending been treated as separate processes, but the expenditure side is handled in 13 major appropriation bills instead of being treated as a whole. Reforms introduced in 1974 attempted to integrate these divergent processes and pieces of legislation, but the system had numerous flaws.[5] Chapter 9 discusses in detail efforts at reforming the congressional budget process.

The legislature holds a series of hearings at which the central budget office and the individual agencies testify. These hearings can be lovefests in which the committees that oversee agencies are eager to recommend increased appropriations for the agencies' programs. Conversely, tensions are common in such hearings.

An executive may emphasize the need to restrain expenses, while legislators may seek expansion of various programs and corresponding increases in expenditures. Tensions were particularly high between Congress and President George W. Bush's budget director, Mitchell Daniels.[6]

In both the preparation and the approval phases, one or two issues often dominate budget deliberations. If a state government is projecting a major decline in revenues due to the economy going south, closing the gap between low revenues and higher expenditures will be a major concern. At the federal level, wrestling with a huge budget deficit was a primary focus in budgeting from the 1980s until the mid-1990s. Since September 11, 2001, when terrorists attacked the World Trade Center in New York City and the Pentagon outside of Washington, D.C., both the president and Congress have been deeply concerned with fighting the war against terrorism on a global scale and increasing domestic security. Proposals to fight terrorism and defend the homeland, then, are far more likely to be funded than other unrelated proposals.

Executive Veto Powers. The final step of the approval stage is signing the appropriation and tax bills into law. The president, governors, and, in some cases, mayors have the power to veto. A veto sends the measure back to the legislative body for further consideration. Most governors have item-veto power, which allows them to veto specific portions of an appropriation bill but still sign it.[7] In no case can the executive augment parts of the budget beyond that provided by the legislature. The president was given a form of item veto that took effect in 1997, but it was invalidated by the Supreme Court the following year (see Chapter 9).

Execution

Apportionment Process. Execution, the third phase, commences with the beginning of the fiscal year — October 1 for the federal government and July 1 for most state governments. Some form of centralized control during this phase is common at all levels of government, and such control is usually maintained by the budget office. Following congressional passage of an appropriation bill and its signing by the president, agencies must submit to the OMB a proposed plan for apportionment. This plan indicates the funds required for operations, typically on a quarterly basis. The apportionment process is used in part to ensure that agencies do not commit all their available funds in a period shorter than the 12-month fiscal year. The intent is to avoid the need for supplementary appropriations from Congress.

The apportionment process is substantively important in that program adjustments must be made to bring planned spending into balance with available revenue. Because an agency most likely did not obtain all the funds requested, either from the president in the preparation phase or from Congress in the approval phase, plans for the coming fiscal year must be revised. To varying degrees, state and local governments also use an apportionment process.

Impoundment. The chief executive may assert control in the apportionment process through an informal item veto known as "impoundment," which is basically a refusal to release some funds to agencies. Thomas Jefferson often is considered the first president to have impounded funds. President Nixon impounded so extensively that it stimulated legislative action by Congress. The 1974 legislation in a sense was a treaty between Congress and the White House allowing limited impoundment powers for the president. As will be discussed later, the Supreme Court largely negated the agreed-upon procedures.

Allotments. Once funds are apportioned, agencies and departments make allotments. This process grants budgetary authority to subunits such as bureaus and divisions. Allotments are made on a monthly or quarterly basis, and, like the apportionment process, the allotment process is used to control spending over the course of the fiscal year. Control often may be extensive and detailed, requiring approval by the department budget office for any shift in available funds from one item to another, such as from travel to wages. Some transfers may require clearance by the central budget office.

Preaudits. Before an expenditure is made, a form of preaudit is conducted. Basically, the preaudit ensures that funds are committed only for approved purposes and that an agency has sufficient resources in its budget to meet the proposed expenditure. The responsibility for this function varies widely, with the budget and/or accounting office being responsible for it in some jurisdictions and independently elected comptrollers being responsible for it in others. Later, after approval is granted and a purchase is made, the treasurer writes a check for the expenditure.

Execution Subsystems. During budget execution, several subsystems are in operation. Taxes and other debts to government are collected. Cash is managed in the sense that monies temporarily not needed are invested. Supplies, materials, and equipment are procured, and strategies are developed to protect the government against loss or damage of property and against liability suits. Accounting and information systems are in operation. For state and local governments, bonds are sold and the proceeds are used to finance construction of facilities and the acquisition of major equipment. An office of federal management, independent of the budget office, has been proposed that would assume many duties, including setting procurement policy, conducting regulatory reviews, overseeing financial management systems, and controlling agency-operated grant programs that allocate funds to state and local governments.

Audit and Evaluation

The final phase of the budgetary process is audit and evaluation. The objectives of this phase are undergoing considerable change, but initially the main goal was to guarantee executive compliance with the provisions of appropriation bills — particularly to ensure honesty in dispensing public monies and to prevent needless waste. In accord with this goal, accounting procedures are prescribed and auditors check the books maintained by agency personnel. In recent years, the scope of auditing has been broadened to encompass studies of the effectiveness of government programs.

Location of the Audit Function. In the federal government, considerable controversy was generated concerning the appropriate organizational location of the audit function. In 1920, President Woodrow Wilson vetoed legislation that would have established the federal budget system on the grounds that he opposed the creation of an auditing office answerable to Congress rather than to the president. Nevertheless, the General Accounting Office (GAO) was established in 1921 by the Budget and Accounting Act and made an arm of Congress, with the justification being that an audit unit outside of the executive branch should be created to provide objective assessments of expenditure practices.

GAO Functions. The GAO is headed by the comptroller general, who is appointed by the president, upon the advice and consent of the Senate, for only one term of 15 years.[8] Despite the GAO's title, the organization does not maintain accounts, but rather audits the accounts of operating agencies and evaluates their accounting systems.

The GAO provides a variety of legal services. It gives Congress opinions on legal issues, such as advising on whether a particular agency acted within the law in some specific instance under consideration. It also resolves bid protests over the awarding of government contracts.

The GAO has been given responsibility for assessing the results of government programs in addition to its traditional responsibility for performing financial audits.[9] Comptroller General David Walker has said that the GAO's "activities [are] designed to determine what programs and policies work and which ones don't. This also involves sharing various best practices and benchmarking information. It means looking horizontally across the silos of government and vertically between the levels of government."[10] This responsibility for evaluating government programs has sometimes led to criticism of the GAO. In particular, some members of Congress have claimed that the office has lost its neutrality and become a policy advocate.

In 2002, the General Accounting Office engaged in a historical conflict with the White House. President George W. Bush had created the National Energy

Policy Development Group (NEPDG) to recommend a new energy policy for the government. Vice President Dick Cheney chaired the group. After the group completed its work, the GAO asked to see important records. Of particular concern was which companies and individuals from industry had supplied advice. The energy giant, Enron, had collapsed, leaving many stockholders with huge losses and company employees without retirement benefits. Some suspected that Enron, which had close ties to President Bush before he left Texas for Washington, had exerted undue influence on the design of the energy policy. The White House refused to release the requested documents, which prompted the GAO to file suit in U.S. district court against Vice President Cheney and the NEPDG.[11] This move marked the GAO's first suit in its history against a high-ranking government official. The GAO contended that taxpayers' dollars were used by the group, and consequently the GAO had a right to know how those dollars were spent. The White House's position was that it had a right to obtain information and advice on a confidential basis and should not be required to release the documents. A U.S. district court ruled that the comptroller general had not been harmed by the withholding of information and therefore lacked standing, namely the right to bring suit.[12] The GAO decided not to appeal the ruling.

State and Local Auditors. At the state and local levels, the issue of organizational responsibility for auditing has been resolved in different ways. The alternatives are to have the audit function performed by a unit answerable to the legislative body, to the chief executive, to the citizenry directly, or to some combination of these. The use of an elected auditor is defended on the grounds that objectivity can be achieved if the auditor is independent of the executive and legislative branches. The opposing arguments are that the electorate cannot suitably judge the qualifications of candidates for auditor and that the election process necessarily forces the auditor to become a biased rather than an objective analyst. States primarily use elected and legislative auditors.

Scrambled Budget Cycles

Although it is easy to speak of a budget cycle, no single such cycle actually exists. Instead, a cycle exists for each budget period, and several cycles are in operation at any given time. The decision-making process is not one that simply moves from preparation and submission to approval, execution, and, finally, audit. Decision making is complicated by the existence of several budget cycles for which information is imperfect and incomplete.

Overlapping Cycles

A pattern of overlapping cycles can be seen in **Figure 3–1**, which shows the sequencing of five budget cycles typical of a large state. Only cycle 3 in the diagram displays the complete period covering 39 months. The preparation and submission phase requires at least nine months, approval six months, execution 12 months, and audit 12 months. The same general pattern is found at the federal level, except that the execution phase begins on October 1, giving Congress approximately eight months to consider the budget. As indicated by the diagram, three or four budget periods are likely to be in progress at any point in time.

Budget preparation is complicated particularly by this scrambling or intermingling of cycles. In the first place, preparation begins perhaps 15 months before the budget is to go into effect. Moreover, much of the preparation phase is completed without knowledge of the legislature's actions in the preceding budget period.

Federal Experience. At the federal level, this problem has proved especially thorny. Congress has historically been slow to pass appropriation bills, and the approval phase was rarely completed by the start of the fiscal year when it began July 1. The usual procedure was to pass a continuation bill permitting agencies to spend at the rate of the previous year's budget while Congress continued to deliberate on the new year's budget. Although the budget calendar adopted in the 1970s gave Congress an additional three months, which was expected to permit completion of the approval phase, agencies' preparation problems for the following year's budget request persisted. In any given year, an agency begins to prepare its budget request during the spring and summer, even as Congress deliberates on the agency's upcoming budget. Despite the additional time granted to Congress to act on the budget, work on the budget generally has not been completed on schedule, which compounds the problem of scrambled budget cycles.

Figure 3–1 Scrambled Budget Cycles

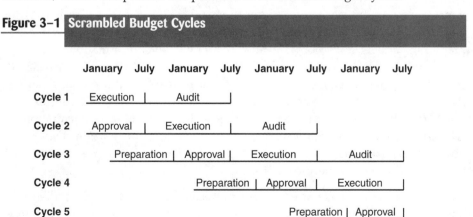

Links Between Budget Phases. While a budget is being prepared, another one is being executed; this budget may be for the immediately preceding budget year, but it can be for the one before. As can be seen in **Figure 3–1**, in the early stages of preparation for cycle 4 the execution phase is in operation for cycle 2. Under such conditions, the executive branch may not know the effects of ongoing programs but is nevertheless required to begin a new budget, recommending changes upward or downward. Sometimes a new program may be created, and an agency must then recommend changes in the program for inclusion in the next budget without any opporunity for assessing its merits.

Length of Preparation Phase. The cycle, particularly the preparation phase, may be even longer than indicated above, especially when agencies must rely upon other agencies or subunits for information. For example, in preparing the education component of a state budget, a department of education will require budget information and requests from state universities and colleges early to meet deadlines imposed by the governor's budget office. The reliability and validity of data undoubtedly decrease as the lead time increases. Therefore, the earlier these schools submit their budget requests to the state capital, the less likely it is that such requests will be based on accurate assessments of future requirements.

Other Considerations

Besides the factors already mentioned, other issues further complicate budget cycles — most notably, intergovernmental considerations and the timing of budget years.

Intergovernmental Factors. Another problem arises from intermingled budget cycles because the three main levels of government are interdependent. For the federal government, the main problem is assessing needs and finding resources to meet these needs. A state government must assess its needs and those of local governments and must then search for funds by raising state taxes, providing for new forms of taxation by local governments, or obtaining federal revenues. In preparing budgets, governors take into account whatever information is available on the likelihood of certain actions by the president and Congress. For instance, the president may have recommended a major increase in educational programs that would significantly increase funds flowing to the states, but considerable doubt might exist as to whether Congress will accept the recommendation. In such a case, how should a governor shape the education portion of the state budget? The problem is even worse at the local level, which is dependent on both the state and federal governments for funds.

Budget Years. Budget cycles are further complicated by a lack of uniformity in the budget period. Although most state governments have budget years beginning

July 1, four states do not: New York's begins April 1; Texas's begins September 1; and Alabama's and Michigan's begin the same day as the federal fiscal year — October 1. Consistency does not even exist within each state. It is common for a state to begin its fiscal year on July 1 but to have to deal with local governments operating with different start dates, such as January 1, April 1, or September 1.

A case can be made for staggering the budget year for different levels of government; this practice might assist decision makers at one level by providing information about action taken at other levels. For example, the federal government might complete action on its budget by October 1; states could then begin a budget year on the following April 1 and local governments on July 1. Under such an arrangement, states could base their budgetary decisions on knowledge of available financial support from Washington. Local governments, in turn, would know the aid available from both Washington and the state capital.

Rearranging the dates for fiscal years is no panacea, however. Information about financial support from other governments is only one of many items used in decision making. Also, any slippage by the legislature in completing its appropriations work by the time a fiscal year begins would void the advantages of staggered budget cycles. In addition, there is no direct translation from appropriations to aid to other governments. Money does not automatically flow to states and communities as soon as an appropriation bill is passed by Congress. Instead, state and local governments must apply for assistance, a process that typically requires many months.

Annual and Biennial Budgets. Not only is there inconsistency in the date on which budget years begin, but the length of the budget period also varies. Whereas the federal government and most local governments operate under annual budgets, 20 states have biennial (two-year) budgets.[13] Under these systems, a governor typically submits the budget in January, and legislative action is supposed to be completed by June 30. The execution phase runs for 24 months beginning July 1. Such a system violates the once-standard principle of annuality.[14] The argument is that annual budgets allow for careful and frequent supervision of the executive by the legislature and that this approach serves to guarantee responsibility in government. The problem with the annual budget, however, is that little breathing time is available; both the executive and legislative branches are continuously in the throes of budgeting. The biennial approach, on the other hand, relieves participants of many routine budget matters and may allow greater time for more thorough analysis of government activities.

The 1993 National Performance Review, conducted by Vice President Al Gore, recommended that the federal government adopt biennial budgeting as a means of eliminating "an enormous amount of busy work."[15] The idea continues to hold interest for some reformers.[16] In 2001, the House Rules Committee recommended passage of a biennial-budget bill.[17] The Bush administration endorsed it, but members of the House Appropriations Committee strongly opposed the measure. The Senate took no action.

One of the greatest dangers of a biennial system is that it may obstruct — if not prohibit — a prompt response to new conditions. The costs of not being able to adjust to changing conditions may far outweigh any benefits accruing from time saved. This consideration may explain why most of the more populous states are on annual budget systems and why many states with biennial budgets make provision for "reopening" the two-year budget at midpoint.

Still another consideration is whether under "normal" conditions sufficient amounts of new information become available to warrant annual systems. If program analysis were a well-established part of the budgetary process, then conceivably new insights into the operation of programs would continually occur; in such instances, an annual process might be preferable. In other cases, in which decision makers operate one year with virtually the same information as was available the preceding year, there seems to be little need for annual budgets. Partially for this reason, proposals have been made for selectively abandoning the annual budget cycle. Under such a system, new programs or proposed changes in existing programs would be submitted in any given year for legislative review, whereas continuing programs would be reviewed only periodically.

Summary

The four phases of the budget cycle are preparation and submission, approval, execution, and audit and evaluation. In general, the first and third phases are the responsibility of the executive branch, and the second is controlled by the legislative branch. The fourth phase in the federal system is directed by the GAO, which is answerable to Congress and not the president. Auditing at the state and local levels often is the responsibility of independently elected officials.

A standard criticism of budgeting, especially at the federal level, is that the budget is seldom considered in its entirety during its preparation phase. Within the executive branch, only the president and his or her immediate staff view the budget as a whole; agencies are primarily concerned only with their own portions of the total. The same disjointed approach has been characteristic of the approval phase at the federal level.

Budget cycles are intermingled. As many as four budget cycles may be in operation at any time in a single government. This phenomenon complicates decision making; for example, budget preparation often is forced to proceed without knowledge as to what action the legislature will take on the previous year's budget. Moreover, the interdependent nature of the three levels of government contributes to a scrambling of cycles. One possibility would be conversion to biennial budgets, a practice that is common at the state level.

Notes

1. G. Michel, The Organizational Structure of City Finance Offices, *Government Finance Review* 16 (June 2000): 21–25.

2. *Budget and Accounting Act*, Ch.18, 42 Stat. 20 (1921).

3. R.M. Nixon, as quoted in the *New York Times*, June 11, 1970; C.G. Dawes, *The First Year of the Budget of the United States* (New York: Harper and Brothers, 1923).

4. A. Wildavsky and N. Caiden, *The New Politics of the Budgetary Process*, 4th ed. (New York: Longman, 2001).

5. *Congressional Budget and Impoundment Control Act*, P.L. 93–344 (1974).

6. D. Baumann, OMB Director Tries to Repair Damaged Relationship with Lawmakers, *Government Executive* (November 30, 2000), *http://www.govexec.com*.

7. Council of State Governments, *Book of the States*, 2000–2001 Edition (Lexington, KY: Council of State Governments, 2000), 260; R.D. Lee, Jr., State Item–Veto Legal Issues in the 1990s, *Public Budgeting & Finance* 20 (Summer 2000): 49–73.

8. General Accounting Office, *http://www.gao.gov*; accessed June 2002.

9. H.S. Havens for the U.S. General Accounting Office, *The Evolution of the General Accounting Office: From Voucher Audits to Program Evaluations* (Washington, DC: U.S. Government Printing Office, 1990).

10. D.M. Walker, *The Role of GAO and Other Government Auditors in the 21st Century*, speech before the 14th Biennial Forum of Government Auditors, Providence, RI, 2002, *http://www.gao.gov*; accessed June 2002.

11. U.S. General Accounting Office, *Decision of the Comptroller General Concerning NEPDG Litigation* (January 30, 2002), *http://www.gao.gov*; accessed June 2002.

12. *Walker v. Cheney*, 230 F. Supp. 2d 51 (D.D.C. 2002).

13. Council of State Governments, *Book of the States*, 255; U.S. General Accounting Office, *Biennial Budgeting: Three States' Experience* (Washington, DC: U.S. Government Printing Office, 2000).

14. J.W. Sundelson, Budgetary Principles, *Political Science Quarterly* 50 (1935): 236–263.

15. National Performance Review, *From Red Tape to Results: Creating a Government That Works Better and Costs Less* (Washington, DC: U.S. Government Printing Office, 1993), 17.

16. U.S. General Accounting Office, *Budget Process: Biennial Budgeting for the Federal Government* (Washington, DC: U.S. Government Printing Office, 2000).

17. H.R. 981, proposed Budget Responsibility and Efficiency Act (2001); B. Ghent, House Rules Committee Votes for Two-Year Budgeting, *Government Executive* (November 2, 2001), *http://www.govexec.com*; accessed November 2001.

Chapter 4

BUDGET PREPARATION: THE REVENUE SIDE

This chapter and the next two describe the budget preparation process. We draw attention first to revenues, then to expenditures, and last to the politics of budget preparation. Our discussion begins with the revenue side. Historically, taxation has been a fundamental concern of the citizenry. Citizens may be less concerned about how government spends its money than about how that money is raised to support programs. The property tax bill, federal income tax filing, and the water bill are more visible events than most of the services citizens receive. In developing a budget package, political leaders are always mindful that program initiatives leading to higher expenditures and, therefore, to higher taxes may have negative effects on the possibility of winning re-election to their offices.

This chapter includes two sections. The first and longer section details various revenue sources; tax equity, tax efficiency, and tax expenditure issues are included in this discussion. The second section considers special concerns about taxation; the discussion concentrates on taxing limitations and revenue estimation.

Revenue Sources

As mentioned in Chapter 2, governments use myriad revenue sources to support their operations, with taxes usually being the most important. In this section, we consider some of the overall concerns about revenue sources and then examine specific sources. Overall concerns focus on the fairness and the efficiency of the tax system. In the discussion of taxes, we deal with three types of tax bases: income, wealth, and consumption. Taxes on income apply to the various types of

income earned during the defined tax period. Taxes on wealth apply to accumulated value regardless of the time period. Real property is considered wealth, for
example. Consumption taxes apply to purchasing transactions, such as retail
sales. We then turn to nontax sources of revenue.

Tax Equity, Tax Efficiency, and Tax Expenditures

Besides the obvious concern that a tax source generate whatever is considered an
adequate amount of revenue, the chief concerns about the tax system are that it
treat taxpayers equitably or fairly and that it achieve revenue objectives efficiently.[1] Fairness as perceived by the taxpayer is a critical element in securing compliance with tax laws and ensuring citizens' general sense of satisfaction with the
political system.[2] One sense of equity relates to the *ability to pay* principle. A tax
should be related to the taxpayer's income or wealth or, more generally, to the
taxpayer's ability to pay the tax. A taxpayer who can afford to pay more should
pay more. Some consider that equitable.

The equity principle is independent of whatever value the taxpayer may
receive, or perceive, from government services. An important facet of efficiency
relates to the second criterion — the *benefit* principle. Payment for public services
or goods should be related to the value of the benefits received from those services. The tax system can be more or less equitable and more or less efficient, not
only in terms of what and how taxpayers have to pay, but also in terms of what
taxpayers do not have to pay. *Tax expenditures*, tax exemptions, and taxes not collected all can have a major impact on equity and efficiency.

Ability to Pay. This principle implies that a tax imposes the same loss of utility for
each taxpayer, or as economists refer to it, the *equal absolute sacrifice*.[3] Equity has
both horizontal and vertical dimensions. *Horizontal equity* refers to charging the
same amount to different taxpayers whose ability to pay (usually measured by
income levels) is the same. *Vertical equity* refers to the principle of charging differently those with different income levels or ability to pay. Confusion immediately develops over whether it is fair for all taxpayers to pay equal absolute
amounts, to pay an equal proportion of their incomes, or to pay according to their
ability to pay.

A tax or other revenue source can be *regressive, progressive*, or *proportional*. In
the last instance, all taxpayers pay the same percentage, such as a 5 percent state
tax on personal income. A progressive tax charges a higher percentage to wealthier taxpayers than to poorer ones, whereas a regressive tax does the opposite. A
tax may seem proportional when it is, in fact, regressive. A sales tax on purchases seems to treat all taxpayers equally but is often actually regressive in that poorer families may spend a greater proportion of their incomes on taxed items than

wealthier families do. Overall, the entire U.S. system of revenue has fallen in a range from slightly progressive to proportional.[4] The revenue system cannot be judged independently of certain government programs. Transfer payments, such as various forms of aid to poor families, are somewhat like "negative" taxes in their effect and increase the progressivity of the tax and transfer system considered together. A Congressional Budget Office study of the incidence of federal taxes — individual income, social insurance, corporate income, and excise taxes — found that the overall result of tax law changes in the 1980s and 1990s was to increase the proportion of household income paid in federal taxes for the highest-income families and to reduce the proportion paid in federal taxes for the lowest-income families. Thus, the total federal tax system became more progressive. In 1979, the highest-income group in the United States paid 46 percent of its household income in federal taxes, compared with 53 percent in 1997. The lowest-income group, by contrast, changed from 2 percent to 1 percent.[5] The 2001 tax cut does not seem to have materially affected the progressivity of the tax system.

Benefit Received. Another concept to keep in mind is that of *benefit received*. Some revenue is derived from payments by recipients for services rendered or benefits received. User charges or fees are notable examples, as in municipal parking garage fees, bus fares, and water and sewer charges. People who park in the garage pay for that service. The principle of payment for services results in an efficient allocation of public sector resources, because people will use only the amount of a particular service for which they are willing to pay. This process is similar to the way in which the private market works. That is, the private market produces no more of those goods than people are willing to purchase.

However, if all government services were paid for by fees, some people would be unable to pay and necessarily would be excluded. Elementary and secondary education, for example, is the most expensive local government service. If government provided this service entirely by charging parents and students the cost of providing education, many parents would be unable to send their children to school. This situation would lead to large segments of the society being uneducated and unable to secure employment that required the ability to read, write, and the like. Because of the *spillover effects* (the fact that lack of education would adversely affect others in the society), many government services cannot be appropriately supported solely through user fees. In addition, the public supports education for equity reasons. Similarly, public goods have positive externalities — that is, they benefit all citizens regardless of whether one actually uses the service. Education, for example, benefits the entire community by making it more attractive to businesses making location decisions, and it benefits the entire economy by increasing the productivity of the work force. The benefit received principle simply cannot be applied uniformly to all government services.

According to the related concept of *efficiency*, an efficient tax is one that does not appreciably affect the allocation of resources within the private sector, such as between consumption and saving or among competing items for consumption. Taxes on alcohol, for example, seem to have no appreciable effect on consumption of alcoholic beverages. However, taxes can be used for regulatory purposes, as opposed to purely efficient revenue-raising purposes. Increased taxes on tobacco have been shown to reduce smoking among youth, precisely as intended.[6] Other tax provisions that exclude some items from taxation, such as selected tax deferrals on personal income saved for retirement, are designed to influence behavior and may not be neutral or simply efficient. Tax systems that are progressive can be inefficient and have unintentional consequences. If tax rates are particularly high for wealthy persons, for instance, then the system may encourage them to spend more time on leisure and less on working and earning more income.

Tax system design generally tries to consider both equity and efficiency objectives. Use of taxes to regulate behavior, as in increased tobacco taxes, is generally not considered in the overall design of a tax system, but rather is typically legislated separately. Extensive research has focused on how to consider both principles simultaneously while devoloping optimal tax structures that are designed to achieve an optimal balance between efficiency and equity objectives.[7]

Tax Expenditures. Revenues that could be, but are not, collected constitute tax expenditures and can aid or hinder attempts to achieve an optimal balance. According to federal law, tax expenditures are "revenue losses . . . which allow a special exclusion, exemption, or deduction from gross income or which provide a special credit, a preferential rate of tax, or a deferral of tax liability."[8] Tax expenditures are not new; home mortgage interest payments (on up to two homes) have been deductible from income since 1910, for example.

Numerous exemptions from taxation or deductions from income for corporations have crept into law over the years as well.[9] The federal budget contains 136 categories of tax expenditures, the largest being exclusion of employer contributions for medical insurance and care, estimated in the fiscal year 2003 proposed budget at more than $99 billion revenue losses. Home mortgage interest deductions are second, with an estimated 2003 impact exceeding $86 billion.[10]

Tax expenditures are not automatically bad. The public policy goal for the home mortgage interest deduction is to encourage and enable individual family home ownership; exclusion of employer pension and medical insurance contributions is meant to increase savings for pensions and reduce the cost of health care. The housing exemption may help make housing affordable to moderate-income families, but it also benefits more affluent taxpayers and may be of no benefit to low-income families. Is the housing exemption, then, a factor that furthers or detracts from equity?

The federal budget presentation includes analyses of the expenditures that the government otherwise would have to incur to achieve the same economic effect as the revenue loss from the tax exemptions and exclusions. For example, the 2003 budget shows an estimated federal outlay equivalent of $2.0 billion for allowing corporations and others to take credits against their tax liability for research and development expenditures. As the analysis noted, "The outlay-equivalent measure allows the cost of a tax expenditure to be compared with a direct Federal outlay on a more even footing."[11]

Since the 1970s, tax expenditures have become an important issue in debates over tax reform. These measures reduce the revenue flowing into government treasuries and can represent "loopholes" for the wealthy. Like the federal government, some state governments routinely report estimates of tax expenditures (see Chapter 6). The 2003 budget notes that the U.S. Treasury Department was undertaking a major study of the concept of tax expenditures and its utility as a budget concept.

Personal Income Taxes

As is well known, all levels of government use personal income taxes, but the federal government's income tax is by far the largest in terms of generating revenue. In fact, as noted in Chapter 2, it is the largest revenue source for the federal government.

Tax Base. All taxes begin with identifying what is to be taxed, or the base. In the case of income taxes, not all income is taxable; local governments, for instance, tend to tax earned income as distinguished from other income. For a local government, salary and wages may be subject to an income tax but income from rents and stock investments are not. The federal government includes salaries, wages, commissions and tips, interest, rents, alimony, and unemployment compensation in the income tax base. Excluded are most employee benefits (such as employer-provided health insurance and contributions to pension funds), disability retirement, workers' compensation, food stamps, and interest earned on some state and local bonds. (These lists, of course, are intended only to illustrate which items are included and excluded.)

Generally speaking, the more sources of income included in the tax base, the more equitable the income tax. When the base excludes sizable segments of income, vigorous debates immediately arise over whether some interests are receiving undue favoritism as a result of legislative lobbying.[12] Tax changes introduced in 1993 increased the federal income tax base in two ways: (1) by taxing employer contributions to pension plans for incomes above $150,000 and (2) by decreasing the tax-exempt amounts employers contribute to other benefits, such as health insurance. These changes affecting benefits increase the tax base for wealthier taxpayers but leave the tax base unchanged for lower-income individuals. The 2001 tax law changes left these base increases intact.

Adjustments, Exemptions, and Deductions. Tax codes also provide for adjustments to gross income that typically have the effect of removing portions of income from the base. For example, the federal tax code excludes moving expenses, some job-related educational expenses, and some employer-paid business reimbursements. Individual exemptions may further reduce the individual income tax base. For 2001, the federal government allowed an exemption of $4,550 for an individual filing separately, and $7,600 for married couples filing jointly. The purpose of these provisions is to equalize taxes among families of different sizes.

A final set of adjustments affects the tax base by allowing deductions. Taxpayers usually have a choice between using a standard deduction or itemizing deductions when they exceed the standard deduction. Deductions on the federal income tax include some medical expenses; casualty losses due to theft, fire, and the like; charitable contributions; home mortgage interest; and deductions for some taxes, such as property taxes. Taxes on gasoline and retail sales are not deductible, nor is interest on consumer debt.

These exclusions, inclusions, adjustments, and deductions to the income base are intended to yield income figures for individuals and families that further horizontal and vertical tax equity. These factors together are meant to recognize variations in total income and the circumstances involved in earning that income and meeting living expenses. Individuals earning the same income but having different numbers of family members and expenses will be treated differently, while others with unequal gross incomes ultimately may have the same ability to pay when adjustments and deductions are taken into account.

Rate Structure. The principle of equity is furthered at the federal level by the use of a progressive rate structure. Tax law changes in 2001 altered tax brackets for 2001, and altered future-year tax brackets through 2006. Married taxpayers in 2001 having taxable income of less than $45,201 paid a 15 percent tax, whereas those with income between $45,201 and $109,251 paid at a 27.5 percent rate on the income exceeding $45,201. Taxpayers in the next bracket paid 30.5 percent on income up to $166,501. The next two bracket rates were 35.5 percent and 39.1 percent for incomes between $166,501 and $297,351 and incomes exceeding $297,351, respectively.[13] A new 10 percent rate for the first $6,000 in income for individuals, or first $12,000 for married couples filing jointly, took effect for 2002; the top tax rate will gradually decrease to 35 percent by 2006.

Most personal income taxes levied by the states are modeled on the federal tax. The states sometimes use the federal base or a modification of it. Some state income taxes are simply a proportion of the federal tax owed; other states use flat and graduated tax rates. When the federal government modifies its tax laws, changes inadvertently occur in state taxes. Local income taxes tend to be simple to calculate and involve flat, rather than progressive, tax rates.

Indexing. The federal government and some states use indexing in various forms to adjust income taxes in accordance with changes in price levels. If tax brackets are not altered and prices subsequently rise, then inflation will produce higher tax revenues because rising incomes will place citizens in higher tax brackets without any real increase in buying power. Besides adjusting tax brackets, other indexing techniques include modifying the standard deduction or personal exemption. A controversial issue is the measure of inflation used to adjust tax brackets (and many other revenue and expenditure elements). The consumer price index historically has been used, but many now feel that it overstates inflation, causing taxes to be lower than they should be and, more importantly, causing federal benefit programs to extend benefits greater than should be. We discuss this issue in Chapter 15.

Enforcement. A key income tax issue is enforcement. The individual income tax relies heavily on honest self-reporting by taxpayers. Although employers withhold an important proportion of total individual income taxes paid, thereby enforcing tax collection for the Internal Revenue Service (IRS), enforcement remains a problem — and an especially difficult problem when taxpayers think the tax is unfair. Much income is never identified and thus never becomes part of the tax base. A large underground economy operates in which transactions occur in trade, payments in kind, and unrecorded payments in cash never become part of the income tax base. Measuring the size of that invisible economy is naturally difficult, but one study of 17 countries estimated that the underground or shadow economy may range from 10 to 20 percent of gross domestic product (GDP) in industrialized countries.[14] For the United States, income equal to an estimated 10 percent of GDP is unrecorded and therefore untaxed.

Corporate Income Taxes

Taxes on corporate earnings have been defended as appropriate given the size of corporate economic power and the fact that some individuals might be able to escape taxation by "hiding" their income in corporations. On the other hand, corporate income taxes seem to result in double taxation: First a corporation is taxed, and then individuals are taxed on dividends paid on their corporate stock holdings. There have been proposals to replace the corporate income tax with a tax on net business receipts to avoid this double taxation, but these proposals have not attracted much interest. Proposals to exclude dividends from individual income taxation also have been unsuccessful.

Tax Base. Corporate taxes use net earnings as a base. Whereas the individual income tax base basically considers income before expenses, except for some deductions and exclusions, corporate income taxes apply only to net profit after operating expenses. In addition, some deductions are allowed for capital losses, operating losses, depreciation of capital investments, charitable contributions, and expenditures for research and development. How these deductions are applied is often controversial, such as how rapidly a corporation can depreciate capital investments. The federal corporate tax rates gradually increase from 15 percent to 39 percent. The two lower brackets of 15 and 25 percent apply to relatively small corporate earnings, up to $50,000 and $75,000, respectively.

Tax Incidence. The primary issue as regards corporate taxation is who actually carries the burden of corporate taxes. Corporations may be able to increase prices and, in effect, make consumers pay the tax, or they may limit wage increases to workers and, in effect, have them pay the tax. Another option is to take taxes out of profits, thereby reducing dividends for investors. Corporations probably use some combination of these shifts.

An issue involving state corporate taxes is whether they affect decisions to locate and expand operations in one state over another. Legislators and executives in a state government fear that any increase in their corporate income taxes will discourage corporations from locating in the state and encourage others to move out of the state. For example, several states, (including Iowa, Massachusetts, Nebraska, and Texas) tax manufacturing companies only on in-state sales. This *single-factor* business tax apportions the income manufacturers receive into in-state earnings and earnings from out-of-state sales, and taxes only the former. The expectation is that what a state loses in tax revenue it will gain from companies already there expanding their operations in the state and from companies relocating to the state. In Chapter 15 we discuss interstate (and sometimes interlocal) competition with tax incentives and other benefits to attract business investment, sometimes called *smokestack chasing.*

Property Taxes

Taxes on wealth are based on accumulated value in some asset rather than on current earnings. Personal property, monetary and financial assets, and equipment are important types of wealth that sometimes are subject to taxation. The wealth tax that is most important in the eyes of taxpayers, however, is the real property or real estate tax. The property tax is the one most reviled by taxpayers, being regarded by many as the most unfair.[15] This tax is the almost exclusive domain of local governments. Despite forecasts of its demise, the property tax remains the largest single generator of revenue for local governments, although it has declined in recent years relative to other state and local taxes. It funds almost 75 percent of locally raised school district revenues. Courts in at least 17 states, however, have overturned their states financing systems that relied heavily on local property taxes.[16] The argument is that despite state aid to local school districts, almost sole reliance on the property tax to finance education at the local level means unequal education opportunities across the state (see Chapter 14). The property tax is also the most important source of local revenue for funding urban services in developing countries, although user charges (discussed later in this chapter) are the fastest growing source of local revenue in the more prosperous emerging market economies.[17]

The justification for using the property tax as the major revenue source for local government is that the services provided by local government supposedly increase the economic value of one's property. It is widely thought that people select their place of residence based on the quality of local schools and other public services. In high-quality service jurisdictions, housing costs are typically higher, reflecting higher costs for delivering services and higher expectations of home buyers for quality services. Property taxes reimburse local government for higher-quality services. The argument goes as follows: If more general taxes, such as the sales tax, were used to finance services that benefit property owners, then property owners would be less aware of the costs of those services and therefore insist on more and higher-quality services. Evidence has been found to support this argument in developing countries, where demand for urban services is much higher in cities that do not use property and other local taxes and charges to finance those services.[18] Property is also less susceptible to tax avoidance because it is clearly visible and is immobile. People can order goods over the Internet and easily avoid paying sales tax (see the discussion later in the chapter). Property taxes, by comparison, are difficult to avoid.

One way to tie the benefits of services affecting property values to taxes on property is through *tax increment financing*. Tax increment financing has been used in redevelopment of inner cities to capitalize on the economic and financial gains that stem from a major rehabilitation project for a contiguous area usually characterized by urban blight and abandoned properties. Prior to city government action, many property owners in such areas derive no benefits from their properties, and the city is able to collect little or no property tax. A redevelopment project changes conditions so that the property in the redeveloped area attains new value, and the property tax gains from that new value are set aside to pay for financing the redevelopment. Some use also has been made of tax increment financing in rural areas, but it is not as valuable a tool there. Property tax rates are typically much lower in rural areas, land values are more volatile, and investors in bonds to support rural infrastructure tax increment funded projects perceive higher risks.[19]

The main policy issue with the property tax is its regressive nature. Higher-income taxpayers tend to have a larger proportion of their wealth in assets that are not subject to the property tax. As a consequence, these taxpayers generally pay a disproportionately lower property tax (as a percentage of their income) as compared with middle- and lower-income taxpayers, whose only major asset may be their home. For middle- and lower-income taxpayers, most of their wealth is being taxed each year. For renters, the regressive effects of the property tax depend on the extent to which the landlord can pass on the property tax through the rent. For all these reasons, the regressive nature of the property tax fuels controversy. In addition, the property tax is relatively complicated to implement and to maintain. Updating the tax base for the property tax and updating tax rates are always controversial when carried out.

Tax Base. The base of the real property tax is the market value of the land and any improvements on it, such as homes, factories, and other structures. The value is what the property would sell for if placed on the market. Value for commercial and industrial property sometimes is reflected in the income earned by a corporation from the property or facility.

Property's use and value often do not coincide, with farmland in metropolitan areas being one of the prime examples. As metropolitan areas expand and encroach upon farming areas, the value of the land increases even though the use remains unchanged. Situations emerge in which taxes rise beyond what farmers can afford and create a market incentive for the land to be sold and subdivided for homes and other development. All states provide some form of protection for farmland as a means of preserving rural land and discouraging urban sprawl, with reduced tax assessments for farming and other undeveloped land being the most common method. Often these tax breaks are really postponements. If the land is later sold for subdivision and housing at a value much higher than the land's worth as farmland, the seller must then pay back property taxes reflecting the residential use tax rate. As with other tax preferences, property tax reductions to preserve farmland can have unintended consequences. One study of Pennsylvania's program concluded that it preserved land in rural areas where population pressure is light, so the need for preservation is small.[20] Many states also buy the development rights from property owners as a way of preserving land for open space or other purposes.

Many properties are completely tax exempt in the United States. Federal and state land is normally exempt from local property taxes, for example, although these jurisdictions may make payments in lieu of taxation. Places of worship, such as churches and synagogues, are tax exempt, as are most parsonages and other related properties. Nonprofit hospitals, YMCAs and YWCAs, nonprofit cemeteries, and the like are usually tax exempt as well. When tax-exempt properties account for a large proportion of a jurisdiction's potential tax base, the effects of tax exemption can be severe. Some governments have aggressively challenged the tax-exempt status of some nonprofit organizations. The basis for the challenge is that some nonprofit organizations produce for-profit goods and services. Philadelphia, for example, employs a five-part test. To remain exempt from property and other taxes, a nonprofit has to prove that it: "advances a charitable purpose; gives away a substantial portion of its services; benefits people who are legitimate subjects of charity; relieves government of some of its burden; and operates entirely free of profit motives."[21] However, Philadelphia lacks the authority to force those nonprofits that do not meet the tests to pay property taxes. Instead, it asks, with some success, for voluntary payments in lieu of taxes.

Another challenge is keeping property market value assessments current. The sale of a property offers an opportunity to measure directly its market value and to revise the assessment, but many properties do not go on sale for decades. Therefore, assessments are revised by using market data regarding similar properties and by periodic assessment surveys in which each property in the jurisdiction receives a direct inspection. Adjustments may be done annually or only once every several years.

Fractional Assessment. Property assessments usually are stated as a percentage or fraction of the full market value. A home whose market value is $120,000 would be assessed at only $24,000 if the assessment ratio were 20 percent. In practice, it should make no difference whether the full value or a fraction of it is used; fractional assessment simply requires a higher tax rate than market value assessment to produce the same revenue. Taxpayers may find some psychological solace in fractional assessment, but the opportunity exists for some taxpayers to have their properties overassessed and therefore taxed more than their share. Fractional assessment often is not uniform. If some properties are assessed at one percentage of market value and other properties at a different percentage, then the tax burden is no longer proportionate to the value of the property. To address that problem, the trend is to assess all properties at 100 percent of market value to ensure that all properties are on an even basis, except where fractional assessment is used to differentiate types of properties. For example, rural property may be assessed at a lower fraction than highly developed property.

Tax Rates. Property tax rates are a percentage of assessed value. The rate is expressed in mills, with one mill being one-tenth of one percent. As applied to property taxes, a one-mill rate yields $1 of revenue for every $1,000 of assessed value. A property tax rate of 68.5 mills as applied to a $120,000 property assessed at 20 percent of market value would yield $1,644 (120 x 0.2 x 68.5 = 1,644).

Local jurisdictions often determine the annual property tax rate by calculating backward from projected expenditures minus other revenues. The property tax then is expected to make up the budget gap. The community's decision makers simply determine how many additional mills will be needed to close the gap. Of course, attempts are made to avoid such tax increases by keeping expenditures as low as considered possible. The process of adjusting the tax rate to match expenditure requirements probably accounts for the great popularity of the property tax among local officials. This tax is one over which officials have considerable control, unlike other taxes that depend on the economy (income and sales taxes) or intergovernmental aid.

Circuit Breakers. As taxes rise, some property owners may encounter considerable difficulty in paying their tax bills and may even be forced to sell their homes and move into rental housing. To alleviate this problem, several states use circuit breaker systems that set a limit on taxes, particularly for low-income elderly persons. A qualified homeowner pays an amount up to the limit, and the state pays any additional amount owed. Often a state bases the limit on some income criterion: when property taxes exceed a specified percentage of the taxpayer's income, the state pays the difference.[22]

Databases for Tax Administration. For a local government instituting the property tax for the first time, the valuation process is almost overwhelming. Traditional valuation procedures involve comprehensive tax mapping to locate every property; an assessor also must visit each property, measuring the foundation to determine square footage, noting construction details, and recording information about the condition of the structure. This type of comprehensive process is now occurring in many developing countries, where property taxes are being newly applied or where existing records are incomplete and largely useless.[23]

For most jurisdictions in the United States, properties have been constructed under building permits that require supplying information about construction details to the local jurisdiction. Periodic inspections of the property when under construction, conducted by a local code enforcement officer or building inspector, provide additional information. A database, then, can be devised using existing building records and information about sales of properties when deeds are transferred. As new structures are built, they can be added to the database.

Orange County, North Carolina, has what is considered a model property tax valuation system. It is fully computerized and includes diverse information about each property in the county (**Table 4–1**). Besides information about the location of each lot, the size of the structure, and the number of baths in it, a drawing of the lot and the location of the structure on it are included in the computerized file and can be displayed on screen. Of course, printed maps of properties are available as well.

Table 4–1	Property Tax Registration Information Base, Orange County, North Carolina

- Property address
- Plot map and reference to deed register
- Area of lot (square footage)
- Occupancy (single-family dwelling, two-family, multifamily)
- Size of dwelling (square footage of living space)
- Number of structures
- Number of stories of each structure
- Basement, slab, or crawl space
- Foundation construction method
- Exterior construction method
- Roof type and roofing materials
- Number of rooms
- Number of bathrooms
- Number of bedrooms
- Year built
- Number of fireplaces
- Interior finish
- Floor type
- Built-in appliances
- HVAC system
- Special features (spas, etc.)
- Landscaping
- Land topography
- Utility connections
- Paved or unpaved driveway
- Last sale price and date

Source: Courtesy of Office of the Tax Assessor, 2002, Orange County, North Carolina.

Techniques such as those used in Orange County help to foster a perception of fairness among taxpayers. Property owners conclude that they are paying their fair share and are not being overcharged while other taxpayers are being undercharged. If these equity considerations are met, then the likelihood of a taxpayer revolt is minimized. However, it does not make the property tax popular; it remains the most hated tax in the country.

Personal Property. Besides taxing real property, some jurisdictions tax personal property. For individuals, such property includes furniture, vehicles, clothing, jewelry, and the like. Intangible personal property includes stocks, bonds, and other financial instruments such as mortgages. For corporations, personal property includes equipment, raw materials, and items in inventory. Taxes on personal property are unpopular and subject to considerable evasion.

Retail Sales and Other Consumption Taxes

Sales taxes are one of the most important sources of revenue for state governments. Forty-five of the 50 states levy a general sales tax, and it is the largest state-generated source of revenue for many of them. All states have at least some selective sales taxes. Overall, the general and selective sales taxes account for nearly 21 percent of total state general revenues from all sources; the second largest single general revenue source is the income tax, which accounts for nearly 18 percent of general revenues. However, all taxes account for slightly less than 50 percent of state general revenues. User charges are the fastest-growing source, approaching 13 percent of general revenue.[24] If one looks at the sales tax as a proportion of tax revenues only, sales taxes account for 36 percent of state tax revenue.[25]

Tax Base. While all three levels of government rely on some form of consumption tax, state governments are the most dependent, particularly on retail sales taxes. The base of any consumption tax is a product or class of goods (sometimes services) whose value is measured in terms of retail gross sales or receipts. The base is a function of which products and services are included and excluded. Almost all states exclude prescription medicines, and many states exclude food, except for that sold in restaurants. The number of states excluding food from the sales tax has been growing, but at considerable expense to state revenues. Some states have opted for reducing the sales tax rate on food, compared to other taxed items, rather than eliminating it altogether.

Other commonly excluded items are clothing, household fuels, soaps, and some toiletries. Some items may be exempt from the general sales tax only because they are subject to another sales tax; cigarettes, gasoline, and alcoholic beverages are examples. However, states generally are not precluded from levying two taxes on one sale, such as a general and a specific sales tax placed on cigarettes.

The most notable items not included in most sales tax bases are services, such as the professional services of doctors and lawyers. A Council of State Governments study found that consumption expenditures for tangible goods are less than those for services; states that exclude services from the sales tax base forgo considerable revenue. However, applying the sales tax to services is so unpopular that few states have implemented that option.

States currently have only limited authority to tax mail-order sales and have been lobbying Congress to pass legislation allowing such taxation. The reason is a simple one. Mail-order sales vastly increased starting in the 1980s and constitute a potentially lucrative source of revenue. U.S. Supreme Court interpretations of the due process and interstate commerce clauses have been fairly restrictive on states' ability to tax interstate sales. A 1967 case (*National Bellas Hess, Inc. v. Department of Revenue, State of Illinois*) concluded that the mail-order firm had to have a substantial nexus of business in the state, in the form of a physical presence. A 1992 case (*Quill Corporation v. North Dakota*) relaxed the so-called nexus doctrine, holding that the due process clause of the Constitution does not bar enforcement of North Dakota's use tax on the Quill Corporation, but on other grounds it still refused to overrule *Bellas Hess*.[26]

An additional complication is the growth of sales through cable and satellite television and other electronic commerce. Use of the Internet as a mechanism to place orders shipped interstate has become a significant mode of commerce, and it will continue to grow as more users gain access to electronic sources. Michigan, for example, is estimated to have lost as much as $21 million per year in sales taxes not collected on Internet retail.[27] Although the principle has not been tested in any court case so far, Internet commerce is being treated the same as interstate mail-order and phone sales.

In 1998, Congress passed the Internet Tax Freedom Act.[28] That act placed a moratorium on taxing Internet sales, and Congress appointed an Advisory Commission on Electronic Commerce to deal with the issue.[29] The Commission deadlocked without effectively solving the problem. In its wake, some states have taken matters into their own hands. Michigan and North Carolina attempt to tax Internet purchases by asking taxpayers filing individual income tax returns to report on goods purchased from out of state through on-line sources, but have not created any enforcement mechanisms. More generally, state governments have joined together through the National Governors Association to create the Streamlined Sales Tax Project. This project intends to simplify and make consistent across the states the application and administration of the sales tax. Success with this approach might overcome judicial objections to requiring retailers to collect sales taxes for all 45 states, each of which has a different system, as an undue burden.[30]

Sales taxes are regarded as regressive in that higher-income consumers typically have more discretionary income and may spend it on items not subject to sales taxes. The more the base of the sales tax includes luxury or nonessential goods and services, therefore, the less regressive the tax is likely to be.

Tax Rates. State sales tax rates vary from as low as 2.9 percent (Colorado) to as high as 7 percent (Mississippi and Rhode Island).[31] To avoid levies of a fraction of a cent, bracket systems are used in which a set amount is collected regardless of the specific sale. For example, a 5 percent tax might yield 5 cents on any purchase starting at 81 cents or 90 cents. With computers and electronic scanners at check-out counters in stores, determinations can be quickly made as to whether an item is taxable and how much tax, if any, should be charged.

Other Consumption Taxes. Some taxes are considered to be *luxury excises.* At one time, federal excise taxes were levied on a wide range of luxury goods, such as jewelry, yachts, and expensive automobiles. The logic of these taxes rests on the assumption that the purchase of such goods is prima facie evidence that the consumer can afford the tax.

Sumptuary excises are regulatory in nature. Taxes on alcohol and tobacco have been justified as deterring people from consuming these commodities. In reality, the evidence suggests that the demand for these products is relatively inelastic, casting doubt on whether taxes discourage usage. A substantial tax increase on tobacco was proposed as an important source of financing for health care reform. The rationale was that smokers are one of the major sources of health care insurance utilization and that those who create those costs should be the ones to pay taxes to fund them — a sort of *reverse benefit* principle. The proposal, however, did not get serious review in Congress. Nevertheless, some states have substantially increased tobacco taxes both as a revenue measure and as a health regulatory measure. As noted earlier in this chapter, large increases in tobacco taxes have discouraged youth from smoking.

Benefit-based excises are linked to the benefit received concept discussed earlier. Motor vehicle fuel taxes are the classic case. Revenues from taxes on gasoline and diesel fuels are used for road and bridge construction and maintenance. Other such excises include taxes on airline tickets; the revenues from these taxes are used to maintain airports and airport security.

User Charges

All governments have user charges, and almost all public sector functions are partially supported by user charges. As noted earlier, user charges and fees for services are the fastest-growing state and local revenue source. For example, admission fees are charged to national and some state parks and to local tennis courts, other recreational facilities, and exercise and athletic programs. Some elementary and secondary schools charge for textbooks, and higher-education institutions charge tuition. Hospitals, transit systems, water and sewer operations, and refuse collection revenues come mainly from fees and charges. Some jurisdictions own electric and telephone facilities, which they finance through user fees. Police departments charge fees for fingerprinting and special assignments, such as patrolling at sports events.

Rationale for Fees. The employment of user charges to raise revenues is based on the principle that citizens ought to pay for the cost of public services as a control on the amount of services produced. The more technical argument for their employment holds that the amount of a service provided is closer to the optimal level of service, as determined by consumer preferences, when the cost of service is borne directly by the consumer.[32] If the cost of a service is part of general taxes, then citizens tend to demand more of that service than they are actually willing to pay.

At the federal level, the growth in user charges and fees began with the Reagan administration's opposition to tax increases; with massive annual federal deficits and a president opposed to tax increases, federal agencies in need of additional revenues selectively considered fees as an alternative. The philosophy of federal user charges, that "the service, sale, or use of Government's goods or resources provided by an agency to specific recipients be self-sustaining," is expressed in Office of Management and Budget Circular A-25. During and following the budget surplus years of the late 1990s, presidents have found it financially useful and politically acceptable to increase user fees while holding taxes steady or even cutting taxes. In the 2003 budget, the Bush administration estimated that user fees without any new proposals would increase by approximately 6 percent from 2001 to 2002, and proposed annual user fee increases of an additional 1 percent per year through 2007.[33]

Types of Charges. Fees vary in the extent to which they are voluntary. Charges for entrance into a museum or a municipal swimming pool clearly are voluntary; other leisure options are available if citizens prefer not to pay for these public services. On the other hand, charges for sewers and trash collection usually are mandatory; if a municipal sewer system exists, citizens normally have no choice but to use it and pay the requisite fee. The largest federal user fees are the U.S. Postal Services charges, which may be considered partially voluntary in that alternatives for at least some postal services exist. Other services lie between these extremes. Paying a bus or subway fare may be voluntary, but for many people without other transit options the fees are required. Differentiating between a mandatory fee and a tax is difficult.

Some fees are continuous, whereas others are applied only for special occasions. Transit fares and sewer and water charges are examples of continuous fees. Special-occasion charges include a building permit fee that a contractor has to pay preparatory to erecting an office building. Although many jurisdictions use general tax revenues to repave and improve streets, other communities levy special assessments on the property owners whose streets will be improved. Similarly, when a community installs a sewer system for the first time, property owners are assessed fees. These charges are calculated on a front footage basis — namely, the number of linear feet that a lot faces or fronts a street. User charges increasingly are being seen as effective revenue sources for social and human services as well.

Special assessments are used in more general ways to support municipal services. Firms that construct new office buildings in a city may have an option to provide on-site parking or pay a fee that is used to construct municipal parking facilities. Raleigh, North Carolina, finances much of the cost of lengthening streets, extending water and sewer lines, and expanding parks in new developments through the imposition of *impact fees* on developers. Other communities use impact fees to fund low- and moderate-income housing and environmental programs.

Charges and Tax Subsidies. Although user charges can be substantial, they often fail to cover the costs of the services they support. Entrance fees to a municipal swimming pool usually do not provide adequate funds to operate the pool; therefore, tax revenues are used. An important example of such a subsidy is in the operation of municipal transit systems. If transit fares were set high enough to generate the required operating revenues, the rates would be so high that poor commuters could not afford to use the system and higher-income commuters would shift to alternative modes of travel — private vehicles and taxicabs. Pricing policies for some services can be quite complicated, making it difficult to determine whether the actual costs are fully recovered by the tariff structure.[34]

Subsidies, however, have the effect of aiding all who use a service. If transit fares remain artificially low because of a tax subsidy, then both the wealthy and the poor who use the system benefit. Alternative mechanisms include providing free service to the poor, such as free bus tokens, or setting fees on a sliding scale. For example, a government-operated mental health clinic might charge poor and moderate-income families little or nothing for services while charging higher-income families at a rate that covers costs.

Some local governments that own profitable utilities, such as public electricity companies and sometimes water enterprises with substantial industrial customers, use utility fee revenue to decrease the taxes otherwise needed to finance other, unrelated services. For those local governments owning such profitable enterprises, the overall cost of other government services to citizens is often lower per capita than for other comparable local governments.[35] Austin, Texas, is an example of a city that uses sales of electricity from its municipally owned utility to subsidize the costs of other services. Caution is in order before one automatically assumes that local governments should seek to become utility owners. The sometimes hidden costs of diverting public management talent to the operation of an essentially private business could adversely affect the municipality's overall management efficiency, although that may be difficult to quantify.[36]

Insurance Trust Revenues

Insurance trust funds, which are separate accounts set up to hold certain earmarked revenues (see Chapter 11), are financed by means of charges on salaries and wages (the charges are paid by employees, employers, or both). These charges are not taxes in as much as they do not generate revenue to be used to pay for services; instead, the programs provide insurance to the people who are covered by them. Employers and employees pay into these systems, and people earn benefit credits through contributions made during their working careers. Social insurance receipts rose as a percentage of gross domestic product (GDP) from 4.5 percent in 1971 (as low as 2.1 percent in the 1950s) to nearly 6.6 percent in 2000, while corporate income and excise tax revenues fell from 2.5 percent to 2.1 percent and 1.6 percent to 0.7 percent of GDP, respectively.[37]

Social Security and Supplemental Security Income. Social Security is a trust program of vast proportions. Its complexities far exceed the scope of this book; all that can be done here is to sketch its overall structure.

Three major programs are administered directly by the Social Security Administration. The first, Old Age and Survivors Insurance, is a benefits program for retired workers and their survivors. Chapter 13 discusses the program as it pertains to retired government employees. The second program, Disability Insurance (DI), provides benefits for covered workers who are disabled and cannot work. In 2000, more than 38.7 million retired workers, dependents, and survivors received benefits under the old-age and survivors program and almost 7 million disabled workers and dependents received benefits. Benefits paid out from those two programs totaled $3,524 billion and $55 billion, respectively.[38] The third major program under Social Security provides monthly benefits to people who are aged, blind, and disabled; this program is known as Supplemental Security Income (SSI).[39] SSI funds come from general tax revenues, rather than from employer-employee contributions. Unlike disability insurance, SSI does not require work credits for eligibility but does require that recipients be needy. It is possible to qualify for both programs, although qualifying for DI has the effect of reducing SSI benefits. In 1999, 4.9 million people received $31.0 billion in benefits under the SSI program.[40]

Medicare. In addition to the three main Social Security programs, a fourth one, Medicare, is administered by the Centers for Medicare and Medicaid Services (CMS) in the Department of Health and Human Services. Medicare provides basic health insurance to the elderly, with a separately funded catastrophic coverage component, and is funded by contributions through Social Security, premiums paid by persons covered under the program, and general revenues. Medicare has become one of the major contributors to rapidly rising federal expenditures for health care. More than 38 million persons received benefits from the Medicare program in 2000.[41] The major issue facing Medicare is providing a prescription drug benefit, as senior citizens living on fixed incomes find the cost of prescription drugs to be a rapidly increasing burden.

Medicaid. A fifth program often mentioned in conjunction with these other programs is Medicaid; it is funded by federal and state tax revenues as opposed to payroll taxes earmarked for the Social Security Trust Fund. The federal government pays about 70 percent of the costs of Medicaid, with the states and local governments paying the remainder. From 1970 through 1998, total federal Medicaid spending increased from $5 billion to $100.1 billion, with the state and local share increasing from $2 billion to $77.2 billion.[42] Medicaid provides medical care to the poor and the medically indigent (persons who are not classified as poor but who cannot afford medical care). Medicaid and SSI are not trust programs as defined earlier, because their funds come from general tax revenues and not revenues earmarked for special trust funds.

Insurance Trust Programs

Employee Retirement. The largest type of insurance trust fund at the state and local levels is for government employee retirement. These retirement programs, as well as the federal government's pension plan, are discussed at length in Chapter 13.

Unemployment Insurance. The second largest insurance trust for state governments is unemployment compensation. This program is administered by the states within in a framework imposed by the federal government. A floor on benefits is set nationally, although states have the option of exceeding the floor. The program is supported by payroll taxes paid mainly by employers, although in a few states employees are required to make supplementary payments. It is expected to generate sufficient revenues during prosperous periods to cover payments to unemployed workers during recessionary periods. Sometimes state programs can run into a deficit situation, such as during a sustained recession or occasionally because of temporary timing differences between payments into the funds and payments out. In such cases, the federal government loans money to the states but expects repayment with interest. Obviously, a state with a declining tax base can face severe problems in financing its unemployment insurance program. The economic downturn of the early 2000s underscored this problem for many states.

Workers' Compensation. Another important insurance trust at the state level is workers' compensation, which provides cash benefits to persons who, because of job-related injuries and illnesses, are unable to work. Accidents at work may disable people temporarily or permanently; working conditions can cause physical and mental health problems. In addition to cash benefits, the program pays for medical care and rehabilitation services.

Social Security and Medicare Reform

Legislation passed in 1983 greatly modified the financing of Old Age and Survivors Insurance to make it solvent for the long term; estimates then were that the trust fund would be insolvent before 1990 unless corrective actions were taken. While the increases in both the employer and the employee contribution rates and an increase in the amount of annual income subject to the tax will satisfy the fund's needs for some decades, the consensus is that the program will need revising again, and that the longer reform is postponed, the more dramatic will be the changes required. Different scenarios place the date at which annual disbursements from the Social Security Trust Fund will exceed annual revenues anywhere from 2025 to 2065. The wide variance in estimates is caused by assumptions about retirement age, employment rates that swing with economic fluctuations, and labor force participation rates coupled with population age shifts.

The Advisory Council on Social Security, which in 1997 considered alternative reforms to the system, developed both low-growth and moderate-growth scenarios for population and labor force growth. The low-growth scenario shows the trust fund in deficit sometime after 2050; the moderate-growth scenario shows no deficit through the next 75 years – through the 2070s at least.[43] The Bureau of Labor Statistics and the Census Bureau, however, have cautioned that the Advisory Council used extremely pessimistic assumptions about shrinkage in the population birth rate. If birth rates do not fall as rapidly and as far as the Advisory Council assumed, then the work force paying into the Social Security Trust Fund will be larger in mid-century, and the fund will still show a surplus in 2050. Immigration rates also can have a substantial effect, as generally immigrants to the United States are likely to be participants in the labor force for quite some time after immigration.

Several issues have fueled the debate over Social Security reform, and the motivations for reform among many groups are not necessarily consistent. First is the issue we might label "violation of trust." This issue is based on an emotional (mis)understanding that the fund is supposed to be a trust fund exclusively for financing Social Security benefits. Many citizens assume that the funds they and their employers contribute to the system are being held in trust, invested much like pension funds to yield the benefits that will be paid out to them in the future. Politicians make a similar claim in their criticisms of Social Security. In reality, each year's payments into the Social Security Trust Fund are used to pay claims to beneficiaries in that year. For some time to come, the payments into the fund will exceed payments to beneficiaries out of the fund. Those excess payments create a surplus in the fund, and that surplus in turn is lent to the U.S. Treasury at the equivalent of the 30-year Treasury bond to finance part of federal spending. The alternative to the Treasury borrowing from the Social Security fund is to force the Treasury to borrow from the U.S. and overseas capital markets. Under such a scheme, the surplus Social Security funds would need to be invested some place rather than sit idle — perhaps the stock market (discussed below)?

Thus, one motivation for reform is the political point of view that the fund should behave as a revolving fund, with proceeds paid into the fund being invested as in most pension funds. That view somewhat naively assumes that private pension funds pay out benefits commensurate with the results of investment of funds paid in. That statement is true of defined contributions plans, but defined benefit plans pay out defined benefits regardless of whether the fund investments are sufficient to meet those benefit payouts (see Chapter 13 for a more detailed discussion of defined benefits and defined contributions pension programs). Just as an employer with a defined benefits pension fund is obligated to meet the benefit payouts defined in the plan, from business net profits if necessary, so the federal government is obligated to meet whatever Congress determines will be the benefit structure, first from the trust fund itself and then from other federal revenues as necessary. Unless Congress fails to appropriate funds to meet legislated benefits (if and when the surplus in the fund turns into a deficit) or passes legislation so as to lower benefits, then the trust fund issue really is not an issue. Instead, it is a convenient political football for both parties to kick around.

A second motivation for reform is closely linked to the debates on the federal budget surplus or deficit. Because the fund shows a surplus, and all revenue to the fund counts as part of the federal government's revenue total, the size of the federal deficit is disguised. The more fiscally conservative believe that the practice of using the trust fund surplus to finance part of other spending is inappropriate. The less conservative position was articulated in the Bush administration's 2003 budget, which noted that unlike private "trust" custodians who legally must manage the assets on behalf of the beneficiary, the federal government owns the assets and earnings and can legally change collections, payments, and even the purposes of the funds.[44]

A third issue involved in demands for reform is that the funds being paid into Social Security according to many should be earning more than the implicit 30-year Treasury bond rate. The bull market of the 1990s particularly fueled this aspect of the debate, as stocks earned dramatic returns — two and three times the rate of the 30-year Treasury bond. Proposals have been advanced to invest the funds flowing into the trust fund in the stock market, so as to earn higher benefits for future pensioners. In 1996, the Advisory Council on Social Security, unable to reach a consensus, presented three options for reforming the way Social Security funds are invested.

One option, favored by six of the Council's 13 members, was that 40 percent of the trust fund's money should be invested in the stock market. A second option, favored by two members, recommended that workers put 1.6 percent of their pay (slightly less than one-third of their own contributions) into personal retirement accounts, with the rest of the employee contributions and all of the employer contributions going into the Social Security Trust Fund as they do now. Individuals would have some say in how the personal retirement accounts would be invested, although Social Security would administer the accounts. The third option, favored by the remaining five members of the Council, would replace the current guaranteed benefit system with a system in which workers would be required to put 5 percent of their pay into personal accounts, and individuals would bear all the responsibility for determining investments.[45] The president of Chile, during a state visit to the United States in 1997, even got into the act, recommending that the United States fully privatize the entire Social Security system, much as Chile has done. That a nonpartisan council after two years of deliberations could not agree to support any single reform indicates how difficult it will be to make a major change in the way Social Security funds are invested.

In 2001, the Bush administration appointed a new, nonpartisan advisory panel with a prominent Democrat and a prominent Republican as co-chairs.[46] The Commission concluded that "Social Security will be strengthened if modernized to include a system of voluntary personal accounts."[47] However, the drastic decline of the stock market starting in 2001, though not ending discussions of investing Social Security funds in the stock market, greatly diminished the enthusiasm for proposals to invest Social Security funds in the stock market. The corporate accounting scandals that swept the stock market in 2002 further dramatized the risks of investing Social Security funds in the stock market. If Social Security funds had been invested in a portfolio that had invested half of its funds in Enron, WorldCom, and Tyco, it would have lost 50 percent of its value. It is highly likely that the federal government would have been called upon to bail the fund out.[48]

A final important proposed reform in the system is tied up with a broader proposal to recalculate the consumer price index, which would affect a variety of federal revenue and expenditure programs, as noted previously in this chapter.[49] Currently, Social Security benefits change annually, as does the calculation of income tax brackets, to take into account the effects of inflation as measured by changes in the consumer price index. The 1996 Advisory Council noted that increasing the payroll tax by 0.3 percent and changing the formula to produce what many feel is a more accurate and lower estimate of inflation would ensure Social Security system solvency through the next century, without changing the employer and employee contribution rates or modifying the age at which people may begin drawing Social Security benefits. A Senate Finance Committee–appointed commission recommended that the consumer price index be cut 1.1 percent per year. This recommendation met with substantial opposition from groups such as the American Association of Retired Persons and died without being enacted.[50]

Medicare reforms also have been an important part of the Social Security system reform debate. In 1997, estimates were that Medicare would become insolvent before the end of the decade. That prediction did not materialize, as the payroll tax rate was increased. The hospital insurance portion of Medicare, in particular, would have run at a deficit by 1995 had premium increases not shored it up. Reform proposals especially have aimed at reducing the incentives for physicians and hospitals to order expensive treatments for Medicare patients and to reduce the possibilities for fraudulent charges. Holding down reimbursement rates slowed the slide toward a Medicare deficit, and on the agenda for longer-term reform is moving more people into managed care organizations and away from individual physicians. Almost inevitable is eventually raising the age at which one becomes eligible for Medicare from 65 to perhaps 67. The program's reform is tied up in debates over budget surpluses and deficits. The program's impact on the budget has become so significant that most agree that it can tip the budget into deficit or surplus, especially as the eligible population increases when the baby boom generation becomes eligible.

Private Sector Production of Services

Governments that are feeling the pinch from deficits and taxpayer reluctance to support tax increases have increasingly turned to the private sector to finance many services traditionally thought to be the province of the public sector. Harnessing the entrepreneurial spirit of the private sector to provide services and thereby reduce the need for public taxes has become virtually nonpartisan. This trend was especially pronounced during the 1980s and 1990s. The financial collapse of Asian markets, which spread rapidly to Russia and Latin America, did cause some hesitation as a number of large private investments in power and water systems in mega-cities such as Jakarta, Manila, and Buenos Aires got into financial difficulties when contract terms could not be met. Furthermore, the complexities of managing private contractors and concessionaires have proved to be more complicated than was thought when contracting out and granting service concessions were in their heydey.[51]

The span of public services considered for privatization is almost unlimited. Private police and fire services are not exempt. Use of toll roads and turnpikes is increasing. Privatization of water and wastewater utilities is seen by some as the only way to finance badly needed new investment.[52] In addition, numerous local school districts have turned to the private sector to operate either entire schools or elements of schools on a contract basis. Because it is not really a revenue-raising measure but more a case of turning over a formerly public service to the private sector, we discuss privatization in a separate chapter (Chapter 10).

Tools for achieving private sector participation that do involve private sector financing include concession contracting and various forms of build-operate-transfer (BOT) and build-operate-own (BOO).[53] Under contracting arrangements, a private organization or consortium contracts with a public agency to rehabilitate, build, operate, and perhaps at a specified future time transfer a facility to the public agency. In the concession contract, the private party operates the facility under a long-term concession and may be required to make significant capital investments in the facility, but it never assumes ownership. In BOT/BOO arrangements, at least for some period of time, the private party has legal ownership of the facility. In Sydney, Australia, for example, a BOO contract was awarded in 1996 to a consortium led by the French water company Lyonnaise des Eaux, calling for a $200 million capital investment on the part of the private consortium. The consortium constructs and rehabilitates facilities, is the outright owner of the facilities built during the concession period, and is the fully responsible operator for the 25-year period.[54] The issue for Sydney was the cost to the city and taxpayers of financing the needed capital investments, the ability of public officials to manage those investments as efficiently as the private consortium could, and the need to expand services much more rapidly than the city could manage.

Concession projects increasingly have been used in many developing and emerging market countries, including Cameroon, Chile, Colombia, Morocco, Peru, the Philippines, Poland, and South Africa for water, wastewater, and solid waste treatment services. Buenos Aires turned over the entire city water system on a concession basis, resulting in the removal of thousands of employees from the city payroll.[55]

BOT/BOO and other concession contracting approaches to private sector participation benefit the public sector primarily by eliminating or reducing the need for additional public sector debt to construct expensive infrastructure facilities and by reducing or holding constant the size of the public sector payroll. The latter advantage is particularly important where public sector employees tend to be paid higher wages and better benefits than employees of comparable private operations.[56] Research has shown that U.S. cities that experience fiscal distress are characterized by larger numbers of municipal employees and higher-than-average wages for municipal employees (these cities typically increased hiring and pay rates when large federal grants were plentiful during the 1960s and 1970s).[57]

Private concession contracting must bring management expertise, new technology, and operating efficiencies to bear to actually reduce the cost of a service, given that private parties will require a profitable return on their investment over and above cost recovery.

Other Revenue Sources

Besides the various revenue sources discussed so far, there are still others that can be mentioned only briefly here. Governments operate revolving loan programs that produce revenue as borrowers make principal and interest payments. Licenses are issued that usually require fees; the purpose of these fees may be to cover costs (for example, building permit fees are used to pay the salaries of building inspectors) or to raise revenues beyond costs. Charitable contributions constitute another revenue source, such as gifts to municipal hospitals, county nursing homes, state universities, and the like.

Borrowing also must be mentioned — not literally as a revenue source, but as a temporary means to obtain revenue while waiting for other revenues to enter the city or state coffers. As will be seen later in discussions of congressional budgeting and budget execution, the federal government's budget is often out of balance, and deficits are routinely financed through the issuance of debt instruments. State and local governments sometimes obtain revenues through borrowing to cover short-term cash flow problems. These governments borrow on a long-term basis to fund capital projects such as highways and government buildings (see Chapter 12).

Lotteries, Casinos, and Other Gambling. Since 1963, when New Hampshire began the first modern state lottery, all but 13 states have launched lottery programs. Lotteries typically produce 3 to 4 percent of total state revenues, but their contribution ranges from as little as 1 percent of revenues in Nebraska to more than 10 percent for Massachusetts.[58] Revenues generated from the programs can vary considerably from year to year, depending upon lottery activity in adjacent states, the size of jackpots, and the extent to which a lottery has "matured" and lost the public's interest. State lottery revenues rose rapidly in the late 1980s and early 1990s, then leveled off by mid-decade. In recent years, there has been a resurgence in interest due in part to very large, multistate payouts and the serious state fiscal trouble resulting from the economic downturn of the early 2000s. Lotteries can be regressive in that lower-income individuals are more likely to participate than middle- and upper-income individuals.[59]

In addition to lotteries, a number of states have legalized casino gambling. Although in some states, such as Louisiana, casino gambling has cut into state lottery revenues, other states are generating significant revenues from such ventures. Illinois has found casino gambling and lottery revenues to be reinforcing, earning more than $1 billion in revenues in less than a year in 2002.[60] Mississippi has one of the highest per capita gambling revenue rates among states, with revenues in 1999 topping $180 million, or about $67 per capita (a rate exceeded only by Nevada).[61]

Overall, however, the enthusiasm for tax and economic benefits from lotteries, casinos, and other legalized gambling has waned somewhat, except in those states where neighboring states seem to be attracting residents of nonlottery states to cross state borders to purchase lottery tickets. For example, one argument often used in 2002 in North Carolina to support a lottery proposal was the amount of money that North Carolina residents were spending in the neighboring Virginia and South Carolina lotteries. The economic benefits in terms of employment and increased tax revenues have been less than expected, though definitely positive. Hard evidence of social consequences has been difficult to find, although anectdotally opponents of legalized gambling argue that the social costs exceed the economic benefits.[62] One estimate showed the state of Maryland may have lost as much as $1.5 billion in reduced productivity, unpaid taxes, and other losses due to its lottery operation. Even the benefits promised to specific public services have not always materialized; in some states where lottery earnings are earmarked exclusively to support education, state legislatures have cut other state education spending by commensurate amounts.[63]

Tobacco Settlement Windfall. During the 1990s, more than 40 states sued various large tobacco companies over the costs to state government of health care costs and related losses to states due to tobacco usage. When a few individual states reached settlement agreements with individual tobacco companies, it became apparent that damage recovery was possible and would be upheld in the courts. The tobacco companies realized that individual settlements would drag litigation out over decades, likely bankrupting most of them, and efforts began to reach a uniform settlement. In 1998, a majority of states reached a setttlement agreement with the largest companies in which the companies agreed to spend more than $300 billion to compensate states for health care costs due to tobacco usage.[64] The estimated payout is based on the agreement to pay forever to the states involved in the settlement a share of profits from tobacco products sales. Estimates of $300 billion to $350 billion are based on the 1999 present value of the future stream of payments.[65]

Some states focused their settlement payments on one core issue. Michigan committed to invest in developing the biotechnology industry in the state. Other states decided to devote their share of the settlement to tobacco-related economic and health issues. North Carolina, which has numerous tobacco farmers and a large tobacco industry, focused on assisting the industry to overcome the economic downturn brought on by tobacco sales declines in the United States, economic development programs in tobacco-impacted areas, and health programs. Still other states, including Virginia, committed the settlement funds to tax relief. As the state revenue shortfalls mounted, states increased the diversion of tobacco settlement funds to budget relief and away from health and economic development programs.

Overall, the settlement funds do not add large amounts as a proportion of total state revenue, though those states that have focused on a few problems have been able to add significant funding to those areas. A few states have explored with the investment community the possibility of issuing bonds based on the future revenue stream from settlement payments. Other states have used the settlement funds to help fill the gap between revenues and expenditures as state revenues started to fall during the 2001–2002 economic downturn.

Value-Added Tax. Increased concerns about the robustness of the U.S. tax system, especially the intergovernmental system of taxation and revenue transfers (see Chapter 14), have led some to advocate adoption of a value-added tax (VAT).[66] The United States is one of the few industrialized countries without a VAT. As its name implies, a VAT is a consumption tax on the value added by producers and distributors at every stage in the production, distribution, and sales process. Interest in the VAT in the United States seemed to peak in the early 1990s. Proposed during the 1992 election by then-candidate Clinton, the VAT did not get serious attention in Congress. During the 1996 campaign, it was not mentioned at all, but instead was superseded by various candidates' proposals for fundamental income tax reform, including various flat-tax alternatives. Tax professionals argue that it is superior to many other forms of consumption taxation, but it just has not generated much enthusiasm in the United States.[67]

Special Concerns

This section addresses two topics of special interest. The first topic is the limitations that have been imposed on state and local taxes, and the second is the ongoing problem of revenue estimating.

Taxing and Spending Limitations

Although citizens seemingly have had little opportunity to affect taxes and spending other than through the process of selecting elected representatives, 1978 changed all that. In that year, California voters approved Proposition 13, an initiative that limited the property tax rate to 1 percent of market value. That provision by itself would have required a rollback in taxes, but an additional provision further cut taxes. Property assessments were to be returned to their values in 1975, when property was considerably less expensive. Although tax limitation measures were not new, Proposition 13 began a new era in which government officials were forced to consider taxpayer reaction and to limit taxes and spending.[68] Many state and local governments followed California's lead during the late 1970s and early 1980s by passing statutory limits or, in some cases, adding restrictions to state constitutions. California voters approved Proposition 4 in 1979, which limited both state and local government expenditures. In the following years, restrictive measures were adopted in about half of the states. Massachusetts, which had come to be known as "Taxachusetts," gained notoriety in 1980 as a result of its passage of Proposition 2 1/2. This measure required that local governments reduce taxes by 15 percent each year until they equaled 2.5 percent of market value.[69] "By 1990, 21 states had enacted potentially binding limitations and 13 had enacted nonbinding limitations on the finances of their local governments."[70] The elections of 1994 and 1996 brought more conservative control to many state legislatures and ushered in a new round of tax limitation proposals.[71] In 1996, California passed Proposition 218, the most severe limitation to date.[72] Oregon, Colorado, and Missouri also passed tax or spending limitations in the mid- to late 1990s.

Causes and Types of Limitations. The original stimulus behind what came to be known as the taxpayers revolt was the sharp rise in property values and, consequently, tax bills, but a more generally negative attitude emerged — the attitude that government officials have an insatiable appetite for spending. Besides taxing too much, governments allegedly use the revenues to interfere needlessly in the lives of citizens and the operations of corporations. Property taxes remain one of the most criticized forms of taxation. This is probably because of dissatisfaction with the results school systems are producing, which are funded almost entirely by the property tax.[73] The result has been several types of tax and expenditure limitations. One review classified them into five categories:

1. Overall property tax limitation (for example, limit to maximum annual percent increase)
2. Specific property tax limitation (for example, limit on use of property tax to finance education)
3. Property tax levy limit (for example, ceiling on amount of tax)
4. General revenue or general expenditure increase limit (for example, limit annual expenditure increase to a specific limit)
5. Property tax assessment increase limit[74] (limit on the assessed value increase)

In addition, taxpayer concern has caused many state and local governments to increase communication with the public on what is accomplished with taxpayer dollars and how taxes are kept to a minimum. Minnesota, for example, enacted a law requiring the construction of an overall index calculating the cost of everything residents pay to the government as a percentage of personal income. Not only are taxes included, but so are all fees, charges, and any other payment to government.[75] The index is kept for different state departments and individual local governments so that citizens throughout the state can compare their own government with others and with limitation guidelines.

Tax Revolt Impact. The effect of these limitations has varied, but in most cases local governments made up for the revenue loss through other sources, usually non–general-revenue sources. In some cases, state governments almost immediately made up for the shortfall.[76] Overall, spending may have declined in some jurisdictions but not enough to show up in aggregate figures for individual states. The main effects seem to have been fourfold.

First, state legislatures and local governments are much more reluctant to initiate new programs and especially to propose tax increases or new taxes.

Second, combined with major cutbacks in federal aid to states and localities in the 1980s, the limitation movement set these governments on an imaginative hunt for alternative finance measures. The significantly greater use of impact fees, discussed earlier, and other direct charges to those benefiting from services was an outgrowth of the tax revolt.

Third, states provided increased financial assistance to hard-pressed local governments. For example, when Michigan ran into problems with property tax funding for education, the state increased the sales tax and, in turn, used state funds for formerly local education funds. Sometimes that state aid has come at a price — namely, various strings attached by states for their aid. One simple example is that local governments were forbidden from giving their employees salary increases greater than those given to state employees.

Fourth, overall expenditures have been cut somewhat and some services have been reduced, either in quality or quantity, as a means of curbing spending.[77] Essential services such as law enforcement and fire protection have been maintained, albeit at decreased levels. Budget problems forced cutbacks in maintenance of buildings and purchase of new vehicles and equipment.[78] Overall, however, tax and expenditure limitations did not materially change the relative amounts that state and local governments spent on government functions.[79] Some evidence indicates that spending cuts have produced long-term quality decline, at least in some services. For example, public school student performance has declined in several states that have imposed expenditure limitations, even after controlling for a number of other possible influences.[80]

Starting in the late 1980s, enthusiasm for the enactment of restrictive measures on government waned, and concern grew among citizens that the reductions imposed over the preceding decade had cut too severely into the level of services. At the same time, there was continued citizen consciousness about tax and expenditure matters. At the federal level, the Budget Enforcement Act of 1990 added the requirement that any additional mandatory expenditure proposed in Congress had to be matched with either an equivalent expenditure reduction or a revenue increase (see Chapter 9). The congressional elections of 1994 and the Republicans' Contract with America provided renewed focus on controlling the size of government. Similarly in state governments, more fiscally conservative legislators continued to focus on reducing the size of government or limiting its growth. Federal and state budget surpluses achieved by the late 1990s caused a virtual disappearance of talk about tax and spending limitations, though the fiscal crises states started experiencing in 2001 may stimulate new activity.

Revenue Estimating

Little imagination is required to appreciate the importance of revenue estimating. If a government is required to have a balanced budget, as state and local governments are, then accurate revenue forecasts become critical. Estimates that are too high can create major crises during the execution phase, at which time expenditures must be cut so as not to exceed revenues. Low estimates also cause problems, in that programs may be needlessly reduced at the beginning of the fiscal year.

Deterministic Models. Perhaps the easiest method of revenue forecasting involves deterministic models that manipulate the revenue base and tax rate to produce a desired level of revenue. Property tax forecasts are deterministic in that a government can adjust assessments and tax rates to meet desired revenue levels. The main problems to address in such forecasting are the extent that (1) overall property values will rise or possibly decline, (2) new properties will be added to the tax rolls, and (3) old and deteriorating properties will fall into default. Deterministic models are useful for revenue sources over which a jurisdiction has substantial control; they are not useful for taxes on such items as personal income and retail sales, which depend on economic trends.

Simple Trend Extrapolations. Both formal and informal trend extrapolations are used in revenue estimating. In an informal situation, an assumption may be made that a particular revenue source will increase by 5 percent because that is what has occurred for the last several years. In most cases, of course, revenues do not increase or decrease by a set percentage or remain constant. Revenue growth may increase on average by 5 percent, but in some years the growth may be 10 percent and in others only 1 or 2 percent. Given this information, what percentage estimate should be used for the upcoming budget year?

One method of dealing with this problem is to use simple linear regression, a statistical technique that fits a straight line to a series of historical data. The formula used is $y = mx + b$. In the equation, y, the forecast revenue, is a function of a coefficient m multiplied by a known value x plus a constant b. In the formula, m is the slope of the straight line, x is the actual revenue generated the previous year, and b is a scale factor that adjusts for orders of magnitude differences between values. Computer software is readily available for making the appropriate calculations, but such projections also can be made using simple calculators.

The straight-line calculation of linear regression, however, may not parallel the actual historical series; the fit of the regression can be gauged by calculating the correlation coefficient known as R. When the data are random, R is 0.00. The closer R is to 1.00, the more likely it is that the regression accurately forecasts revenue.

Besides linear regression, other techniques exist for smoothing out fluctuations in a historical series into a straight line. The method called moving averages calculates an average value for each point in the historical series. Starting with a series of, say, 8 years, the revenues for years 1, 2, and 3 are averaged. This average becomes the new smoothed value for year 2. Then actual values for years 2, 3, and 4 are averaged to create a new "smoothed" year 3. Similar averages are calculated for the remaining years. A variant of this technique weighs the most recent years more heavily than the early years in calculating the moving average, on the grounds that recent years are better predictors.

Underlying these techniques is the premise that the future will be like the past. The purpose of any projection technique is to reduce historical information to a discernible pattern and then extend that pattern into the future. One way of testing how well the technique works is to "predict" several recent time periods and compare those predictions with what actually occurred. Most local governments, except large cities, still rely on one form or another of trend extrapolation. Chesterfield County, Virginia, adds the expert judgment of the county government's program managers, business leaders, state tax experts, and expertise from the Federal Reserve Bank of Richmond convened in a semi-annual forum to discuss underlying trends. This addition of expert judgment allows the county to adjust the results of trend extrapolation methods.[81] Evidence suggests that when used in combination with other tools, trend extrapolations produce reliable estimates for local governments,[82] as long as there are no significant and abrupt changes in economic conditions such as the rapid economic decline that began in late 2000, causing rapid reversal from state and local budget surpluses to severe fiscal pressures.

Econometric Models. Several types of econometric models exist.[83] One of the most popular is multiple regression. In multiple regression models, independent variables are sought that can serve as predictors of revenue yield. The assumption is that a linear relationship exists between each predictor and the dependent variable of forecast revenue. Another assumption is that each independent variable is unrelated to the others. A model for sales tax receipts might include the independent variables of population, personal income, and the consumer price index. As each of these variables increases, revenues increase.

Multiple predictor variables are used in simultaneous equation models (multiple regression models rely on a single equation). In simultaneous equation models, individual equations relate each independent or predictor variable to the revenue to be forecast. These individual equations are solved simultaneously. The advantage of simultaneous equation models is that, unlike multiple regression models, they do not assume that each predictor variable is independent of each other predictor variable. Because many of the variables one would use to make a revenue forecast would be expected to be related to each other, the simultaneous equation approach is both more realistic and computationally more valid.

Revenue forecasts can be made using microsimulation models that are dependent on large databases manipulated by computers. Individual taxpayers and corporations are included in the models and exhibit behavior changes in response to projected changes in the economy, tax laws, price levels, personal income, and the like. Data based on the historical performance of actual taxpayers in the jurisdiction are used.

All of these models necessarily use variables that are sensitive to changes in economic conditions. Sales and income tax receipts rise and fall according to economic trends. Many user charges are affected, too; when people are unemployed, they curtail their use of public transportation, parking facilities, museums, and zoos. Therefore, these models are most vulnerable with regard to the assumptions made about future economic trends. Also critical are basic demographic shifts. Changing population patterns due to shifting birth rates and migration can undermine the effectiveness of forecasting models that previously had shown themselves to be extremely accurate.[84] Projecting national trends is extremely difficult, and state and local trends are no easier to predict, especially given that each subnational jurisdiction has its own economic characteristics and is influenced by national trends.

Politics. Revenue estimating has its political aspects. Presidents, governors, and mayors are loathe to forecast economic hard times and low revenue levels. Political executives tend to campaign for election in part on the promise that they will strive for economic growth. Presidents have the additional problem that the forecast of a recession may be a self-fulfilling prophecy. State and local executives must limit expenditures to available revenue; pessimistic estimates force executives to make difficult choices as to where to cut programs so as to reduce overall expenditures. In general, there seems to be a tendency to underestimate revenues more often than to overestimate them. Apparently, politicians feel the political risks of underestimating and producing a surplus at the end of the year are less dire than the consequences of overestimating and having to make program cuts or raise taxes unexpectedly during the year.[85] Since revenue estimates can rarely, if ever, be guaranteed to come true, establishing *contingency reserves* or *rainy day funds* may be a useful method of protecting against possible shortfalls and the political problems that ensue from them.

Summary

Governments use numerous revenue sources to support their operations, with taxes obviously being one of the most important types. In devising a tax system, governments need to consider whether horizontal and vertical equity standards are met. One important consideration is whether to have a person pay based on the benefits received or on his or her ability to pay. Taxes on personal and corporate income, property, and retail sales are the largest generators of tax revenue. Each tax has a base, and then a rate or rates are applied to it. Other important revenue sources include user charges; reliance on such charges and fees has increased since the late 1970s. There is also increasing reliance on the private sector to initiate or take over needed services as a means of reducing public payrolls and avoiding an enlargement of public sector debt for capital facilities. Insurance trusts constitute another important source of revenue; they include Social Security, government employee retirement systems, unemployment insurance, and workers' compensation.

Two topics of special concern are limitations imposed on taxing and spending and the procedures used in revenue estimating. Many state and local governments have adopted tax and/or expenditure limitations. Citizens and political leaders alike remain concerned that taxes and spending be kept to a minimum. The 1997 balanced budget agreement between the White House and the Congress and the record-low federal budget deficit compared with recent decades have not diminished the attention focused on limiting taxes and spending.

Revenue estimating is an ongoing process. Deterministic models, trend extrapolation techniques, and econometric models are among the tools used to forecast future revenues. Increasingly sophisticated merging of mathematical tools with expert judgment can improve the accuracy of budget forecasts.

Notes

1. R.A. Musgrave, Fairness in Taxation, in *The Encyclopedia of Taxation and Tax Policy*, J.J. Cordes, ed., (Washington, DC: Urban Institute Press, 1999), 117–120.

2. N. Magner, et al. Tax Decision Making in Municipal Governments: Citizens' Reactions to Outcomes and Procedures, *Journal of Public Budgeting & Financial Management* 9 (1998): 552–570.

3. P. Burgat and C. Jeanrenaud, Do Benefit and Equal Absolute Sacrifice Rules Really Lead to Different Taxation Levels?, *Public Finance Quarterly* 24 (1996): 148–162.

4. M.L. Whicker, P.L. Julnes, and D.W. Williams, Making Tax Policy: A Variance Ratio Approach to Measuring Tax Incidence, *Journal of Public Budgeting, Accounting & Financial Management* 13 (2001): 83–102.

5. U.S. Congressional Budget Office, *Effective Federal Tax Rates, 1979–1997.* (Washington, DC: Congressional Budget Office, 2001), xvii.

6. F.J. Chaloupka and M. Grossman, Price, Tobacco Control Policies and Smoking Among Young Adults, *Journal of Health Economics* 16 (1997): 359–373.

7. C.E. McClure, Jr., and G.R. Zodrow, The Study and Practice of Income Tax Policy, in *Modern Public Finance*, J.M. Quigley and E. Smolensky, eds., (Cambridge, MA: Harvard University Press, 1994), 185.

8. *The Congressional Budget and Impoundment Control Act*, P.L. 93–344, 88 Stat. 297, 299 (1974).

9. J.G. Gravelle, Tax Expenditures, in *The Encyclopedia of Taxation and Tax Policy*, 379–380.

10. Office of Management and Budget, *The Budget of the United States Government: Fiscal Year 2003, Analytical Perspectives* (Washington, DC: U.S. Government Printing Office, 2002), 107.

11. *The Budget of the United States Government: Fiscal Year 2003, Analytical Perspectives*, 109.

12. S. Pollack, *The Failure of U.S. Tax Policy: Revenue and Politics* (University Park, PA: Pennsylvania State University Press, 1996).

13. Internal Revenue Service, *1040 Forms and Instructions* (Washington, DC: U.S. Government Printing Office, 2001).

14. Light on the Shadows, *The Economist* 343 (May 3, 1997): 63–64.

15. G.W. Fisher, *The Worst Tax? A History of the Property Tax in America* (Lawrence: University of Kansas, 1996).

16. W.A. Fischel, School Finance Litigation and Property Tax Revolts: How Undermining Local Control Turns Voters Away from Public Education, *Developments in School Finance: Fiscal Proceedings from the Annual State Data Conference*, July 1999 and July 2000 (Washington, DC: National Center for Education Statistics, 2002): 79–127.

17. R.W. Johnson and J.S. McCullough, Case Study on Urban Local Government Finance (Paper presented at the Asian Development Bank seminar on Urban Infrastructure Finance in Asia, Research Triangle Institute, Research Triangle Park, NC, April 17, 1996).

18. R.W. Bahl and J.F. Linn, *Urban Public Finance in Developing Countries* (New York: Oxford University Press, 1992); R.M. Bird, *Tax Policy and Economic Development* (Baltimore: Johns Hopkins University Press, 1992).

19. J.E. Petersen, TIFs in the Hinterlands, *Governing* 13 (August 2000): 68.

20. T.W. Kelsey and K.S. Kreahling, Preferential Tax Assessments for Farmland Preservation: Influence of Population Pressures on Fiscal Impacts, *State and Local Government Review* 28 (Winter 1996): 49–57.

21. P. Lemov, Tin-Cup Taxation: Local Governments Are Pressuring Nonprofits to Chip in to Cover the Costs of the Services They Use, *Governing* 8 (October 1995): 25–26.

22. D.H. Monk, *Educational Finance: An Economic Approach* (New York: McGraw–Hill, 1990), 158–160.

23. C.K. Zorn, et al., Diversifying Local Government Revenue in Bosnia–Herzegovina through an Area–Based Property Tax, *Public Budgeting & Finance* 20 (Winter 2000): 63–86; R. Kelly, Designing a Property Tax Reform Strategy for Sub-Saharan Africa: An Analytical Framework Applied to Kenya, *Public Budgeting & Finance* (Winter 2000): 36–51.

24. U.S. Bureau of the Census, *Statistical Abstract of the United States: 2001* (Washington, DC: U.S. Government Printing Office, 2001), 279–280.

25. D. Hoffman, ed., *Facts and Figures on Government Finance*, 36th ed. (Washington, DC: Tax Foundation, 2002): 178; W.A. Fischel, School Finance Litigation and Property Tax Revolts: How Undermining Local Control Turns Voters Away from Public Education, *Developments in School Finance: Fiscal Proceedings from the Annual State Data Conference*, July 1999 and July 2000 (Washington, DC: National Center for Education Statistics, 2002): 79–127.

26. H.A. Coleman, Taxation of Interstate Mail-Order Sales, *Intergovernmental Perspective* 18 (Winter 1992): 9–14; *Quill Corporation v. North Dakota*, 504 U.S. 298 (1992).

27. C. Swope, E-conomics Problem, *Governing* 13 (March 2000): 20–23.

28. *Internet Tax Freedom Act*, P.L. 107–75 (1998) and extended by P.L. 107–75 (2001).

29. A. Goolsbee and J. Zittrain, Evaluating the Costs and Benefits of Taxing Internet Commerce, *National Tax Journal* 52 (1999): 413–428.

30. C. Swope, E-Tax Outrage Turns into Action, *Governing* 13 (September 2000): 86.

31. Sales Tax Institute, June 15, 2002: *http://www.salestaxinstitute.com/sales_tax_rates.html*; accessed June 2002.

32. Johnson and McCullough, *Case Study on Urban Local Government Finance.*

33. U.S. Office of Management and Budget, *Budget of the United States Government: Fiscal Year 2003, Analytical Perspectives* (Washington, DC: U.S. Government Printing Office, 2002), 87.

34. B.D. Foster and G. Fujita, Rate Setting for Municipal Utilities: Detroit's Combined Sewer Overflow Facilities, *Government Finance Review* 16 (June 2000): 33–40.

35. A. Khan and T.J. Stumm, The Tax and Expenditure Effects of Subsidization by Municipal Utility Enterprises, *Municipal Finance Journal* 15 (1994): 68–81; T.J. Stumm and A. Khan, Effects of Utility Enterprise Fund Subsidization on Municipal Taxes and Expenditures, *State and Local Government Review* 2 (Spring 1996): 103–113.

36. Johnson and McCullough, *Case Study on Urban Local Government Finance.*

37. U.S. Bureau of the Census, *Statistical Abstract of the United States: 2001* (Washington, DC: U.S. Government Printing Office, 2001), 305, 422.

38. U.S. Bureau of the Census, *Statistical Abstract of the United States: 2001*, 347.

39. M.C. Daly and R.V. Burkhauser, *The Supplemental Security Income Program*, (San Francisco: Federal Reserve Bank of San Francisco, 2000).

40. U.S. Bureau of the Census, *Statistical Abstract of the United States: 2001*, 340, 342.

41. U.S. Bureau of the Census, *Statistical Abstract of the United States: 2001*, 99.

42. U.S. Bureau of the Census, *Statistical Abstract of the United States: 2001*, 344.

43. A. Bernstein, Social Security: Is the Sky Really Falling? *Business Week* (February 10, 1997): 92.

44. U.S. Office of Management and Budget, *Budget of the United States Government: Fiscal Year 2003, Analytical Perspectives*, (Washington, DC: U.S. Government Printing Office, 2002), 351.

45. American Survey: The Pensions Conspiracy, *The Economist* 341 (December 14, 1996): 20, 27–28.

46. W. Duka, AARP's Deets Sees Flaws in Social Security Panel, *AARP Bulletin* 42 (June 2001): 19.

47. The President's Commission to Strengthen Social Security, *Strengthening Social Security and Creating Personal Wealth for All Americans* (White House: U.S. Government Printing Office, 2001): *http://www.ssa.gov/commission/Final_report.pdf*; accessed August 2002.

48. Author's calculations.

49. J.L. Norwood, The Consumer Price Index, the Deficit, and Politics, *Government Finance Review* 13 (February 1997): 32–33.

50. R. Lewis, AARP Disputes Panel's CPI Call, *AARP Bulletin* 38 (January 1997): 6–7, 13.

51. Y.K. Kodrzycki, Fiscal Pressures and the Privatization of Local Services, *New England Economic Review* (January/February 1998): 39–50; S.M. Emerson, Promises and Pitfalls of Contracting for Public Services: The LAWA Case, *Journal of Budgeting, Accounting & Financial Management* 12 (2000): 307–332.

52. D. Haarmayer, Privatizing Infrastructure: Options for Municipal Systems, *Journal of the AWWA* 96 (March 1994): 43–55.

53. R.W. Johnson and N.J. Walker, Financing Municipal Infrastructure through Direct Private Investment (Paper presented at Southeastern Conference for Public Administration, Research Triangle Institute, Research Triangle Park, NC, October 7, 1993).

54. *International Water Development: Annual 1997* (World Congress, LLC, 1996), ix.

55. D. Rivera, *Private Sector Participation in the Water Supply and Wastewater Sector: Lessons from Six Developing Countries* (Washington, DC: World Bank, 1996).

56. K. Slattery, Water Concessions Worldwide Promise Healthy Market in 2001, *Waterworld* 6 (2000): 16–21.

57. A.M. Sullivan, Urban Economics (Homewood, IL: Irwin, 1990), 500.

58. U.S. Bureau of the Census, *Statistical Abstract of the United States: 2001*, 278, 289.

59. C.T. Clotfelter and P.J. Cook, On the Economics of State Lotteries, *Journal of Economic Perspective* 4 (Fall 1990): 105–119.

60. Gambling Revenues Exceed $1 Billion, *Chicago Tribune*, August 24, 2002: *www.chicagotribune.com*; accessed August 2002.

61. U.S. Bureau of the Census, *Statistical Abstract of the United States: 2001*, 21, 289.

62. U.S. General Accounting Office, *Impact of Gambling: Economic Effects More Measurable Than Social Effects*, (Washington, DC: U.S. Government Printing Office, 2000). *http://www.ssa.gov/commission/Final_report.pdf*.

63. C.J. Spindler, The Lottery and Education: Robbing Peter to Pay Paul? *Public Budgeting & Finance* 15 (Fall 1995): 54–62.

64. D.W. Winder and J.T. LaPlant, State Lawsuits against "Big Tobacco": A Test of Diffusion Theory, *State and Local Government Review* 32 (2000): 132–141.

65. D.G. Swaine, Will the Tobacco Settlement Payments Go Up in Smoke? *New England Fiscal Facts* (Boston: Federal Reserve Bank of Boston, Spring 2000): 1–5.

66. A.M. Rivlin, *Revising the American Dream: The Economy, the States and the Federal Government* (Washington, DC: Brookings Institution, 1992).

67. G.R. Zodrow, The Sales Tax, the VAT, and Taxes in betweeen – or, Is the Only Good NRST a "VAT in Drag"?, *National Tax Journal* 52 (1999): 429–442.

68. K. Rueben, The Impact of Initiatives on State and Local Government Finance, *Muncipal Finance Journal* 20 (2000): 20–25.

69. H.F. Ladd and J.B. Wilson, Who Supports Tax Limitations: Evidence from Massachusetts' Proposition 2 1/2, *Journal of Policy Analysis and Management* 2 (1983): 256–279; E. Moscovitch, Proposition 2 1/2, *Government Finance Review* 1 (October 1985): 21–25.

70. D.R. Mullins and P.G. Joyce, Tax and Expenditure Limitations and State and Local Fiscal Structure: An Empirical Assessment, *Public Budgeting & Finance* 16 (Spring 1996): 75–101.

71. S.D. Gold, State Tax Cuts of 1995: Is Something New Afoot? *Public Budgeting & Finance* 16 (Spring 1996): 3–22; National Association of State Budget Officers, 1996 State Tax Initiatives, *http://www.nasbo.org/pubs/infobrf/taxib.htm*; accessed December 1997.

72. Proposition 218, *Government Finance Review* 13 (February 1997): 3.

73. K.L. Bradbury, et al., School Quality and Massachusetts Enrollment Shifts in the Context of Tax Limitations, *New England Economic Review* (July/August, 1998): 3–20.

74. Mullins and Joyce, *Tax and Expenditure Limitations and State and Local Fiscal Structure*, 77.

75. J. Dunn, A Tax-and-Spend Report Card on Governing in Minnesota, *Governing* 8 (April 1995): 48.

76. T.J. McGuire, Proposition 13 and Its Offspring: For Good or for Evil? *National Tax Journal* 52 (1999): 129–138.

77. T. Brown, Constitutional Tax and Expenditure Limitation in Colorado: The Impact on Municipal Governments, *Public Budgeting & Finance* 20 (2000): 29–50.

78. T. King-Meadows and D. Lowery, The Impact of the Tax Revolt Era State Fiscal Caps: A Research Update, *Public Budgeting & Finance* 16 (Spring 1996): 102–112.

79. P.G. Joyce and D.R. Mullins, The Changing Fiscal Structure of the State and Local Public Sector: The Impact of Tax and Expenditure Limitations, *Public Administration Review* 51 (May/June 1991): 244–245.

80. T.A. Downes and D.N. Figlio, Do Tax and Expenditure Limits Provide a Free Lunch? Evidence on the Link between Limits and Public Sector Service Quality, *National Tax Journal* 52 (1999): 113–128.

81. J.J.L. Stegmaier and M.J. Reiss, The Revenue Forum: An Effective Low-Cost, Low-Tech Approach to Revenue Forecasting, *Government Finance Review* 12 (April 1994): 13–16.

82. G.A. Grizzle and W.E. Klay, Forecasting State Sales Tax Revenues: Comparing the Accuracy of Different Methods, *State and Local Government Review* 26 (1994): 142–152.

83. C. Cirincione, et al. Municipal Government Revenue Forecasting: Issues of Method and Data, *Public Budgeting & Finance* 19 (1999): 26–46.

84. D.R. Mullins and S. Wallace, Changing Demographics and State Fiscal Outlook: The Case of Sales Taxes, *Public Finance Quarterly* 24 (1996): 237–262.

85. R. Rodgers and P. Joyce, The Effect of Underforecasting on the Accuracy of Revenue Forecasts by State Governments, *Public Administration Review* 56 (1996): 48–56.

Chapter 5

BUDGET PREPARATION: THE EXPENDITURE SIDE

In the budget preparation phase, important decisions about expenditures are made simultaneously with decisions concerning revenues. The two general types of information relevant for budgeting are program and resource information (see Chapter 1). Program information consists of data on what government does and what those activities accomplish; resource information consists of the inputs necessary to perform those activities. The input side, which includes dollars, facilities, equipment, supplies, and personnel, has long been an established feature of budgetary systems. The use of program information, on the other hand, has slowly emerged as an integral part of budgeting.

The critical argument relating to these two types of information is that they must be considered in combination if budgeting is to be a sensible process of allocating resources. The budget is expected to relate the accomplishments of government to the costs of resources. The history of budgetary reform can be viewed as a struggle to create such budget systems.

This chapter examines the various approaches used in assembling the expenditure side of budgets, with the following chapter considering the political concerns of budget preparation. The first section of this chapter discusses early reform efforts. The second section describes the types of program information used to varying degrees in budget systems. The last section explores the numerous budget systems that have been used, including performance, program, zero-base, and hybrid budgeting systems.

Early Developments

As noted in Chapter 1, budgeting can focus on expenditure control, management control, and planning control.[1] While the development of these three emphases follows a historical pattern to some extent, they are not rigidly fixed to specific time periods, and both the management and planning phases have involved greater utilization of program information. Not only is there a blurring of distinctions between these stages in terms of the dates of their popularity, but use of planning coupled with program information also was advocated at least as far back as the early part of the century. (By *planning*, we mean an effort to associate means with ends in an effort to attain goals and objectives in the future.)

Program Information

1910–1939. Before the establishment of the federal budgetary system, budgeting often was advocated as a means of allocating resources to obtain program results. Two of the most notable proponents were President Taft[2] and the 1912 Taft Commission on Economy and Efficiency. At one point in its report, the commission stated, "In order that he [the administrator] may think intelligently about the subject of his responsibility he must have before him regularly statements which will reflect *results in terms of quality and quantity;* he must be able to measure quality and quantity of results by units of cost and units of efficiency"[3] (emphasis added). Although there was an obvious interest in economizing — in saving dollars — there was also an interest in obtaining the best return in program terms for resources spent.

Other important spokespersons for program results in budgeting in the 1910s included Frederick A. Cleveland[4] and William F. Willoughby.[5] The 1920s and 1930s brought Lent D. Upson,[6] A. E. Buck,[7] Wylie Kilpatrick,[8] and the 1937 President's Committee on Administrative Management.[9] A. E. Buck's classic *Public Budgeting* (1929) admittedly lacked a strong program information orientation, but Buck did express interest in reforms that would concentrate upon measuring the products of government activities.

1940–1960. Although the use of program information and planning was advocated throughout the first four decades of the century, this issue received far greater attention beginning in the 1940s. V. O. Key, Jr., challenged previous budgetary literature as largely mechanical and criticized it for failing to focus on the "basic budgeting problem" of comparing the merits of alternative programs: "On what basis shall it be decided to allocate X dollars to activity A instead of activity B?"[10] The 1949 Commission on the Organization of the Executive Branch of the Government, commonly known as the First Hoover Commission, recommended that the federal budget be "based upon functions, activities, and projects; this we designate as a performance budget." Budgeting should be in terms of "the work or the service to be accomplished."[11]

More proponents of the same viewpoint emerged in the 1950s. Noted scholars included Verne B. Lewis,[12] Frederick C. Mosher,[13] Catheryn Seckler-Hudson,[14] and Arthur Smithies.[15] The Second Hoover Commission supported the recommendations of its predecessor.[16] Smithies suggested the use of program information in budgeting as a primary means of improving both executive and legislative decision making. Jesse Burkhead's *Government Budgeting*, while basically descriptive rather than normative, devoted considerable discussion to performance and program budgeting.[17]

By the 1950s the use of program information in budgeting had become a mainstream reform issue. At the same time, another school of thought, led by Charles E. Lindblom, Aaron Wildavsky, and others, challenged the budget reform movement on the grounds that political decision systems were not readily adaptable to program planning. Lindblom advanced the "muddling through" model of decision making (see Chapter 1), which ran counter to budgetary reform efforts. Wildavsky was to become the most outspoken skeptic of the feasibility of using program information in budgeting. In 1969 he concluded, "No one knows how to do program budgeting."[18]

Nonbudgetary Developments

An alternative school of thought led by David Novick, Charles J. Hitch, Roland McKean, and others was rooted in a set of theoretical and technological fields that developed after World War II. These fields and technologies were highly compatible with the budget reform movement and served as the theoretical foundation for planning-programming-budgeting (PPB) systems attempted in the 1960s. Of central importance were the following six:[19]

1. Operations research, a technique that involves specifying objectives, designing a model representing the situation under investigation, and collecting and applying relevant data[20]

2. Economic analysis, a process of determining whether benefits exceed costs of a current or contemplated program[21]

3. General systems theory, an approach that focuses on how components of a system relate to one another[22]

4. Cybernetics, the science of control and communication[23]

5. Computer technology, the growth of which made possible a variety of analytic processes that required the manipulation of large amounts of data[24]

6. Systems analysis, an eclectic form of analysis that draws upon the previous five items[25]

These fields and technologies were developed outside of the budget reform movement but were highly compatible with it. The six constituted the theoretical and technological foundation for what became the PPB system in the Department of Defense in the 1960s.

The reform efforts from the early 1900s to 1960 that emphasized the use of program information, coupled with this series of other nonbudgetary developments, constitute the foundation for more recent budget system innovations and for contemporary budget systems.

Structuring the Request Process

Except in the smallest organizations, the central budget office alone cannot prepare a budget. As noted in Chapter 3, budget preparation begins with the almost simultaneous amassing of supporting information in the operating agencies and the issuance of budget instructions from the central budget office. The information developed at this stage depends in part on how each agency chooses to make its case and in part on the way decisions are expected to be made. If only dollar requests are prepared, obviously no information will be available with which to make judgments on program effectiveness. On the other hand, a central budget office may not necessarily use program information in its deliberations even if it requires its submission. Still another factor determining what information will be prepared is the known information demands from other budget participants — most notably, the legislative body. Much data may be amassed, not because the agency or the chief executive has any intention of using them for decision purposes, but simply because each year the legislative body demands that information.

Preparation Instructions

Budget preparation practices vary considerably within agencies. Different degrees of participation by field office staff and other line personnel occur, but while such variation exists, the overall process is guided by a set of instructions issued by the central budget office of a government.

At the federal level, such instructions are contained in Office of Management and Budget (OMB) Circular A-11, *Preparation and Submission of Budget Estimates*. This document, issued annually, contains considerable detail and, counting text and supporting illustrations, runs more than 600 pages in length. The circular is available on the Internet, and agencies can submit much of their budget requests through a computer template system.[26] **Table 5–1** indicates the vast array of materials that agencies must submit. Much of this information is mandated by various statutes, such as performance information being required by the Government Performance and Results Act of 1993.[27] (Explanations of various items in **Table 5–1** are provided in other chapters.)

Instructions such as those contained in Circular A-11 include forms to be completed, reducing uncertainty among agencies as to what the budget office

Table 5–1 Selected Materials That Federal Agencies Must Submit as Part of Their Budget Requests

Type of Material	Description
General	
Summary and highlight statement	Summarizes major changes that are being proposed
Budget justification	Compares program benefits and program costs; includes information on program evaluations
Baseline budget estimates	Shows the effects of projecting the current-year budget into the future
Financial management	Reports plans for improving financial management (accounting), including discussion of any material weaknesses or nonconformance with requirements
Resources for financial management activities and systems	Reports planned expenditures for asset management, accounting and reporting, financial auditing, and financial management systems
Financial management systems	Indicates proposed spending for upgrading financial systems in compliance with the Chief Financial Officers Act
Technology management	Reports how planned improvements in financial management are linked with improvements in information technology (computers) and electronic government
Rental payments for space and land	Provides information on costs for rent
Receipts estimates	Shows monies that the agency expects to collect

Tax expenditures	Estimates the effect of proposed exclusions from tax laws, including justifications for those proposed exclusions
Credit liquidating accounts	Indicates monies to be carried forward into next fiscal year to cover current obligations
Impact of full funding of capital assets	Shows the amount of budget authority needed to fund completely projects that are currently being funded incrementally
Energy costs	Reports agencies' spending for energy when paid directly to utilities
Drug control programs	Gives information about drug abuse prevention and treatment and drug law enforcement and prosecution
Annual performance plan	Gives information required by the Government Performance and Results Act, indicating linkage between the strategic plan and the annual performance goals, and linkage between the annual goals and the budget

Computer and Print Materials

Budget authority and outlays	Compares proposed authority to commit government to expenditures and expected expenditures
Character classification	Reports investments in physical assets, research and development, and the conduct of education and training
Program, financing, and object class	Shows program activities and finances according to the annual performance plans required by the Government Performance and Results Act; shows expenditures according to the standard accounting structure for specific object classes (personnel, travel, and the like)
Federal credit	Reports existing credit programs and proposals for extending new credit to potential beneficiaries
Contract authority	Indicates the status of contract authorities such as the amount obligated and the amount expiring

Personnel	Indicates full-time equivalents for personnel and their proposed compensation
Operations/balance sheet	Provides information on assets, liabilities, and net position for programs with revolving funds
Status of funds	Shows balances, cash income, and cash outgo of main trust funds
Budget plan	Reports for military expenditures multiyear obligations in the year that the appropriation is granted
Appropriations requests	Displays net resources included in the proposed appropriations language for accounts requesting new spending authority
Unavailable collections	Reports monies received that are unavailable due to limitations in the law

Print Materials

Appropriations language	Proposes wording that Congress may eventually use to appropriate funds for each account within the agency
Narrative statements on program and performance	Describes each account with activity in the past, current, or budget year in terms of planned objectives and past performance

Additional Information

Grants to state and local governments	Indicates grants going to each state
Motor vehicles	Reports obligations for purchasing, leasing, and operating motor vehicles
Baseline estimates of budgetary effects of major regulations, management initiatives, and administrative actions	Projects resources, outlays, and receipts into future years based on existing laws (current services projections)
Risk categories	Reports risks associated with federal credit programs

Source: Adapted from U.S. Office of Management and Budget, *Preparation and Submission of Budget Estimates*, Circular A-11, 2002.

expects of them. Typically, a calendar will be provided explaining when requests are due for submission to the budget office and indicating a period when agencies may be called for hearings with the budget office. The instructions, then, determine the type and amount of information that will be required of the agencies, although the budget office may request additional information from particular agencies.

No matter what the jurisdiction, standard items can be found in virtually all budget instruction manuals. Where appropriate, agencies are asked to submit revenue data (e.g., an agency operating a loan program with a revolving fund). Most of the instructions, however, concentrate on expenditures. The expenditures are keyed with the accounting system, using objects of expenditures such as personnel and supplies (see Chapter 11). There also may be detailed breakouts on the number of persons in a given unit, their job titles, and their current salaries. The instructions usually allow for the agencies to provide narrative statements to justify their requests.

Separate sets of instructions may be provided for the operating and capital fund budgets. Instructions for the latter, which are used extensively at the state and local levels, are meant primarily for requests on major fixed assets such as buildings and equipment. Federal agencies are required to separate out their investments in fixed assets (see Chapter 12). The federal government, under Executive Order 12837 issued by President Clinton in 1993, at one point attempted to separate administrative expenses from other expenses that provide direct benefits to program participants. According to the executive order, administrative expenses were to be reduced over a multiyear period while other expenses could increase. The Executive Order covered only fiscal years 1994 through 1997 and is not currently in effect.

Program Information

Budget systems are making increased use of program information, and therefore request instructions specify which types of program data are to be supplied. The measures typically will have been negotiated between the budget office and the agencies before budget preparation time. In other words, when the agencies receive the request instructions, they already know what program information they need to submit. Determining what information to collect and present in budget requests is of concern at all levels of government in the United States and abroad. As of the early 2000s, the umbrella term used to describe the overall field of program information was *performance measurement*.[28] Such measurement is seen as a means for holding agencies accountable for the expenditure of tax dollars and other public resources.[29]

Social Indicators. Of the variety of program information, social indicators are the broadest or most general type. These measures of the physical, social, and economic environments are intended to reflect what sometimes is called *quality of life.* The percentage of the work force unemployed broken out by age, sex, race, and income constitutes a set of important social indicators. OMB lists several social indicators in its annual report, *Analytical Perspectives.* This report includes such measures as the median annual family income of female householders with no husband present and infant mortality per 1,000 live births.[30] Measures of this type are useful in assessing past and current trends and provide decision makers with some insights into the need for programs. One volunteer network in the Seattle area has developed 40 such indicators to determine whether the region is maintaining "sustainability" — namely, preserving its "cultural, economic, environmental and social" conditions. In the 1990s, the group found that the region was declining in sustainability in such areas as wetlands, energy use, and children living in poverty.[31]

One limitation of the Seattle measures and other social indicators is their lack of direct linkage with any given government service, meaning that the indicators are of little use for making yearly budget decisions. Children live in poverty as a result of many factors, and no government program alone could be expected to solve the problem.[32] At the same time, social indicators about communities in a state may give rise to decisions about how to help each of the communities in need.[33]

Impacts. Measures of more direct relevance to budgeting are impacts (sometimes called outcomes). Measures of this type concentrate on *effectiveness* — whether desired effects or consequences are being achieved. When a government service has affected "individuals, institutions [or] the environment," an impact has occurred.[34] In the case of employment, an impact measure might be the average earnings of nonwhite men who completed a job training program or, even more narrowly focused, the average increase in hourly earnings after completion of the program compared with prior earnings. Such a measure needs to be assessed carefully, because earnings may have increased in a given time period mainly as a result of inflation or an upturn in the economy. Impacts can be seen as a method of gauging the value of government services or determining whether expenditures for services are investments.[35]

Sometimes myths or doctrines lead to problems in the selection of impact measures. In providing funds to police departments, for example, the assumption is often made that crime will be controlled. This assumption leads to the selection of crime rates as impact measures despite the fact that police have only limited control over crime.

Outputs. In contrast with impact measures, output measures reflect the immediate products or services being provided. Returning to the employment example, the number of graduates of the training program would be the output. The percentage of persons enrolled who graduate — the completion rate — can be calculated from year to year. Such measures are far easier to calculate than many impact measures because the data sources are within the organization. One needs simply to keep accurate records of who enrolled and who graduated. Impacts, on the other hand, are external. In the case of earnings of graduates, a monitoring or follow-up system for the graduates is necessary to obtain the appropriate data.

One drawback of using output measures alone is that an erroneous assumption can be made about causal relationships. Focusing on the graduation rate of the training program makes sense only if it is assumed that training improves employability. Unless data are collected to verify anticipated results, however, the program is being maintained strictly on faith or doctrine. Outputs, then, may encourage *suboptimization,* or the improvement of operations for attaining subobjectives while risking the possibility of moving away from, rather than toward, larger values.

Activities and Workload. Activities are the work that is done to produce outputs. The total hours of instruction could be a measure for a job training program, or the measure might be more tightly focused, such as hours of instruction in lathe operations. Activities are sometimes measured as workload. The number of applications processed and the number of enrollees in a program are both workload measures. If the number of applicants increases even though enrollments are kept constant because of space limitations, the workload will still increase, because more applications must be screened. Both activities and outputs are far easier to measure than impacts, a factor that contributes to the extensive use of the former and more limited use of the latter in budgeting.

Management by Objectives. Workload is often the focus of management by objectives (MBO) and other participative management techniques.[36] Although many diverse activities have been carried out in government under the rubric of MBO, a common theme tends to be prescribing objectives for organizational units, managers, and workers in terms of the work they are expected to accomplish. Participative management systems such as MBO emphasize involvement of all strata of the bureaucracy in the development of objectives.

Productivity. Another term having many different meanings is *productivity.*[37] This term is sometimes used to cover virtually all forms of program measurement. A different approach is to limit the concept of productivity to comparisons of resource inputs and work. Ratios are typically used for productivity measurement, such as the total cost of a job training program divided by the number of graduates, yielding an average cost per graduate. If average cost remains constant from one year to another despite increases in salary rates and various supplies, then the assumption is made that the unit is more productive. Emphasis is placed on making government operations increasingly more efficient. OMB Circular A-11 provides that agencies should report gains in productivity, especially when justifying staffing and other resource needs.

Productivity measures often require extensive recordkeeping. If a group of employees together performs several different activities, then a reporting system is needed to account for the hours committed to each activity by each employee. This accounting is sometimes accomplished by means of daily report forms. State and local police often must submit daily reports on hours spent patrolling, investigating, testifying in court, and report writing itself. Less complicated systems may use weekly, monthly, or quarterly report forms. On the cost side, accounting systems need to capture nonpersonnel expenditures related to activities.

Total Quality Management or Continuous Quality Improvement. Total quality management (TQM) — also called continuous quality improvement — is not a budget system but, as envisioned by its creator, W. Edwards Deming, is a management system that focuses on the end products or results of organizations.[38] Available space does not allow a thorough discussion of TQM, but it should be noted that the system relies heavily on program measurement and that one of Deming's 14 TQM recommendations is to avoid management by objectives. The latter management system is seen as setting quotas for workers rather than empowering them to think creatively and allowing them to achieve results that might well be beyond any expected quotas.

Need. A final type of measure gauges the need for a program. The need measure indicates the gap between the level of service and the need for it. In the case of the job training program, one need measure would be the number of persons who are without adequate job skills and therefore require training.

In discussing need, we have come full circle back to social indicators, prompting a few words of caution. We have relied here on several examples to show differences among types of measures, but it should be understood that the differences might not always be so obvious. For example, the dollar value of fire damage in a city might be considered a social indicator, an impact of the fire department, and an indicator of fire service need.

Using Program Measures. A major challenge facing any budget system is deciding how to use these diverse types of information. Which types will be used, in what combination, and to what extent? An initial temptation is to decide to use every imaginable measure of government operations. Such an approach is doomed to failure. If carefully and thoroughly executed, it would produce massive amounts of data that could not be comprehended by decision makers. Indeed, such data produce what is called "noise" rather than information.

Reformers for decades have been concerned that budgeting keep its focus on the missions of government and on the goals and objectives to be achieved. Osborne and Gaebler's popular work *Reinventing Government* stresses the need to keep mission primarily in mind when making decisions in government.[39] *Mission* refers to the fundamental reasons why a government program exists. Although scholars and practitioners in the field of budgeting have yet to reach any consensus on what constitutes a goal as distinguished from an objective, one approach is to think of goals as broadly stated ideal conditions, such as the absence of crime. *Goals*, under this definition, are unlikely to be achieved but function as desired states that governments can continuously work toward attaining. *Objectives*, on the other hand, are more focused and immediate, and impact data are used to gauge whether a program is moving toward achieving its objectives. A jurisdiction might focus on reducing burglaries and could specify a quantitative target for the future, such as a 10 percent reduction in burglaries. In setting goals and objectives, decision makers must understand that some desired results can be achieved in a comparatively short period, such as a year, whereas other results will require many years of effort to acheive.[40]

The program measures that agencies develop may be a reflection of their overall types of missions. Four such types may exist: distributive, redistributive, regulatory, and market emulators.[41] *Distributive* encompasses the provision of services such as defense and transportation. *Redistributive* refers to making transfer payments, as with rent subsidies, and programs targeted at special groups, such as health benefits for the needy. *Regulatory*, as the term suggests, concentrates on control, such as controlling would-be air polluters or controlling food producers as a means of protecting the nation's food supply. *Market emulators* are those government operations that are run like a business, such as public utilities. To some extent, operations such as municipal golf courses and institutions of higher education may operate somewhat like businesses.

Selecting measures for any given program depends on perceptions about the program's mission, and individuals may differ widely on what they consider to be a specific program's mission. In a broad sense, the vision one has of a program is related to one's perception of what the public interest is. In a narrow sense, individuals may have specific expectations of what government programs should accomplish. Renters may want a city housing program to focus on affordable rental housing, while homeowners may be largely concerned with city policies that will protect property values and keep taxes low. Owners of rental properties, in contrast, may be chiefly interested in achieving substantial returns on their financial investments. Ultimately, then, the success of many, if not most, government programs will be evaluated in terms of several measures rather than only one or two. The need to use multiple measures makes analysis of a program's achievements more challenging than if a single measure is used (see Chapter 7).

Interpreting measures, especially social indicators and impacts, poses an additional problem. Because conditions in society result from a wide assortment of variables, isolating government's contribution to any given situation is difficult. One of the most difficult tasks in developing program measures is to select those that reflect what a particular government accomplishes. The federal government faces considerable challenges in this arena, because national programs are carried out through a variety of means, such as through state and local government and nonprofit organizations. If a given program is successful, to what extent is the success due to partial funding by the federal government?[42]

Choosing among Program Results. Inevitably some tradeoffs occur when trying to decide among programs. Consequently, *equity* becomes a concern — are different segments of the citizenry benefiting according to some standard of fairness? The perceived severity of a problem to be addressed by government enters into such deliberations, such as the perception that a community has a major illegal drug problem or that the nation must address the problem of conquering acquired immune deficiency syndrome (AIDS). In both of these examples, a tempering factor is whether government programs are able to use infusions of resources effectively. Large budget allocations for combating drugs or AIDS will not necessarily resolve these problems.

Governments are at a disadvantage in making these difficult choices in comparison with private corporations, which have the profit motive as their primary concern. Put simply, a private corporation will invest in those product lines that are expected to yield the highest rate of return on investments. Governments utilize some combination of the types of program information discussed here but cannot readily convert them into a single measure of profit. Instead, they must choose among disparate commodities such as fire protection, air pollution reduction, and public transit. Making comparisons may help in this situation. Cost-benefit studies, discussed in Chapter 7, can provide insights into the return on public investments.

▮ Systems of Budgeting

If the central budget office simply instructed agencies to request budgets for the coming year, the result most likely would be several different types of responses based on different assumptions about the coming budget year. One agency might respond by requesting what it felt was needed. Another might respond in light of what resources it thought were available, resulting in a much lower request. Others might use combinations of these and other approaches. The consequences would be budget requests based on varied assumptions, and these requests would require different reactions by the budget office. To avoid such disparities in the assumptions made by requesting agencies, budget instructions often provide guidance to agencies.

Preparation Assumptions

Current Services Budgeting. One type of guidance is to assume essentially no change in programs. A department's current budget is considered its *base*, and any increases are to be requested only to cover additional operating costs, such as increased costs for personnel, supplies, and so on. An assumption is made that the government is committed or obligated to continue existing programs. This base approach often has been used only implicitly, but since the 1960s and 1970s many governments have had their budgets explicitly indicate levels of commitment for agencies and programs. The federal budget has included current services estimates since the 1970s. For the federal government, current services estimates are frequently referred to as "baseline" budget estimates. A baseline budget, like a current services budget, estimates the effects of continuing current tax and spending policies into the future.

Explicitly determining the current commitments is difficult because programs often are created without any forthright statement of commitment. In the easiest cases, there is an obligation to serve all claimants on the system. School districts, for example, are obligated to serve all eligible children, and therefore budget requests from units within the school district would be based on the expected number of enrolled children. In other cases, the commitment may be in terms of the level of service, specifically outputs and workload. Using job training as an example again, the unit could have a commitment to maintain the same number of graduates or, alternatively, the same number of students. Budgeting, then, can be seen as adding increments to or subtracting them from the base.

Fixed-Ceiling Budgeting. An alternative to the current commitment approach is fixed-ceiling budgeting. Under this system, a dollar limit is set government-wide, then factored into limits for departments, bureaus, and other subunits. The advantage is that budget requests are created that do not, when totaled, exceed the desired ceiling. The disadvantage is that some organizational units may receive inadequate funding and others may be overfunded in terms of program priorities. This imbalance can result from the unavailability of adequate information about program requirements when limits are set. Fixed-ceiling budgeting is most useful during periods of stability.

A weakness of both the base and fixed-ceiling approaches is that by themselves they offer no suggestions for program changes. If the budget office and chief executive have only these types of budget requests, they lack information about alternative resource allocations. In response to this lack of information, several "what-if" approaches to budget requests have been devised. These approaches ask agencies to develop alternatives by asking, for example, What if more dollars were available? Or what if program improvements were to be made in specific areas?

Open-Ended Budgeting. One of the most common what-if approaches is openended or "blue-sky" budgeting. The question is asked, What if resources were available to meet all anticipated needs? Agencies are expected to ask for what they think they need to deal with problems assigned to them. This approach should not be confused with the absence of guidance, in which some agencies might request "needed" funds and others might ask for lesser amounts. The advantage of the open-ended approach is that it brings perceived needs for services to the surface. The open-ended budget, in contrast with the current services budget, can serve as the basis for discussions of preferred funding levels. The disadvantage is that open-ended requests may exceed the economic and political capabilities of the jurisdiction, making the requests seem like fanciful wish lists. Such has been the case in the Department of Defense and its use of the Joint Strategic Objectives Plan (JSOP), which is based on the assumption that defense forces should be as strong as necessary to meet all potential threats simultaneously.[43]

Performance Budgeting

A flurry of budget reform activity aimed at bringing greater program data into the budget decision-making process occurred in response to the First Hoover Commission (1949), which proposed the use of performance budgeting. In response to the commission's recommendation, Congress specifically provided in the National Security Act Amendments of 1949 that performance budgeting be used in the military.[44] The following year saw passage of the Budget and Accounting Procedures Act, which in essence required performance budgeting for the entire federal government.[45] State and local governments followed suit.

Among federal, state, and local agencies, performance budgeting was geared mainly toward developing workload and unit cost measures of activities. For the postal service, the number of letters that could be processed by one employee was identified. Armed with this knowledge and an estimate of the number of letters to be processed, postal officials could calculate the personnel required for the coming budget year.[46] In the name of performance budgeting, the Department of Defense in 1950 adopted a single set of budget categories that were applied to all services. These categories, most of which were still in use in the 2000s, included personnel, maintenance and operation, and research and development.

Applying performance budgeting to all aspects of government is difficult. For instance, there is no easy method for determining how much defense is enough. The problem is that defense is mainly a matter of deterrence and preparedness. The military is expected to have sufficient strength to deter an attack by a potential aggressor and to be sufficiently prepared for war or other emergencies if they do occur. The deterrent strategy is working when no attack has been launched. Preparedness, on the other hand, can be tested only in real combat and other military situations. When the nation is not fighting a war or deploying troops in emergency situations at home or abroad, it is difficult to prove conclusively that the nation is or is not sufficiently prepared.

Although reconstructing the past is difficult, little evidence suggests that performance budgeting ever became the basis upon which decisions were made in federal, state, or local budget processes. Nevertheless, some lasting effect is evident. Performance budgeting did introduce on a wide scale the use of program information in budget documents as well as the use of performance information for various purposes. Both program and performance information gained increasing attention in later years.

Planning-Programming-Budgeting and Program Budgeting

The origin of the term *planning-programming-budgeting* is uncertain. Mosher used it in his 1954 book on Army program budgeting.[47] During the early 1960s in the Department of Defense, PPB stood for program package budgeting, because a package was presented in terms of the resource inputs (personnel, equipment, and so forth) and outputs.[48] By 1965, when President Lyndon Johnson extended the system to civilian agencies, PPB had come to mean planning-programming-budgeting. It should be recognized that planning and programming are not distinct from each other but differ only in degree. They have been defined as follows:

> *Planning* is the production of the range of meaningful potentials for selection of courses of action through a systematic consideration of alternatives. *Programming* is the more specific determination of the manpower, material, and facilities necessary for accomplishing a program.[49]

Today, PPB is generally used to refer to a series of budgetary reform efforts in the 1960s. The term program budgeting is more generic and applies to systems intended to link program costs with results.

Defense. There are several reasons why PPB started in the Department of Defense. Probably the most important one was that, despite having the authority to manage the military, the secretary of defense did not have the necessary management support. Secretary Robert S. McNamara in 1961 had the determination to initiate change. In coming to the Pentagon, he brought with him several people from the

RAND Corporation who earlier had done extensive work related to program budgeting. David Novick of RAND published reports in the 1950s recommending such a system for the Department of Defense.[50] The key person for program budgeting under McNamara was Charles J. Hitch, who became assistant secretary of defense (comptroller). McNamara, Hitch, and others made use of the development of operations research, computers, and systems analysis, all of which were complementary to the mainstream of budgetary reform.

The central component of the Department of Defense system is the Future Years Defense Program (FYDP), which projects costs and personnel according to missions or programs. The programs form the *program structure*, a classification system that begins with broad missions and factors them into subunits and activities. The structure groups like activities together regardless of which branches of the service conduct them, thereby allowing for analyses across organizational lines. The major programs within the FYDP are as follows:

- Strategic forces
- General-purpose forces
- Intelligence and communications
- Airlift and sealift
- Guard and reserve
- Research and development
- Central supply and maintenance
- Training, medical, and other general personnel activities
- Administration and associated activities
- Support of other nations
- Special operations forces

Changes in terminology and process have occurred since the 1960s, but overall the main approach in the Department of Defense has remained constant. Changes in the FYDP are accomplished by the Office of the Secretary of Defense issuing guidance, to which the services respond by preparing program objective memoranda, which contain budget proposals for modifying the FYDP.[51] The program objective memoranda suggest programmatic and resource incremental changes to the base established in the FYDP. In addition to this elaborate process, the Department of Defense undergoes a Quadrennial Defense Review every four years, following the presidential election. While the PPB system is organized around programs, Congress has continued to appropriate funds for defense based on object classifications, with the main ones including military personnel; operation and maintenance; procurement; research, development, test, and evaluation; and military construction.

The Department of Defense's PPB system has been in operation for about four decades, but the system clearly has not proved a panacea for all defense-related problems. During that period the department was subjected to extensive and severe criticism regarding its conduct of the Vietnam War. Since then, major cost overruns and failures of various weapons systems have occured, along with scandals involving alleged corruption in weapons contracting. Clearly, budget systems may provide useful information for decision makers but do not guarantee that wise decisions will be made.

In 1995, the Commission on Roles and Missions of the Armed Forces, created by the National Defense Authorization Act for Fiscal Year 1994, issued a wide-sweeping set of recommendations, including a call for a major overhaul of the defense budget process. Earlier, the National Performance Review (NPR) had suggested changes in the process, but the 1995 Commission made recommendations that would fundamentally revise the system.[52] The report stated, "The current PPB system reexamines the entire multiyear defense program annually, uses too many people, takes too long, goes into too much detail, and leaves little time for reflection and creativity."[53] The revised system, if adopted, would have two phases: the first concentrating on the broad decisions about defense and the second focusing on how to meet those needs through the budget process. The powers of the secretary of defense would be enhanced and the individual armed services would be brought into closer linkage with one another. Any new system needs to take into consideration the fact that defense is organized simultaneously by type of weapons system (missiles, aircraft, naval ships, and the like), geography (Western Europe, Pacific, and so on), and mission. The latter has changed dramatically since the end of the Cold War, so that today there is less concern about nuclear attack. Instead, there is an increased emphasis on the use of the military to combat terrorism throughout the world, coupled with other missions such as selectively serving to bring stability to various regions and providing humanitarian relief for civilians caught in the middle of conflict.[54]

Despite much discussion during the Clinton administration, the defense decision-making system remained largely unchanged and was passed to the George W. Bush administration in 2001. Secretary Donald Rumsfeld wrestled with the question of how to structure defense so as to meet contemporary challenges, such as civil wars in the Balkans or (particularly) the war on terrorism. Even before the events of September 11, 2001, the General Accounting Office indicated that the Defense Department faced "major performance and accountability challenges."[55]

Federal Civilian Reforms. Turning to the civilian side of government, use of PPB by federal agencies was announced in 1965 by President Johnson, who had been impressed with the Department of Defense budget system. This action sparked massive reform efforts throughout all levels of government in the United States.

The federal civilian system was intended to be similar to the Department of Defense model. Multiyear plans, known as program and financial plans, were to be devised for each department. Changes were to be made through the submission of program memoranda. However, by 1969, when Richard M. Nixon became president, PPB had not been fully implemented by the civilian agencies. In 1971, OMB relieved agencies of the duty to prepare program and financial plans and program memoranda. As a major budget system, PPB was allowed to die a quiet death.[56]

A study conducted by the Bureau of the Budget (now OMB) found six factors that characterized the more successful efforts to introduce PPB: [57]

1. The number of analysts was sufficient.

2. Analysts were well qualified.

3. Analysts had formal access to agency heads and managers.

4. Analysts had informal access.

5. Agency heads and managers gave strong support for use of analysis.

6. Analysis was viewed as a valuable tool by agency heads and managers.

This study and others found that lack of understanding of and commitment to program budgeting on the part of leadership tended to deter success, as did an agency's general "underdevelopment" in the use of analytic techniques. Agencies administering "soft" social programs had difficulty devising useful program measures. Bureaucratic infighting also reduced the chances of successful implementation. These findings are instructive for any government that undertakes to restructure the operations of its budget system.

State and Local Reforms. The use of PPB did not revolutionize state and local decision making in the 1960s any more than it revolutionized federal decision making. Most of the states that experimented with PPB emphasized the development of program structure, multiyear plans, and program memoranda, while only a few concentrated on analysis as their main thrust. By the mid-1970s, the emphasis had swung away from the structural features of PPB to the use of measures of effectiveness and efficiency and program analysis. In the 1960s, many states and municipalities took only cautious first steps and established no timetable for completion of the installation process. Others began the effort on a pilot basis, attempting PPB in one department before expanding its use.

By the close of the 1960s, it was difficult to identify many ongoing PPB systems at the state and local levels. The reasons for failure or lack of major success were similar to those already mentioned for federal agencies. State and local governments usually did not have sufficiently sophisticated management practices to be able to undertake the expected transformation. Additionally, people simply expected too much to result from conversion to PPB and did not realize the financial and administrative costs associated with the conversion. Legislative bodies often showed little support for the new budget system, and this fact was interpreted by some as legislative hostility toward change.[58]

Change, however, did occur as a result of efforts to introduce PPB systems. Perhaps the biggest single achievement was that governments began to make greater use of program information in budgetary decision making, albeit information largely of the output variety.[59] This pattern continued through the 1980s but, as discussed later, may have waned somewhat in the 1990s.

Zero-Base Budgeting

Zero-base budgeting (ZBB) is another form of "what-if" budgeting. "Traditional" ZBB — that is, not the type used by the federal government during the Carter administration — asks, What if a program were to be eliminated? Rather than assuming that a base exists, the approach asks what would happen if a program were discontinued. Each program is challenged to justify its very existence in every budget cycle.

Early Use. The U.S. Department of Agriculture engaged in an experiment with ZBB in the early 1960s, and the results were disappointing.[60] ZBB, it was found, wasted valuable administrative time by requiring the rehashing of old issues that had already been resolved. The system was unrealistic; many programs were mandatory within the political arena and could not be dismantled no matter how compelling the available data and analysis. Decision makers within the agency could not adequately review the excessive paperwork that was generated.

The disadvantage of ZBB is analogous to that of open-ended budgeting. Both approaches make basically unrealistic assumptions. Whereas open-ended budgeting assumes unlimited resources, the zero-base approach assumes that decision makers have the capacity to eliminate enough programs to justify the time spent in evaluating them. In reality, the political forces in any jurisdiction are such that few programs in any given year can be abandoned. For this reason, ZBB may be better applied to selective programs in any one year rather than government-wide. A cycle of reviews can be established such that some programs are thoroughly reviewed each year using ZBB, and all programs are reviewed in any five-year period.

The 1970s. ZBB gained new popularity in the 1970s.[61] Much attention focused on Georgia and its governor, Jimmy Carter, who subsequently brought a new version of ZBB to the federal government upon becoming president in 1977.[62] The

Carter administration's version had three major characteristics: [63]

1. *Decision units* were identified for which budget requests, called decision packages, were to be prepared. Approximately 10,000 of these were prepared each year.

2. Alternative funding levels were used for each package:

   - The *minimum level,* which entailed providing services below present levels;

   - The *current level,* which maintained existing services and reflected increased costs for personnel, supplies, and the like; and

   - An *enhancement level,* which provided for upgraded services.

3. Alternative funding levels of decision packages were to be *ranked* by importance.

The ZBB experiment at the federal level was criticized on several counts. The most frequently heard complaint related to the amount of time required to prepare requests and the corresponding deluge of paperwork. The ZBB system, contrary to what President Carter had promised, did not require agencies to justify every tax dollar they received. Administrators puzzled over how a minimum level below current operations could exist when the statute under which an agency operated specified benefits, as in the case of Social Security.

ZBB rarely eliminated unnecessary programs, curtailed their growth, or resulted in reassigning priorities among programs.[64] In some isolated instances, savings were achieved by funding programs at the minimum level, but that produced agency resentment. Administrators of these programs saw themselves as being punished because they had identified how their programs could operate with less than the current budget. More often, however, the system was seen as involving excessive paperwork that ultimately had little or no impact on policy making. Shortly after President Reagan took office in January 1981, the new administration announced that ZBB would no longer be practiced.

The experience at the state and local levels was comparable to that of the federal government. ZBB initially seemed to hold great promise but ultimately was abandoned, although some governments continued to describe their budget systems as founded on the concept.

One observation was that ZBB efforts in the 1970s were doomed because of the immense amount of data that needed to be processed with technology that would seem ancient compared with today's standards. An extension of such reasoning is that today's technology may make possible ZBB and other reforms that failed in earlier times.[65]

Strategic Planning and Guidance

Planning. Some governments, in part following the lead of private sector organizations, have engaged in strategic planning efforts, which focus attention on missions, goals, and objectives.[66] In *strategic planning*, options are identified and chosen in light of fundamental values and purposes. Annual budgeting is then used to allocate resources according to the established priorities. Some have called budget systems that use strategic planning and performance measurement *performance-based budgeting* (PBB).[67] Performance-based budgeting is not to be confused with *performance budgeting* (mentioned earlier). PBB differs, as did program budgeting, in that it focuses on results rather than on workload or activity.

Strategic planning can be an extremely time-consuming process in which various plans, often presented in great detail, are drafted, reviewed, and then modified. This process usually involves developing an overall plan and then revising the plan annually to reflect new information and revised priorities. Comparisons can be drawn here with the Department of Defense's JSOP and FYDP, mentioned earlier. The process of devising and revising plans is sometimes considered as valuable as the actual written plans themselves, in that the process fosters extensive thinking within a government about its core values in serving the citizenry.

Policy and Program Guidance. A less ambitious but nevertheless useful approach is to provide broad policy guidance or more narrowly focused program guidance to departments and agencies before they begin to prepare their budget requests. At the federal level, the OMB often instructs specific agencies regarding which program funding proposals are likely to receive favorable review and instructs them to prepare issue papers on specific programs for which concern exists about the efficacy of resource utilization. Some state and local budget offices provide program guidelines that indicate to agencies the concerns of their governors or mayors — namely, the issues that have high priority for the coming budget year.

In response to such guidance, agencies prepare detailed program requests. A discussion of the range of available alternatives is likely to take place, possibly with detailed costing and the expected results of each. Where guidance is not directed at any one agency, two or more may submit competing requests, each attempting to show how its proposed alternative would deal with a problem. For example, both the city police and the recreation departments might submit budget proposals for dealing with juvenile delinquency.

The advantage of such guidance is that agencies prepare requests that are likely to be favorably received by the chief executive and are spared many hours of needless work in preparing requests that are fated for rejection. Policy or program guidance, however, does not ensure executive approval of agency requests.

The requests may be rejected simply because of inadequate funds or because the arguments for the proposed changes fail to persuade decision makers.

Multiyear Requests

All budget requests are multiyear in that they at least cover the current year plus the coming budget year and probably the past year as well. States with biennial budgets obviously have multiyear requests. One issue is whether budget requests should extend beyond the budget year and, if so, how a multi-year perspective is to be included in the budget. The argument for multiyear requests is simple: Without looking beyond the budget year, commitments of resources may be made that were never intended. This argument applies particularly to proposed expansions and new programs (see Chapter 12). The budget directors of the 29 member countries of the Organization for Economic Cooperation and Development (OECD) have agreed that results-oriented budgeting using multi-year forecasting needs to be adopted.[68]

Time Horizons. In theory, the time horizon of a budget request should be geared to the life cycle of each program. This life cycle is clearest in specific projects or programs that have an obvious beginning and conclusion. A weapons system is one of the best examples. The cycle begins with research and concludes when the system is judged to be obsolete.

On the other hand, many government programs have no foreseeable conclusion. The need for education, roads, law enforcement, recreation, and the like will always exist. Each may have unique properties that suggest possible time horizons. Given the length of time required to design and construct schools, projections of several years are needed. Multiyear requests can reveal when roads will require major repairs, redesigns, and expansions. Indeed, the necessity for multiyear planning is often part of the justification for the separate capital budgeting processes pursued by many governments.

Because an appropriate life cycle for multiyear requests often is not obvious, an arbitrary set of years may be imposed. The most common is the budget year plus the four succeeding years, known as a five-year projection. The federal government, for example, makes such projections. Making projections beyond five years is difficult because of the many unknowns. Using the road example, it may be largely unknown what the typical commuting pattern will be 10 or more years from now. Further, political leaders have limited incentives to focus on costs or benefits that occur many years in the future, because these future costs and benefits will likely arise outside of their electoral window (see Chapter 8).

Cost and Program Projections. Assuming they can be made, projections can be limited to finances or can include program data projections. The state of the art tends to limit projections to finances, showing anticipated future financial requirements. When program impacts and outputs are projected, the requests show what resources will be needed in future years as well as the benefits that will be accrued.

Multiyear projections using cost and program data can prove helpful in coping with severe economic conditions. Where program reductions are necessary, agency requests can illustrate the consequences over a longer time period. Cuts in an agency's budget made this year may seem essential but produce undesirable future consequences. To live within available revenues, a city may reduce its road maintenance program, with no noticeable reduction in road quality in the first year; however, by the second or third year following these cuts, the city may have a road network of substantially lower quality than before.

Use of Budget Techniques

Hybrid Techniques. Many of the techniques discussed here can be used in combination to form hybrid systems. ZBB, for example, can be used selectively for some agencies undergoing intensive review even as others use a fixed-ceiling approach. A government may use fixed-ceiling budgeting to allocate monies among major departments but then allow each department to use *entrepreneurial budgeting* — namely, allocating funds within the department with only a minimum of control from the central budget office.[69] *Target-base budgeting* is also sometimes used. In this type of budgeting, agencies prepare budget requests based on fixed ceilings but then may propose budget increases above the ceilings.[70] Governments can use a current services budget in conjunction with priority listing of decision packages in an approach akin to the Carter administration's version of ZBB. The base approach can be combined with open-ended budgeting, in which agencies request funds for what they perceive to be their needs. Program guidance can be linked with priority listings.

Federal Initiatives — National Performance Review. Upon taking office in 1993, President Clinton established NPR under the direction of Vice President Gore. NPR's initial report, issued in 1993, contained a host of recommendations intended to streamline all aspects of the government.[71] Prompted by the work of this group, President Clinton issued Executive Order 12862 in 1993, requiring that federal agencies devise *customer service standards,* intended to establish levels of performance by agencies. The executive order instructed agencies to determine what services customers demand and what complaints customers have, and to allocate resources — make budget decisions — based on customer satisfaction. Some standards that have been adopted simply indicate that an agency will perform a certain task, such as the National Park Service committing itself to keeping the "Great Smoky Mountains visitor center open every day but Christmas."[72] Other standards are time-specific, such as the Highway Traffic Safety Administration committing to mailing a registration form for hazardous material within 10 days of receiving a request for the form.[73]

NPR, which continued through President Clinton's second term, became known as the National Partnership for Reinventing Government and had as its focus the *reengineering* or *reinvention* of government.[74] *Benchmarking* was an important component in which best practices elsewhere, whether in government or the private sector, were identified and used as a guide for revising how government operates. As NPR reported, benchmarking was "stealing shamelessly" from the best, as in the case of the Social Security Administration learning about toll-free telephone service from American Express, AT&T Universal Card, Citibank, and the like.[75] Other aspects of NPR included an emphasis on regulatory reform and seeking opportunities for privatizing government services.

At the end of the Clinton administration in 2001, those involved in NPR claimed great results. Savings were said to amount to $137 billion.[76] Others, including the U.S. General Accounting Office and federal employees who were surveyed, said that NPR had not been as successful as some had claimed.[77] The contention was sometimes made that reinventors were taking the unrealistic position that administration should be removed from politics.[78] When George W. Bush became president, he allowed NPR to fade into history but kept some activities, such as a government-wide survey of customer satisfaction. For example, agencies surveyed visitors to national parks, participants in state Medicaid programs, and Army personnel receiving new equipment.[79]

Federal Initiatives — Government Performance and Results Act. Occurring coincident with the NPR was congressional passage of the Government Performance and Results Act (GPRA, pronounced "gip-ra") of 1993 and the law's ensuing implementation. This law resulted from a congressional and presidential concern about "waste and inefficiency" in government and "insufficient articulation of program goals and inadequate information on program performance." It is based on the premise that agencies (1) need to define their missions and desired outcomes, (2) measure performance, and (3) use the performance information to revise programs.[80] All aspects of GPRA are under the direction of the OMB and the Chief Financial Officers (CFO) Council, consisting of the top financial officers of major federal agencies.[81] OMB Circular A-11, which instructs agencies on how to prepare their budgets, provides guidance on the implementation of GPRA. This law is part of a series of legislative initiatives aimed at improving the management of the federal government .[82]

Federal agencies were required to have strategic planning processes and plans in place by the end of fiscal 1997. Each plan covers at least five years and includes a mission statement, outcome-related goals and objectives, a discussion of factors that are beyond the agency's control and could affect its ability to achieve the goals and objectives, and an explanation of how program evaluations were used in developing the plan. **Exhibit 5–1** illustrates a system in which mission and desired outcomes lead to performance measures, and the use of performance information helps redefine missions and desired outcomes.

Beginning with fiscal year 1999, annual performance plans were prepared as outgrowths of the multiyear strategic plans. The OMB did not prescribe a specific format for the annual plans, but Circular A-11 gives agencies overall guidance for what information the plans must contain. The performance plans must include information about outcomes, outputs, and activities. By March 31, 2000, each agency was required to submit its annual program performance plan to the president and Congress.

Given the diversity of agencies within the federal government and the immensity of the task of implementing GPRA, unevenness in the quality of the annual plans was inevitable. In its review of the first draft plans, GAO said that

Exhibit 5–1 Implementing GPRA: Key Steps and Critical Practices

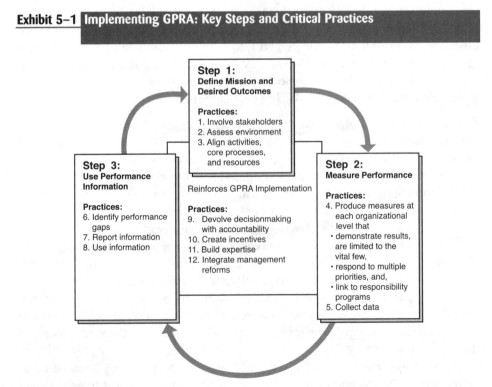

Step 1:
Define Mission and
Desired Outcomes

Practices:
1. Involve stakeholders
2. Assess environment
3. Align activities,
   core processes,
   and resources

Step 3:
Use Performance
Information

Practices:
6. Identify performance
   gaps
7. Report information
8. Use information

Reinforces GPRA Implementation

Practices:
9. Devolve decisionmaking
    with accountability
10. Create incentives
11. Build expertise
12. Integrate management
    reforms

Step 2:
Measure Performance

Practices:
4. Produce measures at
   each organizational
   level that
   • demonstrate results,
     are limited to the
     vital few,
   • respond to multiple
     priorities, and,
   • link to responsibility
     programs
5. Collect data

Source: Reprinted from *Executive Guide: Effectively Implementing the Government Performance and Results Act*, p.10, 1996, U.S. General Accounting Office.

"a significant amount of work" needed to be done for agencies to meet GPRA's requirements.[83] Goals were said to be vague, such as the Veterans' Affairs' goal to "improve benefit programs." Objectives and goals as stated often could not be measured. Social Security, for instance, said it aimed "to promote valued, strong, and responsive social security programs." The OMB's own plan was critized for such weaknesses as failing to show a clear results orientation of goals and objectives and failing to show how the unit's strategies would move toward the attainment of goals and objectives.[84] In a later evaluation of the linkage between performance and budget data, GAO stated that 75 percent of agencies required by the CFO Act to produce audited financial statements "were able to show a direct link between expected performance and requested program activity funding levels" for fiscal year 2002. This level represented an increase from the 40 percent of agencies showing similar linkages in 1999.[85] The agencies' plans are available on the Web through FirstGov (see Chapter 11).

In 1997, the leadership in the Republican-controlled House of Representatives graded the plans using 10 factors.[86] The two top agencies, Transportation and Education, received grades of "C." Of the other 22 agencies, four were said to have minimally acceptable reports, with the rest being deemed failures. The report criticized "low-ball" goals, meaning that agencies were setting easy targets for themselves. The Agriculture Department, for example, intended to resolve any Y2K (Year 2000) computer problems by 2002. Agencies were criticized for reaching beyond their missions, such as the Small Business Administration being concerned with the welfare-to-work program when it supposedly should be interested only in helping small businesses.

By the early 2000s, the plans had been improved, but considerable work remained. A group of scholars at George Mason University ranked as the best plans those from Veterans Affairs, Transportation, and the Agency for International Development.[87] Critics, however, contended that the plans failed to reflect the Bush administration's priorities, such as cost cutting and expanded outsourcing of operations.[88]

Another review of agency experience in "managing for results" in general reviewed 27 agencies between 1999 and 2002. The Federal Performance Project (FPP) was carried out by The George Washington University and *Government Executive* magazine under the sponsorship of The Pew Charitable Trusts. The FPP found some impressive examples of results-based management in places such as the U.S. Coast Guard and the National Weather Service, both of which received "A" grades. It also uncovered some examples of agencies that still have substantial progress to make, including the Immigration and Naturalization Service and the Bureau of Indian Affairs, recipients of overall "D" grades. The overall average across the federal government was a "B minus" over the 27 agencies evaluated.[89]

The new Bush administration emphasized that it planned to go forward with GPRA. OMB Director Mitchell E. Daniels, Jr., and Deputy Director Sean O'Keefe spoke publicly in support of the effort. O'Keefe said, "First and most critically is the president's very clear signal that he wants his administration and our government to be results-oriented."[90]

The Bush administration's interested in performance-based budgeting is probably most clearly manifested in its emphasis on "budget and performance integration" as one of the president's five management initiatives. (The others are strategic human capital, competitive outsourcing, financial management, and electronic government.) The administration subjected 26 departments, including all cabinet agencies, to a review of the linkage between performance and the budget as a part of the fiscal year 2003 budget process. It awarded "green lights" to agencies that had satisfied all of the administration's core criteria, "yellow lights" to those with a mixed record, and "red lights" to those with the most significant remaining impediments to results-based budgeting. The administration believed that substantial obstacles remained to full implementation, as reflected in the initial set of "scores" published in February 2002 — no green lights, three yellow lights (Environmental Protection Agency, Department of Transportation, and Small Business Administration), and 23 red lights.[91] The scores reported in the Fiscal Year 2004 budget demonstrated some progress, with five more agencies joining these three with "yellow" scores, and 18 agencies rated as "red." The five new yellow-light agencies were the departments of Commerce, Defense, Labor, and Veterans Affairs, and the National Aeronautics and Space Administration.[92] The administration promised that the executive branch budget process would continue to focus on results for future fiscal years. Specifically, OMB Director Daniels unveiled a new analytical device called the Program Assessment Rating Tool (PART), which was used for the first time in the fiscal year 2004 budget process. PART is designed to evaluate the extent to which federal programs are achieving desired results. Initially, more than 200 programs, representing 24 percent of federal spending, were to be reviewed.[93]

OMB Circular A-123, the Paperwork Reduction Act of 1995, and the Information Technology Management Reform Act of 1996 further strengthen the federal government's commitment to program measurement and government reengineering. A-123, which was revised in 1995, requires that agencies establish management controls to "ensure that (1) programs achieve their intended results, (2) resources are used consistent with agency mission, (3) programs and resources are protected from waste, fraud, and mismanagement, (4) laws and regulations are followed, and (5) reliable and timely information is obtained, maintained, reported, and used for decision making."[94] The Paperwork Reduction Act of 1995 requires that the OMB ensure that agencies share information through the

Government Information Locator Service (GILS).[95] Through the sharing of information, agencies can reduce the demands they make on state and local governments, corporations, and individuals to supply information needed for program measurement. The Information Technology Management Reform Act of 1996 requires that agencies use appropriate information technology when setting goals and establishing program measures.[96]

Rather than discussing many of the problems with implementing GPRA here, that discussion is deferred until state and local efforts and those in other countries are first discussed. The problems of implementing budgeting systems based on a results-based orientation are immense, although not necessarily insurmountable.

State Techniques. Various surveys of state budget offices shed light on state budgetary practices. In a longitudinal study of state budgeting, the use of effectiveness measures in budget documents increased from 29 percent of the states in 1970 to 88 percent in 2000, and the use of productivity measures increased from 45 percent to 88 percent.[97] About three-fourths of the states (79 percent) reported that agencies, when requesting approval of new programs or revisions in existing programs, are required to submit data on estimated program effectiveness. This figure, while substantial, was down considerably from the 95 percent figures of 1985 and 1990, perhaps suggesting some backsliding among the states.[98] In 2000, a majority of the states (78 percent) reported using written policy guidance (up from 30 percent in 1970). Only 39 percent reported using written program guidance. More than half of the states (62 percent) used a current services budget, and 87 percent used priority ranking. About half of the states (53 percent) said they use fixed ceilings expressed in dollars.[99]

Other surveys have shed additional light on state techniques. One study found that 10 states used performance measures and then tied appropriations to the measures: Arkansas, Hawaii, Illinois, Louisiana, New Hampshire, New Jersey, Texas, Virginia, Washington, and Wisconsin.[100] Intriguingly, a survey of state executive and legislative budgeters found disagreement in eight states regarding whether performance-based budgeting (PBB) had been implemented. These states were Alabama, Georgia, Idaho, Minnesota, New Hampshire, Ohio, Vermont, and Washington. Nine states reported not implementing PBB, and 29 states reported implementing PBB.[101] On the plus side, the vast majority of the respondents said that PBB had improved their understanding of state government operations (82 percent); on the minus side, a substantial majority said the system had increased their workload (75 percent). More than half (61 percent) said that PBB could not be traced to even some changes in appropriations.[102]

The Government Performance Project, an activity of the Maxwell School at Syracuse University in cooperation with *Governing* magazine, has been studying management capacity in both state and local governments. Using a letter-grade system, the project found a wide range of performance in managing for results in 1999 and 2001. The top-ranked states in 2001, all with grades of "A-", were Iowa, Missouri, Texas, Virginia, and Washington. The lowest-ranked states were New Hampshire and South Dakota, with "D" grades. Alabama, which had been the only "F" state in 1999, received a "D+" grade in 2001.[103]

Local Techniques. Use of program information at the local level is more limited than at the state level. A mid-1990s study of members of the Government Finance Officers Association found that 51 percent of local governments still used line-item budgeting.[104] Performance budgeting and zero-base/target-base budgeting were used by 2 to 3 percent, while program budgeting was used by 10 percent of the local governments. Thirty-five percent reported using a hybrid system. In another 1990s study, this one of medium-size cities (population of 25,000 to 1 million), 41 percent of the cities used program budgeting and 30 percent used ZBB, with the latter being down 15 percentage points from a survey of five years earlier.[105] Surveys of local governments — specifically, cities — have found that from 30 percent to more than 60 percent used performance measurement and monitoring in the budget process.[106]

Some studies have focused specifically on the use of performance measures. One survey of cities with 25,000 population or more found that 38 percent reported using performance measures.[107] Usage of measures increased with population size, with more than 75 percent of the largest cities (250,000 population or more) reporting usage of performance measures. Usage also varied by functional area. For example, workload or output measures were employed in 72 percent of fire departments of the cities that used such measures, compared with only 45 percent of housing departments. Variation was noted among the types of measures. Of the police departments using measures, 78 percent used workload or output measures, 64 percent used outcomes or effectiveness measures, and 53 percent used client or citizen satisfaction measures, but only 32 percent used unit cost or efficiency measures.

A similar study was done of counties with more than 50,000 population.[108] One-third of the counties (34 percent) reported using performance measurement. Of those cities reporting usage, 80 percent or more reported usage in personnel, finance, corrections, parks and recreation, code enforcement, street maintenance, and animals. Police came in at 79 percent and fire at 54 percent.

In addition to grading the states, the Government Performance Project has graded the nation's largest cities and counties on several factors, including managing for results.[109] The highest-ranked city, with an "A", was Phoenix. "A-" cities were Austin, Indianapolis, Milwaukee, and San Diego. The lowest-graded cities, with scores of "D+", were Buffalo and New Orleans. Milwaukee, which had a high grade, has attracted attention as to how a city can undergo comprehensive management and budget reform.[110] At the county level, the highest grades went to Fairfax, Virginia, and Maricopa, Arizona, with "A-" grades. The lowest-rated were Nassau, New York ("D-"), and Allegheny, Pennsylvania ("D").[111]

Although a substantial number of local governments continue to use traditional line-item budgeting, which emphasizes resources consumed rather than results, other local governments have been experimenting by including various types of program information in their budget processes.[112] In *Reinventing Government*, Osborne and Gaebler discuss local governments that have adopted mission-driven budgeting, which empowers managers by freeing them from many restrictions of line-item budgeting.[113] Charlotte, North Carolina; Dallas, Texas; Dayton, Ohio; Phoenix, Arizona; Portland, Oregon; St. Petersburg, Florida; and Sunnyvale, California, all have received national attention for their budget systems.[114] Cities such as these may be in the forefront of budget reform, ahead of both the states and the federal government.[115] A study of counties found that of those reporting usage of performance measurement in budgeting, 78 percent said measures were used in preparing departmental budget requests, 68 percent said measures helped county commissioners review the executive budget, and 80 percent said measures were used for monitoring the efficiency and effectiveness of services.[116]

Techniques in Other Nations. Efforts to include performance measurement in budgeting are common in other countries. In the mid-1990s, New Zealand was said to be furthest along in developing a resource allocation system that relies heavily upon quantified performance.[117] Australia, Canada, and the United Kingdom received worldwide attention when they embarked on performance measurement projects as means for curtailing budget deficits and for holding government agencies accountable for achieving results.[118] Local governments in the United Kingdom have undergone a performance management initiative known as "Best Value."[119] A survey of local governments in the Australian state of Victoria found that 50 percent of the respondents thought budget reforms changed attitudes in favor of planning and 47 percent thought the reforms influenced resource allocations.[120]

Management reforms, including those in the budgeting arena, in Australia, New Zealand, the United Kingdom, and, to a lesser extent, Canada have been called the *New Public Management* (NPM).[121] Over time, this movement has spread throughout Europe, especially into Austria, Germany, and Switzerland. NPM has reached the United States from the standpoint of scholars trying to understand what constitutes NPM, whether it has accomplished anything in other countries, and whether it is on the upswing or downswing. It should be noted, at a minimum, that NPM is more than a budgeting reform. It typically covers myriad other changes, including privatization and increased flexibility for managers. The debate about the content and effects of NPM is too complex to be covered here, but reforms such as those introduced by the National Performance Review (see above) and the Grace Commission of the 1980s, which sought to bring business best practices to the federal government, are seen as being compatible with the thrust of NPM.

Multiyear Techniques. Making multiyear projections is difficult, and as a consequence some governments choose not to engage in them. A survey of state budget offices found that 79 percent of the states project measures of program effectiveness and half (51 percent) project measures of productivity.[122] In a study of local governments in Florida, problems cited as deterring the use of expenditure forecasting included the difficulty of anticipating new state mandates, anticipating the impacts of court rulings, and anticipating the cost of employee wage agreements.[123] In a study of cities with populations of 25,000 or more, about two-thirds reported using revenue and expenditure forecasting.[124]

Reasons for Adopting Reforms. Why do some governments adopt budget reforms while others do not — or adopt them at a slower pace?[125] Researchers have identified several factors:

- Fiscal stress caused by the inability of governments to finance all programs at what seems to be a minimal standard stimulates searches for alternative budget techniques. Improved budgeting is seen as a means for improving the "health" of the government and the economic health of the economy.[126]

- Governments search for techniques that facilitate dealing with the knottiest of problems and provide them with the sense of being in control of current and future operations. Emphasis is on increasing the efficiency and effectiveness of operations.[127] The concern is to link programmatic goals with results.[128]

- Government structure is sometimes important; cities with professional managers are more likely to adopt program and performance budgeting than are those with strong mayor systems.[129]

- Having an elected and appointed political leadership that is committed to budget reform is another important ingredient, because reforms that are generated exclusively from lower levels in the bureaucracy are unlikely to be effective. Leadership not only must be committed but must also have the leadership skills necessary to forge ahead.[130]

- Governments need trained professional staffs and computer capabilities to undertake many budget reforms. Any such changes that are undertaken should be expected to take time. Expectations of quick results are likely to lead to disappointments.

- A desire on the part of legislators for enhanced information as an aid in exercising oversight of the executive branch is another important factor.[131]

- Legal requirements, such as the 1993 federal legislation instructing agencies to prepare strategic and annual performance plans, and other mandates and incentives are important.

- Another potential influence of major proportions relates to professions. The professional accounting field has shown interest in mandating that accounting systems be linked to program measurement. The Governmental Accounting Standards Board (GASB) intends to adopt a requirement that governments link service efforts and accomplishments to their accounting systems. The Government Finance Officers Association, in opposing the GASB proposal, favors a voluntary system and maintains that the GASB, as an accounting organization, would overstep its bounds and area of expertise were it to require service efforts and accomplishments reporting.[132]

This listing is in no way exhaustive but simply illustrates some of the factors that can be important in whether a government successfully implements some form of budget reform that is results-oriented.

Impediments to Reform. Perhaps one of the most difficult barriers to reform is overcoming the past. So-called new management practices arise with great frequency. Governments may feel pressure to jump on the most current bandwagon, but then later they jump from that bandwagon to another. Any person involved in policy making and administration can easily become cynical about the prospects for any new management practice actually being implemented. Experienced administrators inevitably question whether the latest technique will have any real effect upon how decisions are made and what outcomes they produce.[133]

Other factors that complicate or deter reform include the following:

- Major difficulties can be expected in setting goals and measures and gaining acceptance of those goals.[134] For example, environmental and conservation interests hold differing views on which goals the U.S. Forest Service should pursue.[135] This lack of clarity would be much less of a problem for an agency such as the U.S. Weather Service, which operates with the luxury of an agreed-upon mandate — to forecast the weather in an accurate and timely manner.

- Another concern is whether strategies lead to accomplishment of goals. Do the efforts of the Immigration and Naturalization Service really influence the influx of illegal aliens entering the United States?[136] Is an integrated comprehensive approach to strategic planning possible?[137]

- More generally, producing believable data presents a major problem. Simple errors can occur in collecting and tabulating data. Organizations may be tempted to falsify or misrepresent their accomplishments. For example, road crews in Houston seemingly inflated their numbers when reporting how many potholes they filled. If a pothole was large, it might be reported as five potholes.[138] As the General Accounting Office has observed, data need to be valid (measures are appropriate) and verified (completeness, accuracy, consistency, and the like).[139]

- Agencies have overlapping missions, and consequently any outcomes or impacts may actually result from several agencies' work. Managing for results suggests prospects for collaboration across agencies but can work in the other direction, leading to battles over administrative "turf."[140]

- Measuring the accomplishments of regulatory agencies is particularly challenging, and much of what the federal government does is of a regulatory nature.[141] The regulatory units are located both in departments, such as the Food and Drug Administration in the Department of Health and Human Services, and in stand-alone bodies, such as the Securities and Exchange Commission and the Federal Communications Commission.

- Obtaining accurate data in a uniform format and on a timely basis can be a nightmare for federal agencies that depend upon information from state and local governments and private enterprises.[142] The same problem arises for state agencies in obtaining data from local governments.

- Some governments have used adjusted performance measures that attempt to take into account the extent to which external factors (i.e., those outside of an organization's control) influence outcomes. These techniques are themselves subject to criticism.[143]

- Linking program data with cost data is complicated by the limited abilities of accounting systems and inconsistencies across accounting systems (see Chapter 11). Accounting systems may track financial transactions in formats that do not match up well with the needs of a program manager.[144] Comparisons between units may be thwarted because the units use different accounting system rules.

- The lack of incentives can doom efforts to use performance measurement in budgeting. If high-level executives and legislators show little or no interest in using performance data for decision making, lower-level administrators will consider data collection and program planning to be merely a paper exercise.[145] Equally as troublesome is holding executives and managers accountable for results but not giving them the means to accomplish the desired outcomes. Due to revenue declines, budgets may be cut, but departments may be expected to accomplish what was originally planned.

- Managers often find it unpleasant, if not downright repulsive, to have their operations compared with operations in other departments or in other governments.[146] Yet, benchmarking is frequently regarded as a desirable technique. As discussed earlier, benchmarking involves comparing one's operations with those of others. Serious problems of comparison arise in that governments operate in different environments, may measure their activities differently, and may account for their use of resources differently. Therefore, a city roads department will be wary of comparing its operations with those of other cities, unless there are assurances that variations taken into account, such as variations in weather, amount of traffic, and terrain.[147] Benchmarking holds the prospect of being able to compare schools as to which are performing better in educating children but in doing so threaten those who run the schools.[148] The federal government's No Child Left Behind Act, for example, requires testing of individual students to hold teachers and administrators accountable for educational outcomes. Citizen satisfaction can be measured across governmental boundaries, such as determining whether one community is more satisfied with its recreation services than other communities.[149]

If all of these problems were not enough, additional factors could become influential. The public sector routinely borrows management ideas from the private sector, and one that is emerging is the "balanced scorecard," developed and popularized by Robert S. Kaplan and David P. Norton.[150] Its underlying premise is that the private sector has been too focused on the "bottom line" of profit and loss and needs to be concerned with other matters, such as customer satisfaction and employee satisfaction. While public sector performance measurement often includes customer satisfaction, employee satisfaction may be of limited concern. The balanced scorecard suggests that government should step back and rethink how it measures its activities and results.

Summary

One of the main themes running through budgetary literature has been the need to use the budgetary process as a vehicle for planning. In particular, this need has facilitated an attempt to incorporate program data into the system along with resource data, such as dollar and personnel costs.

During and after World War II, a set of theoretical fields and technologies emerged that had a great influence on budgetary reform. These include operations research, economic analysis, general systems theory, cybernetics, computer technology, and systems analysis.

Budget requests are prepared by agencies in accordance with instructions provided by the central budget office. In addition to data on finances and personnel, request instructions increasingly require program data, including social indicators, impacts, outputs, workloads, and activities, as well as data on the need or demand for services. Productivity measures are used to relate resource consumption, as measured in dollars and personnel, to the work accomplished and the product of that work.

Budget request manuals take varied approaches to providing guidance on how agencies should request resources. These approaches include current commitment, fixed-ceiling, and open-ended budgeting. Reform efforts since the 1960s have focused on PPB systems, or more generally program budgeting, as well as on zero-base budgeting. Strategic planning and policy and program guidance also have proved popular. Current emphasis is on performance measurement. Governments tend to use hybrids of these systems.

Notes

1. A. Schick, The Road to PPB: The Stages of Budget Reform, *Public Administration Review* 26 (1966): 243–258.
2. W.H. Taft, *Economy and Efficiency in the Government Service*, House Doc. No. 458, January 1912, 16.
3. Commission on Economy and Efficiency, *The Need for a National Budget*, House Doc. No. 854, 1912, 4–5.
4. F.A. Cleveland, Evolution of the Budget Idea in the United States, *Annals* 62 (1915): 15–35.
5. W.F. Willoughby, *The Problems of a National Budget* (New York: Appleton, 1918).
6. L.D. Upson, Half-Time Budget Methods, *Annals* 113 (1924): 69–74.
7. A.E. Buck, *Public Budgeting* (New York: Harper and Brothers, 1929).
8. W. Kilpatrick, Classification and Measurement of Public Expenditures, *Annals* 183 (1936): 19–26.
9. President's Committee on Administrative Management, *Report* (Washington, DC: U.S. Government Printing Office, 1937).
10. V.O. Key, Jr., The Lack of a Budgetary Theory, *American Political Science Review* 34 (1940): 1138–1144.
11. Commission on Organization of the Executive Branch of the Government, *Budgeting and Accounting* (Washington, DC: U.S. Government Printing Office, 1949), 8.

12. V.B. Lewis, Toward a Theory of Budgeting, *Public Administration Review* 12 (1952): 42–54.

13. F.C. Mosher, *Program Budgeting: Theory and Practice with Particular Reference to the U.S. Department of Army* (Chicago: Public Administration Service, 1954).

14. C. Seckler-Hudson, Performance Budgeting in the Government of the United States, *Public Finance* 7 (1952): 327–345.

15. A. Smithies, *The Budgetary Process in the United States* (New York: McGraw–Hill, 1955), 198–225.

16. Commission on Organization of the Executive Branch of the Government, *Final Report to Congress* (Washington, DC: U.S. Government Printing Office, 1955); Commission on Organization of the Executive Branch of the Government, *Budgeting and Accounting* (Washington, DC: U.S. Government Printing Office, 1955).

17. J. Burkhead, *Government Budgeting* (New York: Wiley, 1956), 133–182.

18. A. Wildavsky, Rescuing Policy Analysis from PPBS, *Public Administration Review* 29 (1969): 193.

19. The early thinking on this topic was suggested by Robert J. Mowitz, Director of the Institute of Public Administration, The Pennsylvania State University.

20. C.W. Churchman, et al., *Introduction to Operations Research* (New York: Wiley, 1957).

21. For an early survey of the economic analysis field, see A.R. Prest and R. Turvey, Cost-Benefit Analysis: A Survey, *Economic Journal* 75 (1965): 683–735.

22. L. von Bertalanffy, General System Theory: A New Approach to Unity of Science, *Human Biology* 23 (1951): 303–361.

23. N. Wiener, *The Human Use of Human Beings* (Garden City, NY: Doubleday, 1956).

24. W.G. Ouchi, A Short History of the Development of Computer Hardware, in *Information Technology and Organizational Change*, T.L. Whisler, ed., (Belmont, CA: Wadsworth, 1970), 129–134.

25. G.H. Fisher, *The Analytical Bases of Systems Analysis* (Santa Monica, CA: The RAND Corporation, 1966).

26. U.S. Office of Management and Budget, *Preparation and Submission of Budget Estimates*, Circular A–11 (2002), *http://www.whitehouse.gov/omb/circulars/index.html*; accessed August 2002.

27. Government Performance and Results Act, P.L. 103–62 (1993).

28. H.P. Hatry, *Performance Measurement: Getting Results* (Washington, DC: Urban Institute, 1999); J. Walters, *Measuring Up: Governing's Guide to Performance Measures for Geniuses (and Other Public Managers)* (Washington, DC: Congressional Quarterly, 1998).

29. I. Rubin, Budgeting for Accountability: Municipal Budgeting for the 1990s, *Public Budgeting & Finance* 16 (Summer 1996): 112–132.

30. U.S. Office of Management and Budget, *Budget of the United States Government, Fiscal Year 2002: Analytical Perspectives* (Washington, DC: U.S. Government Printing Office, 2001), 29.

31. Sustainability Seattle, *Indicators of Sustainability Community*, 1998 (Seattle: Sustainability Seattle, 1998).

32. M.P. Aristigueta, et. al., The Role of Social Indicators in Developing a Managing for Results System, *Public Performance & Management Review* 24 (2001): 254–269.

33. D.A. Murphey, Presenting Community-Level Data in an "Outcomes and Indicators" Framework: Lessons from Vermont's Experience, *Public Administration Review* 59 (1999): 76–82.

34. R.J. Mowitz, *The Design and Implementation of Pennsylvania's Planning, Programming, Budgeting System* (Harrisburg: Commonwealth of Pennsylvania, 1970), 17.

35. J. Brizius, et al., *Deciding for Investment: Getting Returns on Tax Dollars* (Washington, DC: National Academy of Public Administration, 1994).

36. G. Odiorne, *Management by Objectives* (New York: Pitman, 1965); T.H. Poister and G. Streib, MBO in Municipal Government: Variations on a Traditional Management Tool, *Public Administration Review* 55 (1995): 48–56.

37. See current issues of *Public Performance and Management Review*, a quarterly journal.

38. W.E. Deming, *Quality, Productivity, and Competitive Position* (Cambridge, MA: Massachusetts Institute of Technology Center for Advanced Engineering Study, 1982); T.H. Poister and R.H. Harris, Service Delivery Impacts of TQM: A Preliminary Investigation, *Public Productivity and Management Review* 20 (1996): 84–100.

39. D. Osborne and T. Gaebler, *Reinventing Government: How the Entrepreneurial Spirit Is Transforming the Public Sector* (Reading, MA: Addison–Wesley, 1992); D. Osborne and P. Plastrik, *Banishing Bureaucracy: The Five Strategies for Reinventing Government* (Reading, MA: Addison–Wesley, 1997); see also D.F. Kettl and J.J. DiIulio, Jr., eds., *Inside the Reinvention Machine: Appraising Governmental Reform* (Washington, DC: Brookings Institution, 1995).

40. R.S. Kravchuk and R.W. Schack, Designing Effective Performance-Measurement Systems under the Government Performance and Results Act of 1993, *Public Administration Review* 56 (1996): 348–358.

41. M.L. Whicker and C. Mo, Impact of Agency Mission on Agecny Budget Strategy, Paper presented at the national conference of the Association for Budgeting and Financial Management in Washington, DC, November 5–7, 1998.

42. U.S. General Accounting Office, *Managing for Results: Analytic Challenges in Measuring Performance* (Washington, DC: U.S. Government Printing Office, 1997).

43. W.A. Lucas and R.H. Dawson, *The Organizational Politics of Defense* (Pittsburgh: International Studies Association, University of Pittsburgh, 1974), 87.

44. National Security Act Amendments, Ch. 412, 63 Stat. 578 (1949).

45. Budget and Accounting Procedures Act, Ch. 946, 64 Stat. 832 (1950); U.S. General Accounting Office, *Performance Budgeting: Past Initiatives Offer Insights for GPRA Implementation* (Washington, DC: U.S. Government Printing Office, 1997).

46. Schick, The Road to PPB: 252–253.

47. Mosher, *Program Budgeting*, 34–47.

48. R.J. Massey, Program Packages and the Program Budget in the Department of Defense, *Public Administration Review* 23 (1963): 30–34.

49. D. Novick, *The Department of Defense*, in D. Novick, ed., *Program Budgeting: Program Analysis and the Federal Budget* (Cambridge, MA: Harvard University Press, 1965), 91.

50. D. Novick, *Efficiency and Economy in Government through New Budgeting and Accounting Procedures* (Santa Monica, CA: RAND Corporation, 1956).

51. L.R. Jones, Policy Development, Planning, and Resource Allocation in the Department of Defense, *Public Budgeting & Finance* 11 (Fall 1991): 15–27.

52. National Performance Review, *Creating a Government That Works Better and Costs Less: Department of Defense* (Washington, DC: U.S. Government Printing Office, 1993).

53. Commission on Roles and Missions of the Armed Forces, *Directions for Defense* (Washington, DC: U.S. Government Printing Office, 1995).

54. F. Thompson and L.R. Jones, *Reinventing the Pentagon* (San Francisco: Jossey–Bass, 1994).

55. U.S. General Accounting Office, *Major Management Challenges and Program Risks: Department of Defense* (Washington, DC: U.S. Government Printing Office, 2001), 16–71. Also see W.C. Banks and J.D. Straussman, Defense Contingency Budgeting in the Post–Cold War World, *Public Administration Review* 59 (1999): 135–146; U.S. General Accounting Office, *Future Years Defense Program: Risks in Operation and Maintenance and Procurement Programs* (Washington, DC: U.S. Government Printing Office, 2000).

56. A. Schick, A Death in the Bureaucracy: The Demise of Federal PPB, *Public Administration Review* 33 (1973): 146–156.

57. E.L. Harper, et al., Implementation and Use of PPB in Sixteen Federal Agencies, *Public Administration Review* 29 (1969): 634.

58. R.C. Casselman, Massachusetts Revisited: Chronology of a Failure, *Public Administration Review* 33 (1973): 129–135.

59. D. Sallack and D.N. Allen, From Impact to Output: Pennsylvania's Planning-Programming-Budgeting System in Transition, *Public Budgeting & Finance* 7 (Spring 1987): 38–50.

60. A. Wildavsky and A. Hammann, Comprehensive versus Incremental Budgeting in the Department of Agriculture, *Administrative Science Quarterly* 10 (1965): 321–346.

61. P.A. Phyrr, *Zero-Base Budgeting: A Practical Management Tool for Evaluating Expenses* (New York: Wiley, 1973).

62. T.P. Lauth and S.C. Rieck, Modifications in Georgia Zero-Base Budgeting Procedures: 1973–1981, *Midwest Review of Public Administration* 13 (1979): 225–238.

63. U.S. General Accounting Office, *Streamlining Zero-Base Budgeting Will Benefit Decision Making* (Washington, DC: U.S. Government Printing Office, 1979).

64. A. Schick, The Road from ZBB, *Public Administration Review* 38 (1978): 177–180.

65. J. Metzgar and R. Miranda, Bringing Out the Dead: Can Information Technology Resurrect Budget Reform?, *Government Finance Review* 17 (April 2001): 9–14.

66. T.H. Poister and G.D. Streib, Strategic Management in the Public Sector, *Public Productivity & Management Review* 22 (1999): 308–325; J. Rabin, et al., eds., *Handbook of Strategic Management*, 2nd ed. (New York: Marcel Dekker, 2000).

67. K.G. Willoughby and J.E. Melkers, Implementing PBB: Conflicting Views of Success, *Public Budgeting & Finance*, 20 (2000): 105–120; J.S. Wholey, Performance-Based Management, *Public Productivity & Management Review* 22 (1999): 288–307.

68. Budgets Should Look to the Future, *Focus: Public Management Newsletter* 17 (September 2000): 1.

69. P. Kobrak, The Social Responsibilities of a Public Entrepreneur, *Administration and Society* 28 (1996): 205–237.

70. I.S. Rubin, Budgeting for Our Times: Target Base Budgeting, *Public Budgeting & Finance* 11 (Fall 1991): 5–14.

71. National Performance Review, *From Red Tape to Results: Creating a Government That Works Better and Costs Less* (Washington, DC: U.S. Government Printing Office, 1993), 16–17; U.S. General Accounting Office, *Management Reform: Implementation of the National Performance Review's Recommendations* (Washington, DC: U.S. Government Printing Office, 1994).

72. National Performance Review, *The Best Kept Secrets in Government* (Washington, DC: U.S. Government Printing Office, 1996), 31.

73. National Performance Review, *Putting Customers First '95: Standards for Serving the American People* (Washington, DC: U.S. Government Printing Office, 1995), 69.

74. D. Osborne and P. Plastrik, *Banishing Bureaucracy: The Five Strategies for Reinventing Government* (Cambridge, MA: Perseus, 2000).

75. National Performance Review, *Common Sense Government: Works Better and Costs Less* (Washington, DC: U.S. Government Printing Office, 1995): 59–60. See also D.N. Ammons, *Municipal Benchmarks*, 2nd ed. (Thousand Oaks, CA: Sage, 2001).

76. K. Lunney, NPR Director Touts Reinvention's Results, *Government Executive*, *http://govexec.com*, January 9, 2001.

77. U.S. General Accounting Office, *NPR's Savings: Claimed Agency Savings Cannot All Be Attributed to NPR* (Washington, DC: U.S. Government Printing Office, 1999); U.S. General Accounting Office, *Reinventing Government: Status of NPR Recommendations at 10 Federal Agencies* (Washington, DC: U.S. Government Printing Office, 2000); J. Peckenpaugh, Employee Survey Finds Mixed Progress in Reinvention, *Government Executive*, *http://www.govexec.com*, December 15, 2000.

78. D. H. Rosenbloom, History Lessons for Reinventors, *Public Administration Review* 61 (2001): 161–165.

79. J. Peckenpaugh, Customer Survey Release Delayed until December, *Government Executive*, *http://www.govexec.com*, April 11, 2001.

80. U.S. General Accounting Office, *Executive Guide: Effectively Implementing the Government Performance and Results Act* (Washington, DC: U.S. Government Printing Office, 1996).

81. U.S. Office of Management and Budget and Chief Financial Officers Council, *Federal Financial Management Status Report and Five-Year Plan* (Washington, DC: U.S. Government Printing Office, 1995); Johnny C. Finch, Assistant Comptroller General, *Managing for Results: Status of the Government Performance and Results Act* (Washington, DC: U.S. Government Printing Office, 1995).

82. U.S. General Accounting Office, *Managing for Results: The Statutory Framework for Performance-Based Accountability* (Washington, DC: U.S. Government Printing Office, 1998).

83. U.S. General Accounting Office, *Managing for Results: Critical Issues for Improving Federal Agencies' Strategic Plans* (Washington, DC: U.S. Government Printing Office, 1997): 3. Also see U.S. General Accounting Office, *The Results Act: An Evaluator's Guide to Assessing Agency Annual Performance Plans* (Washington, DC: U.S. Government Printing Office, 1998).

84. P.L. Posner and J.C. Mihm, U.S. General Accounting Office, *Managing for Results: Observations on OMB's September 1997 Strategic Plan,* testimony before House Committee on Government Reform and Oversight, U.S. Congress, 1998.

85. U.S. General Accounting Office, *Managing for Results: Agency Progress in Linking Performance Plans with Budgets and Financial Statements* (Washington, DC: U.S. Government Printing Office, 2002): 6.

86. Dick Armey, et al., *Clinton Administration Fails Accountability Review,* *http://freedom.house.gov/results/final report;* accessed November 6, 1997.

87. K. Lunney, Agencies' Performance Reports Show Modest Improvement, *Government Executive, http://www.govexec.com,* May 17, 2001.

88. R.N. Ballard, House Chairman Sends Agencies Back to Drawing Board on Strategic Plans, *Government Executive, http://www.govexec.com,* March 26, 2001.

89. A. Laurent, Management Counts, *Government Executive* 23 (May 2002): 8–16.

90. S. O'Keefe, as quoted in K. Lunney, OMB Deputy Says Performance-Based Budgeting Is Top Priority, *Government Executive, http://www.govexec.com,* June 20, 2001.

91. Office of Management and Budget, *Budget of the United States Government: Fiscal Year 2003* (Washington, DC: U. S. Government Printing Office, 2002).

92. Office of Management and Budget, *Executive Branch Management Scorecard* (June 30, 2002), *http://www.whitehouse.gov/omb/budget/fy2003/score1.html.*

93. Office of Management and Budget, *Memorandum for Heads of Departments and Agencies, Program Performance Assessments for the FY 2004 Budget* (July 15, 2002), *http://www.whitehouse.gov/omb/memoranda/m02–10.pdf.*

94. U.S. Office of Management and Budget, *Management Accountability and Control,* Circular A–123 (1995), Section II.

95. *Paperwork Reduction Act,* P.L. 104–13 (1995).

96. *Information Technology Management Reform Act*, P.L. 104–106 (1996).

97. R.D. Lee, Jr., A Quarter Century of State Budgeting Practices, *Public Administration Review* 57 (1997): 133–140.

98. R.D. Lee, Jr. and R.C. Burns, Performance Measurement in State Budgeting: Advancement and Backsliding from 1990 to 1995, *Public Budgeting & Finance* 20 (2000): 38–54.

99. R.D. Lee and R.C. Burns, unpublished data from Survey of State Budget Offices (2000).

100. M.M. Jordan and M.M. Hackbart, Performance Budgeting and Performance Funding in the States: A Status Assessment, *Public Budgeting & Finance* 19 (1999): 68–88.

101. K.G. Willoughby and J.E. Melkers, Implementing PBB: Conflicting Views of Success, *Public Budgeting & Finance* 20 (2000): 105–120.

102. J.E. Melkers and K.G. Willoughby, Budgeters' Views of State Performance-Budgeting Systems: Distinctions across Branches, *Public Administration Review* 61 (2001): 54–64.

103. K. Barrett and R. Greene, Grading the States: A Management Report Card, *Governing* 14 (February 2001): 20–108.

104. D.E. O'Toole, et. al., Current Local Government Budgeting Practices, *Government Finance Review* 12 (December 1996): 25–29.

105. T.H. Poister and G. Streib, Municipal Management Tools from 1976 to 1993: An Overview and Update, *Public Productivity and Management Review* 18 (1994): 115–125.

106. J.R. Fountain, Are State and Local Governments Using Performance Measures?, *PA Times Supplement* (January 1997): PM–2, PM–8; Poister and Streib, Municipal Management Tools from 1976 to 1993; P. Tigue, Use of Performance Measures by GFO Members, *Government Finance Review* 10 (December 1994): 42–44; D.N. Ammons, ed., *Accountability for Performance: Measurement and Monitoring in Local Government* (Washington, DC: International City/County Management Association, 1995).

107. T.H. Poister and G. Streib, Performance Measurement in Municipal Government: Assessing the State of the Practice, *Public Administration Review* 59 (1999): 325–335.

108. E. Berman and X. Wang, Performance Measurement in U.S. Counties: Capacity for Reform, *Public Administration Review* 60 (2000): 409–420.

109. K. Barrett and R. Greene, Grading the Cities: A Management Report Card, *Governing* 13 (February 2000): 22–88.

110. R. Hendrick, Comprehensive Management and Budgeting Reform in Local Government: The Case of Milwaukee, *Public Producitivy & Management Review* 23 (2000): 312–337.

111. K. Barrett and R. Greene, Grading the Counties: A Management Report Card, *Governing* 15 (February 2002): 22–88.

112. C. Tyer, ed., Symposium on Local Government Performance Measurement and Budgeting, *Journal of Public Budgeting, Accounting & Financial Management* 12 (2000): 43–164.

113. Osborne and Gaebler, *Reinventing Government*, 117–124, 161–165.

114. F. Fairbanks, Managing for Results: The Path That Phoenix Has Followed, *Public Management* 78 (January 1996): 12–15; A. Chan and D. Rich, Sunnyvale's Outcome Management: Taking Performance Budgeting One Step Further, *Government Finance Review* 12 (December 1996): 13–17; P.B. Scheps, Linking Performance Measures to Resource Allocation, *Government Finance Review* 16 (June 2000): 11–15. Also see U.S. General Accounting Office, *District of Columbia Government: Progress and Challenges in Performance Management* (Washington, DC: U.S. Government Printing Office, 2000); R. Calia, S. Guajardo, and J. Metzgar, Best Practices in Budgeting: Putting NACSLB Practices into Action, *Government Finance Review* 16 (April 2000): 9–17.

115. Brizius et al., *Deciding for Investment*.

116. X. Wang, Performance Measurement in Budgeting: A Study of County Governments, *Public Budgeting & Finance* 20 (2000): 102–118.

117. Organization for Economic Cooperation and Development, *Budgeting for Results: Perspectives on Public Expenditure Management* (Paris: Organization for Economic Cooperation and Development, 1995): 55.

118. U.S. General Accounting Office, *Managing for Results: Experiences Abroad Suggest Insights for Federal Management Reforms* (Washington, DC: U.S. Government Printing Office, 1995); R.C. Mascarenhas, Searching for Efficiency in the Public Sector: Interim Evaluation of Performance Budgeting in New Zealand, *Public Budgeting & Finance* 16 (Fall 1996): 13–27.

119. J.L. Harris, Best Value and Performance Management: Lessons Learned from the United Kingdom, *Government Finance Review* 16 (August 2000): 27–33.

120. R. Kluvers, An Analysis of Introducing Program Budgeting in Local Government, *Public Budgeting & Finance* 21 (2001): 29–45.

121. M. Barzelay, *The New Public Management* (Berkeley, CA: University of California Press, 2001); N.M. Riccucci, The "Old" Public Management Versus the "New" Public Management: Where Does Public Administration Fit In?, *Public Administration Review* 61 (2001): 172–175; discussion on International Public Management Network Listserv, *http://www.willamette.org/ipmn/*.

122. Lee and Burns, Survey of State Budget Offices.

123. S.A. MacManus, Forecasting Frustrations: Factors Limiting Accuracy, *Government Finance Review* 8 (June 1992): 7–11.

124. R.K. Goertz, Target-Based Budgeting and Adaptations to Fiscal Uncertainty, *Public Productivity and Management Review* 16 (1993): 425–429.

125. U.S. General Accounting Office, *Managing for Results: State Experiences Provide Insights for Federal Management Reforms* (Washington, DC: U.S. Government Printing Office, 1994); J.P. Forrester and G.B. Adams, Budgetary Reform Through Organizational Learning, *Administration and Society* 28 (1997): 466–488.

126. J. Walters, Raising Alabama, *Governing*, 14 (October 2000): 28–32.

127. J.F. Smith, The Benefits and Threats of PBB: An Assessment of Modern Reform, *Public Budgeting & Finance* 19 (Fall 1999): 3–15.

128. U.S. General Accounting Office, *Managing for Results: Opportunities for Continued Improvements in Agencies' Performance Plans* (Washington, DC: U.S. Government Printing Office, 1999).

129. G.H. Cope, *Juggling Dollars and Making Sense: Budgeting in Local Government*, paper presented at 1992 Conference on Budgeting and Financial Management, American Society for Public Administration, Arlington, VA, October 1992.

130. U.S. General Accounting Office, *Managing for Results: Federal Managers' Views Show Need for Ensuring Top Leadership Skills* (Washington, DC: U.S. Government Printing Office, 2000).

131. J.C. Mihm, U.S. General Accounting Office, *Using GPRA to Assist Oversight and Decisionmaking*, testimony before the House Subcommittee on Government Efficiency, Financial Management and Intergovernmental Relations (Washington, DC: U.S. Government Printing Office, 2001); J. Walters, Deeds, Data, and Dollars, *Governing* 14 (November 2000): 98–102.

132. Governmental Accounting Standards Board, *Concept Statement No. 2: Service Efforts and Accomplishments Reporting* (Norwalk, CT: Governmental Accounting Standards Board, 1994); D.K. Clancy and T.K. Patton, Service Efforts and Accomplishments Reporting: A Study of Texas Public Schools, *Public Budgeting and Financial Management* 8 (1996): 272–302.

133. J. Walters, Fad Mad, *Governing* 9 (September 1996): 48–52.

134. X. Wang, Conditions to Implement Outcome-Oriented Performance Budgeting: Some Empirical Evidence, *Journal of Public Budgeting, Accounting & Financial Management* 11 (1999): 535–552.

135. J. Peckenpaugh, Linking Performance Goals to Budgets Won't Be Easy, Experts Say, *Government Executive*, March 22, 2001, *http://gov.exec.com/daily/fed*.

136. U.S. General Accounting Office, *Managing for Results: Challenges Agencies Face in Producing Credible Performance Information* (Washington, DC: U.S. Government Printing Office, 2000).

137. N. Roberts, The Synoptic Model of Strategic Planning and the GPRA, *Public Productivity & Management Review* 23 (2000): 297–311.

138. R. Graves, Pothole Crew's Reports Scrutinized by Officials, *Houston Chronicle*, April 23, 2001, *http://www.chron.com*.

139. U.S. General Accounting Office, *Performance Plans: Selected Approaches for Verification and Validation of Agency Performance Information* (Washington, DC: U.S. Government Printing Office, 1999).

140. P.L. Posner and C.J. Mihm, U.S. General Accounting Office, *Performance Budgeting: Initial Agency Experiences Provide a Foundation to Assess Future Directions*, testimony before the House Subcommittee on Government Management, Information and Technology (Washington: DC: U.S. Government Printing Office, 1999); U.S. General Accounting Office, *Managing for Results: Emerging Benefits from Selected Agencies' Use of Performance Agreements* (Washington, DC: U.S. Government Printing Office, 2000).

141. U.S. General Accounting Office, *Managing for Results: Strengthening Regulatory Agencies' Performance Management Practices* (Washington, DC: U.S. Government Printing Office, 1999).

142. U.S. General Accounting Office, *Managing for Results: Measuring Program Results That Are under Limited Federal Control* (Washington, DC: U.S. Government Printing Office, 1999).

143. L. Stiefel, et al., Using Adjusted Performance Measures for Evaluating Resource Use, *Public Budgeting & Finance* 19 (Fall 1999): 67–87; A.C. Brooks, The Use and Misuse of Adjusted Performance Measures, *Journal of Policy Analysis and Management* 19 (2000): 323–328.

144. J. Peckenpaugh, Better Cost Data Is the Key to Performance Budgeting, Expert Says, *Government Executive*, May 18, 2001, *http: www.govexec.com*.

145. U.S. General Accounting Office, *Managing for Results: Federal Managers' Views on Key Management Issues Vary Widely across Agencies* (Washington, DC: U.S. Government Printing Office, 2001).

146. J. Walters, Performance and Pain, *Governing* 10 (June 1997): 26–29, 31.

147. D.N. Ammons, C. Coe, and M. Lombardo, Performance-Comparison Projects in Local Government: Participants' Perspectives, *Public Administration Review* 61 (2001): 100–110.

148. C.J. Wheelan, Why National Standards and Tests? Politics and the Quest for Better Schools, *Journal of Policy Analysis & Management* 18 (1999): 519–521.

149. D. Swindell and J.M. Kelly, Linking Citizen Satisfaction Data to Performance Measures, *Public Performance & Management Review* 24 (2001): 30–52.

150. R.S. Kaplan and D.P. Norton, *The Balanced Scorecard* (Boston, MA: Harvard Business School Press, 1996); R.S. Kaplan and D.P. Norton, *The Strategy-Focused Organization* (Boston, MA: Harvard Business School Press, 2001); J. Walters, The Buzz over Balance, *Governing* 13 (May 2000): 56–62.

Chapter 6

BUDGET PREPARATION: THE DECISION PROCESS

Preparing a budget in an executive budget system involves having agencies prepare requests and then assembling those requests. However, the process also involves much more. Indeed, the request process is simple compared with the difficult task that remains — making decisions on the recommended levels for revenues and expenditures. Is a tax increase needed? Which programs should be expanded and which should be reduced? In systems that do not centralize budget preparation in the executive, the same concerns prevail. A legislative committee or a joint group of executives and legislators may be responsible for weighing the citizens' joint demands for increased services and possibly lower taxes and for proposing a budget package that balances these competing demands.

This chapter includes two sections. The first section considers how a proposed executive budget is assembled; deliberations on the revenue and expenditure sides of the budget are examined. The second section reviews the products of budget preparation — namely, the various types of budget documents and their formats.

Decisions on Budget Requests

Budget preparation involves participation by a variety of individuals and organizations, which have myriad values regarding taxing and spending. In an executive budget system, the chief executive has the overall responsibility for the preparation process. Numerous other actors play roles as well, including, of course, the central budget office and other units such as the treasury office. Not all governments have executive systems. Many county governments do not have a county executive or manager, for example. As a consequence, their budgets are prepared jointly by several different executive and legislative officials. In other systems, such as some local governments in Russia, finance departments have reporting responsibilities to both the mayor and the legislative council, and municipal finance officers and/or treasurers sometimes are appointed by the central government, such as in Ukraine.

Legislators or their staffs may be involved in budget preparation. On occasion, state legislative staff members may be allowed to attend executive budget hearings that review the proposed budgets of line agencies. This practice helps the legislative branch become aware of the budget proposals being developed and the rationales behind these proposals prior to the budget actually reaching the legislature. In small local governments, budget preparation may be a relatively fluid process that is characterized by close links between executive and legislative officials. Even when legislative officers are not involved, their views on taxing and spending are taken into account.

In some other systems, such as in Egypt, agencies make their recommendations to a ministry of finance, which has the final decision authority but is not subject to significant legislative review. Subunits of other ministries, without the presence of their superiors, may be called to defend budget requests before the finance ministry, creating a situation in which heads of ministries may have only limited input into their budgets.

Concerns of the Chief Executive

The chief executive — president, governor, mayor, county executive, and the like — may have official responsibility for budget preparation but usually will have only limited direct involvement until the later stages of preparation. This system allows the chief executive extra time to take care of other duties. Having the budget office and other units, such as treasury, involved early in the process provides for the application of professional administrative talent in analyzing problems and options that will later come before the chief executive for review. A professional budget staff endeavors to take preliminary actions on budget requests that are in keeping with the policy objectives of the chief executive, thereby allowing the chief executive to avoid dealing with minor problems and reserving time to deal with major ones.

Strategic Concerns. The chief executive needs to convey to the units involved, and especially to the central budget office, a sense of priorities so that effort is not needlessly wasted on proposals that he or she will later reject. Several concerns arise, with a major one being the overall philosophy of the role of government in contemporary society. What is the overall public interest, and how large should the public sector be in the total economy?

Another concern for many chief executives is the effect that the budget may have on the economic environment. Cities, counties, states, and the national government are concerned about budgetary influences on the economy. For local and state chief executives, their concern tends to focus on whether current or proposed taxes will deter businesses from locating or expanding operations in their jurisdictions. Perhaps equally important is the quality of government services. While school districts and special districts may have little or no official role in economic development, the quality of education, water systems, sewers, and so on are critical in the location decisions of corporations. The national government has these same concerns and others as well, including international implications and price stability (see Chapter 15).

The chief executive sets ground rules on policies and program priorities. A president conveys an overall sense of priorities to the Office of Management and Budget (OMB) regarding defense and domestic spending and a sense of priorities within each of these categories. Election campaign promises are important in that chief executives usually attempt to pursue the objectives outlined in their bids for voter approval. For many chief executives, the budget serves as a vehicle for strategic planning for the government. For example, President George W. Bush wanted to advance his faith-based intiative in which religious organizations would be enlisted to help combat social problems. That initiative, however, was eclipsed by the disasters of September 11, 2001. His administration subsequently placed much greater emphasis on national and homeland security concerns.

Program priorities also can be viewed from the perspective of achieving some degree of social justice or equity.[1] While space constraints prohibit any extensive discussion of what constitutes social justice, it can be said that budget deliberations include an overall assessment of how different segments of the society will benefit or be burdened by governmental actions. One way of viewing this situation is to think of government as redistributing income among the various segments of society. Funding one set of programs at a high level obviously will benefit those programs' clients. If, for example, the elderly benefit from a program, then the young do not. Providing income maintenance checks to the needy redistributes money from the middle and upper classes to the poor. Redistribution also occurs through tax measures, including tax expenditures, such as the policy of not taxing home mortgage interest payments (see Chapter 4).[2]

A major concern of Southern and Western border states is social justice as it pertains to illegal immigrants. When taxes are high but available revenues cannot keep pace with funding needs, one view holds that illegal aliens should be denied access to government services, including health care and various social services.

Complaints from citizens arise in such instances as when most mothers giving birth at the Los Angeles County Hospital are illegal aliens.[3] Providing free services to illegal immigrants is seen by many people as imposing an unfair burden on taxpayers.

Another suggestion whose popularity is growing is that budgeting should be concerned with its generational effects — the extent to which current actions will improve or harm the conditions that older, younger, and future generations must confront.[4] The federal government has reported generational effects in terms of taxes and transfers, for example.

Surplus or Deficit? The dynamics of decision making are greatly affected by whether a current services budget would be expected to yield a surplus or a deficit. In other words, if current revenue sources and spending patterns continue, will a surplus or a deficit result? In budget preparation, the projection of a budget deficit becomes an overriding issue that cannot be ignored. For state and local governments, chief executives are often required to submit balanced budgets, so any projections of a deficit must be resolved.[5] For the federal government, deficits loomed so large between 1981 and the mid-1990s that most discussions about the budget seemed to focus on how to reduce the deficit. Instead of being concerned with which alternatives were more likely to bring positive results in the operation of a program, decision makers worried almost exclusively about the cost of the alternatives and their potential for increasing or decreasing the deficit. Deficits can incapacitate decision makers, who presume they are unable to deal with society's problems for lack of funds.

In the latter half of the 1990s and into 2000, a robust national economy greatly altered budgetary decision making. Federal, state, and local governments experienced surpluses as incomes rose and people paid greater income taxes and, at the state level, sales taxes. The federal government used some of its additional resources to pay down a portion of the national debt. Probably most governments used some of their surpluses to create new programs or enhance existing ones.[6] Other approaches were to cut taxes and to put some of the surplus monies into rainy day funds (Chapter 10). Exercising fiscal discipline is difficult during surplus times. There is a temptation to act as though surpluses will continue indefinitely, when that surely is not the case.[7]

By 2001, budgetary decision making had flip-flopped from being oriented toward surpluses to being oriented toward deficits. The economy weakened and eventually entered a recession, resulting in a sharp decline in revenues at all levels of government. By January 2002, 39 states had officially declared budget shortfalls and other states soon followed suit.[8] To some extent, the states may have created problems for themselves by overspending and reducing revenue through tax cuts during the budget surplus years.[9]

The situation was even more complicated at the federal level. When President Bush came into office in January 2001, he succeeded in getting Congress to enact a tax cut. The administration's position was that the cut would help stimulate the economy, but critics contended that it simply worsened the budget situation by reducing revenues.

An additional problem was that while money was lacking in the general fund budget, a surplus existed in Social Security. President Bush, however, had vowed not to "raid" Social Security to meet government's expenses. To get around that problem, the administration chose to change long-standing accounting practices so that some Social Security money could be used without being accounted for as such. One critic called this "Rose Mary Woods accounting," referring to President Nixon's secretary who claimed she mistakenly erased key portions of oval office discussions pertaining to Watergate.[10]

The events of September 11, 2001, changed everything. The attacks on the World Trade Center in New York City and the Pentagon outside of Washington D.C., unleashed enormous spending demands. War was begun in Afghanistan and later Iraq and military troops were dispatched to other parts of the globe. The intelligence and law enforcement communities at all levels of government stepped up their activities. Immense clean-up costs were encountered in New York and at the Pentagon. Adding to the situation was the mailing of anthrax-laced letters that contaminated post offices, led to massive vaccination programs, and ended up with some people dying of the disease. The anthrax crisis under-scored the vulnerability of the country to terrorist attacks and spurred government efforts and expenditures to identify risks and increase security. The president's fiscal 2003 budget proposed large increases for defense and homeland security. Bioterrorism initiatives resulted in large proposed increases for such agencies as the Centers for Disease Control and Prevention and the National Institute of Allergy and Infectious Disease. Given this situation, the federal budget inevitably went into a deficit mode, and great uncertainty arose as to when the situation might be reversed. (See Chapter 9 for additional details on federal budgetary politics.)

Tactical Concerns. In addition to a "philosophical" approach to taxation and expenditures, the chief executive conveys a tactical view. An assessment must be made of political reactions to any possible proposed tax increase or cut. Of course, increases are more likely to produce negative reactions than are tax cuts.

For governors and the president, intergovernmental relations constitute an important component of budget preparation deliberations. Presidents may prefer, where possible, to carry out policies through state and local governments rather than directly through federal agencies. Likewise, governors may prefer to work through local governments. Mandating that state and local governments deliver services, adopt standards, or otherwise implement federal programs is seen by some as a way of achieving a federal policy goal without paying for it. These *unfunded mandates*, of course, are extremely unpopular with governors, state legislatures, mayors, and city councils (see Chapter 14).

Another set of considerations involves relationships with the legislative body. Stated simply, the chief executive assesses the chances of various recommendations receiving the approval of Congress, the state legislature, or the city council. Executives must decide whether to push for proposals that will meet with certain opposition from some legislators in alliance with interest groups. In making such calculations, chief executives do not recommend only policies likely to be approved. A doomed recommendation may be put forth as a means of preparing the legislature to approve the proposal in some future year, or the chief executive may be strongly committed to a proposal despite legislative opposition. There was speculation in 2002 that President Bush took a somewhat hands-off approach on the budget with Congress because, in part, he wanted to avoid any skirmishing that might harm the high public approval rating that had resulted from his handling of the September 2001 crisis.[11]

Perceived citizen preferences regarding service and tax levels constitute another consideration. Chief executives have a keen sense for what the general citizenry and interest groups desire. What services do citizens demand and what are they willing to pay for those services through either taxes or fees? Results from national and state polls are watched in an effort to identify important trends. Some cities conduct surveys of citizens and hold public hearings at which citizens may testify as a means of identifying prevailing attitudes about existing and desired services.

In preparing a budget for the upcoming fiscal year, the executive must also consider the current budget. Supplemental appropriations are standard at the federal level, in which agencies' budgets are selectively augmented during the fiscal year to meet unanticipated needs. These supplemental apppropriations may throw the existing budget out of balance (or further out of balance) as the president and the budget office begin preparing a deficit budget for the new year. This kind of situation can play into the hands of the president's political opponents.

Revenue Deliberations

Revenue Estimates. Central to deliberations on the revenue side of budget preparation are revenue estimates. Chapter 4 dealt with some of the technical problems associated with revenue estimating. Here we note that several important bureaucratic considerations apply. Sometimes revenue estimating is assigned to the organization responsible for collecting revenues, most often a treasury or revenue department. Such an arrangement may place that unit in competition with the budget office, because the latter may offer different revenue projections. The budget office may be essentially forced into developing a budget package that is perceived to be unnecessarily constrained because of an estimate that anticipates little or no growth in revenue or even a downturn. This problem is especially troublesome in some developing countries where the local treasurer is a central government appointee. At the federal level, the revenue-estimating function is handled jointly by OMB, the Council of Economic Advisers, and the Treasury Department. The Congressional Budget Office makes independent revenue estimates for congressional consideration.

Taxing Limitations. Since the 1970s, taxing limitations have constituted a major consideration at the state and local levels (see Chapter 4).[12] Government officials, in assembling a budget proposal, may be constrained by having to present a balanced budget that allows for no increases in tax revenues. One commonly used alternative to raising taxes is raising user fees.

During the first year of President George W. Bush's administration, some members of Congress proposed "triggers" for tax cutting. Although not enacted, the idea was that some automatic trigger would be placed in law that would reduce taxes either to stimulate the economy or to reduce an excessively large surplus. President Bush opposed the concept, preferring that tax cuts take effect regardless of the level of the surplus or deficit.[13]

Balanced Budgets. For state and local governments, revenue estimating is particularly critical because of the standard requirement that they have balanced operating budgets. Indebtedness is possible but is typically used only for capital investments and other selected expenses. If a budget is built on revenue estimates that are too high, crises will ensue during execution as the government attempts to bring expenditures down so as to balance them against actual revenues.

In addition to legal restraints, the bond markets impose a norm of budgetary balance on state and local governments. The fact that states or localities lacking a structural balance between revenues and spending may experience lower bond ratings and higher borrowing costs creates strong incentives for sound fiscal management (see Chapter 12).

Although most states have requirements for a balanced budget, the requirements are not uniform across all states. In the first place, "balance" means that expenditures may not exceed revenues, but not all available revenues must be appropriated and spent. Coverage is not all-inclusive, and trust funds and capital expenditures are often excluded. Thus as little as half of all state funds may be covered by the balanced budget requirement. Balancing requirements also vary as to when they apply in the budget process, such as when the budget is presented to the legislature or when it is adopted.[14] Similar variations are found at the local level.

Achieving balance in a state budget is a political process. The obvious alternatives are to seek revenue increases or impose spending decreases, but balance can also be attained through other means. Budget reserves, rainy day funds, or savings from previous years may be drawn upon to increase available revenues.[15] It is possible that some governments may continue spending at high levels, helped by rainy day funds, when budget cuts are really needed. Sometimes payments from one fiscal year may be shifted to the next, even though resources are actually used in the earlier year. Political leaders use this technique and others to make budgets appear to be balanced when the opposite is true.

Elimination of tax expenditures can yield additional revenues without officially raising tax rates; for instance, adding products or services to the list of items subject to a state sales tax can increase revenues. Decision makers are concerned with whether each tax expenditure serves any major public purpose, and all tax expenditures are particularly subject to challenge when revenues are needed to balance a budget.[16]

Budget gimmickry also is used during economic boom-times. By estimating revenues to be lower than are most likely to occur, decision makers later in the year can "discover" that a budget surplus exists and then use the money for some combination of tax relief and new spending.

Tax earmarking often constrains efforts to balance budgets without necessarily helping the programs officially decreed to be beneficiaries. Receipts from state lotteries, for instance, are often earmarked for such good causes as public education or aid to senior citizens. Available evidence indicates that programs with such earmarked revenues do not receive proportionately greater overall funding than other programs. Indeed, earmarking is sometimes used as an excuse for not providing more funds to a program, because it is expected to operate within available revenue from the earmarked source. The supposed program that benefits from a lottery, then, may receive no greater funding than it would have without the lottery. Earmarking in effect "Balkanizes" a government's finances and can greatly hamper efforts to resolve budget problems when revenues decline, because monies are compartmentalized and cannot be treated as part of the total resources available for creating an overall balanced budget.

In addition, revenue gaps are sometimes closed with public employee pension monies. A government may simply not make its full contribution to the employee pension funds or may even have the freedom to withdraw monies in an effort to balance the budget. Typically, financial penalties must be paid for such actions, including negative reactions by the financial markets for municipal bonds issued by jurisdictions engaging in such practices. More subtle methods involve adjusting actuarial assumptions. By making an assumption that retired employees will die comparatively early in life, fewer dollars will be needed to cover expected retirees when benefit levels are predetermined. Also, by assuming that investments on retirement monies will result in comparatively high returns, more dollars will become available to cover expected retirement benefits and the government will need to contribute less to the retirement fund.[17]

Another revenue source used by the states is the money received from the negotiated settlement with the tobacco industry (see Chapter 4). After states filed suit for compensation for the costs they incurred through treating smokers, tobacco companies agreed to pay the states billions of dollars. This money was intended to cover the states' costs and to be used in antismoking campaigns, to discourage people from starting to smoke and to encourage smokers to quit. However, when budget crunches arose, the states turned to these monies for budget balancing purposes.[18]

Whereas the decision makers responsible for state and local budgeting spend substantial time and energy balancing their budgets, the situation is quite different at the federal level. Whether to require a balanced federal budget has long been a controversial issue, but a law requiring an annually balanced budget has yet to be adopted (see Chapters 9 and 15).

Spending Deliberations

Entitlements and Other Commitments. Much of the spending side of any budget is determined in advance of budget preparation deliberations. Interest on the debt must be paid, and prior commitments to employees, such as set levels of contributions to retirement plans, must be met. Entitlement programs that guarantee benefits to various groups, such as the needy, the elderly, and the ill, determine much of the spending side of a budget, where the amount spent is a function of the numbers of people qualifying for various programs and the amount each would be paid under existing law. Increased spending for these entitlements is often pegged to increases in the consumer price index, which has been criticized as overstating the rate of inflation. Nevertheless, as long as a law is mandated to use the consumer price index, budget makers must use its projected increases as the basis for calculating entitlement costs.[19]

Organizational Competition. Just as central administrative organizations compete in trying to influence revenue decisions, so organizations vie with one another on the spending side of the budget. At the top level of a government, personalities become important. The roles of various participants at the federal level depend upon a president's administrative style, his or her confidence in the abilities of key figures, and the roles that these figures seek for themselves. A president is not obligated to rely on the advice of any individual and may seek guidance from anyone inside or outside government.

The international policy arena includes many participants, such as the president's national security advisor, the State Department, the Department of Defense, the National Security Agency, and the Central Intelligence Agency (CIA), and each may resist major exercise of control by the central budget office. In addition, the National Security Council (NSC) exists to advise the president on "domestic, foreign, and military policies relating to national security."[20] The NSC is headed by the president and includes among its members the vice president and the secretaries of state and defense; the director of the CIA and the chair of the Joint Chiefs of Staff serve as statutory advisers to the council. Also included is the president's national security advisor.

OMB is notably not part of the NSC, although it can be invited to meetings at the president's discretion. OMB can be eclipsed in this arena, performing the largely routine function of assembling budget materials rather than influencing how much money is to be allocated to defense and foreign affairs and for what purposes.

In the domestic arena, the competition is also fierce. Cabinet officers seek to gain acceptance and financial support for their agencies' programs. Central advisers to the president are other contenders for attention. In addition to advice provided by the White House Office staff, advice is available from the Office of Policy Development (consisting of the Domestic Policy Council and the National Economic Council) and the Council of Economic Advisers.

Some have suggested that at this level of government, but also at lower levels, misrepresentation and other ethically questionable behavior prevails.[21] The competitive nature of budgeting may emphasize self-interest, both personal and collective, to the detriment of the public interest. As C. W. Lewis notes, "The process depends on and rewards deceit."[22] Agencies may misrepresent their situations to budget offices — for example, by claiming dire consequences unless budgets are increased for programs that are highly visible and favored by the public. At a higher level, political leaders may deceive the public — for example, by downplaying the importance of budget deficits and rationalizing the need for greater spending on pet projects even though the budget is out of balance.

Budget Office Roles. The central budget office has numerous roles to perform. Not only does it recommend policies on spending, but it participates in the review of legislative proposals, economic policy, administrative regulations, evaluation of programs, collection of data by agencies, and agency management studies and management improvement efforts (see Chapter 10). When OMB examines an agency's budget request, all of these forces come into play. Agency budget proposals will be seen in the context of what legislative changes will be necessary, what regulatory actions will be required by the agency, and whether the agency is perceived as well managed.

Agency Expectations and Deliberations. In approaching the budget process, including the preparation phase, agencies have expectations about what constitutes success. Until the latter half of the 1970s, success often was measured in terms of budget increases approved by the executive and ultimately by the legislative body. This approach of adding increments to a base has since been discarded in many locales. Where taxing and spending limits have been imposed at the state and local levels, agencies have been forced instead to concentrate on defending their bases and minimizing the extent of cuts imposed on their budgets. The period from the late 1970s to the early 1990s has been dubbed the *decremental age.*[23]

By the time a budget request reaches the central budget office, an extensive series of discussions has been completed within the line agency. In large agencies having several layers of organizational units, those at the bottom will have attempted to persuade their superiors to approve requests for additional funding. The force being exerted from the top downward tends to be negative — in the sense that pressure is applied to limit the growth of programs and the corresponding rise in expenditures. Yet this does not mean that there is simply a set of petitioners and a set of rejecters who do battle within each agency or department. Middle managers up through department heads are required to take positive and negative positions, rejecting many of the proposals brought to them by subordinates and, in negotiating with their superiors, advocating those proposals that they accept.

Part of the influence within an agency is a function of superior levels attempting to determine what is likely to be salable to the budget office and the chief executive. Agencies are aware that they are likely to get less than they request. Therefore, they will avoid requesting too little but will not ask for exorbitant sums unless an open-ended budget system is in use.

The amount eventually requested by the department is necessarily a function of the type of budget system in place. As discussed in Chapter 5, some systems provide for a base budget and then permit requests for additions to that base. Others use a current services budget and require that an agency include information about possibly funding activities below and above the current services level. Some budget systems may require reductions. For example, President Clinton issued Executive Order 12837 in 1993, requiring federal agencies to segregate their administrative expenses from other budget items and to reduce these expenses (when adjusted for inflation) each year through fiscal 1997. The executive order was intended to force agencies to improve their productivity — that is, to meet their statutory mandates to provide services but with reduced resources.

Budget Office and Agency Relations. Just as the interplay within an agency is extensive and vociferous during budget preparation, so is the interplay between the central budget office and the agencies.[24] The central office, serving as the agent of the chief executive, must assert a unifying influence over the diverse interests of administrative units; these, on the other hand, can be expected to favor greater autonomy. Operating departments and agencies will, of course, favor the advancement of their particular programs (seeking greater funds or defending programs against cuts), while the budget office usually will be forced to say no to program growth and even sometimes to say yes to cutbacks.

When the budget office receives agency budget submissions, examiners are assigned to review these documents. The examiners serve as the main link between the budget office and line units. With the passage of time, examiners gain considerable knowledge about their agencies, providing substantive expertise within the budget office. They often become advocates for the agencies they review and frequently even shift to an operating agency. Still, the accusation is commonly made by the agency officials that budget examiners are not program-oriented and are insensitive to the needs of operating units.

The structure of budget offices varies from government to government and from time to time. One key concern is whether the central function of examining agency budget requests should be integrated with other functions, notably management functions (discussed in Chapter 10), program analysis, and planning. The argument for their integration is that it gives budget analysts much broader exposure to the operations of government and enhances the analysts' opportunities to make valuable inputs into budget deliberations. The argument against integration is that all too often budget examination activities take top priority, leaving all other activities on the sidelines.

OMB is organized into four resource management offices:

1. Natural resources (including agriculture, energy, science, and space)
2. National security (including international affairs)
3. Human resources (including education, health, and labor)
4. General government (including housing, justice, transportation, and treasury)

Each resource management office is responsible for budgeting, management, and planning/policy issues within its particular arena.

Budget office discussions with agencies will involve how services are to be delivered to the citizenry, as well as the funding for those services. The deliberations will include whether services should be provided directly by agencies, by private corporations operating under contract with government, or through some combination of these and other modes.

The nature of the dialogue between the budget office and the agencies hinges in large measure on the extent to which the latter consider the former to be an important ally or an opponent. Only minimal information can be expected from an agency that is suspicious of the central budget office. A common concern is that an agency will not release data that could be used to its detriment. On the other hand, if an agency can win the confidence and support of the examiner, then it in effect gains a spokesperson for its program on the chief executive's staff.

The budget office holds hearings with agency representatives. Whereas earlier in the process the examiners may have contacted agencies by phone, e-mail, facsimile, or in person to clarify detailed items included in requests, hearings tend to focus on broader concerns. The budget office must decide whether agencies can accomplish what they propose and whether the anticipated accomplishments are worth seeking. The burden of proof rests with the agencies. The operating agency that has a reputation for requesting excessive sums and for overpromising on results will be suspect.

The George W. Bush administration, coming into office in 2001, sought to utilize much of the earlier work accomplished due to the Government and Performance Results Act of 1993. Agencies were pressed by OMB to justify their budget requests based upon performance data, and the budget office threatened cuts justified on performance reviews. The Bush administration's management agenda explicitly promised that "high-performing programs will be reinforced and non-performing activities reformed or terminated."[25] Of course, what the budget office and the president recommend is subject to approval by Congress, which may be loathe to cut some programs for political reasons.

At the same time, winning budget office approval does not guarantee success for the agency. The resistant or recalcitrant agency may, indeed, be able to increase the caution with which the examiner makes recommendations to reduce the agency's budget. At the federal level, the significance of OMB action is mitigated by the fact that Congress retains the power to pass appropriations. It has even been suggested that opposition by the budget office to any agency's request for funds may sometimes be helpful in winning legislative support.

The agencies, not OMB, have had major responsibility for defending their budget requests before Congress, and therefore the office's utility to the agencies has been greater in the preparation phase than in the approval phase of the budget cycle. Some organizational units, such as the Federal Bureau of Investigation in the 1950s and 1960s, were able to secure extensive support within Congress, thereby providing them with some autonomy vis-à-vis their departments and OMB. Of course, agencies, including the FBI, can fall out of favor when their heads lose public and congressional confidence, making the agencies more vulnerable to OMB control. Beginning in the 1980s, OMB gained greater responsibility for explaining and defending the president's budget before Congress; this role, however, often was negative in the sense that the main task was to explain how and why reductions should be made in agencies' budgets.[26]

Legal requirements and court decisions may force increases in expenditures and preclude some decision making by agencies and the central budget office. For instance, state government mandates may require local governments to establish recycling programs for solid waste. Federal officials may require a city to upgrade its sewage treatment facilities. Federal and state court decisions may force a state government to expand prison facilities to accommodate increased numbers of prisoners or may overturn programs. Court cases may be filed against governments, forcing them to spend considerable sums on legal representation. Such suits may be filed by private citizens or corporations or by one government against another, as in the case of a state challenging a city school voucher program.[27]

War on Terrorism and Homeland Security. The terrorist attacks on September 11, 2001, dramatically changed budgetary priorities in the federal government. Suddenly the primary focus was on defending the nation at home and abroad. President Bush created the Homeland Security Office and then recommended that Congress create a Department of Homeland Security that would be composed largely of units that were housed in other departments. Congress created this department when it passed the Homeland Security Act following the November 2002 elections.[28]

OMB Director Mitchell Daniels issued a memorandum to department and agency heads stating clearly that homeland security had top priority in preparing the fiscal 2004 budget and, by implication, suggested that all else was of secondary importance.[29] The budget office indicated that agencies that did receive increased funding for security would be scrutinized carefully to make certain that results were forthcoming from that funding. Conversely, agencies not directly involved in homeland security might well experience budget cutbacks. Given this situation, then, agencies had a clear incentive to show how their operations were in some way related to security.

Budget Office Recommendations. The response of the budget office to agency requests is, in part, a function of the office's assessment of its own powers and responsibilities in relation to the operating agencies and other central units. Few would deny to a budget office the ministerial or bookkeeping functions of assembling requests and carrying out the mechanical duties of designing, tabulating, and overseeing the printing of the budget. At the same time, how many additional responsibilities the budget office has depends largely on the competition from other units and the management style of the chief executive.

In an executive budgeting system, the chief executive has the final say on what to recommend to the legislative body. Thus, the budget office attempts to formulate recommendations thought to be in keeping with the executive's priorities. As part of the calculation of what to recommend, it assesses the chances of agencies' making direct appeals to the chief executive, or in the extreme case to the legislature, and thereby overturning the budget office's recommendations. If this strategy — making an end-run around the budget office — is successful, it can severely weaken the budget office's role. If an agency knows it can get what it wants by appealing directly to the chief executive or the legislature, the agency is likely to consider the budget office as merely a bookkeeper that can be largely ignored.

As a staff unit of the chief executive, the budget office is expected to develop recommendations that are compatible with executive priorities. On the other hand, as professionals, budgeters have a responsibility to report to the chief executive their views on the worthiness of programs. To report that a given program is operating well simply because the chief executive wants to hear that message does a disservice. So does recommending severe budget cuts to the chief executive when the budget office knows that these cuts could have devastating results on the affected programs. *Neutral competence* has been proposed as the appropriate role for the budget office: The office should retain its professional approach in developing its budget recommendations but simultaneously should develop recommendations in tune with executive priorities.[30]

As the budget is being developed by the budget office and when it is released, the budget office may engage in a public relations campaign that is intended to reach not only the public but also administrative agencies. At the federal level, the OMB director may issue press releases, hold press conferences, appear on Sunday television talk shows, and speak before such groups as the National Press Club. In this way, the budget director communicates on a broad scale the priorities of the administration and in effect warns agencies to beware of pushing for other priorities.

Downsizing, Rightsizing, and Spending Cutbacks

For many government programs, the 1980s marked the beginning of a new era that continued into the 1990s — an era of downsizing, rightsizing, and spending cutbacks. A brief respite from this trend occured in the second half of the 1990s and into 2000 when a robust economy produced budget surpluses and eased some pressure on cutbacks. The ensuing recession, however, brought a return to cutback management.

Government sometimes has been viewed as bloated by years of excessive budget increases, and the response has been to reduce the size of operations. Whether this process is called downsizing or rightsizing, the result is the same: Agencies must try to provide the same or even more services with fewer personnel and other resources.

Fiscal Stress. State and local governments experience periods of both short and prolonged fiscal stress or distress.[31] Some of these governments' problems derive from extended economic declines in their economies. Other problems stem from a temporary lack of robustness in the national economy. When the economy slumps, state and local sales and income tax revenues fall. So-called Rust Belt states and communities face a different set of economic woes — namely, a long-term erosion in their tax bases. Additional fiscal stress sometimes is caused by major reductions in aid from the federal government. During the 1980s, the national government permanently reduced funding of many grant programs and totally eliminated general revenue sharing (see Chapter 14).

The tax revolt movement discussed in Chapter 4 imposed additional constraints on spending. In some instances, a jurisdiction's economy may have been vibrant, but the government was precluded from taxing that economic base to the extent it perceived was needed to fund government programs.

Cutback Management. In response to their financial problems, governments sometimes engage in cutback management, retrenchment, downsizing, or rightsizing. (Note that governments in other countries have experienced similar problems.) Also, sometimes retrenchment programs are undertaken not because of fiscal stress but because of the preferences of the political leadership — that is, a desire on the part of officials to reduce the size of government.[32]

The tactics used to deal with a budget shortage depend in part upon its perceived duration. If the shortage is considered to be short term, perhaps lasting only for the current year, then modest adjustments can be made, such as imposing temporary cuts on programs and drawing on *budget reserves* or *rainy day funds.*

When long-term budget retrenchment is seen as necessary, then decision makers must manage the immediate problems of the current and upcoming budget years and anticipate problems in future years. Where budget cuts must be imposed several years in a row, then decision makers must be prepared to make extraordinarily difficult choices. Sometimes across-the-board cuts are ordered. These uniform cuts can have the effect of inappropriately freezing current priorities in place rather than taking a hard look at which lower-priority programs deserve larger reductions. Which budget cuts will be made ultimately hinges on the extent to which various groups in the society will suffer from program reductions or eliminations. Budget cuts are less likely to be imposed on groups that are politically organized and vocal than on other, less visible groups. Applying the budget knife to programs for the elderly is often politically dangerous, for instance, whereas cutting programs for the poor, who tend to be politically less active, may seem "safer" for decision makers. In relatively homogeneous communities, budget cutback procedures do not pit one segment of the community against another.

Budget Office Roles during Cutbacks. When jurisdictions confront fiscal stress, the decision process initially tends to be centralized. After all, without central instruction to begin a process of cutting, agencies might well submit budget requests based on unrealistic assumptions. The central budget office, working with the chief executive, attempts to instruct departments as to priorities for funding. Efforts are made to avoid across-the-board cuts in all programs because such an approach can cause severe harm to essential services.

If programs are set aside as immune from budget cuts, they may have few incentives to be efficient in their spending. Moreover, achieving the level of budget reductions needed to balance a budget may be impossible if many key programs are protected from cuts. This problem existed at the federal level during the Reagan administration, where Social Security and the Department of Defense were protected from cuts.

In a retrenchment environment, agencies normally can expect budget office approval of no more than their projected current services budgets. In other situations, the central budget office may provide specific budget ceilings to each department. These figures, which most likely are below the current services levels, are used in preparing budget requests. This process has all the strengths and the weaknesses of fixed-ceiling budgeting. Where such approaches are taken, the process of cutting often starts earlier in the calendar than in a budget situation where growth, rather than reduction, predominates.[33] More time may be needed to determine which programs will be cut than to introduce new programs or expand existing ones, although some governments may find themselves in crisis situations in which cuts must be imposed immediately to avert a collapse of their financial situation.

Legislative Roles. If legislative preferences can be identified at the beginning of budget preparation, then cuts can be planned that are ultimately likely to meet with legislative approval. Some communities have used confidential questionnaires and other techniques for soliciting legislative input when budget cutting must be part of the preparation phase. Members of local legislative bodies, however, may prefer not to reveal their preferences until later, when more is known about the options for cutting and about citizens' attitudes. Of course, legislatures are not always on the "cutting" side of the budget process, in that sometimes legislatures are in the position of restoring cuts proposed by the executive.

Items to Cut. When reductions in expenditures become necessary, certain standard areas are considered. One of them is personnel costs. Because much of any government's operating budget covers personnel costs, it is difficult to make any appreciable reduction in expenditures without reducing personnel numbers. Holding down general pay increases for workers is a common practice, although this technique can make compensation for government jobs noncompetitive with that for private sector jobs. Commonly used techniques for reducing personnel expenditures include delaying filling vacant positions, leaving other positions empty as they become vacant, and, if necessary, laying off workers. Financial incentives may be offered to senior workers to encourage them to retire early, nonpaid furloughs of one day per week may be required of all employees, and, depending on legal restrictions, some workers may be required to accept pay cuts. Governments must be cautious in instituting personnel and other cutbacks because intergovernmental aid can be reduced accordingly, especially if grants include matching provisions.

Equipment and facilities are other areas in which cutting can occur. Decisions may be made to delay the purchase of major equipment and to defer maintenance, such as postponing the repair of city-owned sidewalks, roofs on government buildings, and potholes in city and state roads. The savings here can be short-lived: The failure to repair a roof, for example, might result in water damage costing many thousands of dollars. There may be a tendency to use the deferred maintenance approach on less visible facilities, especially water and sewer lines, although highways and bridges have suffered notably due to state and local fiscal problems.

In so-called tight budget periods, major emphasis is given to making operations as efficient as possible. The expectation is that organizational units should be able to operate with fewer resources while maintaining existing service levels. On the other hand, no single agency is eager to relinquish resources through increased efficiency if other agencies are not compelled to take the same route. Each agency is fearful of being the first to show how savings can be accomplished in its operations. This same attitude prevails in the approval phase among legislators, who are not eager to agree to budget cuts in their favored programs even though it is well understood that major cuts will be necessary.

Governments sometimes allow agencies to carry forward unspent money into the next fiscal year. This technique is seen as giving agencies incentives to use their resources efficiently. In a cutback period, however, the budget office and the legislature may be tempted to cancel out any carryover monies. Agencies mindful of such possible action, then, may avoid carrying forward any monies during economic recessions.

Budget cutting creates havoc, low morale, and some inefficiencies in agencies. Personnel rightfully become concerned that their positions will be eliminated in the agency's budget request. Political appointees in an agency may be at odds with career personnel over which activities are essential and which are expendable. Some budget cuts necessitate agency reorganization, which disrupts operations. Uncertainty in funding can require stretching out the completion of projects. Defense is a major example of this problem, where changes in project schedules can result in billions of dollars of increased costs.

Budget Systems and Cutbacks. A final consideration regarding cutback budgeting is how the various budget systems discussed in Chapter 5 assist in retrenchment efforts. As already noted, central budget offices use variations on fixed-ceiling budgeting to indicate to agencies what funding levels are acceptable in the budget preparation process. Perhaps most other budget systems have been developed on the stated or unstated premise that budgets will increase from year to year and, therefore, these budget systems are less central to decision making when budget cuts must be imposed. At the same time, program budgeting and various forms of zero-base budgeting in theory should be highly useful in budget-cutting situations. During prosperous times, budgeting may be largely a process of considering possible incremental additions to the budget bases of programs. During declining times, the process may become one of subtracting increments from the base.

Credit and Insurance Liabilities

In assembling a proposed budget, both obvious and not-so-obvious expenditures must be anticipated. Much of any budget will be committed to funding the operations of government, either for direct services provided by the government's departments or through grant programs, as in the case of state aid to local school districts. Monies also must be set aside for making payments on the principal and interest for any outstanding debt. As is discussed in subsequent chapters, sustained federal budget deficits have yielded an increasingly large total federal debt that requires massive interest payments every year — so massive that they now constitute one of the most important components of federal expenditures. In addition to debt accumulated through borrowing by the U.S. Treasury Department, federal debt has grown through borrowing by federal agencies such as the U.S. Postal Service and the Tennessee Valley Authority.

Beginning in the late 1980s, political leaders, public administrators, leaders in private financial institutions, and the citizenry became painfully aware that the federal government had other liabilities that until then had seemed innocuous or almost nonexistent.[34] Hundreds of savings and loan institutions failed, forcing the federal government to meet its financial commitments to depositors. The Resolution Trust Corporation was established, as a temporary agency, to manage the resources of thrifts going into receivership at a staggering cost to taxpayers. Further liabilities were encountered when the government had surviving banks acquire many of the failed thrifts.[35]

Types of Liabilities. Appreciating the nature of government liabilities is difficult due to the complex nature of the institutions involved. At least three methods for differentiating these institutions and the programs that they administer are possible: (1) the ownership of the institution, (2) the purpose that it serves, and (3) the type of service that it provides.

Figure 6–1 indicates how ownership can vary from an agency within a regular department of government, to a separate government corporation, such as the Rural Telephone Bank, to a government-sponsored enterprise, such as the Federal National Mortgage Association (Fannie Mae), and finally to a privately owned corporation. As the figure illustrates, a government corporation is owned by the public but may be only partially funded by government, may be largely independent of any government department, and is usually created for a business purpose. A government-sponsored enterprise is a "federal chartered, privately owned, for-profit corporation designed to provide a continuing source of credit nationwide to a specific economic sector."[36] As might be expected, institutions in this obscure realm do not always fit nicely into one of the four categories suggested by **Figure 6–1**. Indeed, Congress has recognized in legislation that some government corporations have mixed ownership, including the Federal Deposit Insurance Corporation (FDIC) and Amtrak.[37]

A second way of viewing these institutions is to consider them in terms of the purposes that they serve. They bolster and foster growth of the financial system of the nation, housing, education, agriculture, and the like.

A third approach is to consider the methods the institutions use in serving these purposes. Here, four approaches are used, as outlined in **Table 6–1**. As can be seen, the instruments used and the consequent categories of liabilities are direct loans, guaranteed loans, insurance, and government-sponsored enterprises.

Before discussing these instruments, we should note that other major liabilities are omitted from the table, such as the costs of environmental clean-up of nuclear weapons production plants, defense installations that are being abandoned both in the United States and overseas, and other federal agency facilities. Other exclusions include federal research and development centers, such as the RAND Corporation, which are primarily the creations of the Departments of Defense and Energy, and congressionally chartered, nonprofit corporations, such as the American Red Cross.

Direct loans involve operations at home and abroad. Monies are available to help farmers acquire homes, electrify their farms, and engage in overseas commerce. International operations include loans to support the defense and economic development of other nations and to stimulate the growth of the private sectors in these countries. Immense political risks exist with such instruments, because a change in a government may lead to the renunciation of previous commitments to repay loans. In other situations, developing countries may be too poor to repay loans so that these become de facto grants.

Guaranteed loans entail agreement by the government to pay loans when customers default. A major segment of the housing mortgage market in the United States is backed by federal government loan guarantees. The category has also

Figure 6–1 Comparison of Public and Private Entities

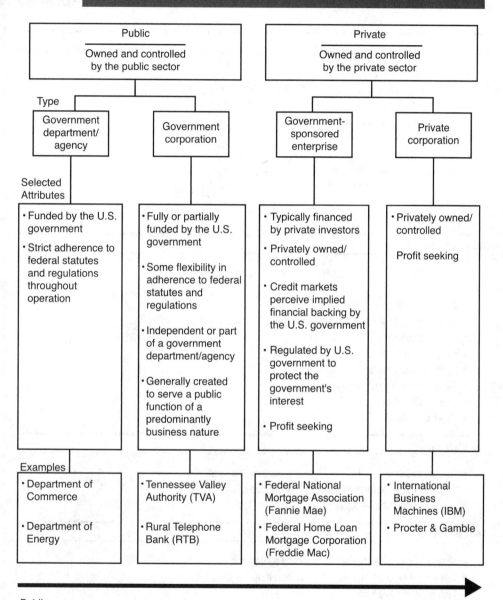

Source: Reprinted from U.S. General Accounting Office, *Government Corporations: Profiles of Existing Government Corporations* (Washington, DC: U.S. Government Printing Office, 1995), 5.

Table 6-1 Long-Term Federal Government Obligations and Risks

1. Direct Loans

- Federal student loan programs
- Farm Service Agency (excluding CCC), Rural Development, Rural Housing
- Housing and Urban Development
- Agency for International Development
- P.L. 83-480 — Agriculture
- Export-Import Bank
- Commodity Credit Corporation
- Federal Communications Commission spectrum auction
- Disaster assistance
- Other direct loan programs

2. Guaranteed Loans

- Federal Housing Administration — mutual mortgage insurance
- Veterans housing
- Federal family education loan
- Federal Housing Administration — general and special risk
- Small business
- Export-Import Bank
- International assistance
- Farm Service Agency and Rural Housing
- Commodity Credit Corporation
- Other guaranteed loan programs

3. Insurance

- Deposit insurance — Federal Deposit Insurance Corporation
- Pension guarantees — Pension Benefit Guaranty Corporation
- Disaster insurance — flood, crop

4. Government-Sponsored Enterprises

- Federal National Mortgage Association (Fannie Mae)
- Federal Home Loan Mortgage Corporation (Freddie Mac)
- Federal Home Loan Banks
- Student Loan Market Association (Sallie Mae)
- Farm Credit System

Source: Adapted from U.S. Office of Management and Budget, *Analytical Perspectives, Budget of the United States Government, Fiscal Year 2003* (Washington, DC: U.S. Government Printing Office, 2002) 197–203.

included student loans, which have had a history of high rates of default.[38] In the international arena, the federal government has guaranteed billions of dollars of loans made by U.S. financial institutions to developing countries under the Housing Guaranty Loan Program and other programs such as Development Credit Authority.

Federal insurance programs cover deposits in financial institutions and private pension deposits. While the huge bank failures of the 1980s have been mopped up, bank failures continue to occur.[39] Pension guarantees present other problems. Corporate failures, as in the case of Enron, leave pensioners and employees with credits into pension plans that lack adequate financial backing. The Pension Benefit Guarantee Corporation deals with these problems, with the support of the federal government. Other programs include crop insurance for farmers.

Government-sponsored enterprises are another source of liability. The institutions listed in **Figure 6–1**, including Freddie Mac and Fannie Mae, involve largely secondary credit markets, in which these institutions purchase debt instruments, such as mortgages, and in turn release funds to lending institutions for further loan activity.[40]

Federal Liability Reforms. Efforts are under way to bring some clarity to what liabilities the government has, and proposals exist for reforming this immense area of finance.[41] The concerns about such liabilities are not new but rather date back to 1945, when Congress passed the Government Corporation Control Act.[42] At the time, there was concern that government corporations were operating without sufficient guidance and control by the government. The argument can be made that, despite the numerous revisions Congress has made in the law over the years it remains inadequate in controlling these major institutions.

The Financial Institutions Reform, Recovery, and Enforcement Act of 1989 dealt with failed thrift institutions and required the General Accounting Office (GAO) to investigate the financing of government-sponsored enterprises.[43] The GAO has designated some programs, such as farm loan programs, as "high risk."[44] The GAO's intent is to train attention on those programs that have the potential for creating large economic losses for the government.

The Federal Credit Reform Act of 1990 required the government to upgrade its accounting for credit programs.[45] OMB issued Circular A-129 (1993), which provides a uniform set of procedures for agencies engaged in loan programs, both direct and guaranteed. The procedures indicate how agencies should estimate the costs of loans and loan guarantees, a function that is difficult to accomplish. The purpose of Circular A-129 is to reduce risks and place the federal government's credit operations on a better financial foundation. Agencies that guarantee loans must estimate potential defaults and include those estimates in their current appropriations requests. This reform places potential defaults in direct competition with current spending requests, a practice expected to make decision makers more cautious in extending loans and loan guarantees.

Efforts are now under way to improve the collection of debts rather than simply writing off bad debts. The Debt Collection Improvement Act of 1996 strengthened the government's ability to retrieve monies owed.[46] Agencies may refer bad debts to private collection companies and may share information with one another in locating those borrowers who are in arrears.

These significant changes, however, have not addressed the main issue — namely, what should be the federal government's responsibilities in this area and how can liabilities and risks be curtailed? One line of criticism states that the federal government has been too generous. Fostering a credit market is important to national economic growth, but should the federal government assist three-fifths of all nonfederal credit in the nation, as is currently the case? Agencies, under pressure to justify their continued governmental support, have issued reports explaining how their operations contribute to the well-being of the nation.[47]

Credit programs subsidize risk taking on the part of individuals and corporations. When the federal government provides full backing for a venture, then it assumes 100 percent of the risk. Crop insurance, for example, is available at comparatively low cost to farms. Only about one in four farms uses the insurance, however, because when droughts, floods, and other conditions destroy crops, the government usually passes legislation that fully covers all damage. Prescriptions for reform, therefore, tend to favor increasing the risk of the private sector and decreasing that of the public sector. Such action was taken in 1996 with the passage of the Student Loan Marketing Association Reorganization Act, which provides for the privatization of Sallie Mae (student loans) and Connie Lee (college construction loans).[48] The student loan program was one that the GAO identified as a high-risk program.[49]

Another reform theme insists that structural changes should bring greater coordination among the various institutions involved and greater oversight of their operations. It may be desirable to have a single regulatory body that would oversee many government-sponsored enterprises and related institutions. An oversight board specifically dedicated to this function might be more energized than OMB, which must oversee the operations of these varied institutions as well as all of the regular departments and agencies of the government.[50]

Although one line of concern insists that credit and insurance institutions have become burdensome on government, perhaps suggesting that they should be totally privatized, the reality is that they serve important functions. Proposals exist for creating still more of these bodies. Government corporations have been proposed for air traffic services, management of petroleum reserves, and development of national infrastructure.[51]

State and Local Governments. Similar liability and risk problems exist at the state and local levels. The Governmental Accounting Standards Board has prescribed how these governments should report risks and insurance (see Chapter 11). Potential losses can be due to "torts; theft of, damage to, or destruction of assets; business interruptions; errors or omissions; job-related illnesses or injuries to employees; acts of God; and any other risks of loss assumed under a policy or participation contract issued by a public entity risk pool."[52] *Torts* are civil wrongs that occur independent of contract, as when a city refuse truck accidentally backs into a person's vehicle and causes personal harm and property damage. Among the greatest liabilities of state and local governments are their pension systems, which are sometimes actuarially unsound (see Chapter 13).

Final Preparation Deliberations

The chief executive becomes most active in the budget preparation phase during its final weeks, a frustrating period for the budget office. Decisions are seemingly reached but then may be reversed. The chief executive may instruct the budget office to include an agency's proposed change in the budget but later reject the proposal after considering revenue estimates. The chief executive may tentatively decide to recommend tax increases and then reverse that decision. Materials prepared during evenings and weekends by the budget office may find their way to the paper shredder as decisions are changed. The process may seem haphazard — and it probably is in many respects — but it is necessarily complicated because of the numerous factors being evaluated simultaneously.

A common complaint about the preparation phase is that only the chief executive and the director of the central budget office consider the budget as a whole. An organizational unit within a department or agency is concerned primarily with its own piece of the budget, and the same is true of a department vis-à-vis other departments and the rest of the budget. Even within the central budget office, budget examiners focus mainly on one or a few segments of the budget and not on the total package. The chief executive, assisted by the budget director, must pull together pieces of information and intelligence provided by various sources into a set of decisions that can be defended as a whole. The budget that is to be submitted to the legislative body is the chief executive's creation.

The decision process necessarily involves tradeoffs. A $1 million increase in a city police department's budget means there is that much less available for other departments in the government. A one-mill increase in property taxes makes more money available to provide services that citizens want but at the same time may anger those same citizens who face an increase in their tax bills. Planning personnel layoffs may seem a reasonable choice for avoiding tax increases, but will layoffs be imposed on all agencies, including highly visible units such as the police and fire departments? Chief executives take seriously the justifications that agencies make for increasing budget amounts or for avoiding budget cuts, and perceptions about the effectiveness of agencies' programs and activities influence executive decisions in the preparation phase of budgeting.

In this final stage of preparation, the chief executive must decide to what extent to include intiatives that may be ill-received by the legislature. For example, with the end of the Cold War and the advent of worldwide terrorism, the Defense Department has insisted on the need for a "transformation" and a corresponding budget.[53] The argument is made that the military needs to invest in new technologies and scrap old ones. Closing unneeded military bases is part of this argument, but it runs counter to the interests of key members of Congress, who want to preserve bases in their jurisdictions. The president, then, must decide what to include in the budget on this sensitive matter, balancing the needs of national security with the reality of politics.

Chief executives often include items in their budgets that they do not wholeheartedly support, because they know that the legislature is likely to fund the initiatives in any event. In this type of situation, an executive may include the item to get a more realistic picture of ultimate expenditures and budget tradeoffs.

▮ Budget Documents

The final product of the preparation phase of budgeting is a budget document (or documents) that contains the decisions reached during the months of agency requests and executive reviews. The budget at this point is only a proposal, a set of recommended policies and programs set forth by the chief executive. It remains a proposal until the legislative body acts on it.

Number and Types of Documents

The budget for any government may consist of one or several documents. Small jurisdictions often have one-volume budgets, whereas larger governments usually package their budgets in several volumes. The size of a jurisdiction's budget, as measured in receipts or expenditures, does not always determine the size of its documents, however. Documents are printed on different sizes of paper and vary considerably in their graphics. Some volumes contain mainly text and tables, while others include charts, graphs, photographs of citizens and government buildings, and magazine-style articles on special topics — for example, nursing home care for the elderly.

The preparers of budget documents are paying increasing attention to making the documents more "user friendly," reflecting the fact that these documents are expected to communicate the proposals contained within not only to technical budget analysts but also to executive and legislative political leaders, the news media, and the general citizenry. Budget documents often include glossaries that define technical terms in everyday language. Explanations are provided as to how tables should be read. Sections are sometimes color-coded and tabbed or have markings on page edges to help readers find the topics of interest to them. Since 1984, the Government Finance Officers Association has given its Award for Distinguished Budget Presentation to hundreds of state and local governments.[54]

A government may produce one main document as well as one or more additional documents. A *budget-in-brief* may be prepared for general consumption that places emphasis on graphics and readability. The government can enhance its documents' interest to general readers by using attractive formats made possible by the widespread availability of affordable desktop publishing computer software. Of course, many governments have their budgets online, which increases their accessibility.

Federal Documents. In some years, the federal government publishes numerous budget documents; in other years, it provides far fewer documents. The main budget document is the *Budget of the United States Government*, which is backed up by a second and much larger document — the *Budget Appendix*. In addition to preparing these documents, OMB prepares *Analytical Perspectives*, which provides more detailed information about specific aspects of the budget. Topics in this document include the government's balance sheet, expenditures for research and development, federal credit and insurance, aid to state and local governments, borrowing and debt, current services estimates, and compliance with the Budget Enforcement Act (see Chapter 9). *Historical Tables* provides multiyear financial data on a variety of subjects. *Budget System and Concepts* gives an overview of federal budgeting. *Performance and Management Assessements* provides a wealth of performance information about federal programs and evaluates them on the basis of green, yellow, and red standards (see Chapter 5). OMB produces other important documents, such as budget circulars (for example, Circular A-11 describes budget preparation) and annual publications covering procurement and the midyear status of the budget. Some documents may be prepared for a few years but then are replaced or superseded by other documents. For instance, sometimes separate annual volumes have been prepared that describe the policy initiatives being advocated by the president and the information being collected by federal agencies.

The *Economic Report of the President* is prepared by the Council of Economic Advisers and is released at about the same time as the other main budget documents. The *Economic Report* discusses expected economic trends for the coming fiscal year and is the basis upon which the president's economic policy is formulated. The economic assumptions reflected in this report are used for estimating revenues and expenditures for the budget year.

The Treasury Department has an extensive publishing program and produces several documents specifically related to budgeting. The *Combined Statement of Receipts, Outlays, and Balances of the United States Government* reports on the financial condition of the government (see Chapter 12). The *Treasury Bulletin*, issued quarterly, reports information about the economy, government receipts and outlays, and federal debt. This document provides details on the various forms of federal securities. In addition to these documents, the Treasury Department publishes monthly and daily reports on the government's financial transactions and separate reports on trust funds, such as the unemployment, highway, and disability insurance trust funds.

Other Specialized Documents. Governments sometimes publish specialized budget-related documents in addition to those already mentioned. Some states and many local governments publish capital budgets, showing planned construction projects and major pieces of equipment to be purchased (see Chapter 12), and some publish separate volumes on personnel (see Chapter 13).

The federal government and some states publish discussions of tax expenditures, which are losses in government revenue due to tax provisions that exempt some items from taxation or provide favorable tax rates. In its annual publication *Analytical Perspectives*, OMB provides an extensive itemization of tax expenditures and projects each into the future for five years. California and Massachusetts have published separate volumes on tax expenditures. **Figure 6–2** presents two types of tax expenditures that are part of the Pennsylvania tax code. If the state chose to tax some forms of retirement income and employers' contributions to retirement plans, then tax revenues would increase.

Budget Messages. Another feature of budget documents is the budget message, in which the chief executive highlights the major recommendations in the budget. This message sometimes is presented orally to the legislature. The president's budget message is included in the *Budget of the United States Government* itself. State governments vary widely in this regard, with some having no message and others having lengthy ones, sometimes as long as 100 pages. State and local jurisdictions occasionally publish their budget messages as separate documents.

Approved Budgets. Some jurisdictions publish their approved budgets (i.e., budgets that reflect action taken by the legislative bodies). North Carolina, for example, publishes a *Post-Legislative Budget Summary*. The federal government does not provide such a volume.

Coverage

Budget documents vary with regard to the extent of their coverage. All report information about government receipts and expenditures. Likewise, intergovernmental transactions are reported. A state budget highlights the funds it receives from the federal government and the funds it provides local governments within the state. Issues arise over how much detail to provide on these items.

General and Special Funds. Confusion is common in the handling of funds in budget documents. State and local governments are major users of special funds,

Figure 6–2 **Pennsylvania Personal Income Tax Expenditures, Exclusions from Income, 2000–2007**

Retirement Income

Description: Payments commonly recognized as old age or retirement benefits paid to persons retired from service after reaching a specific age or after a stated period of service are exempt from taxation.

Purpose: The exemption limits the impact of the tax on retired persons. It also prevents taxation of previously taxed employee contributions to retirement plans.

(Dollar Amounts in Millions)

Estimates:	2000–01	2001–02	2002–03	2003–04	2004–05	2005–06	2006–07
	$1,388.6	$1,490.6	$1,600.0	$1,717.5	$1,843.6	$1,978.9	$2,124.2

Beneficiaries: As many as 1.9 million retired residents benefit from this tax expenditure.

Retirement Contributions By Employers

Description: Payments made by employers for programs covering employee retirement and employer Social Security contributions are exempt from taxation.

Purposes: This provision lessens the burden of the tax on Pennsylvania wage-earners and maintains fairness, because the employee often does not have the right to possess the funds in the retirement plan except upon retirement or separation from the company after a set number of years of service.

Estimates:	2000–01	2001–02	2002–03	2003–04	2004–05	2005–06	2006–07
	$ 495.1	$ 519.6	$ 545.8	$ 577.5	$ 604.3	$ 625.9	$ 648.6

Beneficiaries: As many as 5.7 million employees benefit from this tax expenditure.

Note: This exhibit does not include all exemptions listed in the budget document.
Source: Office of the Budget, Commonwealth of Pennsylvania, *2002–03 Governor's Executive Budget,* Harrisburg, PA, 2002, D56–D57.

which basically are financial accounts for special revenue sources, such as the Casino Revenue Fund in New Jersey, and which can be used only for specific purposes. A jurisdiction's general fund consists of revenue that can be used for all functions of the government. These different types of funds are discussed elsewhere in this book in conjunction with accounting issues (Chapter 11), but here we note that many jurisdictions have a general fund budget document plus one or more documents for special funds. One result of having separate budgets can be confusion over the size of the total budget and the amount spent by any given agency, because the agency may be receiving support from several funds.

Federal Coverage Prior to 1969. The coverage issue at the federal level is similar. Until the late 1960s, there were really three types of federal budgets: the administrative budget, the consolidated cash statement, and the federal sector of the national income accounts. The differences among these need not bother us here. What is important to understand is that using three types of budgets resulted in much confusion. Because each type had a different coverage, total revenues and expenditures varied from one to another, leading to different statements of budget surpluses and deficits. Different pictures of federal finances — gloomy or bright — could be painted by choosing to discuss one budget statement and ignoring the other two. In response to this problem, President Johnson in 1967 appointed the President's Commission on Budget Concepts, whose eventual recommendation for a unified budget was incorporated into the budget document beginning with fiscal year 1969.[55]

Unified or Consolidated Budget. In the revised format, all federal agencies and programs are included, with some important exceptions noted below. Receipts, budget authority (appropriations), outlays (expenditures), and the resulting deficit or surplus are shown. Information is supplied for the means of financing the deficit and about the size of the federal debt.

Off-Budget. Since adoption of the unified budget, important changes have occured. One trend was toward greater use of what is known as the *off-budget.* Congress determined what was included in this budget, which varied somewhat from year to year. The postal service, for example, was placed in the off-budget, because it was expected to operate like a business, largely independent of the government. Other federal entities were removed from the budget because they operated largely with revolving funds rather than annual appropriations and made direct loans to the public. For example, the Rural Telephone Bank, the Federal Financing Bank, and the U.S. Synthetic Fuels Corporation were placed in the off-budget. The Gramm-Rudman-Hollings Act of 1985, however, required that all federal entities be placed in the budget, with some exceptions. As of the early 2000s, Old Age and Survivors Insurance, Disability Insurance, and the

Postal Service constitute the off-budget. Determination of what is part of the off-budget is almost exclusively a political decision.

Exclusions from the On-Budget and Off-Budget. Government-sponsored enterprises are included in neither the on-budget nor the off-budget. The same is true for the Board of Governors of the Federal Reserve System. Information about these bodies, however, is provided in OMB's *Analytical Perspectives.*

Alternative Budget Presentations. The decades of debate about how best to present the overall budget of the federal government have made clear that probably no single format is ideal. As a result, OMB attempts to satisfy the needs of different participants in the budget process by presenting information in a variety of formats. The exact coverage of the *Budget of the United States Government* varies from year to year. The document may show outlays divided into mandatory and discretionary categories, along with revenues and the deficit or suplus. Mandatory outlays include deposit insurance, federal retirement, Medicaid, Medicare, and the like. An alternative presentation is usually provided using national income and product accounts (see Chapter 15). Presentations may be based on a format suggested by the GAO or on one similar to a typical state government format. The budget may be displayed so as to highlight its effects upon various age groups or generations. Although the federal government does not have a capital budget, a presentation usually is provided to show federal investment expenditures as distinguished from operating costs.

Information Displays

Revenues. Budget documents present both revenue and expenditure data. The coverage of receipts or revenues usually is substantially less extensive than the coverage of expenditures. Budgets show receipts from taxes, such as individual and corporate income taxes; from user charges, such as water service fees; and from other governments, such as state grants to local government. **Table 6–2**, taken from a Tennessee budget, shows the state, federal, and other revenues that support the state's Housing Development Agency. Budget documents also typically discuss proposed changes in tax laws, especially proposed tax rate changes. For the federal government, some revenues are treated as expenditures. OMB treats receipts generated by an agency as an "offsetting collection" and deducts them from outlays rather than treating the amount as revenue.

Expenditures. The bulk of the budget document is devoted to the expenditure side of government finance, with the main classification usually based on organizational unit. Each department presents a budget within which subunits are given separate treatment. A generally uniform format is used for each subunit, including a brief narrative description of the subunit's responsibilities and functions.

Table 6–2 Base and Improvement Budget, Tennessee Housing Development Agency, 2000–2003

	Actual 2000–2001	Estimated 2001–2002	Base 2002–2003	Improvement 2002–2003	Recommended 2002–2003
Full-time	171	174	174	6	180
Part-time	0	0	0	0	0
Seasonal	0	0	0	0	0
Total	171	174	174	6	180
Payroll	6,340,700	7,675,700	7,675,700	243,200	7,918,900
Operational	73,814,900	256,034,300	256,034,300	36,500	256,070,800
Total	$80,155,600	$263,710,000	$263,710,000	$279,700	$263,989,700
State	0	0	0	0	0
Federal	66,454,600	247,766,300	247,766,300	279,700	248,046,000
Other	13,701,000	15,943,700	15,943,700	0	15,943,700

Source: Budget Division, State of Tennessee, *The Budget, Fiscal Year 2002–2003*, Nashville, TN, 2002, B-344.

Narratives contained in the federal appendix section also contain proposed appropriations language that may be quite specific: For the Commodity Futures Trading Commission's budget of nearly $83 million, not more than $2,000 was to be used for "official reception and representation expenses."[56]

In addition to the narrative are various tabular displays. Expenditures are reported by object classes, such as personnel, equipment, and travel (see Chapter 11). These financial tables may be primarily for informational purposes or they may later be incorporated into the appropriation bill. When this practice is used, the legislative body is said to have adopted a line-item budget, which reduces the president's, governor's, or mayor's flexibility in executing the budget.

Budget presentations sometimes show for the past fiscal year the budgeted amounts and actual amounts, for both receipts and expenditures. This information is important in understanding the accuracy with which the government is able to estimate its revenues and keep its expenditures within budgeted amounts.

Current Services. Governments sometimes provide current services budget data, which are intended to show decision makers what receipts and expenditures will be without any changes being made in tax laws, other revenue sources, and spending levels. **Table 6–3** shows current services projections for the federal government from 2001 through 2007. In addition to receipts, the table reports out-lays subdivided into discretionary spending and mandatory or entitlement spending. It also shows the differences between receipts and outlays for the on-budget and the off-budget for each year. The surplus in the off-budget is due to the Social Security system bringing in more revenue than it pays out.

Table 6–3 Current Services Estimates, Baseline Category Totals, U.S. Budget, 2001–2007 (in Billions of Dollars)

	2001	2002	2003	2004	2005	2006	2007
Receipts	1,991	2,011	2,121	2,234	2,366	2,461	2,581
Outlays							
Discretionary:							
Defense	309	336	347	359	371	377	383
Nondefense	348	382	402	413	420	429	439
Subtotal, discretionary	657	718	749	772	791	806	822
Emergency response fund	0	22	19	20	21	21	21
Mandatory:							
Social Security	429	456	472	491	515	542	571
Medicare	214	223	229	237	252	260	279
Medicaid	129	145	159	171	185	202	219
Other mandatory	228	279	277	272	278	290	294
Subtotal, mandatory	1,000	1,102	1,136	1,172	1,231	1,294	1,363
Net interest	206	177	175	178	174	168	160
Total outlays	1,864	2,020	2,080	2,142	2,218	2,289	2,366
Unified surplus	127	-9	41	92	148	172	215
On-budget surplus	-33	-165	-138	-102	-69	-56	-29
Off-budget surplus	161	155	179	195	217	228	244
Memorandum:							
Alternative baseline that assumes emergency response fund spending is temporary:							
Emergency response fund	0	22	9	5	2	1	*
Unified surplus	127	-9	51	109	169	196	240

*$500 million or less.

Source: Reprinted from U.S. Office of Management and Budget, *Analytical Perspectives, Budget of the United States Government, Fiscal Year 2003* (Washington, DC: U.S. Government Printing Office, 2002) 295.

Program Information. Since World War II, program data have become increasingly common in the budget documents of most governments. Federal program data are presented in the *Appendix* volume of the *Budget of the United States Government*, but only for a small number of agencies, and the information tends to be presented in terms of workload or outputs rather than impacts. **Table 6–4** illustrates the workload of the Food Safety and Inspection Service of the U.S. Department of Agriculture. The table shows the numbers of different types of plants inspected and the millions of pounds of meat and eggs inspected. With regard to state governments, 88 percent reported in 2000 that their documents contained effectiveness and productivity measures for some or most agencies.[57]

While the extent of program data in the federal budget has remained largely unchanged for decades, the budget's format was changed to give it a more programmatic thrust starting with the budget for fiscal year 2003. In particular, the budget was organized according to departments. Within each department, the discussion began with the president's proposals, such as enhancing teacher recruitment and retention by the Department of Education. That was followed by

Table 6–4 Food Safety and Inspection Service Workload, U.S. Department of Agriculture, 2001–2003

	2001 Actual	2002 Estimate	2003 Estimate
Federal inspected establishments:			
Slaughter plants	230	222	210
Processing plants	4,201	4,175	4,120
Combination slaughter and processing plants	933	912	890
Talmadge-Aiken plants	242	235	230
Import establishments	120	115	110
Egg plants	72	70	68
Other plants	478	459	423
Federal inspected and passed production (millions of pounds):			
Meat slaughter	47,397	47,900	48,400
Poultry slaughter	46,728	47,500	48,500
Egg products	3,134	3,150	3,200

Note: This table does not show all food safety and inspection workload information listed in the budget document.
Source: Reprinted from U.S. Office of Management and Budget, *Budget of the United States Government, Fiscal Year 2003—Appendix* (Washington, DC: U.S. Government Printing Office, 2002) 90.

a status report on selected programs within the department, including a blunt assessment of the programs. For example, the Education Department's statistics and effectiveness program was rated as effective but most other programs were rated ineffective. This overall departmental summary was followed by sections on specific programs. Overall, there was more discussion or narrative than detail about finances. The detail was provided in the budget's *Appendix*.

Program Structure. An alternative to arranging the budget document by organizational unit is to arrange it by program structure. The structure consists of a number of broad programs that are subdivided into more narrowly focused subprograms, which are themselves subdivided. Terminology varies, but one approach divides programs into program categories, which are divided into subcategories and then into elements.

The federal government does not have a program budget but does use broad functional classifications to summarize the budget: national defense, natural resources and environment, agriculture, transportation, and the like. The functional classifications are useful for highlighting the changing character of government expenditures over time, such as changes in the proportion of the budget committed to social services, but these classifications are not linked explicitly to program descriptions or specific agency activities.

Using a program structure for the main outline of a budget has both advantages and disadvantages. On the positive side, the budget shows how the activities of different programs relate to each other, regardless of the agency location of the activities, since they are juxtaposed with one another in the document. As a result of being placed in the same program, agencies are forced to recognize their dependence on each other and the need for cooperation. For example, a city transportation department and police department must acknowledge that they both influence traffic safety.

On the negative side, the "pure" program structure type of budget disperses parts of agencies throughout the budget, making it difficult to identify the budget for any one agency. One solution to this problem is known as *crosswalking,* in which information organized by program is reconfigured into an organizational format. Crosswalking, while a successful technique when computer technology is employed, is cumbersome and may force a government to produce two budgets — a program budget and an agency budget.

It is possible to reach a compromise between these two methods. A budget can be divided into major programs first, such as the protection of persons and property program and the human services program, and then each program can show the departments within it.

Figure 6–3 displays the programmatic format used by Long Beach, California. It shows the mission statement, customers served, and primary activities of the city fire department. For fire prevention and fire operations, information is supplied on the services provided and service improvement objectives. Quantitative measures of service are shown for the past year, current year, and budget year.

Program Revisions. Chief executives often wish to use the budget to highlight the programmatic initiatives they are recommending to their respective legislative bodies. Budget documents frequently contain a section that sets forth themes that summarize the major recommendations being made. The federal government's budget for fiscal year 2003 had three such themes: protecting the homeland, winning the war on terrorism abroad, and returning to economic vitality.

Figure 6–4 illustrates another type of information display provided in budget documents. It first shows that the Pennsylvania budget has four program revision "themes," with one being "sustaining economic opportunity." Next, it shows that two departments (the Department of Community and Economic Development and the Department of Labor and Industry) plus an independent agency are part of this set of revisions. Program measures are then presented along with recommended spending levels for each activity within each department. The information is displayed on a multiyear basis.

Future Years. Budget reformers have tended to advocate multiyear projections as a method for helping decision makers understand the long-term implications of policy and program issues.[58] However, given the uncertainty of the future, one might expect few governments to attempt to make projections beyond the budget year or biennium. Perhaps somewhat surprisingly, the use of multiyear projections has steadily increased. A longitudinal study of state budgeting found that while only 2 percent of the states responding in 1970 said they projected effectiveness measures in budget documents, 79 percent reported they made such projections in 2000; comparable figures for the use of productivity measures were 8 percent and 51 percent, respectively.[59]

Space Limitations. Not all available program and resource information can be presented in budget documents without making the documents unwieldy. The budget formats of some jurisdictions rigidly prescribe allowed space — one page, for example, for each bureau, program, or activity. This type of format may increase the readability of the document. Its disadvantage is that not all subunits are of equal importance, in terms of either budget size or political interest. Therefore, many jurisdictions use more flexible formats, providing more information on some agencies and programs and less information on others. With this type of format, larger agencies commonly receive more extensive coverage because they are more complex and engage in more varied activities. Agencies that are particularly popular or unpopular may receive more extensive coverage regardless of their size.

Figure 6–3 Fire Prevention and Operations, City of Long Beach, California, 2000–2002

FIRE DEPARTMENT

Mission Statement:

We prevent loss of life, injury, and property loss within the community through aggressive prevention, education, and enforcement; quick response to emergency situations; and effective action including fire suppression, medical care, and rescue.

Customers Served:

The residents and visitors to Long Beach, Signal Hill, and surrounding jurisdictions.

Primary Activities:

To protect our residents and visitors, our environment and property, from unanticipated dangers resulting from fire and/or medical emergencies.

To deliver our services in a timely, professional, and user-friendly manner.

To interact with the community to educate them to the perils that surround them so that they may participate in protecting themselves.

Fire Prevention

Services Provided:

To provide a safe community for the residents of the cities of Long Beach and Signal Hill through the proactive enforcement of fire, life safety, and environmental code requirements.

Service Improvement Objectives:

To review 1,500 building plans and return 98 percent to submitter within two weeks of receipt.

To implement a fueling station inspection and hazardous material business plan review program.

To inspect 100 percent of all occupancies requiring an annual code enforcement inspection.

To implement a computerized records management system (RMS).

Quantitative Measures of Service	Actual FY 00	Adopted FY 01	Estimate Actual FY 01	Adopted FY 02
Number of plans received and reviewed within two weeks	1342	7	1375	1500
Implementation date for hazardous material business plan review	N/A	N/A	N/A	4/1/02
Percentage of occupancies inspected	99%	100%	98%	100%
Implementation date for RMS	New	9/30/01	Not Implemented	1/1/02

continues

Fire Operations

Services Provided:

To protect lives, the environment, and property by responding to all emergency incidents. Provide rescue, lifeguarding, and paramedic services throughout the city, including beaches and waterways.

Service Improvement Objectives:

Respond to calls for emergency service.

Implement an electronic data management system to track the Marine Safety Rescue Boat services.

Determine the need to place an additional paramedic rescue ambulance in service.

Update and enhance shipboard firefighting training to the Suppression Divisions.

Quantitative Measures of Service	Actual FY 00	Adopted FY 01	Estimate Actual FY 01	Adopted FY 02
Number of calls for emergency service	52,759	7	53,500	54,000
Implementation of new software	N/A	N/A	N/A	03/01/02
Completion of needs assessment	N/A	N/A	N/A	04/01/02
New program implementation and training provided	N/A	N/A	N/A	08/01/02

Source: *Fiscal Year 2002 Adopted Resource Allocation Plan*, City of Long Beach, California, 2001, 116, 120, 121.

 ## Summary

In beginning the preparation phase, the chief executive conveys to agencies some sense of priorities, either formally in writing or by more subtle means. The executive's view of the role of government in society is indicated to agencies, along with more specific priorities.

The revenue side of the budget is examined carefully, especially because state and local governments are not permitted to have operating budgets that exceed available revenues. Requiring the federal government to balance its budget annually is a proposal that has gained considerable acceptance but has not been put into law (see Chapter 9).

Budget preparation begins in agencies and involves extensive debate; similar debate develops between agencies and the central budget office, which in turn must compete with other central staff units. Because little formal authority is granted to a central budget office, it must always be concerned with being overruled by the chief executive.

The 1980s ushered in a new era in budgeting, where the focus is on budget cutbacks rather than program expansion. Fiscal stress, taxing and spending limitations, and an increase in anti–big government attitudes among political leaders have resulted in retrenchment efforts. A respite in cutbacks occurred in the second half of the 1990s, when the booming economy produced budget surpluses. With the recession of the early 2000s, cutback management returned.

Figure 6–4	**Pennsylvania Program Revisions: Sustaining Economic Opportunity, 2000–2007**

Program Revision Themes

Sustaining Economic Opportunity

Improving the Quality of Life

Ensuring Public Safety

Health Care Cost Containment

Sustaining Economic Opportunity Theme

Community and Economic Development:

TANFBG-Critical Job Training

Workforce Leadership Grants

Higher Education Assistance Agency:

SciTech and Technology Scholarships

Labor and Industry:

WIA — Statewide Activities

WIA — Dislocated Workers

Program Measures for Community and Economic Development (Based on Program Revision)

	2000-01	*2001-02*	*2002-03*	*2003-04*	*2004-05*	*2005-06*	*2006-07*
Number of critical job training providers	0	0	122	0	0	0	0
Number of Pennsylvanians receiving critical job training	0	0	6,075	0	0	0	0
Students receiving SciTech and Technology Scholarships	0	0	4,200	4,300	4,400	4,500	4,600

Program Revision Costs by Appropriation (in Thousands of Dollars)

	2000-01	*2001-02*	*2002-03*	*2003-04*	*2004-05*	*2005-06*	*2006-07*
General Fund							
Community and Economic Development Workforce Leadership Grants	$ 0	$ 0	$ 5,000	$ 0	$ 0	$ 0	$ 0
Higher Education Assistance Agency							
SciTech and Technology Scholarships	0	0	6,200	6,200	6,200	6,200	6,200
General Fund Total	$ 0	$ 0	$ 11,200	$ 6,200	$ 6,200	$ 6,200	$ 6,200

Source: *2002–03 Governor's Executive Budget*, Office of the Budget, Commonwealth of Pennsylvania, Harrisburg, PA, 2002, A33, E11.14, E11.15.

Decision makers have come to realize that they can be forced to deal with immense problems associated with credit and insurance liabilities. The collapse of hundreds of federally backed thrift institutions amply demonstrated the risks that are involved.

The product of the preparation phase is a budget or a set of budget documents that reflect executive decisions on policies and programs. The federal government has what is called a *unified budget*. Revenue and expenditure data are treated in all budgets, but the latter receive much more extensive treatment. One common budget format has a structure based on organizational units and includes supporting narratives and tabular displays that present costs, personnel, and program data.

Notes

1. G. Hampton, Environmental Equity and Public Participation, *Policy Sciences* 32 (1999): 163–174; U.S. General Accounting Office, *Gender Equity: Men's and Women's Participation in Higher Education* (Washington, DC: U.S. Government Printing Office, 2000).

2. A.L. Franklin and B. Carberry-George, Analyzing How Local Governments Establish Service Priorities, *Public Budgeting & Finance* 19 (Fall 1999): 31–46.

3. C. Mahtesian, Immigration: The Symbolic Crackdown, *Governing* 7 (May 1994): 52–57.

4. J.B. Williamson, D.M. Watts-Roy, and E.R. Kingson, *The Generational Equity Debate* (New York: Columbia University Press, 1999).

5. H.R. Balanoff and C.W. Pinto, What Do You Do When Your City Is Looking at a Million-Dollar Deficit in the Current Fiscal Year?, *Public Productivity & Management Review* 23 (1999): 83–88.

6. R.D. Picur, Managing Fiscal Slack: You Have a Surplus . . . Now What?, *Government Finance Review* 16 (June 2000): 7–10.

7. P.L. Posner and B.S. Gordon, Can Democratic Governments Save? Experiences of Countries with Budget Surpluses, *Public Budgeting & Finance* 21 (Summer 2001): 1–28.

8. S. Pattison, Fiscal State of the States, presentation at the national conference of the Association for Budgeting and Financial Management, Washington, DC, 2002.

9. J. White, Are States to Blame for Their Fiscal Woes?, *Stateline.org* (March 13, 2002), *http://www.stateline.org*.

10. Gene Sperling, as quoted in C.M. Yang, Bush's Budgetary Two-Step, *ABCNEWS.com* (August 16, 2001), *http://www.abcnews.go.com*.

11. S. Collender, Backing Off, *Government Executive* (January 23, 2002), *http://www.govexec.com*.

12. D. Figlio and A. O'Sullivan, The Local Response to Tax Limitation Measures, *Journal of Law and Economics* 44 (2001): 233–256.

13. S. Collender, Trigger Happy, *Government Executive* (March 28, 2001), *http://www.gov.exec.com*; Bush Team Focusing on Anti-Deficit "Triggers," CNN.com, (March 19, 2001), *http:www.cnn.com*.

14. Council of State Governments, *Book of the States, 2000–01 Edition* (Lexington, KY: Council of State Governments, 2000).

15. P.G. Joyce, What's So Magical About Five Percent? A Nationwide Look at Factors That Influence the Optimal Size of State Rainy Day Funds, *Public Budgeting & Finance* 21 (Summer 2001): 62–87.

16. K.I. Jen, Tax Expenditures in Michigan: A Comparison to Federal Findings, *Public Budgeting & Finance* 22 (Spring 2002): 31–45.

17. M. Schneider and F. Damanpour, Determinants of Public Pension Plan Investment Return, *Public Management Review* 3 (2001): 551–573.

18. State Budgets Burn through Anti-Tobacco Funds (Reuters), *FindLaw* (January 15, 2002), *http://www.news.findlaw.com*.

19. J. White, Entitlement Budgeting vs. Bureau Budgeting, *Public Administration Review* 58 (1998): 510–521.

20. National Security Act of 1947 and Amendments of 1949, 50 U.S.C. § 401–402.

21. L.R. Jones and K.J. Euske, Strategic Misrepresentation in Budgeting, *Journal of Public Administration Research and Theory* 1 (1991): 437–460.

22. C.W. Lewis, Public Budgeting: Unethical in Purpose, Product, and Promise, *Public Budgeting and Financial Management* 4 (1992): 667–680.

23. A. Schick, Incremental Budgeting in a Decremental Age, *Policy Sciences* 16 (1983): 1–25.

24. C. Barrilleaux, Governors, Bureaus, and State Policymaking, *State and Local Government Review* 31 (1999): 53–59; J.W. Douglas, Agency Strategies and Determinants of Agency Success under Redirection in Georgia, *State and Local Government Review* 31 (1999): 31–42.

25. U.S. Office of Management and Budget, *The President's Management Agenda: Fiscal Year 2002* (Washington, DC: U.S. Government Printing Office, 2001), 29.

26. D.A. Stockman, *The Triumph of Politics: How the Reagan Revolution Failed* (New York: Harper & Row, 1986); A. Wildavsky and N. Caiden, *The New Politics of the Budgetary Process*, 4th ed. (New York: Longman, 2001).

27. L. Sidoti, State Asks U.S. Supreme Court to Review Voucher Program, *FindLaw* (May 24, 2001), *http://www.findlaw.com*.

28. J. Peckenpaugh, Bush Proposes Massive Overhaul of Homeland Security Agencies, *Government Executive* (June 6, 2002), *http://www.govexec.com*; Homeland Security Act, P.L. 107–296 (2002).

29. M.E. Daniels, Jr., Memorandum for Heads of Executive Departments and Agencies (M–02–06), Office of Management and Budget, April 24, 2002.

30. H. Heclo, OMB and the Presidency: The Problem of "Neutral Competence," *Public Interest* 38 (1975): 80–98.

31. M. J. Dougherty and K.A. Klase, The Relationships between Public Finance Issues, Financial Management Issues, and Conditions of Fiscal Stress in Small and Rural Governments: The Case of West Virginia, *Journal of Public Budgeting, Accounting and Financial Management* 12 (2000): 545–565; R.C. Feiock, et al., Political Conflict, Fiscal Stress, and Administrative Turnover in American Cities, *State and Local Government Review* 33 (2001): 101–108.

32. D.J. Kraan, Cutback Management in the Netherlands, *Public Budgeting & Finance* 21 (Summer 2001): 46–61.

33. A. Schick, Macro-Budgetary Adaptations to Fiscal Stress in Industrialized Democracies, *Public Administration Review* 46 (1986): 124–134.

34. Committee on the Budget, U.S. House of Representatives, *Hidden Exposure: The Unfunded Liabilities of the Federal Government: Hearing*, 102nd Cong., 1st sess. (Washington, DC: U.S. Government Printing Office, 1991).

35. R. Feldman, How Weak Recognition and Measurement in the Federal Budget Encouraged Costly Policy: The Case of "Supervisory Goodwill," *Public Budgeting & Finance* 16 (Winter 1996): 31–44.

36. U.S. General Accounting Office, *Government-Sponsored Enterprises: A Framework for Limiting the Government's Exposure to Risk* (Washington, DC: U.S. Government Printing Office, 1991), 16.

37. Government Corporations, 31 U.S.C.§ 9101.

38. U.S. General Accounting Office, *Student Loans: Direct Loan Default Rates* (Washington, DC: U.S. Government Printing Office, 2001).

39. J. Jagtiani and C. Lemiux, Market Discipline Prior to Bank Failure, *Journal of Economics and Business* 53 (2001): 313–324; U.S. Congressional Budget Office, *U.S. Banks' Exposure to Foreign Financial Losses* (Washington, DC: U.S. Government Printing Office, 2002).

40. U.S. Congressional Budget Office, *Assessing the Public Costs and Benefits of Fannie Mae and Freddie Mac* (Washington, DC: U.S. Government Printing Office, 1996).

41. D. Torregrosa, Credit Subsidy Reestimates, 1993–99, *Public Budgeting & Finance* 21 (Summer 2001): 114–118.

42. Government Corporation Control Act, Ch. 557 (1945).

43. Financial Institutions Reform, Recovery, and Enforcement Act, P.L. 101–73 (1989).

44. U.S. General Accounting Office, *Major Management Challenges and Program Risks: Department of Agriculture* (Washington, DC: U.S. Government Printing Office, 2001).

45. Federal Credit Reform Act, P.L. 101–508 (1990), as part of the Omnibus Budget Reconciliation Act of 1990.

46. Debt Collection Improvement Act, P.L. 104–34 (1996); also see Federal Debt Collection Procedures Act, P.L. 101–647 (1990).

47. U.S. Department of Treasury, *Government Sponsorship of the Federal National Mortgage Association and the Federal Home Loan Mortgage Corporation* (Washington, DC: U.S. Government Printing Office, 1996).

48. Student Loan Marketing Association Reorganization Act, P.L. 104–208, 3009–275 (1996), as part of the Omnibus Consolidation Appropriations Act of 1997.

49 U.S. General Accounting Office, *High Risk Series: Student Financial Aid* (Washington, DC: U.S. Government Printing Office, 1995).

50. R.C. Moe, Congressional Research Service, *Managing the Public Business: Federal Government Corporations* (Washington, DC: U.S. Government Printing Office, 1995).

51. U.S. General Accounting Office, *Government Corporations: Profiles of Recent Proposals* (Washington, DC: U.S. Government Printing Office, 1995).

52. Governmental Accounting Standards Board, *Accounting and Financial Reporting for Risk Financing and Related Insurance Issues*, Statement No. 10 (Norwalk, CT: Financial Accounting Foundation, 1989).

53. M.M. Peterson, Pentagon Balances Anti-Terrorism Efforts, Transformation Plans, *Government Executive* (April 10, 2002), *http://www.govexec.com*.

54. Government Finance Officers Association, *http://www.gfoa.org*; accessed June 2002.

55. President's Commission on Budget Concepts, *Report* (Washington, DC: U.S. Government Printing Office, 1967).

56. U.S. Office of Management and Budget, *Budget of the United States Government, Fiscal Year 2003—Appendix* (Washington, DC: U.S. Government Printing Office, 2002), 1085.

57. R.D. Lee, Jr., and R.C. Burns, Survey of State Budget Offices, unpublished survey data (University Park, PA: The Pennsylvania State University, 2000).

58. L.F. Jameson Boex, J. Martinez-Vazques, and R.M. McNab, Multi-Year Budgeting: A Review of International Practices and Lessons for Developing and Transitional Economies, *Public Budgeting & Finance* 20 (Summer 2000): 91–112.

59. Lee and Burns.

Chapter 7

POLICY AND PROGRAM ANALYSIS

The use of policy and program analysis is part of a long-standing trend toward linking financial and program decision making. As preceding chapters have shown, reformists since the early 1900s have advocated decision systems that focus on the results of public expenditures. Analysis, though in no sense new, has gained recognition as a means of relating what government does and costs to what government accomplishes. Measuring, monitoring, and analyzing governmental performance is as much a part of the landscape of modern public budgeting systems as financial tracking and accounting. Today, there is little issue over whether analysis is useful. Instead, the issues are: How should we conduct analysis, and How should we use analysis in the decision-making system?

We discuss three main topics in this chapter. The first section considers the purposes or roles of analysis, the second section reviews analytical techniques, and the third section discusses the limitations of analysis within a political framework.

Focus of Analysis

There are as many types of analysis as there are potential subjects for analysis and persons to conduct the analyses. In budgeting and finance, financial analyses can focus on revenue projections, the expected costs of proposed program changes, alternative methods for financing debt, and so on. The concern in this chapter, however, is less with financial matters and more with serving public policy and program goals and objectives. Although the main emphasis here is on government expenditures, the revenue side should not be forgotten. Important policy goals, such as redistributing income among groups in society and encouraging increased retirement savings, can be achieved through tax measures, such as progressive income tax rates and expanded individual retirement account incentives, respectively, in addition to expenditure programs that provide benefits to lower-income families or individuals or increased Social Security benefits.

Intellectual Roots

Analysis has many intellectual roots.[1] Chapter 5 noted some of these as they relate to the beginning of program budgeting in the 1950s and 1960s. Several disciplines and cross-disciplinary perspectives have influenced the development of the analysis techniques and perspectives that typically are applied to public sector programs.

Economics. Some argue that analysis of public policies and government programs has its roots in the discipline of economics. Cost-benefit analysis, whose origins lie in economics, is an early example of an attempt to improve public policy or program choices by applying an analytical perspective.[2] The tools and concepts of microeconomics, including resource allocation efficiency and the role of government in correcting market failures, have contributed greatly to the increased use of analysis to decide which programs to fund at what levels. The welfare economics branch of microeconomics particularly concerns identifying and evaluating alternative decisions. Since Keynes, macroeconomic analysis of government's effects on the economy also has played a major role in government policy decisions (see Chapter 15).[3]

Policy Sciences. In the broadest perspective, policy and program analysis is simply using knowledge in public sector decision making. The main question is, How can information or knowledge improve the quality of decision making? We can call this broad perspective *policy sciences,* a term that includes a wide range of types of intellectual inquiry.[4] *Public choice* is another possible unifying term that encompasses numerous forms of analysis. Generally, public choice refers to collective decisions made on behalf of societal interests as distinct from individual choices made in market situations.[5]

Social Sciences. Political science, sociology, and public administration are social science disciplines relevant to policy and program analysis. Political science studies government institutions and processes, including policy formulation and implementation, and individual political behavior. Sociology examines group behavior, including decision making in governments and related bodies.

Public administration or management, of course, is deeply committed to analysis. Whether this field is another social science discipline or is an applied specialty of the traditional social sciences is open to question, however. Also debatable is whether distinctions can be made between a public management approach to analysis and a public administration approach. Whatever the case, public administrators engage in a wide range of analyses intended to affect policy and program deliberations.

Policy Analysis. Another elusive term is *policy analysis*; it is elusive in the sense of defying simple definition. Policy analysis sometimes refers to the application of rational thought processes to political decisions, but that perspective seems to ignore the fact that analysis and political argument about policy choices cannot be separated so easily.[6] Despite varying formal definitions, the heart of policy analysis is in its product, which is "advice relevant to public decisions."[7] This definition distinguishes policy analysis from academic policy research, social criticism, journalistic investigation, and other activities that may analyze public programs and government successes and failures but do not purport to provide information deliberately to policy makers to aid them in making choices.

A broader term often used in conjunction with policy analysis is *systems analysis* (discussed later in this chapter). One may conduct a systems analysis in the course of policy analysis, but systems analyses also may be carried out in technical, engineering, and other arenas in which *policy* is not relevant. No single, widely accepted paradigm clearly differentiates among policy analysis, systems analysis, and the numerous other terms that are used regularly in the discussion of analysis.

Uses of Analysis

Policy Formulation. One way of reducing confusion is to think of how analysis is used. Several types of uses are possible, the first being policy formulation. Sometimes analysis starts when a problem is identified, but sometimes analysis itself identifies what the real problem is. Involvement of citizens — the *constituents, stakeholders, or beneficiaries* of public programs — often serves to clarify the real problem that government might be attempting to address.[8] One useful form of analysis might focus on the causes of the problem, whereas other analyses might identify tradeoffs among different options for handling the problem and the probable consequences of selecting among those options. These types of analyses are prospective in that they look at possible events and outcomes in the future. New presidents often initiate a major policy proposal with a broad-gauge approach to seeking technical information and public opinion. President Ronald Reagan emphasized his commitment to downsize government with the appointment of a special study commission, the Grace Commission. Early in his first term, President Bill Clinton appointed a broad-based group to examine the entire array of problems preventing many Americans from gaining access to adequate health care. Initially the advisory group considered a wide array of possible solutions, ranging from modest improvements in the private health insurance system to radical changes in methods for reimbursing costs. Ultimately, no recommendation by the group was found acceptable in Congress and no major policy changes came out of the broad-based policy exercise. The George W. Bush administration relied on previous policies implemented when he was the governor of Texas for his first major education reform proposal at the federal level, though numerous evaluations of the Elementary and Secondary Education Act of 1965 aided in the formulation of the No Child Left Behind Act of 2001.[9]

Another broad type of policy problem is the illegal use of narcotics; conceivable responses may include a variety of law enforcement and preventive options, such as public education programs aimed at increasing general awareness of the health hazards of drug use. Policy issues associated with this type of social problem might include weighing the merits of law enforcement strategies against the value of strategies to reduce demand for illegal drugs. Other analyses might be more narrowly focused — targeting only options that relate to law enforcement, for example. Similarly, analysis can be limited by the costs of options, as in the case of examining only drug treatment program options that cost no more than some specified maximum amount.

The uses of policy analysis in broad policy formulation, or policy reform, often are cited as accomplishing major turnarounds in national economic performance. After two decades of dictatorial rule and poor economic performance, Ghana began early in 2000 to experience significant economic gains as a result of a democratically elected regime adopting significant policy reforms to liberalize trade and open up the country's financial system. These policy reforms were supported in important ways by international assistance agency–funded policy analysis. In March 2002, the George W. Bush administration announced a proposal to significantly expand U.S. economic assistance to developing countries, to reward those countries that had made significant policy changes to open up their economies, and to address the health and education needs of their citizens.[10] Contemporary theory guiding development assistance programs for such international agencies as the World Bank and bilateral assistance agencies such as the U.S. Agency for International Development recognizes that the mere transfer of funds, even accompanied by technical assistance, is not sufficient to promote sustainable development in the absence of sustained policy change.[11]

Program Monitoring. A second general type of analysis measures or monitors program results.[12] In 1924, Lent D. Upson wrote, "The budget should be supplemented by an operation audit that will measure the effectiveness of expenditures as thoroughly as the financial audits measure the legality of expenditures."[13]

Program monitoring, especially when used in conjunction with a budget system, often focuses on keeping agencies honest in the sense of seeing that promised results are indeed produced with the resources provided. The U.S. General Accounting Office has an important program monitoring function, providing Congress with the data necessary for exercising its legislative oversight responsibilities.[14]

One important consideration, in addition to performance, is the actual implementation process itself. Considerable congressional attention centers on whether programs, once enacted, are implemented as Congress intended. Another term is *accountability*, which indicates that agencies should be held answerable for promised results.

Program Evaluation. The third type of analysis is evaluation of ongoing programs.[15] This type of research can involve a host of research questions. One task of an inquiry may be to look at the intended goals and objectives of a program, as sometimes these are not stated clearly. Former Director of the Budget Charles Schultze suggests, "Systematic analysis does not simply accept objectives as immutably given and then proceed to seek the most effective or efficient means of achieving these objectives. One of its major contributions to the complex decision-making process lies precisely in its consideration of both objectives and means, allowing analysis of each to influence the other."[16] Schultze warns that he does not mean that analysts determine objectives for those individuals in decision-making positions. Analysts may suggest objectives previously not considered, and a good analyst may argue for their importance, but decision makers still have the final choice.

Analysts, of course, have their own values and cannot be totally neutral in dealing with goals and objectives. At the same time, analysts are "scientific" in their pursuit of knowledge. Social scientists sometimes unrealistically expect greater objectivity of themselves than is possible even in the physical and biological sciences. This has led to some criticism and rethinking in the policy analysis profession, acknowledging that value-free scientific analysis ignoring the political nature of the process is an unrealistic aspiration.[17]

When the objectives of a program are unknown or not clearly delineated, the nature of the analysis becomes more qualitative and less quantitative. This type of research has been called *social evaluation*, as distinguished from *technical evaluation*. An example of technical evaluation might be the examination of an air pollution control program's impact on the environment given the agreed objective of reducing pollutants to a specified maximum level. Social evaluation, in contrast, might include interviewing policy makers and administrators in regard to their objectives in creating and maintaining the pollution program.

Program evaluation as a rigorous analysis of ongoing program costs and results became institutionalized in the federal government in the 1960s. Some legislation, such as the No Child Left Behind Act of 2001, contains requirements for a portion of program funds to be spent on research and evaluation. Even congressional critics of many social programs endorse requirements for evaluating program costs and program results. Congressional interest often is expressed in provisions requiring specific, quantitative information on how federal programs are being used, how many beneficiaries are actually receiving service, and what results are being attained. The National Center for Education Statistics, part of the U.S. Department of Education, carries out several longitudinal surveys in response to congressional mandates. Congressional interest focuses, for example, on how students finance their post-secondary educations, what they study, and what subsequent employment results they attain.

Service Delivery Alternatives. Analysis also can consider the delivery mechanism for meeting objectives. Obvious choices are the direct delivery of services, delivery in conjunction with another organization (called coproduction), contracting with a private for-profit firm or nonprofit agency, leaving it up to private parties without government involvement, and policy setting through regulation.[18] Achieving policy goals by regulation had become such a concern among many advocates of smaller government by the early 1980s that President Reagan ordered agencies to consider the expected costs of regulations before adopting them. Executive Order 12291 required evaluation of costs imposed on the federal government, state and local governments, individuals, and corporations along with the benefits derived for all major regulations. President Clinton strengthened that position on limiting regulation only to that "made necessary by compelling public need . . ." in Executive Order 12866. The Paperwork Reduction Act of 1995 requires federal agencies to analyze the costs and benefits of collecting information from the private sector and from state and local government. President George W. Bush amended Executive Order 12866 with Executive Order 13258, which further controlled the impact of regulatory activity (see Chapter 10).

Criteria for Judgment in Analysis

Analysis gathers information intended for use in policy and program decision making. The analytical tools of analysis typically organize such information around key concepts that focus attention on the judgments that decision makers have to make. Adoption of a policy change, introduction of a new program, modification of an existing program, and similar decisions may be based on several criteria, including efficiency, effectiveness, productivity, and equity.

Effectiveness and Efficiency. Policy analyses and program evaluations commonly deal with issues of effectiveness and efficiency. The use of resources is considered effective if, in fact, it has the impact on persons or the environment that was intended. Using effectiveness as a criterion for evaluating a program involves determining that the program does, in fact, achieve its goals and objectives. In effectiveness analysis, the focus is on program outcomes. For example, health outcomes may be described "in terms of generic health states (including death)."[19] Impact assessments are common types of program evaluations and are designed to help decision makers decide on program continuation or program change. For example, one prenatal health care effort may be favored over another because it achieves a greater reduction in infant mortality.

Judgments of *efficiency* always imply comparison. The focus may be on operational efficiency, such as how best to reduce the cost of a particular activity, or it may be on broader questions, such as how to allocate societal resources to best advantage. Operational efficiency criteria may be used, for example, to choose the most efficient routes for different sizes and types of garbage trucks. Focusing on different ways of allocating resources can aid in determining whether it is really better overall for the economy to undertake a particular public sector expenditure. An expenditure is considered optimally efficient from the total economy's point of view if it results in an excess of benefits over costs that is greater than the excess that would result from spending the same amount in any other way.[20] This concept is known as *opportunity cost*. An efficient expenditure is one that does not cause us to forgo an opportunity that would have greater benefits in either the public or the private sector.

Efficiency analysis always involves either direct comparisons among alternatives or indirect comparisons in which the rate of return from a particular public expenditure is compared with the typical rate of return for private investments. A public sector expenditure is considered efficient if the economic rate of return for the program is equal to or greater than the interest rate that could be earned if the expenditure were simply left to the private sector to invest.[21] We will discuss the concept of *discount rate* in this context in the following section.

Sometimes the questions framed for analysis may be too narrowly defined, with the result that decisions seem efficient or effective within the frame of the question but when considered in a broader framework appear questionable. This is often the case in debates about spending funds for managing a problem after it has occurred versus spending funds for preventing the problem in the first place. Foreign assistance funds for improving the health of children in poor countries increasingly focus on preventive actions, such as immunizations, because prevention consumes fewer resources than dealing with the effects of diseases later.

Federal emergency management programs focus mainly on addressing disasters after they occur, whereas more funding spent on prevention may be more efficient and effective in terms of both budget impact and in human consequences.[22]

Productivity. The terms *productivity analysis* and *performance measurement* have received much publicity in recent years. Sometimes they are used interchangeably and encompass effectiveness and efficiency concerns, though most regard productivity analysis to be a narrower subset of performance measurement. On other occasions, the term *productivity* is restricted to the efficient use of resources in conducting work, with little or no consideration given to results or impacts. The concepts of *reengineering* and *reforming*, at least as they have been applied to government, mainly refer to improving productivity without much focus on the value of results achieved.[23]

Equity. Another concern of evaluation is equity — namely, whether program benefits are distributed according to some concept of fairness.[24] An analysis of special low-interest mortgages subsidized by the government might consider how various income groups benefit from the program. Or an analysis might focus on the delivery of city services to poor, middle-income, and upper-income neighborhoods to determine whether the distribution of services is fair.

Methods and Techniques of Analysis

Some policy and program analysis techniques are relatively simple; others are extremely complex. Depending on the precision of policy definition, the susceptibility of the problem to quantification, and the questions asked of the analysis, an analysis might be primarily qualitative in nature or it might be highly quantitative.

Approaches to Analysis

Numerous formulations of analysis describe it as a basic methodology consisting of a number of steps. One basic text divides those steps into two stages: problem analysis and solution analysis.

Problem Analysis

1. Understanding the problem
   a. Receiving the problem: assessing the symptoms
   b. Framing the problem: analyzing market and government failures
   c. Modeling the problem: identifying policy variables
2. Choosing and explaining relevant goals and constraints

3. Choosing a solution method

Solution Analysis

4. Choosing evaluation criteria
5. Specifying policy alternatives
6. Evaluating: predicting impacts of alternatives and valuing them in terms of criteria
7. Recommending actions[25]

Throughout these seven steps, analysts find and organize relevant data and theories and use them to estimate future consequences of current and alternative actions. The ultimate step is the communication of recommendations to policy makers. Any reduction of a complex analysis process to a series of steps inevitably oversimplifies matters. The most important oversimplification is perhaps the implication that analysis is always an ordered process performed by rational analysts, which ignores the reality that analysis takes place in a disorderly, highly political process. Analysis and argumentation over normative issues are entwined. In formulating the problem, in articulating the goals, in choosing evaluation criteria, and in recommending actions, the analyst inevitably is a part of the political argument about what should, and should not, be done.[26] Nevertheless, the above outline is useful in calling attention to the several phases of the research process that should not be overlooked.

Analytic Models

Operations Research. Most techniques of analysis predate program budgeting, being derived in large part from such antecedent fields as systems analysis and operations research (OR) (see Chapter 5). Although some have considered OR synonymous with the application of the scientific method to problem solving,[27] in the narrower sense in which it was defined in Chapter 5, OR actually refers to a set of algorithms, generally mathematical, for solving recurrent problems that can be expressed quantitatively. Several types of quantitative problems recur with such frequency in private business applications that prototype models have been developed to solve them. These include problems in allocation, inventory, replacement, queuing, sequencing and coordination, routing, and search. The task of routing overnight express packages efficiently is a good example. Specific techniques for solving these problems include linear programming, queuing theory, Monte Carlo or randomizing methods, and gaming theory.

When government programs involve similar problems, such as problems in transportation scheduling, warehousing, inventory, or other routine tasks, OR techniques readily apply. Problems associated with routing garbage trucks or with mail service, for example, are susceptible to such analytic techniques. The basic requirement for applying them is that a single objective be stated in a quantifiable form. The usual form is to maximize some specific measure of production (output) or to minimize a measure of cost (input). Numerous linear and nonlinear programming techniques also exist for solving *optimization problems* involving multiple inputs and multiple outputs, although interpreting the results is still largely an art rather than science, as these methods yield numerous mathematical solutions as opposed to a single optimal solution.[28]

Systems Analysis. The techniques of OR as well as techniques associated with economics may be used in systems analysis, but a distinguishing feature of systems analysis is that it may deal with issues that go beyond quantitative techniques. For example, OR may aid in designing methods for providing logistical support to combat troops. Systems analysis might go beyond this issue to ask, Are there other means of handling a situation that would reduce the need for logistical support? Systems analysis tries to avoid the danger of myopic vision in which techniques are emphasized over purpose and takes a more holistic view of both problem definition and solution.[29]

Cost-Benefit and Cost-Effectiveness Analysis. We can distinguish between cost-benefit and cost-effectiveness analysis. Both attempt to relate costs of programs to performance, and both quantify costs in monetary terms. They differ, however, in the way they measure the outcomes of programs.

Cost-effectiveness analysis measures outcomes in quantitative but nonmonetary form. For example, it might focus on the number of students who achieve or exceed the standard on end-of-grade achievement tests.

Cost-benefit analysis, by contrast, measures program outcomes in monetary form, thereby allowing for the development of ratios or other measures of the extent to which returns exceed costs, or vice versa. For example, cost-benefit analysis would estimate the dollar value of time to travelers and would use that figure to calculate the dollar value of the time saved by flying on the supersonic aircraft. Attaching monetary value to some things, however, can be controversial. The final report to the Federal Aviation Administration on introducing nitrogen or other inert gases into empty fuel tanks to reduce the chance of explosions that caused the 1996 crash of TWA Flight 800 off Long Island recommended against the proposal given current technology because the costs exceed the benefits.[30] The benefit calculation included an estimate of the value of potential lives saved, along with other monetary benefits. The report also recommended continuing study of new technologies to reduce the costs of inserting inert gases into fuel tanks.

The potential technical merit of cost-benefit analysis over cost-effectiveness analysis is that the former allows for analysis across subject areas. When the expressed ratio of benefits to costs of a program is 1.0, costs are equal to benefits. As the ratio increases, the benefits accruing have increased. In theory, if a supersonic transport program yielded a ratio of 1.7 and a highway traffic control program yielded a ratio of 2.5, then, based on the standard of economic efficiency (and assuming the difference in the magnitude of the programs was not great), government would be advised to favor the traffic control program over the air transportation program. Cost-effectiveness analysis, in contrast, would not allow such direct comparisons because the effects would be expressed in time saved for one program and lives saved for the other.

As noted in Chapter 5, cost-benefit analysis was seen at the time of planning-programming-budgeting's (PPB) introduction into government budgetary decision making as a key analytical tool for making rational budget allocation decisions. With the demise of PPB, cost-benefit analyses increasingly were applied only to a limited set of analysis problems. However, both cost-benefit and cost-effectiveness analysis have gained some new stature in federal program and policy analyses. Environmental regulations particularly have sparked interest in cost-benefit analysis. Both presidents and Congress have imposed requirements aimed at ensuring that the economic benefits of proposed regulations exceed the economic costs. Executive Order 12866, issued by President Clinton, and various statutes, including Title II of the Unfunded Mandates Reform Act, impose broad requirements for demonstrating that costs exceed benefits before imposing a regulatory requirement.[31] Similarly, cost-effectiveness analysis is widely used in regard to medical devices and pharmaceutical products. In Australia, Canada, and the United Kingdom, drugs are placed on the national health system approved list (*formulary*) only after they are shown to be safe, efficacious, and cost-effective. The influenza treatment drug Relenza, though meeting U.S. Food and Drug Administration efficacy and safety tests, failed the cost-benefit/effectiveness test in the United Kingdom. As a result, it was not approved for reimbursement in the U.K. national health service list of drugs approved for prescription, except for more extreme health risk cases.[32] That does not mean the drug cannot be produced, but merely that it will not be provided through the national health service. While not required in Western European countries with national health systems, cost-effectiveness analyses of drugs and medical products are becoming the norm. In the United States, managed care organizations are prodding pharmaceutical companies to use the techniques of cost-benefit and cost-effectiveness analysis to evaluate which drugs and products will be put on their approved lists.[33]

Strategic Analysis. Not all analyses will be as quantitative as the preceding examples suggest. One analytic approach engages decision makers in the process of *scenario writing*. Scenario writing may be an analytic tool itself, or it may be the first stage in a more extensive policy formulation process. It requires policy makers, typically assisted by analysts, to engage in speculative consideration of a plausible sequence of events leading from a current state to alternative end states. A now relatively famous example of scenario planning was undertaken by the Royal Dutch Shell company in the mid-1970s. Although many within the company thought the scenario preposterous, the organization considered what steps should be taken if the major oil producers in the Middle East and Latin America formed a cartel to control the world oil supply. Extensive analysis did not produce a set of firm prescriptions, but did prepare Shell decision makers to react quickly and decisively when the seemingly unlikely event actually happened.[34]

Military policy analysts commonly use scenario writing to help identify the circumstances that might lead to committing troops to a hostile situation. The purpose of this exercise is to describe a logical sequence of events or circumstances that then would require a response. While thinking out the scenario, the decision-making team may decide to explore ways to prevent the sequence of events from occurring. Or based on the logical outcomes of the scenario exercise, an existing plan for response may be rethought because it may seem, in light of the scenario, to be too drastic a response to a likely sequence of events. Of course, some scenarios seem so far-fetched that even scenario planning exercises cannot formulate the problem as an exercise. The type of event that occurred on September 11, 2001, seemed so improbable that it is unlikely to have received careful consideration in any scenario planning process. Of course, various threats including the introduction of biological weapons have been subjected to various scenario planning exercises. September 11 likely increased the range of possibilities taken into account during such activities.

A related perspective looks on analysis not as a process directed toward finding an optimal allocation of resources but as an extension of the policy-making institution's strategic planning process. According to this view, the problem definition phase should be more holistic, examining the organization's ability to adapt to its changing environment. A variety of OR and cost-benefit techniques could be used, but the problem would be framed more in systems terms so as to focus on the interaction between the organization and the environment. This approach is useful in directing attention to how the organization might implement a policy change to achieve the desired results. The other analytic approaches tend to stop at the selection of a "best choice" and assume that implementation will follow.[35]

Problems in Conducting Analysis

Even though there are different approaches to analysis, several problems are common to most.

Multiple Goals. One common problem in policy and program analysis is that people expect most policies, and even most individual programs, to serve more than one goal. Even when a program's goal is stated in narrow terms, such as reducing the morbidity from childhood diseases through an immunization program, people may have different reasons for supporting that goal. For example, some may compare the immunization program with other health measures as a means of decreasing future health costs, but others may evaluate the program as one among several poverty alleviation alternatives. The clearly stated goal, morbidity reduction, in reality reflects more than one goal. In this case, the policy analyst either may have to guess which goals are more important or may attempt to get explicit weights from the client decision makers to carry out the analysis.

The problem of assigning weights among multiple goals reflects the reality that decision makers use different criteria to make policy choices. The political process in most systems deliberately pits various groups against each other, relying on advocacy and checks and balances to protect the public interest. This is the basis for the separation of powers among the executive, legislative, and judicial branches in the U.S. system, and similar checks and balances are built into most constitutional systems. This political reality requires policy analysis to consider multiple criteria and to consider multiple perspectives on what is the best choice.

Causal Relationships. Closely related to the multiple goals problem is the problem of understanding the pattern of causal relationships. In examining alternative programs, the analyst must make some assumptions about causation in order to proceed. In reality, many effects have multiple causes, and sorting out the subset of causes that are under the program's control is not easy. The analyst can rely somewhat on earlier experiences or evaluations of existing programs of similar character for guidance. For example, in analyzing a possible advertising program to persuade smokers to quit, available research on advertising programs aimed at reducing drunk driving may be useful.

Another problem analysts face in understanding the causal relationships involved in a program is that a single evaluation study, unless it is extensive, may be unable to detect relatively small effects. One strategy for addressing this problem is to pool data from many different studies and evaluations of the same program. Called *meta-analysis*, this approach takes advantage of numerous smaller studies to create a larger data set. This helps point out small increments in the program's impact and identify causal relationships.

One of the widely publicized examples of a meta-analysis is a study of the DARE program, a popular drug-use prevention program in which police officers work closely with elementary school children. Many specific evaluations of different DARE sites have had difficulty in detecting any results. A meta-analysis of many of these evaluations revealed that DARE seems to have little effect on drug use but does increase positive attitudes toward police and improve youngsters' social skills.[36]

In some cases, there may be little available information from which to assess causal relationships. This is the case particularly when new technologies and materials must be developed as part of the project being analyzed or when the problem is new. Early attempts to understand the means by which human immunodeficiency virus (HIV) infections are transmitted offer a good example of a new problem. The analysis of a new fighter aircraft might require an assessment of the person-hours, materials, and equipment needed to develop new light-weight metals and design new instrumentation. Estimates must be made of the relationships between resource inputs and technological breakthroughs.

Study design has a great influence on the ability to attribute cause and effect. In the George W. Bush administration, the Department of Education shifted its focus in evaluating education programs somewhat to stress more scientific research on what works best in various education intervention efforts. In reporting positive results in educational attainment as measured by the National Assessment of Educational Progress, a major federally sponsored test and measurement program, the Assistant Commissioner for Educational Research and Improvement noted that the department must address gaps in scientific knowledge of what works.[37] The No Child Left Behind Act even specifically defines scientific research and requires scientific evidence of the effectiveness of programs funded by the Department of Education before mandating or even recommending their more widespread use.[38] The 2003 budget cited examples of the kinds of programs that had been found to work, such as the 21st Century Community Learning Centers that "improve student behaviors and possibly boost achievement."[39]

Identifying Costs and Benefits. Another issue is the decision as to what counts as a cost and as a benefit. Determining the financial costs of existing programs is often difficult because accounting systems are designed to produce information by organizational unit and not necessarily by program. Only if a program is unique to an organizational unit specified in the accounting system will the financial costs be easy to measure. Even when this matter is resolved, all that is produced are the direct financial expenditures of government rather than costs as would be derived by a cost accounting system (Chapter 11). Indeed, critics often charge that analyses overlook the costs imposed on others. Failure to consider all costs tends to weight the analysis in favor of the proposed project under review.

Related problems are that the financial accounts for a program agency may not distinguish between capital and current costs and may not include services provided to that agency by a central service unit. For example, many evaluations of federal programs involve collecting data on costs and impacts from state, local, and even voluntary agencies that are implementing the program. But in one state's accounting system, all the costs of a facility improvement might show up in the budget outlays in the year in which the improvement is built; in another state, the same costs might show up as a one-year depreciation charge. Similarly, utility costs might be associated with the building that houses the program in one location and might be part of a central account in another location. The analyst must be sure to measure all costs on the same basis across multiple program sites.[40]

Externalities. Indirect costs as well as benefits granted to others are called *externalities*, or *spillover, secondary,* and *tertiary effects*. These costs and benefits affect parties other than the ones directly involved. In the private sector, air and water pollution from industrial plants are externalities. The main concern of a private enterprise is making a profit, but part of the cost of production may be imposed on persons living in the area. Residents of areas downstream and downwind of the plant may pay the costs of discomfort, poor health, and loss of water recreation opportunities. They may also experience an actual decrease in the value of their assets, such as their homes, if the pollution is bad enough to make it difficult to sell property. If a municipality downstream has to treat water that has been polluted by the plant, the costs imposed are relatively easy to identify.

Most government expenditure decisions involve similar spillover effects. The costs of an urban renewal program are not just the financial outlays required for purchasing and clearing land, but also the costs imposed on the families and businesses that must relocate. One government's decision can affect thousands of individuals, businesses, nonprofit organizations, and other governments, including national governments throughout the world.

Some argue that there are no such things as secondary or spillover effects, that all effects of a program should be part of the explicit benefits and costs of that program. This idea is sometimes expressed as the belief that every affected individual or organization should have *standing* and should thus be taken into account in any analysis of the program.[41] Affected parties are said to be *stakeholders* in that they have interests regarding the outcomes of the program and any decisions that may change it.[42]

Redistributive Effects. Related to spillover costs and benefits are redistributive effects, which analysts once tended to ignore. Today, consideration of major policy changes commonly encompasses their potential redistributive effects. For example, the federal budget has in some administrations included a summary table of the redistributive effects of taxing and spending decisions as part of the budget presentation. Involved here is the matter of whether some groups in the society will benefit more than other groups.[43] In the example of a supersonic transport program mentioned earlier, the program presumably would benefit middle- and upper-income groups, who would be the only ones likely to take advantage of this means of transportation. Other criteria for judging redistribution include race, educational level, and occupational class.[44] The effects of programs on different generations in the population have increasingly become a focus of attention.

Common tools for analyzing redistributive effects include *Lorenz curves* and *Gini coefficients of inequality*.[45] A Lorenz curve plots the cumulative percentage of income held by income groups against the cumulative percentage of income groups. For example, in a perfectly equal distribution of income, the lowest population decile in income would have 10 percent of the income, the first and second lowest deciles would have 20 percent of the income, and so forth. That perfectly equal distribution would plot as a straight 45-degree line on an *x, y* graph (**Figure 7–1**). The difference between the actual plotted Lorenz curve and the perfectly equal distribution is measured as the area between the two curves — the Gini coefficient of inequality.

Figure 7–1   Illustration of Lorenz Curve Deviation from Perfect Equality

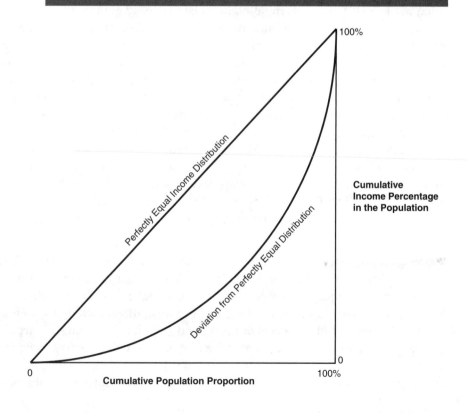

Subjective Information. Analyses often must rely on subjective, attitudinal data as distinguished from data that gauge behavior. One objective measure of a city road program might be the miles of roads resurfaced; an attitudinal measure of the same program might be citizen satisfaction with road conditions. It is indeed possible for citizens (stakeholders) to exhibit no increase in satisfaction even though road conditions may have improved markedly. The same type of situation can develop regarding police protection. Citizens' fear of being burglarized may not decrease despite a decline in the burglary rate. Analytical models such as cost-benefit and cost-effectiveness analyses are based on rational behavior models in which individuals are presumed to respond to choices based on the desire to maximize their personal utility. Behavioral research calls into question these underlying assumptions, with the consequence that a supposedly rational result of policy analysis still may not be the actual preferred result of those affected by the policy. Methodologies to take into account these more subjective perspectives involve surveying preferences of stakeholders or those with presumed interests in a potential program implementation and assessing their subjective values.[46]

Internal Validity. When costs, benefits, and expected relationships among them are defined, analysis must consider whether other possible variables may influence outcomes. Such influence is a threat to internal validity.[47] For example, a school program working to increase employment among disadvantaged teenagers may seem to be effective when, in fact, it may have little influence on employment. Any increase in employment might be attributable not to school district efforts, but to some other program, such as one operated by a nonprofit agency or church. Or a general improvement in the local economy may increase the number of jobs for everyone. This type of problem is common in the area of social services, where several agencies may work with some of the same clients or engage in the joint production of services.

Problems of Quantification

Even if an ideal model is designed displaying all of the relevant types of costs and benefits or effects of a program, the problem of quantifying them remains. What are the monetary costs imposed on families relocated by urban redevelopment activities? Part of the costs will consist of moving expenses, perhaps higher rents, and greater costs for commuting to work. While these items can be measured, it is much more difficult to set a dollar value on the mental anguish of having to move and leave friends behind.

Shadow Pricing. Much of the problem of setting dollar values in the analysis stems from the fact that government programs do not have market prices. Despite various limitations, the private market does provide some standard for measuring the value of goods and services by the prices set for those. Much of analysis in the public sector, however, must impute the prices or values of programs. One such method is known as *shadow pricing*.[48]

Suppose an analyst is given the task of predicting the benefits of a proposed outdoor recreation project. The average hourly value (the shadow price) to a person attending the proposed new public facility can be assumed to be what individuals on the average spend per hour for other similar forms of outdoor recreation. This figure multiplied by the number attending will yield an approximate value of the recreational opportunities to be provided by the facility under study.

More detailed approaches can examine each form of outdoor recreation — hiking, swimming, tennis, golfing, picnicking, and so forth. In the case of swimming, the average spent per person for one hour of swimming at a private beach can be imputed to be the value of swimming at a public beach. One danger of such an assumption, however, is that it ignores the possibility that the quality of swimming may be different at the two beaches. If such a difference exists, the shadow price should be adjusted accordingly. Another danger is that building the new public swimming facility will change the overall market value of swimming in the area. In that instance, the shadow price must take into account the changes in demand.

Shadow pricing becomes increasingly difficult and the analysis more tenuous when the subject matter for study involves functions that are primarily governmental. There is no apparent method by which a dollar value can be set for the defense capability of killing via intercontinental missiles x million people of an aggressor nation within one hour. Similarly, it is difficult to calculate the dollar value of avoiding one traffic fatality. The calculations employed require assessing what kinds of people are killed in automobile accidents, how old they are, and what income they would have earned in their lifetimes.

Given the questionable assumptions that must be made in estimating the dollar value of saving a life, the argument can be made that cost-effectiveness analysis is preferable to cost-benefit analysis. The former does not attempt to place a dollar value on life but leaves the estimation of that value to decision makers. The disadvantage is that cost-effectiveness analysis, unlike cost-benefit analysis, seldom will yield a single measure of effectiveness. A traffic safety program might be measured by the number of lives saved and by the dollar value of property damage caused by crashes. Like apples and oranges, these benefits cannot be added together.

Contingent Valuation. The amount the public is willing to pay for a particular benefit or to avoid a particular cost also can be measured by means of formal surveys. The methodology, known as *contingent valuation*, describes to survey respondents a particular service or government action and asks through various contingency statements what the respondent would be willing to pay. For example, "Would you be willing to pay a $0.75 per day per family fee to avoid the smoke and other pollution emitted by a nearby power plant?" Guidelines for federal government cost-benefit analysis, contained in Office of Management and Budget (OMB) Circular A-94, recommend willingness to pay as an appropriate concept for measuring costs and benefits. A contingent valuation survey includes a series of questions gradually increasing the price the respondent is asked to consider to determine at what price point the survey respondent no longer would be willing to pay. Contingent valuation is used by both government and private industry in the valuation of resource losses due to damages, such as in the *Exxon Valdez* oil spill, and by government to assess the benefits of projected recreational and natural resource preservation programs.[49] Contingent valuation studies are now almost universally required in designing multilateral donor agency–funded infrastructure construction projects that are predicated on user fees to ensure project financial viability.

Discount Rates. Another problem for analysis involves the diversion of resources from the private to the public sector and from current consumption to investment in future returns. From an economic point of view, investment in a public project or program is warranted only if the returns are greater than they would be if the same funds were left to the private sector and if the future returns are worth the current sacrifice. Thus, the relevant concept of the cost of a public expenditure is the value of the benefits forgone by not leaving the money in the private sector to be consumed or invested.

A dollar diverted from the private sector to the public sector is not just an equivalent dollar cost or dollar benefit forgone. Presumably, had the dollar not been collected as taxes, it would have been available for the private citizen's use in some enjoyable, immediate consumption. Or it would have been available for the private citizen to invest in some kind of interest-bearing security. If the tax is used to finance a public project that produces a benefit to that citizen, or to citizens in general, then the benefit may offset the sacrifice the taxpayer had to make in private consumption or investment. But what if the public benefit occurs at some future time, whereas the private consumption would have been in the more or less immediate time period? The future public benefit, even if it could be said to be exactly equal to the benefit of private consumption, will not be as valuable because of the simple fact of its being postponed into the future. Some charge must be made against that dollar removed from consumption to arrive at the current value of future consumption forgone. This charge is known as the *discount* or *interest rate*.

The discount rate serves two purposes. First, it is similar to an interest charge that reflects the cost of removing a dollar from private sector use and diverting it to the public sector. If a dollar could earn 6 percent in the private sector, investment in the public sector would be warranted (in an economic sense) only if the rate of return from the public investment would be at least 6 percent. Second, the discount rate must take into consideration the time pattern of expenditures and returns. In general, people prefer present consumption to future consumption. A dollar that might be spent for current consumption is worth more than a dollar that might be consumed 10 years from now. Normally people do not willingly save unless they receive interest in compensation for the temporary loss of consumption. A discount rate, then, provides a means of showing the present value of dollars to be spent or returned in the future.

The relationships among costs, returns, and time are depicted graphically in **Figure 7–2**. Most investment projects involve heavy capital costs early on, followed by a tapering off to operating costs. Returns are nonexistent or minimal for the first few years and then increase rapidly. The shape of the return curve after the initial upturn depends on the nature of the particular investment and is drawn arbitrarily for illustrative purposes in the figure. The comparison of costs to benefits over time makes the necessity for discounting obvious. Higher costs occur earlier in most projects. The higher benefits that occur later are valued less because they occur later in time.

Figure 7–2 Relationship of Costs and Benefits to Time

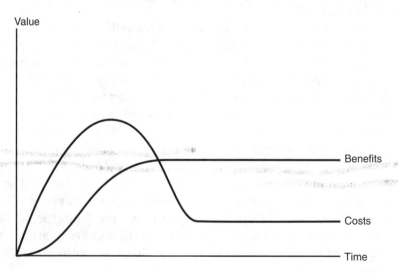

The value scale is expressed in common units, usually dollars. The time scale goes from one unit, such as one year, through the expected life span of the project.

Costs and benefits must therefore be compared for each time period (usually each year), and the differences summed over the life span of the project. That is, in essence, what a discount rate accomplishes. The longer it takes for returns to occur, the more their value is discounted. In effect, the situation involves compound interest in reverse. Costs occurring earlier are subject to less discounting. Thus, for a project to be economically feasible, total discounted benefits must exceed total discounted costs. This excess of discounted benefits over discounted costs is known as the *net present value* (NPV). Government expenditures are efficient allocations of a society's resources when the net present value is positive. Any spreadsheet software contains built-in functions for calculating the net present value, the internal rate of return, and similar concepts useful in assessing the value of benefits occurring over time in comparison with the costs of the investment.

Clearly, the choice of a discount rate has an important influence on investment decisions. Too low a rate understates the value of current consumption or of leaving the money to the private sector. Too high a rate uneconomically favors current consumption over future benefits and results in less investment than is worthwhile. The choice of a discount rate may thus determine the outcome of the analysis.

Selecting appropriate discount rates is difficult. Private market rates are inappropriate because they include calculations of the risks of loss involved in making loans. On the other hand, interest rates charged governments often are artificially low because of various guarantees against defaults and sometimes the loans' tax-exempt status. The appropriate discount rate lies between these extremes. OMB annually provides guidance to federal agencies on the discount rates that should be used for federal projects (Appendix C, Circular A-94). In 2002, the discount rate for costs and benefits ranged from 4.1 percent for a three-year period to 5.8 percent for a 30-year period, the equivalent nominal interest rate for federal Treasury bonds with three- and 30-year maturities, respectively.[50]

Several discount rates may be applied to program alternatives to determine the *sensitivity* of the analysis to discounting. If the cost-benefit ratios of a project are well above 1.0 regardless of the discount rate used, little problem occurs. A different situation arises if some plausible discount rates yield results well below 1.0. In other situations, one discount rate might result in a favorable cost-benefit ratio for alternative A and another ratio for alternative B. The point is that an arbitrary choice of a discount rate without consideration of other ranges can produce misleading results. Some evidence also shows that discount rates and net present value calculations are used less frequently by public sector managers than by private sector managers, attributable presumably to the greater influence in the public sector of political variables.[51]

Problems of Implementation

Analyses that are conducted with due regard paid to all the preceding issues mentioned will not ensure that the intended effectiveness, efficiency, or equity gains are, in fact, achieved. Cost-effectiveness analysis, cost-benefit analysis, and other analyses conducted at the policy formulation or program design stage are worthless unless the implementing public agency is capable of carrying out the program. For that reason, analysts now pay increased attention to the various factors that will influence implementation once the program starts. One of the more consistent findings from research on implementation is that involvement of the intended clients or beneficiaries of the program in its design is one of the most important factors affecting the achievement of intended results.[52] Involvement of the client at the design stage helps ensure that factors affecting success are accounted for and helps mold the program to the needs as perceived by the beneficiaries rather than by the bureaucrats. Continued involvement of the program beneficiaries in modifying the design of the program as it is implemented is one aspect of the application of concepts such as total quality management to government programs.[53]

Organizational Locus and Use of Analysis

Analytic Units

With the increasing interest in analysis has come a proliferation of analytic units. Central budget offices and other central units such as planning departments, line agencies, and offices of inspectors general have all developed analytic capabilities. Legislative analytic units have been established. The 1974 Congressional Budget and Impoundment Control Act specifically empowered standing committees and the comptroller general to "review and evaluate the results of Government programs and activities." The Congressional Budget Office, which initially restricted its work to economic trend analysis, has broadened its scope to include policy and program analysis. State legislative staff units, such as Florida's Office of Program Performance and Government Accountability and the Virginia Joint Legislative Audit and Review Commission, have gained national prominence in the field of program evaluation. Just as with the U.S. General Accounting Office transition, many state audit agencies have incorporated analyses of economy and efficiency into their traditional auditing roles. While federal line agencies led the way in formal impact or results-oriented evaluation in the 1970s, the subsequent years have seen a decline in executive-branch impact evaluations.

Part of the decrease in federal program evaluation can be attributed to a shift in focus. In the 1970s, the major federal anti-poverty programs were the focal points of large-scale, longitudinal studies. Some of the largest social science research projects ever conducted were evaluations of the income maintenance and housing allowance experiments funded in the 1970s by the Departments of Health and Human Services and Housing and Urban Development, respectively. Then, along with significant reorientation of the role played by the federal government, the Reagan administration shifted the focus from the impacts of federal programs to more management-oriented studies of administrative efficiency — how to reduce the costs of federal programs. This emphasis resulted in a significant decrease in executive agency use of large-scale program evaluation research studies; it was countered by growth in the role of offices of inspectors general as they performed more management-oriented program reviews and growth in the role of the General Accounting Office in program reviews, program audits, and even specific evaluation studies.[54]

Analysis had become widespread at the state level by the beginning of the 1990s, but may have declined somewhat, as revealed by surveys of state budget offices. Whereas in 1970 only 18 percent of state budget offices reported that they conducted effectiveness program analysis, by 1990 66 percent reported engaging in such analysis. Ten years later, in 2000, that figure had dropped to 57 percent. Similar patterns are observed for conducting productivity analysis — 31 percent in 1970, a whopping 94 percent in 1990, and a drop to 58 percent in 2000.[55] To some extent, the decline in state government budget agencies' conduct of analysis has been offset by increased program analysis in other central agencies, but clearly state executive agencies have decreased their reliance on analysis in the budgetary process. Local governments also engage in analysis, but many are too small to be able to afford large analytic staffs.

Greater dissemination of analyses may allow more than one community to benefit from the findings of a given study. While some cities may be reluctant to apply the results achieved in other cities, comparison with comparable communities is irresistible to many local politicians. Popularized in the management literature as *benchmarking*, the idea of seeing what other communities have achieved as an aid in one's own local decision-making process is now entrenched. Comparisons with other school districts' capital expenditures for school construction, for example, changed one county commission's near-unanimous opposition to a bond issue for school construction to near-unanimous support for putting the bond issue on the ballot.[56] Performance measurement has become so commonplace in governments at all levels that the demand for comparative information on both results and the ways that those results were attained is high.[57]

Universities and contract research organizations also perform analyses of various kinds. Faculty and staff in a wide range of research and academic units conduct research that is of direct relevance to policy deliberations in government. Contract research organizations conduct research relevant to policy issues for a wide variety of clients. Whereas the evaluation-related work that the GAO and CBO carry out is performed largely with in-house staff, most of the program evaluation work in federal executive branch agencies is contracted to outside parties. Policy analysis, on the other hand, is a more sensitive topic. Executive branch agencies may contract for policy analytical work, but the agency and the contractor/consultant must draw a careful line between policy analysis and actual policy formulation. The GAO periodically reviews work performed by outside contractors when that work has some kind of policy or policy analysis label or title to ensure that the agency has not effectively delegated the policy formulation process to an outside contractor.

A key management weakness in many developing countries is lack of a strong analytic unit capable of evaluating the possible consequences of alternative policy decisions. Somewhat greater institutional capacity for conducting project analyses to assess the financial and economic impact of pending projects exists in most developing countries, but even that capacity is plagued by lack of coordination among different agencies. Considerable donor agency assistance, such as that of the U.S. Agency for International Development (USAID), is devoted to helping developing countries' public institutions to develop strong policy analysis and evaluation capabilities. As an example, USAID has assisted South Africa by providing policy analysis advisors, training, formal education, and technical assistance to develop policy analysis capacity in the Department of Education, beginning even before the transition government actually replaced the apartheid government.

Regardless of the location of the analytic unit, it necessarily has limited resources and must choose carefully the targets of analysis. If an analytic unit in a government commits all of its resources to one study each year, then many programs will go unreviewed. At the opposite extreme, numerous "quick-and-dirty" studies can be conducted in a year, but at the risk of excessive superficiality. Central analytic units may use a mixed strategy of conducting brief analyses and more thorough analyses and diversifying them over a wide range of programs and departments. Criteria used in selecting targets for analysis include the dollar magnitude of programs and the political feasibility of changing them.

Analysis in Decision Making

Producing reports and studies is not the same as using them in policy deliberations. In the state budget office survey mentioned earlier, 30 percent of the states reported that executive budget decisions were based substantially on effectiveness analyses, and 39 percent used productivity analyses to a substantial degree. Another 51 and 45 percent of the states, respectively, reported analyses being used somewhat in executive decision making, also down from previous years.[58] The complaint from analysts that their findings and recommendations often go unheeded is common.

One reason for the limited use of analyses may be the analyses themselves. Any decision maker needs to examine an analysis report before using it. Of course, the analytic process requires an initial selection of possible causal relationships to consider and benefits and costs to count, and this obviously occurs before the decision maker sees the analysis results. The decision maker needs to maintain a healthy skepticism and be aware of the technical difficulties, discussed in the preceding section, that might influence or determine the outcome of a study. The database of a study may have been weak, resulting in highly qualified and tentative conclusions; in such a case, the decision maker will probably rely on his or her hunches more than on those of the analysts. Further, the analysts themselves are acutely aware of the political realities involved in budgetary decisions. For this reason, they may blend both political and economic issues in their analyses, leading decision makers to treat the analyses not as answers to their policy questions but as additional data to be considered.

Some analyses may be self-serving, produced by analysts eager to secure funding for their departments. A state department of transportation study that concludes that the department needs more funds may be the product of overzealous analysts eager to serve the needs of their department. Analysts face serious ethical conflicts over loyalty to their agencies and loyalty to some degree of objectivity.

Many other factors can render an analysis of limited use. The topic may be politically too hot or excessively trivial for decision makers to act upon. If research reports are not relevant to decision makers, the reports will not be used. Sometimes "windows" open on program areas in which major decisions can be made — at which time analyses can be influential. At other times, these same program areas are unlikely to be influenced greatly by analyses because of political conditions. Some criticism has been leveled at the policy analysis profession as being too focused on unrealistic positivist assumptions of value-free neutrality and nonpolitical rational approaches. Policy analysis now is much more likely to incorporate political factors into the analysis, involve decision makers in assigning weights to those factors, and link evaluation researchers more closely to the program and policy issues they are being asked to address.[59] The corrective measure advocated is that policy analysis be seen less as analytical problem solving and more as one of the tools in the consensus-building, political process of reaching agreement on an action.[59] Beyond the analyses is the nature of the decision system. It may be that a program budget system, for instance, is more likely to use available analyses because the decision structure is specifically geared toward that possibility. However, most budget systems are likely to be biased largely in favor of maintaining existing programs and organizations. It is possible that analyses often are directed toward revising and perhaps salvaging existing operations rather than toward exploring alternative opportunities for dealing with society's problems.

Analyses of major projects have far greater appeal than more mundane operational analyses of ongoing activities. It is much more satisfying to analysts to undertake a major study of a controversial new program than to conduct detailed analyses of costs and outputs of a necessary but long-standing program. However, much of what government does consists of day-in, day-out continuation of basic operational processes, such as cleaning out and maintaining the city's storm sewers, and analyses of these operational activities can discover important economies of operation.

The organizational location of analytic units can sometimes virtually ensure visibility or obscurity for their products. An analytic unit buried in an agency is unlikely to have much influence on decision making. Having an analytic unit within a budget office can give it visibility but, conversely, can result in analysts' being regularly assigned to deal with "brush fires" so that no time is left for analysis. The Department of Education in the George W. Bush administration significantly strengthened the role of the Office of Educational Research and Improvement, giving it the responsibility of expanding the scientific base of knowledge on what works to improve education and transferring to OERI some evaluation functions that were previously performed by other parts of the department. This was a rare elevation of evaluation research, due most likely to the administration's education focus, as it was not paralleled by a similar elevation of evaluation research in other executive departments and agencies.

The political and administrative cultures of a government and the agencies within it influence the use of analysis. Some units operate in an environment where analysis and the use of information are taken as a given, whereas other organizations find analysis to be a new commodity. The use of analysis is related to the incentives for conducting it. An inherent tension exists between the manager's job and the evaluator's job. The program manager feels that the evaluator demands unreasonable standards of social scientific rigor to "prove the program is working," while the evaluator often feels the manager is too quick to rely on unscientific anecdotal evidence.[60] Furthermore, analytical studies can identify ways to reduce costs. If such studies result in agency budget cuts, however, then agencies have little incentive to perform them.

Evaluations may be mandated by legislatures, but executive agencies may be reluctant to conduct these with vigor, because most, if not all, analyses are regarded as threats. Negative findings are seen as indicators of administrators' failures and can be used as the rationale for budget cuts. This tendency is related to a more general observation that program managers should have permission to experiment and to fail. Managers will resist analysis as long as any admission that a program is not working as it was originally intended is taken as evidence that the program should be eliminated rather than as an opportunity to redesign or to learn from failures.[61]

Implementation of analysis is further complicated by interagency and intergovernmental relations. The benefits of an improved municipal law enforcement program may not be realized if courts are unable to cope with increased numbers of arrests and prosecutions (assuming that increased arrests yield reductions in crime). Moreover, societal problems do not respect political boundaries, and problems do not coincide with each other. One mix of government units may be appropriate for dealing with air pollution problems and another for dealing with physical health. The increasing partnership between government and community groups such as volunteer associations further complicates analysis, as the number of actors involved in a program and the actions they take may be difficult to determine during the course of a program evaluation.

Institutionalizing the Use of Analysis

In addition to institutionalizing analysis through the creation of analytic units within agencies, within central budget offices, and within groups supporting legislatures, increasing use of analysis can be seen in the trend to make performance measures as integral a part of government reporting as financial statements.[62] Long recommended by the GAO, the inclusion of program performance measures as part of federal agency financial reporting practices now is mandated by the Government Performance and Results Act of 1993 (see Chapter 5). To encourage federal agency personnel to take performance measurement and management seriously, some agencies establish performance agreements with senior agency personnel aligning their own individual performance goals with achieving the agency's performance goals.[63] Similarly, the Governmental Accounting Standards Board has recommended performance reporting standards for state and local governments.

The adoption of formal standards and the imposition of regular reporting requirements for government financial accounts (see Chapter 11) contributed to the increase observed in cost analysis and other financial analysis of government programs. Regular reporting on the service accomplishments of government agencies could similarly lead to an increase in the analysis of the results of government expenditures. To the extent that performance indicators measure program outputs, these analyses will focus on government productivity or operational performance. To the extent that performance indicators highlight the impacts on the intended beneficiaries, the types of analysis will focus on governmental effectiveness.

The more extensive the regular capture of information on the outputs and outcomes of government programs at the time the events occur, the less costly the analysis. Prospective analyses of the potential results of pending programs typically rely on analytical models to extrapolate the results from similar programs to the new programs. Research in this type of prospective analysis tends to review previous analyses. Evaluation of program outcomes, after programs are already operating, can be both expensive and time-consuming. Often external contractors are hired by government agencies to send teams to collect extensive field data, frequently after some records are no longer maintained or after the opportunity to structure recordkeeping related to program results has been missed. Designing evaluations into a pilot or demonstration program as part of program implementation brings the evaluation contractor, the implementing agency, and the sponsoring funding source together at the beginning of program implementation and allows these parties to structure data collection that will be useful for evaluating the program's operations and results on a continuing basis.

These trends undoubtedly will increase the use of analysis in decision making. They will not, however, cause analysis to supplant political judgment. Government will continue to weave analysis into the fabric of public sector decision making — but as a tool to enhance judgment rather than as a substitute for it.

Summary

Several related but divergent fields of study impinge upon analysis. Included are policy science and public choice and the disciplines of political science, sociology, economics, and public administration or management. Operations research and systems analysis are included as well.

Much of this chapter focused on cost-benefit and cost-effectiveness analyses. These types of analysis are similar, but cost-benefit analysis quantifies program outcomes in monetary terms whereas cost-effectiveness analysis quantifies outcomes in programmatic terms, such as the number of lives saved. Many of the problems associated with analysis relate to the assumptions that must be made to derive cost and benefit data, particularly through the use of shadow prices and discount rates.

Numerous political and institutional factors limit the use of analysis. Because analysis is part of the political process, some analyses will undoubtedly be designed to produce the desired conclusions. Even when studies conclude that existing programs are not yielding the intended impacts, these studies can serve as justification for expanding rather than shrinking the programs. Beyond the politics of the situation are institutional constraints that deter the translation of analytic findings into program decisions for the coming budget year. Analysis is now a maturing field; gone is the era in which it was viewed as a novel activity.

Notes

1. B.A. Radin, *Beyond Machiavelli: Policy Analysis Comes of Age* (Washington, DC: Georgetown University Press, 2000).

2. Prest and Turvey, in their survey of cost-benefit analysis, date program analysis in the United States back to the River and Harbor Act of 1902, which required analysis of the costs of river and harbor projects undertaken by the Army Corps of Engineers in comparison with the amount of commerce benefited by these projects. A.R. Prest and R. Turvey, Cost-Benefit Analysis: A Survey, *The Economic Journal* 75 (1965): 683–735.

3. J.E. Stiglitz and C.E. Walsh, *Economics*, 3rd ed. (New York: W.W. Norton, 2002).

4. Credit for "inventing" the term *policy sciences* often goes to H.D. Lasswell, The Policy Orientation, in *The Policy Sciences*, D. Lerner and H.D. Lasswell, eds., (Stanford, CA: Stanford University Press, 1951), 3–15.

5. J.M. Buchanan and R.A. Musgrave, *Public Finance and Public Choice: Two Contrasting Views of the State* (Cambridge, MA: MIT Press, 1999).

6. E. Bardach, *A Practical Guide for Policy Analysis: The Eightfold Path to More Effective Problem Solving* (New York: Chatham House, 2000).

7. D.L. Weimer and A.R. Vining, *Policy Analysis: Concepts and Practice*, 3rd ed. (Englewood Cliffs, NJ: Prentice Hall, 1998), 1.

8. Radin, *Beyond Machiavelli*, 2–5.

9. No Child Left Behind Act, P.L. 107–110 (2001).

10. George W. Bush, White House press release, March 14, 2002, *http://www.whitehouse.gov/news/releases/2002/03/images/20020314-7.html*; accessed July 15, 2002.

11. L.A. Crouch, E. Vegas, and R.W. Johnson, *Educational Policy Dialogue in Latin America* (Research Triangle Park, NC: Research Triangle Institute, 1992).

12. U.S. General Accounting Office, *Program Evaluation: Studies Helped Agencies Measure or Explain Program Performance* (Washington, DC: U.S. Government Printing Office, 2000).

13. L.D. Upson, Half-Time Budget Methods, *Annals* 113 (1924): 74.

14. U.S. General Accounting Office, *Determining Performance and Accountability Challenges and High Risks* (Washington, DC: U.S. Government Printing Office, 2000).

15. E. Vedung, *Public Policy and Program Evaluation* (New Brunswick, NJ: Transaction, 1997); P.H. Rossi, et al., *Evaluation: A Systematic Approach* (Thousand Oaks, CA: Sage, 1999).

16. C.L. Schultze, *The Politics of Economics of Public Spending* (Washington, DC: Brookings Institution, 1968), 65.

17. D. Durning, The Transition from Traditional to Postpositivist Policy Analysis: A Role for Q-Methodology, *Journal of Policy Analysis and Management* 18 (1999): 389–410.

18. C.C. Barnett and R.W. Johnson, *Urban Services Delivery in Central and Eastern Europe and the Newly Independent States* (Research Triangle Park, NC: Research Triangle Institute, 1996); R.W. Johnson and J.S. McCullough, *Case Study on Urban Local Government Finance* (paper presented at the Asian Development Bank seminar on Urban Infrastructure Finance in Asia, Research Triangle Institute, Research Triangle Park, NC, April 17, 1996).

19. M.R. Gold, et al., Identifying and Valuing Outcomes in *Cost-Effectiveness in Health and Medicine*, M.R. Gold, et al., eds., (New York: Oxford, 1996), 83.

20. T.F. Nas, *Cost-Benefit Analysis: Theory and Application* (Thousand Oaks, CA: Sage, 1996).

21. A. Wildavsky, The Political Economy of Efficiency: Cost Benefit Analysis, Systems Analysis, and Program Budgeting, *Public Budgeting and Financial Management* 1 (1989): 1–41 (originally published in *Public Administration Review*, December 1966, 292–310).

22. A.K. Donahue and P.G. Joyce, A Framework for Analyzing Emergency Management with an Application to Federal Budgeting, *Public Administration Review* 61 (2001): 728–740.

23. P.F. Drucker, Reinventing Government, in *P.F. Drucker, Managing in a Time of Great Change* (New York: Truman Talley Books, 1995), 285–306; P.F. Drucker, *Managing in the Next Century* (New York: St. Martins, 2002), 93–110.

24. J. Rawls, *Political Liberalism* (New York: Columbia University Press, 1993).

25. Weimer and Vining, *Policy Analysis*, 194.

26. L.E. Lynn, Jr., A Place at the Table: Policy Analysis, Its Postpositive Critics, and the Future of Practice, *Journal of Policy Analysis and Management* 18 (1999): 411–424.

27. R.L. Ackoff and M.W. Sasieni, *Fundamentals of Operations Research* (New York: Wiley, 1968).

28. R.C. Nyhan and L.L. Martin, Assessing the Performance of Municipal Police Services Using Data Envelopment Analysis: An Exploratory Study, *State and Local Government Review* 31 (1999): 18–30.

29. P.M. Senge, *The Fifth Discipline: The Art and Practice of the Learning Organization* (New York: Doubleday, 1990); K.E. Kendall and J.E. Kendall, *Systems Analysis and Design*, 5th ed. (New York: Prentice-Hall, 2001).

30. Federal Aviation Administration, *Aviation Rulemaking Advisory Committee Harmonization Working Group Final Report: Fuel Tank Inerting, 2001*, *http://www.faa.gov/avr/arm/fueltank/docs/13%20Section%2013.pdf*; accessed July 2002.

31. Unfunded Mandates Reform Act, P.L. 104–4 (1995); T. Croote, *Cost Benefit Analysis of Environmental Regulations: An Overview* (Congressional Research Service: U.S. Government Printing Office, 1999), *http://www.cnie.org/nle/crsreports/risk/rsk42.cfm#WhatAnalysisofRegulationsisEPARequiredtoPerform?*; accessed July 2002; Rogelo Garcia, *Federal Regulatory Reform: An Overview* (Congressional Research Service: CRS Web, 2001), *http://www.cnie.org/nle/crsreports/risk/rsk-3.pdf*; accessed July 2002.

32. IMS Health, NICE Refusal on Relenza (London: IMS Health Service, 1999), *http://www.ims-global.com/insight/news_story/news_story_991103b.htm*; accessed August 2002.

33. M.F. Drummond and Alistair McGuire, *Economic Evaluation in Health Care: Merging Theory with Practice* (New York: Oxford, 2002).

34. P. Schwartz, *The Art of the Long View* (New York: Doubleday, 1991).

35. A.L. Franklin, et al., Renovations and Innovations in Program Evaluation, *Public Productivity & Management Review* 22 (1998): 88–106.

36. S.T. Ennett, et al., How Effective Is Drug Abuse Resistance Education? A Meta-Analysis of Project DARE Outcome Evaluations, *American Journal of Public Health* 84 (1994): 1394–1401.

37. G.J. Whitehurst, *Foundations for Learning*, testimony before the House Subcommittee on Labor/HHS/Education Appropriations, April 17, 2002, *http://www.ed.gov/Speeches/04–2002/20020417b.html*; accessed July 2002.

38. Title IX, No Child Left Behind Act.

39. Office of Management and Budget, *Budget of the United States Government: 2003* (Washington, DC: U.S. Government Printing Office, 2002), 109.

40. B.J. Hayward, *A Longitudinal Study of the Vocational Rehabilitation Service Program: Third Interim Report* (Washington, DC: U.S. Department of Education, 1997).

41. D. Whittington and D. MacRae, Jr., The Issue of Standing in Cost-Benefit Analysis, *Journal of Policy Analysis and Management* 5 (1986): 665–682; W.N. Trumbull, Who Has Standing in Cost-Benefit Analysis? *Journal of Policy Analysis and Management* 9 (1990): 201–218.

42. T.A. Steelman and L.A. Maguire, Understanding Participant Perspectives: Q-Methodology in National Forest Management, *Journal of Policy Analysis and Management* 18 (1999): 361–388; L.C. Walters, et al., Putting More Public in Policy Analysis, *Public Administration Review* 60 (2000): 349–359.

43. A. Wildavsky, Political Implications of Budget Reform: A Retrospective, *Public Administration Review* 52 (1992): 597.

44. R.W. Johnson and J.M. Pierce, The Economic Evaluation of Policy Impacts: Cost-Benefit and Cost Effectiveness Analysis, in *Methodologies for Analyzing Public Policies*, eds. F.P. Scioli, Jr., and T.J. Cook (Lexington, MA: Lexington Books, 1975), 131–154.

45. R. Hemming and D.P. Hewitt, The Distributional Impact of Public Expenditures, in *Public Expenditure Handbook: A Guide to Public Policy Issues in Developing Countries*, eds. K. Chu and R. Hemming (Washington, DC: International Monetary Fund, 1991), 119–129.

46. D. Durning, The Transition from Traditional to Postpositivist Policy Analysis.

47. D.T. Campbell and J.C. Stanley, *Experimental and Quasi-Experimental Designs for Research* (Boston: Houghton Mifflin, 1963).

48. R.N. McKean, The Use of Shadow Prices, in *Problems in Public Expenditure Analysis*, ed. S.B. Chase, Jr. (Washington, DC: Brookings Institution, 1968), 33–65; T. Boeri, *Beyond the Rule of Thumb: Methods for Evaluating Public Investment Projects* (Boulder, CO: Westview Press, 1990).

49. R. Carson, *Contingent Evaluation: A Comprehensive Bibliography and History* (London: Edward Elgar Publishing, 2002).

50. OMB Circular A–94, Appendix C, *Discount Rates for Cost-Effectiveness, Lease Purchase, and Related Analyses, http://www.whitehouse.gov/omb/circulars/a094/a94_appx-c.html*; accessed August 2002.

51. K. Richardson, The Effect of Public Versus Private Decision Environment on the Use of the Net Present Value Investment Criterion, *Journal of Public Budgeting, Accounting & Financial Management* 10 (1998): 21–52.

52. N. Shulock,The Paradox of Policy Analysis: If It Is Not Used, Why Do We Produce So Much of It?, *Journal of Policy Analysis and Management* 18 (1999): 226–244.

53. D. Osborne and P. Plastrik, *Banishing Bureaucracy: The Five Strategies for Reinventing Government* (New York: Addison-Wesley, 1997).

54. K.E. Newcomer, Opportunities and Incentives for Improving Program Quality, *Public Administration Review* 54 (1994): 148; U.S. General Accounting Office, *Program Evaluation: Agencies Challenged by New Demand for Information on Program Results*, (Washington, DC: U.S. Government Printing Office, 1998).

55. R.D. Lee, Jr., and R.C. Burns, Survey of State Budget Offices, unpublished data (University Park, PA: The Pennsylvania State University, 2000).

56. L.S. Stewart and R.W. Johnson, *Can Vance County Afford a New School Bond? An Independent Analysis of Vance County's Comparative Ability to Finance School Improvements* (Research Triangle Park, NC: Research Triangle Institute, 1995).

57. S. Nagel, ed. *Handbook of Public Policy Evaluation* (Thousand Oaks, CA: Sage, 2001).

58. R.D. Lee, Jr., and R.C. Burns, Survey of State Budget Offices.

59. D. Durning, Review of I. Mayer, *Debating Technologies: A Methodological Contribution to the Design and Evaluation of Participatory Policy Analysis* (Tilburg, Netherlands: Tilburg University Press, 1997) in *Journal of Policy Analysis and Management* 18 (1999): 339–343.

60. E. Albaek, Between Knowledge and Power: Utilization of Social Science in Public Policy Making, *Policy Sciences* 28 (1995): 79–100.

61. D.E. Ellingson and J.R. Wambsganss, Modifying the Approach to Planning and Evaluation in Governmental Entities: A "Balanced Scorecard" Approach, *Journal of Public Budgeting, Accounting & Financial Management* 13 (2001): 103–120.

62. National Academy of Sciences, *Implementing the Government Performance and Results Act for Research* (Washington, DC: National Academy Press, 2001).

63. U.S. General Accounting Office, *Managing for Results: Emerging Benefits from Selected Agencies' Use of Performance Agreements* (Washington, DC: U.S. Government Printing Office, 2000).

Chapter 8

BUDGET APPROVAL: THE ROLE OF THE LEGISLATURE

The struggle over the budget has only begun when the budget document goes to the legislative body. Executive budget preparation at the state and federal levels will have consumed months, but the product of the process is simply a proposal. The distinction between preparation and approval is alluded to by the phrase, "the executive proposes and the legislature disposes." The process differs from that used in parliamentary governments such as the British one, in which the executive and legislative functions are controlled by the same political party. In such systems, the approval phase is largely pro forma. Parliaments generally can alter the government's budget but often are prohibited from increasing it. Party discipline generally ensures that the changes made by a parliament are typically minor. In the United States, in contrast, the legislative body may approve a budget that diverges in important respects from the budget proposed by the executive.

In this chapter, major emphasis is given to the similarities in the approval phase across levels of government—local, state, and federal. The next chapter focuses exclusively on Congress, because that body is unique in the American political system and has unique budgetary roles, procedures, and problems.

This chapter has two main sections. The first discusses the parameters that constrain how legislative bodies operate and the processes used in approving government budgets. The second section examines the relationships between the legislative and executive branches and the changing role of the legislature as an overseer of the executive branch.

Parameters

Legislative Characteristics

Legislative bodies — city councils, school boards, state legislatures, and Congress — sometimes have had a reputation for being relatively weak, ineffective bodies, but that perception has changed in recent times. Legislative bodies at all levels of government are reasserting their authority to set policy and are taking measures to increase their ability to wield the powers granted to them.

Economic Environment. As with all human enterprise, legislative bodies must operate within a set of parameters, which greatly constrain how they approve the budgets. One of the most important constraints is the economic environment, both in the short and the long term. How a legislative body approaches the task of passing a budget is influenced greatly by whether a surplus of revenues is projected or whether sizable cuts must be made to bring expenditures down to meet anticipated reductions in revenues.

Previous Decisions. Before a local legislative body commences considering the budget, many decisions already will have been made. As explained in previous chapters, the state will have imposed a variety of mandates. A school district will be told how many days it must operate in a school year, possibly what the minimum salaries should be for teachers at different levels, and what courses must be taught. More than half of a school district's budget typically comes from state aid, which greatly reduces what the school district can decide on its own. The state also will have imposed limits on the taxation and borrowing authority for each type of local government and may deny taxing power to some jurisdictions, as is sometimes the case with special districts.

Just as many decisions already will have been made before a local legislative body begins its deliberations, so will many decisions have been made for state legislatures and Congress. Entitlement laws that provide open-ended benefits to individuals, such as guaranteed payments to all persons qualifying for disability benefits under Social Security, greatly curtail what Congress can do in a given year.[1] Similarly, some federal grant programs to state and local governments have been on a permanent appropriation basis, providing for no input from Congress over a period of several years. Federal highway funding is an example. State legislatures face this same situation, most notably in the case of aid to local school districts. Additionally, courts force legislative bodies to take actions, as in such situations as legislatures having to revise state funding formulas for school districts to comply with court orders (see Chapter 4).

Representation of Interests. Socioeconomic and political diversity both influence legislative behavior. At the national level, Congress must deal with a broad range of issues and associated interest groups. States tend to be less diverse and therefore tend to have fewer interest groups that press their preferences upon legislatures; this situation can allow for a relatively small number of interests to influence legislation.[2] The concentration of influence can be even greater at the local level, as in the case of a town that is dominated by a single employer.

Citizen initiatives, allowable in many states, constitute another set of parameters that can have major impacts on the legislative bodies responsible for approving budgets.[3] Under the initiative process, citizens have the power to legislate changes, often by making amendments to state constitutions; if citizens become dissatisfied with tax rates, as was frequently the case in the 1970s, voters may approve new limits on taxes that force jurisdictions to cut tax rates and spending.

The news media are also important influences on legislatures. The media bring issues to the public's attention, help frame those issues and their solutions, and focus attention on legislatures in their efforts to resolve issues. However, newspapers, local radio and television stations, and news networks vary in their abilities to understand complex budget matters and to convey information to the public.[4] As a consequence, the media can be important sources of misinformation as well as information regarding public budgeting and finance.

A responsibility — if not the chief responsibility — of legislators is to represent their constituents. Decisions on the budget can have major positive and negative effects on a legislator's constituents, and therefore on the legislator's prospects for re-election. Although a legislator may generally favor reduced government spending, one common exception arises with any budget reduction proposed for the legislator's district. Positive budget decisions — increases in government spending or fending off possible decreases in spending — are seen by every office-holder as essential for gaining re-election, which itself is seen as of paramount importance.

Representation sometimes can be considered along generational lines. Most legislative bodies include new, younger members who may have a zeal for reforming existing processes, including budgeting. Younger members may see their elections as mandates for representing their generation's needs.[5] They may also be less likely to see legislating as a "career," particularly given that many legislative bodies now operate under term limits, as discussed later in this section.

Legislative Apportionment. How the duty of representation is met is influenced by how legislators are elected to their jobs. In the 1960s, the U.S. Supreme Court ruled that state legislatures must draw district lines that are proportional to population. The effect of this ruling has been to apportion legislative election districts on a population basis and, in turn, to reduce substantially what was once over-representation of rural interests and to increase representation of urban and sub-urban areas in states.[6]

Local governments are undergoing similar changes. City councils are chang-ing from using at-large seats, because this procedure tends to result in under-rep-resentation of minority interests. Instead, the movement is toward *single-member districts* based on neighborhood populations, or a combination of these and at-large seats.[7] Legislative bodies are increasingly diverse in terms of gender and minority representation, although the distinct influence that women and minori-ty legislators have on the legislative process is uncertain.[8]

Race is of great concern regarding how district boundaries are drawn. In an earlier time when efforts were made to deliberately under-represent the interests of minorities, boundaries were drawn such that minority neighborhoods were carved into small segments and then apportioned to several districts. This approach ensured that a minority candidate would never be elected to represent any of the districts. In contemporary times, efforts have been made to help ensure minority representation by drawing boundaries to encircle minority neighbor-hoods. The Supreme Court has held through a series of rulings that when race becomes the dominant factor in deciding on district boundaries that action is a violation of the Equal Protection clause of the Fourteenth Amendment.[9] The result has been considerable confusion when state legislatures have redrawn district boundaries for their own election districts or for congressional districts.

Redistricting plans are frequently challenged in courts for any number of rea-sons, and federal courts have been very active in ruling on state redistricting plans.[10] Some plans are viewed as being unfair to minorities or as over-represent-ing them.[11] The U.S. Supreme Court, for example, which had initially found that the state of North Carolina violated the Constitution because it used race as a "predominant factor" in redrawing its congressional boundaries, later overruled a state court decision that a subsequent redrawing of the boundaries was racially (rather than politically) motivated.[12] In short, the Court seems now to be content to side with boundaries that are redrawn primarily for partisan political reasons, even if that results in a district that consists mostly of minority people where one had not existed before.[13]

Term Limits. A related concern regarding legislators is that they not become so entrenched in their positions that they lose a sense of responsibility to the citizens who elected them. One response to this concern has been a move to impose term limits that curtail the number of years a person may serve.[14] The limits typically involve consecutive years of services, such as no more than two terms of four years in a state senate and no more than six terms of two years in a state house. Limits also can be on a lifetime basis, such as limiting the total number of years a person may serve in the house or senate for one's entire life. As of 2000, six states had lifetime limits for membership in their state legislative bodies.[15]

Term limits have been proposed at all levels of government, and many governments now have such limits. Eight of the largest cities in the country, such as New York City and Los Angeles, along with smaller cities such as Honolulu, Omaha, and Spokane, have term limits.[16] There are currently legislative term limits on the books in 17 of the 50 states; by 2004, these limits will have forced legislators to retire in 14 of these 17 states, and in all of them by 2008.[17] As for the federal government, the Supreme Court has ruled that term limits to be imposed on the Congress must be carried out through a constitutional amendment.[18] Proponents of term limits, convinced that the two-thirds vote necessary for the Congress to pass such an amendment is unlikely to happen without substantial prodding, have taken to using the initiative to adopt state term-limits accountability laws. These laws require the states' delegations to Congress to support a term-limits constitutional amendment and require members of the state legislatures to ratify the amendment. If a member of Congress or the state legislature fails to vote in favor of the amendment or if a candidate for office fails to pledge support for term limits, the ballot indicates that fact. The constitutionality of such laws is being challenged in the courts.

In the meantime, many state legislatures are in the midst of implementing term-limits requirements. One view is that the reform has led to more women and Latinos being elected. In 1997, members of the California Assembly chose the state's first-ever Latino speaker, a feat that would have been highly unlikely without term limits.[19]

Term-limits reform has its downside. Political bodies are automatically denied the experience that can be gained only from long years of service in a legislature. People do not automatically change their family doctors and dentists every six years, so why should they do so with their elected representatives? Effective representatives presumably should be retained in office, while ineffective ones should not be re-elected. Reducing the length of time that someone may stay in office may deter some more-qualified people from running for office in the first place. Term limits, in addition to denying a legislative body experienced legislators, may also increase the influence of staff who know vastly more about particular issues than inexperienced members. In fact, given the complexity of government, many legislators find that their learning curve begins to get more shallow at the precise moment that their legislative career is drawing to an end. To counter this problem, some states have established "training" and "mentoring" programs for new legislators to try to increase their effectiveness.[20] Citizens may support term limits less because of any dissatisfaction with their representatives and more because of a general cynicism about government itself.[21]

Fragmentation. An overriding characteristic of state legislatures and Congress is fragmentation in budgeting. Constitutionally imposed bicameralism divides the legislature into two chambers, a house and a senate, which seek to establish their own identities and powers but which must be coordinated if a budget is to be approved. Local governing bodies, in contrast, usually are unicameral and do not face this fragmentation problem. Fragmentation also is apparent within each chamber of a legislative body and between the executive and legislative branches.

Political parties can serve as a unifying force between branches, between legislative chambers, and within chambers. According to conventional practice, whichever party wins a majority of seats in a chamber controls the leadership positions, has a majority of its members on each committee, and has each committee chaired by a member of the party. In theory, if the Democrats hold a majority of the seats in a state senate, then the Democratic party has control of that chamber in handling all legislative matters. Sometimes a ruling party may have the narrowest possible majority or no majority at all. In 2000, Washington, New Hampshire, and Virginia each had at least one legislative chamber whose members were evenly divided between Republicans and Democrats.[22]

Political Party Leadership. In the United States, political parties are weak, and their leaders cannot control their own party members. On any given issue there may be no guarantee that all or even most of the party's members will vote as a block. Many members of the legislative body, especially those who have gained seniority through numerous re-elections, are not always amenable to supporting the policies pursued by their party's leadership, whether in the legislature or in the executive branch. Further, in term-limited legislatures, the assistance that leaders can offer rank-and-file members with re-election is much less important. For this reason, leaders do not have as much to offer these members in exchange for toeing the party line. In addition, regional differences sometimes trump partisan differences. In the Illinois Senate, for instance, a Republican from the Chicago area may be as likely to vote with a Chicago Democrat on some issue that affects the Chicago area as to vote with a Republican from "downstate" Illinois. Studies have also found evidence that interpersonal ties influence legislators' votes independent of partisanship.[23] In a situation where party control is weak, leaders must try to persuade members to win their votes, unlike in earlier times when legislative leaders may have ruled with iron fists.[24]

Parties attempt to exert influence on their legislators by providing or withholding privileges or by taking party positions in caucuses. Legislative leaders have different levels of insitutional control over rank-and-file members; they may, for example, differ substantially in terms of their ability to appoint members to key committees or to provide resources.[25] Republicans in a state house of representatives, for example, will meet periodically to develop party positions on issues and then attempt to exert their influence on party members to vote accordingly. The positions approved in caucus meetings do not always coincide with the views of the party's leadership.

The situation is further complicated by the fact that the two chambers can be controlled by different parties. Even if both are controlled by one party, the chief executive might be of another party. In 2000, for example, 27 states had divided governments in which the governor, the lower legislative chamber, and the upper legislative chamber were not all controlled by the same political party.[26] This condition is sometimes seen as leading to *gridlock*, which is one oft-cited cause for the inability of government to deal with pressing problems. Divided government, however, as will be seen in this chapter and later ones, should not be considered the sole explanation of why governments sometimes fail to address major problems.[27]

Legislative Committees. The extensive use of legislative committees is essential in that acting as a committee of the whole is impractical, but committee structures add to fragmentation. Committees become little legislatures in their own right.[28] Given that the U.S. House of Representatives has 435 members and the Senate has 100 members, a committee structure is inevitable. Among the states, New Hampshire has the largest legislature, with 424 members, and Nebraska the smallest, with 49 members in one chamber. Most states have more than 100 legislators.[29]

In a bicameral legislative body, legislation is handled by parallel committees in each chamber. These committees report out bills that are acted upon by the full membership of the house and senate. When differences exist in the two bills, a *conference committee* is usually appointed, which reports a revised bill that again is acted upon by both houses. The conference committee consists of members from the two committees that prepared the legislation. Once the chambers have passed identical bills, the legislation is ready for signing or vetoing by the governor or president.

At the local level, where unicameralism prevails, a budget committee often assumes the main responsibility for reviewing and amending the executive's proposed budget and for submitting a set of recommendations to the full legislative body, such as a city council or school board.

Committees that continue on a permanent basis are known as *standing committees*, whereas ad hoc committees are usually created to deal with specific problems and are then disbanded. Most standing committees consist of selected members of one house of a legislature, but standing committees can be joint in nature, consisting of selected members from both chambers. State legislatures usually have 15 to 20 standing committees in each chamber; in 2000, the range was six (Rhode Island Senate) to 46 (Missouri House).[30]

Legislators seek to serve their district's or state's interests by gaining appointment to appropriate legislative committees. Someone from a farming community may seek appointment to a state senate's agriculture committee, and a member of the U.S. House of Representatives from a district that includes major military installations may seek appointment to the Armed Services Committee to help ensure that military funds continue to flow into the district. Similarly, members of the House and Senate will seek appointment to key subcommittees (organized in line with key constituencies — defense, agriculture, transportation, and so forth) of their chamber's appropriations committee.[31]

Availability of Time. How a legislative body operates is greatly influenced by whether it continues in session throughout the year. City councils usually hold meetings once, twice, or even more times per month throughout the year. Congress is in session much of each year except for holidays and recesses during election periods.

State legislatures vary widely. While about a dozen states have no limits on the length of legislative sessions, the rest control whether the legislature can meet each year, for how many days, and whether the legislature may call itself back into session after adjournment. The legislatures in California, Illinois, Massachusetts, Michigan, New Jersey, New York, Ohio, Pennsylvania, and Wisconsin hold sessions that run during much of the year.[32] When legislatures have time limitations, procedural limits are used to "budget" the available time. For example, a common practice is to set a cutoff date for the introduction of bills, as late submission would carry deliberations beyond the required adjournment.

Similarly, time limits are set on the budget process. Some states allow their spending and taxation committees only a few weeks to consider their relevant portions of the budget, while other states allow 20 or more weeks. In some states, the entire budget approval process must be completed by the legislature within six weeks or less; other states allow 20 weeks, 30 weeks, or even more.

A major problem facing Congress is not that it has limits on the time that it may be in session, but rather that it has difficulty approving the budget within the available time. Until legislation was adopted in 1974, Congress faced a situation in which the president's budget was delivered to it shortly after the first of the calendar year and work was to be completed by July 1, then the beginning of the fiscal year. Although the beginning of the fiscal year was shifted to October 1, which gave Congress an additional three months to complete its work, Congress's track record in completing its work on time often has been poor. In fact, between fiscal year 1977 (the first year covered by the new budget timetable) and fiscal year 2002, it passed all appropriation bills prior to the start of the fiscal year only three times.[33] This trend continued with the fiscal year 2003 budget, when 11 of the 13 appropriation bills were not completed when the 107th Congress adjourned in November 2002. Part of the problem lies in the lack of positive incentives for finishing its work on time, or the lack of negative consequences for failing to do so. In practice, only external pressures, such as the desire to return home to campaign or the desire to spend time with family, tend to spur the Congress to complete its work.[34] A separate external force may govern states and localities. They may discover that the failure to enact bills on time can have an adverse effect on bond ratings and, therefore, increase borrowing costs.

Part of the problem is that every two years Congress has to reorganize itself and, in the process, loses valuable time. In January and February of odd-numbered years, Congress must reorganize because all members of the House of Representatives and one-third of the members of the Senate will have been elected (or re-elected) the previous November. New memberships result in new committee assignments, new chairs of some committees, some new leadership, and a reassignment of offices. When party control of a chamber changes, the disruptions are compounded. Under these conditions, Congress simply has immense difficulty finding sufficient time to act on the budget.

Compensation and Staff. Closely associated with time limits on legislatures is the issue of compensation for their members. Annual compensation is low in many states. For example, in 1999, Arkansas, Georgia, Indiana, Mississippi, Nebraska, New Hampshire, Rhode Island, South Carolina, and Texas paid their legislators $13,000 or less.[35] In these states and others, however, members might be eligible for per diem payments, travel expenses, and other payments. Nevertheless, pay for state legislators overall is low, so most legislators need other income sources, such as from law practices. In contrast, members of Congress earn incomes and receive other benefits, such as travel expenses, that allow the legislative job to be a full-time occupation. One of the most important forms of compensation afforded members of Congress is generous pension benefits, which can be an incentive for continuing to stand for re-election. Fees for speeches and other appearances are lucrative for some legislators.

Staffing is another factor that influences legislative behavior. Staff dedicated to assist legislators presumably can help them perform more effectively and reduce their reliance on the executive branch and lobbyists for information. Although local bodies, such as county commissioners or city council members, rarely have sizable staffs at their disposal, Congress does. So do many state legislatures, although some states have small staffs. A predominantly rural state, such as Wyoming, will have a legislative staff numbering less than 100, while a large state, such as New York, will have a staff numbering in the thousands. These personnel serve individual members, committees, and persons holding leadership positions, as in the case of the speaker of a state house of representatives. In addition, some legislative staff units serve a variety of individuals and committees in both chambers. The Congressional Budget Office is a notable example of such a unit. Since the 1960s, staffs in state legislatures and Congress have greatly increased their professional training. Many staff members now have graduate degrees, including doctorates.

Legislative fiscal committee staffs provide a host of services. For example, most state legislatures' fiscal committee staffs conduct fiscal research studies, prepare reports on revenues and taxes, and prepare reports on expenditures and the budget. Other important staff functions include making revenue projections, analyzing budget trends during the fiscal year, and preparing reports on economic conditions. States also differ as to whether they maintain separate fiscal staffs for each house or one joint legislative fiscal office that serves both houses.[36]

A study published in 2000 identified the following as the most "professional" of state legislatures: Alaska, California, Florida, Illinois, Michigan, New York, Ohio, and Pennsylvania. This study measured professionalism according to several factors. Those legislatures judged to be the most professional were those with the highest level of compensation, those that spent the greatest number of days in session annually, and those that spent the most money on staff and other services.[37] Professionalism, however, is no guarantee of a smoothly operating legislature, as has been evident in such states as California and New York. One view is that professionalism attracts better-informed individuals who inevitably clash with one another, yielding conflict that is not necessarily productive.[38]

The Legislative Process

Members of the legislature or their staff often participate in budget preparation deliberations by the executive branch. When the budget reaches the legislature, therefore, it may contain relatively few surprises in terms of proposals being advanced; that is, many of the key legislators already will be familiar with the budget's main proposals. Legislative involvement during preparation can help build support for executive budget recommendations.

Committee Responsibilities. When a budget reaches a state legislature or Congress, the document is divided into numerous pieces and sent to committees. Proposals that require new substantive legislation to implement them will be sent to substantive standing committees. These committees exist for areas such as environmental protection, education, recreation, welfare, and, at the federal level, defense and international relations. For programs to be implemented, these committees must report bills that will be approved eventually by the two chambers of the legislature. Legislation of this type authorizes the existence of programs, while appropriations provide the necessary funding.

While deliberations proceed on these substantive matters, other committees deal with the financial aspects of the budget. A regular practice is to assign taxing and other revenue matters to one group of committees and spending or appropriations to another. In Congress, taxation is handled by the Ways and Means

Committee in the House of Representatives and by the Finance Committee in the Senate; spending is dealt with by each chamber's appropriations committee. These committees actually conduct much of their work at the subcommittee level (see Chapter 9).

Coordination problems and terrain battles among committees are common. A person achieves the position of chair of a committee by serving on the committee for a long time and hence, once made chair, is unlikely to look favorably on threats to the committee's powers. The Appropriations Committee of the U.S. House of Representatives was once considered the College of Cardinals, and while the committee has lost the prestige and power that such a title suggests, it remains powerful and its members work to retain its powers.[39] Nevertheless, some coordinating mechanisms are essential to ensure that realistic budgets are adopted. For example, if separate revenue and expenditure committees are free to act independently, then there may be little relationship between how much income comes into the government and how much is spent. It was precisely this situation that led the federal government to enact the Congressional Budget and Impoundment Control Act of 1974, creating the Budget Committees and budget resolution to better coordinate action on the budget (see Chapter 9). The budget resolution, which is under the jurisdiction of the Budget Committees, sought to address the fragmentation of the budget process at the federal level by requiring the Congress to vote on the whole budget, rather than considering it only in pieces.

Local governments are much less likely to have particular budget committees. In local governments with elected boards or councils, hearings and budget reviews are typically conducted with the entire legislative body present. Directors of city or county departments are asked to defend budget proposals in the same way that similar officials defend their budget requests at the state and national levels. The public, however, may be much more involved in local budget issues at a much greater level of detail than is the case for national or state budgets, because citizens are likely to be more knowledgeable about local issues and more directly affected by the budget.[40]

Fiscal Notes. One important mechanism that has been adopted is the requirement that fiscal notes be developed for most draft legislation. A fiscal note is a report that addresses the current and future costs of implementing a proposed bill. It may include analysis of the purpose of the legislation, the proposed sources of funding, and the impact on other governments, as in the case of a state law affecting local government budgets. Fiscal notes are typically prepared by legislative staff. At the state level, appropriations committees often have this responsibility. At the federal level, the Congressional Budget Office (CBO) prepares fiscal notes to any bill that is reported out of a House or Senate Committee. CBO is required to estimate the cost of the proposed legislation to the federal government relative to the baseline (which is the estimate of costs under current law). It also estimates the costs of legislation to state and local governments; the State and Local Government Cost Estimate Act of 1981 requires that fiscal notes be prepared to estimate the impact of proposed legislation affecting these governments.[41] The Unfunded Mandates Reform Act of 1995 requires that Congress consider the possible financial effects of draft legislation on state and local governments and create hurdles to considering legislation that does not include an estimate of potential unfunded mandates (see Chapter 14).[42]

The fiscal note is intended to help decision makers be better informed about the implications of draft legislation. For example, if a proposal provides for revising a state program for teenagers to include 13-year-olds, whereas only those 14 years old and older are currently included, the revision could greatly increase the number of clients served and heighten the demand on resources. Fiscal notes also are prepared for revenue proposals, as in the case of forecasting the extra income that would be generated by increasing a state sales tax by one percentage point.

Fiscal notes are particularly important at the state and local levels, where balanced budgets are required. Indeed, the revenue estimates prepared by the chief executive, coupled with any fiscal note on proposed revenue increases, will greatly influence what spending programs the legislature will be able to approve. While nearly all states require that fiscal notes be prepared,[43] the content and thoroughness of fiscal notes varies widely from state to state. Some states, for example, require that fiscal notes be prepared for tax expenditure proposals (see Chapter 4), while others do not.[44] The failure to prepare thorough fiscal notes may be a function of short deadlines that are impossible to meet and the lack of qualified staff in sufficient numbers to prepare the notes.[45]

In addition to fiscal notes, other mechanisms are devised to link together the work of committees and ensure that "reasonable" budgets are developed. Some states have used a system by which lump-sum amounts are assigned to program areas, and these funds then are distributed among programs within each area by standing committees and reported back to the appropriations committee for inclusion in their budget bills. Congress uses a variation of this approach. Local governments generally have less of a coordination problem, because most of the budget work is handled by a single committee.

Legislative Roles

Legislative–Executive Interactions

In this section, we turn to how the executive branch relates to the legislative branch. Because legislatures are not integrated wholes but rather consist of numerous subunits, this section considers how the executive branch relates to those subunits, especially to the two legislative chambers and their committees.

Authority. The executive and legislative branches of government in the United States are typically said to be coequal.[46] The separation of powers — in this case, between the executive and legislative branches — is a fundamental feature of U.S. governments. Therefore the two branches tend to be wary of possible diminution of their powers and may seek strategies for demonstrating their independence. Confrontations between the two are sometimes akin to tests of strength, with each branch showing it is not subservient to the other.

In earlier days, the legislature was considered to be responsible for setting policy. Today, both the legislative and executive branches are inextricably engaged in policy making. Conflicts arise, not over whether the executive should be involved in policy making, but rather to what extent and in what ways. The movement toward executive budget systems has placed the executive four-square in the policy-making process, because the preparation of budget proposals by the executive is, in effect, the drafting of proposed policies. Congress, state legislatures, and city councils have often found themselves in the position of having to react to executive recommendations instead of formulating policy. To demonstrate their independence, then, legislators may feel a compulsion to alter a proposed budget no matter how compatible its recommendations are with their own preferences.

Not all governments have executive budgeting systems. In some governments, budgeting powers overlap between the branches; in others, legislatures dominate the budgeting process. In fact, in a study of 13 states in terms of their budget practices, only three were characterized as states where the executive is dominant, while four were judged as states where the legislature is dominant. In the rest, budgetary power was viewed as relatively equal between the branches.[47] Regardless of the distribution of powers, tensions will exist between the branches of government.

Constitutional and legal constraints greatly affect the extent of executive and legislative powers in budgeting. The Budget and Accounting Act of 1921 and comparable legislation at the state level have granted substantial budgetary powers to the president and governors. Yet, in some states, the governor must share budget-making authority with other relatively independent executive officers or legislative bodies. In most states, the legislature is free to adjust the governor's budget either upward or downward, but in a few states (Maryland, Nebraska, New York, and West Virginia), the legislature has limited or no authority to appropriate amounts above those recommended by the governor.

Relationships between the branches change over time. Changes in political leadership have both short- and long-term effects. When a new executive takes office, inevitable discontinuities occur during the transition period, which can last from a few weeks to months.[48] In addition, personalities and the political clout of leaders influence executive–legislative relations. The election of a highly popular political leader in the legislature can lead to diminished executive powers. A newly elected governor who is more assertive than his or her predecessor, may succeed in demanding that the legislature yield some of its budgetary powers. When either the executive or the legislative branch changes its partisan makeup (as occurred, for example, when several southern states elected Republican legislatures for the first time since Reconstruction, or in 1995 when the U.S. House was taken over by the Republicans for the first time in 40 years), it can create a period of instability while new relationships are forged. In periods of fiscal crisis and other challenging times, the executive may tend to garner greater budgetary powers at the expense of the legislature.[49]

Constituency Differences. The legislative and executive branches have different constituencies and, as a result, have different perspectives on the budget. One common interpretation has been that the chief executive, being elected by the jurisdiction's entire constituency, has a broader perspective on the budget; a governor will attempt to satisfy the diverse needs of citizens throughout the state. Legislative bodies, on the other hand, have been seen as consisting of parochial individuals who may be less impressed with government-wide problems and, therefore, more likely to cut budgets. The legislature, then, is seen as a protector of the treasury and as a budget cutter.

A competing view of legislative bodies is that, in their desire to represent constituents, they tend to be eager to spend resources far beyond what is financially sound and that, while the requirement for a balanced budget keeps that desire to spend in check at the state and local levels, few constraints are evident at the national level. *Pork barrel*, a basic term of U.S. politics, refers to legislatively approved government projects that are aimed at helping home districts and states.[50] In fact, some prominent political scientists have suggested that pork barrel spending and constituent casework (intervening on behalf of constituents with administrative agencies) have become more valued than legislating because they offer a more certain path to re-election.[51] A standard complaint of pork barrel projects is that they have limited utility beyond winning votes for legislators seeking re-election. The item veto, discussed below, may help to reduce the wastefulness of pork barrel spending.

Recent presidents have attempted to advance their own legislative programs while minimizing the gap between high spending and lower revenues. For example, budgets submitted during the Reagan administration were intended to support a buildup in defense; to minimize deficits, sizable reductions in domestic programs were proposed. In this type of situation, almost regardless of political party positions, legislatures tend to be supportive of efforts to restore budget cuts proposed by the executive. Selective cuts may cost the executive few votes in a bid for re-election, whereas those same cuts can have dire effects on the political futures of many legislators.

Deadlock between the branches is a common phenomenon. When the two cannot agree on a budget, commuters can be greatly inconvenienced due to shutdowns in public transit, welfare recipients can be forced to eke out an existence without their checks, and public employees may have to endure payless paydays. Requirements at the state and local levels that balanced budgets be adopted, while imposing fiscal discipline on decision makers, can lead to delays in adopting budgets, because neither the executive nor legislative branch wishes to take the first step toward compromise lest it be viewed as a sign of weakness. In 1992, California state government operated for months without a budget, during which time employees were issued scrip rather than dollars.

Executive Fragmentation. An executive budget system provides the chief executive with control over budget preparation, but there is no guarantee that all units within the executive branch will subscribe fully to the budget's recommendations. The chief executive will not be uniformly in support of all portions of the budget; some recommendations will have been approved because of political considerations. Typically, the chief executive will single out a few major recommendations for which approval is sought, with other recommendations being considered a low priority. The budget office will be expected to make general presentations on the overall recommendations contained in the budget, even though it may be lukewarm toward many of those recommendations.

Detailed defense of specific recommendations is normally the responsibility of the operating agencies. Because the heads of the agencies in a strong executive system are the appointees of the chief executive, they have an obligation to defend the budget recommendations, even though higher funding levels may be preferred.[52] Agency representatives, however, may have little enthusiasm for defending budget proposals that call for deep cuts in programs. As a result, agencies attempt to calculate the extent to which they can reveal their preferences for greater resources to the spending committees in the legislature and still remain "faithful" to the chief executive. They do not always calculate correctly. In 2002,

President George W. Bush's appointed director of the Army Corps of Engineers, former Representative Mike Parker, was fired for being a bit too honest in his responses to questions from the Congress about the adequacy of the Corps' budget.[53] Agencies also seek to head off any budget cuts being contemplated by the appropriations committee and are willing to engage in conflict if necessary to protect their budgets.[54]

During the approval phase, central budget offices may have responsibility for exercising some control over agencies that might seek to garner financial support beyond what the executive is recommending to the legislature and may serve as a major negotiator for the executive in sensitive discussions with legislative leaders. Since the early 1980s, the Office of Management and Budget (OMB) has played a much more prominent role in legislative relations. This role includes activities not just of the OMB director, but also of individual budget examiners.[55]

Budget offices commonly perform a *clearinghouse function* by reviewing all proposed legislation and bills that have been passed by the legislature and forwarded to the chief executive for signing. OMB Circular A-19 prescribes for federal agencies that they submit to OMB an annual set of proposals for legislation. If these proposals are not submitted in time for consideration at budgeting time in the latter part of the year, then they are excluded from the president's budget and therefore not endorsed by the president and his administration. Circular A-19 provides that when Congress passes a bill, OMB distributes copies of the *enrolled bill* to affected agencies for their comments. The agencies must respond promptly, either endorsing or opposing the enrolled bill, to be considered within the president's limit of ten days. If the president does not act within the ten days (including holidays but excluding Sundays), the bill automatically becomes law.

Influence of Bicameralism. One set of calculations from both the executive and the legislative branch perspectives involves the relative roles of the two chambers. At the federal level, the Constitution requires that revenue or tax bills begin in the House of Representatives — in particular, the Ways and Means Committee (Article I, Section 7). Until the 1974 reform legislation, the normal procedure was for the Senate Finance Committee to wait until the House completed action before taking up the tax bill. Appropriations were handled in a similar manner, although the practice was based on custom and not the Constitution; appropriation bills began in the House and later were referred to the Senate. Under that system, strategists were able to concentrate their attentions on first one committee and then another as the legislation worked its way through Congress. Since 1974, the House and Senate have simultaneously commenced work on the budget.

Where appropriations are handled sequentially (that is, beginning in the lower chamber and then moving to the upper chamber), the two chambers tend to take on different roles. Since a house of representatives tends to have more members than a senate, a house appropriations committee tends to have more members than its counterpart in the senate. As a result, house committee members can specialize in segments of the budget, whereas senators must attempt to become informed on a larger number of areas and consequently may be viewed as amateurs. Members of the senate committee, on the other hand, might consider themselves to have a broader awareness of total budget needs than house members. Also, given the sequencing of one chamber acting followed by the other, the house appropriations committee tends to focus on the proposed budget, whereas the senate committee focuses on what the house did to the proposed budget.[56]

Federal Aid to States. One particular area of executive–legislative contention at the state level has been control over federal assistance. Historically, legislative bodies did not appropriate federal funds coming into state treasuries. Governors contended that they acted as custodians over federal dollars and were bound by federal regulations that established how and for what purposes monies were to be spent; the conclusion followed that the legislature had no role in deciding about the use of these funds. Occasionally, governors were able to use federal grants to finance services that state legislatures opposed. The legislative view of this situation was and is that, once received, federal dollars become state dollars and can be spent only when approved by an appropriation bill adopted by the legislature. Although the Supreme Court has not ruled on this issue, in 1979 it let stand a lower court's ruling in favor of the legislature.[57]

The issue of state appropriation of federal funds became more important in 1981, when Congress passed legislation creating large block grants to be administered by the states (see Chapter 14). Under these grant programs, the states were given increased flexibility in how they spent some of the grant monies and how they distributed the remainder to local governments. The response has been for state legislatures to require that appropriations be passed before federal dollars can be spent. The legislatures in Florida, Ohio, and Washington, for example, determine in considerable detail how monies are to be spent on programs and subprograms.

Strategies. Regardless of what level of government is considered, executive–legislative relationships inevitably can be characterized as cat-and-mouse games, although it is not always clear who is the cat and who is the mouse. Strategies are devised in each branch to deal with the other. On the executive side, an almost ubiquitous general strategy is to cultivate clientele who will support requests for increased funding. Agencies are sensitive to where they locate buildings and other facilities; a new facility in a key legislator's district may gain the support of that legislator. Agencies pursue such strategies continuously as a matter of course.[58]

Contingent strategies, on the other hand, are limited to particular situations. No comprehensive cataloging of them is possible, because they vary from agency to agency and from circumstance to circumstance. They arise out of perceptions of what is possible in a given budget period. In growth periods, when revenue surplus or slack is evident, agencies may seek to expand existing programs or gain approval for the creation of new ones. Even when revenues are scarce, agencies whose areas are favored by the chief executive may seek expansion, as occurred with defense and homeland security in the aftermath of the September 11, 2001, terrorist attacks. Sometimes obtaining approval for a new program may be easier than obtaining approval for expansion of an existing one; executives and legislators alike prefer being able to take credit for creation of a new program over simply improving an existing one. A ploy that may be used is to start a new project with a small appropriation, get the legislature accustomed to the program, and then seek much greater appropriations in subsequent years.

When funds are less plentiful, one strategy is to defend programs against cuts and to maintain what is called the *base.* An agency's existing budget is often regarded as the base, with the budget process adding or subtracting increments to the base. Agencies have been known to warn that the slightest of budget cuts would necessarily diminish popular programs and thereby erode electoral support of legislators.

When cuts are perceived as inevitable, often because of declining tax revenues, one strategy is to minimize cuts in the base and to obtain *fair share* funding. An agency will argue, on the one hand, that its programs are essential and should not be cut at all; on the other hand, it will insist that, if cuts must be made, they be no greater than cuts imposed on programs in other agencies.

Strategies used by proponents of government programs can be highly situational. A thorough study of the strategies used by federal agencies in dealing with OMB and the Congress catalogued 35 different stategies used at various times. These included some that have been well documented in the budgeting literature, such as establishing earmarked funding sources, portraying the disastrous consequences of failing to spend money, or stressing the needs of a particular group that will be served. They also include many more arcane strategies that have been less well documented: establishment of a government-sponsored enterprise; creation of a loan guarantee program; establishment of a tax expenditure (see Chapter 4); and leasing instead of purchasing a capital asset.[59] There are, in short, many different "tools" available to governments to satisfy the desire for social action. Increasingly, these tactics involve less direct means than government expenditures, for strategic as well as substantive reasons.[60] Some changes in the budget process, such as federal credit reform (see Chapter 11), have occurred specifically to lessen the incentives to provide resources through less direct and apparently less costly means.

While various strategies may be influential, there are limits to their effectiveness. Legislatures are influenced by personal values and committee role expectations as well as by agency budget strategies and presentations. Agency strategies may also backfire and create negative feelings on the part of members of the appropriations committees, perhaps because they suspect they are being exploited.

In response to agency pressure, legislators devise a number of strategies for dealing with their budgetary responsibilities. A major problem is the capacity of agencies to produce vast amounts of information in support of their requests — more information than the legislature can process. Legislative strategies, then, may be seen as methods to simplify complex choices.

For example, an appropriations committee or subcommittee may find it difficult, if not impossible, to decide rationally if $83.6 million is the exact amount that should be granted to an agency. As a consequence, legislators in appropriations committees may look for other ways to determine what should be granted an agency. They may place much of the burden for calculation on the executive branch and demand that an agency justify its need for certain funds in response to probing questions. Detailed questions, which to outsiders may seem petty and trivial, are designed to determine how much confidence the subcommittee can place in the executive's testimony. Legislators have "discernible patterns" in their line of questioning, suggesting that they have their own strategies for dealing with different agencies and that these strategies depend in part upon changes in fiscal conditions.[61] How the various strategies affect the outcomes of appropriations is uncertain and no doubt varies among jurisdictions and over time.

Item Veto. Once appropriation and revenue bills are adopted by the legislature, the approval phase is not completed. In more than 40 states, governors have item-veto power, which permits reductions in amounts that have been appropriated. In some cases, governors may eliminate selected language in appropriation bills, which can have substantial effects on policy. State legislatures may seek to override these vetoes; usually a two-thirds vote is required for an override. As with the general veto power, the threat of the item veto may be as important as its eventual use, in that legislators may avoid including some measures in an appropriation bill on the assumption they would be excised eventually by the governor. The item veto has three uses:[62]

1. It allows chief executives to keep total expenditures within the limits of anticipated available revenue.

2. The executive can reduce or even eliminate funds for projects or programs considered to be unworthy. The item veto can help curtail the excesses of pork barrel projects mentioned earlier.

3. The veto can be used for partisan purposes. This kind of use often occurs in situations where the governor is of one political party and one or both chambers of the legislature are of another party.

Studies have found that the item-veto power sometimes — but not always — has a negative effect on spending, especially for pork barrel highway projects, and can be particularly important when at least one chamber is under the control of a political party that differs from the governor's party.[63] From a practical standpoint, the item veto allows action by the governor without forcing the legislature to react unless it chooses to do so. Indeed, legislators may be privately pleased to have the governor veto some projects that were included in an appropriation bill to satisfy strong lobbying pressure. In spite of the Constitutional foundations underlying state item vetoes, state courts have been very active in interpreting their application, and these court decisions can have a substantial effect on the potential "reach" of a governor's item-veto power.[64]

At the federal level, the president has always been able to exercise the standard veto power, meaning that he can veto an entire appropriation bill. When this power is exercised, the House and Senate may override the veto by a two-thirds vote. Should the veto be sustained, the legislation is referred back to committee for further review. The disadvantage of the veto power for both Congress and the president is that much time and energy may be consumed in redrafting the legislation and negotiating an agreement between the two branches.

Every president since Ulysses S. Grant, including President Clinton, requested the item-veto power.[65] In 1996, Congress granted that wish by passing the Line Item Veto Act.[66] The law, which was ultimately declared unconstitutional by the Supreme Court in 1998, is discussed in Chapter 9, which deals with congressional budget processes.[67]

Legislative Oversight

Not only are the executive and legislative branches typically separated in U.S. governments, but each branch is also provided with powers that can be used to limit the powers of the other. The basic structure of this *checks-and-balances system* is set forth in the U.S. Constitution, state constitutions, and city charters. However, constitutional and statutory provisions must be implemented on a daily basis, and the extent to which one branch limits the other may fluctuate over time. In this section, we consider the increasing interest being given to the legislative body's overseeing of executive operations.[68]

Influences on Oversight. When revenues are limited and the demands for expenditures are seemingly limitless, legislators perceive a need for greater efficiency and effectiveness in government operations. Such perceptions increase the interest in oversight operations, which in turn increases the pressure on administrative agencies to improve their operations while curtailing or even reducing expenditures. Agencies are required to provide masses of information to legislative committees to support their quest for ferreting out mismanagement and saving taxpayers' dollars.[69]

There are, of course, other reasons for the current legislative oversight movement. Financial crises in major cities have contributed to the interest in oversight. The Watergate scandal during the Nixon administration and subsequent scandals and abuses of government funds by federal agencies have stimulated interest in greater legislative oversight. Legislators have not been immune from their own scandals, raising the question of whether they have the appropriate credentials to oversee executive branch operations.

Legislators are sincerely interested in using government to alleviate societal problems. Frustrated by what is perceived as inept administration, they are attracted to the idea of expanding their oversight roles in the hope of improving government operations. Of course, oversight of the executive branch can also provide an opportunity for legislators to score political points. In fact, legislatures have often been criticized for engaging in oversight designed to take an agency to task for some particular perceived offense, rather than using this opportunity to attempt to understand programs in detail so that they can be reformed constructively.

This legislative interest in oversight occurs at a time when executives feel increasingly frustrated with their own efforts to control public bureaucracies. Elected executives often complain that they lack the authority needed to control and redirect agencies. Merit systems that protect civil service employees are often cited as weakening executives and protecting lazy and incompetent employees from disciplinary actions. Tensions exist between the White House and Congress over control of the chief financial officers in federal agencies, with the White House seeing the officers as a means of exerting executive influence and Congress being concerned with extending its oversight function (see Chapter 11).[70]

Methods. Legislative oversight can be performed using numerous methods. Legislation that provides authorizations, revenues, and appropriations constitutes one set of methods. Other familiar devices are laws that prescribe the structure of executive agencies and personnel policies regarding hiring, promotion, and dismissal. An informal type of oversight occurs when a legislator or a legislative staff member contacts an agency about specific day-to-day operations; although legislators may have no official power to command any action by an agency, their wishes will be treated carefully and with some urgency by agency personnel. Oversight is important in advise-and-consent proceedings in which a senate committee screens a nominee for an executive position; the questions asked a nominee can influence that person's actions once in office.

Legislative investigations and just the simple threat of investigation are other instruments of oversight. A legislative committee chair may greatly influence an agency by suggesting that investigative hearings will be scheduled unless certain practices are changed within the agency.

Greater specificity of *legislative intent* is being used to reduce executive discretion. In the past, ambiguous language was used as a deliberate tool for delegating responsibilities to the executive and increasing executive flexibility in carrying out policies. The opposite is common today. State legislatures attempt to establish legislative intent through the use of wording contained in line items, footnotes, and concluding sections to appropriation bills; the use of committee reports; and the use of letters of intent delivered to the governor.

Legislatures often find it difficult to enforce legislative intent. What if an agency stays within the legal prescriptions of legislative intent but violates its spirit? The punitive action of cutting the agency's budget often is not possible; citizens benefiting from agency programs would be harmed as well as the agency itself. Therefore, the main punitive alternative may be to impose more restrictions on the agency, such as making legislative intent more explicit, specifically prohibiting various practices, and perhaps increasing the number of line items in the agency's budget to hamstring its flexibility.

The legislature may also attempt to enforce legislative intent by requiring agencies to collect and provide specific information to the legislature. This practice denies agencies the tactic of confessing ignorance about their own programs; if legislation indicates that an agency is to collect specific data, the agency will be expected to deliver it at designated times every year.

Congress often adopts appropriation bills that have detailed language. In particular, the foreign assistance program is said to be hamstrung by crosscutting legislative requirements built into appropriations. For example, appropriations specify how much each country will receive. In addition, appropriations specify the amounts that will be spent on programs such as child survival, population, the environment, and natural resources. Executives of the Agency for International Development must plan their expenditures within a matrix that links programs with nations, even though more flexible planning might better serve foreign policy objectives.

Sunset Legislation and Zero-Base Budgeting. Another type of oversight mechanism consists of sunset legislation coupled with zero-base budgeting. Programs are authorized to exist for a given period, after which they expire (the sun sets on them). Before a program's expiration date, an agency may be required to present a zero-base budget indicating the achievements of the agency's program and the projected consequences if the program is not renewed. Depending on how these proposals are implemented, they can provide greater leverage for the legislature. For these reasons, sunset legislation is used widely by state legislatures.

Information and Analysis. Program budgeting and analysis constitute another approach to legislative oversight. Legislatures are increasingly demanding impact and output data from agencies; such demands have reinforcing effects on chief executives' efforts to install program budgeting. At the federal level, the Government Performance and Results Act of 1993 and President George W. Bush's initiative to better integrate budgeting and performance measurement are expected to result in increased programmatic information being presented to the Congress as well as to the president (see Chapter 5).

Tensions exist over which organizational units should conduct analyses. Legislatures have sometimes given little attention to oversight, and the function has fallen to audit agencies, which at the state level are often headed by independently elected auditors. When legislative bodies later develop their own analytic capabilities, turf issues arise.[71] Virginia's Joint Legislative Audit and Review Commission and Florida's Office of Program Performance and Government Accountability are examples of state legislative analysis units.

At the federal level, the General Accounting Office (GAO) has an extensive ongoing research agenda that examines the full gamut of government programs.[72] The fact that the GAO works for Congress often brings it into conflict with the executive branch. The most high-profile recent case involved the GAO's desire to obtain records of Vice President Cheney's contacts with outsiders in the process of developing the administration's energy policy. This issue became particularly salient politically after the collapse of Enron, which had ties to some high-ranking officials in the Bush administration.[73] Information technology also makes possible greater legislative oversight. Congress and state legislatures have developed their own information systems that allow them to tap into a variety of databases, including those maintained by agencies. However, the application of this technology is limited by the quality of data being maintained; computer hardware and software cannot compensate for agency neglect in collecting important information.

Legislative Veto. Legislatures are making increased use of their power to veto proposed executive actions. For instance, an agency may be granted authority to issue regulations, but a stipulation in the legislation can require the agency to obtain legislative approval prior to implementing the regulations.[74] Depending on the governing legislation, a proposed action can be vetoed by a vote in either house or both houses of a legislature, or it can be implemented only with a vote of approval from both houses. Sometimes legislative committees have veto powers. More than 40 state legislatures exercise some form of legislative veto over executive agency regulations.[75]

The legislative veto is used as a means of furthering policy. Legislative intent is served presumably by allowing the full legislature or designated committees to oversee executive implementation. The veto process can steer executive agencies away from actions that are contrary to what the legislature wishes to see implemented.

Not surprisingly, executives have a less positive view of legislative vetoes. The process often delays implementation of actions because the legislature is assured a given number of weeks to consider whether to support or veto a proposal. These vetoes are seen as giving authority to legislatures to meddle needlessly in the details of administration and, more significantly, to infringe upon the constitutional administrative powers of the executive.

A crisis seemed to develop in 1983 when the Supreme Court handed down one of its most controversial decisions in *Immigration and Naturalization Service v. Chadha*.[76] The case dealt with congressional veto power involving the deportation of aliens. What was significant was not that the Court struck down that legislative veto, but rather that it struck down most, if not all, such vetoes at the federal level. The Court's reasoning was simple: The Constitution provides for the House and Senate to set policy subject to veto by the president and does not allow for the opposite procedure.

Following the *Chadha* decision, Congress did not rush to adopt statutory measures or seek constitutional revisions that would reinstate the legislative veto. Instead, it dealt with matters as they arose and, in some instances, largely ignored the Court's ruling. For example, subsequent appropriation bills have included legislative vetoes. In 1996, Congress passed the Congressional Review Act, which provides a form of legislative veto of agency draft regulations (see Chapter 10).[77]

Oversight Limitations. While numerous methods of oversight are available, the organizational locus of oversight remains a problem because of the fragmentation discussed earlier. A coherent approach to oversight is not possible when committee powers overlap. Every federal agency must deal with at least one substantive committee, the Appropriations Committee, and the Budget Committee (discussed in Chapter 9) in each chamber of Congress. These committees may disagree with each other and may not have the backing of the full legislative body. Turf battles among committees are routine. For instance, the Chief Financial Officers Act of 1990 (see Chapter 11), by creating chief financial officers in agencies, enhanced the oversight powers of the House Government Reform and Oversight Committee and the Senate Governmental Affairs Committee at the expense of the Appropriations Committees.[78]

One approach to overcoming fragmentation might be to concentrate oversight in a staff unit of the legislature. For example, GAO at the federal level could be given greater oversight responsibilities. Another option would be to give oversight duties to committee staffs. The problem with these suggestions is that they tend to conflict with legislators' desire to have staffs act in subordinate and inferior capacities. For a staff unit to evaluate a program enacted by the legislative body, to find the program inadequate, and to suggest means of improving it is likely to be viewed by many legislators as an affront to their authority in setting policy. For this reason, legislative analytic units tend to be cautious in program analysis and tentative in reaching conclusions and recommendations.

A final limitation on oversight is the priorities that legislators set for themselves. Re-election is always paramount, and legislators often regard oversight activities as not contributing appreciably to their prospects for winning voter approval. In that sense, the limited oversight role performed by legislatures is seen as a completely rational response to the incentives facing them. If voters are more supportive of legislators who initiate new programs than of those who serve as watchdogs over the executive branch, legislators will respond accordingly.

Summary

A variety of factors constrain the budgetary role of legislatures. The availability of revenue greatly influences how the legislature approaches budget approval. Previously reached decisions, such as established entitlement programs, limit action, as do numerous socioeconomic and political factors, such as the influence of interest groups. Fragmentation that results from bicameralism and the use of committees complicates the approval phase of budgeting, although political parties can help to overcome some of the problems.

The budget is approved through the work of substantive standing committees, appropriations committees, and revenue or finance committees. Fiscal notes have become important tools for tracking the financial implications of proposed legislation.

In recent years, a movement has emerged that seeks to revitalize the role of legislatures vis-à-vis executives in the budgetary process. In years past, legislatures sometimes had a reputation for being budget cutters. More recently, however, their role has been to represent constituents who would be harmed if proposed budget cuts were implemented. Many executives have the power to item-veto appropriations that seem excessive.

Agencies use numerous strategies in seeking approval of their budgets. An administrator's initial objective may be to obtain increased funding for a program. If that is not possible, then the administrator will concentrate on protecting the base and preventing budget cuts beyond those that constitute a fair share.

Legislative oversight has become increasingly popular. Prior legislative approval of some administrative decisions may be required. Legislative investigative hearings serve the oversight function, along with detailed specification of legislative intent. Sunset legislation and zero-base budgeting are other oversight techniques.

Notes

1. A. Wildavsky and N. Caiden, *The New Politics of the Budgetary Process*, 4th ed. (New York: Longman, 2000), 187–223.

2. W.J. Keefe and M.S. Ogul, *The American Legislative Process: Congress and the States*, 10th ed. (Upper Saddle River, NJ: Prentice-Hall, 2000).

3. R. Kurfirst, Direct Democracy in the Sunshine State: Recent Challenges to Florida's Citizen Initiative, *Comparative State Politics* 17 (August 1996): 1–15.

4. D.P. Swoboda, Accuracy and Accountability in Reporting Local Government Budget Activities: Evidence from the Newsroom and from Newsmakers, *Public Budgeting & Finance* 15 (Fall 1995): 74–90.

5. T. Loftus, *The Art of Legislative Politics* (Washington, DC: Congressional Quarterly Press, 1994), 6.

6. *Baker v. Carr*, 369 U.S. 186 (1962); *Reynolds v. Sims*, 377 U.S. 533 (1964).

7. *Reno v. Bossier Parish School Board*, 117 S.Ct. 1491 (1997).

8. A.J. Nelson, *Emerging Influentials in State Legislatures: Women, Blacks, and Hispanics* (New York: Praeger, 1991).

9. *Shaw v. Reno*, 509 U.S. 630 (1993); *Miller v. Johnson*, 115 S.Ct. 2475 (1995); *Shaw v. Hunt*, 116 S.Ct. 1894 (1996); *Bush v. Vera*, 116 S.Ct. 1941 (1996).

10. Federal Court Involvement in Redistricting Litigation, *Harvard Law Review* 878 (January 2001).

11. *Abrams v. Johnson*, 117 S.Ct. 1925 (1997); *Lawyer v. Department of Justice*, 117 S.Ct. 2186 (1997).

12. *Hunt v. Chromartie*, 532 U.S. 234 (2001).

13. D.G. Savage, High Court Flexible on Redistricting, *State Legislatures* 27 (June 2001): 21.

14. J.L. Sundquist, *Constitutional Reform and Effective Government*, rev. ed. (Washington, DC: Brookings Institution, 1992), 144–198.

15. State Legislative Term Limits, U.S. Term Limits Home Page, *http://www.termlimits.org/Current_Info/State_TL/index.html*; accessed June 2002.

16. Local Term Limits, U.S. Term Limits Home Page; accessed June 2002.

17. See State Legislative Term Limits, U.S. Term Limits Home Page. See also A. Greenblatt, Term Limits: Crash Course, *Governing Magazine* (November 2001), *http://www.governing.com/archive/2001/nov/term.txt*. It is interesting to note that Idaho, which had passed term limit legislation in 1994, repealed term limits in 2002. The Oregon term limits law was found to be unconstitutional in 2001.

18. *U.S. Term Limits, Inc. v. Thornton*, 115 S.Ct. 1842 (1995).

19. M. Katches and D.M. Weintraub, The Tremors of Term Limits, *State Legislatures* 23 (March 1997): 21–25.

20. Greenblatt, Crash Course.

21. J.A. Karp, Explaining Public Support for Legislative Term Limits, *Public Opinion Quarterly* 59 (1995): 373–391.

22. Council of State Governments, *Book of the States, 2000–2001 Edition* (Lexington, KY: Council of State Governments, 2000): 70–71.

23. L.W. Arnold, R.E. Deen, and S.C. Patterson, Friendship and Votes: The Impact of Interpersonal Ties on Legislative Decision Making, *State and Local Government Review* 32 (2000): 142–147.

24. M.E. Jewell and M.L. Whicker, *Legislative Leadership in the American States* (Ann Arbor: University of Michigan Press, 1994).

25. R.A. Clucas, Principal-Agent Theory and the Power of State House Speakers, *Legislative Studies Quarterly* 26 (May 2001): 319–338.

26. Included in the 27 is Nebraska, which has a unicameral legislature, and Maine and Minnesota, which had independent governors as of 2000. Data on legislatures from Council of State Governments, *Book of the States*, 70–71; Data on governors from National Governors Association, The Governors, Political Affiliations, and Terms of Office, 2002 (*www.nga.org*), and K. Barrett and R. Greene, Grading the States 2001, *Governing* (February 2001).

27. C.W. Cox and S. Kernell, eds., *The Politics of Divided Government* (Boulder, CO: Westview Press, 1991).

28. G. Goodwin, Jr., *The Little Legislatures: Committees of Congress* (Amherst: University of Massachusetts Press, 1970).

29. Council of State Governments, *Book of the States*, 70–71.

30. Council of State Governments, *Book of the States*, 70–71.

31. G.S. Gryski, The Influence of Committee Position on Federal Program Spending, *Polity* 23 (1991): 443–459.

32. Council of State Governments, *Book of the States*, 66–68.

33. S. Streeter, *Continuing Appropriations Acts: Brief Overview of Recent Practices, CRS Report for Congress* (Washington, DC: Congressional Research Service, January 11, 2002).

34. See R.T. Meyers, Late Appropriations and Government Shutdowns: Frequency, Causes, Consequences, and Remedies, *Public Budgeting & Finance* 17 (Fall 1997): 25–38.

35. Council of State Governments, *Book of the States*, 83–84.

36. A Chadha, et al., The Consequences of Independence: Functions and Resources of State Legislative Fiscal Offices, *State and Local Government Review* 33 (Fall 2001): 202–207.

37. J.D. King, Changes in Professionalism in U.S. State Legislatures, *Legislative Studies Quarterly* 25 (May 2000): 327–343.

38. C. Mahtesian, The Sick Legislature Syndrome, *Governing* 10 (February 1997): 16–20.

39. J. Shear, Power Loss, *National Journal* 28 (1996): 874–878.

40. R.L. Bland and I.S. Rubin, *Budgeting: A Guide for Local Governments* (Washington, DC: International City/County Management Association, 1987).

41. State and Local Government Cost Estimate Act, P.L. 97–108 (1981).

42. Unfunded Mandates Reform Act, P.L. 104–4 (1995).

43. Council of State Governments, *Book of the States*, 106–107.

44. D.R. Snow, Do Legislative Procedures Affect Tax Expenditures?, *Journal of Public Budgeting, Accounting and Financial Management* 11 (1999): 357–385.

45. J.M. Kelly, Fiscal Noting Reconsidered: The Experience of the States with Mandate Cost Estimation, *Public Budgeting and Financial Management* 6 (1994): 1–27.

46. Loftus, The Art of Legislative Politics, 61–75; J. Gill, Formal Models of Legislative/Administrative Interaction: A Survey of the Subfield, *Public Administration Review* 55 (1995): 99–106.

47. E.J. Clynch and T.P. Lauth, eds., *Governors, Legislatures, and Budgets: Diversity across the American States* (New York: Greenwood Press, 1991).

48. K. O'Lessker, The New President Makes a Budget: From Eisenhower to Bush, *Public Budgeting & Finance* 12 (Fall 1992): 3–18.

49. Clynch and Lauth, *Governors, Legislatures, and Budgets*.

50. J.L. Payne, *The Culture of Spending: Why Congress Lives beyond Our Means* (San Francisco: ICS Press, 1991).

51. M. Fiorina, *Congress: Keystone of the Washington Establishment*, 2nd ed. (New Haven: Yale University Press, 1989).

52. J.P. Dobel, Managerial Leadership in Divided Times, *Administration and Society* 26 (1995): 488–514.

53. D. Rosenbaum, Official Forced to Step Down After Testifying on Budget Cut, *New York Times*, March 7, 2002, A22.

54. C.M. Johnson, *The Dynamics of Conflict Between Bureaucrats and Legislators* (Armonk, NY: M.E. Sharpe, 1992).

55. B. Johnson, The OMB Budget Examiner and the Congressional Budget Process, *Public Budgeting & Finance* 9 (Spring 1989): 5–14.

56. R.F. Fenno, Jr., *Power of the Purse: Appropriations Politics in Congress* (Boston: Little, Brown, 1966); S. Horn, *Unused Power: The Work of the Senate Committee on Appropriations* (Washington, DC: Brookings Institution, 1970).

57. *Shapp v. Sloan*, 480 Pa. 449, 391 A.2d 595 (1978); *Thornburgh v. Casey*, 440 U.S. 942 (1979).

58. Wildavsky and Caiden, *The New Politics of the Budgetary Process*, 47–55, 59–64.

59. R.T. Meyers, *Strategic Budgeting* (Ann Arbor: University of Michigan Press, 1994).

60. L.M. Salamon, *The Tools of Government: A Guide for the New Governance* (Baltimore: Johns Hopkins Press, 2002).

61. K.A. Stanford, State Budget Deliberations: Do Legislators Have a Strategy?, *Public Administration Review* 52 (1992): 16–26.

62. G. Abney and T.P. Lauth, The Line-Item Veto in the States, *Public Administration Review* 45 (1985): 372–377; T.P. Lauth, The Line-Item Veto in Government Budgeting, *Public Budgeting & Finance* 16 (Summer 1996): 97–111.

63. J. Alm and M. Evers, The Item Veto and State Government Expenditures, *Public Choice* 68 (1991): 1–15; N. Berch, The Item Veto in the States: An Analysis of the Effects over Time, *Social Science Quarterly* 29 (1992): 335–346; P. Thompson and S.R. Boyd, Use of the Item Veto in Texas, 1940–1990, *State and Local Government Review* 26 (1994): 38–45.

64. R.D. Lee, Jr., State Item Veto Legal Issues in the 1990s, *Public Budgeting & Finance* 20 (Summer 2000): 49–73.

65. C. Bellamy, Item Veto: Dangerous Constitutional Tinkering, *Public Administration Review* 49 (1989): 46–51; Sundquist, *Constitutional Reform and Effective Government*, 281–294.

66. Line Item Veto Act, P.L. 104–130 (1996).

67. P.G. Joyce, The Line Item Veto Act: After the Supreme Court Decision, What's Next?, *Public Budgeting & Finance* 18 (Winter 1998): 3–21.

68. J.D. Aberbach, *Keeping a Watchful Eye: The Politics of Congressional Oversight* (Washington, DC: Brookings Institution, 1990); D. Evans, Congressional Oversight and the Diversity of Members' Goals, *Political Science Quarterly* 109 (1994): 669–687.

69. B.J. Lewis and P.V. Ellefson, Evaluating Information Flows to Policy Committees in State Legislatures, *Evaluation Review* 20 (1996): 29–48.

70. C.C. Lawrence, New Chief Financial Officers Straddle Branches of Power, *Congressional Quarterly Weekly Report* 49 (1991): 2286–2287.

71. K.S. Walton and R.E. Brown, State Legislators and State Auditors: Is There an Inherent Role Conflict? *Public Budgeting & Finance* 10 (Spring 1990): 3–12.

72. H.S. Havens, U.S. General Accounting Office, *The Evolution of the General Accounting Office: From Voucher Audits to Program Evaluations* (Washington, DC: U.S. Government Printing Office, 1990); National Academy of Public Administration, *The Roles, Mission and Operation of the U.S. General Accounting Office* (Washington, DC: U.S. Government Printing Office, 1994).

73. L. Denniston, GAO Sues for Access to Cheney Records, *Boston Globe*, February 23, 2002, A1.

74. M.L. Gibson, *Weapons of Influence: The Legislative Veto, American Foreign Policy, and the Irony of Reform* (Boulder, CO: Westview Press, 1992).

75. Council of State Governments, *Book of the States*, 121–123.

76. *Immigration and Naturalization Service v. Chadha*, 462 U.S. 919 (1983).

77. Congressional Review Act, P.L. 104–121 (1996).

78. L.R. Jones, Counterpoint Essay: Nine Reasons Why the CFO Act May Not Achieve Its Objectives, *Public Budgeting & Finance* 13 (Spring 1993): 87–94.

Chapter 9

BUDGET APPROVAL: THE U.S. CONGRESS

The preceding chapter examined the budget approval process across levels and types of government. This chapter examines the special case of Congress, which is of unique importance in the U.S. governmental system and has unique procedures. Whereas Chapter 8 emphasized similarities among governments, this chapter considers the special budgetary processes used by Congress and the problems it faces.

As will be seen in the following discussion, the process by which Congress acts on the budget has become increasingly complex. In one illustration of the complexity, the Congressional Research Service issued a report that included eight single-spaced pages that simply itemized all of the actions that were taken by Congress to pass the budget for fiscal year 2002; that report did not include a listing of the various actions taken by the subcommittees of the House and Senate Appropriations Committees.[1] This chapter tries to bring some clarity to understanding this intricate budget system.

The chapter has four sections. The first section reviews the historical development of the modern budget process, from the passage of the Congressional Budget and Impoundment Control Act of 1974 to the deficit-based budget reforms embodied in the Gramm-Rudman-Hollings reform and the Budget Enforcement Act of 1990. The second section reviews the timetable for the resulting budget process, from presidential budget submission to budget resolution to committee action, including reconciliation, authorizations, and appropriations. The third section chronicles the movement of the federal budget from deficit to surplus and then back to deficit again, by discussing the Omnibus Budget Reconciliation Act of 1993, the Balanced Budget Act of 1997, and developments during the George W. Bush administration (including the tax cut and the war on terrorism). The last section discusses a variety of possible reforms.

Evolution of the Federal Budget Process

The federal budget process has evolved over the past 80 years as it has been used to achieve particular objectives and to solve particular problems. For that reason, understanding this history is crucial to demystifying the budget process. Most of the current procedures result from three sets of laws — the Budget and Accounting Act of 1921, the Congressional Budget and Impoundment Control Act of 1974, and the deficit-based budget reforms (such as Gramm-Rudman-Hollings and the Budget Enforcement Act) that were enacted in the 1980s and 1990s. The first of these laws, the Budget and Accounting Act of 1921, was discussed in Chapters 1 and 6. It had three main purposes. First, it created a requirement that the president submit a budget to Congress each year. Prior to the Budget and Accounting Act, federal agencies submitted their budget estimates directly to Congress. Second, it created the Bureau of the Budget (now the Office of Management and Budget) to assist the president in preparing the budget.[2] Third, it created the General Accounting Office (see Chapter 8), initially to help control agency spending but later to do programmatic and performance audits of federal agencies and programs.[3]

The Congressional Budget and Impoundment Control Act of 1974

An axiom to remember is that Congress conducts its work in committees. One group of committees, as explained in Chapter 8, has responsibility for substantive legislation. Some committees develop authorizing legislation, which establishes departments and agencies and the programs they operate. An *authorization* provides a dollar amount as a ceiling for spending. Approval to commit the government to spend, however, is given through the appropriation process.[4]

Another set of committees provides the wherewithal for the government to operate.[5] The Ways and Means Committee in the House and the Finance Committee in the Senate fashion legislation that generates revenue for the government. In addition to being responsible for tax legislation, these committees are responsible for some substantive measures, such as Social Security and Medicare. They handle legislation permitting increases in the federal debt; such legislation is necessary because the government accumulates debt by spending more than it collects in revenues. Raising the debt is a sensitive matter because members of Congress fear that their votes for debt increases can be cited by their political rivals as evidence of fiscal irresponsibility.

The Ways and Means Committee includes about 40 of the 435 members of the House, and the Finance Committee includes about 20 of the 100 members of the Senate. The number of seats held by each party on the committees is generally proportional to total party membership in the chambers.

Discretionary (non-entitlement) spending is under the aegis of the Appropriations Committee in each house.[6] There are more than 60 members on the House committee and approximately 30 on the Senate committee. The spending side of the budget is divided among 13 subcommittees in the House and the Senate that report out appropriation bills. Appropriations permit agencies to commit the government to expenditures, with some spending occurring in subsequent budget years as a result of contracts signed in the current year.

Starting in the 1940s, two major problems with this process became abundantly apparent. First, because Congress dealt with the budget through a variety of bills, the budget was handled piecemeal, making it difficult to set overall comprehensive policy. Second, the piecemeal approach meant that various subcommittees, committees, and the two chambers had to exercise discipline over themselves to complete their work in time for the beginning of the fiscal year.

When appropriation bills are not passed on time, agencies financed through the appropriations process no longer have the funds to operate and are forced to shut down. To avoid this situation, Congress passes one or more continuing appropriation bills that permit the affected agencies to operate for a specified time period, usually spending at the same level as they did in the just-completed fiscal year. When the federal government's fiscal year began on July 1, it was common for many or most appropriation bills not to have cleared Congress by the deadline, and agencies often operated for an entire fiscal year with continuing rather than regular appropriations.

Early Reforms and the Emergence of Backdoor Spending. Congress first attempted to deal with these problems by passing the Legislative Reorganization Act of 1946.[7] The law allowed Congress to agree on an overall budget package before detailed tax and spending bills were developed and approved. In 1947, the House and Senate could not reach agreement; in 1948, the chambers reached agreement but ignored it. The law's requirement for an overall budget was ignored in subsequent years.[8] Next, Congress experimented with using a single omnibus appropriation bill as a means of controlling total spending. The process seemed to work well for fiscal year 1951, but neither the Appropriations Committees nor the White House supported its continuation.[9]

During the 1960s and 1970s, the situation was complicated by what became known as *backdoor spending*, in which spending authority was provided outside of the appropriation process.[10] Backdoor spending may take several forms, including direct actions by substantive committees, such as contract authorizations that allow agencies to commit the government to spend and later may force the Appropriations Committees to provide the necessary funds. Substantive commit- tees have given agencies borrowing authority, which allows them to borrow from the Treasury and spend debt receipts. Entitlement programs (Medicare and Medicaid, for example) that provide *direct or mandatory spending* constitute anoth- er form of backdoor spending in that the government obligates itself to provide benefits to all qualifying applicants.

The effect of backdoor spending was that virtually all committees in Congress came to play important roles in financial decisions, with no mechanism existing to coordinate their diverse activities. Many observers and participants believed that the budget was becoming increasingly uncontrollable, meaning that, barring any major readjustment in commitments to programs, much of the budget could not be altered in a given year. Contributing to this situation were multiyear gov- ernment contracts with government suppliers, multiyear grants to state and local governments, entitlement programs, and interest on the national debt.[11] As a means of controlling spending, President Nixon vetoed appropriation bills on the grounds that they included too much spending, but that action pleased neither Congress nor the agencies that were covered by the bills. Later in his administra- tion, Nixon went ahead and signed the bills but refused to spend all of the money, a process known as *impoundment*. The lack of a coordinating mechanism for the budget, combined with a desire to limit impoundments, led to passage of the Congressional Budget and Impoundment Control Act of 1974.[12]

The 1974 Budget Reform. Many objectives underlie the 1974 reform legislation.[13] One goal was to provide Congress with a means for controlling the budget as a whole, namely, linking appropriation bills with each other and linking these with revenue measures. Controlling the budget as a whole was seen as essential if Congress was to influence economic policy. Resolving conflict between Congress and the president was another important objective that required dealing with the impoundment problem. Members of Congress wished to assert their policy-mak- ing role vis-à-vis the presidency. A process was needed by which Congress could complete its work on the budget by the beginning of the fiscal year.

Taken as a whole, the Budget Act of 1974 had four main effects. First, it creat- ed a new mechanism, the budget resolution, to express the overall will of Congress on budget issues. Second, it created the Budget Committees to marshal the budget resolution though Congress. Third, it created the Congressional Budget Office, a new agency intended to provide Congress with information on the budget and the economy. Finally, it established a new procedure for dealing with presidential impoundments.[14]

The Budget Resolution. Under the procedures established by the Budget Act of 1974, Congress would adopt a concurrent budget resolution that established the overall outline of the budget (a concurrent resolution is an action that is taken by both houses of the Congress that does not require the president's signature). The resolution would represent a "blueprint" for the budget, showing aggregate budget numbers — revenues, budget authority (the authority to commit the government to spend money), outlays (the actual spending of funds out of the Treasury), the overall target (budget deficit or surplus, if any), and government debt.

Following passage of the concurrent resolution in the spring, Congress then reverted to its old procedures. Committees in Congress needed to adopt individual pieces of legislation affecting revenues and spending within the constraints imposed by the budget resolution. Subcommittees of the Appropriations Committees considered specific appropriation bills, and the revenue committees considered their portion of the budget. To allow for accommodating changes in policy, a second resolution was to be adopted by September 15. That resolution could be used for *reconciliation*, a process in which committees were instructed to adjust spending and revenue measures upward or downward to conform with the overall budget plan. The beginning of the fiscal year was shifted from July 1 to October 1, thereby giving Congress three additional months for its annual budgetary work.

The Budget Committees. To provide for coordination among the various components of Congress, the 1974 law established House and Senate Budget Committees, whose members are representatives from the chambers' leadership and relevant committees — the four major money committees and the substantive committees that provide authorizations. As of 2003 (108th Congress), there were 43 members on the House Budget Committee and 23 on the Senate Budget Committee. The Budget Committees were to serve two functions. First, they had jurisdiction over the development of the budget resolution itself, putting them in the center of macro-level budget policy. Second, they were to serve as watchdogs, making sure that legislation was not substantially at variance with the resolution, although they lacked authority to overrule other committees. The resolution could be enforced through *points of order*, which would make legislation not consistent with the resolution more difficult to enact.

The Congressional Budget Office. The law also provided Congress with additional staff support by creating the Congressional Budget Office (CBO) to serve as overall staff to the Budget Committees, the other four money committees, and any other committees or individuals in Congress that need assistance in the area of budgeting. CBO's charge was to serve the Congress in a nonpartisan manner, presenting "just the facts" and not providing policy recommendations. It was to:

- Develop the budget baseline (a current services estimate) that would prove to be the starting point for the resolution;

- Estimate the costs of proposed legislation; and
- Conduct policy research on issues before Congress.[15]

The CBO currently has a staff of about 230. It has had six directors from its creation through 2003 — Alice Rivlin, Rudolph Penner, Robert Reischauer, June O'Neill, Dan Crippen, and Douglas Holtz-Eakin.

Impoundment Control. Prior to the passage of the 1974 legislation, the Nixon administration claimed it was simply following in the footsteps of virtually every president since Thomas Jefferson in deciding not to spend all of the funds that were appropriated.[16] The Anti-Deficiency Act of 1950, allowing the executive to establish agency reserves in the apportionment process (see Chapter 10), was used as further justification for impounding monies.[17]

Not only did the Nixon administration use impoundment to control total spending, but the process also was used to halt spending on grant programs that the president wanted consolidated into block grants (see Chapter 14). Several court suits were filed, which generally were decided in favor of releasing funds, but the Supreme Court never addressed the issue of whether the president has the constitutional power to impound monies.

The Congressional Budget and Impoundment Control Act represented a compromise between the legislative and executive branches, albeit one that the Nixon administration was forced to accept. Two forms of impoundments were permitted: *rescissions* and *deferrals*. When in the judgment of the president part of or all funds of a given appropriation were not needed, a rescission proposal was to be made to Congress; the rescission would not take effect unless approved by Congress within 45 working days. The other type of impoundment, deferral, was a proposal to delay obligations or expenditures. Like rescissions, deferral proposals had to be submitted to Congress, but they became effective unless either the House or the Senate passed a resolution disapproving them.

The impoundment process was dealt a major blow by the Supreme Court in *Immigration and Naturalization Service v. Chadha* (1983), which prohibited most uses of the legislative veto (see Chapter 8).[18] In effect, the 1975 law had given the president a form of item veto coupled with a legislative veto, in which Congress had an opportunity to veto actions taken by the president, but those provisions were nullified by the *Chadha* decision. The president, then, has been forced to request congressional action on policy rescissions and deferrals. The *Chadha* decision did not deal with the constitutionality of the item veto, a topic addressed later in this chapter.

The Arrival of Large Deficits, 1981–1985

The Budget Act of 1974 established procedures and institutions to govern priority-setting in the Congress, but was largely silent concerning budget outcomes. That is, no assumptions were made about the appropriate size of the federal budget or budget deficit. The focus of the budget process changed substantially in the 1980s, however, largely in response to the unprecedented large deficits ushered in during the administration of President Ronald W. Reagan.[19] Reagan came into office in January 1981 following a major victory at the polls during the previous November. The 1980 election created a phenomenon not seen since the 83rd Congress of 1953 — the Senate dominated by a Republican majority, the House remaining under the control of the Democrats, and a Republican president. Reagan submitted a set of budget proposals that provided for severe budget cuts in domestic programs, a shift toward the use of block grants to state and local governments (see Chapter 14), an increase in defense spending, and a massive set of cuts in the personal income tax that became law in the Economic Recovery Tax Act of 1981.[20] Although the House of Representatives was under the control of the Democrats, Reagan was so popular that few political leaders dared to speak out against his recommended policies.

During the early Reagan years, OMB began to play an increasingly important role.[21] Previously, it had the job of making overall presentations on the budget before congressional committees, but the defense of specific recommended appropriations was left to the affected departments. After Reagan's election, major realignments in policies were being recommended on both the revenue and the expenditure sides of the budget, and the defense of these recommendations became the job of OMB.[22]

The Deficit. A cloud soon developed that ended the euphoria of early 1981: The budget deficit began to grow at an alarming rate.[23] As early as 1983, Reagan budget director David Stockman famously predicted "$200 billion deficits as far as the eye can see."[24] The administration had championed the 1981 massive tax cuts as a means of stimulating the economy and thereby increasing revenues. The economy *was* stimulated — but not enough to avoid large deficits. Subsequently, Congress used various tactics to escape having to vote on budget resolutions that would show the budget badly out of balance and avoided voting directly on increases in the federal debt by embedding the provision in an overall budget package. The debt limit had to be raised to $1.1 trillion in 1981 and $2.1 trillion in 1985.

Stalemate. Substantive issues were partially to blame for Congress's inability to adhere to the prescribed timetable. During these years, President Reagan took a firm stand on priorities. He wanted the tax cuts that had been approved in the 1981 law, wanted a buildup in defense capability, insisted that programs such as Social Security be protected from budget cuts, and at the same time sought a balanced budget.[25] All of those objectives simply could not be met simultaneously. If the budget were to be brought into balance by reducing its unprotected areas, which included an array of social programs such as Aid to Families with

Dependent Children, decimation of the remaining part of the federal government would be required. As a consequence, a stalemate between the president and Congress developed, with the two occasionally reaching agreement on actions that only marginally improved the situation.

Reconciliation. As noted earlier, reconciliation was intended to provide in one resolution directed guidance to committees on how they should alter authorizing, taxing, and spending legislation. The process was envisioned as coming at the end of the budget approval phase. However, in the years following the 1974 reforms, the House and Senate Budget Committees were reluctant to use reconciliation because it would have been seen as an infringement on the domains of powerful committees and as a personal affront to the committee chairs.

The reconciliation process was used for the first time in 1980, the last year of the Carter administration, and from that time forward it became a prominent feature of congressional budgeting.[26] Significantly, reconciliation was used early in the 1981 approval process, with the bill clearing Congress in July rather than in September, as originally intended. Early action was needed to give affected committees sufficient time to adhere to the reconciliation instructions, such as reducing amounts in a given appropriation bill. The current use of reconciliation is discussed below as a part of the discussion of the general budget timetable.

Controllability and Policy Making. The deficit situation during the 1980s imposed constraints on Congress in regard to what it could and could not fund. The Reagan administration proposed numerous program cuts that were unpopular in Congress. While Congress had every right to reject the president's recommendations, in rejecting the proposed savings and trying to avoid adopting a budget more out of balance than that recommended by the president, Congress was forced to find offsetting measures to raise revenues, cut expenditures, or both.

The result was a tendency to impose across-the-board budget cuts on programs. As a consequence, programs became smaller and smaller; advocates of programs struggled to maintain the existence of programs no matter how small they might become. "Staying alive" became an objective, as it would be extremely difficult to revive a program once cut out of the budget. Whether Congress made substantive policy during this period is difficult to determine.[27] While what Congress approved is different from what Reagan recommended, that does not necessarily mean Congress had a great influence on policy. It should be understood, of course, that each branch takes the other into account when advocating policy.

Impact on Departments. The uncertainty of a department's programs, given recommended cuts by the president, is unsettling; the uncertainty is compounded when Congress delays taking action and resorts to continuing appropriation bills.

Congressional budgeting problems resulted in workers being briefly sent home in both November 1981 and October 1986. In numerous other cliffhangers, Congress narrowly met a deadline before workers had to be sent home for lack of government funding. Such crises are administratively disruptive and increase citizen discontent with government.

The Gramm-Rudman-Hollings Era, 1985–1990

The situation came to a head in the latter part of 1985. Democrats agreed with Republicans and representatives agreed with senators that the deficit situation had become intolerable. The White House did not exhibit the same level of concern but concurred that something should be done to remedy the situation.

By October 1, 1985, the beginning of the fiscal year, not a single appropriation bill had cleared Congress; a stopgap continuing appropriation bill was passed to keep the government operating. The budget resolution had been adopted on August 1 despite the official deadline of May 15. By November, both the stopgap appropriation bill and the debt-limit ceiling were expiring, forcing another stopgap appropriation bill and an increase in the debt ceiling to be rushed through Congress.

Enactment of the Law. It was in this politically charged atmosphere that Congress adopted the Balanced Budget and Emergency Deficit Control Act of 1985.[28] The chief authors were Senators W. Philip Gramm (Republican of Texas), Warren B. Rudman (Republican of New Hampshire), and Ernest F. Hollings (Democrat of South Carolina). As an indication of how Congress had changed, both Gramm and Rudman were serving their first terms in the Senate. In an earlier time, only more senior senators would have authored legislation of such importance.

The main objective of Gramm-Rudman-Hollings was simple: to reduce the size of the budget deficit annually until expenditures were in balance with revenues. Target figures were set, and if the president and Congress could not reach agreement on a budget package that met the target figure for a given fiscal year, then automatic across-the-board reductions in expenditures were to occur — a process known as sequestration. Senator Rudman described the law as "a bad idea whose time has come."[29]

Legal Challenge and Revision. As soon as the law was enacted, it was challenged in court. The case was brought on appeal to the Supreme Court, which ruled in July 1986 that one key provision violated the Constitution.[30] The comptroller general, who heads the General Accounting Office and as such is an officer of Congress, was found to have been granted executive powers in violation of the Constitution.

After much debate, Congress in September 1987 adopted the Balanced Budget and Emergency Deficit Control Reaffirmation Act, which modified the original Gramm-Rudman-Hollings legislation.[31] In the interim between the Supreme Court's ruling and the 1987 revisions, the Republicans lost control of the Senate in the November 1986 elections. When Congress convened in January 1987, the Democrats controlled both chambers while the White House was still occupied by President Reagan.

Timetable. Gramm-Rudman-Hollings, as amended, provided a new timetable for Congress to act on the budget and set new target figures for annual budget reductions until the budget was supposed to be balanced in fiscal 1993. The Gramm-Rudman-Hollings process began with the president's submission of the budget in early January. Provisions were made for calculating a baseline, which is analogous to current services calculations. The baseline projects budget authority, outlays, revenues, and the resulting unifed budget deficit or surplus for the budget year and subsequent ones. Congress then was to prepare its budget resolution in response to the president's recommendations. Reconciliation was to be completed in June, after which the president was to prepare a midsession budget due in July.

Sequestration. Gramm-Rudman-Hollings created a new procedure — called *sequestration* — that was to impose budget reductions if the procedures were not followed. Some cuts were to be taken from appropriated spending and some from mandatory spending. Of the appropriated cuts, half were apportioned to defense and the other half to domestic programs. On the mandatory side, special rules applied to some domestic programs, such as Medicare and guaranteed student loans; the rules generally limited the severity of sequestration. Other programs, projects, and activities (PPAs) were totally protected from sequestration. These included the basic retirement program under Social Security, Aid to Families with Dependent Children, civil service retirement funds, and the like. The budgets of Congress and the courts were subject to sequestration.

Gramm-Rudman-Hollings was overtaken by events in 1987. Less than a month after Congress passed the Reaffirmation Act of 1987, the stock market crashed. On Tuesday, October 19, the Dow Jones Industrial Average dropped 23 percent (508 points), a greater drop than the 13 percent decline on October 28, 1929.[32]

The crash, as would be expected, startled private and public sector leaders. Although a feared depression did not materialize, the situation served as a catalyst to force an agreement on budget deficit reduction. In November a two-year agreement was reached by the president and Congress on cutting the deficit, but by no means eliminating it. After four stopgap measures, Congress on December 22 passed a huge continuing appropriation bill, along with a reconciliation bill, for the remainder of the fiscal year.

Gramm-Rudman-Hollings and the 1987 budget accord contributed to the trend toward centralization mentioned earlier. Both provided for decision making to be handled by central players, with lesser figures being told what the parameters of the budget would be.

The 1980s closed without Gramm-Rudman-Hollings having appreciably affected the overall budget deficit situation of the government.[33] In fact, the Gramm-Rudman-Hollings targets were routinely met by basing presidential budgets and congressional budget resolutions on unrealistically optimistic economic assumptions. Nothing in the act required the president and the Congress to do anything when (invariably) these projections did not come true.

The 1990 Budget Summit and the Budget Enforcement Act

President George H. W. Bush was elected in 1988 and almost immediately faced a rapidly deteriorating budget outlook. While the process limped along under the Gramm-Rudman-Hollings act during 1989, by late summer 1990 the budget situation had reached another crisis stage. If Congress were to live within the constraints imposed by Gramm-Rudman-Hollings, it would have required a massive reduction in the deficit in a single year. Because this result was not credible or possible, political leaders of both parties became convinced that another approach to deficit reduction was necessary. A budget "summit" was held between Bush administration officials and key members of Congress in late 1990, which ultimately resulted in the passage of the Omnibus Budget Reconciliation Act of 1990 (OBRA 1990). OBRA 1990 included a combination of revenue increases, reductions in mandatory spending, and budget enforcement procedures estimated to reduce cumulative deficits by almost $500 billion between fiscal year 1991 and fiscal year 1995.[34]

The Budget Enforcement Act. The Budget Enforcement Act, which was established by Title XIII of OBRA 1990, provided for a new budget process that officially only temporarily replaced Gramm-Rudman-Hollings. The 1990 law shifted emphasis away from fixed annual targets for the budget deficit. In effect, it was based on the premise that Congress had little control over the total annual deficit and that the emphasis should therefore be on those areas over which control was possible. Entitlement program expenditures were allowed to fluctuate according to shifts in the eligibility pools. The law also exempted the budget from emergencies. The Persian Gulf War and the bailout of failed savings and loan institutions were to fall under this heading.[35] Spending limits, or caps, were set for the discretionary portion of the budget. These caps were considered to be reductions in the deficit because they did not allow discretionary spending to grow as fast as inflation.

The Budget Enforcement Act established so-called *firewalls* for discretionary spending, separating the three areas of defense, international aid, and domestic spending. Spending caps were set for each area for fiscal 1991, 1992, and 1993, and overall budget caps were set for 1994 and 1995. The significance of the firewalls was that each area was protected from possible budget cuts in response to budget increases in one of the other areas. For instance, the rules prevented defense advocates from trying to avoid cuts by proposing extra cuts in domestic programs. When the Soviet Union crumbled and Eastern European nations dismantled their communist governments, the existence of a single cap after 1994 allowed the targets to be reached through cuts in the defense budget (the "peace dividend").

The BEA also created a *pay-as-you-go* (PAYGO) process affecting laws governing revenues and entitlement programs. The PAYGO system required that, in a given Congress, the overall effect of policies that would expand entitlement spending or decrease revenues relative to the baseline should be deficit-neutral. In practice, it was intended to focus attention not only on the cost of the policy change but also on tradeoffs with existing tax or spending programs. PAYGO gave an advantage to those programs already budgeted and made difficult the inclusion of new or expanded initiatives. The Budget Enforcement Act, along with its companion the Omnibus Budget Reconciliation Act of 1990, were successful inasmuch as they limited the growth in programs, but they were not intended to eliminate the annual deficit and had no such effect. The laws successfully kept the budget process under control through the 1992 presidential election, a primary objective of many political leaders. Members of Congress came to the realization that whatever proposals they wished to advance, a price was to be placed on them. Neither tax cuts nor spending increases could be advocated without taking into account their effects on the overall deficit.

The Resulting Congressional Timetable

When put together, these four laws — the Budget and Accounting Act, the Budget Act of 1974, Gramm-Rudman-Hollings, and the BEA — prescribe the rules and the timetable for enacting the federal budget each year. This section of the chapter summarizes the steps in the budget process as a chronology of events. Each year, the budget process begins (not quite in earnest, but it begins) with the president's budget submission in early February. It continues (with luck) only until October 1, with all appropriations enacted prior to the start of the fiscal year. More frequently, the process continues beyond October 1, as one or more bills fail to become law by the statutory deadline. **Table 9-1** shows the timetable for budgetary action as applied to the fiscal year 2003 budget process.

Submission of the President's Budget Request

As noted in Chapter 6, chief executives submit their budget proposals hoping that the legislature will "rubber stamp" the plans, but expecting (except in cases where the legislature is very weak) that significant changes will be made. Congress is an extremely strong and professional legislative body, so the president's budget is viewed as only the "first shot" in what is almost invariably an annual budgetary war. The law provides that a president submit his budget to Congress no later than the first Monday in February. In practice, this schedule has been complied with except for cases where new presidents have just taken office on January 20. In this case, OMB normally submits current services estimates by the February deadline, and the new president submits policy proposals, in the form of amendments to the budget, within two months.

| Table 9–1 | Federal Budget Process Timetable, Fiscal Year 2003 |

Date	Action to Be Completed
Between the first Monday in January and the first Monday in February	President transmits the budget, including a sequester preview report
Six weeks later	Congressional committees report budget estimates to Budget Committees
April 15	Action to be completed on congressional budget resolution
May 15	House consideration of annual appropriation bills may begin
June 15	Action to be completed on reconciliation
June 30	Action on appropriations to be completed by House
July 15	President transmits mid-session review of the budget
August 20	OMB updates the sequester preview
October 1	Fiscal year begins
15 days after the end of a session of Congress	OMB issues final sequester report, and the president issues a sequester order, if necessary

Source: Reprinted from The Budget System and Concepts, *Budget of the United States Government Fiscal Year 2003: Analytical Perspectives* (Washington, DC: U.S. Office of Management and Budget, 2002), 434.

The Budget Resolution and Reconciliation

Congress responds to the president's budget request by producing its overall plan for the budget, in the form of its budget resolution. As noted earlier, the budget resolution, created as a coordinating mechanism by the 1974 Budget Act, serves as the overall blueprint for the budget. It also may result in reconciliation, an optional process used to make changes in revenues and mandatory spending.

The Budget Resolution. Under the current timetable, Congress is to complete work on the budget resolution by April 15 of each year. The groundwork for the development of the budget resolution is typically done by CBO, whose annual report *The Budget and Economic Outlook* presents baseline budget estimates 10 years into the future.[36] This is designed to give Congress a reasonable idea of the starting point for its deliberations. The budget resolution ultimately includes aggregate budget targets (total revenue, total budget authority, and the like), functional budget targets, and allocations of budget authority and revenue authority to congressional committees. Committees are not permitted to exceed these targets — called *Section 302(a) allocations* — and face procedural points of order on the House and (particularly) Senate floor if they attempt to do so.[37]

The budget resolution, in practice, is a tricky annual spring ritual in which the House and Senate Budget Committees must each work with other committees and members to forge an agreement that will withstand later challenges as the details of the budget are prepared. In many years, the budget resolution has not been adopted by the statutory deadline because of difficulties in reaching agreement within one house or (in particular) between both houses. An extreme version of this problem would be the failure to adopt a budget resolution at all; for example, no budget resolution was enacted for either fiscal year 1999 or fiscal year 2003.[38] The current budget timetable provides that, if the Congress has not enacted a budget resolution prior to May 15, the appropriation committees can begin to act on appropriation bills without any limits that would have been imposed by the budget resolution.

Reconciliation. Reconciliation, an optional procedure, has been used since 1980 primarily during years when some major change is anticipated affecting either mandatory spending or revenues. When the procedure is used, reconciliation instructions are included in the budget resolution that will tell committees to produce legislation that has the effect of reducing spending and increasing revenues.[39] At least six major observations can be made about the use of reconciliation.

1. The size and complexity of these bills defy individual comprehension. When these bills are assembled, even the members of the originating committees may not be familiar with all the details spread across hundreds of pages.

2. Large bills are open invitations to pork barrel politics. Some members will succeed in adding pet projects or programs that, if required to stand by themselves for approval, might not be accepted by Congress.

3. Large bills place presidents at a distinct disadvantage in that they must either accept or reject the bills in their entirety. On the other hand, reconciliation bills differ from appropriations in that they do not need to pass, and Congress has sometimes been hard-pressed to get the president to go along with them on reconciliation.

4. Large bills are compatible with congressional desires to avoid blame. Members of the House or Senate cannot be held accountable for their votes supporting any one aspect of a bill, because they can say they felt compelled to vote for the bill even though it admittedly was flawed in numerous respects.

5. The use of large bills and Congress's preoccupation with budgeting in the 1980s contributed to centralization of decision making at a time when Congress had been democratized. Power was redirected to those members of Congress most closely associated with the budget process. Further, because reconciliation bills cannot be filibustered, some have argued that they have changed the operations of the Senate in a way that no longer gives sufficient protection to legislative minorities.[40] In fact, the protections offered by reconciliation caused the George W. Bush administration to consider the use of multiple reconciliation bills as a means to ease passage of its legislative agenda (including tax cuts, which were passed as a result of reconciliation) without the normal hurdles that such changes would face, particularly in the Senate.[41]

6. Sometimes members of the Appropriations Committees have expressed concern that their powers are diminished through the reconciliation process, which is under the direction of the Budget Committees. In reality, reconciliation involves other members of Congress besides those who serve on the House and Senate Budget Committees. In working out a conference bill between the two chambers, the numerous subconference committees created include conferees who are not members of either the House or Senate Budget Committees. Nevertheless, the Appropriations Committees see the situation as centralizing power in the hands of the Budget Committees.

The Authorization Process

Theoretically, federal programs must be authorized and appropriated. Authorizations play an important role in federal budgeting. They establish or change federal programs, and they create the terms and conditions under which those programs operate. Authorizations can be provided for one year (as is common for defense programs), for multiple years (the Congress passes an agriculture authorization — or "farm bill" — every four to five years), or permanently (many mandatory spending programs). In the case of mandatory spending programs, authorizations provide spending directly. Major entitlement programs are authorized and appropriations are provided simultaneously. An entitlement such as Social Security, for example, is created by an authorization and the authorization itself creates the obligation for the federal government to spend money that goes to program beneficiaries.[42] For discretionary spending, the authorization does not provide the appropriation directly, but rather creates a program that may or may not later be funded in the appropriations process. These authorizations typically include what are called "authorizations of appropriations," which are intended to provide guidance to the appropriations committees but are not binding on them. In fact, the appropriations committees routinely enact approprations for programs that have no authorization at all. In fiscal year 2001, Congress appropriated $91 billion for programs whose authorizations had expired.[43]

The Appropriations Process

While the reconciliation process is optional and the authorization process does not happen for all programs in all years, there is nothing optional or episodic about the process of enacting annual appropriations. In fact, enacting the 13 regular appropriations bills is the only budget action that the Congress has to take each year. Without appropriations, federal agencies cannot pay staff or contractors and cannot deliver basic benefits. For this reason, in most years the main focus of the budget process is on the fate of appropriations. The appropriations process itself involves several kinds of activities, including action in committee, action by the full House and Senate, conference committee action, and negotiation with the White House.

Committee Action. Both the House and the Senate have Appropriations Committees. In each house, the Appropriations Committee is divided into 13 subcommittees, which do the substantive work of crafting the detailed bills that fund each individual budget account. Each subcommittee produces a bill that funds various cabinet departments and (sometimes) related agencies. The jurisdiction of the subcommittees (that is, which federal agencies and programs are financed by which subcommittee) are identical between the House and the Senate. **Table 9–2** lists the appropriations subcommittees in both bodies of Congress.

As noted earlier, the Appropriations Committees receive a 302(a) allocation as a part of the budget resolution. It effectively tells the committees how much

Table 9–2 **Appropriations Subcommittees in Houses of Congress**

Agriculture and Rural Development

Commerce, Justice, State and Judiciary

Defense

District of Columbia

Energy and Water

Foreign Operations

Homeland Security

Interior

Labor, Health and Human Services, Education

Legislative Branch

Military Construction

Transportation, Treasury, and Independent Agencies

Veterans, Housing and Urban Development, Independent Agencies

money they have to divide up in aggregate. At an early stage of the process, the committees divide these allocations by subcommittee. These *Section 302(b) allocations* tell the Congress how much money will be available to divide among the various agencies funded as a part of each subcommittee's bill. In other words, the 302(a) allocations establish the size of the appropriated pie, while the 302(b) suballocations tell each subcommittee how large a slice it will have.

After the suballocations have been set, the subcommittees work to produce appropriation bills. Appropriation bills become law in the same way that other bills become law. They must ultimately be passed by both houses in identical form and approved by the president.[44] For appropriation bills, getting to this point involves a lengthy process:

- Subcommittee action — where hearings are held (see Chapter 8) and initial allocations are made to each account in each appropriation bill. Each subcommittee is headed by a chairperson who exercises substantial influence over the operations of agencies under the subcommittee's jurisdiction.

- Full committee action — where typically the actions of the subcommittee are ratified with very little change.

- Floor action — where procedural limitations in each house restrict what amendments may be proposed, and where amendments that add money normally need to be offset by reductions.

- Conference action — where selected members of appropriations subcommittees in each house convene to work out differences between bills.

- Presidential action — where the president exercises his constitutional authority to approve or veto appropriation bills.

The process of getting through these steps is frequently time-consuming, and often one or more appropriation bills does not become law prior to the beginning of the fiscal year. As noted in Chapter 8, there were only three years between 1977 and 2002 when all appropriations cleared the Congress prior to the start of the fiscal year.[45] In a recent example, Congress failed to complete 11 of the 13 fiscal year 2003 appropriation bills before adjourning in November 2002. Appropriations can be a source of great conflict within Congress, or between Congress and the administration. Perhaps the clearest recent case of this conflict was between President Clinton and Congress in 1995 and 1996, leading to two separate lengthy government shutdowns. This case is discussed in more detail in the next section.

Another source of conflict in the appropriations process has to do with items that are added to the budget by Congress but were not in the president's budget. The incentives facing the Congress and the president lead them to pursue different types of priorities. While not confined to the appropriations process, "pork barrel politics" (see Chapter 8) is perhaps most visible in the appropriations process. The pursuit of these special-interest priorities has led to the effort to provide the president with the line-item veto, as discussed in the last section of this chapter.[46]

From Deficit to Surplus to Deficit, 1991–2003

The Omnibus Budget Reconciliation Act of 1990, while it did not promise a balanced budget, was projected to put the budget on a path to reaching that budgetary promised land. But, while a CBO analysis done immediately after the passage of OBRA 1990 projected a deficit of only $29 billion by fiscal year 1995, an analysis done only 13 months later projected a deficit in excess of $200 billion by mid-decade.[47] This deterioration resulted from the effects of economic recession, not because of any policy actions. It meant, among other things, that the deficit was a salient issue in the 1992 presidential campaign, which saw the election of Bill Clinton. The same election also featured the strong showing of third-party candidate Ross Perot, who was able to garner enough votes that Clinton was elected with only 43 percent of the popular vote. Because many of Perot's supporters had been advocates of greater deficit reduction, both political parties needed to appeal to these voters by embracing deficit reduction as a policy goal.[48]

Coming into office in January 1993, President Clinton attempted to follow through on his campaign promise to bring the budget deficit under control. In fact, the Clinton administration embraced deficit reduction as a top priority only after it failed to gain congressional approval of a proposed stimulus package to bolster a weak economy. Critics, who claimed the package was unnecessary because the economy was already on the rebound and because the government could not afford more spending at a time when the deficit was high, were successful in defeating the proposal in the Senate. The administration then turned its attention to a comprehensive deficit reduction proposal.[49]

The 1993 Budget Agreement

The Omnibus Budget Reconciliation Act, adopted in August 1993, was approved by the narrowest of margins — 218 to 216 in the House and 51 to 50 in the Senate (Vice President Gore cast the tie-breaking vote).[50] The measure was passed without any Republican votes (neither on the reconciliation bill nor on the budget resolution that preceded it) and with considerable pressure applied by Republican members to have their Democratic colleagues join them in the opposition. The Clinton administration knew that the vote would be close, so the White House lobbied members with great intensity. As a result, all members had ample opportunity to be involved in the process of adopting the budget, unlike in earlier situations, such as in 1990, when the rank and file complained that the leadership had made all of the decisions.

The 1993 law included four types of actions:

1. Tax increases, particularly increases in individual income taxes for the wealthiest Americans, gasoline taxes, and corporate taxes
2. Spending cuts, notably cuts in Medicare, Medicaid, and defense, but in other programs as well
3. Spending increases, such as for empowerment zones, which are designated urban and rural areas that are provided with increased social services to attract business
4. Tax expenditures, such as tax credits for lower-income workers and tax incentives for businesses operating in empowerment zones

Overall, the law was expected to shrink, but in no way eliminate, the deficit. The spending caps and the PAYGO process from the Budget Enforcement Act were revised and extended through fiscal 1998.[51] Annual deficits under the law were expected to approach $200 billion. Because nearly $500 billion in deficits was to be eliminated over five years, the debt was expected to increase by "only" $1.1 trillion. The total deficit reductions were expected to be equal to or somewhat less than the reductions that resulted from the Budget Enforcement Act of 1990. If the administration wanted to tackle the budget deficit in earnest, then another round of spending cuts and tax increases would be necessary. Further, the budget would need to be revisited if the president and Congress could reach agreement on a plan for revising health care and its financing, a high priority of the first Clinton administration and one that failed to win congressional approval.

The 1995–1996 Debacle

The November 1994 elections set up a situation ripe for intense executive–legislative conflict that would benefit few, harm many, and add to the skepticism of the citizenry about the worthiness of government and its political leaders. The elections produced victories for the Republicans, giving them the control of both the Senate, which had been under Republican control for six years during the Reagan administration, and the House of Representatives, which had not been under Republican rule for 40 years. The House's new Speaker, Newt Gingrich (Republican of Georgia) had championed a Contract with America in the elections. Gingrich, along with a sizable group of newly elected Republican members, felt deeply committed in legislating the various components of the contract.[52] Their extensive package of proposals included a balanced budget amendment to the Constitution, the line-item veto, and the requirement of a three-fifths majority vote to raise taxes. The new House majority was also committed (at least on paper) to shrinking the size of domestic government.

The new Republican Congress and the Democratic president found themselves on an unavoidable collision track. The Republicans managed to produce a reconciliation bill in spring 1995 that included substantial reductions in many federal programs, including a $270 billion reduction over seven years (from the baseline) for Medicare spending.[53] This proposal was projected to result in a balanced budget by fiscal year 2002. When Congress sent this bill to President Clinton, however, he vetoed it as "extreme." Congress responded by holding appropriation bills hostage until or unless Clinton capitulated on reconciliation. In the resulting "train wreck," portions of the government were forced to shut down for two extended periods (November 14 to 19, 1995; and December 16, 1995, to January 8, 1996).[54] People were inconvenienced in innumerable respects, such as not being able to visit the Grand Canyon and not being able to obtain a passport for overseas travel. While the government continued to distribute Social Security payments, processing was halted on new applications for benefits. Businesses in Washington, D.C., which relied on patronage from business travelers and tourists, were hurt financially as people stayed away from the city.

Eventually, the congressional Republicans capitulated; there was no reconciliation bill and a compromise was reached on discretionary spending that did not cut appropriations by as much as was desired by the Republicans. All participants were eager to have the battles resolved, if for only a short period, to avoid having this situation continue into the 1996 presidential election. As it was, Republicans probably were blamed by the electorate for the shutdowns and overall chaos, partially explaining their losses in the House of Representatives, albeit not enough to lose control, and the win by President Clinton in his bid for re-election.[55]

The 1997 Balanced Budget Act

January 1997 ushered in the 105th Congress, with a new collective mindset, and was the beginning of President Clinton's second and final term in office. The congressional leadership realized that a balanced budget could not be achieved without Clinton's support, as it would be virtually impossible to gain enough votes to override any presidential veto. A balanced budget would inevitably involve budget cuts, which are always unpopular with anyone affected by them. As a consequence, Republicans were eager for a bipartisan budget agreement as a means for spreading the blame for cuts in programs. President Clinton, who had earlier championed the idea of a balanced budget, may well have seen 1997 as an opportunity to achieve this goal and consequently to enhance his record of achievement. Working behind the scenes were a group of largely conservative Democrats in the House, who billed themselves as the "Blue Dogs," eager to find some middle-road compromise that would avoid elimination of programs as a budget reduction effort and yet bring spending under control to balance the budget.[56]

In May 1997, President Clinton and the Republican leadership in Congress agreed on the outline for a package of decisions that was supposed to balance the budget by 2002.[57] The agreement was followed by passage of two key laws — the Balanced Budget Act and the Taxpayer Relief Act — both of which were signed by President Clinton at a special ceremony on August 5, 1997. At the ceremony, President Clinton said:

> We come here today, Democrats and Republicans, Congress and President, Americans of goodwill from all points of view and all walks of life, to celebrate a true milestone for our nation . . . . I will sign into law the first balanced budget in a generation — a balanced budget that honors our values, puts our fiscal house in order, expands vistas of opportunity for all our people, and fashions a new government to lead in a new era.[58]

At the same ceremony, Speaker of the House Gingrich said:

> We have proven together that the American constitutional system works, that slowly, over time, we listen to the will of the American people, that we reach beyond parties, we reach beyond institutions, and we find ways to get things done.[59]

The Balanced Budget Act is an immense piece of legislation covering such topics as food stamps, housing, communications, welfare, education, civil service retirement, and much, much more; the Taxpayer Relief Act provides tax benefits for college education, capital gains tax cuts, family tax credits for children, and other relief measures.[60] Cuts in domestic programs were included, and Medicare expenditures were shaved back. Although spending for Medicaid, which serves the needy, was reduced, the cuts were not as severe as some had advocated.

The Balanced Budget Act included important "budget enforcement" provisions. The law made permanent the requirement that budget resolutions cover a five-year period. Discretionary spending limits, to be enforced through sequestration, were extended through fiscal year 2002, as were PAYGO requirements.

The Arrival – and Disappearance – of Surpluses

The Balanced Budget Act projected that the federal budget would move into surplus in fiscal year 2002. The sustained growth of the economy that continued into the late 1990s merely accelerated this timetable. Fueled in large part by increases in federal revenues (which grew by an average of 8.4 percent per year between fiscal years 1995 and 2000), the budget surplus arrived a full four years earlier than had been projected. The federal government ran a unified budget surplus of $69 billion in fiscal year 1998. The surplus, which was the first since fiscal year 1969, grew to $129 billion in 1999 and to $236 billion in 2000.[61] Attention then turned from the question of "How do we get rid of the deficit?" to "What do we do with the surplus?"

George W. Bush assumed the presidency in January 2001. In the same month, the Congressional Budget Office projected cumulative surpluses of $5.6 trillion between fiscal years 2002 and 2011.[62] Three competing uses of the surplus were debated in the spring of 2001. One group wanted to use the surplus to pay down the debt as quickly as possible. A second group advocated spending the surplus on key domestic programs, including (in particular) a prescription drug benefit for Medicare. A third group advocated a tax cut. Many supported a combination of these three approaches.

Ultimately, the Economic Growth and Tax Relief Reconciliation Act (EGTR-RA), a tax cut estimated to amount to $1.3 trillion over 10 years, was enacted by Congress in June 2001.[63] The tax cut alternative was given substantial legs by Federal Reserve Board Chairman Alan Greenspan, who reversed his earlier opposition to tax cuts in light of the large projected surpluses.[64] The bill created a new 10 percent tax bracket, redefined the 15 percent bracket, and effected a gradual reduction in other marginal rates. By fiscal year 2006, the rates for the other brackets will be 25 percent, 28 percent, 33 percent, and 35 percent. In addition, the act will eventually make a number of other changes, such as repealing the current restrictions on itemized deductions and personal exemptions, doubling the child tax credit (to $1,000) over a 10-year period, and phasing out the estate tax over a

10-year period. All estate and "generation-skipping" taxes will be repealed by 2010.[65] The estimate of $1.3 trillion probably understates the magnitude of the cut, since various provisions were "turned off" in later years so as not to exceed the allowable cost of the tax cut under reconciliation. The CBO estimated that, if some future Congress and future president do not allow these provisions to expire (which seems likely), this action would cost another $553 billion between fiscal year 2003 and fiscal year 2012.[66]

The tax cut is one of several factors that have contributed to a substantially deteriorating budget outlook for the federal government. Revenues and spending were affected by the continuing weakness of the economy in 2001. Further, the terrorist attacks of September 11, 2001, occasioned a response that will have continuing budgetary ramifications. CBO estimated that the 10-year effect of increases in discretionary spending already agreed to in the fiscal year 2002 budget would worsen the budget outlook by $550 billion over this period.

By January 2002, CBO had released a revision of its budget outlook that was substantially more pessimistic than its projections made a year earlier. It estimated that cumulative surpluses had declined to $1.6 trillion over the 10 years; this amount represents a total reduction of more than $4 trillion in "lost" surpluses in one year.[67] A CBO estimate done in March 2003 was even more pessimistic, projecting deficits through fiscal year 2007, under current policies (see **Table 9–3**).[68]

In the immediate term, the urgency of the war on terrorism has moved fiscal discipline to the back burner. While from the mid-1980s to the late 1990s the norm of the balanced budget prevailed, no similar fiscal target has emerged to replace it. The budgetary impact of the terrorist attacks has been largely to drive budgetary considerations underground. As an example, a battle that had been brewing over fiscal year 2002 appropriations that some observers felt offered the best chance of a "government shutdown" scenario since 1996 fizzled immediately in light of the need for both parties to appear to work together directly after September 11.[69] Until some consensus is reached on a norm to replace "the balanced budget" as a macrobudgetary goal, the process is likely to remain adrift.[70]

Proposed Reforms and Their Prospects

The Congress, the President, and the nation face a complex set of interwoven problems. The overall fiscal picture is much brighter today than it was in the mid-1990s, but tremendous uncertainty remains concerning budget priorities and the proper role of government.

The movement of the budget from deficit to surplus and back to deficit again has policy makers struggling to establish the correct goals for the budget. In addition, the nation faces what is perhaps a fundamental (and expensive) shift in priorities to confront threats to security both at home and abroad. In the short run, the aftermath of September 11 seems to have given the Defense Department a blank check. However, a perennial question is, How much defense is enough? Defense policy must be rethought given the absence of the threat of nuclear attack by Russia, the potential threat of terrorism, and the instability in particular regions of the world, such as the Middle East, India and Pakistan, and the Korean Peninsula.

The budget also faces a lurking fiscal time bomb: The baby boomers will begin to retire in droves by 2020 and beyond, placing major strains on programs for senior citizens, such as Social Security and Medicare. Mounting costs for entitlements drive up the size of the budget, but the current demands are nothing compared to the demands that an aging population will put on the budget.[71]

Can Congress better organize itself to deal effectively with this daunting set of problems?[72] If Congress's primary role is to set policy and provide leadership in furthering the nation's interests, then do means exist for improving the processes of that august body to help it meet its responsibilities? Since the budget process is at the very center of policy making, it attracts much attention from reformers, raising fundamental questions. For example, how should power be distributed between the leadership and the individual members? Placing power

Table 9–3 Federal Deficits and Surpluses, Fiscal Year 1985 to Fiscal Year 2007

Fiscal Year	Surplus or Deficit	Fiscal Year	Surplus or Deficit
1985	-212	1997	-22
1986	-221	1998	69
1987	-150	1999	125
1988	-155	2000	236
1989	-153	2001	127
1990	-221	2002	-158
1991	-269	2003	-246
1992	-290	2004	-200
1993	-255	2005	-123
1994	-203	2006	-57
1995	-164	2007	-9
1996	-107		

Sources: Fiscal years 1985 through 2001 actual figures are from U.S. Congressional Budget Office, *The Budget and Economic Outlook: Fiscal Years 2003–2012* (Washington, DC: U.S. Government Printing Office, January 2002). Fiscal year 2002 actual and 2003 through 2007 estimated figures are from U.S. Congressional Budget Office, *An Analysis of the President's Budgetary Proposals for Fiscal Year 2004* (Washington, DC: U.S. Government Printing Office, March 2003).

in the hands of those in leadership positions can help facilitate decision making but at the same time can subjugate the voices of individual members, who have been chosen by their voters to represent them.[73] How should responsibilities be distributed between new members and those with seniority? How should power be shared by the two chambers of Congress? To what extent should or must Congress delegate powers to the president and to others in the executive branch of government?[74]

These questions of process cut to the core of any congressional member's future. For example, getting appointed to the "right" committee — any committee in a position to divert funds to one's home district — is considered critical, and any plan to reorganize the committee structure is necessarily regarded as threatening.[75] One view is that Congress will never be able to deal with fundamental problems as long as campaign funds must be obtained largely through contributions from constituent organizations. Those organizations are likely to donate substantial funds only on the condition that members provide pork barrel spending and other immediate benefits.

Budget process reform proposals are hardy perennials in Congress. Many members, convinced that the current process is fundamentally broken, propose changes in budget procedures or institutions as solutions to fiscal problems. There are many more of these proposals than can be catalogued on these pages, but among the most common are reforms that would give the president a line-item veto, would amend the Constitution to require a balanced budget, would reorganize Congress as it deals with the budget, and would convert Congress to a biennial budget process.

The Item Veto

As discussed in Chapter 8, most governors have item-veto power, allowing them to reduce or eliminate line items in appropriation bills. The president of the United States has historically lacked such power. The power could be provided in a statute or, as many would advocate, in an amendment to the Constitution. Ulysses S. Grant may have been the first President to ask for the item-veto power.[76]

Pros and Cons of the Item Veto. One of the main justifications cited for the item veto is that the president needs the authority to reduce or eliminate funding of pork barrel projects that have little merit other than pleasing specific constituent groups of individual members of Congress. However, what constitutes excesses in spending is necessarily a function of one's values and priorities, and the executive branch is not immune from advocating spending for programs and projects of questionable utility. One aspect that is clearly *not* a purpose of the item veto is to reduce the budget deficit. The spending cuts that might be made by a president would be unlikely to have any appreciable effect on total spending.[77]

Critics of the item veto contend that it gives the president an unwarranted increase in power, allowing for presidential policy preferences to supplant congressional preferences. If a president needed to muster senatorial votes for an initiative, he could privately threaten to item-veto favored projects of individual senators. When the White House was controlled by one political party and the Congress by the other, White House priorities might prevail. One can speculate that if Presidents Reagan and George H. W. Bush had been able to wield item-veto power, then several agencies and programs would have been eliminated, such as the Economic Development Administration, the Appalachian Regional Commission, and urban mass-transportation formula grants.

The Rescission Process. Procedures, as initially established by the Congressional Budget and Impoundment Control Act of 1974, provide that the president submit packages of proposed rescissions in appropriations enacted by Congress. Congress has 45 days in which it is in session to approve each package or approve its own set of cuts. Before adopting an appropriation bill, Congress is made aware of what items are likely to be cut by the president; presidential priorities are reported to Congress through budget submissions and statements of administration policy, which indicate White House opposition to provisions in draft appropriation bills. When the president does propose rescissions, a consistent pattern has been that Congress makes greater cuts than recommended by the president, albeit using a different set of priorities to determine which items will be cut.[78]

Enhanced Rescission and the Line Item Veto Act. After decades of debate, the Republican-controlled Congress enacted the Line Item Veto Act of 1996, which was part of the Contract with America. The act took effect in January 1997, giving President Clinton a tool to use against the Congress during the 1997 legislative session. A general consensus exists that a "true" item-veto power could be provided to the president only through a constitutional amendment and, therefore, the 1996 law is best viewed as *enhanced rescission power*. The law gave the president power to cancel three types of provisions: (1) new items of discretionary spending (which, significantly, were defined to include not only items in appropriation bills but also items alluded to in committee reports accompanying these bills); (2) new entitlements or increased entitlement; and (3) tax provisions that would benefit 100 or fewer individuals or corporations. The president was required to veto an entire item and not just reduce an amount, and he could not veto existing entitlement programs and other forms of mandatory spending. Any savings achieved through this process could not be reappropriated for other purposes but rather would be used to reduce the budget deficit. This *lockbox* provision was important to those who wanted the veto power to be used for deficit reduction. The law had a sunset provision, withdrawing this power from the president on January 1, 2005.[79]

In an effort to circumvent the Supreme Court's ban on legislative vetoes (see the earlier discussion of the *Chadha* decision), the 1996 measure provided a convoluted form of veto. The president was to submit a set of proposed budget cuts. Congress then had 30 calendar days, during a time when it is in session, to consider passing a *disapproval bill*. If Congress did not act, the proposed vetoes would take effect. The disapproval bill would be on an expedited schedule but would go through the standard procedure of passage in both houses and, most likely, a conference committee procedure for working out the differences between the houses. The president could then either sign or veto the disapproval bill. A veto of the disapproval bill would mean he was standing behind his original set of decisions to cut items in the budget. Congress could override the president's veto only by a two-thirds vote.

The item veto was first used by President Clinton to cut three items from the Balanced Budget Act of 1997 and the Taxpayer Relief Act of 1997, just five days after signing these laws. The vetoes covered (1) tax shelters for financial service companies, (2) a Medicaid provision that specifically would benefit New York State and New York City, and (3) a tax benefit that would go to a small number of agribusinesses, including large corporations that in his view did not need such a tax advantage. Clinton noted that many items were protected from his veto on the grounds that the White House had an obligation to act in good faith in retaining items that had been explicitly approved as part of the bargaining process with the Republican-controlled Congress.[80] He agreed with suggestions from the press that the vetoed items were relatively minor but noted that he expected more significant vetoes to arise when appropriation bills began to reach his desk for approval.

President Clinton also used the line-item veto power in the appropriations process. By far the most aggressive use of this power was on the military construction appropriation bill, where the President cancelled 38 projects totaling $287 million. Congress used the procedures contained in the act to pass a disapproval bill, which was ultimately vetoed by President Clinton. His veto was overridden by Congress, thereby restoring funding for these projects. Clinton was much more restrained in his use of the veto on other appropriation bills, cancelling only $190 million in total budget authority from those other 12 bills.[81]

The law included a section for judicial review, allowing for members of Congress and others to file suit in the U.S. District Court for the District of Columbia, with its decision being appealable directly to the Supreme Court. Well before President Clinton had an opportunity to use this new set of powers, the law was challenged in court by Senator Robert C. Byrd (Democrat of West Virginia), who had been the law's most outspoken critic, calling it "a malformed monstrosity."[82] The district court agreed with Byrd that the law had unconstitutionally delegated congressional powers to the president. That decision was appealed to the Supreme Court, which ruled on a procedural rather than substantive basis. In *Raines v. Byrd* (1997), the Court decided that Byrd and others lacked *standing*, a condition in which the party bringing suit shows an injury has occurred or is about to occur.[83] The Court found that an injury had not occurred, as the president had not yet exercised the new power granted to him. Standing was said to be especially important in cases involving conflict between two branches of the government — in this case, between Congress and the president.

Ultimately, the constitutionality of the Line Item Veto Act was challenged on its merits by individuals with standing who had suffered injury as a result of its application. In late 1997, two suits were brought — one by the city of New York and the other by the Snake River (Idaho) Potato Growers over Clinton's cancellation of items in the Balanced Budget Act and the Taxpayer Relief Act, respectively. The law was found unconstitutional in U.S. District Court, and in 1998, the Supreme Court, in a 6 to 3 decision, sided with the District Court in the case of *Clinton v. City of New York*.[84] The Court ruled that the act ran afoul of the Presentment clause of the Constitution, because it permitted the president to unilaterally unmake law that had been made by both houses of Congress in concert with the president. The majority argued that providing the president with the kind of power envisioned in the act would require an amendment to the Constitution. Thus, the Line Item Veto Act was relegated to a one-year experiment — a blip on the federal budgeting radar screen.[85]

Proposed Balanced Budget Requirement

A persistent proposal has been for the federal government to adopt a balanced budget requirement.[86] Proponents typically refer to the successful use of this requirement at the state level — all states except Vermont and Wyoming currently require some form of balanced budget.[87] Governors or budget boards in 43 states are required to submit balanced budgets, legislatures in 36 states are required to enact balanced budgets, and 39 states have a requirement for a balanced budget at year's end. In 35 states, the requirement is embedded in the state constitution, with the remaining 13 states having statutory requirements. Note that balanced budget requirements in most states do not preclude borrowing for capital investments, and few state budgets are annually balanced when both current and capital expenditures are taken into account. Many states also have limitations on revenue raising and spending, stemming from the Proposition 13 movement of the 1970s.

A major concern regarding implementation of a balanced budget requirement at the federal level is that the measure might impose unwarranted restrictions in times of economic hardship or national security emergencies.[88] Some form of override mechanism must be included for situations when the federal government needs to spend more to counteract economic recessions and to wage war. For the override to occur, both houses might be required to have votes of 60 percent, two-thirds, or a majority of all members (rather than a majority of those voting).

Having some set of enforcement mechanisms is regarded as essential for successful implementation, although such mechanisms do not exist at the state level, where the balanced budget process is regarded as generally successful. The states, however, have an externally imposed imperative for bringing revenues and expenditures into structural balance: Failing to do so would have an adverse effect on their bond ratings and borrowing costs. Skeptics of congressional abilities to reach agreement on a set of revenue and spending programs that are balanced fear that Congress would resort to "smoke and mirror" techniques that merely give the illusion of a balanced budget. Such devices might include overestimating revenues to be collected and moving some expenditures off-budget so that they would be excluded from official total spending (these are, of course, precisely the kinds of tricks that resulted under Gramm-Rudman-Hollings, the federal government's prior failed experiment with fixed deficit targets). Attempting to prohibit such practices by outlawing them in the constitutional amendment would be cumbersome, and creative minds might always be able to find loopholes in the amendment's language. In addition, detailed provisions in the amendment could create an inflexibility that later might prove detrimental to the nation's best interests.

Critics of the balanced budget proposal contend that it would unduly enhance the powers of the president. A typical requirement of balanced budget proposals is that the president would have to submit a balanced budget, thereby setting the agenda from which Congress might have little latitude to veer. One line of reasoning states that for the proposal to be effective, an item veto for the president would be essential. Another criticism is that an annually balanced budget is not an appropriate goal for federal fiscal policy. The federal government has routinely, and appropriately, engaged in deficit spending during times of recession or when it needs to deal with other emergencies.[89]

Once the budget moved from deficit to surplus in 1998, the interest in a balanced budget amendment waned. But with the reemergence of budget deficits and the potential search for a new consensus for an overall goal of fiscal policy, it is possible that the amendment will surface again.

Proposed Congressional Reorganization

A perennial topic of discussion in Congress is how it could better organize itself to fulfill its responsibilities, especially its budget responsibilities. Important changes did occur as a result of passage of the Legislative Reorganization Acts of

1946 and 1970 as well as other reorganizations that affected either the House or the Senate.[90]

Committees. One typical proposal is to reduce the number of congressional committees and subcommittees. These various bodies create problems in coordination, because their domains often overlap and subject areas are needlessly segmented among committees and subcommittees. Power becomes diffuse, and setting overall policy is complicated by the split jurisdictions. The greater the number of committees, the greater the number of committee assignments members have, meaning that they can easily be scheduled to attend two or more committee meetings at the same time. This problem is even more acute in the Senate, where 100 members must handle the same work that is done by the 435 members in the House.

The large number of committees and subcommittees poses problems for the executive branch as well as for Congress. Agency administrators complain that valuable time is wasted in having to prepare for and testify before these panels. The defense area is particularly subject to comprehensive congressional involvement, with Defense Department officials having to testify before dozens of committees and subcommittees.

The size of committee membership is a related concern. Memberships are often large because members want to be placed on committees of relevance to their home districts and states. However, the larger the committee size, the greater the number of committees on which members serve and the greater the number of meetings they are unable to attend. The result is a proxy system in which another member, often the chair, votes for absent members on the committee.

Although considerable agreement may exist that Congress needs to reduce the number of committees and subcommittees, the task is difficult. Chairing one of these committees provides power, prestige, and perquisites, so any chairperson or other senior member on the committee is likely to defend continuance of the committee and repel efforts to diminish the committee's powers.[91] Members in both houses have historically sought seats on committees dealing with the various aspects of the budget, as a means of gaining power over congressional actions.

One controversial suggestion has been that the budget process could be streamlined by eliminating the two Appropriations Committees and assigning their duties to the committees that handle authorizations. Rather than appropriation bills emanating from one committee, they would arise from the standing substantive committees in each chamber. Critics of this proposal contend that such a reform would worsen the budget situation, because the Appropriations Committees are far more likely to restrict government spending than the substantive committees, which are often seen as having been captured by the executive branch agencies that they oversee. Further, the Appropriations Committees currently wield great power, and they vigorously oppose any efforts to reduce that power. They would not be abolished without a fight.

Other committee-related proposals involve reconfiguring the House and Senate Budget Committees, and possibly even merging them into a joint committee. Another option would be to eliminate these committees on the grounds that they have merely added to the complexity of congressional budgeting, and have recently failed to accomplish their major objective in any event. During the five years between fiscal year 1999 and fiscal year 2003, Congress twice failed to adopt a budget resolution.

Leadership. Strengthening the powers of the Speaker of the House is another possible reform of how Congress conducts its business.[92] One recommendation is to increase the Speaker's power in determining who chairs committees and how long they retain these roles. Increased power would enhance the abilities of the Speaker to coordinate the diverse components of the chamber and develop a unified set of policies but might stifle the independence of individual members.

Term Limits. Growing interest in limiting the length of time a member may serve continuously in Congress is evident.[93] Imposing term limits, as noted in Chapter 8, is seen as a way to remove encrusted members who have lost touch with the real world and infuse "new blood" into the system. However, term limits by themselves would not resolve the serious financial problems facing the government. Term limits, if imposed, would need to be applied to all members: If only some states adopt this approach, their members will have less seniority than those in other states and consequently will have less influence on policy making. In 1995, the Supreme Court ruled that states could not impose qualifications for federal offices beyond what was contained in the Constitution.[94] The Court rejected the view that the Reserve Powers clause of the Tenth Amendment gave states the power to set term limits on congressional elections. The Republicans in Congress have sought to initiate a constitutional amendment that would set term limits but have been unable to gain the necessary two-thirds vote.

Biennial Budgeting

One frequently mentioned proposal is to change over to a biennial budget.[95] Since Congress has such difficulty acting on a budget, why not simplify the problem by requiring action only every other year? The idea of moving the federal government from an annual to a biennial process is not a new one. Representative Leon Panetta (Democrat of California) introduced the first bill proposing such a change in 1977, and the proposal has been more or less an annual entry in the budget reform sweepstakes since then. Most biennial budgeting proposals would have the president submit his budget biennially and would also feature biennial budget resolutions and appropriations. Perhaps the high-water mark for biennial budgeting came in 1993, when both the Joint Committee on the Organization of Congress and Vice President Gore's National Performance Review recommended that the federal government adopt a biennial timetable for the process. Despite this long history of support, however, no bill to create a biennial process has ever passed either the House or the Senate.[96] Biennial budgeting is still a perennial proposal. In fact, the House Rules Committee reported out a bill recommending biennial budgeting in 2001.[97] This bill was not considered on the floor of the House because of intercommittee disputes between the Rules Committee, the Budget Committee, and the Appropriations Committee.[98]

Proponents of biennial budgeting argue that the current annual process features repetitive votes on many fiscal issues that eat up valuable committee and floor time. For example, there may be three votes on the budget for defense — one associated with the budget resolution, one associated with the annual defense authorization bill, and one on the annual defense appropriations bill. Second, in a related issue, supporters note that time spent on budgeting cannot be spent on other activities, particularly detailed oversight of federal programs. In particular, these advocates of a biennial process indicate that the need for Congress to review agency performance under the Government Performance and Results Act necessitates spending more time on such detailed oversight. Third, supporters point to the dismal record of Congress and the president in enacting appropriation bills prior to the start of the fiscal year. Finally, executive branch officials decry the time-consuming nature of the annual process from their perspective. The sequence of developing an agency budget request, having that budget undergo review by the Office of Management and Budget and the president, and justifying the budget to Congress is continuous in an annual process.[99]

There are also numerous arguments offered by opponents of biennial budgets. First, the federal government has a rather checkered history of budget forecasting. Producing a budget every two years would increase the probability that budgets would be based on erroneous information. A two-year budget resolution adopted in April, for example, would be adopted a full 30 months before the end of the second fiscal year of the biennium. The agencies would have begun developing their budgets for that fiscal year at least 10 months prior to the passage of the budget resolution, or more than three years from the end of the second fiscal year of the biennium. Second, opponents argue that the benefits of biennial budgeting (decreased time on budgeting, more time for oversight) are overstated. The biennial process may degenerate into an annual process, given the uncertainties associated with budgeting for a $2 trillion enterprise (Congress already engages in an annual process of adopting supplemental appropriations) and the likelihood that Appropriations Committee members will want to act on the budget every year. Third, an increase in oversight under biennial budgeting would occur only if the current lack of oversight results from a lack of time. Opponents argue that even if members of Congress had more time to do oversight, they would not be likely to do more of it simply because they do not have any incentives to do so. Understanding more about how federal programs work in great detail is not sexy, nor does it offer any specific benefits in terms of helping members get re-elected.[100]

Other Proposed Revisions in the Budget Process

While the previously mentioned changes have been the most frequently debated, they are by no means the only reform proposals put forth. One whole set of reforms, to include more performance information in the budget process, is discussed in Chapter 5. Another reform, to bring more accrual accounting concepts to the federal government, is discussed in Chapter 11. At least three other reforms are also worthy of discussion — automatic continuing resolutions, making the budget resolution into a joint resolution, and capital budgeting.

Automatic Continuing Resolutions. Under this proposed reform, the institution of automatic continuing resolutions for appropriations would become another possible strategy. If Congress failed to pass an appropriation bill, the agencies affected would operate with a continuing appropriation without Congress's having to act. Since congressional failure to act on the budget in a timely fashion has become the norm, the obvious advantage of an automatic continuing resolution is that it would eliminate the crisis handling of appropriation bills. The disadvantage of the proposal is that incentives for Congress to adopt regular appropriation bills would be reduced.[101]

Joint Budget Resolutions. A more far-reaching proposal would eliminate the concurrent nature of budget resolutions, which do not require presidential signature, and substitute a joint resolution or law to be signed by the president.[102] In effect, budget summitry would be employed at the outset of the budget process. The hope is that the president and key congressional leaders would develop an annual budget resolution that all would support, thereby helping to ensure more timely action as the details of the budget are worked out at a later time. Budget summits bind all participants so that a president who endorsed a summit agreement could not later renege when Congress passed appropriation bills in conformance with the agreement. The down side of a joint budget resolution is that conflict would be "front loaded." Obtaining the agreement of both houses without having the president involved has often proved difficult; allowing the president to have a veto over the budget resolution might be the practical equivalent of ensuring that no budget resolution will occur in many years.[103]

Capital Budgeting. Adoption of a capital budgeting system is yet another possibility. It is advocated as a way of helping to put the deficit into perspective, because it would show that much of federal spending is of an investment nature and not simply annual consumption. Capital budgeting presumably would encourage better planning of expenditures. On the negative side, capital budgets could be used to downplay the true magnitude of federal budget deficits and total debt (see Chapter 12). More and more of the budget could be "capitalized" as a method of making desired spending appear to be less costly. Further, if a balanced budget constitutional amendment were adopted, Congress most likely would move capital expenditures off-budget, just as states permit indebtedness for investments but not for operating expenses.[104]

Summary

Congress has an elaborate system for approving the budget. An authorization process exists independently of appropriations. Meanwhile, the House Ways and Means Committee and the Senate Finance Committee have power to deal not only with tax measures but also with some spending. The Appropriations Committees in the two houses operate by developing a series of bills through subcommittees.

The current budget process resulted from several different laws. The Budget and Accounting Act of 1921 prescribes the president's budget process. The Congressional Budget and Impoundment Control Act of 1974 attempted to deal with several problems, including congressional tardiness in adopting the budget, impoundments, and piecemeal handling of the budget. A budget resolution process, Budget Committees, and the Congressional Budget Office were established. The Gramm-Rudman-Hollings law was a failed attempt to bring the deficit under control. Later efforts that coupled "budget summits" with a new change in process, codified in the Budget Enforcement Act, have proved much more successful.

The budget process resulting from these laws has several stages. First, the president submits his budget on or before the first Monday in February. Congress then adopts a budget resolution that establishes a blueprint for the budget. Committee action follows the constraints established by the budget resolution. In some years, reconciliation bills, which make changes to government revenue and entitlement legislation, are enacted. In each year, much of the budget process focuses on the fate of the 13 regular appropriation bills.

During the presidency of Bill Clinton, the budget finally moved from deficit into surplus. The improvement in the budget outlook resulted from a series of legislative actions coupled with the continued strong growth of the economy (fueling an increase in federal revenues). Fiscal year 1998 was the first year since 1969 that the federal government had a budget surplus. These surpluses lasted through fiscal year 2001, but in 2002 a combination of a tax cut advocated by President George W. Bush, a weakening of the economy, and the after effects of the terrorist attacks of September 11, 2001, signaled the return of deficits.

Numerous proposals exist for further revising how the federal government adopts the budget. Major proposals include giving item-veto power to the president, passing a constitutional amendment requiring that the budget be balanced, restructuring congressional committees, amd moving the government to a biennial budget cycle. Other proposals involve establishing automatic continuing resolutions, changing the concurrent budget resolution to a joint resolution or law, and separating the budget into capital and operating components.

Notes

1 J. Murray for the Congressional Research Service, *Budget FY2002: A Chronology with Internet Access, Updated January 17, 2002* (Washington: Congressional Research Service, 2002).

2. S.L. Tompkin, *Inside OMB: Politics and Process in the President's Budget Office* (Armonk, NY: M.E. Sharpe, 1998).

3. J.W. Hughes, General Accounting Office, *International Encyclopedia of Public Policy and Administration*, J.M. Shafritz, ed. (Boulder, CO: Westview Press, 1998), 969–972.

4. L. Fisher, *The Politics of Shared Power: Congress and the Executive*, 2nd ed. (Washington, DC: *Congressional Quarterly Press*, 1987), 91–217; A. Schick, *The Federal Budget: Politics, Policy, Process*, 2nd ed. (Washington, DC: Brookings Institution, 2000), 105–240.

5. J.F. Manley, *The Politics of Finance: The House Committee on Ways and Means* (Boston: Little, Brown, 1970).

6. R.F. Fenno, Jr., *The Power of the Purse: Appropriations Politics in Congress* (Boston: Little, Brown, 1966); H.E. Shuman, *Politics and the Budget: The Struggle between the President and the Congress*, 3rd ed. (Englewood Cliffs, NJ: Prentice-Hall, 1992); A. Wildavsky and N. Caiden, *The New Politics of the Budgetary Process*, 4th ed. (New York: Longman, 2000).

7. Legislative Reorganization Act, ch. 753 (1946).

8. L. Fisher, Experience with a Legislative Budget (1947–1949), in Senate Committee on Government Operations, *Improving Congressional Control of the Budget: Hearings*, Part 2, 93rd Cong., 1st sess. (Washington, DC: U.S. Government Printing Office, 1973), 237–239.

9. R.A. Wallace, Congressional Control of the Budget, *Midwest Journal of Political Science* 3 (1959): 151–167.

10. S.K. Kim, The Politics of a Congressional Budgetary Process: "Backdoor Spending," *Western Political Quarterly* 21 (1968): 606–623; A. Schick, Backdoor Spending Authority, in Senate Committee on Government Operations, *Improving Congressional Control over the Budget: A Compendium of Materials*, 93rd Cong., 1st sess. (Washington, DC: U.S. Government Printing Office, 1973), 293–302.

11. A. Schick, *Congress and Money* (Washington, DC: The Urban Institute Press, 1980).

12. Congressional Budget and Impoundment Control Act, P.L. 93–344 (1974).

13. L. Fisher, Ten Years of the Budget Act: Still Searching for Controls, *Public Budgeting & Finance* 5 (Autumn 1985): 3–28.

14. A. Schick, *The Federal Budget*; P.G. Joyce and R.D. Reischauer, Deficit Budgeting: The Federal Budget Process and Budget Reform, *Harvard Journal on Legislation* 29 (1992): 429–453.

15. D. Crippen, Informing Legislators About the Budget: The History and Role of the U.S. Congressional Budget Office, speech to parliamentary officials of the OECD, Washington, D.C., June 7, 2002.

16. L. Fisher, The Politics of Impounded Funds, *Administrative Science Quarterly* 15 (1970): 361–377.

17. Anti-Deficiency Act, Ch. 510, §3, 34 Stat. 49 (1950).

18. *Immigration and Naturalization Service v. Chadha*, 462 U.S. 919 (1983).

19. P.G. Joyce, Congressional Budget Reform: The Unanticipated Implications for Federal Policy Making, *Public Administration Review* 56 (1996): 317–325.

20. Economic Recovery Tax Act, P.L. 97–34 (1981).

21. B.E. Johnson, From Analyst to Negotiator: The OMB's New Role, *Journal of Policy Analysis and Management* 3 (1984): 501–515; B. Johnson, The OMB Budget Examiner and the Congressional Budget Process, *Public Budgeting & Finance* 9 (Spring 1989): 5–14; Tompkin, 1998.

22. D.S. Stockman, *The Triumph of Politics: How the Reagan Revolution Failed* (New York: Harper & Row, 1986).

23. L.T. LeLoup and J. Hancock, Congress and the Reagan Budgets, *Public Budgeting & Finance* 8 (Autumn 1988): 30–54.

24. A Plea from David Stockman, *Washington Post*, April 20, 1983, A20.

25. D.S. Ippolito, *Uncertain Legacies: Federal Budget Policy from Roosevelt through Reagan* (Charlottesville: University Press of Virginia, 1990).

26. R. Doyle, Congress, the Deficit, and Budget Reconciliation, *Public Budgeting & Finance* 16 (Winter 1996): 59–81.

27. M.L. Mezey, The Legislature, the Executive and Public Policy: The Futile Quest for Congressional Power, *Congress and the Presidency* 13 (1986): 1–20; J. Cooper, Assessing Legislative Performance: A Reply to Critics of Congress, *Congress and the Presidency* 13 (1986): 21–40.

28. Balanced Budget and Emergency Deficit Control Act, P.L. 99–177, Title II, (1985); H.S. Havens, Gramm-Rudman-Hollings: Origins and Implementation, *Public Budgeting & Finance* 6 (August 1986): 4–24; L.T. LeLoup, et al., Deficit Politics and Constitutional Government: The Impact of Gramm-Rudman-Hollings, *Public Budgeting & Finance* 7 (Spring 1987): 83–103.

29. W. Rudman, as quoted in E. Wehr, Congress Enacts Far-Reaching Budget Measure, *Congressional Quarterly Weekly Report* 43 (1985): 2604.

30. *Bowsher v. Synar*, 478 U.S. 714 (1986); Symposium: *Bowsher v. Synar, Cornell Law Review* 72 (1987): 421–597.

31. Balanced Budget and Emergency Deficit Control Reaffirmation Act, P.L. 100–119, Title I, (1987).

32. T. Metz, et al., Stocks Plunge 508 amid Panicky Selling, *Wall Street Journal*, October 20, 1987, 1, 22.

33. S.E. Schier, *A Decade of Deficits: Congressional Thought and Fiscal Action* (Albany: State University of New York Press, 1992); R. Thelwell, Gramm-Rudman-Hollings Four Years Later, *Public Administration Review* 50 (1990): 190–198.

34. U.S. Congressional Budget Office, *The Economic and Budget Outlook: Fiscal Years 1994–1998* (Washington, DC: U.S. Government Printing Office, January 1993), 85.

35. The Budget Enforcement Act was a component of Omnibus Budget Reconciliation Act, P.L. 101–508 (1990); Joyce and Reischauer, Deficit Budgeting, 1992.

36. U.S. Congressional Budget Office, *The Budget and Economic Outlook: Fiscal Years 2003–2012* (Washington, DC: U.S. Government Printing Office, January 2002).

37. A. Schick, *The Federal Budget*, 105–138.

38. L. Caruso, House, Senate Face Budget Maze, *Congress Daily*, March 4, 2002; L. Caruso and B. Ghent, Senate Pushes to Avoid Budget "Chaos," *Congress Daily*, April 30, 2002.

39. Doyle, Congress, the Deficit, and Budget Reconciliation.

40. W. Dauster, The Monster That Ate the United States Senate, *Public Budgeting & Finance* 18 (Summer 1998): 87–93.

41. S. Collender, Repeated Reconciliation, January 10, 2001, *Government Executive*, *www.govexec.com/dailyfed/0101/011001bb.htm*; accessed January 10, 2001.

42. Senate Appropriations Committee, Authorizations and Appropriations: What's the Difference?, *www.senate.gov/~appropriations/process.htm*; accessed July 2, 2002.

43. U.S. Congressional Budget Office, *Expiring Authorizations and Unauthorized Appropriations* (Washington, DC: U.S. Government Printing Office, January 2002); D. Baumann, Lacking Authorization, *Government Executive*, March 27, 2002, *www.govexec.com/dailyfed/0302/022702bb.htm*; accessed March 27, 2002.

44. A. Schick, *The Federal Budget*, 186–240.

45. S. Streeter, Continuing Appropriations Acts: Brief Overview of Recent Practices, *CRS Report for Congress* (Washington, DC: Congressional Research Service, January 11, 2002).

46. Budget "Pork" Riles White House, *Findlaw Legal News and Commentary*, July 6, 2001, *http://news.findlaw.co..s/s/20010705/budgetpoliticsdc.html*; accessed July 6, 2001; Citizens Against Government Waste, Introduction to the Pig Book, 2000, *www.cagw.org/publications/pigbook/index/phtml*; accessed April 6, 2000.

47. U.S. Congressional Budget Office, *The 1990 Budget Agreement: An Interim Assessment* (December 1990); Congressional Budget Office, T*he Economic and Budget Outlook: Fiscal Years 1993–1997* (Washington, DC: U.S. Government Printing Office, January 1992).

48. B. Woodward, *The Agenda: Inside the Clinton White House* (New York: Simon and Schuster, 1994).

49. B. Woodward, *The Agenda: Inside the Clinton White House*

50. Omnibus Budget Reconciliation Act, P.L. 103–66 (1993).

51. D.P. Oak, An Overview of Adjustments to the Budget Enforcement Act Discretionary Spending Caps, *Public Budgeting & Finance* 15 (Fall 1995): 35–53.

52. J.B. Bader, *Taking the Initiative: Leadership Agendas in Congress and the "Contract with America"* (Washington, DC: Georgetown University Press, 1996); J.G. Gimpel, *Legislating the Revolution: The Contract with America in Its First 100 Days* (Boston: Allyn and Bacon, 1996).

53. P.G. Joyce and R.T. Meyers, Budgeting During the Clinton Presidency, *Public Budgeting & Finance* 21 (Spring 2001): 1–21.

54. R.T. Meyers, Late Appropriations and Government Shutdowns: Frequency, Causes, Consequences, and Remedies, *Public Budgeting and Finance* 17 (Fall 1997): 25–38.

55. Joyce and Meyers, Budgeting During the Clinton Presidency.

56. J. Shear, The Tale of the Dogs, *National Journal* 28 (1996): 18–22.

57. G. Hager, Clinton, GOP Congress Strike Historic Budget Agreement, *Congressional Quarterly Weekly Report* 56 (1997): 993, 996, 997.

58. W.J. Clinton, Remarks by the President at Signing of the Balanced Budget Act of 1997 and the Taxpayers [sic] Relief Act of 1997 (August 5, 1997), *http//www.whitehouse.gov/WH/html/ briefroom.html*; accessed December 1997.

59. N. Gingrich, Remarks at Signing Ceremony for Budget Agreement (August 5, 1997), *http://speakernews.house.gov/signing.html*; accessed December 1997.

60. Balanced Budget Act, P.L. 105–33 (1997) and Taxpayer Relief Act, P.L. 105–34 (1997).

61. U.S. Congressional Budget Office, *The Budget and Economic Outlook: Fiscal Years 2003–2012*, Table F–1, 158.

62. U.S. Congressional Budget Office, *The Budget and Economic Outlook: Fiscal Years 2003–2012*, xiv.

63. Economic Growth and Tax Relief Reconciliation Act, P.L. 107–16 (2001).

64. J.M. Berry, Greenspan Supports a Tax Cut, *Washington Post*, January 26, 2001, A1.

65. L. Nitschke and W. Boudreau, Provisions of the Tax Law, *Congressional Quarterly Weekly Report* (June 9, 2001): 1390.

66. U.S. Congressional Budget Office, *The Budget and Economic Outlook: An Update* (Washington, DC: U.S. Government Printing Office, August 2002), Box 1–1: 7.

67. U.S. Congressional Budget Office, *The Budget and Economic Outlook: Fiscal Years 2003–2012*.

68. U.S. Congressional Budget Office, *The Budget and Economic Outlook: An Update*.

69. S. Collender, Budget Battles: No More Lockbox, September 18, 2001, *Government Executive, www.govexec.com/dailyfed/0901/091801bb.htm*; accessed September 19, 2001; S. Collender, Spending Surge, September 26, 2001, *Government Executive, www.govexec.com/dailyfed/0901/092601bb.htm*; accessed September 26, 2001.

70. P.G. Joyce, Federal Budgeting After September 11th: A Whole New Ballgame, or Is It Deja Vu All Over Again?, paper presented at the Woodrow Wilson Center Seminar *Budgeting During Wartime: Dueling Priorities*, September 13, 2002.

71. G. Burtless, et al., The Future of the Social Safety Net, in *Setting National Priorities: Budget Choices for the Next Century*, R.D. Reischauer, ed., (Washington, DC: Brookings Institution, 1997), 75–122; Congressional Budget Office, *The Looming Budgetary Impact of Society's Aging* (Washington, DC: U.S. Government Printing Office, July 2002).

72. L.N. Rieselbach, *Congressional Reform: The Changing Modern Congress* (Washington, DC: Congressional Quarterly Press, 1993).

73. B. Sinclair, *Legislators, Leaders and Lawmaking: The U.S. House of Representatives in the Post-reform Era* (Baltimore: Johns Hopkins University Press, 1995).

74. J. Marini, *The Politics of Budget Control: Congress, the Presidency and the Growth of the Administrative State* (Washington, DC: Crane Russak, 1992).

75. G.S. Gryski, The Influence of Committee Position on Federal Program Spending, *Polity* 23 (1991): 443–459.

76. W.J. Clinton, Statement on Signing the Line Item Veto Act, *Weekly Compilation of Presidential Documents* 32 (1996): 637–638.

77. U.S. General Accounting Office, *Line Item Veto: Estimating Potential Savings* (Washington, DC: U.S. Government Printing Office, 1992).

78. U.S. General Accounting Office, *Impoundments: Historical Information and Statistics on Proposed and Enacted Rescissions, Fiscal Years 1974–1995* (Washington, DC: U.S. Government Printing Office, 1996).

79. Line Item Veto Act, P.L. 104–130 (1996); P.G. Joyce and R.D. Reischauer, The Federal Line-Item Veto: What Is It and What Will It Do? *Public Administration Review* 57 (1997): 95–104.

80. W.J. Clinton, Remarks by the President on the Line Item Veto (August 11, 1997), *http://www.whitehouse.gov/WH/html/briefroom.html*; accessed December 1997.

81. P.G. Joyce, The Line-Item Veto Experiment: After the Supreme Court Ruling, What's Next?, *Public Budgeting & Finance* 21 (Spring 2001): 3–22.

82. R.C. Byrd, as quoted in A. Taylor, Congress Hands President a Budgetary Scalpel, *Congressional Quarterly Weekly Report* 54 (1996): 866.

83. *Byrd v. Raines*, 65 LW 2660 (DDC 1997); *Raines v. Byrd*, 521 U.S. 811 (1997).

84. *Clinton v. City of New York*, 524 U.S. 417 (1998).

85. P.G. Joyce, The Line-Item Veto Experiment.

86. G. Hager, Country Comes Full Circle on Balancing the Budget, *Congressional Quarterly Weekly Report* 55 (1997): 278–285.

87. U.S. General Accounting Office, *Balanced Budget Requirements: State Experiences and Implications for the Federal Government* (Washington, DC: U.S. Government Printing Office, 1993).

88. D.W. Kiefer, et al., *A Balanced Budget Constitutional Amendment: Economic Issues* (Washington, DC: Congressional Research Service, 1992).

89. U.S. Congressional Budget Office, *The Economic and Budget Outlook: Fiscal Years 1994–1998*.

90. Legislative Reorganization Act, Ch. 753 (1946); Legislative Reorganization Act, P.L. 91–510 (1970).

91. J. Shear, Power Loss, *National Journal* 28 (1996): 874–878.

92. T.E. Mann and N.J. Ornstein, *Renewing Congress: A Second Report* (Washington, DC: Brookings Institution, 1993).

93. E. Garrett, Term Limitations and the Myth of the Citizen Legislator, *Cornell Law Review* 81 (1996): 623–697.

94. *U.S. Term Limits, Inc. v. Thornton*, 115 S.Ct. 1842 (1995).

95. R. Meyers, Biennial Budgeting in the U.S. Congress, *Public Budgeting & Finance* 8 (Summer 1988): 21–32.

96. P.G. Joyce, Testimony Before the Subcommittee on Legislative and Budget Process Committee on Rules, United States House of Representatives, *Biennial Budgeting: A Tool for Improving Government Fiscal Management and Oversight*, March 20, 2000, 268–274; National Performance Review, *From Red Tape to Results: Creating a Government That Works Better and Costs Less* (Washington, DC: U.S. Government Printing Office, 1993).

97. A. Ghent, House Rules Committee Votes for Two-Year Budgeting, *Government Executive, www.govexec.com/dailyfed/1101/110201cdam3.htm*; accessed November 3, 2001.

98. D. Baumann, Death by Commission, *Government Executive, www.govexec.com/dailyfed/0901/091001ff.htm*; accessed September 10, 2001; L. Caruso, Appropriators Lash Out Against Biennial Budgeting, *Government Executive, www.govexec.com/dailyfed/1101/110101cdam3.htm*; accessed November 2, 2001.

99. P.G. Joyce, Testimony before Subcommittee on Legislative and Budget Process.

100. P.G. Joyce, Testimony before Subcommittee on Legislative and Budget Process.

101. H.R. 853, Comprehensive Budget Process Reform Act, Reported in House August 1999.

102. R.T. Meyers, The Budget Resolution Should Be a Law, *Public Budgeting & Finance* 10 (Fall 1990): 103–112; R.T. Meyers, *Strategic Budgeting* (Ann Arbor: University of Michigan Press, 1994).

103. A. Fulton, Budget Reform Bill Faces Opposition in House, *Congress Daily*, May 16, 2000.

104. U.S. General Accounting Office, *Budget Issues: Budgeting for Capital* (Washington, DC: U.S. Government Printing Office, 1998).

Chapter 10

BUDGET EXECUTION

Once the budget has been approved, the execution phase of the budget cycle begins. Of course, at the federal level it is common for many agencies to enter the execution phase with only a continuing resolution to spend at the previous year's rate rather than to spend under a new appropriation. This same practice sometimes occurs at the state level. In contrast, local governments usually are required by state law to complete the budget approval phase by the beginning of the new fiscal year.

This chapter has five sections. The first section deals with interactions between the central budget office and the line agencies. Then four subsystems of the execution phase are discussed — tax administration, cash management, procurement, and risk management.

Budget Office and Agency Relations

As would be expected, relationships — both direct and indirect — are extensive between the central budget office and the line agencies during the execution phase of the budget. In this section, we examine these relationships as they pertain specifically to the budget. We then consider a variety of other activities that bring the budget office into contact with agencies.

Interactions on Budgeting

Execution is the action phase of budgeting, in which the plans contained in the budget are put into operation. Every budget either explicitly or implicitly contains plans for the work to be done and the achievements to be made. Execution, then, involves converting those plans into operations. During this phase, budget office personnel gain important insights into the operations of agencies and this knowledge later becomes important during the next round of budget preparation.[1]

Legislative Intent. In acting on the budget, the legislature provides some indication of legislative intent. Such intent may be expressed in terms of the dollars to be available for an organizational unit. The greater the specificity of these appropriations, the less flexibility afforded agencies and the budget office in how funds will be spent. Some flexibility is essential, if for no other reason than the legislative body is unable to readily specify all aspects of all operations of all agencies. Most legislative action, therefore, leaves the door open to further decision making.

Apportionment and Allotments. At the state and federal levels, an apportionment process is used in which line agencies submit plans to the central budget office for how appropriated funds will be used; the plans often indicate proposed expenditures for each month or quarter of the fiscal year. Office of Management and Budget (OMB) Circular A-11 governs this process at the federal level. According to OMB, "Apportionment means a distribution made by OMB of amounts available for obligation in an appropriation or fund account in amounts available for specified time periods, program[s], activities, projects, objects, or any combinations of these. The apportionment amount limits the obligations that may be incurred."

A primary purpose of apportionment is to ensure that agencies spend at a rate that will keep them within limits imposed by their annual appropriations. Another purpose is to guide agencies so that the desired program accomplishments are achieved. The apportionment plan, therefore, should seemingly be linked closely with performance plans, although that is not always the case. Agencies should be required to defend their proposed apportionment plans in terms of the work that they expect to accomplish over the course of the fiscal year. A third purpose may be to guide agencies in using resources efficiently.

The budget office may require modification of agency proposals and eventually approves apportionments for each agency. Following the approval of apportionments by the budget office, allotments are made within departments. This process grants expenditure authority to subunits. At the local level, this process may be relatively informal.

In the apportionment process, chief executives and their budget offices have greater power to deny authority than to grant authority to agencies. The executive cannot approve apportionments for projects prohibited in the appropriation but may be able to reduce or eliminate some appropriated items. As noted in

Chapter 9, presidents have impounded appropriated funds. Another executive means of denying spending authority is to exercise the item veto, which is common among the states and also is used in some local governments.

Initial Planning. At the outset of the fiscal year, agencies must accommodate differences between the actual appropriations and the original requests for funding. In addition, some substantive changes may be specified in the appropriations, or an informal understanding may have developed between an agency and legislators over how a program will be redirected.

For agencies that were fortunate enough to obtain increased funds for improving or expanding existing programs or for new programs, the budget office plays a key role. Mindful that the legislature will expect a detailed reporting of how these funds were used, the budget office exercises oversight in implementing the program revisions or new programs.

Control of Agencies. From the perspective of the central administration, agencies must live within their budgets; otherwise, the budget process becomes an empty exercise. Therefore, various controls are imposed upon agencies, including the *preaudit*. After approval of an apportionment plan and granting an allotment, an agency still is not free to spend but rather must submit a request to obligate the government to spend resources. The request is matched against the unit's budget to determine whether the proposed expenditure is authorized and whether sufficient funds are available in the agency's budget.

Several different units may carry out the preaudit function. Not only the budget office, but also an accounting department, may be involved. At the state and local levels, independent comptrollers, controllers, or auditors general often have preaudit responsibilities. These officials have the duty of providing another, presumably independent, check on financial transactions.

In the case of an agency proposing to hire new staff, not only will the usual preaudit procedure be used, but a central personnel office also may review the request. Such a review, known as *personnel complement control*, is used in part to avoid increasing personnel commitments and corresponding increases in budget requirements over what has been appropriated.

Midyear Changes. As the year progresses, the budget office conducts reviews of agency operations. One problem that often emerges is that resources in some agencies' budgets are insufficient to meet the demand for services. One alternative is for the budget office to approve a request for supplemental appropriations from the legislative branch. In other circumstances, the budget office will work with agencies to stay within funding limits. Each summer OMB issues the *Mid-Session Review of the Budget*, which discusses economic trends and the ways in which these trends are affecting receipts, spending patterns, the activities of credit programs, and whatever sequester and other procedures are in place to attempt to limit the budget deficit. At about the same time, the Congressional Budget Office updates its *Budget and Economic Outlook* (first issued in January), a document that covers some of the same ground as the OMB document. The General Accounting Office, which is an arm of the Congress, issues its analysis of the OMB mid-session review.

Midyear crises may arise because of an unfavorable revenue situation. Government budgets that depend heavily on a single commodity export (as Venezuela's budget relies on oil) may experience severe fluctuation during the year as the world price of the commodity fluctuates. In the United States, a downturn in a state's economy can have devastating effects on sales tax and income tax receipts, forcing across-the-board cutbacks in spending, as happened in the recession of 2001–2002. Because personnel costs usually are the largest single item in operating budgets, these costs must be curtailed when revenue receipts fall below projected levels; personnel hiring freezes are common in government. Another, more extreme technique is to furlough employees. Some governments have expected all employees to share in the problem by each working, and being paid for, a four-day week rather than a five-day week, thereby creating a 20 percent savings. Depending on the chief executives' authority, they may be able to cut back on agency spending to bring outgo in line with income or they may need approval from the legislature to take such action.

The September 11, 2001, terrorist attacks on the World Trade Center and Pentagon, followed by the spread of anthrax through the mail system, had enormous impacts on budgets at all levels of government. Decision makers ordered increased security for airports, bridges, water systems, and the like. Health officials at all levels of government stepped up activities to be prepared for possible widespread bioterrorism. The Defense Department began a war on the Taliban regime in Afghanistan and sent troops to Yemen and the Philippines, resulting in expenses not previously anticipated in the department's budget. These threats to the health and safety of society had to be met and necessarily forced the midyear approval of major budget changes.

The 2001 catastrophes pushed the then-weak economy into a recession, resulting in decreased revenues at a time when the need for government spending had risen sharply. State governments found themselves having to rework their budgets as a result of massive revenue shortfalls. Meanwhile, Congress had to pass supplemental appropriations to authorize increased spending for federal agencies in the thick of the fight against terrorism.

When an agency wishes to shift existing resources to meet new needs during the fiscal year or when an agency receives a supplemental appropriation, it must prepare a revised apportionment or reapportionment plan. The budget office then has an opportunity to exercise some guidance over how the agency will spend its monies.

Just because a government is experiencing a downturn in revenues and needs to cut expenditures, it does not mean there will be no need for supplemental appropriations. For example, many state government departments may be having their budgets trimmed, while the state's labor department budget is being augmented to cope with an increased caseload of unemployed workers.

End-of-Year Spending. As the fiscal year approaches its end, agencies will attempt to zero out their budgets. An agency having unexpended funds at the end of the fiscal year may be considered a prime candidate for cuts in the upcoming budget. Agencies with budget surpluses at the end of the year may have their budget bases reduced in the next fiscal year. Also, unexpended or unencumbered funds often lapse at the end of the budget year. From the agency's perspective, it is a now-or-never situation for spending the available money. Another factor is that an agency may have delayed some expenditures, saving a portion of its budget for contingencies. This delay results in a spurt in expenditures at the end of the year, with some spending being highly appropriate and other spending being utterly wasteful. Congress has reduced this last-minute spurt by limiting the proportion of an agency's funds that may be spent in the final quarter of the fiscal year.

An alternative is to allow surplus funds to be transferred to the agency's new budget without requiring a reappropriation. Some jurisdictions allow this kind of transfer within limits, such as a small percentage of each unit's total budget. Advocates of an entrepreneurial spirit in government argue that agencies should be rewarded for efficiency by being allowed to carry over funds into the next fiscal year.[2] The National Performance Review recommended that agencies be able to carry as much as 50 percent of their internal operations budgets into the next fiscal year.[3]

Reorganization, Downsizing, Privatization, and Outsourcing

The Taft Commission on Economy and Efficiency is best known for its 1912 report recommending the establishment of a federal budget process under the direction of the president. The title of the commission is significant in that a primary goal was a better use of government resources (see Chapter 1). More than nine decades later, the same concerns of the Taft Commission remain prevalent at all levels of government. Incentives for economy and efficiency are created by taxing and spending limitation measures, by fiscal stress or distress resulting from the erosion of tax bases of many jurisdictions, and by the increased popularity of a form of conservatism dedicated to reducing the role of government in society.

Budget offices historically have played central roles in examining the structures of departments and agencies, with an eye toward possible reorganization as a means for increasing the efficiency of operations.[4] In addition to structural arrangements, budget offices often seek improvements in management processes as a means of garnering savings. Outside experts are used, as was the case of the Grace Commission during the Reagan administration. The commission, whose full title was the President's Private Sector Survey on Cost Control, consisted of chief executive officers from private corporations.[5] The National Performance Review (NPR), during the Clinton administration, was an in-house effort to improve all aspects of government and recommended the reorganization of several government offices and the elimination of others. OMB was deeply involved in all of these efforts, although its participation was not always synchronized with NPR efforts.

In 2002, President George W. Bush recommended to Congress that it create a new Department of Homeland Security consisting of several units already in existence and located throughout the federal bureaucracy. Using Executive Order 13267, he created a transition unit in OMB that was to be in charge of overseeing this major reorganization. The OMB would have the task of merging dozens of agencies and programs into the new department.[6] Congress approved creation of the Department of Homeland Security immediately following the November 2002 elections.

A phenomenon that gained special momentum in the 1980s and continued since is that of cutback management, downsizing, or "right-sizing" (see Chapter 6).[7] Much of the focus of such efforts is on reducing government employment, with the budget offices often in charge of implementing such initiatives. At the federal level, the Clinton administration adopted the NPR's recommendation to reduce personnel levels. The George W. Bush administration provided continued support for cutbacks by recommending major reductions in the supervisory ranks of government workers and by outsourcing government jobs to the private sector.[8] OMB included as part of the budget preparation process a requirement that agencies specify target reductions in personnel and show how they planned to meet these targeted figures (described in OMB Circular A-11). Defense Department downsizing over the years has included closure of numerous installations as well as a "drawdown" in personnel.[9]

While definitions vary, the core of any definition of privatization is the reassignment of government activities to the private sector. *Privatization* typically involves the selling of government assets to the private sector and turning the operation of these facilities over to private companies. In the United Kingdom during the Thatcher administration, for example, British Overseas Airways Corporation became a private company and some public water companies were sold off. Privatization is sometimes coupled with close regulation — namely, while a company is privately owned, it must continue to comply with extensive government regulations.

The delivery of governmental services can be carried out to a considerable degree with the cooperation of private for-profit and nonprofit enterprises. A common mechanism used for this is *contracting* or *outsourcing*, in which a private firm provides a product or service at an agreed quantity, quality, and price.[10] Other means of encouraging private sector involvement in the provision of public services include grants, loan guarantees, tax expenditures, social regulation, and government corporations.[11] Outsourcing of government services is intended to increase government efficiency and reduce government spending. It should be kept in mind that outsourcing may result officially in a reduction in the number of government employees but that many private sector employees have jobs only because of government contracting.

Although the procedures used in contracting are reviewed later in this chapter, we note here that OMB Circular A-76, Performance of Commercial Activities, provides for a review process to determine when activities of the government should be contracted out. Two main criteria apply: that the activity be a "commercial" one and not "governmental," and that the cost be lower in the private sector than in government. Examples of commercial activities include guarding public buildings and providing cafeterias for employees. Policy-making activities are not to be contracted out.

Contracting out has at least two types of supporters. One group wants to increase the efficiency of government operations through utilization of the private sector.[12] Circular A-76 uses an efficiency standard — namely, contracting out should be used when the unit cost for a service is lower outside of government than inside it. The second group of supporters adheres to the view that the population is better served if service delivery is left, where possible, to the private sector. These advocates of outsourcing contend that government should be proactive in seeking opportunities for turning over functions to the private sector.

Although critics contend that sometimes too much faith is placed in private enterprise and that outsourcing supports non-unionized firms that pay low wages, private sector contracting has become a familiar form of service delivery in the United States and abroad.[13] Contracting out is routinely used for such services as refuse pickup and towing of illegally parked vehicles. Private sector firms under government contract now handle services once thought to be exclusively the responsibility of the public sector, such as welfare services and the operation of prisons.[14] Ports, such as the one in Miami, are being largely privatized, so that a port authority leases much of its property to private firms, which in turn operate the facilities.[15] There has been discussion of outsourcing both the air traffic control function and Social Security.[16]

Several lessons have been learned as governments have ventured into out-sourcing, with one of the most important being the need to conduct a thorough analysis before taking the plunge.[17] There is a need to consider whether cost effi-ciencies will be attained, whether the private firm will be held accountable for its performance, whether any cost efficiency is attained at the expense of quality, and whether equity or fairness in treating citizens and employees will be achieved.[18] Another important question is whether companies in the market can provide the agreed-upon services in a timely fashion and can respond to unforeseen problems that may arise. Do any legal barriers prohibit privatizing a given service? And what liability risks may be created by having a private firm deliver a government service?

The analysis needs to include projected costs for monitoring a firm in its delivery of a service. A government must be able to assure itself that a firm is abiding by its commitments and be able to respond when citizens complain about a service. Part of the monitoring process includes determining whether the cost savings that were predicted in the original analysis did, indeed, materialize.[19]

A dogmatic stance that services should be contracted out wherever possible is unwarranted in that government may well be able to provide some services at costs lower than private firms can deliver. Competitive bidding on contemplated outsourcing projects can include not only private firms but government agencies as well. Phoenix, Arizona, and Fort Lauderdale, Florida, have been leaders in developing and using this approach.[20] Contracting out to private firms to operate a school system also has been adopted in some jurisdictions, both to save money and to improve student performance on testing programs. The evidence as to whether school districts are getting what they intended, however, is uncertain. Further, a mix in service delivery may be more cost-effective than strict outsourc-ing. In other words, any given service may be delivered in a cooperative arrange-ment that includes a combination of government agencies, for-profit firms, and nonprofit organizations.[21]

The aftermath of the September 11, 2001, catastrophes is instructive. One patently obvious fact was that airport security had been breached so that terror-ists were able to commandeer and crash four airliners. To that point, security had been the responsibility of private companies, whose expenses were paid by the airlines. There was consensus that this private sector system failed and that gov-ernment involvement was warranted. A vigorous debate developed in the U.S. House of Representatives between Democrats, who wanted the government to take over airport security, and Republicans, who wanted the government to over-see private security operations. The decision ultimately was to convert airport screening jobs to the public sector, at least for the short term.

Management Controls

Budget offices have been assigned a variety of management-related duties beyond the core activities of assembling proposed budgets and overseeing their execution. For instance, budget offices may be partially responsible for establishing standards to be used in accounting systems (OMB Circular A-127). Of course, other units such as the General Accounting Office (GAO) at the federal level also play major roles in this area. Information systems and procurement are other important areas in which budget offices have key roles. Procurement is discussed later in this chapter.

Some budget offices have responsibility for studying agency procedures and for recommending or prescribing new procedures. These organization-and-management (O & M) studies can recommend changes in the department's management processes.

Budget offices set ground rules for many of the routine activities of line organizations. For example, limitations are set for paying employee travel costs. Centrally imposed standards also circumscribe the use of consulting services.

Some budget offices are charged with performing a *legislative clearinghouse* function. Before an agency may endorse a proposal for new or revised legislation, the proposal must be cleared through the budget office. This practice helps ensure that what is proposed is consistent with the views of the chief executive, both substantively and financially (see OMB Circular A-19).

Because corruption in government often involves finance, budget offices sometimes have major responsibility for protecting the government against fraud, waste, and abuse of government resources. The Inspector General Act of 1978 created relatively independent inspector general offices in major federal departments and gave these offices responsibility for investigating possible cases of fraud and other wrongdoing. The inspectors general meet as the President's Council on Integrity and Efficiency, which is chaired by the OMB.[22] In addition, agency-appointed inspectors general meet as the Executive Council on Integrity and Efficiency. This body includes representatives of independent agencies, such as the Federal Trade Commission and the Corporation for Public Broadcasting.

The OMB also oversees agency compliance with the Federal Managers' Financial Integrity Act of 1982, which requires safeguarding financial systems, particularly accounting and payroll, from fraud.[23] OMB Circular A-123, which is used to implement the law, was revised in 1995 to emphasize that managers should be held accountable for producing government services that yield desired results as well as for providing these services free of fraud and abuse of resources. The revision is in keeping with OMB's responsibility to oversee implementation of the Government Performance and Results Act of 1993 (see Chapter 5).

Presidents frequently assign OMB responsibility for improving the management of government operations. In 2001, his first year in office, President George W. Bush issued the *President's Management Agenda*.[24] Three of the five government-wide initiatives in the agenda were specifically related to budgeting: competitive sourcing (contracting), improving finanical performance (correcting errors in government payments; see Chapter 11), and integrating budgeting and performance (see Chapter 5). The other two were strategically managing human capital (see Chapter 13) and expanding electronic government (see Chapter 11). To implement the management agenda as well as other management initiatives, President Bush reconstituted the President's Management Council, a body that had been created by President Clinton in 1993. The council consists of chief operating officers, who have the status equal to that of deputy secretary. In other words, these COOs are expected to have authority to implement management reforms within their respective units.

To bring pressure to bear on departments and agencies, OMB initiated a scorecard system using "traffic light" grading on the five initiatives of the management agenda. In early 2002, the first year that the system was used, the color red for "unsatisfactory" dominated the ratings. The only agency to receive a green rating in any category was the National Science Foundation for its financial management system.[25] By early 2003, several agencies had moved out of the red zone and into the yellow zone.[26]

President Bush asked Congress in 2001 to pass two bills related to management of agency operations. The Freedom to Manage legislation would expedite congressional action in reviewing presidential requests to amend or eliminate statutory provisions that present barriers to efficient management. The contention was that some statutory provisions were well intentioned when originally passed but had outlived their usefulness. The second bill, the Managerial Flexibility Act, would ease many restrictions imposed by personnel management systems. Agencies would have greater flexibility in recruiting workers, compensating them (including the use of bonuses), and retaining workers.[27]

Another function of OMB is to deal with alleged instances of postemployment conflicts of interest in which former government employees may be illegally benefiting from their previous experience in government. Of course, OMB is not the sole central agency responsible for handling problems in this area. Other important offices include the Office of Personnel Management, the Merit Systems Protection Board, the Department of Justice, and GAO.

Another significant executive order was 12857, issued by President Clinton in 1993, in response to complaints that spending on entitlement programs was out of control. The order required federal agencies to develop targets for direct spending; when these targets were exceeded, the agencies were required to submit recommendations for bringing expenditures down to the targeted levels. For many entitlement programs, Congress would need to amend current legislation to reduce spending.

OMB, along with the Council on Environmental Quality, which is a unit of the Executive Office of the President, is responsible for devising means for cleaning up environmental conditions on federal land. Extensive environmental pollution exists on military installations, facilities of the National Aeronautics and Space Administration, and other federal properties.[28]

Agencies must report to OMB on several other matters. According to law, OMB must be given reports on agency activities and expenditures pertaining to crime control and drug control. Agencies must report on how they are complying with the Federal Advisory Committee Act of 1972, Executive Order 12838 (1993), and Circular A-135 (1994), which require agencies to reduce their use of advisory committees.[29] The premise here is that while the government benefits from external advice, such advice often costs more than it is worth.

Besides these areas mentioned, budget offices may have some responsibility for other management controls over agencies. For example, budget offices may be involved in implementing government-wide affirmative action plans. Some states have right-to-know laws that require employers, both public and private, to inform their employees whether they are working with hazardous materials; measures aimed at reducing dangerous conditions obviously have budgetary implications. Budget offices may have some responsibilities in implementing freedom-of-information laws.

Control of Information Collection, Quality, Security, and Dissemination

Government collection and dissemination of information has constituted another problem area in which budget offices are involved. A chief concern is that federal agencies heap huge burdens on individuals, corporations, and state and local governments in requiring them to submit information. The Paperwork Reduction Act, originally passed in 1980 and thoroughly rewritten in 1995, provides an elaborate process by which the government handles information.[30] The process is under the supervision of OMB's Office of Information and Regulatory Affairs (OIRA). The law is implemented by OMB Circular A-130 and strengthened by requirements in Executive Order 13011, Federal Information Technology, issued in 1996. The order provides for the establishment of the Chief Information Officers (CIO) Council. The council, consisting of representatives from all major federal agencies, provides a forum for improving the management of information. In 2000, the council prepared a *Strategic Plan* that contained six information technology goals. For example, one goal dealt with the connection of citizens with information about government, and another dealt with security and the reliability of information.[31] The General Accounting Office has been critical, voicing doubts that the plan was either effective or comprehensive.[32]

The Paperwork Reduction Act required agencies to reduce the information collection burden by 5 to 10 percent each year through 2001. Agencies were required to submit plans to OIRA showing the kinds of information they collect, the estimated thousands of "burden hours" that the collection process demanded of those required to submit the information, and the agencies' plans to meet the law's requirement to reduce paperwork. This has become an annual process, and each year the OMB publishes an information collection budget. The document indicates both reductions and increases in burden hours. For instance, an agency may have made an administrative decision to cut back on some of the information it collects for a specific program, but that same agency may be required to increase its collection of other information due to provisions in laws passed by Congress. Despite efforts to reduce the paperwork burden, the pattern has been for burden hours to increase each year.[33] **Table 10–1** shows the burden hours imposed by federal agencies.

Any new collection of information must be approved by OIRA, but before that can occur, an agency must go through an elaborate analytic process. Factors to consider include the importance to the agency in collecting the information (the practical utility of the information), a realistic assessment of the burden imposed on those who would be required to submit the information, and a determination that the information does not exist already in some other form or in another agency. The agency might be expected to implement a pilot program as a means of evaluating the collection process and the utility of the information collected. Once all of this activity ends, the agency must post a notice about the proposed collection process in the *Federal Register* and then go through a period in which it accepts comments from the public. Only after these steps are completed may the proposal be submitted to OIRA. That office can reject the agency's proposal on grounds such as that the information is nonessential, that the information already exists, that the process would impose an undue burden, or simply that the proposed forms are unacceptable.

At any point in time, OIRA has many agency proposals under review, and action may take up to several months on each. One example of the type of approval that must be sought is the Department of Agriculture's proposal for "recordkeeping requirements for certified application of federal restricted use of pesticides."[34] A listing of OIRA paperwork reviews is available on the OMB home page.

In addition to controlling the collection of information, OIRA regulates the quality of information. Its authority in this area was strengthened in 2000 by a provision in its appropriation; the rider is commonly called the Information-

Quality Act.[35] OMB has subsequently published "Guidelines for Ensuring and Maximizing the Quality, Objectivity, Utility, and Integrity of Information Dissemination by Federal Agencies." Agencies, including OMB, also have published quality guidelines for the information that they disseminate.[36]

Another concern for OMB in this area is the use of electronic signatures as a way of eliminating paperwork. The Government Paperwork Elimination Act of 1998 required federal agencies to have their most important forms on-line by 2003 and stated that individuals and corporations could submit such forms electronically and verify their authenticity through electronic signatures.[37]

The process of disseminating information also is of concern. OMB provides guidance so that the dissemination process does not invade the privacy of citizens

Table 10–1 **Fiscal Years 2000 and 2001 Information Collection Totals for the Federal Government (Millions of Hours)**

	Total Hours Needed	
	Fiscal Year 2000	Fiscal Year 2001
Government Total	**7,361.72**	**7,651.42**
Agency		
Agriculture	75.19	86.72
Commerce*	38.57	10.29
Defense	93.62	92.05
Education	41.98	40.49
Energy	2.92	3.85
Health and Human Services	173.71	186.61
Housing and Urban Development	12.46	12.05
Interior	5.64	7.56
Justice	36.82	40.53
Labor	181.59	186.11
State	29.19	16.56
Transportation†	117.65	80.34
Treasury	6,156.80	6,415.85
Veterans Affairs	5.98	5.31
Environmental Protection Agency	128.75	130.77

* Note that a large portion of Commerce's decrease in burden is attributed to the periodic nature of census collections.

† Due to a PRA violation, the program change total for fiscal year 2001 includes a reduction of 42,464,327 hours. DOT inadvertently allowed OMB's approval of a federal motor carrier safety administration collection, driver's record of duty status, to expire on September 30, 2001. DOT continued to use this collection in violation of the PRA until it obtained a reinstatement of OMB's approval on March 4, 2002.

Source: Modified from Office of Management and Budget, *Managing Information Collection and Dissemination* (Washington, DC: U.S. Government Printing Office, 2002), 65.

or reveal trade secrets of corporations. Circular A-130 provides guidance on when and how much agencies may charge for their information. The Paperwork Reduction Act requires that information be made available in a timely fashion.

Since September 11, 2001, a major concern is that information not be disseminated that could be used by terrorists, such as information about nuclear power plants that could be used to create a nuclear catastrophe. Terrorism also could come in the form of computer hackers destroying major databases. Earlier, Congress had passed the Government Information Security Reform Act of 2000, which gave OMB responsibility for increasing computer security.[38] In October 2001, President George W. Bush issued Executive Order 13231, which created the President's Critical Infrastructure Protection Board. To some extent, there is a conflict in purpose — one set of policies encourages the dissemination of information and another set discourages such dissemination in the interest of national security and cybersecurity.

OMB has other important roles in the information arena. The office influences how much information is collected by controlling agencies' budgets, particularly those agencies whose primary mission is information collection. If budgets are cut for the Census Bureau in the Commerce Department or the Bureau of Labor Statistics in the Labor Department, the immediate results are less information being collected or being made available to the public. An agency might collect information but lack the staff needed to make it available in usable form, whether in paper, electronic, or another format.

Control of Regulations

In addition to relief from paperwork, budget offices may be responsible for providing regulatory relief to businesses and governments. Critics of regulations view them as imposing needless expenses on corporations, which in turn pass these costs on to consumers, or to taxpayers in the case of state and local governments. On the other hand, one should keep in mind that regulations are issued pursuant to statutes and that both the regulations and the statutes presumably have important public purposes, such as ensuring the safety of a polio vaccine or the nation's food supply.

Beginning in the Reagan administration, OMB was given increased powers over the regulatory process, and those powers have been greatly expanded in subsequent years. Part of this movement has probably had political motivations in which presidents have sought to show their concern for keeping a potentially runaway bureaucracy in check. In 1992, the year he sought re-election, President George H. W. Bush imposed a moratorium on issuing new rules on the premise that regulations harm the economy and that the economy was already suffering needlessly from over-regulation.[39]

In 2001, President George W. Bush, acting through his White House Chief of Staff, imposed a moratorium on the regulatory process on his very first day in office.[40] The official reason cited was to give new Bush appointees in the departments an opportunity to review the regulations that were in the pipeline. Another reason was concern over the flurry of regulations that had been released at the end of the Clinton administration. After the suspension period, some regulations were permanently canceled and others were allowed to go into effect.

A central line of reasoning is that thorough analysis is needed to determine whether regulations should be issued and then whether they should be retained. The current executive order governing this field at the federal level is 12866, issued in 1993 by President Clinton. President George W. Bush amended that order in 2002 by issuing Executive Order 13258. Orders 12866 and 13258, coupled with the Paperwork Reduction Act of 1995 (discussed earlier), give OIRA a veto power over most agency regulatory activity.

Executive Order 12866 provides for a regulatory planning and review process under OIRA. Each year agencies must submit to OIRA their proposed plans for revising, issuing, and rescinding regulations. Any proposals for new or revised regulations must be evaluated in terms of their costs and benefits. John D. Graham, administrator of OIRA in the George W. Bush administration, was at the center of considerable controversy over the unit's oversight of the regulatory process. He had founded Harvard University's Center for Risk Analysis and was a champion of requiring that government regulations be cost-effective. In his first seven months in office, Graham rejected more regulations than the Clinton administration had done in its entire eight years; the rejections are known as "return letters."[41] He created a new device called "prompt letters," which instructed agencies to consider writing, rewriting, or rescinding regulations. Graham also created a "target list" of regulations that needed to be reviewed. OIRA made it clear that it was directing the regulatory process on behalf of the president and that line agencies needed to be alert to White House priorities.

A major thrust for reformists has been the idea that regulations should exist only if their benefits outweigh the costs they impose on society. OIRA has established ground rules for the conduct of evaluations so that some degree of standardized procedures exist from one agency to another.[42] There are major technical and political issues over what gets counted as a cost and what as a benefit (see Chapter 7).[43] The budget office was charged by the Regulatory Right-to-Know Act of 1999 with reporting to Congress on the "annual costs and benefits (including quantifiable and nonquantifiable effects) of federal rules and paperwork."[44] The estimate for annual costs of regulations for major federal departments and agencies in 1999–2001 was between $16 billion and $19 billion and benefits were between $33 billion and $54 billion.[45] OMB's annual *Analytical Perspectives* typically reports on the costs and benefits of regulations, especially in areas of health and safety. The report considers the costs imposed by government on industry in saving lives in such areas as automobile head-impact protection and petroleum refining.

Graham also sought to increase what is referred to as government "transparency" by placing on the OMB Web site increased information about regulation and paperwork review.[46] The site provides extensive information about the regulations under review and the actions taken on them. In addition, it indicates meetings held with agency and industry representatives.

Controversy often arises over the fact that many regulations are written for large entities and, as a result, small organizations experience major burdens in attempting to comply with the regulations. In response to that view, Congress passed the Regulatory Flexibility Act of 1980 and made important changes in the law in 1996 through passage of the Small Business Regulatory Enforcement Fairness Act.[47] The 1980 law encourages the use of flexible regulations that require lesser amounts of information from smaller entities, including small businesses and local governments. The 1996 law, supplemented by Executive Order 13272 issued in 2002, instructs agencies to prepare guides to show small businesses how they can comply with regulations. The Small Business Administration was assigned the role of ombudsman in assisting small businesses when they encounter regulatory problems with agencies. In the name of "regulatory relief," agencies may selectively waive the application of regulations to small businesses and waive penalties when these businesses violate the regulations. When small businesses think an agency has failed to comply with the law, they may file suit, claiming the regulation in question is invalid.

The 1996 law also includes within it the Congressional Review Act.[48] This law provides a form of legislative veto of administrative regulations. Before a proposed rule can take effect, it must be submitted to Congress. Congress then has 60 days, excluding days when it is in recess for four days or more, to review the regulations and can pass a joint resolution disapproving or vetoing the regulations. The president may veto the resolution, and Congress may consider overriding the president's veto.

The Truth in Regulating Act of 2000 strengthened congressional influence over the regulatory process. When Congress receives an "economically significant rule, a chairman or ranking member of a committee of jurisdiction of either house of Congress may request the Comptroller General of the United States to review the rule."[49] The Comptroller General, then, has up to six months to submit a report on the proposed rule. As an example, the Comptroller General submitted a report on the Justice Department's proposed rule for administering the September 11, 2001, Victim Compensation Fund.[50]

The most controversial regulations in recent times have dealt with ergonomics in the workplace. The Occupational Safety and Health Administration in the Department of Labor had been planning regulations that would require corporations to rectify worker–machine situations that resulted in injuries. Of particular concern were repetitive motions that stressed the human body. President Clinton, at the end of his term, authorized the issuance of the regulations, resulting in a firestorm from industry and many members of Congress.[51] When George W. Bush became president and a new Congress was seated, Congress overturned the regulations.[52]

Given all of the items discussed here, some observers have suggested that such management tasks are too great to be left to budget offices. One suggestion is to create a separate office of management that would have nonbudgetary duties ranging well beyond what OMB currently has. The argument against creating an office of management hinges mainly on the fact that the issues addressed have budgetary implications and to assign them to a different agency would automatically create coordination problems.

In addition to relations between the central budget office and the line agencies, several other subsystems are in operation during budget execution. Taxes and other debts must be collected, the cash needs of the government must be met, items must be purchased, and the vulnerability of the government to loss of property and other problems must be managed. These topics are discussed next.

Tax Administration and Debt Collection

Tax administration, which is discussed here, and cash management, which is discussed in the next section, are two functions that usually are under the same administrative officer, typically a secretary of treasury or revenue. Having the two functions linked together administratively facilitates sharing information. The cash manager uses information generated by the tax administrator. At the federal level, the Treasury Department handles these tasks.

Besides taxes, numerous other revenue sources must be administered. User charges are common at the local level. State lotteries have become important sources of revenue. Administrators responsible for lotteries focus on marketing to increase sales; as the dollar value of sales increases, the unit cost of administration declines. Governments loan billions of dollars, and loan payments frequently are delinquent.

Main Steps

Tax administration has four main steps:

1. Determining the objects or services to be taxed. Using the local property tax as an example, parcels of land and structures, along with their owners, must be identified.

2. Applying the tax. In the case of the property tax, this is an annual process; in contrast, sales tax calculations are made each time a sale occurs. Governments make property tax calculations, and bills are sent to property owners. Individuals have the responsibility to calculate their income taxes.

3. Collecting the revenues. Funds are paid either directly to the government, as in the case of a corporation's paying income tax, or through a third party, as in the case of employers' remitting individual income tax withholdings to the government.

4. Enforcing the law. Audits are conducted selectively of taxpayers to verify compliance, and some taxpayers are prosecuted for tax evasion.

Tax administration is less concerned with the policy issues of tax equity (see Chapter 4) and more concerned with generating the revenue that is expected and with gaining compliance from the vast majority of taxpayers. The Internal Revenue Service (IRS), located in the U.S. Treasury Department, has a tax compliance measurement program that samples tax returns in an attempt to judge overall how well taxpayers are complying with the tax laws.[53]

Organizational Structure

In response to extensive criticism of the IRS extending over decades, Congress passed the Interal Revenue Service Restructuring and Reform Act of 1998.[54] The law instructed the commissioner to reorganize the agency to reflect the types of taxpayers rather than continue with its then-existing structure organized around geography — nation, region, and district. This "modernization" effort was aimed at achieving a balance between meeting taxpayers' needs and having taxpayers comply with the tax laws. The agency now has four operating divisions: (1) Wage and Investment for individual taxpayers, (2) Small Business/Self-Employed, (3) Large and Mid-Size Business, and (4) Tax Exempt and Government Entities. In addition to restructuring, IRS has initiated other reforms, such as updating work processes and procedures, improving data management, strengthening its customer focus, and improving its use of performance measures. [55]

Another important structural change made by the 1998 legislation was to move the Office of the Chief Inspector out of the IRS and redesignate it as the

Treasury Inspector General for Tax Administration (TIGTA). This office is in addition to to the Inspector General for Treasury and is responsible for ferreting out fraud and abuse in IRS, promoting efficient and effective administration of the tax laws, evaluating the security of IRS technology, and protecting IRS workers from corrupt influences.

The same law created the Internal Revenue Service Oversight Board. This permanent body consists of nine members, six of whom are not employed by the government. These individuals plus one government employee are appointed by the president. The other two members are the Treasury Secretary and the Commissioner of the IRS. The board has the power to review and approve strategic plans prepared by IRS and to review and approve budget requests before they are forwarded to the president.

Enforcement

Numerous tax enforcement measures are used, and well-trained and ethical personnel are essential for effective enforcement practices.

- The IRS verifies mathematical accuracy through the use of optical scanning. Proper design of forms and clearly written instructions contribute to improved taxpayer accuracy in filing returns.[56]

- Tax return information supplied by individuals is compared with information supplied by banks and employers.[57]

- Governments share computer-based data to compare information on income being reported (or not reported).

- Taxpayer services are provided to help in preparing tax returns. Services may be available at designated government offices, at other facilities, and by telephone.[58]

- Governments draw samples of taxpayer returns to audit. Regression models are designed to identify cases that are most likely to involve noncompliance with the tax laws.

- One of the most common groups singled out for tax auditing includes individuals and corporations for which "leads" have been given. Undercover operations may be used in these situations.

- Delinquent accounts are investigated, as are accounts in which taxpayers have stopped complying altogether.[59]

- Some taxpayers are prosecuted in court, depending on the "seriousness" of the cases and the availability of resources to pursue the cases in court.

- Special enforcement is reserved for sources of illegal income, such as gambling, prostitution, narcotics, and, more generally, organized crime.

Any government must decide how many resources to commit to these various activities and how resources should be distributed among them. The IRS has been criticized for not having a firm idea of the relative yield in tax revenue generated from these activities.[60] Decisions must be made not only about the type of activity to conduct, but also about the distribution of tax enforcement resources across different forms of taxes. For example, a state needs to decide how many resources to commit to tax cheating on personal income, corporate income, and motor fuels taxes.[61]

Complaints often arise that some taxpayers are being audited more intensively that others. Increased auditing may be warranted where it is known that certain types of taxpayers are more likely to cheat on their returns than others. Politics also come into play. Congress expects the IRS to give special audit attention to people filing for earned income tax credits in which the claim is made that their incomes are so low that they owe little or no taxes.

One of the most prominent objectives in enforcement of income tax laws is to have taxpayers comply with the law and to identify taxpayers who fail to report some of their income. The federal government would gain billions of dollars annually if the gap between reported and actual income were closed.[62] Major categories of unreported income are sole proprietors' income and nonwage/nonsalary income.

Determining how to detect unreported income is a difficult task. The IRS has decided that its super-audits that required a sample of taxpayers to substantiate every item on their tax returns was ineffective in detecting unreported income and identifying unauthorized or fraudulent claims for tax deductions and tax credits. Between 1995 and the early 2000s, IRS reduced its audit rate — that is, the percentage of tax returns that it audits in one form or another. The reduction was due to cutbacks in IRS staff, the shifting of staff from auditing to assisting taxpayers, and the need for more time in conducting a single audit. The impact that this cutback had on revenue collection remains unknown.[63] In 2002, the IRS announced it was launching the National Research Program, in which 50,000 individual tax returns would be audited each year out of the approximately 132 million returns. The IRS commissioner noted, "We have found new ways to use existing information to measure tax compliance. The process is substantially less intrusive on taxpayers, but will help us catch tax cheating and improve tax administration."[64] The complexity of tax laws greatly hinders the effectiveness of audits both for personal and for corporate income taxes.[65]

Greater revenue can be achieved through a variety of means, including levies on government payments and abatement programs. With regard to levies, government sometimes is in the situation of making payments to taxpayers — both individuals and corporations — for one purpose, while those entities are simultaneously in arrears on their taxes. Levies can be imposed to recoup the taxes owed.[66] As for abatements, tax administration offices may have the authority to negotiate payments from taxpayers and forgive some taxes that are owed. Abatement programs may obtain revenues from sources that otherwise would have paid nothing or almost nothing. On the other hand, attempts to negotiate tax payments can have the unintended consequence of forcing taxpayers into bankruptcy.[67] Liens can be placed against properties as a means of forcing the payment of taxes.[68] The 1998 IRS Restructuring and Reform Act provided new guidance to the agency on liens, levies, and the seizure of property.

Another consideration is that tax administration would be far less complicated if most, or even all, taxpayers were relieved of having to file tax returns. At least 36 countries have tax withholding systems that free taxpayers of the onerous task of preparing and filing tax returns.[69]

Beginning in the 1980s, tax amnesty became popular as a means of retrieving unpaid state taxes. Amnesty programs became especially popular during the 2001–2002 recession, when states were particularly in need of revenue. Taxpayers who were delinquent in their income taxes could file returns during a specified time period in a state without fear of prosecution; the taxpayers, however, were expected to pay all back taxes and interest. The amnesty programs have been successful in getting many taxpayers back on the tax rolls. One possible drawback is that taxpayer compliance declines somewhat following an amnesty program, suggesting that taxpayers feel that government is likely to be less vigilant in ferreting out evaders after having enticed many people to return to the tax rolls. Also, taxpayer evasion is related to tax rates — as tax rates increase, evasion increases.

Tax administration usually focuses upon generating revenue but on occasion includes distributing revenue. In 2001, Congress passed a tax rebate program that resulted in considerable expense for both the rebates and their administration. Individual taxpayers received $300 each, while heads of households received $500 and married couples filing jointly received $600.

Computers in Tax Administration

It should come as no surprise that computers are playing increasingly important roles in tax administration:

- Besides routine recordkeeping, computers are used for drawing samples for tax auditing and for cross-checking information between different sources.
- Many businesses are required to make federal tax payments through the Electronic Federal Tax Payment System.

- State and local governments electronically submit federal income tax and Social Security withholdings.

- Answers to frequently asked questions (FAQs) pertaining to tax laws are commonly available on government home pages on the Internet.

- Some local governments have automated tax systems that can make monthly withdrawals for property taxes from taxpayers' bank accounts, providing that taxpayers preapprove such withdrawals.

- In some locales, taxpayers use the telephone to pay their taxes.

- Some governments accept credit and debit cards for payment of taxes, fees, parking tickets, and the like. The cards, of course, are possible only because of today's computer technology. Some states accept electronic fund transfers for corporations making tax payments.

- Electronic auctions are used by governments to sell delinquent tax properties.[70]

- Auditors on field assignments use portable computers. Computers can be used to manage tax cases, providing on any one case a variety of information and prompting the case manager with reminders about the status of the case.

One of the most important developments in this area relates to on-line tax filing and payments. The 1998 IRS Restructuring and Reform Act mandated the rapid development of electronic filing. In 2001, the Internal Revenue Service unveiled its Electronic Federal Tax Payment System–Online Service for use by individual taxpayers and businesses. This system is much more user-friendly than the system originally developed for businesses. By the early 2000s, about one-third of all taxpayers filed electronically. The expectation was that electronic filers would rise to 80 percent by the mid-2000s.[71] Electronic filing posed and continues to pose important challenges in safeguarding the security of data.[72] Whether it reduces the unit cost of processing returns compared with paper filing remains an open question.[73]

The conversion of various aspects of tax administration from paper files to computer systems or from one computer system to a more advanced one can result in problems for both tax administrators and taxpayers. The IRS became well aware of this problem starting in the late 1980s, as it engaged in a multibillion-dollar Tax Systems Modernization project. The system was intended to aid IRS agents, citizens (through more timely tax refunds), corporations, and executive and legislative decision makers through the provision of more accurate and timely information.[74]

In the late 1990s, the IRS halted much of its modernization work after spending $3.4 billion[75] and developed a new plan that would rely more heavily upon a prime contractor for modernizing the agency's operations. Congress, painfully aware of the deficiencies in IRS technology and the false and expensive starts made in updating the technology, created a special Information Technology Investment Account.[76] By 2000, the IRS commissioner reported that the agency was on track for upgrading its technology by using a consortium of consulting firms, known as the PRIME Alliance.[77] Nevertheless, the task remaining was still daunting, what with 20 mainframes, nearly 900 mid-range computers, and about 200,000 desktop personal computers.[78]

Personnel in Tax Administration

Tax administration involves several personnel-related problems, with one being the sheer number of employees. As long as tax recordkeeping and tax filing remain largely paper-based processes, treasury departments need large numbers of employees, especially at tax filing time (often April 15). Even with the conversion to on-line filing, personnel are still needed, especially for auditing and investigating tax returns. Because these employees typically generate far more revenue than their salaries, the argument can be made that such units should be immune from budget cuts that result in furloughing employees. Nevertheless, treasury departments often are expected to suffer with all other departments when across-the-board layoffs occur.

Treasury departments often encounter difficulties in training their workers. One of the best forms of training is for new employees to be instructed by senior ones. If senior employees are used to train new employees, however, then important resources are diverted away from the main duty of collecting revenue.

Opportunities abound for unethical and illegal activities by employees. As the IRS has improved its computer operations, employees have gained wide access to the tax files of most private citizens, and some employees have been found browsing out of curiosity through the income tax returns of prominent citizens. In response, Congress passed the Taxpayer Browsing Protection Act of 1997.[79] In other instances, employees have been able to have tax refund checks illegally sent to themselves. Other employees may have important conflicts of interest, such as reviewing tax returns of corporations in which they have financial holdings, making obvious the need for financial disclosure systems in which employees must report their financial investments.

Congress, in passing the 1998 IRS Restructuring and Reform Act, made several changes in personnel management at the IRS. Management was given greater flexibility in personnel matters, incentives were provided for encouraging people to resign or retire, and the agency was directed to improve its training operations. Among the most controversial components of the law are what IRS employees refer to as the "Ten Deadly Sins." All employees found to have committed one or more must be fired, unless the IRS commissioner specifically intervenes. The "sins" include not getting the proper signatures when a taxpayer's home is to be seized for back taxes or threatening a tax audit for personal gain, such as an agent threatening a personal enemy with an audit. Hundreds of IRS agents have been fired because of the law and thousands more have been subjected to lengthy investigations. On the one hand, these "sins" have encouraged employees to work more conscientiously and particularly to avoid abusing taxpayers. On the other hand, the "sins" have caused morale problems among workers.[80]

Intergovernmental Relations in Tax Administration

There are intergovernmental aspects to tax administration. As already noted, some governments share information with each other to help detect noncompliance with tax laws. Local governments sometimes work together in joint billing, such as when a county, city, and school district prepare a single bill for property taxes. Tax provisions of governments are sometimes related to each other, which can unintentionally create policy and administrative problems. Changes in the federal income tax laws can affect provisions in state taxes, necessitating adjustments in those laws. The tax package adopted by Congress in 2002 mandated federal tax cuts that also resulted in state tax cuts, unless the states adjusted their laws accordingly. The federal government and the states have cooperated somewhat in tax administration.[81] As noted earlier, governments may expect tax and Social Security holdings to be submitted electronically. When a local government submits state income tax withholdings by check, the local government can be fined for failing to meet state requirements for electronic filing.

Debt Collection and Taxpayer Rights

One of the biggest debts owed government is taxes, but individuals and corporations also may owe several other types of debt to government. Loans, both direct and guaranteed, result in some defaults. Federal loan programs exist for college students, low-income housing, ship construction, development in other nations, and small businesses recovering from disasters, to name only a few. Various business transactions with government result in debts, such as farmers owing on crop insurance payments and foreign countries owing on purchases of agricultural commodities. Fines are another form of debt, as in the case of a corporation being fined for not meeting environmental standards for its mining operations.

The National Performance Review recommended that agencies be allowed "to use some of the money they collect from delinquent debts to pay for further debt collection efforts, and to keep a portion of the increased collections" as a form of incentive.[82] The review also recommended the use of private collection agencies in cases where their services would be cost-effective. Private collection agencies may be particularly useful regarding delinquent accounts, but it should be noted that these agencies often charge as much as a 50 percent commission for what they collect.

The federal government, as discussed in Chapter 6, is attempting to deal with the "hidden liabilities" of federal credit programs. General information on credit is contained in the *Budget of the United States Government,* and more detailed information is available through other documents produced by OMB and the Treasury Department.

OMB Circular A-129, Policies for Federal Credit Programs and Non-Tax Receivables, requires that agencies review their credit programs in terms of the costs and benefits to society. The circular establishes requirements for "sound" credit programs. As noted in Chapter 6, federal agencies must calculate expected credit losses on both direct and guaranteed loans. These losses can reduce the amount of funding available for future loans.

The Debt Collection Act of 1982, the Debt Collection Improvement Act of 1996, and OMB Circular A-129 further require that agencies take steps to improve their credit programs.[83] Loan applications must be examined with an eye toward uncovering the risks that government would take in approving the loans. Delinquent cases can be turned over to collection agencies and can be reported to consumer credit agencies. Salary offsets can be used in the case of federal employees who owe the government, and individuals may have income tax refunds withheld up to the amount owed. State governments also have used this latter technique.

In their zeal to extract as many tax dollars as possible from the public, tax administrators must keep in mind that the citizens are ultimately responsible for setting tax laws and for paying the salaries of tax administrators. In other words, administrators are employees of the citizenry. To this end, governments have adopted laws that declare a set of rights for taxpayers.

The 1998 Internal Revenue Service Restructuring and Reform Act contains more than 70 provisions that protect taxpayers and give them rights in dealing with the IRS.[84] The law includes such important provisions as altering the burden of proof in taxpayer cases. If the IRS challenges a taxpayer on reported income tax deductions, for example, the taxpayer need only provide some credible evidence, which then shifts the burden to the IRS to disprove the evidence. An important provision is that innocent spouses can be relieved of tax fines and other penalties. Restrictions are imposed on liens and on the seizing of taxpayer property for back taxes. The IRS, as prescribed by the 1998 legislation, maintains a taxpayer advocate office, which assists taxpayers in dealing with the agency.

Taxpayers' privacy needs to be protected, and taxpayers need to be treated equally. As noted earlier, some government workers have been found browsing the tax returns of celebrities and other prominent figures. Also, access to files needs to be restricted to ensure security and avoid record tampering. The audit process should not be politically motivated, as has sometimes been the case.

Cash Management

Cash management is the process of administering monies to ensure that they are available over time to meet expenditure needs and that, when temporarily not needed, they are invested at a minimum risk and a maximum yield. Cash management involves both short- and long-term investments; the latter are used mainly in the case of pension funds, which try to build up reserves for future years when employees retire. The state of the art of cash management is necessarily dependent on the state of the larger financial system.

Cash Flow

An essential aspect of cash management is forecasting when revenues will be received and in what amounts (see Chapter 4), and when expenditures will occur and in what amounts over the course of the fiscal year and beyond. A cash management plan will strive to accelerate the receipt of revenues and delay or minimize expenditures. Chapter 11 discusses cash flows statement as one form of financial reporting.

Inflow of Revenues. Enforcement of tax laws is viewed as one means of maximizing inflow. Other techniques involve depositing government receipts as soon as possible into interest-bearing accounts. For example, when tax payments accompany tax returns, these checks can be deposited immediately in banks and processing of the returns can occur later. Governments attempt to minimize the *float time* between when checks and currency are received and when they are deposited. Accounts receivable, involving payments due from citizens, corporations, and other governments, are kept to a minimum. Inflow can be accelerated by prompt invoicing — for example, airlines are invoiced on a monthly basis for their gate space at an airport terminal.

Lockboxes. Another technique used selectively by the federal government and some state governments is the lockbox system, which uses post office boxes that are under the control of banks. Taxpayers send their payments to designated post office boxes that are opened by banking officials, and the receipts are deposited promptly. The process reduces the amount of float time between when a check is written and when government deposits it and begins earning interest.

The Internal Revenue Service, however, learned that some risks are associated with having private contractors operate lockboxes that receive income tax returns. In 2001, employees of Mellon Bank destroyed or misplaced 40,000 returns, with the lost payments estimated at nearly $1 billion. The motivation may have been that workers feared they had fallen behind their quotas in processing returns.[85]

Expenditure Planning and Prompt Payment. Some techniques deal not with inflow, but with outflow. Here the concern is keeping money in interest-bearing accounts until it is needed to cover expenses and avoiding the need to borrow funds to cover expenses when revenues, such as tax receipts, are unavailable in the projected amounts. Cash flow planning is one reason that agencies are required to submit apportionment plans to the central budget office. Agencies may be instructed to shift expenditures in apportionment plans from one month or quarter to another. One rule is to pay promptly — that is, when bills are due and not before or after. This procedure is mandated at the federal level by the Prompt Payment Act of 1982, as amended.[86] Paying bills promptly saves money for the government, such as avoiding payment of late fees, and reduces a common problem encountered by government's suppliers — namely, not knowing when they will be paid. Although the vast majority of the federal government's payments to vendors are on time, that still leaves many millions of other payments that are late.

Of course, another concern is that not only should bills be paid on time, but that they also should be paid to the right party and in the right amount. Lax disbursement systems increase the chances that errors are made in paying vendors and that fraud occurs. Fraud can happen without a government officer being aware of the situation or in conjunction with the officer's assistance.

Borrowing. If forecasted expenditures cannot be adjusted downward to be no greater than expected revenues, then short-term borrowing becomes an important option. State and local governments borrow from banks for up to one year in cases where expenditures are considered essential and funds are unavailable to cover the expenses. The backing of these bank notes consists of future receipt of revenues, and the instruments are known as BANS, RANs, and TANs — *bond, revenue, and tax anticipation notes.*

Governments also may spend from their own reserves and borrow from themselves. *Unrestricted fund balances*, which are in effect contingency funds, may be drawn upon to meet unanticipated expenditure needs. Short-term borrowing from one fund to meet the cash needs of another also occurs, as in the case of a local government's borrowing from its pension funds. State laws, however, may greatly restrict such borrowing as a protection against depleting the funds.

Some governments have established *rainy day funds* or *budget stabilization funds* that can be used during years when revenues decline. Statutes or state constitutional provisions require that monies be placed in these funds when the economy improves and revenues rise and that monies may be withdrawn only when revenues decline by some set percentage. It is common for governments to have in these funds something in excess of 5 percent of their general funds.[87] These funds can reduce fiscal stress during recessions, such as occurred in the early 1990s and the early 2000s.[88] A state that dipped heavily into its rainy day fund in 2002 to balance its budget might then face major problems in 2003 if the economy had not recovered, perhaps forcing decision makers to increase taxes.

Investment Planning

When forecasts show periods during the year when revenues will exceed expenditures, plans are made for investment. Virtually all governments encounter this situation. Often there are spurts in revenue receipts, such as when property taxes are due or when state sales tax receipts are paid following the Christmas shopping period.

At least seven factors must be taken into account when devising an investment strategy:

1. *Security.* Financial institutions insure some deposits up to only $100,000.

2. *Maturity date.* Some instruments mature in a few months, while others mature in 30 years.

3. *Marketability or liquidity.* If cash is needed before the maturity date, may an instrument be sold to a third party or will the issuer convert the instrument to cash?

4. *Call provisions.* May the issuer repay the investor before the date of maturity?

5. *Denominations.* Minimum amounts for investing range from $1,000 to $100,000 or more.

6. *Yield or return on investment.* Yield is measured in terms of a percentage of the investment and often expressed as an interest rate.

7. *Legal authority.* State laws may prohibit the state government and local governments from making some types of investments.

Since the collapse of many savings banks in the 1980s, the security of investments has been a prominent concern of cash managers. When a government deposits funds with a bank, a typical requirement is that the bank set aside funds as collateral on the deposits as a means of protecting the investment in the event that the bank fails. An alternative that was developed in the 1990s is for the bank to purchase private deposit insurance. This insurance, known as ASSURETY, is available through the Municipal Bond Investors Assurance Corporation, which is the largest insurer of municipal bonds.[89]

Investment Instruments

The instruments available for state and local investments consist of three general types: federal government securities, corporate securities, and money market instruments. Any government must decide to what extent it wishes to invest in each type.

Federal Securities. Fully guaranteed federal securities include Treasury bills (T-bills), notes, and bonds. T-bills mature in 4, 13, 26, and 52 weeks.[90] They are sold at a discount by auction and consequently have no set percentage return. Treasury notes and bonds, which range in maturity from 1 to 30 years, have coupons that mature every six months. In 2002, the Treasury Department eliminated the sale of 30-year bonds, opting for securities with shorter maturities, such as 25 years. However, previously issued 30-year bonds remain in circulation.

Other securities issued by the federal government may or may not be guaranteed. Bonds issued by the Small Business Administration and participation certificates issued by the General Services Administration are guaranteed, unlike bonds issued by the Tennessee Valley Authority and the Postal Service.

In the 1990s, the Treasury Department launched two new instruments that are sensitive to inflation. When inflation occurs, the yield rate increases. Treasury inflation-indexed securities, known as TIPS, have their interest rate set at the time of auction. Their principal rises or falls based upon the U.S. city average of the consumer price index. If the consumer price index rises in a time period, the value of the note rises and then the interest is calculated based on the new principal. If deflation occurs, investors at the time of maturity are guaranteed the original purchase price.

The other inflation-sensitive instrument is the Series I savings bond. I bonds are purchased at face value, which ranges between $50 and $10,000, and have a fixed rate of return. Inflation rates, then, are added to the calculations. TIPS and I bonds have yield rates that are somewhat lower than instruments that lack the inflation protection.

Other Federal-Related Securities. Other securities are issued by credit institutions created by the federal government and may have full, limited, or no backing or ambiguous backing of the government. Instruments backed by the federal government include Farmers Home Administration insured notes and Ginnie Maes of the Federal Home Loan Mortgage Corporation. Instruments that do not have the expressed guarantee of the federal government but could be backed in emergency situations include Federal Home Loan Bank bonds, Federal Land Bank bonds, and Federal Intermediate Credit Bank bonds.

Many of these federal-related securities involve mortgages, including mortgages on homes, farms, cooperatives, and overseas investments (Asian

Development Bank notes and bonds and Export Import Bank debentures). Collateralized mortgage obligations, which are pools of mortgages held by financial institutions, constitute a relatively recent development in the mortgage market and provide high security and yields exceeding those of U.S. Treasury instruments.

Corporate Securities. Corporations are another possibility for the investment of state and local monies. Corporate bonds are essentially loans made to the issuers. Stocks, in comparison, represent ownership of the corporation. In the event that a corporation goes into bankruptcy, creditors such as bondholders are paid first. Whatever assets remain, if any, are then distributed among stockholders.

Money Market Instruments. Banks and savings and loan institutions provide numerous investment opportunities. Interest is paid on *negotiable order of withdrawal* (NOW) checking accounts and on savings accounts. Not only can government earn interest on these deposits, but other benefits also may be negotiated through *linked deposit agreements*. In these situations, banks, as a condition of receiving government deposits, may agree to make available more loans for housing in a community or for industrial development in a targeted area.

Monies also can be invested in money market instruments, with *certificates of deposit* (CDs) being one of the most popular. Issuers include banks, offshore subsidiaries of U.S. banks, and U.S. branches of foreign banks. The latter two issue what are known as Eurodollars and Yankee CDs, respectively, which are not guaranteed by the federal government. Some, but not all, CDs are negotiable. Issuers may charge interest penalties for early withdrawal of monies.

Other instruments include *bankers' acceptances, commercial paper,* and *repurchase agreements.* Bankers' acceptances are agreements to purchase a bank's agreement to loan money on a short-term basis to a corporation (one usually involved in international trade); the largest banks in the nation issue these instruments. Commercial paper, also available through banks, is a corporate promissory note. A repurchase agreement (repo) is a pool of U.S. government securities held by a financial institution and sold temporarily to state and local governments and other purchasers; the institution agrees to repurchase the securities at a later date.

Repurchase agreements are controversial because a few major firms specializing in repos went bankrupt in the mid-1980s. Some governments, including the local governments of Beaumont, Texas, and Toledo, Ohio, lost many millions of dollars. In response, Congress passed the Government Securities Act of 1986, which brought these securities dealers under the regulation of the Treasury Department and the Securities and Exchange Commission.[91]

State and local governments may purchase combinations of various money market instruments. One technique is to invest in a money market fund, which is a pool of securities; the Securities and Exchange Commission regulates these funds in an attempt to reduce the risks undertaken by investors. Despite these regulations, however, laws preclude many governments from investing in money market funds because they often include higher-risk investments such as Eurodollars.

Derivatives. One of the most controversial financial instruments is known as a derivative.[92] Derivatives are highly complex devices, which often are poorly understood by both those who sell them and the state and local governments that buy them. A derivative's value depends upon some underlying security or a market index; in other words, the derivative is a bet on what future interest rates will be. Governments purchase swaps that trade in variable rates for fixed rates, with the underlying gamble by the government being that the return on investment will be better with the fixed rate. Some derivatives take the form of collateralized mortgage obligations, which entail investing in a pool of mortgages with the return being based on changes in interest rates and changes in mortgage prepayment rates. As is discussed below, governments have lost large sums of money in these investments.

Investment Pools. Another money management technique that has become popular is for jurisdictions to combine their investments into a state-authorized investment pool. By pooling resources, smaller jurisdictions can take advantage of higher-yield investments that require larger investments than passbook savings or CDs. Liquidity is improved in that jurisdictions often can withdraw some of their monies from these pools without the financial loss that would be involved if they held securities themselves and had to liquidate them.

Yield Rates. **Table 10–2** provides a snapshot of yield rates for some of the instruments discussed here. As can be seen from the table, the rates varied considerably between the two years reported. Rates increase with risk and time. Bankers' acceptances, which involve risks, pay a higher return than generally risk-free T-bills. Bonds usually pay a higher rate than notes, and notes pay a higher rate than bills, because of the time factor involved.

Use of Investment Instruments. Most of the money (more than 90 percent) in state and local government trust funds, such as employee retirement systems and workers' compensation, is invested and little is kept on hand. In contrast, the money for the rest of state and local governments is kept much more fluid (one-third in cash and deposits and two-thirds invested). Retirement systems invest mainly in corporate stocks and bonds (52 percent), federal securities (13 percent), and foreign and international securities (13 percent).[93]

   As noted earlier, legal constraints affect investment programs. The state of Washington, for example, allows its treasurer to invest only in federal securities, repurchase agreements, commercial paper, certificates of deposit, and bankers' acceptances. In 2001, the state's two largest investments were in federal securities (71 percent) and repurchase agreements (14 percent).[94]

In many emerging market economies, newly developing pension systems impose generally strict regulations on investment instruments. It is common to require that at least 50 percent, and sometimes as much as 80 percent, of pension funds be invested in central government securities. Restrictions limiting investments outside the country are often tight, with no more than 10 percent being a common limitation. The motivations are partly to protect pension funds that have not previously existed from investing in too risky a portfoloio as a result of inexperience, and partly to ensure a flow of investment funds into central government securities.

Investment Risks

Investments are not risk-free. One type of risk involves the creditworthiness of the issuer of a security. Bonds issued by the federal government are nearly risk-free in this sense, and bonds issued by major corporations, such as General

Table 10–2 Yield Rates of Selected Investment Instruments, April 1997 and 2002

Instrument	1997	2002
Federal Securities		
4-week Treasury bills	NA	1.74
13-week Treasury bills	5.27	1.79
26-week Treasury bills	5.52	2.08
52-week Treasury bills	5.95	2.61
10-year Treasury notes	6.86	5.30
30-year Treasury bonds	7.08	5.88*
Other Deposits and Securities		
3-month certificates of deposit	5.70	1.87
3-month bankers' acceptances	5.57	1.92
3-month commercial paper	5.70	1.94
3-month Eurodollars	5.69	1.94

* Rate is for 25 years or longer.

Sources: Data from Federal Reserve Board, *Selected Interest Rates* (April 7, 1997, and April 4, 2002) and Moneyline Telerate (April 5, 2002), http://www.telerate.com.

Electric, are low risk. Another aspect of risk, however, is whether a particular instrument is volatile in terms of the yield it may produce. In this context, fixed-rate, long-term government bonds are risky investments. If a government's portfolio contains high-yield securities at a time when yield rates are declining, then the situation is generally positive. If trends reverse and yield rates climb above those in the portfolio, however, the government may have difficulty selling low-bearing securities. In that situation, a government's investments might fail to keep pace with inflation. Derivatives often are singled out as one of the most high-risk investments due to their volatility, even though the issuers of the derivatives may be creditworthy.

Orange County, California, the home of Disneyland and the fifth largest county in the United States, experienced a painful lesson in the risks of investing when it was forced to file for bankruptcy protection in 1994.[95] The county had been hailed as a shrewd investor, earning close to double the rate of return on investments compared with other governments and investment pools. The county had been so successful that 180 other local governments had deposited money with Orange County with the expectation of reaping the benefits of an investment policy that was more aggressive than the typical one. In 1994, reality hit hard: This approach resulted in a loss of nearly $2 billion.

What went wrong in Orange County? First, heavy investments were placed in derivatives, which as noted earlier are gambles on what will happen to interest rates. When rates went in the opposite direction than what was expected, the county was in trouble. Second, the situation was exacerbated by the use of *reverse repos*. As noted previously, a repurchase agreement (repo) is an instrument for investing money. A reverse repo, on the other hand, is a means for a government to borrow against securities that it holds; the instrument is a form of temporary debt for the issuer. Orange County used reverse repos to obtain additional money that was used in turn to purchase additional risky instruments. Subsequently, the Governmental Accounting Standards Board (GASB) issued Interpretation No. 3, Financial Reporting for Reverse Repurchase Agreements, which is intended to force governments to disclose their dealings in reverse repos and presumably rein in their use.

The Orange County debacle underscores the need for careful management of risk in developing a portfolio of investments. Derivatives may be a hedge against other investments that have low yields, but the derivatives themselves clearly entail substantial risks.

GASB has issued important directives regarding investments of government monies.[96] Statement No. 3, Deposits with Financial Institutions, Investments (including Repurchase Agreements), and Reverse Repurchase Agreements, mandates that governments report high-risk investments in their comprehensive annual financial reports (CAFRs). While an annual report showing such investments is helpful, more short-term reporting is needed. One option is to mark or report the value of each item in a portfolio on a daily basis. GASB Statement No. 31, Accounting and Financial Reporting for Certain Investments and for External Investment Pools, specifies that governments account for and report "fair value" for their investments in (1) interest-earning investment contracts, (2) external investment pools, (3) open-end mutual funds, (4) debt securities, and (5) equity securities, option contracts, stock warrants, and stock rights.

Federal Cash Management

The federal government's cash management system is considerably different from those of state and local governments. Federal monies are kept with the Federal Reserve System (see Chapter 15), which pays a form of interest for deposits, and banks, which also pay interest. The Financial Management Service (FMS) of the Treasury Department handles transactions. FMS provides extensive information on its Web site about the overall aspects of cash management and about specific operations.[97] For example, the FMS "Green Book" provides detailed instructions to financial institutions as to how they are to process federal monies. The agency's "Gold Book" gives specifics on how federal checks are to be reclaimed as when they have been forged or have been issued to persons no longer eligible for payment. Other departments and agencies handle many cash management transactions in accordance with instructions issued by the Treasury Department.

The inflow of federal receipts comes from taxes and other payments and from the sale of T-bills and other instruments discussed earlier. These sales are handled through the Federal Reserve and are limited according to the total debt ceiling set by Congress (Chapter 9). T-bills are auctioned off weekly and other instruments are sold less frequently; there is, of course, a secondary market for these securities.

Like state and local governments, the federal government is concerned about having needed cash on hand and minimizing the costs of money, such as avoiding late payment fees on government purchases and avoiding paying out funds any earlier than required. An additional consideration at the federal level is that the government's cash operations affect markets (see Chapter 15).[98] During the second half of the 1990s, the government ran surpluses. Unlike private individuals who could pay off credit card debt or pay down mortgages, however, the government was limited in its ability to use surplus monies to pay off debt. Because federal debt instruments remain in circulation for specified time periods, the government must wait for maturity dates to pay off debt. By 2000, there was speculation that the government might need to invest its money in corporate securities as a means of getting a return on the surplus.

That situation was reversed almost overnight with the disastrous attacks on the New York World Trade Center and the Pentagon in Washington, D.C., on September 11, 2001. The surplus quickly turned to deficit spending as the government rushed to fight terrorism. By 2002, the concern was how to have sufficient cash and stay within the congressionally mandated debt ceiling. By taking temporary action in the handling of government retirement monies, the government was able to borrow sufficient funds to meet its operating expenses and make its debt payments. Later that year, Congress had little choice but to raise the debt ceiling. Other contributing factors to the return to deficit spending included the 2001 tax cut and the deteriorating economy.

Another important consideration is that the federal government must meet its cash needs on a global basis. Sufficient amounts of money must be available at specific times in specific countries. For example, the Defense Department must handle large sums of foreign currency and, in doing so, exposes itself to potential problems in the value of such currency, particularly in the currency's devaluation.[99]

Currency and Coins. Since the 1990s, the federal government has been introducing redesigned currency.[100] The bills use color-shifting ink, security threads, watermarks, and microprinting that greatly deter counterfeiting. Nevertheless, counterfeiting remains a concern, given the sophistication of contempory photocopying equipment.

The U.S. Mint in the Treasury Department has used coinage literally as a "money-making" business.[101] By making coins that are collected and therefore taken out of circulation or never put into circulation, the government in effect makes money. The 25-cent pieces (quarters) that commemorate each state are examples. The Treasury was selling two quarters from the first day of mintage for $19.95, when the face value was only $0.50. The $1 golden Sacagawea coin was similarly marketed but in addition was available as a holiday ornament, a bolo tie, a key fob, and a chain pendant. In 2002, the Mint even had a clearance sale, its first ever.

Checks. In addition to redesigning currency and introducing a redesigned $1 coin, the government redesigned its checks. The punch-card checks that had been used for decades were replaced by checks that have counterfeiting protections and can be read by high-speed processing equipment. Despite advances made in checks and their processing, Congress decided in 1996 to phase out most check writing by January 1, 1999 (Debt Collection Improvement Act of 1996).[102] Nevertheless, the government continues to issue many millions of checks every year. The Treasury Department issued 86 million checks in 2001 as part of the tax rebate program adopted by Congress. Other major issuers of checks include the Social

Security Administration, Veterans Administration, and the Office of Personnel Management.

Electronic Fund Transfers. Advances in computer technology have made possible extensive use of electronic fund transfers (EFT). Through the use of electronic fund transfers, monies are moved via computer communication from bank to bank and from account to account. Monies received at one bank through a lock-box system, for instance, can be moved to other accounts in distant banks. Another advantage of electronic fund transfers is that they can be used for recurring payments, such as making direct deposits of Social Security payments into retirees' bank accounts. A form of electronic fund transfer is the *electronic benefit transfer*, which can be used to transfer funds through automatic teller machines; some governments use electronic benefit transfers to make payments to welfare recipients. EFTs also are used by governments to transfer funds for alimony and child support in cases of divorce. The transfers, which are processed nationally by a few large banking systems, cost much less per transaction than do conventional checks. In 2001, the Treasury Department disbursed $1.2 trillion, of which 72 percent was accomplished through EFTs.[103]

Letters of Credit. An important cash management technique, especially for the federal government, is the use of letters of credit. As mandated by the Cash Management Improvement Act of 1990, these letters are provided to governments and nonprofit corporations that are awarded grants and contracts.[104] The letters allow recipient organizations to establish credit at banks without the federal government having to provide money until it is needed. Funds then are transferred electronically into these accounts by the federal government. The procedure allows the government to delay until the last moment the transfer of funds, thereby saving it money. Recipients benefit because they can draw down on their letters of credit as soon as payments are due. The University of Massachusetts, for example, reports that most federal dollars it receives come through this mechanism.[105]

Other Cash Management Considerations

Computer Usage. New computer technology has greatly altered how financial institutions operate and how governments handle cash. As already noted, electronic fund transfers have greatly modified how government does business. The World Wide Web, which was in its infancy in the early 1990s, is today a commonly available source of information about investment opportunities.[106] Another example of computer applications involves municipal water systems. Experiments are being conducted in which electronic water meters are connected to customers' telephone lines, with the meters being programmed to call in billing information at specified intervals.[107]

Intergovernmental Relations. Cash management has important intergovernmental aspects. States, as noted earlier, have passed laws setting standards for their local governments, which often view these laws as unnecessarily restrictive. Several states have established *investment pools* for their local governments.[108] Some states provide assistance to local governments in the development of cash management plans. One important issue is the timing of grant payments that the federal government makes to state and local governments; the former, for cash management reasons, attempt to provide grant installments at the last possible moment. The Cash Management Improvement Act of 1990 provides that states are to pay interest on federal grant monies if the monies are received earlier than required and that the federal government must pay interest if it is tardy in providing promised grant monies.

Cash and Investment Managers. As is obvious, cash management involves a complex set of interdependent activities that require extensive expertise. For that reason, governments do not attempt to operate solely with their own capabilities. A state or local government will select one or more financial institutions to provide a range of services. Banks will receive checks, clear them, and deposit them in government accounts. A government may have a *bank concentration account* into which monies are first entered and then disbursed to others; each day the bank will move money into accounts requiring deposits to cover checks, and any remaining funds will be placed in overnight interest-bearing instruments. Banks offer EFT services, lockbox services, armored cars, safety deposit boxes, lines of credit, and more. These institutions can provide a wide range of investment services and can handle the registration of government bonds and payments to bondholders. A preferred method for selecting a bank for everyday transactions or a securities dealer for managing an investment portfolio is to request bids from competing institutions.

▆ Procurement

Procurement entails the acquisition of resources required in providing government services.[109] While this function is not at the core of budgeting, it has major budgetary implications. "In fiscal year 1998, the federal government spent $177 billion (or roughly 10 percent of its budget) on contracted goods or services, while state and local governments spent about $1.6 trillion (or 40 percent of state/local budgets) in the same year."[110] Some government agencies, such as the Defense Department and the National Aeronautics and Space Administration, spend a majority of their resources on contracted products and services rather than delivering services directly on their own. In addition, most other federal agencies accomplish their missions through the actions of other parties, usually through grants and other transfers of funds. The U.S. Department of Education, for example, delivers little direct education but provides grants to state and local education agencies in support of congressionally approved federal education objectives.

Procurement, of course, is extremely big business. The top five companies in federal contracting in fiscal 2000 were Lockheed Martin, Boeing, Raytheon, Northrop Grumman, and General Dynamics. All of these companies play major roles in defense and the aerospace industries. However, also included in the top 100 were the University of California (ranked 6th), California Institute of Technology (17th), Johns Hopkins University (38th), the University of Chicago (43rd), and Federal Express (49th).[111]

Organizational Configurations

Most jurisdictions have procurement systems that blend centralized and decentralized services. A central purchasing agency may be responsible for acquiring commonly used materials, such as office furniture and supplies, while line agencies have authority to purchase items used primarily by themselves. Centralization, at least in theory, has the advantage of providing overall controls to ensure that appropriate procedures are followed, resulting in fair competition among government suppliers and the purchase of quality goods and services at the lowest possible prices. Decentralization, on the other hand, presumably reduces red tape, allowing individual agencies to make purchases as needed and to custom-tailor purchases to their specific needs. The National Performance Review, in recommending greater decentralization in federal procurement, cited instances where buying in bulk through central purchasing cost the government more than it would have spent purchasing smaller quantities on a decentralized basis.[112] A survey of cities and counties found that 46 percent were centralized, only 3 percent were decentralized, and 51 percent were mixed.[113]

At the federal level, several major organizational units are responsible for procurement. The General Services Administration (GSA) provides overall support to departments by procuring buildings, equipment, motor vehicles, computer systems, telephone systems, supplies, day care centers for employees' dependents, and the like. Its operations are immense. In any given year, the agency buys about 55,000 vehicles, spends several billions of dollars every year on construction, manages more than 300 million square feet of building space (excluding parking), and keeps many thousands of items on hand in its warehouses.[114]

Although GSA has numerous components, the main ones are the Public Buildings Service, the Federal Supply Service (FSS), and the Federal Technology

Service (FTS). The Public Buildings unit operates with appropriated funds, while the other two units operate with revolving funds by buying goods and services and then selling them to federal agencies. FSS maintains a wide range of catalog items, whereas FTS concentrates on information technology and telecommunications. To some extent, FTS and FSS have competed with one another in selling to federal agencies.[115]

All federal line departments and agencies carry out procurement, with the Department of Defense having one of the largest procurement operations. Defense hires the equivalent of 700,000 workers through its contracting operations.[116] The Defense Logistics Agency purchases many items centrally for the department, while the individual services also have purchasing authority.[117]

Having many procurement offices can result in a hodgepodge of operations, each with its own peculiar set of regulations. In 1974, Congress attempted to deal with this problem by creating the Office of Federal Procurement Policy (OFPP) within OMB.[118] President Clinton strengthened the OFPP's role in 1994 by issuing Executive Order 12931, which charged the unit with providing "broad policy guidance and overall leadership" in procurement. The OFPP, while not conducting purchasing activities, is responsible for coordinating the activities of purchasing offices.

Procurement Objectives. A procurement program has several objectives. One chief concern is having the materials and supplies available when needed and avoiding stock outages. Every agency must keep focused on its mission and use procurement as a means of meeting that mission in a timely fashion. The September 11, 2001, attack on the Pentagon, the headquarters for the Defense Department, led to the issuance of a reconstruction contract in which a primary objective was to restore the damaged portion of the building within one year — that is, by September 11, 2002.

Keeping unit costs as low as possible is another objective; often the lowest costs for acquiring items are obtained by ordering large quantities, whether large amounts of office stationery or entire fleets of automobiles. Ordering large quantities, however, conflicts with another concern — namely, keeping stocked items to a minimum. Procurement specialists strive to determine *economic ordering quantities*, or when to purchase particular types of items and in what quantities. Some purchasing offices have shifted to *just-in-time ordering*, in which items are received from vendors when needed, thereby eliminating the cost of warehousing these items. The widespread use of computer systems has greatly increased the ability of organizations — both public and private — to implement just-in-time ordering.

Procurement objectives often conflict with one another. On the one hand, procurement policies may include numerous specific requirements that are viewed as red tape and unnecessarily hinder executives in managing their operations. On the other hand, such red tape may be important in preventing fraud and waste. President George W. Bush recommended a Freedom to Manage program that included giving greater flexibility in managing government property, such as agencies exchanging properties with one another and leasing underutilized government building space to private corporations.[119]

Choices also must be made between *purchasing*, *leasing*, and *privatizing*. In some instances, there may be financial and other advantages to leasing a building rather than purchasing it. The federal government, however, may rely too heavily on leasing office space, as ownership presumably is less expensive in the long run. A wide range of equipment can be leased, including photocopying machines, computers, and dump trucks. The Defense Department even has considered leasing rather than buying its most expensive weapons systems.[120] *True* or *operating leases* are those in which the government pays for the specified period and gains no ownership of whatever is being leased, whereas *lease-purchase agreements* provide for ownership after a specified period.

Outsourcing, as discussed earlier, is another option and may involve contracting with a private firm to use its facilities, personnel, and other resources to deliver a service. In many cases, private contractor employees and government employees work side by side to produce services in government facilities. Federal agencies must follow the guidance in Circular A-76, which covers contracts for commercial (nongovernmental) activities. While many services can be contracted out, policy making is regarded as a core activity that cannot be privatized. This possibility becomes a concern in situations where government relies heavily on consulting firms to the extent that they seem to be responsible for setting policy or conducting other inherently governmental functions. A blurring of organizational boundaries occurs when a government agency works not with just one but two or more contractors on a particular program or project. In making a choice among these options, a paramount concern must be to use tax dollars efficiently.

The process prescribed by Circular A-76 is a complicated one. OMB provides a "Supplemental Handbook" detailing the procedure to be used. Each year OMB issues guidance on cost figures to be used in calculating anticipated pay raises and changes in the costs of supplies and equipment. An agency must identify an activity that can be contracted out, must establish a process for accepting bids from both private entities and the public organization that currently is providing the service, must review the bids and select the winner, and then must implement the outcome. In the Defense Department, this process often takes 18 months or longer. These competitions tend to result in cuts in the federal work force either because the work is contracted out or because the government unit won the bid by being more cost-effective — namely, operating with fewer workers.[121]

Part of the Circular A-76 process involves setting performance targets or standards so that it is clear what work is to be accomplished. At issue has been the fact that sometimes the same people who set the standards were the ones who prepared the in-house bids to retain operations within the government. The General Accounting Office ruled that this situation involves a conflict of interest and that the two functions need to be performed by different individuals.[122]

In 2001, the General Accounting Office, as mandated by Congress, created a special panel to evaluate the Circular A-76 process and more generally to study the government's policy in regard to commercial activities.[123] The panel's final report recommended scrapping this process and substituting one contained in the Federal Acquisition Regulation (FAR).[124] The FAR process focuses on selecting the contractor that offers the "best value" rather than simply the one with the lowest bid.

In addition to Circular A-76, the Federal Activities and Inventory Reform (FAIR) Act of 1998 gives priority to outsourcing. Each year federal agencies, under OMB's guidance, must report what actitivites are "not inherently governmental in nature."[125] Upward of 50 percent of all jobs analyzed have been identified as potentially being outsourced. The law does not require that some or all of these jobs actually be contracted out, but certainly there is an implication that maybe they should be contracted out. The lists can be challenged, however. Contractors usually contend that jobs that should have been included were not. Employees and unions typically contend the opposite.

The George W. Bush administration, in its *President's Management Agenda*, identified "competitive sourcing" as one of its five government-wide initiatives. The administration has used FAIR to further that initiative. Agencies were instructed to outsource 5 percent of their jobs by October 2002 and an additional 10 percent by October 2003. This effort would result in tens of thousands of jobs being transferred to the private sector.[126] The administration said it would someday like to have half of all of these jobs outsourced.[127]

In late 2002, OMB released a draft revision of Circular A-76. The administration maintained that the competitive process within Circular A-76 was workable and that a shift to the best-value approach was unnecessary for most competitions. A major change was that most competitions were to be completed in no more than 12 months.

The Contracting Process

Steps. Standard procedures are normally followed when contracting for products or services. Specifications for what is to be purchased are determined. For example, a truck might be required to have a specified ground clearance, load capacity, passenger capacity, and the like. Then, bidding procedures begin through the issuance of *invitations for bid* (IFBs), *requests for proposal* (RFPs), and *requests for quo-*

tation (RFQs). An IFB is used when a government has a reasonably detailed conception of what is to be purchased, such as the painting of the exterior of a building. An RFP or RFQ is used in a situation where some latitude exists on the part of the bidder in terms of what is to be offered. Once bids are received, they are analyzed and, in the case of IFBs, awards are made to the lowest responsible bidder. In a competition involving an RFP, an award might be made to a higher bidder, one that was thought to have the best approach to dealing with a problem. When the government selects a firm using an RFQ, bilateral negotiations are required before a final selection may be made. In contrast, with an RFP the government may select a firm without further negotiations. The receipt of a product or service follows the signing of a contract or the award of a grant. Additional steps include inspecting the product or service received and paying the contractor.

Not all spending is handled through the bidding process. As discussed later, many small purchases can be handled through government credit cards and no bids are required. Although restricted to small purchases, the credit card transactions amount to many billions of dollars each year and pose major challenges for auditors.

In some situations, contracts are awarded not to one company but to several firms. The federal government, because it serves the entire nation, finds it advantageous to contract with several suppliers in the same industry. This *multiple-award schedule system* makes goods and services available on a standby basis, allowing agencies to order them when needed. All forms of construction, ranging from simple repair and maintenance to the construction of an entire building, can be handled through a job order contracting mechanism in which suppliers agree to provide services at specified costs when needed. For example, a painting firm might sign a contract agreeing to charge a set amount per square foot; and any agency could then hire the firm for painting services.

The federal government has experimented with *reverse auctioning*. This technique allows bidders during the open bidding period to see the bids made by competing firms but not the identities of the firms themselves. If a company finds its bid has been undercut by another bidder, then the first bidder may consider lowering its bid to meet the competition.

Another feature of some procurement programs is specification of performance in terms of timeliness and quality. For example, a contract for a highway construction project may stipulate that the project must be completed by a specified date, with financial penalties being imposed for each day beyond the deadline.

The 1994 Federal Acquisition Streamlining Act instructs federal agencies to develop *results-oriented* or *performance contracts* for acquisitions other than standardized commercial items.[128] In other words, when an agency buys a service, such as using a firm to process grant applications from local governments, standards should be set for evaluating the firm's performance. Measurable performance is increasingly a part of federal contracts for research and development. These contracts contain award fee incentives in which contractors can achieve higher or lower fees or profits based on their performance. To engage in such contracting, agencies must be able to specify what work to accomplish, at what time, and with what degree of quality. The George W. Bush administration set as a goal to have a majority of all contracts valued at $25,000 or more to be on a performance basis within five years.[129]

Competition. Competition in procurement is considered one of the best means of ensuring quality products or services at minimum cost. Lack of competition may result from blatant favoritism in awarding contracts or from somewhat more subtle ploys, such as specifying a named product brand and model in the IFB. At the state and local levels, corporations have become more aggressive in challenging contract awards when they seem to violate legal requirements for competition.

The Competition in Contracting Act of 1984 was passed to encourage greater competition in federal contracting and specifically enhanced the powers of losing bidders in mounting legal challenges to the awards.[130] In addition to filing a protest with the contracting agency itself or with the GAO, a losing bidder may be able to appeal to the General Services Board of Contract Appeals, the Court of Federal Claims, or a federal district court.[131]

The 1994 Federal Acquisition Streamlining Act contains important provisions that limit bid protests, which often are perceived as needlessly delaying the awarding of contracts. President Clinton's Executive Order 12979 of 1995 instructs agencies to devise alternative dispute resolution (ADR) procedures, such as the use of neutral third parties.

Several factors discourage competition among would-be contractors. Lack of knowledge about how contracts are awarded and how to prepare a bid excludes some companies from bidding, although that problem is somewhat mitigated today given the vast amounts of information on contracting available on government Web sites. The Defense Department has established Procurement Technical Assistance Centers in many states. These centers assists business firms in understanding the process by which they can sell their goods and services to the government.[132] Many procurements are so large and complex that companies would have to make major investments in personnel and technology just to become competitive in the bidding process. *Design-and-build contracts*, in which several contract awards may be made for the design phase, with the best design being selected for the build or implementation phase, enable more firms to compete for such larger, more complex contracts.

Competition is restricted in other ways as well. A close and long-term relationship between a government agency and a contractor can develop over time. When a contract is to be rebid for a new time period, the company already holding the contract usually has a decided advantage.

Contract bundling tends to prohibit smaller companies from competing for contracts. In contract bundling, several would-be small contracts are put up for bid as a single, large contract. The advantages to government are at least twofold. First, the administrative costs of handling the bidding and contracting processes are reduced. Second, the item or service being purchased often is less expensive when it is ordered in bulk as in a bundled contract than when it is purchased in several smaller contracts. However, such bundled contracts can involve a diverse set of products and services, many of which are beyond the scope of a single small company, thereby making the company unable to bid. OMB has instructed agencies to limit their use of the bundling procedure.

Companies become reluctant to participate in competitions when, if they win, they might have to wait for weeks or months to receive the money owed them. Delays in payments can bankrupt a small firm. Even when payments occur promptly, small firms may face other problems. If payments are made but then later the funding agency demands greater documentation on transactions, the small firm may be unable to comply due to weak recordkeeping. Whatever the situation, it will be costly from the standpoint of the time consumed in trying to comply with the government's requests.

Government contracting also opens up contractors to liability over their compliance with various employment laws, such as equal employment opportunity based on race, gender, and the like. The Rehabilitation Act of 1973 requires affirmative action in government hiring of people with disabilities, and this law is extended to private companies when they become government contractors.[133] Similarly, affirmative action is required in the hiring and promoting of veterans under the Vietnam Era Veterans' Readjustment Assistance Act of 1974.[134] Requirements such as these may discourage companies from bidding on federal contracts, not because the companies oppose equal opportunity or hiring veterans but because they fear lawsuits or the threat of lawsuits.

The widespread use of the Web beginning in the 1990s has posed major challenges in the procurement arena. Expectations have developed that procurement should be an essential component of what is known as e-government (electronic government). Governments at all levels have worked diligently to convert their paper-based processes for procurement to ones that include electronic processing.[135] These efforts are complicated by the massiveness of procurement programs in large governments, by statutory restrictions that specify processes to be used, and by rapidly changing technology.

At the federal level, the center of attention is the Acquisition Reform Network (AcqNet).[136] The network's Web site includes a link to Federal Business Opportunities or FedBizOpps, which is to be the single portal into federal procurement for purchases of more than $25,000.[137] AcqNet includes links to e-government initiatives and the Federal Acquisition Management Information System (FAMIS). The latter is expected to become a central repository of information about government purchasing data. Departments will enter data into FAMIS on a real-time basis, when purchase contracts are signed.

Computer technology is as important to government agencies that consume products and services as it is to firms that sell to government. The General Services Administration operates GSA Advantage!, an on-line shopping center.[138] Agencies can not only compare prices on products and place orders, but also configure products and add accessories. GSA offers to agencies similar services in the information technology realm.

Contract management is another critical component of the procurement process.[139] What good is a contract if government procurement officers fail to follow up to be sure that a business met its obligations under the contract? One problem has been for contractors to meet their obligations but for government to overpay the contractors. Congress has required agencies to use *recovery auditing* to identify overpayments and recoup money that was misspent.[140]

Reforms. Numerous efforts have been made to improve procurement practices. Each year Business Solutions in the Public Interest Awards are made to acquisition personnel and teams that demonstrate effective and creative approaches to contracting problems. The awards are administered by the Council for Excellence in Government and *Government Executive* magazine in cooperation with the Office of Federal Procurement Policy.

Procurement procedures become increasingly complex as additional, well-intended requirements are imposed. Three presidential executive orders are instructive. Executive Order 12843 places restrictions on purchasing that in any way involves ozone-depleting substances. Executive Order 12845 requires that computer equipment be energy efficient. Executive Order 12873 mandates recycling and waste prevention in the acquisition process. While each of these orders has laudable purposes, each requires administrators to establish procedures to ensure compliance with the orders, and the steps that are imposed translate into time and cost demands.

One prescription might be to simplify the government procurement process. Off-the-shelf purchasing of commercial items may be less expensive than specifying items that then might require special designs and types of construction. As an example of the rigidity in government purchasing, the General Services Administration had elaborate specifications for the design and durability of "ash receiver[s], tobacco (desk type)" when commercially available ashtrays probably would have been suitable, especially given that smoking is banned in most government buildings. Simplification was one of the chief objectives of the 1994 Federal Acquisition Streamlining Act and President Clinton's Executive Order 12931 of 1994. The law eliminated many contracting procedures for purchases amounting to less than $100,000 and, in purchases of commercial items, waived more than 30 laws that required bidders to collect and submit detailed information of limited utility as part of their bids. The Federal Acquisition Reform Act (FARA) or Clinger-Cohen Act of 1996 broadened the definition of commercial services, bringing more purchasing activities under the simplified procedures.[141] A study by the General Accounting Office of simplified acquisition in defense, however, was unable to document any important benefits achieved through the process.[142]

Another reform frequently mentioned is a move to upgrade the quality of the procurement work force. High-quality workers need to be recruited into government and rewarded for creativity in improving contracting practices. The 1994 legislation provided for the establishment of incentives for purchasing personnel. Training in ethics and technical knowledge also has been prescribed. The National Institute of Government Purchasing makes courses available to purchasing officials, as do private firms. During the Clinton administration, OMB had a regulation that blacklisted from future contracts any company that had engaged in illegal or unethical practices. The potential is great for conflicts of interests developing between government workers who are responsible for contracting and companies that sell to the government.

Despite sustained efforts to improve procurement practices, the field has been plagued with scandals involving waste (as in the case of toilet seats that cost the military hundreds of dollars) and charges of bribery and other forms of collusion between government contractors and purchasing offices. The scandals that occur periodically in the Defense Department are especially notable in that military contracts often involve billions of dollars. Defense, of course, has not been the only area subject to such scandals. Unethical and illegal practices in purchasing arise with some degree of frequency in all federal domestic agencies and throughout state and local governments. Contract auditing is an important mechanism for revealing and presumably deterring such illegal practices. In the final days of the Clinton administration, the Federal Acquisition Regulatory Council adopted regulations that strengthened requirements against contracting with companies that had unsatisfactory records on integrity and business ethics. One year later, the Bush administration repealed the regulations on the ground that adequate safeguards existed without the 2000 regulations.[143] The repeal may have been ill advised given the major accounting irregularities and alleged fraud by major government contractors, such as WorldCom, that came to light in 2002.

A long-standing problem is how to allow for indirect costs or overhead in government procurement. When government purchases a service, for example, costs include direct expenses, such as the materials and personnel needed to provide the service, and indirect or overhead expenses, such as costs associated with central administrative offices, including the budgeting and accounting office, personnel office, computer operations, and the like. Other indirect costs include the heating, electricity, and janitorial services used in the building that houses the employees working on the project. These costs, while legitimate, can become large and can greatly inflate the cost of a project. Consequently, government procurement offices have repeatedly attempted to place limits on indirect costs. Part of the problem involves determining what is and is not appropriately assigned to the indirect category. Universities as well as most other types of organizations have been challenged by federal authorities for inflating indirect expenses as a means of increasing their federal grant and contract monies. Several of the larger federal departments have what are called *cognizant audit agencies*, such as the Defense Contract Audit Agency, that focus entirely on auditing, negotiating, and approving contractors' indirect rates. The Department of Health and Human Services is the cognizant agency for approving overhead rates for many universities and nonprofit grantees and contractors.

Problem Areas and Innovations

Procurement is undergoing extensive changes too numerous to discuss here, but a few can be noted. One major change is the growing importance of contracting for services as distinguished from acquisition of products. At the federal level, services contracting accounts for more than 40 percent of all acquisitions.[144] Service contracting presents special challenges of determining what services of what quality and what quantity are to be delivered and then monitoring the process to assure that the contract requirements are met and that only appropriate expenses are charged for those services. Measuring the costs of services is particularly troublesome due to variations in accounting rules used in the private and public sectors. This situation complicates efforts to compare the costs of producing a service by a corporation with those of a government agency. Further, when such service contracts are awarded to nonprofit entities, important problems may arise over how government expects operations to be managed and how the nonprofits normally manage themselves.[145] Legislation has been proposed that would extend the acquisition simplification process of the Clinger-Cohen Act (see above) to the services arena of the federal government.

The General Services Administration has expanded its role in procuring services through the use of its Management, Organization, and Business Improvement Service (MOBIS). GSA negotiates with contractors and develops a list of approved consulting and other service providers. Then, agencies can procure these services at pre-established hourly rates. The mechanism has become controversial as there is concern that agencies may use the MOBIS mechanism to avoid requirements for competition in procurement.[146]

Government-issued credit cards have become standard components of acquisition systems. Some governments now provide employees with credit cards so that they may charge their travel expenses and be reimbursed later rather than use travel advances or their personal funds to cover costs until being reimbursed. Credit cards also are being used for small purchases, $2,500 or less in the case of the federal government. The cards are helpful in remote areas that lack ready access to General Services Administration supply centers. Today's technology allows credit cards to work or not work at specific stores; for example, the cards would not work at liquor stores. With more than 3 million cards in circulation in the federal government, abuse can be expected. The Defense Department was sharply criticized when it came to light that employees had used the cards to purchase hundreds of dollars worth of cosmetics and compact discs.[147] Senator Grassley (Republican of Iowa) said, "We have found government employees using their cards to make mortgage payments and pay closing costs, to buy cars, an engagement ring, racetrack betting, Elvis photos from Graceland, a framed John Elway jersey, a trip to the Rose Bowl game, and even Caribbean cruises. You name it. They're doing it."[148]

A continuing problem is the extent to which procurement should support affirmative action to assist minority-owned businesses and women contractors. In 1995, the Federal Acquisition Streamlining Act set nonbinding goals of contracting with minority-owned businesses, and President Clinton issued Executive Order 12928 calling upon agencies to develop methods for encouraging minority businesses and historically black colleges and universities to bid on contracts with the government. To avoid charges of reverse discrimination, agencies do not use quotas but rather pursue outreach and other programs to help make minority businesses aware of contracting opportunities and provide advice on how to prepare procurement proposals.

The Supreme Court has ruled that set-aside programs for minority businesses in state and local procurement is permissible only when there is documentation of discrimination against such businesses.[149] That ruling was later extended to the federal government.[150] The court was expected to make a definitive ruling on federal procurement in 2001 but then decided the case had been "improvidently granted" certiorari and dismissed it.[151]

Acquisition programs often are expected to provide special opportunities to small businesses that otherwise might be locked out of selling to the government by large corporations. Executive Orders 13169 and 13170 require federal agencies to increase opportunities for small businesses, especially disadvantaged ones.

In the contracting process, labor–management issues may arise, such as whether a contractor will enter into agreements with labor unions. Executive Order 12871 established the National Partnership Council and required federal agencies to work cooperatively with unions. In 2001, President George W. Bush revoked this order by issuing Executive Order 13202. The new order called for "neutrality towards government contractors' labor relations on federal and federally funded construction projects."

Other potential procurement problems involve energy, the environment, and immigrants. Agencies are expected to purchase equipment that is efficient in the use of energy and minimizes pollution. Executive Order 12969 of 1995 states that federal agencies should contract only with firms that comply with federal requirements for reporting the use of toxic chemicals. A study by the General Accounting Office found that federal agencies do poorly in determining whether their purchases are "environmentally friendly."[152] Executive Order 12989 of 1996 prohibits agencies from contracting with companies that the Attorney General has determined to have violated immigration laws by hiring illegal alien workers.

Security has emerged as a vast new area of purchasing. Although security-related purchasing has long existed, the attacks of September 11, 2001, dramatized the need to reevaluate security in all aspects of government. All levels of government are concerned with increasing the level of security for buildings, other structures such as bridges and dams, computer networks, and the like.

Some important aspects of procurement involve intergovernmental relations. States, through laws and regulations, set standards for purchasing conducted by their local governments. Cooperative purchasing is used to increase the "buying power" of governments. These agreements are forged among local governments or sometimes between local governments and their state government. The Federal Acquisition Streamlining Act permits state and local governments to make purchases through the General Services Administration, but the Federal Acquisition Reform Act of 1996 temporarily suspended that provision.

Contracting of services is an important form of intergovernmental relations. *The Lakewood Plan* in Los Angeles County, California, is probably the oldest and most extensive such program in the United States. Cities within the county may contract with the county for virtually all of their services, which are provided at cost and at the same level of quality as the county provides to unincorporated areas. Some states contract with each other, as when one state contracts to have another state house some of its prisoners.

▮ Risk Management

To provide services, governments must have property and personnel. Arising from this simple fact are a series of *exposures* or *risks*, such as the risk of property being damaged or lost owing to natural disasters, employee error, and fraud by employees and others. Property damage can lead to major repair or replacement costs and to loss of income (e.g., structural problems in a municipal stadium may force its closing). The Chicago flood of 1992, in which water from the Chicago River entered buildings throughout the downtown area, is an example of how inattention to a problem — in this case, leakage into a tunnel system caused by faulty construction under government contract — can have disastrous consequences.

Risk management considers what disasters might occur and the probability of each happening. Until September 11, 2001, the probability of commercial aircraft being used as devices to destroy major landmark buildings would have been considered quite low. Since then, risk managers have had to reexamine the vulnerability of food supplies, water systems, nuclear power plants, ports, and the like to deliberate acts of terrorism.

Other risks pertain to financial guarantees. As discussed in Chapter 6, the federal government strives to identify the extent of its exposure in loan programs and other activities, such as mortgage guarantees.

Liability

Governments are vulnerable to suits brought by employees or by corporations and private citizens. Negligence is often the basis of suits in which government is alleged not to have acted the way a "reasonable" person would and inflicted harm as a result. Local governments have been sued for allowing the leakage of harmful chemicals from landfills into privately owned water wells. Governments also may be sued for violating antitrust legislation, as in the instance where a city favors one cable television operator over another. Court-awarded financial settlements can be extraordinarily large; in some suits against local governments, the awards have been greater than the governments' total annual budgets.

Laws, of course, govern liability cases.[153] The federal government may be sued only in federal court. One of the most important federal laws is the Federal Tort Claims Act of 1946, which selectively permits suits against the government in cases not arising out of contract.[154] State and local governments sometimes may be sued in federal courts as well as in state courts. Antitrust cases against local governments, for example, are the domain of federal courts. Discrimination cases can be filed in federal and state courts.

Managing Risks

Governments need a management strategy for dealing with liability exposure. Risk management planning begins by identifying risks and, where possible, eliminating them. A faulty woodworking machine in a school shop should be repaired; the repair will improve the safety of the machine, thereby eliminating some risk when students use it. A road intersection widely known to be dangerous can be redesigned. A community that is subject to hurricanes obviously cannot avoid these fierce storms, but it can take steps to be prepared for such emergencies.

Having eliminated or reduced risks, governments must be prepared to deal with the remaining areas of exposure. Commercial insurance is used by governments and awarded through a bidding process similar to any other purchasing arrangement. Another option is self-insurance, where a government sets aside funds on a regular basis to cover awards or simply expends funds from the current budget to cover abnormal expenses (for example, the costs of repairing police cars damaged in the line of duty). In some instances, governments help cover each other's risks through self-insurance pooling. Insurance premiums for liability coverage have become extremely expensive, sometimes so expensive that insurance is beyond the reach of governments — if it is available at all. Costs are a function of the nature of a policy. Salient factors include the number of employees and officials of a government, the services covered, the deductibles included, and the loss experience. The latter is not just the experience of a particular government. A given city might have had no major suits filed against it, but because some cities have encountered major legal problems, as in cases involving landfills, all cities pay heavily for coverage.

The costs of risk management are typically handled centrally. That is, the costs of insurance premiums, court-mandated awards to injured parties, out-of-court settlements, and the like are handled by the central budget and not charged to department budgets. Were line agencies charged for these costs, managers would be more aware of the costs of their operations and would have greater incentives to reduce risks. Faced with staggering insurance premiums, a government may choose to discontinue a service, such as operating a community swimming pool.

According to GASB, governments should report risks in their financial statements. GASB Statement No. 10, as amended by Statement No. 30, covers risks associated with torts, thefts, business interruptions, errors or omissions, job-related illnesses or injuries of employees, and acts of God. Governments, when reporting pension plan risks, are expected to conform with GASB Statement No. 27. As noted earlier, GASB Statement No. 31 covers the reporting of investment risks.

The field of risk management requires special expertise. The Public Risk Management Association is a focal point for the profesional development of this field. The organization has identified a wide set of core competencies that every risk manger needs.[155]

Summary

Execution is the conversion of plans embodied in the budget into day-to-day operations. At stake are factors such as interpreting and complying with legislative intent as prescribed in appropriations and providing the services that have been authorized. Control over line agencies is exercised through apportionment planning and preauditing of expenditures.

Since the 1980s, there has been a resurgence of interest in achieving economy and efficiency. Outsourcing of services has been used as one means of increasing the efficiency of operations.

Budget offices are involved in a host of activities other than preparing budgets. On the federal level, OMB exercises major powers related to information collection and dissemination and to agencies issuing regulations.

Tax administration and cash management, which usually are under the direction of a secretary of treasury, are processes aimed at maximizing revenues and minimizing costs. Numerous mechanisms are used to enforce tax laws, ranging from offering assistance in preparing tax returns to prosecuting delinquent taxpayers.

Cash management is the process of administering monies to ensure that they are available to meet expenditure needs and that monies, when temporarily not needed, are invested at a minimum risk and a maximum yield. Many instruments exist for investing state and local funds. The Treasury Department handles federal cash management through the Federal Reserve System.

Procurement entails the acquisition of resources required in providing government services; risk management is concerned with protecting those resources. Governments often have a central purchasing office but allow individual departments some independence in purchasing products and services. A procurement program attempts to purchase only what is needed, avoid stock outages, and keep unit costs low. Risk management attempts to eliminate or reduce risk exposure and to prepare for such events as damage to government property and liability suits arising out of government operations.

Notes

1. K. Thurmaier, Execution Phase Budgeting in Local Governments, *State and Local Government Review* 27 (1995): 102–117; W.B. Hildreth and A. Khan, eds., Symposium on Budget Execution, *Journal of Public Budgeting, Accounting & Financial Management* 11 (1999): 230–310.

2. D. Osborne and T. Gaebler, *Reinventing Government: How the Entrepreneurial Spirit Is Transforming the Public Sector* (Reading, MA: Addison-Wesley, 1992); D. Osborne and P. Plastrik, *Banishing Bureaucracy: The Five Strategies for Reinventing Government* (Reading, MA: Addison-Wesley, 1997).

3. National Performance Review, *From Red Tape to Results: Creating a Government That Works Better and Costs Less* (Washington, DC: U.S. Government Printing Office, 1993), 19.

4. D. Durning, Governors and Administrative Reform in the 1990s, *State and Local Government Review* 27 (1995): 36–54.

5. U.S. Office of Management and Budget, *Preparation, Submission, and Execution of the Budget* (Circular A–11), June 2002, sec. 20–2.5; President's Private Sector Survey on Cost Control, *War on Waste* (New York: Macmillan, 1984); U.S. General Accounting Office, *Compendium of GAO's Views on the Cost Saving Proposals of the Grace Commission* (Washington, DC: U.S. Government Printing Office, 1985).

6. J. Peckenpaugh, OMB to Manage Homeland Security Reorganization, *Government Executive* (July 17, 2002), *http://www.govexec.com*.

7. S.B. Dewhurst, Downsizing: A View from the Inside, *Public Budgeting & Finance* 16 (Spring 1996): 49–59; D. Kraan, Cutback Management in the Netherlands, *Public Budgeting & Finance* 21 (Summer 2001): 46–61.

8. U.S. Office of Management and Budget, *The President's Management Agenda* (Washington, DC: U.S. Government Printing Office, 2001).

9. R.A. Bernardi, The Base Closure and Realignment Commission: A Rational or Political Decision Process, *Public Budgeting & Finance* 16 (Spring 1996): 49–59.

10. See J.J. Cordes and C.E. Steurle, *A Primer on Privatization* (Washington, DC: Urban Institute, 1999); A. Farazmand, ed., *Privatization or Public Enterprise Reform?: International Case Studies with Implications for Public Management* (Westport, CT: Greenwood, 2001); J.D. Greene, *Cities and Privatization* (Upper Saddle River, NJ: Prentice Hall, 2002).

11. L.M. Salamon, ed., *Beyond Privatization: The Tools of Government Action* (Washington, DC: Urban Institute Press, 1989); David R. Warren, *U.S. General Accounting Office, Defense Outsourcing: Challenges Facing DOD as It Attempts to Save Billions in Infrastructure Costs* (Washington, DC: U.S. Government Printing Office, 1997).

12. E.S. Savas, *Privatizing the Public Sector* (Chatham, NJ: Chatham House, 1982).

13. D.J. Gayle and J.N. Goodrich, eds., *Privatization and Deregulation in Global Perspective* (New York: Quorum Books, 1990).

14. J. Austin and G. Coventry, *Emerging Issues on Privatized Prisons* (Washington, DC: Office of Justice Programs, U.S. Department of Justice, 2001).

15. A. Henderson, The Ports Go Private, *Governing* 8 (April 1995): 37–38.

16. J. Dixon and M. Hyde, eds., *The Marketization of Social Security* (Wesport, CT: Quorum Books, 2001); X. Scheil-Adlung, ed., *Building Social Security: The Challenge of Privatization* (New Brunswick, NJ: Transaction, 2001).

17. G. Avery, Outsourcing Public Health Laboratory Services: A Blueprint for Determining Whether to Privatize and How, *Public Administration Review* 60 (2000): 330–337.

18. W.Z. Hirsch, Contracting Out by Urban Governments: A Review, *Urban Affairs Review* 30 (1995): 458–572; U.S. General Accounting Office, *Privatization: Lessons Learned by State and Local Governments* (Washington, DC: U.S. Government Printing Office, 1997).

19. K. Verma, Covert Costs of Privatization, *Public Budgeting & Finance* 16 (Fall 1996): 49–62; K.S. Eagle, Contract Monitoring for Financial and Operational Performance, *Government Finance Review* 13 (June 1997): 11–14.

20. J. Flanagan and S. Perkins, Public/Private Competition in the City of Phoenix, Arizona, *Government Finance Review* 11 (June 1995): 7–12; T. Sharp, Privatization or Managed Competition? The Fort Lauderdale Experience, *Government Finance Review* 13 (June 1997): 15–18.

21. R. Miranda and A. Lerner, Bureaucracy, Organizational Redundancy, and the Privatization of Public Services, *Public Administration Review* 55 (1995): 193–200.

22. Inspector General Act, P.L. 95–452, (1978); P.C. Light, *Monitoring Government: Inspectors General and the Search for Accountability* (Washington, DC: Brookings Institution, 1992). See also the Inspectors General Web site: *http://www.ignet.gov*.

23. Federal Managers' Financial Integrity Act, P.L. 97–255 (1982); President's Council on Management Improvement, *Streamlining Internal Control Processes and Strengthening Management Control with Less Effort* (Washington, DC: U.S. Government Printing Office, 1985).

24. U.S. Office of Management and Budget, *The President's Management Agenda*.

25. U.S. Office of Management and Budget, *Fiscal 2003 Budget*, *http://www.whitehouse.gov/omb/budget/fy2003/bud09.html*; also see U.S. Office of Management and Budget, *Progress Implementing the President's Management Agenda, Mid-Session Review, http://www.whitehouse.gov/omb/budget/fy2003/msr.html*.

26. U.S. Office of Management and Budget, *Budget of the United States Government: Fiscal Year 2004* (Washington, DC: U.S. Government Printing Office, 2003).

27. Managerial Flexibility Act, S. 1612; 107th Cong. Freedom to Manage Act, S. 1613, 107th Cong.

28. U.S. Council on Environmental Quality and U.S. Office of Management and Budget, *Improving Federal Facilities Cleanup* (Washington, DC: U.S. Office of Management and Budget, 1995).

29. Federal Advisory Committee Act, P.L. 92–463 (1972).

30. Paperwork Reduction Act, P.L. 96–511 (1980); P.L. 104–13 (1995).

31. Chief Information Officers Council, *Strategic Plan: Fiscal Year 2001–2002* (Washington, DC: Chief Information Officers Council, 2000), *http://www.cio.gov;* accessed March 2002.

32. U.S. General Accounting Office, *Information Resources Management: Comprehensive Strategic Plan Needed to Address Mounting Challenges* (Washington, DC: U.S. Government Printing Office, 2002).

33. U.S. Office of Management and Budget, *Managing Information Collection and Dissemination* (Washington, DC: U.S. Government Printing Office, 2002); V.S. Rezendes, U.S. Government Accounting Office, *Paperwork Reduction Act: Burden Increases and Violations Persist* (Washington, DC: U.S. Government Printing Office, 2002).

34. Office of Information and Regulatory Affairs, *http://www.whitehouse.gov/omb/inforeg/index.html*; accessed March 2002.

35. Treasury and General Government Appropriations Act for Fiscal Year 2001, P.L. 106–554 (2000).

36. U.S. Office of Management and Budget, *Guidelines for Ensuring and Maximizing the Quality, Objectivity, Utility, and Integrity of Information Disseminated by Federal Agencies* (Washington, DC: Office of Management and Budget, 2002); 67 F.R. 9797 and U.S. Office of Management and Budget, *Information Quality Guidelines, http://www.omb.gov;* accessed December 2002.

37. Government Paperwork Elimination Act, P.L. 105–277 (1998). See U.S. General Accounting Office, *Electronic Government: Better Information Needed on Agencies' Implementation of the Government Paperwork Elimination Act* (Washington, DC: U.S. Government Printing Office, 2001).

38. Government Information Security Reform Act, P.L. 106–398 (2000). See U.S. Office of Management and Budget, *FY 2001 Report to Congress on Federal Government Information Security Reform* (Washington, DC: U.S. Office of Management and Budget, 2002). The board consists of departmental secretaries and other key government administrators.

39. S.R. Furlong, The 1992 Regulatory Moratorium: Did It Make a Difference?, *Public Administration Review* 55 (1995): 254–262.

40. A.H. Card, Jr., Regulatory Review Plan, memorandum, January 20, 2001; U.S. General Accounting Office, *Regulatory Review: Delay of Effective Dates of Final Rules Subject to Administration's January 20, 2001, Memorandum* (Washington, DC: U.S. Government Printing Office, 2002).

41. R. Adams, Regulating the Rule-Makers: John Graham at OIRA, *Congressional Quarterly Weekly Report* 60 (February 23, 2002): 520–526.

42. Regulatory Working Group, *Economic Analysis of Federal Regulations under Executive Order 12866* (Washington, DC: U.S. Office of Management and Budget, 1996).

43. W. Harrington, R.D. Morgenstern, and P. Nelson, On the Accuracy of Regulatory Cost Estimates, *Journal of Policy Analysis and Management* 19 (2000): 297–322.

44. Regulatory Right-to-Know Act as contained in Treasury and General Government Appropriations Act for Fiscal Year 2000, P.L. 106–58 (2000).

45. U.S. Office of Management and Budget, *Draft Report to Congress on the Costs and Benefits of Federal Regulations* (Washington, DC: U.S. Office of Management and Budget, 2002): 52.

46. U.S. Office of Management and Budget, OMB Expands Use of Internet in Regulatory Review Process, press release, October 18, 2001.

47. Regulatory Flexibility Act, P.L. 96–354 (1980); Small Business Regulatory Enforcement Fairness Act, P.L. 104–121, sec. 201 (1996); U.S. General Accounting Office, *Regulatory Flexibility Act: Implementation in EPA Program Offices and Proposed Lead Rule* (Washington, DC: U.S. Government Printing Office, 2000); U.S. General Accounting Office, *Regulatory Flexibility Act: Clarification of Key Terms Still Needed* (Washington, DC: U.S. Government Printing Office, 2002).

48. Congressional Review Act, P.L. 104–121 (1996); R.P. Murphy, General Counsel, U.S. General Accounting Office, *Congressional Review Act* (Washington, DC: U.S. Government Printing Office, 1997).

49. Truth in Regulating Act, P.L. 106–312 (2000).

50. U.S. Comptroller General, *Department of Justice, Office of the Attorney General: September 11th Victim Compensation Fund of 2001*, B–290094 (Washington, DC: U.S. General Accounting Office, 2002).

51. Ergonomics Program Standard, 65 F.R. 68262 (2000).

52. Congressional Disapproval of the Rule Submitted by the Department of Labor, P.L. 107–5 (2001).

53. U.S. General Accounting Office, *Tax Administration: Status of IRS' Efforts to Develop Measures of Voluntary Compliance* (Washington, DC: U.S. Government Printing Office, 2001).

54. Internal Revenue Service Restructuring and Reform Act, P.L. 105–206 (1998).

55. M. Brostek (U.S. General Accounting Office), *Internal Revenue Service—Status of the Modernized Research Operations* (Washington, DC: U.S. Government Printing Office, 2001).

56. U.S. General Accounting Office, *Tax Administration: IRS Efforts to Improve Forms and Publications* (Washington, DC: U.S. Government Printing Office, 1994).

57. U.S. General Accounting Office, *Tax Administration: Information Returns* (Washington, DC: U.S. Government Printing Office, 1993).

58. U.S. General Accounting Office, *IRS Telephone Assistance: Quality of Service Mixed in the 2000 Filing Season and Below IRS' Long-Term Goal* (Washington, DC: U.S. Government Printing Office, 2001).

59. U.S. General Accounting Office, *Tax Administration: New Delinquent Tax Collection Methods for IRS* (Washington, DC: U.S. Government Printing Office, 1993).

60. U.S. General Accounting Office, *Tax Gap: Many Actions Taken, But a Cohesive Compliance Strategy Needed* (Washington, DC: U.S. Government Printing Office, 1994).

61. M. Hackbart and J.R. Ramsey, Estimating Tax Evasion Losses: The Road Fund Case, *Public Budgeting & Finance* 21 (Spring 2001): 58–72.

62. U.S. General Accounting Office, *Reducing the Tax Gap: Results of a GAO-Sponsored Symposium* (Washington, DC: U.S. Government Printing Office, 1995); U.S. General Accounting Office, *Tax Administration: Billions in Self-Employment Taxes Are Owed* (Washington, DC: U.S. Government Printing Office, 1999).

63. U.S. General Accounting Office, *IRS Audit Rates: Rate for Individual Taxpayers Has Declined but Effect on Compliance Is Unknown* (Washington, DC: U.S. Government Printing Office, 2001).

64. C. Rosotti, IRS Commissioner, as quoted in IRS Plans Audits to Check Tax Compliance, Reuters (January 17, 2002), *FindLaw Legal News*, http://www.findlaw.com.

65. U.S. General Accounting Office, *Information Related to the Scope and Complexity of the Federal Tax System* (Washington, DC: U.S. Government Printing Office, 2001).

66. U.S. General Accounting Office, *Tax Administration: IRS' Levy of Federal Payments Could Generate Millions of Dollars* (Washington, DC: U.S. Government Printing Office, 2000); U.S. General Accounting Office, *Tax Administration: Millions of Dollars Could Be Collected If IRS Levied More Federal Payments* (Washington, DC: U.S. Government Printing Office, 2001).

67. U.S. General Accounting Office, *Tax Administration: IRS' Abatement Process in Selected Locations* (Washington, DC: U.S. Government Printing Office, 1999); U.S. General Accounting Office, *Tax Administration: IRS Can Help Taxpayers Reduce the Need for Tax Abatements* (Washington, DC: U.S. Government Printing Office, 2001); L.P. Weston, Tax Payoff Plan Leads to More Bankruptcies, *Los Angeles Times*, October 20, 2000.

68. F.S. Alexander, Constitutional Questions about Tax Lien Foreclosures, *Government Finance Review* 16 (June 2000): 27–32.

69. U.S. General Accounting Office, *Tax Administration: Alternative Filing Systems* (Washington, DC: U.S. Government Printing Office, 1996).

70. R. Johnson and T. Mullen, Electronic Auctions for Delinquent Tax Properties: E-Government in Riverside County, California, *Government Finance Review* 16 (February 2000): 15–22.

71. J. Dean, Luring Taxpayers Online, *Government Executive Magazine* (July 1, 2001), http://www.govexec.com.

72. U.S. General Accounting Office, *Information Security: IRS Electronic Filing Systems* (Washington, DC: U.S. Government Printing Office, 2001).

73. U.S. General Accounting Office, *Tax Administration: Electronic Filing's Past and Future Impact on Processing Costs Dependent on Several Factors* (Washington, DC: U.S. Government Printing Office, 2002).

74. U.S. General Accounting Office, *Tax Systems Modernization: IRS Needs to Resolve Certain Issues with Its Integrated Case Processing System* (Washington, DC: U.S. Government Printing Office, 1997).

75. Taxed by Technology, *Government Executive Magazine* 31 (February 1999): 97.

76. U.S. General Accounting Office, *Tax Systems Modernization: Results of Review of IRS' August 2000 Interim Spending Plan* (Washington, DC: U.S. Government Printing Office, 2000).

77. Internal Revenue Service, *Progress Report: IRS Business Systems Modernization Program* (Washington, DC: U.S. Government Printing Office, 2000).

78. K.D. Schwartz, Tackling Tax Technology, *http://www.govexec.com* (August 1, 2001).

79. Taxpayer Browsing Protection Act, P.L. 105–35 (1997); U.S. General Accounting Office, *Confidentiality of Tax Data: IRS' Implementation of the Taxpayer Browsing Protection Act* (Washington, DC: U.S. Government Printing Office, 1999); U.S. General Accounting Office, *Tax Administration: Allegations of IRS Employee Misconduct* (Washington, DC: U.S. Government Printing Office, 1999).

80. B. Friel, Treasury Asks Congress to Make IRS "Ten Deadly Sins" Less Deadly, *Government Executive Magazine* (February 7, 2002), *http://www.govexec.com*.

81. U.S. General Accounting Office, *Tax Administration: Federal–State Efforts Offer Opportunities But Programs Need Improvement* (Washington, DC: U.S. Government Printing Office, 1996).

82. National Performance Review, *From Red Tape to Results*, 107.

83. Debt Collection Act, P.L. 97–365 (1982); Debt Collection Improvement Act, P. L. 99–578 (1996); U.S. General Accounting Office, *Debt Collection Improvement Act of 1996: Status of Selected Agencies' Implementation of Administrative Wage Garnishment* (Washington, DC: U.S. Government Printing Office, 2002).

84. U.S. General Accounting Office, *Tax Administration: IRS' Implementatation of the Restructuring Act's Taxpayer Protection and Rights Provisions* (Washington, DC: U.S. Government Printing Office, 2000).

85. Bank Fires Workers for Hiding Returns and Tax Payments, *New York Times*, September 6, 2001.

86. Prompt Payment Act, P.L. 97–177 (1982).

87. P.G. Joyce, What's So Magical about Five Percent? A Nationwide Look at Factors That Influence the Optimal Size of State Rainy Day Funds, *Public Budgeting & Finance* 21 (Summer 2001): 62–87.

88. R.S. Sobel and R.G. Holcombe, The Impact of State Rainy Day Funds in Easing State Fiscal Crises During the 1990–1991 Recession, *Public Budgeting & Finance* 16 (Fall 1996): 28–48; J.W. Douglas and R.K. Gaddie, State Rainy Day Funds and Fiscal Crises: Rainy Day Funds and the 1990–1991 Recession Revisited, *Public Budgeting & Finance* 22 (Spring 2002): 19–30.

89. Municipal Bond Investors Assurance Corporation, *http://www.mbia.com*.

90. D. Dupont and B. Sack, The Treasury Securities Market: Overview and Recent Developments, *Federal Reserve Bulletin* (December 1999): 786–806; M.J. Fleming, The Benchmark U.S. Treasury Market: Recent Performance and Possible Alternatives, *Federal Reserve Bank of New York Economic Policy Review* 6 (April 2000): 129–145.

91. Government Securities Act, P.L. 99–571 (1986).

92. I.G. Kawaller and T.W. Koch, What Government Finance Officers Should Know about Derivatives, *Municipal Finance Journal* 17 (Fall 1996): 48–62; C. Evans, ed. *The Euromoney Derivatives and Risk Management Handbook, 2001–2002* (London: Euromoney Institutional Investor, 2001).

93. U.S. Bureau of the Census, *Cash and Security Holdings of Major Public Employee–Retirement Systems* (Fiscal Year 1999–2000); *http://www.census.gov/govs/retire/ret00tl.txt*; accessed April 2002.

94. Washington State Treasurer's Office, *http://www.wa.gov/tre*; accessed April 2002.

95. K.P. Kearns, Accountability and Entrepreneurial Public Management: The Case of the Orange County Investment Fund, *Public Budgeting & Finance* 15 (Fall 1995): 3–21; J.E. Petersen, Managing Cash: Local Officials and the Slippery Slopes, *Governing* 51 (June 1996): 51–52, 54–56.

96. Governmental Accounting Standards Board, *http://accounting.rutgers.edu/raw/gasb/index.html*.

97. Financial Management Service, U.S. Department of Treasury, *http://www.fms.treas.gov*; accessed April 2002.

98. U.S. General Accounting Office, *Federal Debt: Debt Management Actions and Future Challenges* (Washington, DC: U.S. Government Printing Office, 2001).

99. G.M. Groshek, Foreign Currency Exposure in the Department of Defense, *Public Budgeting & Finance* 20 (Winter 2000): 15–35.

100. Bureau of Engraving and Printing, U.S. Department of Treasury, *http://www.bep.treas.gov*; accessed April 2002.

101. U.S. Mint, U.S. Department of Treasury, *http://www.usmint.gov*; accessed April 2002.

102. Debt Collection Improvement Act, P.L. 104–134 (1996).

103. U.S. Office of Management and Budget, *Budget of the United States, Fiscal Year 2003* (Washington, DC: U.S. Government Printing Office, 2002), *http://www.whitehouse.gov/omb/budget/index.html*; accessed April 2002.

104. Cash Management Improvement Act, P.L. 101–453 (1990).

105. Controller's Office, University of Massachusetts, *http://www.umas.edu/aco/gc/lcr.htm*; accessed April 2002.

106. See *Investors Business Daily* at *http://www.investors.com* and *The Wall Street Journal* at *http:// www.wsj.com*; accessed April 2002.

107. R.D. Harrell, The Soul of a Cash Management Machine, *Governing* 8 (June 1995): 69.

108. T.D. Lynch, H. Shamsub, and C. Onwujuba, A Strategy to Prevent Losses in Local Government Investment Pools, *Public Budgeting & Finance* 22 (April 2002): 60–79

109. R. Grimm and K.V. Thai, Symposium on Government Procurement, *Journal of Public Budgeting, Accounting & Financial Management* 12 (2000): 230–332, 399–496.

110. S. Kelman, Contracting, *The Tools of Government*, L. Salamon, ed. (Baltimore: Johns Hopkins Press, 2002), 287–288.

111. The Top 200 Government Contractors, *Government Executive* (August 1, 2001), *http://www.govexec.com.*

112. National Performance Review, *From Red Tape to Results*, 26–31.

113. C.P. McCue, Organizing the Public Purchasing Function: A Survey of Cities and Counties, *Government Finance Review* 17 (February 2001), 1–5.

114. U.S. General Services Administration, *Annual Report* (Washington, DC: U.S. Government Printing Office, published annually), *http:/www.gsa.gov*; accessed April 2002; U.S. General Services Administration, *Annual Performance Report* (Washington, DC), *http://www.gsa.gov*; accessed April 2002.

115. S. Harris, GSA Lacks Hard Data on Inter-agency Competition, *Government Executive* (April 11, 2002), *http://www.govexec.com.*

116. G. Cahlink, Pentagon Says It Uses 700,000 Service Contractors, *Government Executive* (March 30, 2001), *http://www.govexec.com.*

117. Defense Logistics Agency, U.S. Department of Defense, *http://www.dla.gov*; accessed April 2002.

118. Office of Federal Procurement Policy Act, P.L. 93–400 (1974).

119. Federal Property Asset Management Reform Act (proposed bill), H.R. 3947 (2001) and S. 1612 (2002).

120. G.C. Wilson, Rent-a-Weapons, *Government Executive* (February 5, 2002), *http://www.govexec.com.*

121. J. Peckenpaugh, A–76 Competitions May Not Hurt Federal Workers' Pay, *Government Executive* (April 18, 2001), *http://www.govexec.com.*

122. J. Peckenpaugh, Conflict-of-Interest Rules to Apply Only to New A-76 Studies, Says GAO, *Government Executive* (June 3, 2002), *http://www.govexec.com.*

123. Floyd D. Spence National Defense Authorization Act, P.L. 106–398 (2001).

124. Commercial Activities Panel, *Improving the Sourcing Decisions of the Government: Final Report* (Washington, DC: U.S. Government Printing Office, 2002).

125. Federal Activities and Inventory Reform Act, P.L. 105–270 (1998).

126. K. Lunney, OMB Releases Final Round of 2001 Outsourcing Lists, *Government Executive* (January 3, 2002), *http://www.govexec.com.*

127. J. Peckenpaugh, Outsourcing Target Years Away, OMB Chief Says, *Government Executive* (May 25, 2001), *http://www.govexec.com.*

128. Federal Acquisition Streamlining Act, P.L. 103–355 (1994).

129. J. Peckenpaugh, OMB Memo Boosts Performance-Based Contracts, *Government Executive* (March 21, 2001), *http://www.govexec.com.*

130. Competition in Contracting Act, P.L. 98–369 Title VII (1984).

131. U.S. General Accounting Office, *Bid Protests: Characteristics of Cases Filed in Federal Courts* (Washington, DC: U.S. Government Printing Office, 2000).

132. U.S. Department of Defense, Procurement Technical Assistance Centers, *http://www.dla.mil/db/procurem.htm*; accessed April 2002.

133. Rehabilitation Act, P.L. 93–112 (1973).

134. Vietnam Era Veterans' Readjustment Assistance Act, P.L. 93–508 (1974).

135. K. Mitchell, Instituting E-Procurement in the Public Sector, *Public Management* 16 (February 2000): 9–12; T. Newcombe, E-Procurement Rising?, *Public Management* 14 (July 2001): 38, 40; C. Anderson, The eBuyer Era, *Governing* 72 (September 2000): 66–68.

136. Acquisition Reform Network, *http://www.acqnet.gov*; accessed April 2002.

137. Federal Business Opportunities, *http://www.eps.gov*; accessed April 2002.

138. GSA Advantage!, *http://www.gsa.gov*; accessed April 2002.

139. U.S. General Accounting Office, *Contract Management* (Washington, DC: U.S. Government Printing Office, 2002).

140. National Defense Authorization Act for Fiscal Year 2002, P.L. 107–107 (2001).

141. Federal Acquisition Reform Act, P.L. 104–106, sec. 4001 (1996).

142. U.S. General Accounting Office, *Contract Management: Benefits of Simplified Acquisition Test Procedures Not Clearly Demonstrated* (Washington, DC: U.S. Government Printing Office, 2001).

143. 65 FR 80255 (December 20, 2000) and 66 FR 66986 (December 27, 2001).

144. M. Weinstock, Booming Business in Selling Services, *Government Executive* (August 1, 2001), *http://www.govexec.com*.

145. D.M. Van Slyke, The Public Management Challenges of Contracting with Nonprofits for Social Services, *International Journal of Public Administration* 25 (2002): 489–517.

146. M. Weinstock, OMB to Review Contract Bundling, *Government Executive* (June 7, 2002), *http://www.govexec.com*.

147. T.N. Ballard, Defense Task Force Aims to Clean Up Charge Card Abuse, *Government Executive* (March 27, 2002), *http://www.govexec.com*.

148. C. Grassley, as quoted in T.N. Ballard, Army Personnel Continue to Abuse Government Charge Cards, *Government Executive* (July 17, 2002), *http://www.govexec.com*.

149. *City of Richmond v. J.A. Crosson Company*, 488 U.S. 469 (1989); S.E. Celec, et al., Measuring Disparity in Government Provcurement: Problems with Using Census Data in Estimating Availability, *Public Administration Review* 60 (2000): 134–142.

150. *Adarand Constructors v. Pena*, 515 U.S. 200 (1995).

151. *Adarand Constructors v. Mineta*, 534 U.S. 103 (2001).

152. U.S. General Accounting Office, *Federal Procurement: Better Guidance and Monitoring Needed to Assess Purchases of Environmentally Friendly Products* (Washington, DC: U.S. Government Printing Office, 2001).

153. *Tort Liability Today: A Guide for State and Local Governments*, 3rd ed. (Arlington, VA: Public Risk Management Association, 1998).

154. Federal Tort Claims Act, Ch. 753, 60 Stat. 842 (1946).

155. Public Risk Management Association, *http://www.primacentral.org*; accessed May 2002.

Chapter 11

FINANCIAL MANAGEMENT: ACCOUNTING, AUDITING, AND INFORMATION SYSTEMS

Budget execution requires accounting systems that track projected and actual revenues and expenditures during the budget year. Accounting, as will be seen in the following sections, serves a variety of purposes, but one of the most important has always been maintaining honesty and integrity. Accounting also is important to the functions discussed in the preceding chapter — namely, tax administration, cash management, procurement, and risk management. Accounting systems provide the financial information components of more comprehensive management information systems.

This chapter has three sections. The first and largest is devoted to accounting systems; the second discusses the role of auditing; and the third considers information systems used in accounting and, more broadly, in budgeting and finance.

Governmental Accounting

"A standard definition of accounting is the art of analyzing, recording, summarizing, evaluating and interpreting an organization's financial activities and status, and communicating the results."[1] Accounting, then, is one type of information system and usually contains mostly financial information on the receipt of funds and their expenditure.

In this section, we explore several aspects of accounting systems, beginning with the purposes and standards of accounting and the organizations that shape accounting systems. Fund accounting, the structure of accounting systems, the classification of expenditures, and the bases for accounting are considered. The section concludes with a discussion of the types of reports that are generated by accounting systems.

Organizational Responsibilities and Standards

Purposes. Accounting systems have been devised for a variety of purposes, with the maintenance of honesty being one of the most prominent ones. Through accounting, people who have wrongly intercepted monies being paid to government or have channeled expenditures to their own advantage can be detected. Accounting, then, serves as a deterrent to fraud and corruption as well as prevents inadvertent loss.

A related purpose is to prevent expenditures from straying beyond legal parameters. Illegal expenditures can occur that do not involve graft, as in the case of agency expenditures that exceed an appropriation or are used for purposes other than those permitted in authorizing legislation. Accounting serves to control agencies so that they act in accordance with policy and administrative directives as well as appropriation legislation.

Accounting systems are intended to provide complete, timely, and accurate information concerning receipts and expenditures. The information is used in billing taxpayers and receiving tax payments, paying employees, ordering goods, receiving goods, and paying vendors or contractors. Accounting systems help control inventory by providing accurate records of what items have been purchased.

Another important purpose is to report on the management of funds that are held in custody or trust. For example, accounting systems are used to handle contributions to employee retirement funds and outlays to beneficiaries.

Decision making is facilitated by accounting systems, which report historical data on revenues and expenditures that are essential for forecasting financial transactions. Without accurate information from an accounting system, decision makers are unable to determine whether a gap exists between proposed spending for the budget year and available revenue. Accounting information is important in determining whether a budget deficit exists and in what amount; in determining the size of the government's total debt, including those debts that are part of credit programs; and for estimating funds required for proposed changes in service levels and service quality.

Accounting is used internally to help managers increase efficiency and effectiveness in delivering services. The utilization of resources is monitored so as to avoid waste and to help ensure that desired programmatic outcomes are achieved. Managerial accounting focuses on calculating the costs associated with providing services to citizens. These derived costs also can be used for setting schedules for service charges. Office of Management and Budget (OMB) Circular

A-123, Management Accountability and Control, emphasizes that management should be held accountable for achieving results and not just for using resources efficiently and honestly. One of the five government-wide initiatives in President George W. Bush's Management Agenda was to integrate budgeting and performance. Another was to improve financial management, focusing on the quality of accounting systems and the sufficiency of agency controls against fraud and overspending.[2]

Information from accounting systems is used in communication between a government and its citizens, investors, and other governments. Financial reports derived from detailed accounting information can help citizens gain confidence that the government's resources are well supervised. Investors in such commodities as state and local bonds and federal Treasury bills use accounting-based information to understand the financial condition of governments. The federal government, in making grants to state and local governments, wants to be assured that the recipient governments have accounting systems that will protect the assets being invested.

As will be seen, accounting systems are based on details, but those who operate accounting systems should never lose sight of the main purposes. This is the old familiar problem of losing sight of the forest because of all of the trees. It has been said that the Department of Defense "uses a magnifying glass to check a Tootsie Roll purchase and misses the million-dollar problems."[3] Accounting systems, in meeting the purposes noted here, should create value for an entity.[4]

Accounting Organizations. For accounting systems to serve these purposes, certain conventions or standards must be established, or else chaos would reign as each government or department within a government established its own standards and practices. Numerous organizations establish the ground rules for accounting. Both the General Accounting Office (GAO), which is a branch of Congress, and OMB, which is an arm of the Executive Office of the President, set guidelines for federal agencies and to some extent compete with one another over control of accounting.[5] The Federal Managers' Financial Integrity Act of 1982, amending the Accounting and Auditing Act of 1950, requires that each executive agency establish internal accounting and administrative controls in accordance with standards prescribed by GAO and that the agency conduct annual reviews to determine the extent of compliance with those standards.[6] However, since the Supreme Court has ruled that GAO cannot be in a position of instructing agencies in what they must do (see Chapter 9), OMB has the upper hand in establishing financial management practices.[7]

One position at OMB is the statutorily created post of deputy director for management. Under this deputy director is the Office of Federal Financial Management, which is headed by the controller. The Chief Financial Officers Act of 1990 created similar offices and chief financial officer (CFO) positions within the major agencies of the government.[8] For example, the Treasury Department has more than 10 CFOs heading the financial operations of units within the department.[9] OMB's controller, in accordance with the law's instructions that a five-year, government-wide financial plan be developed, has launched an ambitious program to improve organizational arrangements for finance, accounting standards, systems of accounting, internal controls, financial management, employee training and development, and the like.[10] Agency CFOs have responsibility for all financial operations, including budgeting, and the CFOs, along with OMB's deputy director for management, the controller, and the fiscal assistant secretary of Treasury, meet periodically as the Chief Financial Officers Council for the purpose of coordinating their activities.

In addition to the Chief Financial Officers Act of 1990, that year brought the formation of the Federal Accounting Standards Advisory Board (FASAB). As its title suggests, this entity is strictly advisory, but its recommendations have indeed had an impact on federal accounting.[11] The board consists of representatives of GAO, OMB, and the Treasury Department plus a representative from the Congressional Budget Office, representatives from civilian agencies and the Department of Defense, and nonfederal members. Its mission is to develop consensus on accounting standards that can then be adopted by GAO, OMB, and the Treasury Department. Prior to FASAB, the Joint Financial Management Improvement Program played an important role in developing coordinated financial and other management practices among these three organizations and the Office of Personnel Management.

A concern exists that FASAB's work on accounting be fully meshed with budgeting standards set by OMB. Without complete integration, the budgeting standards become preeminent in that agencies are compelled to answer to OMB.[12] Circular A-134 provides for the adoption of Financial Accounting Principles and Standards.

State and local accounting systems are influenced by several sources. State auditors and comptrollers general set standards for their state and local systems. These systems also are influenced by GAO and OMB, which determine how federal grant monies are handled.

Professional organizations have periodically attempted to establish standards of accounting in the public sector. The former National Council on Governmental Accounting consisted of representatives of such bodies as the Government Finance Officers Association, the American Institute of Certified Public Accountants, and the American Accounting Association. It produced what was known as the "blue book" or GAAFR (*Governmental Accounting, Auditing, and Financial Reporting*). GAAFR currently is published by the Government Finance

Officers Association and is designed to assist governments at all levels achieve what are considered the standards in the field.[13] The Government Finance Officers Association issues a variety of policy statements not only on accounting, reporting, and auditing, but also on cash management, debt management, public employee pensions, and intergovernmental finance.[14]

The private sector has long had a well-established standards-setting organization. The Financial Accounting Standards Board issues authoritative pronouncements on accounting for profit and nonprofit organizations. Also, private accounting firms have major input into determining what constitutes good accounting. The Big 5 accounting firms are Andersen, Deloitte & Touche, Ernst & Young, KPMG, and PricewaterhouseCoopers. The scandal and ensuing lawsuits stemming from Andersen's handling of the accounts for failed energy giant Enron in the early 2000s left in doubt whether the company would survive. Subsequent to this scandal, another high-profile scandal, involving telecommunications behemoth WorldCom, came to light. In this case, the firm was estimated to have overstated its financial health through the use of inappropriate accounting practices, to the tune of approximately $6 billion.[15]

One source of concern arises when accounting firms not only perform auditing functions but also provide consulting services. At the time of the Enron collapse, Andersen was receiving more payments from Enron for consulting than for auditing. Such situations may create conflicts of interest in which the consulting arm of a company is eager to see that the auditing arm finds no serious problems in the manner that accounting is conducted by the client. The Securities and Exchange Commission has authority in this area, and Congress has considered legislation that would create a body dedicated to overseeing the accounting industry.[16]

In 1984, a government counterpart to the Financial Accounting Standards Board was established. The Governmental Accounting Standards Board (GASB, usually pronounced "gas-bee") speaks for accounting practices by government entities. Both the Financial Accounting Standards Board and GASB are under the umbrella of the Financial Accounting Foundation. GASB issues accounting standards, known as statements, first as exposure drafts available for public comment and then in final form. The organization also issues technical bulletins that provide guidance on the implementation of the standards. The Governmental Accounting Standards Advisory Council (GASAC) provides advice to GASB.

While the various organizations discussed here may set standards for accounting, the actual practice of operating accounting systems is typically conducted by individual agencies throughout large governments. The federal government has hundreds of systems, a fact that greatly complicates reform efforts. Efforts to streamline accounting include the merger of systems and the use of *cross-servicing*, in which one agency provides financial services to another agency. In contrast with large governments, small ones, such as a local school district, typically have a single centralized accounting system.

Standards and Principles of Accounting. While GAAFR is useful to state and local governments in evaluating their accounting systems, it is not regarded as an authoritative document. In contrast, GASB has issued a document that is authoritative regarding the standards to be used in public accounting: *Codification of Governmental Accounting and Financial Reporting Standards.*[17] The Government Finance Officers Association has produced a guide showing how GAAFR relates to GASB pronouncements.[18]

GASB and its predecessors have recognized what are considered *generally accepted accounting principles* (GAAP). While space limitations do not allow a discussion of each of the 12 principles, it should be noted that they are intended as guides to establishing and modifying accounting systems. The first principle provides the foundation for the other 11 by requiring that accounting principles should be followed and that the legal requirements of a government should be met. Adhering to this first principle can be difficult in that laws can require accounting practices that are contrary to the generally accepted principles.

At the federal level, the generally accepted accounting principles contained in Title 2 of GAO's *Policy and Procedures Manual for Guidance of Federal Agencies* are being replaced by new standards developed by FASAB. Since FASAB's products are merely advisory, OMB takes authoritative action by issuing statements of federal financial accounting standards (SFFAS, Circular A-127, Financial Management Systems, and Circular A-134, Financial Accounting Principles and Standards).

Organizational Arrangements and Fraud. Creating organizational arrangements that deter fraud is of paramount interest in accounting. Fraud can be committed by workers handling receipts; an employee might hold taxpayer A's money for personal use and use taxpayer B's money to cover A's taxes and subsequently C's money to cover B's taxes. Employees may steal from petty cash or from inventory. Employees may pay vendors who are due nothing or provide travel reimbursement checks to employees who are due nothing.

To prevent these types of fraud from occurring and to reduce other losses due to errors in data entry and the like, internal controls that specify organizational arrangements and procedures are established. Federal Circular A-123, for example, "provides guidance to Federal managers on improving the accountability and effectiveness of Federal programs and operations by establishing, assessing, correcting, and reporting on management controls."[19] Responsibility needs to be assigned to individuals, and any delegations of responsibility need to be detailed in writing. One standard practice is to segregate duties, so that one individual may have only limited authority over monies and two or more people may be required to approve some financial transactions. The presumption is that if two or more individuals are part of a particular process, they will monitor each other's behavior and limit various abuses. For example, two or more signatures may be required in approving the issuance of checks or in transferring money through electronic fund transfers.

Employees are trained in how to enter transactions properly in accounting systems and what their ethical and legal responsibilities are in handling public resources. Individuals who handle funds may be subject to more extensive background checks before hiring and may be bonded. Downsizing can force the elimination of personnel and increase the risk that funds are vulnerable to theft or accidental loss due to the reduced oversight of financial operations.

Auditing bodies are important in preventing and detecting fraud. GAO conducts financial as well as program audits and on occasion finds losses in the billions of dollars. When discrepancies are identified through audits, follow-up is necessary to determine their causes and the corrective measures that need to be initiated.[20]

Fund Accounting

One of the main differences between public and private sector accounting is the definition of the *accounting entity*. For the typical private sector organization, the entity is the organization itself, since accounts are designed to reflect its entire resources. Governments, in contrast, separate financial resources into distinct accounting entities called *funds*. Each fund is set up to record and account for the uses of a specific group of assets or sources of revenue. As provided for in generally accepted accounting principles 2, 3, and 4, there are three general classes of public sector funds and 10 different particular types of funds.[21]

Governmental Funds. The first class, known as *governmental funds*, consists of four types. The most important one is the general fund. Several revenue sources may flow into a government's general fund, such as property tax and income tax receipts at the local level. The resources in the fund are available for expenditure for virtually any purpose that the jurisdiction is legally empowered to pursue. Most municipalities, for instance, may use general fund receipts for police and road services but not schools, since the latter are the domain of independent school districts.

The other fund types within the governmental class are available for what are thought of as normal government operations, but these types have receipt and/or expenditure restrictions. *Special revenue funds* receive monies from special sources and are earmarked for special purposes. Gasoline taxes are typically accounted for in a special revenue fund, with expenditures limited to transportation, especially roads and highways.

Capital project funds account for receipts and expenditures related to projects, such as construction of a new park or city hall, or for major pieces of equipment, such as vehicles for a city fire department. Monies may come into these funds from bond sales that will be paid for with general fund tax receipts.

Debt service funds are used to account for interest and principal on general-purpose long-term debt. The revenue received by this type of fund usually is from the general fund.

Proprietary Funds. The second class of funds consists of those that are proprietary or business-like in nature. *Enterprise funds* operate as businesses whose customers are external to government. Such funds are established for toll roads, bridges, and local water systems. Numerous proposals have circulated recommending that various federal operations be converted to government corporations, which would be run as enterprises.[22] *Internal service funds* operate as businesses whose customers are internal to government. A central purchasing office or a vehicle maintenance garage may operate as an internal service fund, with revenues coming from other departments as services are rendered. When bonds are sold to support the activities of a proprietary fund (for example, bond proceeds might be used to renovate a city sewage system), capital expenditures and payment of debt are handled through the proprietary fund, not through a capital project or debt service fund.

Fiduciary Funds. The third class, known as fiduciary funds, has four types. This class, often called *trust and agency funds*, consists of accounts that are dedicated to a third party. *Expendable trust funds* are used for bequests to government in which both the principal and the interest can be spent. *Nonexpendable trust funds* allow for the expenditure of the interest but not the principal, as in the case of a continuing university scholarship named in memory of someone. Often the largest set of fiduciary funds comprises *pension trusts* for government employees. The fourth type in this class consists of *agency funds*. These pertain to government acting as a conduit for another party, such as a city government collecting taxes for the local school district. GASB proposes to change some of the rules regarding the types of fiuciary funds, but these requirements had not been fully implemented as of early 2003.

Account Groups. According to generally accepted accounting principles 5 through 7, governmental funds use account groups to report fixed assets and long-term liabilities, whereas proprietary and fiduciary funds report these resources and debts within the funds themselves. Governmental funds include only financial assets — namely, assets that will be converted to cash — and therefore the *general fixed asset account group* (GFAAG) is used to report assets that will not be converted to cash, such as buildings, swimming pools, aircraft hangars, and airport terminals. The GFAAG is simply a reporting of assets and does not involve transactions.

The second account group is the *general long-term debt account group*. This group reports government debt that is not part of proprietary or fiduciary funds. In other words, the account group reports liabilities of the entity as a whole, as distinguished from specific funds. This account group and the fixed assets group in effect are memoranda that report assets and liabilities that otherwise would not be reported.

Structure and Rules of Accounting Systems

Ledgers. Accounting systems use ledgers as a means of organization or structure. Each fund has a general ledger and subsidiary ledgers. The general ledger records the overall status of revenues and expenditures, while subsidiary ledgers are established for each revenue source and type of expenditure. In a general fund having several tax sources of revenue, a subsidiary revenue ledger is used for each source. OMB and the Treasury Department have established a U.S. Government Standard General Ledger, which indicates how agencies are to organize their ledgers (Circular A-127).[23]

Expenditure subsidiary ledgers control expenditures by appropriation, organizational unit, object of expenditure, and sometimes purpose or activity. Accounting systems are used to track expenditures according to provisions in appropriations; often these appropriations are specific to organizations, as in the case of $2 million appropriated to a city housing department. The appropriation also may contain limitations on how funds will be spent, such as expenditures for personnel or equipment; this aspect of accounting is explained later. Some jurisdictions track expenditures by program or activity (this is done if a government's program budget structure does not match its organizational structure).

Accounting Formula. Accounting systems use equations that allow systematic recording of transactions and double-checking that the transactions have been properly recorded. The basic equation that is used is:

assets = liabilities + fund balance

In the formula, *assets* can be the revenue in a fund; *liabilities* are the monies owed others, such as suppliers of office equipment and tires for police cars; and the *fund balance* comprises the residual, uncommitted monies. Specific accounts are established for each of the three components of the formula. Asset accounts, for example, can include those showing cash on hand as well as monies owed by taxpayers (taxes receivable). FASAB has recommended standards for assets and liabilities.

Double-entry accounting, in which any single transaction is recorded twice (at a minimum), is used as a cross-check. If taxes are received and no additional obligations are incurred, then both assets and the fund balance increase. The double-entry approach also can be used within one portion of the overall formula. If taxes are received but were already noted in an asset account called taxes receivable, then that account would be reduced while another asset account for cash would be increased; that particular set of transactions would not affect liabilities or the fund balance.

Transactions are recorded in a T in which the left side of the T constitutes *debits* and the right side constitutes *credits*. The terms *debits* and *credits* refer only to the left and right sides of the T and have no connotation of negative and positive. Rules exist as to when an account should be debited and when credited. In any transaction, the amount debited to one or more accounts must equal the amount credited to other accounts.

Specified Procedures. Flowing out of accounting standards and principles are procedures that determine how transactions will be recorded and in what accounts. These procedures are typically specified in manuals or handbooks so that employees involved in whatever aspects of accounting know how to meet their responsibilities. Manuals may begin with such basics as how to log onto the computer system and proceed to cover receipts and purchases, including, for example, overall purchasing policy, purchase orders, contract payments, and emergency purchases. Payroll procedures will be specified in some detail in a manual and are likely to require the approval of specific individuals, possibly including written signatures confirming which employees are to be paid what amounts.

The typical accounting cycle is as follows.[24] An event occurs and a source document is prepared. The event might be a decision to tax property and the document might be a tax bill sent to a citizen; when the citizen pays the bill, another transaction will occur. On the expenditure side of the budget, one event might be the placing of an order for office supplies and a later event might be the receipt of the supplies and the invoice. These types of transactions will first be posted in a *journal*, which is a chronological listing of events or transactions. The journal entry indicates both the credits and the debits involved in the transaction. For example, tax monies received would increase a cash account and decrease a taxes receivable account. Entries once recorded in the journal are posted to ledgers, and from time to time the debits and credits of these accounts are totaled to obtain *trial* and *final balances*. The balances are used in preparing financial reports (which are discussed later).

Classification of Receipts and Expenditures

Receipts and expenditures are classified in a variety of ways, and elaborate coding systems are used to monitor and control financial transactions. Such coding devices help hold government officials responsible for honestly managing the government's business.

Receipts. The monies that government receives need to be recorded according to the source. The money derived from each tax source, such as property and income taxes, needs to be recorded separately and in distinction from user fees, such as charges for using a municipal golf course. The federal government treats user fees as *offsetting collections*. Namely, money derived from fees, as in the case of the Tennessee Valley Authority, are used to offset expenditures for Tennessee Valley Authority operations. The net differences in such transactions are reported in the budget.

Fund and Appropriation. Expenditures are accounted for in a variety of ways. One set of characteristics is the fund and appropriation. An appropriation is a legislative approval to spend from a specific fund. Since several bills may be passed that appropriate out of the general fund, the dollar stipulations in each of these bills must be observed vis-à-vis the total assets available in the general fund. Even if a jurisdiction uses only one appropriation bill, each of the expenditure limits in the bill must be observed and consequently must be monitored by the accounting system. When an expenditure is made, it is charged against the appropriated amount and the remaining available balance is shown. In this way, an accounting system can be used to keep agency expenditures within budgeted figures.

If the legislative body earmarks expenditures in detail, then the accounting system becomes increasingly complex. For example, Congress in its annual foreign assistance appropriation bill typically imposes detailed figures on the level of funding for programs within the Agency for International Development and amounts to be available in each country receiving aid. The accounting system, therefore, must monitor expenditures by program (e.g., child survival) and by country to adhere to the stipulations in the appropriation bill.

Organizational Unit. Expenditures are made by organizational units, and accounting systems must track expenditures accordingly. Appropriation bills usually are specific to agencies so that, instead of the government simply being authorized to spend an amount on forest preservation, a specific unit within a department is granted the money. Large governments, then, account for expenditures not only at the department level but also at the bureau, office, division, or regional unit level.

Objects of Expenditure. Accounting systems invariably account in terms of the objects acquired or the objects of expenditure. Broad groupings of objects are called major objects, and their subdivisions are called minor objects. **Figure 11–1** illustrates the object classes used by the federal government. The object series beginning with the number 11, for example, covers all personnel-related expenditures. Within that series are the three subclasses of direct compensation, benefits for employees, and benefits for former employees.

Accounting systems can become unwieldy in their use of minor objects. For instance, travel as a major object can be subdivided in numerous ways:

- Mode (personal automobile, government automobile, commercial airline)
- Type of person traveling (elected official, political or career executive, employee, client)
- Purpose (meeting, conference, training, inspection)
- Location (in state, out of state, out of country)
- Type of expense (lodging, meals, transportation)

The number of possible permutations is great. When an accounting system uses such detail, the entry of many transactions may be delayed due to classification ambiguities.

Despite the administrative problems of detailed minor objects, legislative bodies often incorporate such details in appropriation bills. These line items in an appropriation allow control when there is concern that funds may be abused. Restrictions may be inserted regarding the purchase of newspaper subscriptions, the number of automobiles, and government employee travel. When minor object restrictions are embedded in appropriations, the limits are legally mandated, and the accounting system must ensure compliance.

Executives also use object classifications in an attempt to control agencies and increase their efficiency. President Clinton's Executive Order 12837 required agencies to reduce their administrative costs, especially travel and other selected objects that often are viewed as luxuries. Of course, many administrative expenses are central to the missions of agencies. Travel is essential for inspectors of meat and poultry processing plants, mines, and workplaces, for example.

Purpose and Activity. Program-oriented budgets that focus decision-making attention on specific program goals and objectives also require accounting-based information on how much each program costs. The federal government uses broad functional categories, such as national defense, energy, and income security, which are divided into subfunctions. For example, energy is subdivided into supply; conservation and preparedness; and energy information, policy, and regulation.[25] If a budget based on program classifications cuts across agency lines, then the

Figure 11–1 Federal Objects of Expenditure Classification

Code	Title

Personal Services and Benefits

11 Personnel Compensation

    11.1   Full-Time Permanent

    11.3   Other Than Full-Time Permanent

    11.5   Other Personnel Compensation

    11.7   Military Personnel

    11.8   Special Personal Services Payments

    11.9   Total Personnel Compensation

12 Personnel Benefits

    12.1   Civilian Personnel Benefits

    12.2   Military Personnel Benefits

13 Benefits for Former Personnel

Contractual Services and Supplies

21 Travel and Transportation of Persons

22 Transportation of Things

23 Rent, Communications, and Utilities

    23.1   Rental Payments to General Services Administration

    23.2   Rental Payments to Others

    23.3   Communications, Utilities, and Miscellaneous Charges

24 Printing and Reproduction

25 Other Contractual Services

    25.1   Advisory and Assistance Services

    25.2   Other Services

    25.3   Purchases of Goods and Services from Government Accounts

    25.4   Operation and Maintenance of Facilities

    25.5   Research and Development Contracts

    25.6   Medical Care

    25.7   Operation and Maintenance of Equipment

    25.8   Subsistence and Support of Persons

26 Supplies and Materials

continues

Code	Title

Acquisition of Assets

31 Equipment

32 Land and Structure

33 Investments and Loans

Grants and Fixed Charges

41 Grants, Subsidies, and Contributions

42 Insurance Claims and Indemnities

43 Interest and Dividends

44 Refunds

Other

91 Unvouchered

92 Undistributed

93 Limitation on Expenses

Source: *Preparation and Submission of Budget Estimates, Circular No. A-11* (Washington, DC: U.S. Office of Management and Budget, 2002).

accounting system needs to cut across agency lines to accumulate the costs according to program. Similarly, preparing a budget that allocates funds according to detailed work activities requires an accounting system that tracks expenditures by those activities. In a 2000 survey of state budget offices, 92 percent reported that their states' accounting systems controlled to some extent expenditures at the specific program level.[26] The problem of accounting for finances by program or activity is discussed more fully in the next section in regard to cost accounting.

Performance Measurement. While practitioners and academics in the field of budgeting have long been concerned about how to measure the results of government programs, accountants only became particularly concerned starting in the 1980s.[27] They came to recognize a need for measuring outputs, impacts, efficiency, effectiveness, and the like (see Chapter 5). What is significant here is that accountants now back the notion that financial accounting should be tied to *performance measurement.* If one wishes to determine the efficiency of an organization in delivering a service over time, then there needs to be a measurement of the service provided (outputs) and the costs (obtained through accounting). GASB is moving toward adopting an accounting statement that may require *service efforts and accomplishments* (SEA) reporting as part of *general-purpose external financial reporting* (GPEFR).[28]

Accounting for performance and then auditing for it require going beyond the boundaries of the organization to where results are produced. In contrast, traditional accounting systems have been structured to capture financial transactions within organizations. Once the accounting system has to take measurements outside the organization, as it must with performance accounting, major problems arise over how to collect information and how to audit it. Measurement errors inevitably occur in such systems, raising issues about their accuracy and utility.

The federal government has taken major steps in the direction of greater utilization of performance measurement. The Chief Financial Officers Act of 1990 instructs agency CFOs to develop reporting systems that provide for "the integration of accounting and budgeting information and the systematic measurement of performance."[29] The Government Performance and Results Act of 1993, as explained in Chapter 5, requires federal agencies to develop strategic plans and annual performance plans that are integral to the budget.[30] Of course, one should keep in mind that achieving change is different than simply mandating change. Efforts to include performance measurement within accounting systems surely face major challenges.

Perhaps equally difficult is the direct challenge that connecting performance and the budget creates for accounting systems themselves. Connecting performance information and cost information implies the ability to appropriately measure both. Proper cost measurement requires a level of accounting sophistication that has proved difficult for governments to achieve. They have attempted to remedy this problem through greater attention to cost accounting, as discussed later.

Basis of Accounting

The *basis of accounting* refers to the timing of transactions, or when a revenue item is recorded as received by the government and when an expenditure is recorded as having occurred. There are several methods for determining when a revenue or expenditure item is recorded, and each has a different purpose.

Cash Accounting. The oldest system is cash accounting, which is still used today, particularly in small governments. In general, all governments have a cash aspect to their accounting systems. In a cash accounting system, tax receipts are recorded when they are actually received by the government and expenditures are recorded when payments are made. Minor variations exist; some systems record expenditures when checks are written, but others record expenditures when checks clear the banking system. The major advantages of the cash system are that it is simple in comparison with alternatives and that it presents an accurate picture of cash on hand at any point in time.

The major disadvantage of the cash system is that it does not provide information about the future — namely, anticipated receipts and expenditures. The cash on hand may seem to suggest that one's financial situation is reasonably secure, but a different picture may emerge when considering obligations that must be met, such as payrolls.

Encumbrance Accounting. A step in the direction of anticipating future transactions is encumbrance accounting. Expenditures are recorded when purchase orders are written or contracts are signed; some of the cash on hand, then, is said to be encumbered and not available for covering other expenditures. In the case of a multiyear contract, all of the expenditures for a year may be encumbered at the outset of the fiscal year, or amounts may be encumbered each month as work is completed by the contractor. An encumbrance system helps ensure that a government unit will not overspend its appropriation.

Accrual Accounting. In accrual systems, financial transactions are recognized when the activities that generate them occur. Revenues are recorded when the government earns the income, as when a local government sends tax bills to property owners. Expenditures are recognized when the liabilities are incurred, regardless of when payment for those goods or services might actually be made during the year.

The accrual basis has been required of federal agencies for more than 30 years, but few federal accounting systems actually use accrual accounting. The obstacle has been the diversity of accounting systems; large departments such as the Department of Defense, for example, have many different accounting systems.[31] Where accrual accounting is used in government, it is normally on a modified basis; not all transactions are accrued and some remain on a cash basis. Full accrual, however, is recommended for proprietary funds (enterprise and internal service funds) and pension trusts.

Despite the obstacles to implementation, the accounting profession continues to endorse strongly the accrual basis of accounting. GASB's Statement No. 11, Measurement Focus and Basis of Accounting: Governmental Fund Operating Statements (MFBA, pronounced "muff-bah"), provides for extending the accrual process to cover items previously not covered. For instance, the costs of employees' vacations are to be recognized when employees earn their vacation time. When employees are allowed to accumulate vacation leave, the accounting system needs to recognize that government's liabilities have increased. Particularly controversial is the provision that employee pension funds should recognize future payments owed future retirees by recording them in the governmental funds rather than as normally reported in the general long-term debt account group. These provisions are controversial in that they negatively affect fund balances, pushing some governments into negative balances. Chapter 13 discusses defined contribution retirement plans, which reduce the liability of governments for pension benefits.

Cost Accounting. While the cash, encumbrance, and accrual bases of accounting focus attention on resources coming into government and being expended, cost accounting is concerned with when resources are used in the production of goods and services.[32] For example, gasoline purchased for a state highway department could be accounted for when the order is made (encumbrance), when the goods are received (modified accrual method), or when the vendor is paid (cash method). The cost approach, in contrast, records the transaction when the gasoline is consumed.

Managerial cost accounting can be viewed as providing key information needed by managers in conducting their operations and, in addition to this internal function, providing information to external parties such as the legislative body, taxpayers, and investors in governmental securities.[33] In a cost accounting system, costs of providing services are matched with measures of those services. For example, a school district might want to know the average cost of graduating someone from the general population compared with the average cost of graduating a student with special needs — for instance, a student with physical disabilities. *Activity-based costing* and *activity-based management* concentrate on collecting costs of delivering services to citizens.[34] The costs of delivering services can be monitored over time, thereby giving an impetus for increased efficiency of operations. Such accounting can determine the costs of producing activities, outputs, and impacts.

The incentives for using cost accounting are markedly different in the private and public sectors. To determine their profitability, corporations need to know the cost of providing each product or service. The costs of production can be subtracted from sales receipts to determine corporations' profit or loss. Governmental programs, such as police and fire departments, obviously do not seek a profit and consequently may see less need for cost accounting. Other programs, particularly enterprise and internal service funds, while not seeking a profit, do endeavor to break even and consequently have an incentive to know the costs of their services. For example, a centralized office supplies agency has an incentive to calculate its costs so as to set appropriate fee schedules for charging departments for products. A central maintenance garage for city vehicles needs an accurate understanding of its costs for maintaining garbage trucks, police cars, and buses. Keeping costs down in each of these areas is important in linking the production of services with costs and is especially important in an era of privatization. In particular, "managed competition," where government agencies and private firms compete to provide services, necessitates the ability to make appropriate cost comparisons between public agencies and private firms. As a means of cutting costs, for example, a police department might be eager to contract out for patrol car repairs rather than use a city maintenance facility. Bureaucratic politics are rampant in such situations.

Besides the reduced incentives to use cost accounting in government, several other impediments to its implementation exist. One such obstacle is that purposes and objectives are not neatly compartmentalized into organizational units, resulting in situations in which one organization may be serving multiple purposes and another organization may be serving some of those same purposes. To resolve this problem, *cost centers* must be used in which the accounting system records financial information for each activity performed within an organizational unit. In a bureau that engages in three activities and that has its personnel working at various times on the three activities, records must be maintained regarding the amount of time each worker spends on each activity. Other bureau costs, such as those for supplies, telephones, and furniture, must be distributed among the cost centers.

Other impediments to cost accounting being used in government pertain to how various financial transactions are currently conducted. Government agencies sometimes provide services to one another at no charge, resulting in a form of subsidy to the recipient agencies and a consequent understatement of the costs of the services that those agencies provide. Salaries, wages, and other personnel expenses, such as pension contributions and health benefits for employees and retirees, may appear in central budgets and not in the budgets of units that deliver services. Likewise, other support services involving budgeting, legal assistance, janitorial services, and computer support may not be charged to line agencies. The result is that organizational budgets typically fall short of fully reflecting the costs of activities.

Cost accounting requires that special attention be given to the acquisition and utilization of *fixed assets* — land, structures, and major pieces of equipment. Fixed assets sometimes are financed centrally and, as a consequence, do not appear in the budgets of the organizational units that actually use these assets. Additionally, the purchase of fixed assets or capital goods should not be considered costs in the year of purchase but rather should be depreciated over the life span of the goods. From a cost standpoint, the cost of police patrol cars might be spread over three years; from a cash standpoint, the purchase will be recorded in the first year when the purchase is made. Buildings and vehicles then are depreciated over time, showing a truer picture of the cost of services than the cash method does. The life cycle of an asset needs to be considered — that is, how long an asset has utility. Federal law and OMB Circular A-131 instruct agencies to use value engineering as a management technique in determining how long assets will be of use.[35] The circular defines *value engineering* as "an organized effort directed at analyzing the functions of systems, equipment, facilities, services, and supplies for the purpose of achieving the essential functions at the lowest life-cycle cost consistent with required performance, reliability, quality, and safety."[36]

Depreciation rules need to be applied differently according to the assets involved. FASAB has identified four types of property, plant, and equipment (PP&E).[37] The *general PP&E* category includes buildings for which a market value can be derived, such as the value of an office building. The category of *federal mission PP&E* is for the uniquely federal functions of defense and space exploration. Depreciating these assets is extremely difficult because it requires estimating the assets' useful lives. How long will a weapons system be of use, or how long will a space satellite continue to operate? The *heritage PP&E* category includes education, culture, and artistic endeavors. The Washington Monument and the White House are in this grouping, as they have special significance and are not just ordinary government buildings. The last category, *stewardship PP&E*, covers government holdings that are entrusted to the government for safekeeping. It includes federal land held by the National Park Service and the U.S. Forest Service.

In addition to fixed assets, other investments pose major challenges for the use of cost accounting in government. When a government bureau pays for several of its workers to attend a training program, is it an investment and, if so, what is the life of that investment? When a state government provides a grant to a local government for construction of a sewage treatment plant, how should the state record the investment given that the new plant will belong to the local government and not to the state?

Given the complexities of cost accounting, one can readily see why it is used in only limited cases in government. It is an open question whether FASAB and its participating agencies will be successful in moving the federal government toward the use of cost accounting. A 2000 survey of state budget offices found that most states were unable to track costs in relation to work or tasks performed.[38] Despite the enormous impediments to applying cost accounting in government, the concept remains very much alive. President George W. Bush has recommended that Congress require costing of programs. One of the Bush administration's five management initiatives is "competitive sourcing," with the goal that 50 percent of appropriate positions be opened up to competition with the private sector. A driving concern underlying this proposal is that were "true" costs identified for current operations, better decisions could be made as to whether operations should be outsourced or contracted out.[39]

Project-Based Accounting. Another option that is not as elaborate as cost accounting is project-based accounting. Accounts can be established on a temporary basis to track costs for selected activities. Private firms, both for-profit and nonprofit, keep detailed accounting records for contracts, including costs at task or subtask levels. If a consulting firm has been awarded a government contract, a separate set of accounts is established showing which personnel worked on which tasks for what length of time within a given reporting period (weekly, biweekly, or monthly). Accounts of this type are important for reimbursement purposes.

Project-based accounting also is used for monitoring internal operations. If a corporation is developing a new product or group of products, separate accounts can be established to gauge the developmental costs of the project. In the quasi-governmental arena, the World Bank uses account codes and employee time report systems to account for project costs, enabling management to evaluate the cost of preparing, negotiating, and supervising a specific loan to a country.

Cost Finding. In some instances, governments may be satisfied with something less than a complete cost accounting system or even project-based accounting. Rather than having an ongoing cost information system, governments sometimes selectively study costs of specific activities that may be contained within a single organization or spread across several units. The cost of delivering family planning services to teenagers might be derived through analysis of expenditure records and a sampling of employee time commitments. A far more elaborate cost-finding endeavor would be to try to derive the costs of HIV/AIDS to a state government; the analysis would attempt to determine the costs of prevention and treatment activities that most likely are not encoded in the accounting system. For example, AIDS may well increase health care costs for prisoners, but such costs would not routinely be segregated in the accounting system.

The analysis of cost data can be useful in identifying fixed costs and variable costs. There may be a minimum or fixed cost for providing a given service up to some particular level, above which costs increase as units of service increase. For example, a preschool program for disadvantaged children begins with a fixed set of costs for essentials such as a school room, a teacher, and some supportive services — costs that are incurred whether one or ten children are taught. As the number of children in the class increases, variable costs increase, such as those for teaching materials and supplies, teacher aides, another teacher, and possibly another classroom.

Allowable Costs. In the awarding of grants and contracts, governments need to determine what costs are allowable. The federal government's Cost Accounting Standards Board has attempted to set parameters for costs in defense and related contracts.[40] OMB Circular A-87 specifies in great detail what costs are allowable in grants to state and local governments. Unallowable costs include entertainment, alcoholic beverages, interest on debt (such as working capital borrowings), and donations, as in the case of volunteer services.

Risk and Credit Accounting. Public sector officials have come to recognize that risks arise in carrying out public duties. Not only are revenues raised and expenditures made, but other factors create conditions that can result in major financial loss and/or expenditures. Risk management involves assessing the risk exposure of a government (see Chapter 10). On the one hand, in making and guaranteeing loans, the federal government assumes risks that can have major financial consequences, as evidenced by the forced bailout of failed savings and loan associations (see Chapter 6). On the other hand, credit programs can yield savings or negative subsidies, particularly at some point in the future. Estimating such savings poses considerable technical problems, plus agencies that administer such programs may be biased in favor of forecasting such savings.[41]

State and local governments are expected to follow the instructions for reporting risks contained in GASB Statement No. 10. That statement covers property and liability, workers' compensation, and employee health care. GASB Statements No. 26 and No. 27 cover health care plans of retirees and pension plans, respectively. GASB Statement No. 3 provides for reporting risks associated with government investments in corporate stocks and bonds and other instruments. GASB Statement No. 31 sets standards for risks involved in cash management.[42] The reporting of investments in derivatives (see Chapter 10) is an important aspect of risk accounting.[43]

Another form of risk involves the imposition of unfunded mandates on state and local governments (see Chapter 14), creating huge financial costs for these governments. GASB Statement No. 18 covers the reporting of costs associated with closing landfills and maintaining them after their closure. These costs have been imposed by the standards of the Environmental Protection Agency.

OMB, as prescribed by the Federal Credit Reform Act of 1990, is overseeing a thorough revamping of how the government accounts for credit programs and how decisions are made about these programs. The law is intended to "place the cost of credit programs on a budgetary basis" so that they will compete with all other programs for scarce resources.[44] OMB requires agencies to supply data on direct loans, loan subsidies, guaranteed loans, and guaranteed loan subsidies as part of the agencies' budget submissions (Circular A-129). Prior to passage of the Federal Credit Reform Act, many federal agencies could borrow from the Federal Financing Bank, but they now must borrow from the Treasury Department to finance their direct and guaranteed loan programs. Federal agencies have encountered considerable difficulty in complying with the law, because their existing accounting systems and supporting staff often are inadequate.[45]

Generational Accounting. Of growing interest are the potential effects of government finances on different generations. Expenditures for elementary and secondary education obviously help children, whereas alcohol programs help adults and programs such as Medicare help the elderly. Generational accounting is important in considering future benefits or costs imposed on different age groups. Although accounting systems have not been devised for identifying the costs or the benefits of government activities for different age groups, some reporting of such effects occurs.

Need for Different Bases. These different approaches to the basis of accounting are not substitutes for one another. Rather, each satisfies a different type of need. From the standpoint of a treasury department, a cash basis for recording receipts and expenditures is necessary because the department has the legal responsibility to receive revenue and issue checks to cover expenses. This responsibility extends to determining that there are sufficient funds to cover checks to be issued. The encumbrance basis is important in showing the current status of assets and liabilities, including liabilities that will place a demand on cash in the future. Cost accounting is valuable in identifying resources consumed, as distinguished from resources acquired and placed in inventory. Risk accounting provides a more comprehensive overview of obligations than is available through accounting systems that cover only revenues and expenditures. Generational accounting provides insights into the implications of government finances for different generations, from the elderly to the young and to those not yet born.

Reporting

Accounting systems generate reports that are used by managers, policy makers, and people outside of government. Generally accepted accounting principle 12 calls on jurisdictions to prepare both interim and annual reports. Interim reports, such as daily and weekly reports, serve internal purposes, as in the case of checking on appropriated funds that are neither spent nor encumbered. These reports are useful in monitoring budget execution and anticipating situations in which agencies might have insufficient funds to operate their programs throughout the fiscal year. A fundamental expectation of all financial reports is that they can be audited, meaning that accounting records back up the data in the reports.

Annual reports are particularly useful to people and organizations outside of government. They can show taxpayers how revenues have been used to support services, for example. Annual reports of local governments are helpful for businesses that are considering locating, relocating, or expanding existing facilities. Such reports are used to help discover the financial condition of governments and decide whether to purchase their bonds. The Government Finance Officers

Association issues certificates of achievement for excellence in financial reporting. The association also issues awards for outstanding *popular annual financial reports* (PAFRs) — namely, reports that are prepared for use by the general public and not accountants and budgeters.[46]

Financial Reports. GASB prescribes a *comprehensive annual financial report* (CAFR) that has three sections: introduction, finances, and statistics.[47] The first section includes a letter of transmittal and general information about the government. It lists the principal officials and provides an organization chart indicating lines of authority and responsibility.

The second section contains a variety of financial statements. As governments make extensive use of funds, several different types of statements may be provided on each fund. These statements by themselves can be confusing in that they do not provide an overall perspective on the finances of the government. For this reason, GASB and other professional accounting organizations prescribe the use of condensed statements that offer a comprehensive picture of a jurisdiction and omit some of the confusing detail.

One particularly troubling aspect of these statements is the use of *transfers* among funds. Monies can be moved from one fund to another without affecting the overall assets of a jurisdiction, but if transfers are not carefully noted, they may appear as expenditures in one fund and as new assets or receipts in another fund. These transfers need to be clearly identified not only to avoid confusion but also to provide important information about a government's operations. Transfers may indicate that enterprises are subsidizing general government operations, as when proceeds from a city airport are used in part to support a city's general fund. This type of transfer may be welcome relief to local taxpayers but may raise concern among holders of airport bonds. Good financial reports clearly label transfers — showing the source of receipts and the recipient of transfers — so that false impressions of asset creation or usage are avoided.

The third section of a financial report contains statistical data. Some tables present trend data assembled from earlier financial reports, such as general revenues by source over the most recent ten-year period. Other tables provide demographic data and indicate the principal taxpayers in the jurisdiction.

Balance Sheets. Of the numerous types of financial statements, balance sheets are one of the most common. A balance sheet can be thought of as a snapshot of a government's finances at a point in time, such as at the end of a quarter or fiscal year.

A balance sheet is organized according to the accounting formula discussed earlier. Assets are first listed, showing cash on hand (bank deposits) and taxes receivable. For proprietary funds and fiduciary funds, fixed assets (buildings, land, and so forth) are also reported as assets. The balance sheet then indicates liabilities — namely, accounts that are payable and bonds outstanding — followed by the fund balance, showing items such as monies that are encumbered. **Table 11–1** is an example of a balance sheet from the State of Connecticut.

GASB's Statement No. 11 on measurement focus and the basis of accounting is of critical importance as to how balance sheets are calculated for state and local governments. Statement No. 11 requires governments to recognize items as liabilities that were previously excluded. As a result of complying with this requirement, balance sheet bottom lines went from positive to negative for many governments. When numerous governments complained about the potential political and economic harm of such balance sheets, GASB allowed governments to use the term *fund equity* for the difference between revised assets and liabilities. The term *fund balance* can be used for calculating balance sheets in the format that preceded Statement No. 11.

Table 11–1 **Governmental Funds Balance Sheet, State of Connecticut, Fiscal Year Ended June 30, 2001 (in Thousands)**

	General	Special Revenue	Debt Service	Capital Projects	Total
Assets and Other Debits					
Cash and Cash Equivalents	$735,755	$553,122	$ 0	$150,875	$1,439,752
Other	50,460	24,123	0	0	74,583
Receivables:					
Taxes	891,171	37,859	0	0	929,030
Accounts, Net of Allowances	234,018	8,336	0	2,270	244,624
Loans, Net of Allowances	1,636	313,684	0	0	315,320
Interest	0	167	5,409	0	5,576
Federal Grants Receivable	62,074	14,094	0	9,732	85,900
Non-federal Grants Receivable	6,554	8,318	0	0	14,872
Due from Other Funds	22,911	25,475	0	13,678	62,064
Advances to Other Funds	4,950	0	0	0	4,950
Receivable from Other Governments	496,585	18,654	0	50,675	565,914
Inventories and Prepaid Items	36,232	13,142	0	0	49,374
Restricted Assets	0	0	562,131	0	562,131
Total Assets and Other Debits	**2,542,346**	**1,016,974**	**567,540**	**227,230**	**4,354,090**

continues

Liabilities, Equity, and Other Credits

Accounts Payable and Accrued Liabilities	1,050,733	55,012	0	109,263	1,215,008
Due to Other Funds	69,435	5,592	5,409	47,985	128,421
Due to Component Units	151	19,209	0	0	19,360
Payable to Other Governments	78,708	0	0	0	78,708
Deferred Revenue	480,893	29,593	7,315	1,547	519,348
Liability of Escheat Property	48,717	0	0	0	48,717
Total Liabilities	**1,728,637**	**109,406**	**12,724**	**158,795**	**2,009,562**
Equity and Other Credits					
Fund Balances:					
Reserved	1,595,555	382,069	554,816	0	2,532,440
Unreserved, Undesignated	(781,846)	525,499	0	68,435	(187,912)
Total Equity and Other Credits	**813,709**	**907,568**	**554,816**	**68,435**	**2,344,528**
Total Liability, Equity, and Other Credits	**2,542,346**	**1,016,974**	**567,540**	**227,230**	**4,354,090**

Note: Table is based on a combined balance sheet for all funds.

Source: Adapted from Connecticut Comptroller, *Comprehensive Annual Financial Report for the Fiscal Year Ended June 30, 2001* (Hartford, CT: State of Connecticut, 2002).

While a compelling case is often made that governments should operate like private businesses, a balance sheet for the federal government modeled strictly on the basis of that used for private corporations would be incomplete in that important resources and needs of the nation as a whole would be excluded. As can be seen in **Figure 11–2**, the government's balance sheet consists of three components. It begins with the familiar listing of assets and liabilities. The second component consists of resources/receipts and responsibilities/outlays. This section of the balance sheet projects long-run receipts (based on the expected growth of gross domestic product) and outlays (notably, those for entitlement programs). The third component reports the assets that have been developed and national needs that require the expenditure of monies.

Operating Statements. A second major type of financial statement is the operating statement, which shows the monies received and expended during a specified period of time. State and local governments refer to these as "statements of revenues, expenditures, and changes in fund balance." Revenues can be reported by source — sales tax and income tax. Expenditures can be reported by major objects, organizational units, or other means. **Table 11–2** is an operating statement for the State of Missouri. Tables such as this one and others shown in the chapter typically have notes that explain what is included and excluded in specific entries in the statements and that are essential components of the statements.

Figure 11–2 A Balance Sheet Presentation for the Federal Government

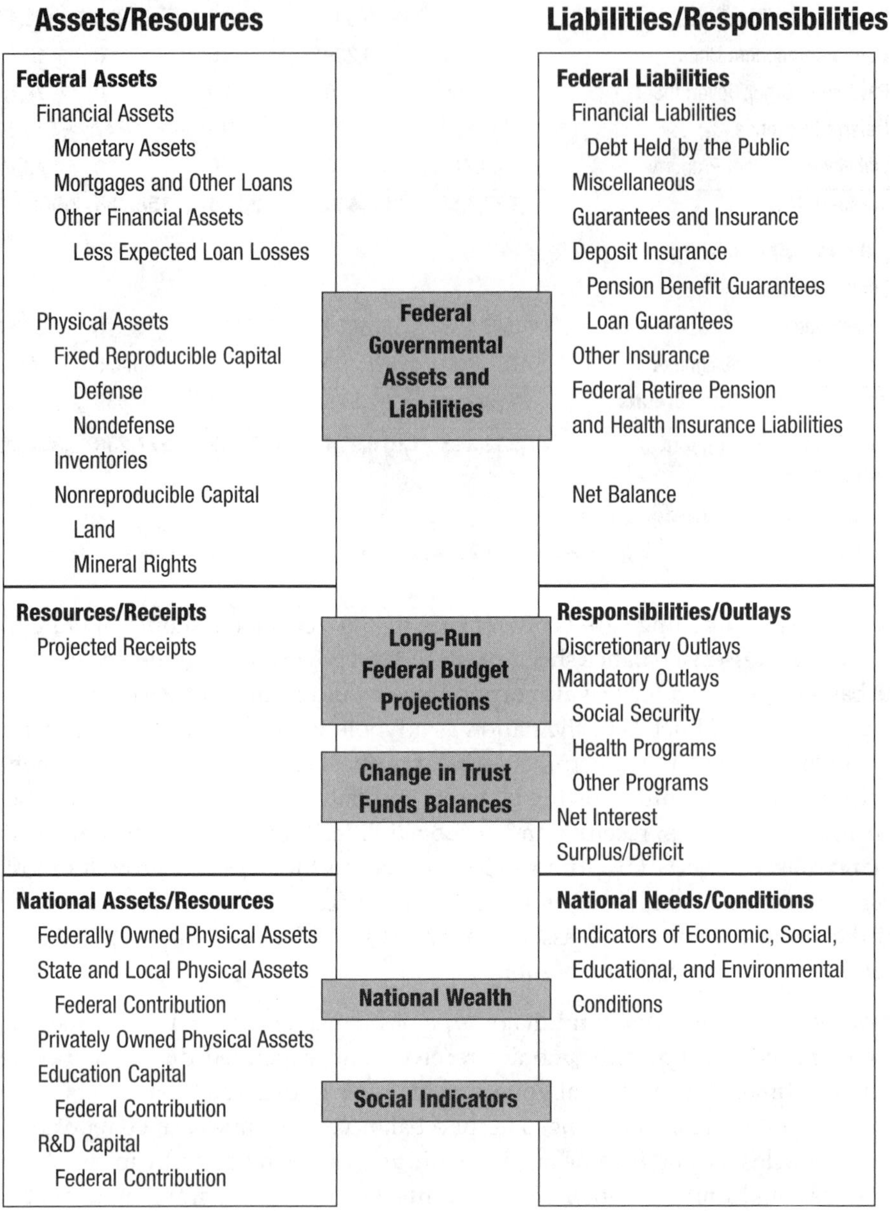

Assets/Resources

Federal Assets
Financial Assets
  Monetary Assets
  Mortgages and Other Loans
  Other Financial Assets
    Less Expected Loan Losses

Physical Assets
  Fixed Reproducible Capital
    Defense
    Nondefense
  Inventories
  Nonreproducible Capital
    Land
    Mineral Rights

Resources/Receipts
  Projected Receipts

National Assets/Resources
  Federally Owned Physical Assets
  State and Local Physical Assets
    Federal Contribution
  Privately Owned Physical Assets
  Education Capital
    Federal Contribution
  R&D Capital
    Federal Contribution

Liabilities/Responsibilities

Federal Liabilities
Financial Liabilities
  Debt Held by the Public
  Miscellaneous
  Guarantees and Insurance
  Deposit Insurance
  Pension Benefit Guarantees
  Loan Guarantees
Other Insurance
Federal Retiree Pension
  and Health Insurance Liabilities

Net Balance

Responsibilities/Outlays
Discretionary Outlays
Mandatory Outlays
  Social Security
  Health Programs
  Other Programs
Net Interest
Surplus/Deficit

National Needs/Conditions
  Indicators of Economic, Social,
  Educational, and Environmental
  Conditions

Center boxes:
Federal Governmental Assets and Liabilities

Long-Run Federal Budget Projections

Change in Trust Funds Balances

National Wealth

Social Indicators

Source: U.S. Office of Management and Budget, *Analytical Perspectives* (Washington, DC: U.S. Government Printing Office, 2002), 36.

Table 11–2 State of Missouri Receipts, Expenditures, and Transfers, August 31, 2001

	August 2001	August 2000
Receipts and Transfers In		
Receipts:		
Sales and Use Tax	$ 203,422,955	$ 211,709,953
Individual Income Tax	327,905,858	311,388,319
Other Taxes	54,940,688	38,260,829
Interest on Deposits, Taxes, and Investments	5,341,858	8,457,633
Licenses, Fees, and Permits	4,327,876	3,343,296
Sales, Services, Leases, and Rentals	6,878,885	6,499,182
Refunds	1,457,674	411,108
Interagency Billings/Inventory	5,807	67,279
All Other Sources	7,044,953	6,308,677
Total Receipts	611,324,554	586,446,276
Total Transfers In	45,945,926	22,357,998
Total Receipts and Transfers In	**657,270,480**	**608,804,274**
Expenditures and Transfers Out		
Expenditures:		
Personal Service	153,845,496	169,172,524
Expense and Equipment	31,856,018	33,344,584
Capital Improvements	4,440,141	20,905,515
Program-Specific	280,320,455	223,228,961
Total Expenditures	470,462,110	446,651,584
Transfers Out:		
Appropriated	247,125,212	271,924,921
Other	0	23,009
Total Transfers Out	247,125,212	271,947,930
Total Expenditures and Transfers Out	**717,587,322**	**718,599,514**
Excess Receipts and Transfers In (Expenditures and Transfers Out)	**$ (60,316,842)**	**$ (109,795,240)**

Source: Adapted from Division of Accounting, Office of Administration, *State of Missouri Receipts, Expenditures and Transfers — All Funds, August 31, 2001* (Jefferson City: State of Missouri, 2002), *http://www.oa.state.mo.us/acct/index.html;* accessed June 2002.

The *pro forma operating statement* represents a particular type of statement. Although used routinely in the private sector, the pro forma is rarely used as such in the public sector. It commonly is prepared in the private sector when a company is considering a capital investment. The statement has three component forecasts: demand and prices, variable expenses, and fixed expenses. The pro forma is used to determine whether a potential capital project, such as the expansion of a hotel, would add to the company's bottom line.[48]

Cash Flows Statements. A third form of financial statement details cash flows. The purpose is to show how cash entering and leaving a fund affects an entity's operations. These statements cover cash and cash equivalents, such as short-term investments (U.S. Treasury bills; see Chapter 10). Controversy exists over how these statements should be organized and whether they should be extended from just covering enterprise funds to include basically all funds.[49] **Table 11–3** is a cash flows statement for the Commonwealth of Pennsylvania.

In addition to balance sheets, operating statements, and cash flows statements, governments issue other important financial reports (e.g., disclosures on securities). For example, they provide statements when issuing bonds and other securities that are intended to help would-be purchasers understand what is being offered for sale in terms of the backing of the securities and what risks are involved.

Table 11–3 **Commonwealth of Pennsylvania Combined Statement of Cash Flows, Proprietary Funds, June 30, 2000 (in Thousands)**

	Enterprise	Internal Service
Cash Flows From Operating Activities:		
Operating income (loss)	$99,112	$774
Adjustments to reconcile operating income (loss) to net cash provided by (used for) operating activities:		
Depreciation	5,480	9,912
Net amortization	0	0
Provision for uncollectible accounts	(4,795)	151
Nonoperating revenues	584	11
Nonoperating expenses	0	(97)
Reclassification of investment income	(54,414)	0
Changes in assets and liabilities	7,875	(215)
Total Adjustments	**(45,270)**	**9,762**
Net Cash Provided by (used for) Operating Activities	**53,842**	**10,536**
Cash Flows from Noncapital Financing Activities:		
Borrowings (repayments under advances from other funds)	(66,094)	9,000
Operating transfers out	(52,320)	0
Increase in contributed capital	10,170	0
Decrease in contributed capital	(86)	0

continues

Net Cash Provided by (Used for)		
Noncapital Financing Activities	**(108,330)**	**9,000**
Cash Flows from Capital and Related Financing Activities:		
Increases in contributed capital	27,000	0
Acquisition and construction of capital assets	(9,454)	(13,811)
Proceeds from sale of capital assets	0	1,648
Net Cash Provided by (Used for)		
Capital and Related Financing Activities	**17,546**	**(12,163)**
Cash Flows from Investing Activities:		
Purchase of investments	(8,493,558)	(194,438)
Proceeds from sale and maturities of investments	8,406,577	185,489
Investment income	125,223	1,570
Net Cash Provided by (Used for) Investing Activities	**38,242**	**(7,379)**
Net Increase (Decrease) in Cash	**1,300**	**(6)**
Cash, July 1, 1999	**13,997**	**410**
Cash, June 30, 2000	**15,297**	**404**

Source: Adapted from Office of the Budget, *Comprehensive Annual Financial Report for Fiscal Year Ended June 30, 2000* (Harrisburg: Commonwealth of Pennsylvania, 2001), 11.

GASB Statement No. 34, issued in 1999, has imposed dramatic changes on state and local government financial reporting, including the following:

- Statements must have "management's discussion and analysis" indicating in an objective way the current financial situation in understandable English.

- Government-wide financial statements must be provided and must show the current and prior year. Full accrual accounting for all government activities is mandated. All capital assets must be shown and depreciated, including infrastructure assets.

- Analysis must be shown of significant changes in fund balance for the various governmental, proprietary, and fiduciary funds.

- Governments must show the originally budgeted amounts, the final budgeted figures, and actual revenues and expenditures.

- Note disclosures are required to show important accounting policies. Disclosures must show changes in long-term liabilities and in capital assets.

- Expendable and nonexpendable trust fund types are eliminated. Trust funds formerly treated as expendable now are to be treated as special revenue funds, while nonexpendable funds are converted to "permanent funds," a new fund type. Another new fund type, the "private purpose trust fund," is to be used to account for trust activities.[50]

Just as state and local governments have had to revise their financial reporting systems, so have federal agencies. The Chief Financial Officers Act of 1990 and the Government Management Reform Act of 1994 required agencies to prepare a series of *auditable* financial statements by March 1, 1997, and every year thereafter.[51] Federal agencies have experienced numerous problems in meeting these congressionally imposed deadlines.

OMB Bulletin No. 01-09, Form and Content of Agency Financial Statements, brought further changes to federal reporting. The bulletin shortened the time periods during which agencies must prepare their reports. Unaudited quarterly financial reports were initiated. Reports must show the relationship between the budget and agency statements known as "statements of budgetary resources." The bulletin provides guidance on preparing balance sheets, statements of net cost, statements of changes in net position, and the like. The Reports Consolidation Act of 2000 gave OMB authority to shift due dates for agency reports and to instruct agencies to consolidate their reports so that the information presented would be more useful.[52]

Government financial reporting has clearly become much more extensive in recent decades, but this expansion has come at a cost. Questions arise regarding whether accounting systems have become overloaded and whether some of the resources spent on financial reporting might be better spent on the delivery of services to citizens. Demands for the streamlining of financial reports are increasing. To date, Congress has authorized OMB to waive some reporting requirements imposed on federal agencies.[53] The accounting profession itself also has shown some awareness that reporting requirements can create overwhelming burdens.

■ Governmental Auditing

Auditing serves a variety of functions and consequently exists in many different forms. One distinction made is between *preaudits* and *postaudits* — that is, between reviewing transactions before and after they occur. The preaudit occurs before the government commits itself to a purchase and is used to verify, for example, that the police department has sufficient funds to purchase a piece of equipment and that the department is authorized to have that equipment. Not only the budget office but also an accounting department may be involved in preaudits; if personnel are to be hired, a personnel office may have some preaudit responsibility. Often at the state and local levels, independent comptrollers, controllers, or auditors general have preaudit responsibilities.

Postaudits generally involve more extensive procedures and often more participants. The following discussion concerns the function of postaudits in government budgeting and finance. This form of auditing has been defined as "a systematic collection of the sufficient, competent evidential matter needed to attest to the fairness of management's assertions in the financial statements, or to evaluate whether management has efficiently and effectively carried out its responsibilities."[54]

Audit Objectives and Organizational Responsibilities

Purposes. Auditing in the private sector is used largely to ensure that the financial statements issued by a firm fairly reflect its financial status, and this same concern exists in the public sector. Auditing provides some assurance to investors in both the private and public sectors that their investments are secure and are being well managed.

Another purpose of auditing is ensuring that funds are not subject to fraud, waste, and abuse or subject to error in reporting. When financial reports cannot be verified by checking accounting records, the opportunities for dishonesty, waste, or just poor management of funds may exist. GAO has been highly critical of the Internal Revenue Service for being unable to reconcile its account records, but in 2002, the agency was lauded for its "extraordinary efforts" so that the financial statements for fiscal 2000 and 2001 received unqualified opinions. These efforts were necessary in part because the IRS, along with many other federal agencies, continues to lack automated accounting systems that will produce timely and accurate financial information. Instead, these agencies must rely on cumbersome manual systems to produce information necessary to generate unqualified opinions.[55]

Auditing in government is used for compliance purposes as well. As has been noted, accounting systems track receipts and expenditures to ensure that they are handled in conformance with restrictions contained in revenue and appropriation bills. Auditing helps ensure that an agency does not spend funds on an activity that, while beneficial to society, simply has not been authorized. Compliance auditing can include ensuring that an agency has accomplished programmatically what it was instructed to do. Another form of compliance auditing involves grants. The federal government, for example, needs to check that only appropriate charges have been made by a state government in the case of a federally funded project or program, such as Medicaid, or by a university in the case of funded research.

Auditing Organizations. Nationally, several organizations influence the practice of governmental auditing. The American Institute of Certified Public Accountants issues *generally accepted auditing standards* (GAAS).[56] GASB, in the process of identifying standards for accounting, inevitably becomes involved in auditing. GASB

Statement No. 34, discussed earlier, has raised questions about how auditing is to be performed in state and local governments.[57] GAO issues *generally accepted government auditing standards* (GAGAS, known as the "yellow book"), which are applied to federal agencies and may be applied to state and local governments that receive federal financial assistance.[58]

Auditing within a government often is performed by several organizations. Audits are conducted periodically by officers within an agency to provide information to management; these internal audits help maintain managerial control over operations. Other audits are conducted by external officers, who can be from a unit answerable to the legislative body (such as GAO being answerable to Congress), a unit headed by an independently elected officer, or an independent private corporation that has a contract to conduct an audit. The federal government augmented the auditing function during the 1970s and 1980s by creating *inspectors general* in major federal agencies. Appointed by the president with the advice and consent of the Senate, inspectors general are located within agencies but can only be removed by the president. According to the Inspector General Act of 1978 and the Chief Financial Officers Act of 1990, inspectors general are responsible for conducting audits and for investigating possible cases of fraud, waste, and abuse of government resources.[59] The Chief Financial Officers Act, by creating CFOs in major agencies, greatly increased the attention that agencies devote to sound accounting practices and to the auditing of accounts. Agencies have redesigned their central staff units, consolidating considerable powers under the CFOs. Other federal agencies not covered by the 1978 legislation also have inspectors general, and legislation has been proposed that would require these agencies to conduct audits.[60]

Executive Order 12993 provides a process for dealing with instances of possible wrongdoing by inspectors general and their deputies. The Federal Bureau of Investigation is authorized to investigate such matters, and the President's Council on Integrity and Efficiency (PCIE) reviews the FBI's findings. The PCIE consists of department inspectors general and selected central administrators, such as representatives from OMB and the Office of Personnel Management.[61]

All levels of government use Big 5 and other accounting firms to conduct or assist in auditing. Depending on the state, a local government may have a choice of paying either the state auditor or a private firm for audit services; state services may be less expensive, but private services may perform audits in a more timely fashion. When a private firm is to be used, a government will employ a bidding process to give competing firms an opportunity to indicate what services they can provide, in what time frame, and at what cost.

A common practice in the private sector, and one often recommended for the public sector, is the use of audit committees. When they exist in government, these bodies typically consist of administrators, legislators, and financial experts from outside of the government. The committees can serve as useful interfaces between finance offices and auditors. Such committees, however, are seldom used. Sometimes the number of organizations involved in auditing in a given situation can seem overwhelming. An agency may have two or more auditors. In the Department of Defense, for instance, audit functions are performed by the Defense Contract Audit Agency (which audits contractors), the inspector general, the comptroller, and the CFO. Large state and local agencies may have similar internal auditors, and all levels of government have their central auditors, such as GAO for the federal government and auditors general for the states. As noted, private accounting firms may have responsibilities as well. Additional auditing occurs because of intergovernmental financial transactions. State government agencies, for example, may be audited by federal funding agencies and GAO, although this level of auditing has changed since passage of the Single Audit Act of 1984 (see below).

Types of Audits and Standards

Audit Types. As already noted, there are preaudits and postaudits, and internal and external audits. Another means of categorizing audits is by considering the purposes to be served. The definition of auditing provided earlier suggests that audits can be directed toward finance and performance.

According to GAGAS, financial audits focus on whether financial statements prepared by a government accurately reflect financial transactions and the government's or agency's status. The standards of auditing provide a framework for conducting an audit.

Financial audits also review how financial matters are handled or whether suitable internal controls exist to protect resources. Auditors are concerned with the vulnerability of a financial management system to potential fraud. Are organizational lines of responsibility clearly established to ensure that whoever is in charge has the authority to protect the government's or agency's finances? Are policies and procedures established for maintaining records, and are those policies and procedures adhered to in practice? Are computer systems that handle financial transactions protected against potential fraud?

Guidelines in this area are established at the federal level by the Federal Managers' Financial Integrity Act of 1982; the Chief Financial Officers Act of 1990; OMB Circular A-123, Management Accountability and Control; Circular A-127, Financial Management Systems; and Circular A-134, Financial Accounting Principles and Standards.[62] OMB, working with federal agencies, has published a list of high-risk situations in which fraud, waste, and abuse are more likely to occur. The Federal Financial Management Improvement Act of 1996 requires that each federal agency be audited and a report be prepared stating whether the agency complies with the financial management systems requirements (Circular A-127) and the Standard General Ledger.[63]

Identification of the risks is the first step in eliminating the problems. Auditors make risk assessments to determine which accounting activities or operations to audit, as only a sample of financial activities can be audited, given the auditors' limited resources. The risk assessment determines which activities are most vulnerable to fraud, waste, and abuse and therefore should be audited.

In 2001, the GAO's list of high-risk situations included 22 items, with some items having been on the list since its inception. For example, student financial aid programs and defense weapon systems acquisition have always appeared on the list.[64]

The other major auditing function served is performance auditing, which deals with whether resources are being used efficiently and whether results or objectives are being achieved (see Chapter 7). Some audit agencies, most notably GAO, have had their traditional duties expanded to include such performance audits.

Any audit agency faces the difficult choice of deciding how much effort and resources should be devoted to the competing functions of financial and performance auditing. If major emphasis is given to performance auditing, fraud and other abuses may become more prevalent; conversely, placing greater emphasis on financial auditing may keep government honest but do little to encourage agencies to fulfill their missions.

Auditing Standards. GAAS provides overall guidelines as well as standards for conducting fieldwork and preparing audit reports.[65] Overall standards call for auditors to be independent of the agencies under review and to be fully trained in the auditing function. The Securities and Exchange Commission oversees accounting firms to ensure that private auditors are independent of the entities that they audit. Fieldwork is to be planned adequately in advance and sufficiently staffed to meet the requirements of the work plan. Auditors must keep accurate records of their fieldwork to answer questions that may arise at a later time.

Field auditing involves verifying sample transactions to ensure that transactions did occur as recorded. For example, an expense report of a trip taken by a city employee to a national conference, among numerous expense reports, might be selected for review. The auditor may (1) call the travel agent or airline to verify the ticket price, (2) check that the trip was an authorized budget expenditure, (3) interview the employee to verify unreceipted miscellaneous expenses, and (4) review other receipts and documents to determine the accuracy of the report. The purpose of this fieldwork is not particularly to find cases of fraud, waste, and abuse but rather to verify that the jurisdiction has procedures in place to protect against them.

The Single Audit Act. A concern of the federal government for many years has been the large volume of federal financial transfers to state and local governments and to nongovernment organizations, and verification of whether these transfers are being suitably audited. OMB has three circulars that detail how these organizations are to organize their accounts: (1) Circular A-21, Cost Principles for Educational Institutions (1996); (2) Circular A-87, Cost Principles for State, Local and Indian Tribal Governments (1995); and (3) Circular A-122, Cost Principles for Non-Profit Organizations (1997).

The Single Audit Act of 1984, as amended, deals with this audit problem by requiring that recipients of federal assistance amounting to $300,000 or more in a fiscal year must undergo a single audit of their accounting systems and the way federal funds are handled.[66] Audits must be submitted within nine months of the audit period's close. The law applies to state and local governments as well as to nonprofit organizations. It has had the effect of requiring tens of thousands of audits annually. These audits, normally conducted by private firms, are intended to help ensure that recipients use federal resources in accordance with federal laws and regulations. The act is implemented through OMB Circular A-133, Audits of States, Local Governments, and Non-Profit Organizations. A survey of accounting/finance offices in state, county, municipal, and township governments found widespread agreement that the Single Audit Act had improved the handling of federal financial assistance, but had less of an impact on overall financial management in these governments. While the law was intended to reduce duplicated efforts, that goal was not always accomplished.[67]

GAAS, GAGAS, and the Single Audit Act set standards for audit reporting. Of course, one of the chief concerns with regard to any report is that financial statements be in accordance with generally accepted accounting principles. Audit reports are expected to indicate deficiencies, such as inconsistent use of accounting procedures. Reports indicate whether internal controls exist to protect against fraud, waste, and abuse.

Four types of conclusions can be drawn by the auditing body:

1. The audit might be unqualified, providing a "clean opinion"— that is, the accounting system meets all standards.

2. The report may be qualified, indicating there are problems but that the system generally meets standards. A qualified audit of a local or state government might be interpreted unfavorably by would-be investors in the government's bonds.

3. A disclaimer audit indicates that the accounting system is inadequate and that conducting an audit is impossible.

4. An audit can be adverse or negative, indicating that the financial statements fail to provide an accurate report of the entity's finances.

For fiscal year 2001, the federal government received a disclaimer on its financial audit by the General Accounting Office, the fifth disclaimer in a row. Of the 24 agencies covered by the CFO Act, 18 received clean opinions.[68] While this news about federal agencies seemed encouraging, OMB was less than sanguine. The budget office on its management scorecard for financial management assigned a code of red, indicating serious flaws, or yellow, indicating not fully complying with financial criteria, to 23 of the 24 agencies. Only the National Science Foundation received a green, indicating it met all standards. The Departments of Energy and Labor, the Environmental Protection Agency, and the Office of Personnel Management showed improvement, but the performance of the Small Business Administration and the National Aeronautics and Space Administration actually deteriorated.[69] On the other hand, in late 2002 the Association of Government Accountants honored eight federal agencies — the General Accounting Office, the Nuclear Regulatory Commission, the National Science Foundation, the Social Security Administration, and the Departments of Energy, Interior, Labor, and State — for excellence in accountability reporting.[70]

Both the Office of Management and Budget and the General Accounting Office identify *material deficiencies* or *material weaknesses* found in federal agencies. Both have been critical of the means by which federal agencies account for their property and the lack of adequate security of computerized financial systems.[71]

Erroneous payments have been one of the biggest problems. Correcting these problems has been identified part of President George W. Bush's Management Agenda. According to the Management Agenda report, "Federal agencies recently identified $20.7 billion in erroneous benefit and assistance payments associated with just 13 programs. That amount represents more than the total annual expenditures of seven states."[72] Of course, the federal government is not the only government subject to wrongful spending. A county treasurer in Iowa was accused, for example, of making hundreds of dollars of phone calls at government expense to a lonely-hearts telephone service.[73]

Follow-up after an audit is essential to ensure that weaknesses are corrected. Without such follow-up, auditing is an empty exercise. OMB Circular A-50, Audit Followup, sets guidelines for checks to be made after audits have been completed at the federal level.

Information Systems

Contemporary approaches to budgeting and accounting obviously require considerable amounts of information for decision making and evaluation. Information systems, then, constitute an effort to bring about greater coordination of organizational units in the collection, storage, manipulation, retrieval, and analysis of information. The following discussion addresses the design of information systems, the use of computers, the information available through the Internet, and the problems and issues that are endemic to information systems.

Management Information Systems/Knowledge Management Systems

The term *management information system* (MIS) is most commonly used to refer to systems of information processing intended to provide assistance to planning, administration, and control functions, and the term *system* suggests a categorizing or ordering of information processing.[74] A distinction is made between data and information; *data* refer to facts and *information* takes into account the usefulness of data. Data that are not information are considered *noise*, in that they detract from, rather than aid, the decision-making process. Thousands of pieces of data about individual welfare recipients, for example, may be of little help in deliberations about changing the funding formula for federal welfare aid to state and local governments. The management of information is commonly referred to as *information resources management* (IRM).

A term related to MIS is *decision support system* (DSS), which usually refers to a computer information system that facilitates nonroutine, semistructured decision making. In other words, routine activities are excluded, such as simple recordkeeping for patient appointments at a mental health clinic, but so are unstructured decision-making processes, such as setting relative funding priorities among mental health services, narcotic law enforcement, and national security interests in Central Asia.[75]

Knowledge management system (KMS) is a related term.[76] Here the focus is on what we understand to be true or what we know. The emphasis, then, is on managing that knowledge to assist in problem solving and planning for the future.

Categorization of Information. We have consistently noted that two basic types of information are used in budgetary and financial decision making: program information and resource information. That typology is manifest in **Figure 11–3**, which provides a schematic representation of the types of information used in the federal government. The figure shows how public concerns and concerns of the legislative and executive branches determine the information requirements of government. Four columns of boxes are depicted. The first column, which represents program information, includes social indicators, impacts, outputs, and other program-related information (see Chapter 5). The other three columns involve resource information — personnel, finances, and property (land, buildings, and equipment).

The illustration also has several rows depicting the nature of the decisions or the types of transactions involved. The highest level includes strategic planning information and programming information. The second level includes operational planning, and the third includes execution and control. The fourth level includes relatively routine transactions, such as employee payroll, debt service, and construction management.

Structure. The design or structure of an MIS or KMS is dependent on the intended users and their information needs. **Figure 11–3** is oriented toward the executive branch and its roles in budget preparation and execution. Other major users are the legislative branch in its budget approval and oversight roles and a comptroller office in its auditing role. In addition to needing information pertaining to appropriations and expenditures, legislatures want information on fiscal notes, the status of bills in each chamber, the receipt of grants, and the like.

The public has come to be recognized as a major set of information users in a variety of ways and at a level of intensity not previously experienced. The Clinton administration popularized the term *national information infrastructure* (NII), referring to linkages between the general public and the information superhighway.[77] Use of the Internet to serve the public is discussed later in this chapter.

As part of this effort to make information available to the public, the Government Information Locator Service (GILS) was developed by the federal government as prescribed by the Paperwork Reduction Act of 1995 and OMB Bulletin 95-01. The objective is to have all federal agencies make known the information in their possession. Much information is available through the Internet, while other information is available by toll-free telephone numbers, fax telephone transmission, hard copy, or CD-ROM. GILS is maintained by the Government Printing Office.[78]

There were high hopes for GILS when it was launched. It was viewed as a major portal for private citizens, corporations, and government agencies to locate necessary data. GILS was seen as a means for government agencies to share information and to reduce redundancy in information collection. Many of those high hopes have not been realized, however. Getting agencies to share data has proved to be a particularly knotty problem.[79] This problem became painfully evident when the lack of information sharing among federal agencies on matters of security and terrorism was revealed.[80] GILS, then, has not fulfilled its mission as an interagency information-sharing mechanism and is simply one of many useful means for obtaining information.

Figure 11-3 | **Federal Information Requirements Planning Chart**

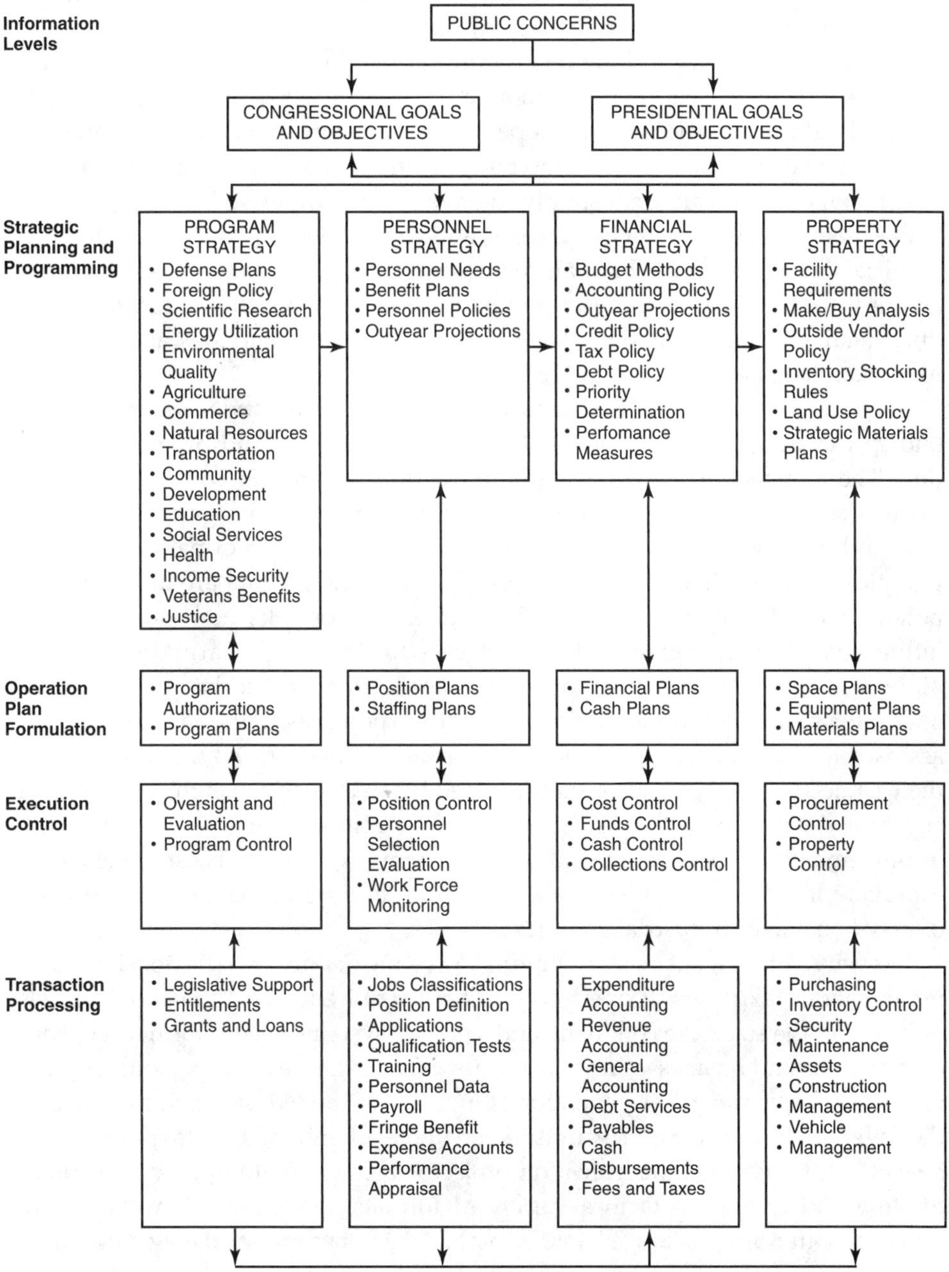

Information Levels				

PUBLIC CONCERNS

CONGRESSIONAL GOALS AND OBJECTIVES

PRESIDENTIAL GOALS AND OBJECTIVES

Strategic Planning and Programming

PROGRAM STRATEGY
- Defense Plans
- Foreign Policy
- Scientific Research
- Energy Utilization
- Environmental Quality
- Agriculture
- Commerce
- Natural Resources
- Transportation
- Community
- Development
- Education
- Social Services
- Health
- Income Security
- Veterans Benefits
- Justice

PERSONNEL STRATEGY
- Personnel Needs
- Benefit Plans
- Personnel Policies
- Outyear Projections

FINANCIAL STRATEGY
- Budget Methods
- Accounting Policy
- Outyear Projections
- Credit Policy
- Tax Policy
- Debt Policy
- Priority Determination
- Perfomance Measures

PROPERTY STRATEGY
- Facility Requirements
- Make/Buy Analysis
- Outside Vendor Policy
- Inventory Stocking Rules
- Land Use Policy
- Strategic Materials Plans

Operation Plan Formulation

- Program Authorizations
- Program Plans

- Position Plans
- Staffing Plans

- Financial Plans
- Cash Plans

- Space Plans
- Equipment Plans
- Materials Plans

Execution Control

- Oversight and Evaluation
- Program Control

- Position Control
- Personnel Selection Evaluation
- Work Force Monitoring

- Cost Control
- Funds Control
- Cash Control
- Collections Control

- Procurement Control
- Property Control

Transaction Processing

- Legislative Support
- Entitlements
- Grants and Loans

- Jobs Classifications
- Position Definition
- Applications
- Qualification Tests
- Training
- Personnel Data
- Payroll
- Fringe Benefit
- Expense Accounts
- Performance Appraisal

- Expenditure Accounting
- Revenue Accounting
- General Accounting
- Debt Services
- Payables
- Cash Disbursements
- Fees and Taxes

- Purchasing
- Inventory Control
- Security
- Maintenance
- Assets
- Construction
- Management
- Vehicle
- Management

Source: Reprinted from U.S. General Accounting Office, *Managing the Cost of Government*, vol. 2 (1985), 21.

Other efforts to serve citizens are under way at the state and local levels. Some states, such as Florida, have their own projects.[81] Numerous communities have created electronic information kiosks located in convenient places, such as shopping malls. Selected Web sites are discussed later.

Organizations vary in how much information they need and how they will use it. A line agency needs much more data about itself than the budget office needs about the agency. Similarly, a personnel department needs much information on agency personnel, while the budget office needs some but not nearly as much. Some users want data simply to have them without necessarily planning to use them. Congress, state legislatures, and city councils often demand detailed financial data that will not be analyzed. Legislative bodies sometimes suspect the executive of hiding something important unless they force the executive to produce detailed expenditure data. The fact that legislators could look at any particular detail helps keep the executive honest.

A budget office needs information for budget preparation, for monitoring budget execution, and possibly for performance auditing and program evaluation. The information needed, as discussed throughout this book, covers such matters as expenditure data based on organizational unit, program, appropriation, and the like. In addition, the budget office may want information on a geographical basis, such as by region or by county. Regional data are important for policy and political reasons — to determine, for example, how programs are influencing different regions or how budget reductions might harm some regions more than others. Local governments may need to have tax data generated by region for special neighborhood assessment purposes, as in the case of a special assessment on downtown businesses. *Geographic information systems* (GISs), as their name suggests, provide data organized by area, such as neighborhoods in a city or counties of a state.[82] A GIS can be helpful in planning for infrastructure improvements, such as water and sewer systems and roads. These systems are especially helpful in considering the impact on utilities of planned construction of new housing or industrial complexes.[83]

Revenue offices, such as the Internal Revenue Service, need extensive information about taxpayers. Property tax systems require information about parcels of land and the structures on them, and sales tax systems need information about corporations and businesses responsible for collecting taxes. The personal income tax, of course, is the major generator of income for the federal government, and the Internal Revenue Service must keep track of millions of taxpayers. The agency's Tax Systems Modernization project was intended to upgrade its ability to store and retrieve data in a variety of formats. IRS efforts, however, were plagued with numerous problems, in part perhaps because of the agency's mismanagement, but also because the complexity of tax laws challenges even the most sophisticated computer systems.[84] The project was ultimately scrapped and replaced by PRIME Alliance, a project led by a consortium of consulting firms.[85]

In addition to central offices such as a budget office and a treasury department, line departments and agencies have a host of information needs and corresponding systems. Agencies that are covered by the Chief Financial Officers Act have hundreds of financial systems, plus hundreds of other systems pertaining to the operations of their programs. Some states have publicly accessible information systems for persons seeking government employment. States on occasion have linked their systems with local governments as another means for making information more readily available. The opportunities for networking information on an intergovernmental basis are seemingly limitless.

Timeliness is another criterion. Some data need to be maintained on a daily basis. An accounting department needs daily reports on the status of funds, cash balances, and the like, whereas some organizational units may need only weekly or monthly reports about their budgets. A central budget office does not need daily reports from agencies on program performance, such as outputs and impacts. Some information may need to be available only upon request, with an acceptable lag time of perhaps a week or more before the requested information is provided.

The quality of information is an additional criterion. Congress instructed the Office of Management and Budget to promulgate guidelines for agencies in making quality information available to the public.[86] The *Guidelines for Ensuring and Maximizing the Quality, Objectivity, Utility, and Integrity of Information Disseminated by Federal Agencies*, as the title suggests, covers the gamut of characteristics that make for data that is useful and worthy of being relied upon.[87]

While numerous approaches to designing an MIS or KMS exist, seemingly one of the most viable approaches is to develop modules or subsystems that can be linked with each other. Each subsystem need not be computer-based, but as computer technology advances, more and more subsystems will be converted from paper and microfiche files to computer files. One essential subsystem of any financially oriented MIS/KMS is an accounting system. As has been noted, large governments may have many accounting systems, and in some such cases there is only limited standardization. Over time, standardization will become more prevalent, given the need to compare and analyze data from different accounting systems.

Other subsystems may exist that are largely independent of the accounting system (or systems). There is no compelling need to have a computer-based system containing program impact and output data as part of a financial accounting system. In fact, having both types of information in the same set of files may unnecessarily complicate data input, storage, and manipulation. On the other hand, computer-supported information systems containing program data can be linked to accounting systems as needed. One approach is to download selected information from various subsystems into a temporary file. A state budget office that wants to examine the economic impact of tourism, for example, might assemble information from a variety of sources both within the state government and from external databases.

Although the modular approach is attractive in concept, it is difficult to implement. The problem lies in linking the modules to each other. In the real world, it is not just a matter of literally plugging one module into another. Although a financial module may be suitable for capturing financial transactions, the problem remains of linking those data to program information. In other words, there might be no easy linkage between information about a city department's expenditures and information about its accomplishments. Similar problems exist in linking tax systems with more general information needed for the revenue side of budget preparation or linking appropriations provided to an organizational unit with procurement data about specific purchases. Interfaces among these systems can be difficult to achieve, and when information must be reentered from one system to another, personnel and time are required, errors occur, and information-processing costs rise.

A more comprehensive approach than this modular system (sometimes called a *legacy system*) is what is known as an *enterprise resource planning system* (ERP). The basic difference between the two is that a legacy system is a preexisting system (usually outdated) with which a new system must interface, wheras an ERP allows a more comprehensive approach to information management. These options are discussed in the next section.

Computers

The rapid advances in computers and related technology are making possible information systems that were merely concepts a few years ago, and they are also making these systems affordable for most governments. Powerful mainframe computers, of course, have been a staple for federal agencies, states, and large cities for decades. With the advent of microcomputers, small governments suddenly had easy access to computer technology. By the early 1990s, probably every government in the United States had at least one computer, and by 2000, computers were prevalent throughout governments. By 1995, all 50 states and the District of Columbia reported using computers for agency budget request preparation, budget request analysis by the central budget office, and preparation of the executive budget.[88] A survey conducted in 2000 of cities having populations of more than 50,000 found that three-fourths had tested or implemented financial budgeting software.[89]

What exists may well be a hodgepodge of hardware and software. Large jurisdictions may continue to use mainframe equipment but also find a need for mini- and microcomputers that run independently of the mainframes. In some instances, agencies may create microcomputer systems that contain duplicates of mainframe files because the central data processing office takes too long to respond to user requests or the mainframe files are not as user-friendly with regard to the manipulation of data. A survey conducted in 2000 asked state budget offices to estimate the extent to which their professional staff relied on various information sources. The budget offices estimated that 33 percent of their information came from client servers, 25 percent from mainframes, 20 percent from local PCs and Macintosh computers, and 20 percent from print media.[90] This hodepodge presents daunting hurdles in attempts to integrate information sources. Differing computer architectures often thwart integration efforts.[91]

Acquisition Planning. While most governments in the United States have at least one computer and probably most have applied computer technology to some or a wide range of their financial processes, governments in other countries are just beginning to undertake the process of applying computers to budgeting and finance. Painful lessons are being learned along the way, such as the cost of conversion, the time required, and the need for skilled personnel.

As governments gain experience in computing, they are expending greater effort in planning computer installations and information systems. Once having entered the realm of computing through the purchase of one or more computers, a government must decide what steps to take next; planning for the introduction of new computer-based financial information systems is essential. Steps include designating a group of individuals to be responsible for overseeing the design and installation of the system, making an assessment of which tasks need to be handled by the system, assessing the volume of work to be processed, determining hardware and software needs, identifying employee training requirements, and selecting appropriate vendors.[92] Traditional purchasing procedures that award contracts to low bidders may be unsuitable in the acquisition of information technology.[93]

The federal government is attempting to take a systematic approach to future acquisition of computer hardware and software. The Information Technology Management Reform Act of 1996 required each federal agency to establish a position of *chief information officer* (CIO) and required the head of the agency to work with the CIO and the CFO in integrating financial and information systems.[94] OMB is responsible for overall implementation of the law, including overseeing the acquisition of information technology. Circular A-130, Management of Federal Information Resources, provides guidance on how agencies are to collect, store, and distribute information. The CIOs meet as a council under the direction of OMB.[95]

The Office of Management and Budget has been highly critical of agencies' approaches to *information technology* (IT) investment. Investments have been said to be duplicative, resulting in wasteful spending. In addition, they have not improved mission performance. Plans generally do not exist that show how IT investments are related to the business needs of an agency. IT projects often fail to meet "cost, schedule, and performance goals."[96] Congress has proposed going even farther to ensure effective IT investment in at least one case. An amendment to the Defense Department's appropriation bill for fiscal year 2003 would have withheld funds from any part of the department that did not comply with specific accounting requirements. These requirements have proved difficult to meet largely because of antiquated and incompatible information systems.[97]

To provide central leadership, OMB has created two key information positions. The associate director for information technology and e-government is commonly referred to as the government's "technology czar." Operating at the direction of this new associate director is the government-wide chief technology officer (CTO). It is significant that these positions are independent of the Office of Information and Regulatory Affairs (see Chapter 10).

At the state level, the National Association of State Chief Information Officers (NASCIO) is providing leadership.[98] The association collects and publishes information about IT usage in the states and has several working groups that provide guidance on best practices in the information arena. NASCIO has worked with the White House Office of Homeland Security in regard to technology security.[99]

In addition to CIOs, some agencies are creating chief knowledge officers (CKO) positions. As noted earlier, knowledge management has become an increasingly popular approach to how government operates. What CKOs do varies from agency to agency, but the emphasis is generally on utilizing the knowledge held by workers and often sharing knowledge through the use of information technology.[100]

Many sources are available to assist governments in making critical decisions about information technology. Numerous informative sites exist on the Internet, such as CNET, "the source for computing and technology."[101] The U.S. General Services Administration has a unit that advises federal agencies on the acquisition of hardware, software, and consultative IT services. The Government Finance Officers Association provide similar services to state and local governments.

Software. In addition to the acquisition of computer hardware, software or programming is needed. One of the most common forms of software in budgeting is the *spreadsheet*. A spreadsheet is a chart in which the rows can be organizational units within a department or, at a more detailed level, major and minor objects within a bureau or office; the columns can be time units, such as last year's actual figures, current-year projected figures, and proposed figures for the budget year and out-years. Other columns can be included, such as expenditures by quarter. Side-by-side columns can be used to show appropriated amounts and actual expenditures. Spreadsheets can be used for budget proposals and for multiyear budget plans.

The advantage of a spreadsheet program is that it can calculate thousands of adjustments in a few seconds. It can quickly adjust personnel costs, for example, to reflect possible pay increases, such as an across-the-board 3 percent pay adjustment, and can recalculate employee benefits based on projected new pay rates. Spreadsheet programs can accommodate numerous assumptions, such as a pay increase at one level and price increases for supplies and equipment at another level. Among the more popular microcomputer spreadsheet programs are Excel and Lotus.

Agency budget requests can be submitted to a central budget office either electronically or by sending the requests on floppy disks and CD-ROMs. If the central budget office decides to reduce a request, the computer can readjust figures, thereby recalculating all subtotals and totals, without having to consume many hours of staff time.

At the federal level, OMB uses the MAX Decision Support System (MAX DSS). This system is used for preparing the budget and various reports and for the ad hoc analysis that commonly arises in any budget office. The system is immense, having more than 100 data tables; the largest has more than 2 million rows of data.[102] Instructions for the use of MAX DSS in agency submissions of budget requests are contained in OMB Circular A-11, Preparation and Submission of Budget Estimates (see Chapters 5 and 6).

One technology that holds great promise for government is *computer imaging.* Paper records can be scanned into a computer, with the data compressed on optical disks, allowing for the elimination of vast amounts of paper records and the warehouses needed to store them. *Optical character recognition* (OCR) and *intelligent character recognition* (ICR) permit the searching of these scanned records as needed. *Word processing* also is an integral part of budget preparation, because substantial textual materials must be drafted each year. Perhaps the biggest advantage offered by any word-processing software package is that it frees staff from having to retype portions of the budget countless times as decisions, such as whether to fund a particular activity and at what level, are made and adjusted. Changes can be made, the computer can be instructed to check for spelling errors, and the new material then is ready to be presented in a variety of formats.

Database managers constitute another type of software widely used in budget and financial operations. These software packages are intended to handle data pertaining to cases, such as characteristics of welfare clients, paychecks issued to employees, and the status of corporations inspected for compliance with air and water pollution regulations. Some agencies and even entire governments have moved to *data warehousing*. In these systems, data that may have been housed in numerous data sets and in numerous computers are merged into one "warehouse." Such a system provides ready access to all available information, avoiding the need to seek selected pieces of information from different databases. The state of Washington, an acknowledged leader in information management, announced in 2002 the creation of a Digital Archives building that would store electronic records from its three branches of government in a common location.[103]

Integrated software or suites are desirable because they allow use of word processing, spreadsheets, database managers, and graphics. With an integrated software package, a budget office can prepare the text for the budget document along with tables, charts, and graphs.

Local area networks (LAN) connect a series of computers to one another, allowing for common access of data. Wireless technology known as *wireless fidelity* (WiFi) allows for high-speed connectivity in a wireless environment. In other words, several computers can can be linked together without stringing cumbersome cables. *Wide area networks* (WAN) link computers over a span of miles.

On a much larger scale than a LAN is an *intranet*. Instead of linking users in the same physical location, it uses Web technology to allow all users within the "net" (who may be separated by hundreds or thousands of miles) to access data, forms, policies, and so forth. The Navy Marine Corps Intranet is being designed to link 350,000 desktop computers and 200 networks.[104]

Studies are under way to evaluate the possibility of implementing an intranet for the federal government as a whole. The idea, called GovNet, is attractive because it offers the prospect of providing a secure set of information, unlike the Internet, which is prone to attack by hackers and possibly terrorists.[105]

An *application service provider* (ASP) distributes software to a government or agency on an as-needed basis. Rather than an entity buying software or leasing it, the entity pays for the software when it is actually used. The ASP provides not only the software but also the technical support. Through such an arrangement, governments can utilize computer applications that otherwise would be beyond their financial and technical capabilities.[106]

Enterprise resource planning (ERP) is a relatively new term in the technology field and might be considered the "ultimate" in computer functionality. "Enterprise" refers to a wide scope, such as an entire local government or a large state agency or group of agencies. "Resource" covers both financial and nonfinancial resources, such as personnel. "Planning" suggests an emphasis on strategic decision making.[107] An ERP system organizes data into a common database, as distinguished from numerous databases located in different computers, and provides the computer software that allows for the manipulation of data to serve the needs of decision makers. ERP systems are seen as being particularly important in efforts to create e-government and e-commerce. ERP systems can be accomplished not only government-wide but also on an intergovernmental basis.[108]

The Internet

The Internet has become an essential tool for budgeting and finance. The "Net," as it is called, is a vast system of interconnected computers, originally designed to connect researchers in national defense with one another. The Net, which provides communication links and access to information, has several components:

- *Electronic mail* (e-mail) is one of the Net's most popular features. It allows people to send messages to one another and attach lengthy documents to those messages.

- *Usenet News* (Netnews) is a bulletin board system that allows people to post inquiries and announcements and then receive comments from others.

- *Mailing lists* (listservs) are similar to bulletin boards, except that one must join a group, usually at no cost. In a listserv, members automatically receive communications from other members, whereas in Netnews a person needs to enter the bulletin board to see posted messages.

- *File Transfer Protocol* (FTP) allows text and data files to be sent at high speed to someone requesting the information.

- *Wide Area Information Service* (WAIS) and *Gopher* are tools that facilitate searches for information that has been posted by organizations and individuals. WAIS and Gopher have become less popular since the advent of the World Wide Web.

- *Internet Relay Chat* (chat rooms) allows people to communicate with others having similar interests. A person can enter a chat room and talk with whoever is in the room at the time. Communication is currently accomplished through the typing of messages but voice communication is becoming available.

- *The World Wide Web* (WWW) is a Windows-based system developed at CERN Research Center in Switzerland. The Web makes a vast array of information available in text, still picture, video, and audio forms.

The World Wide Web is one of the most popular features of the Internet. Begun only in 1991, it includes millions of *Web sites* or *home pages* for individuals, nonprofit groups, for-profit companies, and governments. To deal with the immensity of the Web, devices known as *search engines* have been developed to aid in "surfing" the Web to find information of interest. Popular search engines include AskJeeves, Yahoo!, Google, and HotBot.

Table 11–4 lists selected Web sites in the field of budgeting and finance. The first group of sites is of general interest. The first entry, Governments on the WWW, provides links to government Web sites around the world. The U.S. Library of Congress Web site links to a vast array of information. Statistical Resources on the Web and Government Information Locator Service (GILS) both provide numerous links to data sources of relevance to the budgeting and finance arena.

Federal, state, and local governments maintain numerous sites, as shown in **Table 11–4**. FirstGov is designed as the main portal to federal agencies' home pages. Cross-agency portals are being developed at the federal level. For example, the Department of Housing and Urban Development is developing a Virtual Home Center that will enable citizens to obtain information and purchase housing through several federal agencies.[109]

States can be reached by using such sites as State and Local Governments on the Net, U.S. State and Local Gateway, and GovernmentGuide. Many state Web sites have links to their local governments. Local governments often are troubled by the expense of developing their individualized Web sites. It may be possible to develop more generic systems for local government use, what might be called a "portal in a box."[110] Finding a site and the information one seeks within the site can require much patience, however. Many sites have alphabetical indexes or keyword search features that act as aids in locating information. **Table 11–4** includes some sample state and city sites.

As is indicated in **Table 11–4**, numerous other sites are available. Information can be obtained from professional associations, such as the Association for Budgeting and Financial Management and the National Association of State Budget Officers. Private firms maintain many useful sites, as in the case of the *Wall Street Journal* and the Big 5 accounting firms (PricewaterhouseCoopers is listed in the table). Many sites can be accessed without a fee, while other sites may operate on a fee or subscription basis. Still other sites are maintained by public interest groups. OMB Watch operates a Web home page and listservs that provide members with specific kinds of information as it becomes available, as in the case of action taken by an appropriations subcommittee.

E-Commerce. From a governmental perspective, the Web serves two overlapping functions: *e-commerce* and *e-government*. E-commerce entails government working with businesses, other governments, and nonprofit organizations in carrying out the functions of government. This activity is sometimes referred to as G2B, for "government to business." The Web can be especially helpful in working with government bond buyers and in cash management.[111] As noted in Chapter 10, the Web already is being used extensively in the procurement process. The Colorado and Utah state governments have entered into a joint e-procurement system.[112] The federal government's venerable printed *Commerce Business Daily*, which solicited bids on government procurement, has been replaced by Federal Business Opportunities (FedBizOpps), a Web site that will serve as the single government point of entry for all federal procurement over $25,000.[113] The federal government also has a Web site devoted to finding forms, such as forms that businesses must complete for the Environmental Protection Agency. The Government Paperwork Elimination Act of 1998 mandated that such forms be posted on the Web.[114] Governments in other parts of the world, such as Ireland, are engaging in similar e-commerce projects. [115]

Table 11–4 **Selected World Wide Web Sites Related to Budgeting and Finance**

	Address (http://)
General Sites	
Governments on the WWW	www.gksoft.com/govt
U.S. Library of Congress	www.loc.gov
Yahoo! Government Directory	Dir.yahoo.com/Government/Web_Directories
Statistical Resources on the Web	www.lib.umich.edu/govdocs/stats.html
Government Information Locator Service	www.access.gpo.gov/su_docs/gils/index.html
Federal Government	
FirstGov (links to U.S. government)	www.firstgov.gov
FedWorld Information Network	www.fedworld.gov
FedStats	www.fedstats.gov
Office of Management and Budget	www.omb.gov
Council of Economic Advisers	www.whitehouse.gov/cea
Department of Treasury, including Internal Revenue Service	www.ustreas.gov
U.S. House of Representatives	www.house.gov
U.S. Senate	www.senate.gov
Congressional Budget Office	www.cbo.gov/
General Accounting Office	www.gao.gov

continues

	Address (http://)
State and Local Governments	
State and Local Governments on the Net	piperinfo.com/state/index.cfm
U.S. State and Local Gateway	www.statelocal.gov
GovernmentGuide (to State and Local Government; America Online)	webcenter.government guide.com
Council of State Governments	www.csg.org
State of North Carolina	www.ncgov.com
State of Texas	www.state.tx.us
National League of Cities	www.nlc.org
International City/County Management Association	www.icma.org
National Association of Counties	www.naco.org
Blacksburg (Virginia) Electronic Village	www.bev.net
Chicago	www.ci.chi.il.us
Professional Associations	
American Accounting Association	www.aaa-edu.org
American Institute of Certified Public Accountants	www.aicpa.org
Association for Budgeting and Financial Management	www.abfm.org
Association of Government Accountants	www.agacgfm.org
Financial Accounting Standards Board	www.fasb.org
Governmental Accounting Standards Board	www.gasb.org
Government Finance Officers Association	www.gfoa.org
National Association of State Budget Officers	www.nasbo.org
Private Profit and Nonprofit Organizations	
Barron's	www.barrons.com
Bond Buyer	www.bondbuyer.com
Brookings Institution	www.brook.edu
Comparative International Governmental Accounting Research	www.cigar-network.org
Electronic Policy Network	epn.org
Federal Reserve Board	www.federalreserv.gov
FinanceHub	www.financehub.com
Governing	www.governing.com
Government Executive	www.govexec.com

continues

	Address (http://)
Government Contracting	www.govcon.com
Government On-Line (State and Local Government)	www.gol.org
Moody's Investors Service	www.moodys.com
OMB Watch	ombwatch.org
Pricewaterhouse Coopers	www.pwcglobal.com
Regional Economic Models	www.remi.com
Wall Street Journal	online.wsj.com/public/us

Note: Due to the rapid developments in the World Wide Web, this table was outdated at the moment it was completed.

With regard to government-to-government commerce (G2G), the federal government made great strides when it created the Federal Commons Web site.[116] This site is designed to help state and local governments cut through the morass of federal grant programs and the application process. The site also provides information on the administration of grants, such as payment information and auditing. In another move, Michigan and Pennsylvania have contracted with Standard and Poor's to create Web sites that provide comparative evaluation data to their respective local school districts.

E-Government. To date, the focus of e-government has been primarily that of serving citizens as customers. This effort is called government-to-citizens, or G2C. In information technology, *customer relationship management* (CRM) focuses on applications designed to serve the needs of the customer. In the lingo of free enterprise, "the customer is king." The concept of "lifetime value" is applied, in which one considers a customer to be a resource that has value over time. While businesses may be concerned with customers choosing competitive firms, governments generally have citizens who have no alternatives unless they move out of their respective jurisdictions. That, nevertheless, does not obviate the need for good customer/citizen relations.

Web sites provide different functions. At the most elemental level, government or agency Web sites are static and provide simple information. A site might provide an organization chart, mission statement, and the like. A step up from that level is to provide content-rich information, such as annual reports, budgets, and audit reports. Some degree of interaction between an agency and citizens begins to occur when the agency posts telephone numbers and postal addresses, and greater interaction is encouraged with hot-links to e-mail addresses of agency officials. More extensive interaction occurs when citizens can conduct business through Web sites, such as paying taxes, applying for loans, and applying for social services. Further development includes bringing citizens into the governing process through Web interactions. This latter function is rarely utilized now but may be important one day.[117]

IT leaders recognize that e-government needs to be seamless across governments. When citizens need assistance with housing problems, they want help from whatever sources are available — local, state, or federal. The Government Without Boundaries project is working to further seamless connectivity. The project is sponsored by the National Association of State Chief Information Officers and the Federal Chief Information Officers Council.[118] Also, the U.S. General Services Administration has an Intergovernmental Solutions Office. Other resources include the Center for Digital Government and the Government Online International Network.[119]

At the federal level, President George W. Bush designated e-government as one of his five government-wide management initiatives. The president's report criticized information technology as previously concentrating on serving agencies' needs rather than citizens' needs. OMB's Office of Information and Regulatory Affairs reported in 2002 that major initiatives were under way in facilitating citizens to file their income tax returns electronically, in enabling citizens to obtain information about benefits available through the Labor Department, in providing a one-stop database for recreational information, and in locating potential sources of federal loans.[120] The Treasury Department has created an encrypted Web site for citizens to pay for products and services received from the government; in one year, nearly $900 million was received through this site using the direct debit method of payment.[121] OMB has established the position of Associate Director for Information Technology and E-government, which is attempting to simplify key administrative processes, such as training, travel, and payroll.[122]

State and local governments also are moving swiftly in implementing e-government strategies.[123] Washington was the first state to have its social services programs on-line. One survey ranked the Indiana and North Carolina state governments as tops in Web sites on taxation/revenue, followed by Illinois, Kansas, and Wisconsin.[124]

Both e-government and e-business will inevitably change as technology changes. Government today can be accessed by regular telephone and cellphone, by personal computer, and by WebTV. Some governments have established kiosks in public places, such as public buildings and shopping malls, so that people can interact electronically with government regardless of whether they have their own computer access. Personal digital assistants (PDAs) are becoming "smarter" and can be used to access government. New technologies, as will be seen in the next section, are improving the security of government sites and better protecting the information that citizens supply electronically. One major result of the new information age is that up-to-date information can be provided to citizens and businesses alike. For example, the *Code of Federal Regulations* (CFR), which is the storehouse of all regulations that citizens, corporations, and governments must obey, was once available only in paper format and was updated annually. Today, the CFR is available electronically and is updated daily.[125]

Issues and Problems

Accessibility. Access to information and information systems is one of the most critical problems in the field of information management. The federal government has hundreds of databanks that contain more than a billion records on individuals. Who should have access to these files? The Privacy Act is intended to protect individuals on whom federal agencies maintain files; on the other hand, the Freedom of Information Act opens many federal records to public inspection.[126] Balancing the two objectives of protecting privacy and maintaining freedom of access obviously is difficult. Agencies that collect information about individuals may be reluctant to share that information with other government units and indeed may be legally prohibited from such sharing.

Accessibility problems are of several types. One problem is what has been called the "digital divide," referring to the fact that middle-income and high-income families are likely to have home computers and access to e-government while lower-income families do not. Having Web access readily available in elementary and secondary schools and other public buildings such as libraries and recreation centers helps reduce this problem. Nevertheless, a survey in 2002 found that about one-third of the population lacked access to the Internet.[127] Language can also be part of the problem, as most Web sites are only in English and many Americans speak and read mostly Spanish or another language.

Accessibility is a problem for people with disabilities. People with sight and hearing problems may have problems navigating Web sites. The 1998 amendments to the Rehabilitation Act of 1973 require federal agencies to make available to their employees with disabilities information and computer systems that would be comparable to employees without disabilities.[128] Sites that show an English police officer and say "Bobby Approved" are accessible to people with disabilities.[129]

In addition, the complexity of Web sites creates accessibility problems. Citizen-users often find it difficult to navigate government Web sites to find the information that is sought.

Security. The security of information systems has become a major driving force in government. Lack of security can result in unwarranted invasions of personal privacy, fraud (as in situations involving tampering with financial records), breaches of national security, and the destruction of critical databases due to terrorist attacks. The Federal Managers' Financial Integrity Act requires federal agencies to test their information systems for "integrity," meaning the degree to which unauthorized users are prevented from accessing or altering records. Additionally, the Computer Security Act of 1987 requires federal agencies to develop security plans for computer systems containing sensitive information.[130] The so-called Clinger-Cohen Act of 1996, which created chief information officers in agencies, called for information security. The Government Information Security Reform Act of 2000 requires agencies to evaluate the security of their information systems and to develop agency-wide security plans.[131] Following the disasters at the World Trade Center and the Pentagon, President Bush issued Executive Order 13231, establishing the President's Critical Infrastructure Protection Board, which includes securing information systems. The National Infrastructure Protection Center gathers information on security threats and works to coordinate information gathering across agency lines. The Cyber Warning Information Network (CWIN) was created to help agencies share information about cyberspace attacks.[132]

While improvements in security have undoubtedly occured, significant weaknesses remain. The General Accounting Office concluded that billions of federal dollars are at risk due to lack of adequate computer security, rendering federal computers vulnerable to "hacking" from unauthorized users.[133] The Office of Management and Budget found six common security weaknesses:

- Senior managers gave little priority to information security.
- Performance evaluations of information security personnel failed to focus on the success or failure of security measures.
- Training and education of employees in information security was inadequate.
- Information security funding was insufficiently built into the capital planning and budgeting process.
- Contractor services were inadequately secure.
- Detecting and sharing information on vulnerabilities was insufficient.[134]

In regard to terrorism and information security, President Bush created an information agency that is designed to facilitate the sharing of information among intelligence and law enforcement agencies while simultaneously working to secure that very information.[135] The White House ordered federal agencies to review their Web sites and remove information that might be of use to would-be terrorists. Agencies have developed backup data systems and plans in the event that computer terrorism destroys critical files.[136] Because of the perceived severity of the threats to information security, there has been strong interest in creating a government network that would not be accessible to the public, perhaps to be called GovNet. The Department of Homeland Security is also expected to provide increased attention to cybersecurity.

All of these efforts to increase security come at a cost. Billions of dollars are being pumped into enhanced security measures. Another cost is that of making some information less accessible to the public. Indeed, the trend toward greater information security may be somewhat at odds with e-government efforts.

Privacy. Related to issues of security are ones pertaining to privacy. With the increased amount of data that government maintains on people, corporations, and other organizations comes greater opportunities for invasion of privacy. As noted in Chapter 10, employees at the Internal Revenue Service have been caught browsing the tax returns of celebrities. Government employees having access to Social Security numbers have engaged in identity theft, in which the employees were able to gain access to bank accounts and credit card accounts and effectively rob people. In a competitive environment, one company may attempt to gain secrets about its competitors through government databases. The IRS has taken action to make its systems more secure, establishing a privacy impact assessment procedure for all new information systems.[137]

Another concern about privacy is the use of "cookies" by the agencies that provide Web sites. When people visit a site, they may be unwittingly allowing the site to plant a temporary or permanent cookie on their computers. The cookie can be used to gain information about the user. Sites that use cookies often lack privacy statements that warn that cookies are in use. A GAO study conducted in 2000 found that the Postal Service, the General Services Administration, and other agencies all planted permanent cookies.[138] In 2001, Congress banned federal agencies from collecting personal information about how people used the Internet.[139] A study in 2001 found that half of all state legislative Web sites used one or more cookies and almost none of the sites informed visitors that they did so.[140]

Technological advances are being made in devising means to protect the privacy of Web users. As required by law, the federal government has developed a method of digital signature. The signature can be used, for example, to verify that a document being sent was actually sent by the person named. Other techniques that have applicability are identification of people based on electronic reading of fingerprints, irises of the eye, and voice.

People always need to be taken into account when new technology is introduced. Executives and managers who are unfamiliar with computers may fear having to use them and may resist their introduction. The federal government's information technology czar has said that e-government would be much further developed were senior managers and IT personnel better able and more willing to communicate with one another.[141] Another problem is that of being able to recruit workers with the talents needed in today's information world. Needed skills may be in short supply, and salary levels may be beyond what government typically expects to pay.[142] Related problems occur for government contractors that supply information technology support.

Although the use of information technology may seem quite advanced compared to the situation only a decade ago, the technology is still in its infancy. Major work is needed in the area of *solution-based services*. Government employees, private businesses, and citizens all become quickly frustrated when trying to find the specific information that they need. Solution-based services are intended to guide users in their quests so that they avoid going up blind alleys looking for data or being confronted with a list of dozens of Web sites that might contain the needed information.

Summary

Governmental accounting is characterized by procedures intended to prevent fraud and to guarantee agency conformance with legal requirements. Information from accounting systems is used in decision making and can help improve the efficiency and effectiveness of services. The GASB was established to help improve state and local government accounting systems, and the Federal Accounting Standards Advisory Board has similar responsibilities at the federal level. Generally accepted accounting principles allow the use of several different types of funds, with the general fund usually the most important for any government.

Accounting systems are structured by having a general ledger and subsidiary ledgers. They follow a relatively simple formula: assets equal the total of liabilities and fund balance. Within the ledgers, expenditures are accounted for in a variety of ways, including major and minor objects of expenditures.

Bases of accounting include cash, encumbrance, accrual, and cost. Some jurisdictions use project-based accounting and cost finding instead of the more comprehensive cost accounting methods. Regardless of the basis for accounting, reports summarizing transactions are prepared at specified intervals. Three of the most common types of reports are balance sheets, operating statements, and cash flows statements.

Auditing attempts to determine whether financial statements accurately reflect the status of accounts and/or whether an organization is operating efficiently and effectively. It is used for compliance purposes — namely, to ensure that financial transactions are in accordance with revenue and appropriation legislation. Generally accepted auditing standards constitute the guidelines for auditing in the public sector; in addition, generally accepted government auditing standards are used by GAO.

Management information systems, as applied in budgeting and finance, encompass program and resource information. These systems are used by chief executives, legislatures, and auditors for all four phases of the budget cycle: preparation, approval, execution, and audit. Computers, ranging from mainframes to powerful microcomputers, are greatly increasing the ability to provide the information needed for budgetary decision making. The rapid development of the Internet and especially the World Wide Web have increased the information available to everyone. Unfortunately, new problems have arisen as a result of the introduction and expanded use of computer technology, including problems of accessibility, security, and privacy.

Notes

1. J.W. Norvelle, *Introduction to Fund Accounting*, 5th ed. (Eaton Rapids, MI: RIA Professional Publishing, 1997), 1.

2. U.S. Office of Management and Budget, *The President's Management Agenda* (Washington, DC: U.S. Government Printing Office, 2001); L.R. Jones and F. Thompson, Responsibility Budgeting and Accounting, *International Public Management Journal* 3 (2000): 205–227.

3. T. Harkin, U.S. Senator (Dem., Iowa), as quoted in Report Faults Accounting at Defense Department, *Washington Post*, no. 159 (May 13, 1997): A4.

4. U.S. General Accounting Office, *Executive Guide: Creating Value Through World–Class Financial Management* (Washington, DC: U.S. Government Printing Office, 2000).

5. F.C. Mosher, *A Tale of Two Agencies* (Baton Rouge: Louisiana State University Press, 1984).

6. Federal Managers' Financial Integrity Act, P.L. 97–255 (1982); *Accounting and Auditing Act*, ch. 946, Title I (1950).

7. T.J. Cuny, The Pending Revolution in Federal Accounting Standards, *Public Budgeting & Finance* 15 (Fall 1995): 22–24.

8. Chief Financial Officers Act, P.L. 101–576 (1990).

9. U.S. General Accounting Office, *Financial Management: Status of the CFO Act Implementation at the Department of Treasury* (Washington, DC: U.S. Government Printing Office, 1994).

10. U.S. Office of Management and Budget and Chief Financial Officers Council, *2000 Federal Financial Management Report (Five-Year Plan)* (Washington, DC: U.S. Government Printing Office, 2000).

11. U.S. General Accounting Office, *Accounting Principles, Standards, and Requirements: Title 2 Standards Not Superceded by FASAB Issuances* (Washington, DC: U.S. Government Printing Office, 2001); R.N. Anthony, The Fatal Defect in the Federal Accounting System, *Public Budgeting & Finance* 20 (Winter 2000): 1–14.

12. R.N. Anthony, The FASAB's Dilemma, *Government Accountants Journal* 44 (Spring 1996): 31–39.

13. Government Finance Officers Association, *Governmental Accounting, Auditing, and Financial Reporting* (Chicago: Government Finance Officers Association, 1994); S.J. Gauthier, Then and Now: 65 Years of the Blue Book, *Government Finance Review* 17 (June 2001): 9–11.

14. Government Finance Officers Association, *http://www.gfoa.org*; accessed June 2002.

15. Report: WorldCom's Problems Worsen, Associated Press, August 8, 2002, *http://news/findlaw.com/ap_stories/f/1310/8.../2002080815401_04.htm*; accessed August 9, 2002.

16. U.S. General Accounting Office, *Highlights of GAO's Corporate Governance, Transparency and Accountability Forum* (Washington, DC: U.S. Government Printing Office, 2002); U.S. General Accounting Office, *Oversight, Auditor Independence, and Financial Reporting Issues* (Washington, DC: U.S. Government Printing Office, 2002).

17. Governmental Accounting Standards Board, *Codification of Governmental Accounting and Financial Reporting Standards* (Norwalk, CT: Governmental Accounting Standards Board, published biennially).

18. Government Finance Officers Association, *The GAAFR Review Guide to GASB Pronouncements* (Chicago: Government Finance Officers Association, 1996); G. Allison, GAAFR 2001: A Conversion Tool for GASB 34, *Government Finance Review* 17 (June 2001): 17–19.

19. U.S. Office of Management and Budget, Circular A-123, *http://www.whitehouse.gov/omb/circulars/a123/a123html*; accessed August 12, 2002.

20. U.S. General Accounting Office, *The Accounting Profession: Major Issues, Progress and Concerns* (Washington, DC: U.S. Government Printing Office, 1996), 60–80; U.S. General Accounting Office, *HCFA Extended Its Contract with Accounting Firm Implicated in Major Fraud* (Washington, DC: U.S. Government Printing Office, 2000).

21. Norvelle, *Introduction to Fund Accounting*, 16–18.

22. U.S. General Accounting Office, *Government Corporations: Profiles of Recent Proposals* (Washington, DC: U.S. Government Printing Office, 1995); B.S. Bunch, Changes in the Usage of Enterprise Funds by Large Cities, *Public Budgeting & Finance* 20 (Summer 2000): 15–29.

23. U.S. Government Standard Government Ledger, *http://www.fms.treas.gov/ussgl/tl–s2–01–02.html*; accessed June 2002.

24. Norvelle, *Introduction to Fund Accounting*, 43.

25. U.S. Office of Management and Budget, *Analytic Perspective: Fiscal Year 2003* (Washington, DC: U.S. Government Printing Office, 2002), 450.

26. R.D. Lee, Jr., and R.C. Burns, Unpublished data from Survey of State Budget Offices, The Pennsylvania State University, 2000.

27. A. Roberts, Accounting for Results, 1997: Government-wide Performance Plan, Fiscal Year 1999, *Journal of Policy Analysis and Management* 18 (1999): 187–191.

28. Governmental Accounting Standards Board, *Concept Statement No. 2: Service Efforts and Accomplishments Reporting* (Norwalk, CT: Governmental Accounting Standards Board, 1994).

29. Chief Financial Officers Act, P.L. 101–576 (1990).

30. Government Performance and Results Act, P.L. 103–62 (1993).

31. U.S. General Accounting Office, *Accrual Budgeting: Experiences of Other Nations and Implications for the United States* (Washington, DC: U.S. Government Printing Office, 2000).

32. W.K. Carter and M.F. Usry, *Cost Accounting*, 13th ed. (Cincinnati, OH: Dame/Thomson Learning, 2002).

33. D.R. Geiger, The Emerging Need for Managerial Cost Accounting, *Government Accountants Journal* 44 (Fall 1995): 46–52.

34. Activity-Based Costing and Activity-Based Management Symposium, *Public Budgeting & Finance* 19 (Summer 1999): 3–58; J. Peckenpaugh, Teaching the ABCs, *Government Executive Magazine* (April 2002), *http://www.govexec.com*.

35. National Defense Authorization Act for Fiscal Year 1996, Title XLIII, P.L. 104–106 (1996).

36. U.S. Office of Management and Budget, *Circular A-131: Value Engineering* (1993), *http:// www.whitehouse.gov/omb/circulars/a131/a131.html*; accessed June 2002.

37. M. Ives, A Fresh Look at Capital Asset Accounting: The New FASAB Proposals, *Government Accountants Journal* 44 (Summer 1995): 24–29; U.S. General Accounting Office, *Budget Issues: The Role of Depreciation in Budgeting for Certain Federal Investments* (Washington, DC: U.S. Government Printing Office, 1995).

38. Lee and Burns, Survey of State Budget Offices.

39. J. Peckenpaugh, Legislation Would Force Agencies to Track Costs of Operations, *Government Executive* (May 15, 2001), *http://www.govexec.com*.

40. U.S. General Accounting Office, *Cost Accounting Standards Board: Little Progress Made in Resolving Important Issues* (Washington, DC: U.S. Government Printing Office, 1994).

41. U.S. General Accounting Office, *Credit Reform: Speculative Savings Used to Offset Current Spending Increase Budget Uncertainty* (Washington, DC: U.S. Government Printing Office, 1994).

42. Governmental Accounting Standards Board, *Statement No. 31, Accounting and Financial Reporting for Certain Investments and for External Investment Pools* (Norwalk, CT: Governmental Accounting Standards Board, 1997).

43. Governmental Accounting Standards Board, *Technical Bulletin No. 94–1, Disclosures About Derivatives and Similar Debt and Investment Transactions* (Norwalk, CT: Governmental Accounting Standards Board, 1994).

44. Federal Credit Reform Act, P.L. 101–508, Title XIII (1990).

45. U.S. General Accounting Office, *Federal Credit Programs: Agencies Had Serious Problems Meeting Credit Reform Accounting Requirements* (Washington, DC: U.S. Government Printing Office, 1993).

46. B.R. Hennessy and F.P. Daroca, Popular Annual Financial Reports: Current Trends and Future Prospects, *Government Finance Review* 9 (February 1993): 7–13.

47. Governmental Accounting Standards Board, *Codification of Governmental Accounting and Financial Reporting Systems*, updated periodically.

48. W.A. Andrew and R.S. Schmidgall, *Financial Management for the Hospitality Industry* (East Lansing, MI: Educational Institute of the American Hotel and Motel Association, 1993), 39–41.

49. G.R. Smith, Jr., and R.J. Freeman, Statement of Cash Flows: The Direct vs. Indirect Method, *Government Finance Review* 12 (February 1996): 17–21.

50. R.S. Kravchuk and W.R. Voorhees, eds., Governmental Accounting Standards Board (GASB) Statement No. 34 Symposium, *Public Budgeting & Finance* 21 (Fall 2001): 1–87.

51. Government Management Reform Act, P.L. 103–356 (1994).

52. Reports Consolidation Act, P.L. 106–531 (2000).

53. Government Management Reform Act of 1995.

54. Government Finance Officers Association, *Governmental Accounting, Auditing, and Financial Reporting*, 314.

55. U.S. General Accounting Office, *Financial Audit: IRS's Fiscal Years 2001 and 2000 Financial Statements* (Washington, DC: U.S. Government Printing Office, 2002).

56. L.P. Bailey, *Miller GAAS Guide 2001* (Orlando, FL: Harcourt Brace, 2000). Also available on CD–ROM.

57. J.H. Engstrom and D.E. Tidrick, Audit Issues Related to GASB Statement No. 34, *Public Budgeting & Finance* 21 (Fall 2001): 63–78.

58. U.S. General Accounting Office, *Government Auditing Standards* (Washington, DC: U.S. Government Printing Office, issued periodically).

59. Inspector General Act, P.L. 95–452 (1978).

60. U.S. General Accounting Office, *Financial Management: Extending the Financial Statements Audit Requirement of the CFO Act to Additional Federal Agencies* (Washington, DC: U.S. Government Printing Office, 2002).

61. U.S. General Accounting Office, *Inspectors General: Handling of Allegations Against Senior OIG Officials* (Washington, DC: U.S. Government Printing Office, 1996).

62. Federal Managers' Financial Integrity Act, P.L. 97–225 (1982).

63. Federal Financial Management Improvement Act, P.L. 104–208 (1996).

64. U.S. General Accounting Office, *High-Risk Series: An Update* (Washington, DC: U.S. Government Printing Office, 2001).

65. American Institute of Certified Public Accountants, *Audits of State and Local Governmental Units* (New York: American Institute of Certified Public Accountants, issued periodically).

66. Single Audit Act, P.L. 98–502 (1984); Single Audit Act Amendments, P.L. 104–156 (1996).

67. G.J. Miller and R.P. VanDaniker, Impact of the Single Audit Act on the Financial Management of State and Local Governments, *Government Accountants Journal* 44 (Spring 1995): 55–63.

68. U.S. General Accounting Office, *U.S. Government Financial Statements: FY 2001 Results Highlight the Continuing Need to Accelerate Federal Financial Management Reform* (Washington, DC: U.S. Government Printing Office, 2002); see U.S. General Accounting Office, *Financial Management FFMIA Implementation Critical for Federal Accountability* (Washington, DC: U.S. Government Printing Office, 2001).

69. U.S. Office of Management and Budget, *Federal Financial Management Report* (Washington, DC: U.S. Government Printing Office, 2002).

70. R. Widenoja, Eight Agencies Honored for Accountability Reports, *Government Executive* (September 16, 2002), *http://www.govexec.com*.

71. U.S. General Accounting Office, *Financial Management Service: Significant Weaknesses in Computer Controls Continue* (Washington, DC: U.S. Government Printing Office, 2002).

72. U.S. Office of Management and Budget, *The President's Management Agenda*, 19. See U.S. General Accounting Office, *Financial Management: Improper Payments Reported in Fiscal Year 2000 Financial Statements* (Washington, DC: U.S. Government Printing Office, 2001); U.S. General Accounting Office, *Canceled DoD Appropriations: $615 Million in Illegal or Otherwise Improper Adjustments* (Washington, DC: U.S. Government Printing Office, 2001).

73. K. Kompas, Treasurer Faces Charges for Making Calls at Work, *Des Moines Register* (March 16, 2001).

74. R. McLeod, Jr., and George Schell, *Management Information Systems*, 8th ed. (Upper Saddle River, NJ: Prentice Hall, 2001).

75. H.J. Watson and T.A. Carte, Executive Information Systems in Government Organizations, *Public Productivity & Management Review* 23 (2000): 371–382.

76. R. Maier, *Knowledge Management Systems: Information and Communication Technologies for Knowledge Management* (New York: Springer, 2002).

77. National Information Infrastructure Advisory Council, *Common Ground: Fundamental Principles for the National Information Infrastructure* (Washington, DC: National Information Infrastructure Advisory Council, 1995); see National Biological Information Infrastructure maintained by the U.S. Geological Survey, *http://www.nbii.gov*; accessed June 2002.

78. Government Information Locator Service, *http://www.access.gpo.gov/su_docs/gils/index.html*; accessed June 2002.

79. D. Landsbergen, Jr., and G. Wolken, Jr., Realizing the Promise: Government Information Systems and the Fourth Generation of Information Technology, *Public Administration Review* 61 (2001): 206–220.

80. M.M. Peterson, Agencies Must Undergo "Cultural Change" to Share Data, *Government Executive* (March 20, 2002), *http://www.govexec.com*.

81. Florida Statistics and Reports, *http:/taxonomy.myflorida.com/Taxonomy/Government/ Statistics%20and%20Reports*; accessed June 2002.

82. T. Bernhardsen, *Geographic Information Systems*, 3rd ed. (New York: Wiley, 2001).

83. J.B. Hokanson, Planning and Financing Infrastructure Using GIS Technology, *Government Finance Review* 10 (August 1994): 19–21.

84. U.S. General Accounting Office, *Tax Systems Modernization: Cyberfile Project Was Poorly Planned and Managed* (Washington, DC: U.S. Government Printing Office, 1996).

85. K.D. Schwartz, Tackling Tax Technology, *Government Executive Magazine* (August 2001), *http://www.govexec.com*.

86. Treasury and General Government Appropriations Act for Fiscal Year 2001, P.L. 106–554 (2000).

87. U.S. Office of Management and Budget, *Guidelines for Ensuring and Maximizing the Quality, Objectivity, Utility, and Integrity of Information Disseminated by Federal Agencies* (Washington, DC: U.S. Office of Management and Budget, 2001 and 2002), *http://www.omb.gov*; accessed March 2003.

88. R.D. Lee, Jr., A Quarter Century of State Budgeting Practices, *Public Administration Review* 57 (1997): 133–140.

89. J.P. West and E.M. Berman, The Impact of Revitalized Management Practices on the Adoption of Information Technology, *Public Performance and Management Review* 24 (2001): 233–253.

90. Lee and Burns, Survey of State Budget Offices.

91. M.J. Murdocca and V.P. Heuring, *Principles of Computer Architecture* (Upper Saddle River, NJ: Prentice Hall, 2000); WWW Computer Architecture Page, *http://www.cs.wisc.edu/~arch/www*; accessed June 2002.

92. W. Cats-Baril and R. Thompson, Managing Information Technology Projects in the Public Sector, *Public Administration Review* 55 (1995): 559–566.

93. C. Mathesian, Low Bid Hazards in a High Tech World, *Governing* 8 (March 1994): 64, 67, 70.

94. Information Technology Management Reform Act, P.L. 104–106 (1996).

95. Chief Information Officers Council, *http://www.cio.gov*; accessed June 2002.

96. U.S. Office of Management and Budget, Program Performance Benefits from Major Information Technology Investments, *Analytical Perspectives: Fiscal Year 2003* (Washington, DC: U.S. Government Printing Office, 2002), 392–393.

97. M.M. Peterson, Paying the Price, *National Journal's Technology Daily*, July 16, 2002, *http://www.govexec.co,/dailyfed/0702/071502db.htm*; accessed August 9, 2002.

98. National Association of State Chief Information Officers, *http://www.nascio.org*; accessed June 2002.

99. L. Porteus, State CIOs Aid White House in Homeland Security Plan, *Government Executive* (May 24, 2002), *http://www.govexec.com*.

100. S. Harris, In the Know, *Government Executive Magazine* (July 2001), *http://www.govexec.com.*

101. CNET, *http://www.cnet.com.*

102. A.M. Schoenbach, *MAX Decision System* (Presentation at the annual conference of Association for Budgeting and Financial Management, Washington, D.C., October 1995).

103. S. Peterson, Washington Breaks Ground on Digital Archives Building, *Government Technology* (June 18, 2002), *http://www.govtech/news.phtml?docid=2002.06.18 –303000000001174;* accessed August, 2002.

104. J. Dean, Taking the Plunge, *Government Executive Magazine* (August 2001), *http://www.govexec.com.*

105. D. Clark, White House Computer Expert Says GovNet Is Not a Certainty, *Government Executive* (March 11, 2002), *http://www.govexec.com.*

106. Y. Liang, M. Madden, and R. Roque, The ABCs of ASPs, *Government Finance Review* 16 (December 2000): 29–33.

107. R.A. Miranda, Rise of ERP Systems in the Public Sector, in R.A. Miranda, ed., *ERP and Financial Management Systems* (Chicago: Government Finance Officers Association, 2001), 14.

108. K.A. Hall, Intergovernmental Cooperation on ERP Systems, *Government Finance Review* 17 (December 2001): 6–13.

109. S. Harris, Federal CIO Council to Fund Eight New Government Portals, *Government Executive* (August 13, 2001), *http://www.govexec.com.*

110. National Information Consortium, *http://www.nicusa.com;* accessed June 2002.

111. J.B. Watkins III and L.H. Harris, Using Your Web Site to Enhance Bond Market Disclosure, *Government Finance Review* 18 (June 2002), *http://www.gfoa.org;* accessed June 2002; J.T. Deter, BidOhio: Using Technology to Earn More for Taxpayers, *Government Finance Review* 16 (October 2000): 32–40.

112. Colorado, Utah Will Share E–Procurement System, *Government Technology* (August 8, 2001), *http://www.govtech.com.*

113. Federal Business Opportunites (FedBizOpps), *http://www.fedbizopps.gov;* accessed June 2002).

114. FederalForms, *http://www.fedforms.gov;* accessed June 2002; Government Paperwork Elimination Act, P.L. 105–277 (1998).

115. Business Access to State Information and Services (Government of Ireland), *http://www.basis.ie;* accessed June 2002.

116. Federal Commons, *http://www.cfda.gov/federalcommons;* accessed June 2002.

117. M. Howard, E-Government Across the Globe: How Will "E" Change Government?, *Government Finance Review* 17 (August 2001): 6–9; C. Weare, The Internet and Democracy: The Causal Links Between Technology and Politics, *International Journal of Public Administration* 25 (2002): 659–691.

118. Government Without Boundaries, *http://www.gwob.gov*; accessed June 2002.

119. U.S. General Services Administration, *http://www.gsa.gov*; accessed June 2002; Center for Digital Government, *http://www.centerdigitalgov.com/navigator*; accessed June 2002; Government Online International Network, *http://www.governments–online.org*; accessed June 2002.

120. U.S. Office of Management and Budget, *President's Management Agenda*; U.S. Office of Management and Budget, *Managing Information Collection and Dissemination* (Washington, DC: U.S. Government Printing Office, 2002).

121. PayGov, *http://pay.gov*; accessed June 2002.

122. A Gruber, E-Government Projects Aim to Simplify Paperwork for Feds, *Government Executive* (December 13, 2002), *http://www.govexec.com*.

123. M.H. Sprecher, Racing to E-Government: Using the Internet for Citizen Service Delivery, *Government Finance Review* 16 (October 2000): 21–22.

124. K. Eleveld, Heeding the Call, *Government Technology* 14 (August 2001): 56–61.

125. U.S. Government Printing Office, Code of Federal Regulations, *http://www.access.gpo.gov/nara/cfr/index.html*; accessed June 2002.

126. Freedom of Information Act, P.L. 89–487 (1966); Privacy Act, P.L. 93–579 (1974).

127. J.Dean, E-Government Hits the Mainstream, Survey Says, *Government Executive* (February 26, 2000), *http://www.govexec.com*.

128. Rehabilitation Act, P.L. 93–112 (1973); Rehabilitation Act Amendments, P.L. 105–220 (1998).

129. Bobby, *http://bobby.cast.org*; accessed June 2002.

130. Computer Security Act, P.L. 100–235 (1987).

131. Government Information Security Reform Act, P.L. 106–398 (2000).

132. R.L. Dick, Critical Infrastructure Information Sharing (Congressional statement from the National Infrastructure Protection Center), *http://www.fbi.gov/congress/congress02/rondick050802.htm*; accessed June 2002.

133. U.S. General Accounting Office, *Financial Management Service: Significant Weaknesses in Computer Controls Continue* (Washington, DC: U.S. Government Printing Office, 2002).

134. U.S. Office of Management and Budget, *FY 2001 Report to Congress on Federal Government Information Security Reform* (Washington, DC: U.S. Government Printing Office, 2002).

135. G. Seigle, New Agency Aims to Improve Flow of Anti-Terror Information, *Government Executive* (February 20, 2002), *http://www.govexec.com*.

136. S. Harris, Managing Technology: Information Insurance, *Government Executive Magazine* (June 2002), *http://www.govexec.com*.

137. J. Dean, IRS Sets the Standard for Protecting Privacy, *Government Executive* (April 29, 2002), *http://www.govexec.com*.

138. U.S. General Accounting Office, *Internet Privacy: Federal Agency Use of Cookies* (Washington, DC: U.S. Government Printing Office, 2000).

139. Treasury and Postal Service Appropriation Act, P.L. 107–67 (2001).

140. OMB Watch, Plugged In, Tuning Up (2001), *http://www.ombwatch.org*; accessed June 2002.

141. S. Harris, OMB Official Outlines His Plan for Overhauling E-Government, *Government Executive* (July 27, 2001), *http://www.govexec.com*.

142. Workforce and the Knowledge Economy (special issue), *Government Technology* 14 (May 2001).

Chapter 12

FINANCIAL MANAGEMENT: CAPITAL BUDGETING AND DEBT

Every year, governments spend resources on the construction of facilities or the purchase of equipment that will continue in use for many years beyond the year of purchase. The construction of a new water treatment plant will serve a community for decades, although the actual construction itself may take less than two years. In addition, during the construction phase, the construction costs could equal a large portion of a small community's total budget. Because of the large outlay required in one time period, many communities elect to finance the construction costs over a long period by borrowing or, in fewer instances, by putting aside resources for several years in a capital reserve fund until there is a sufficient amount to pay for the facility.

By constructing the water treatment plant, the community has acquired a capital facility that will operate for perhaps 30 years or more. It has purchased an asset. This chapter focuses on the decision to build that facility or purchase an asset and related decisions on whether and how to finance that investment through borrowing. In this chapter, we examine both the rationale for public sector capital budgeting and the general form of capital budgeting processes. In addition, since state and local governments finance much of their capital spending through borrowing, we examine the various types of bonds and other debt instruments. The chapter concludes with a discussion of debt capacity and debt management. We defer discussion of federal borrowing, which is largely unrelated to capital investments, to Chapter 15.

▇ Capital Planning, Budgeting, and Asset Management

In this section we define capital and capital investments, discuss the reasons for considering capital spending separately from operating budgets, describe the general form for a capital investment planning and budgeting process, and discuss the issues involved in separating capital from operating budgets. We focus mainly on state and local governments. Although there is much discussion in annual federal budgets of investments and capital expenditures, the federal government, as discussed below, has resisted developing and using a capital budget, or a formal capital budgeting process.

Capital Investments Versus Current Expenditures

Capital Investments. The purchase or construction of a long-lasting physical asset or facility is a capital investment. Businesses invest to have new capacity and to replace existing capacity with more efficient methods of production. These investments are intended to increase the businesses' output in the future. Many public sector physical facilities also represent investment in the ability to provide more or higher-quality services in the future. However, public sector assets differ in important respects from private sector assets. In conventional private sector accounting, assets have the capacity to generate future revenues for the enterprise. In contrast, public sector assets typically do not have as a primary purpose the generation of future revenues.

In the private sector, there are three sources of financing capital assets: debt, equity, and retained earnings. Debt is available to both public and private institutions. Equity, in the form of stock issuance in the case of publicly traded companies or of owners' equity investments in the case of privately held companies, is not available to public institutions. Retained earnings, essentially profits not distributed to owners, may be available to public utilities such as water authorities, but typically either are prohibited or are tightly constrained. Retained earnings may be invested or equity investments may be sought by private companies in the expectation that the investment financed will yield higher future profits.

A limited, accounting-based definition of assets is too restrictive for purposes of public sector budgeting. While a government facility that provides a service to citizens, such as a wastewater treatment plant, may not have as an objective generating future revenues, the facility once built does provide a continuing service through many future years. In that sense, an expenditure on a facility that will provide benefits for many years after its construction is an investment. According to Statement 34 of the Governmental Accounting Standards Board (GASB; see Chapter 11), "infrastructure assets are long-lived capital assets that normally are stationary in nature and normally can be preserved for a significantly greater number of years than most capital assets."[1] This long-lived investment aspect helps explain why many governments, like businesses, distinguish capital expenditures from current expenditures and have capital budgeting processes, in addition to budgeting processes for current (operating) expenditures.

For governments, it is useful to distinguish among three types of investments. First, a government may purchase physical assets for its own use over many years in the future — assets such as office buildings and machinery. Second, governments may make investments in physical facilities that enhance private economic development — for example, roads and water systems. Third, governments may invest in intangibles, such as education and research. Capital budgeting processes may assist in deciding how much of each type of investment is necessary, although only physical facility investments typically are included in formal capital budgets.

With or without a formal capital budget, focusing some attention on the investment component of a government budget is politically useful because it draws attention to the fact that many public spending programs build for the future. It also reminds citizens that public assets, like highways, may deteriorate to the point of uselessness if not regularly rehabilitated. A study by the American Society of Civil Engineers (ASCE) estimated that the combined public infrastructure deficit in facilities such as water systems, schools, airports, and highways was a staggering $1.3 trillion in 2000.[2] That figure was close to the total amount of municipal debt outstanding that year. ASCE defined the infrastructure deficit as facilities that have outlived their usefulness as well as facilities needed to address unmet needs of unserved and underserved populations. For example, some sewer systems still in use according to the report were more than 100 years old. A Congressional Budget Office study noted that sewer pipes, for example, have an average asset life of 50 years, and that many systems in major U.S. cities are approaching that age.[3] The American Water Works Association estimated a year earlier that more than $1 trillion in investments was needed to replace older water and wastewater systems and to meet more stringent regulatory standards.[4] **Table 12–1** indicates the number of states requiring different investment levels to meet safe drinking water requirements, according to the U.S. Environmental Protection Agency. As one might expect, the larger and more populous states are those with the greatest needs, such as California, New York, and Texas. Central states such as Illinois and Michigan and eastern states such as Pennsylvania fall into the second category.[5]

State and local governments also stress the importance of public capital investment in stimulating economic growth. Not only are obvious facilities such as convention centers or improved water services for water-intensive industries the focal point of economic development-oriented investments, but increasingly

Table 12–1 **Distribution of Safe Drinking Water Investment Requirements by States, 2000**

Investment required	>$1 billion	$500–$999 million	$100–$499 million	$50–$99 million	<$50 million
Number of states	4	3	24	9	10

Source: U.S. Environmental Protection Agency quoted in *Governing* 15 (December 2001): 49.

state and local governments invest in quality-of-life facilities such as parks and other recreational facilities and even open space to attract companies to locate in the area.[6] States and local governments compete with each other in offering facilities, tax concessions, and other inducements to attract economic growth (see Chapter 15), requiring in many cases significant capital investments. Sometimes it is difficult to draw the line between investment and noninvestment. The federal budget's definition of investment is very broad, including such human capital investments as education, research, and development expenditures, but still it does not include many other elements that it logically could. For example, mental health programs, programs for juveniles, and family counseling programs may be considered investments that help prevent future social and economic problems. A major rationale for the Child Health Insurance Program, which provides federal assistance to states for uninsured children, is that the investment in health helps prevent some future federal expenditures for Medicaid.

While it is useful to think of government expenditures in terms of investment or consumption, for budgeting purposes the distinction is more often in terms of capital versus current or operating expenditures. Capital expenditures differ from current expenditures, and some governments therefore distinguish between capital and current budgets.

Physical Nature and Time Duration. Businesses think of capital expenditures as the purchase of physical assets or the construction of facilities that will be used over a period of several years. Public sector capital expenditures likewise involve the purchase of physical assets whose use extends over a number of years, often 30 to 50 years with proper maintenance, as in the case of sewage treatment plants.

Examples of capital expenditures are easy to find. A school building is physically present and will last for many years. On the other hand, paper, pens, pencils, and staples, although physical, are used up and have to be purchased anew each year. The purchase of the building is easy to classify as a capital expenditure and the purchase of the supplies is clearly a current expenditure. Similarly, water mains extending from a treatment plant to neighborhood lines have a physical presence and will serve for many years. Their construction is a capital expenditure. In contrast, chemicals used in the water treatment process will be used up and need to be purchased again and again. Purchase of these chemicals is an operating or current expenditure. Conventionally, debt service payments for both principal and interest for long-term bonds or loans also are included in the capital budget, as opposed to the operating budget, when the government has a capital budget separate from the operating budget. Debt service accounts may be used to segregate these payments (see Chapter 11), but they are regarded as capital budget items.

Classification Problems. These examples illustrate that capital expenditures normally are for purchases of physical assets that have a long life. Other examples, however, show that the distinction between capital and current expenditure is sometimes ambiguous. A big-city police department may purchase more than 50 vehicles per year, and most of them may replace vehicles purchased the previous year. That city may classify the purchase of the police cars as a current expenditure. A small town may purchase two police cars of the same type as the big city's but expect those two cars to last for three to five years. The small town probably would consider purchase of the police cars to be a capital expenditure.

Even within the same city, some classification problems occur. Books and periodicals bought for a library are expected to be used for many years, and their purchase can be treated as a capital investment. On the other hand, purchase of a periodical by a department of public works, if the periodical has a short useful life, would be an operating expense.

Every government and every business establishes some kind of arbitrary cutoff point that distinguishes current from capital expenditures. In most cases, the cutoff is a combination of the size of the expenditure and the useful life of the asset. Purchase of anything expected to be consumed (or destroyed) during one year normally will be a current expenditure, no matter how large it is. In addition, small expenditures, even for goods that will last several years, also are classified as current. But the size of the government's budget usually determines how small is small. A small town may classify expenditures of less than $1,000 as current regardless of the useful life. A larger city may use $25,000 as a cutoff — below that, anything is a current expenditure regardless of its useful life. Although some purchases may be classified arbitrarily one way or the other, what constitutes a capital purchase and what constitutes a current one usually is not controversial.

Capital Versus Current Decisions

Separate Capital Budgets. The size of the expenditure and the longevity of the asset or facility purchased distinguish a capital expenditure from a current one. A third distinction of importance to decision making, the method of financing the expenditure, leads most state governments and a majority of local governments to pay at least some separate attention to capital expenditures in the annual budget decision-making process. Few states do not distinguish capital from current expenses in the form of either capital improvement plans or budgets or both, and most larger counties and cities as well as some smaller ones make similar distinctions.

Table 12–2 shows state and local capital expenditures for 1996 as a proportion of total expenditures. Considering only direct capital outlays, about 11 percent of state and local expenditures are for capital purposes. That percentage has been more or less constant for several years. The actual expenditures do not tell the whole story, however, since most of the capital outlays are financed by borrowing and hence have interest costs. With interest included, the figure is closer to 16 percent. Local government capital outlays are a slightly higher proportion of total outlays than state government outlays — 18 percent and 14 percent, respectively. However, these gross percentages obscure the real nature of the decisions to undertake capital projects. Capital expenditures cluster in only a few government functions. For local governments, school construction; utilities such as electricity, roads, sewage, and water; and housing construction account for most direct capital outlays.

State government capital outlays also cluster in only a few functional categories, and decisions made in one year affect future-year budgets. More than 80 percent of state public works expenditures in 1996 went to highway construction.

Table 12–2 **Direct Capital Outlays as a Proportion of Total Outlays, by Level of Government, 1996 (Billions of Dollars)**

Government	Total Direct Outlays[*]	Capital Outlays	Capital as Percentage of Total	Interest on Debt[+]	Combined Capital Outlays[++]	Combined Capital as Percentage of Total
All	2866	234	8%	302	303	11%
Federal	1472	75	5%	233	75	5%
State and local	1394	159	11%	69	228	16%
State	608	59	10%	26	85	14%
Local	786	100	13%	43	143	18%

[*] Outlays here exclude duplicative intergovernmental transfers so that the figures shown are for the level of government making the expenditure even if the source of finance is a transfer from another level of government.

[+] Only interest on general debt and interest on utilities' borrowing is included here.

[++] For state and local governments, interest on general debt plus interest on utility borrowing is attributed in this table to borrowing for capital investment. Federal debt is not considered borrowing for capital investments and is not included as capital outlay.

Source: U.S. Bureau of the Census, *Statistical Abstract of the United States: 2001* (Washington, DC: U.S. Government Printing Office, 2001), 302.

That level of capital construction implies significant future-year expenditures for highway maintenance. Combined state and local highway capital expenditures in 1996 were $43 billion, but total expenditures — capital plus operating or current — on highways were $127 billion.[7] More than twice the new capital investments in highways was spent on operations and maintenance of highways built in prior years.

Separate Capital Budgeting Processes. These examples demonstrate that decisions about capital spending at the state and local levels are consequential in the year they are made and can have major consequences for future budgets. As discussed in previous chapters, particularly Chapters 5 and 6, it is difficult to incorporate a long-run perspective into budget decisions, especially when the decisions tend to focus in large part on personnel expenditures and only on the current-year implications of starting new programs. The fact that current-year capital budget decisions have significant implications for future operations and maintenance suggests that the effects of capital decisions on future operating budgets must be taken into account in any capital budgeting process. For state and local governments, the logic of having some kind of process for examining capital spending decisions in more detail seems compelling. That does not necessarily entail separate capital budgets, however. In the next section, we illustrate a general approach to capital investment planning and budgeting that satisfies both the requirement to examine capital decisions in more detail and the requirement to consider implications for future-year operating budgets.

Capital Investment Planning

Multiyear Capital Investment Plans. Many governments that distinguish between capital and current budget decisions have an established process for developing a multiyear capital investment plan (CIP) and incorporating elements of that plan into a capital budget. Five years is a common period for projecting capital expenditures, although a longer period is often included in the statements of long-range programs. For example, the Orange County (North Carolina) Water and Sewer Authority distinguishes between its 15-year capital improvements plan and its five-year capital improvements budget.[8] The long-range plan focuses on the expected needs for water supply and sewage treatment for the next decade and a half, while the capital improvements budget includes detailed cost estimates only for the next five years.

Asset Management. Long-term CIPs may be a part of a larger program of asset management. Concern for the condition of America's deteriorating infrastructure base emerged in the early 1980s. Throughout that decade, spectacular incidents, such as the collapse of the Mianus Bridge in Connecticut, and detailed studies of investment deficits brought heightened attention to the need to rebuild and maintain the nation's physical infrastructure assets.[9] As noted earlier, inadequate maintenance expenditures, plus the fact that investments are not keeping pace with population growth, and more importantly, with changing regulatory requirements, continue to increase the infrastructure deficit. The nation's physical infrastructure asset base exists primarily because of state and local government investments. As far back as the mid-1950s, state and local capital spending greatly exceeded federal capital spending. In 1956, state and local capital spending on infrastructure amounted to almost $28 billion, whereas federal capital spending was less than $10 billion. A gradual climb in federal spending led to its overtaking state and local capital spending in 1976, and it remained higher until significant federal budget cutbacks affected capital spending in 1986.[10] **Figure 12–1** illustrates the pattern for public works facilities specifically, including highways, airports, water transport and terminals, sewage, solid waste, water supply, and mass transit.

Figure 12–1 gives some indication of the relative roles played by federal, state, and local governments in public works funding. The figures for federal, state, and local sources are for all direct spending, both capital investments and maintenance and rehabilitation. By far, local governments exceed both federal and state governments combined. The federal grants figure shows the contribution the federal government makes, for nondefense capital investments only, through intergovernmental grant transfers. Federal grants for physical capital investment historically were a relatively small contribution. Programs introduced in the 1970s caused federal grants to state and local governments for physical capital investments to double between 1975 and 1980, and then remain basically static until the early 1990s. There has been a gradual trend toward higher levels since then. Budget estimates show these investments stabilizing through 2007.[11]

Some state and local governments have adopted elaborate systems for assessing the condition of capital assets and linking these "inventories" with the capital planning and budgeting process. San Diego uses a computerized inventory and mapping system to keep track of maintenance schedules on 3,000 miles of water and sewer pipes.[12] Cities throughout developing countries that have underinvested in both maintenance and reconstruction of such critical urban infrastructure assets as paved roadways, water systems, and drainage also have begun to develop more complete systems for taking inventory of existing assets and developing CIPs based on a schedule of needed improvements.[13] These innovations in public sector asset management have begun to alter the way some cities plan, budget, and manage their finances — capital planning and budgeting are now playing a more important role.[14]

Practices vary considerably from city to city, but it is possible to outline a general format for a capital investment planning process. One such model for capital

Figure 12–1 Federal, State, and Local Roles in Public Works Funding, 1980–1998

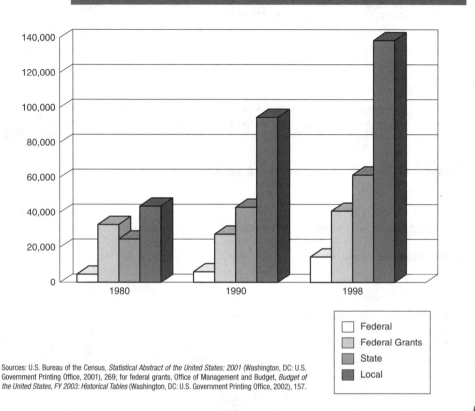

Sources: U.S. Bureau of the Census, *Statistical Abstract of the United States: 2001* (Washington, DC: U.S. Government Printing Office, 2001), 269; for federal grants, Office of Management and Budget, *Budget of the United States, FY 2003: Historical Tables* (Washington, DC: U.S. Government Printing Office, 2002), 157.

investment planning and budgeting, linked to an inventory of existing facilities, consists of eight steps, which are discussed below (see **Figure 12–2**).

Identifying Present Service Characteristics. The first step is to make an inventory of existing physical or infrastructure facilities and to assess the services provided. For a state or local government that has not previously conducted an inventory, this first step is neither simple nor inexpensive, although maintaining the inventory once established need not be burdensome. Such an inventory involves listing all physical facilities and elements of the physical infrastructure and such related information as date of construction, date of last major rehabilitation, type of construction material (such as type of road surface), and, where relevant, characteristics such as size and capacity. For a building, information may be collected on electrical wiring, fiber optics for computer hookups, plumbing, and elevators.

Quantity of service includes such characteristics as the number of people served, the proportion of total population served, the geographic area covered (area, density, and spatial distribution), and various socioeconomic groupings related to coverage, such as number of clients served by a facility. Different quantity measures are appropriate for different services.

Quality of service in part is a function of the level or the type of service provided. For example, water treatment systems that remove only bacteriological contaminants are qualitatively less effective than those that remove toxins and heavy metals as well as bacteria. Quality also may be indicated by such things as

Figure 12–2 | **Capital Facilities Planning and Budgeting**

1. Identify present service characteristics (inventory facilities and service levels)

   a. Coverage (quantity)

   b. Quality

   c. Cost per unit of service (efficiency)

2. Identify environmental trends

   a. Population growth projections

   b. Changing regulatory environment

   c. Employment and economic development trends

3. Develop service objectives

   a. Extension of service to new population or area (coverage)

   b. Improvement in quality of service

   c. Opportunities to stimulate economic growth

4. Develop preliminary list of capital projects and cost estimates

   a. Rehabilitation of existing facilities

   b. Replacement of existing facilities

   c. Addition of new facilities

5. Identify financial resources

   a. External assistance

   b. Projected growth in present revenue base

   c. Potential for direct cost recovery for individual projects

   d. Use of credit

6. Select subset of projects for inclusion in five-year capital investment plan (CIP)

7. Identify future recurrent cost impact of CIP on operating budget

8. Include first year of CIP in annual budget estimate

the age of the facility and its condition. The latter may be measured by the frequency-of-repair record. Qualitative measures of service, including records of citizens' complaints and structured citizen satisfaction surveys, are as appropriate as quantitative measures.

Identifying Environmental Trends. The second step looks toward the future. Most city and state governments develop long-range planning forecasts to estimate future service requirements. These forecasts, which project population growth, commercial and industrial growth, demographic and economic changes, and so forth, are linked to the capital facilities planning process in order to develop plans for required service expansion or contraction. In addition, more detailed analyses of trends in business locations may predict possible shortages or other problems in critical areas, such as the water supply. The capital facilities planning process can provide a means for the jurisdiction to plan expansion of services in an orderly way and can help convince potential investors that the jurisdiction is anticipating future business and residential requirements.

Developing Service Objectives. The process of defining the need for capital investments can take numerous forms. Representation on long-range planning groups, open forums to discuss the need for community facilities, and referendums to approve a specific bond issue to finance a capital investment (see the next section) are typical means for generating citizen input. Even in jurisdictions with established channels for citizen input, a special group often convenes every two to three years just to review the current CIP and establish new priorities. Thus a key step is to determine the service objectives that capital investments will need to satisfy.

Preliminary Listing of Capital Projects and Cost Estimates. Based on the service objectives established in the previous step, a preliminary list of capital projects can be developed, along with a timetable for completing the projects. Typically, the preliminary list includes the rehabilitation of existing facilities to improve the quality and/or efficiency of service; the replacement of existing facilities, also for the purpose of improving quality and efficiency; and the addition of new facilities or expansion of existing facilities to meet expansion objectives. The preliminary list typically will not be screened for financial feasibility at this stage.

Identifying Financial Resources. The fifth step, identifying the financial resources potentially available to carry out the preliminary list of capital projects, involves analyzing the jurisdiction's overall financial condition and some of the individual capital projects for possible sources of financing specific to them. Since the 1980s, an important aspect of overall financial management has been the evaluation of the financial condition of local governments.[15] In the wake of public pressure to hold steady or to cut back state and local taxes, major new revenue initiatives in the form of tax increases often are not possible, even when the need to build up infrastructure and rehabilitate existing facilities is obvious. However, because of the expansion of tax bases, making long-range projections of tax yield increases and assessing the performance of other ordinary revenue sources sometimes reveal potential revenues that will be available at some point in the future for capital investment financing.

More commonly, state and local governments (and particularly the latter) rely increasingly on revenue sources specific to individual capital projects. User fees and property assessments traditionally have been used to finance the major portion of water and other utility capital investments as well as operating expenses. More recently, cities have exacted special impact fees and other charges from residential and commercial developers to pay for roads, water, and sewer lines and drainage intended to serve new developments[16] (see Chapter 4).

Other sources of revenues tied to particular projects include grants from other levels of government and borrowing (typically involving the issuance of bonds). Although federal funding cutbacks were significant starting in the early 1980s, state aid to local governments has in some cases made up for some of the federal cutbacks, and federal funds are still available on a more limited programmatic basis (see Chapter 14).

Selecting Projects for Inclusion in Five-Year Capital Investment Plan. Step 6 involves matching available financial resources with the set of projects included in the preliminary investment plan. Steps 3 through 6 may be iterated to eventually narrow down the list of projects and select a feasible set. Reevaluation of desired service objectives sometimes is necessary during this iterative process, because financial realities can make it clear that some objectives are impossible without major new financial initiatives. For most state and local governments, the application of complex analytical tools such as cost-benefit analysis or rate-of-return analysis plays only a small role in the selection of projects. Further, there is substantial disagreement over the validity of estimates of economic benefits from investments in infrastructure.[17] Instead, the ranking of priorities is often based on the principle that replacing deteriorated facilities should be the first concern, meeting population growth requirements should be the second, and improving quality of services should be last. Contemporary management tools such as the *balanced scorecard* have been adapted to help in the project selection process.[18] This approach emphasizes balancing selection criteria among four factors — financial information, customer requirements, internal management processes, and innovation and learning — with the notion being that a structured process to balance several criteria in different categories can lead to better choices *and* more successful implementation than over-reliance on any one set of factors.

Identifying Implications for Future Recurrent Costs. Decision makers frequently neglect considering the recurrent cost implications of capital investments.[19] It is sometimes difficult to anticipate the costs of keeping a facility operating, and the usually valuable public relations aspects of a new project tend to overshadow the longer-run impact on the general fund's budget. The problem is exaggerated by the fact that the operating and maintenance costs of any new project or facility are lower in the early years of operation, and the heavier costs fall outside the range of normal five-year capital planning cycles. Without an analysis that takes into account this fact, a state or local jurisdiction may find itself 10 or 20 years down the road facing the dilemma of either forgoing new capital investments because of the need to budget greater funds for maintenance or neglecting maintenance in favor of politically more popular capital projects.[20]

The analysis of future operation and maintenance costs is not all negative. If the analysis of the current capital facilities base in step 1 has been carried out well, the jurisdiction will have an idea of the present operation and maintenance costs of existing facilities. Replacing some facilities that require expensive maintenance expenditures may produce significant reductions in operation and maintenance costs in the operating budget.

Including the First Year of the Capital Investment Plan in the Annual Budget. Once a feasible set of investments has been selected and the short- and long-term costs have been determined, the final step is to incorporate the first year of the CIP into the annual budget. To this point, the process, which has been one of planning and programming, may have involved input from the legislative body, but no legal appropriation of funds will have taken place. Some jurisdictions submit the CIP to the legislative body (e.g., state legislature, city council) for formal approval, but the CIP does not necessarily include actual appropriation of funds. Some states appropriate the full costs of capital projects, at least for smaller projects, whereas other states appropriate only the annual costs of each project. In the latter case, only a single year's cost actually shows up in the appropriation act.

Evaluation of Capital Budgeting

Much of the argument over the value of capital budgeting at state and local government levels hinges on whether there should be a separate capital budgeting process. There is little argument over the need to examine the full long-term implications of capital spending and not just focus on a single budget year. But it is possible to have a comprehensive capital planning process that concludes with a capital budget plan or statement without a separate capital budgeting process. The amount the city council or state legislature is then asked to appropriate may be for only one year, but the budget request is made in the context of future-year requirements.

Pros and Cons of Separate Capital Budgeting. Capital budgets and statements indicate the extent to which investments are being made with current expenditures. From a political perspective, this gives capital budgets a certain value, since government officials can show citizens that government funds are being used for the acquisition of useful assets and not solely for the payment of bureaucrats' salaries.

On the negative side, capital budgeting can encourage political logrolling, in which various political interests agree to help each other. A capital budget can be a political grab bag, a fund in which every interest can find a project. A state capital budget may provide highway projects in every county, even though real need is concentrated in a small number of counties. In providing everyone with something, some important needs will not be met while less pressing needs will be satisfied. Furthermore, if capital costs are presented in a completely separate budget, particularly when financed by borrowing, it may appear as if capital decisions are "costless" in the current year.

On balance, however, the arguments in favor of paying special attention to capital spending, at least at the state and local levels, seem overwhelming. While capital budget decisions are no less political than other budget decisions, the logic of focusing attention on long-run financial and economic consequences of spending or failing to spend for capital facilities is compelling. More than current operating budget decisions, decisions to invest in infrastructure help shape the future direction, location, and extent of private economic investments in the community. Local governments' capital investments may in some cases play a leading role in encouraging future local economic development (see Chapter 15). State and local governments compete for location of major facilities, and they sometimes offer large incentive packages comprising infrastructure projects and financial assistance to induce private companies or federal agencies to locate facilities in their jurisdictions.

Once built, major facilities largely will be limited to the uses for which they were designed; inadequate planning of facilities can result in inadequate services, major financial burdens, or the need for expensive alterations. Excess capacity built into a community sewer system cannot be converted into other uses. Too little acquisition of land for parks in a rapidly growing suburban area may later result in a shortage of recreational opportunities or may force the local government to pay far more for space than it might have earlier. These arguments do not mandate that capital budgets be separate from operating budgets. In fact, they suggest the opposite. While capital spending requires attention to some issues that are not germane to operating budgets, capital and operating expenditures are inevitably related. As noted earlier, the mistake governments often make even with separate capital budgets or a distinctive capital planning/budgeting process is not taking into account the much longer-term operation and maintenance costs. And as governments get strapped for funds, as happened in the early 2000s after several years of surpluses at all levels of government, maintenance expenditures begin to be neglected. Capital budgeting, even if formalized and well done, must clearly link back to the operations and maintenance implications in the future for current capital spending.

Federal Capital Budgeting. For the federal government, the logic of capital budgeting is less compelling. First, much of the "capital" side of the federal budget goes toward defense acquisitions — 73 percent in the 2003 budget proposal. These are not investments in the same sense as state and local expenditures for water systems or highways. This statement does not mean that the purchase of nuclear-powered aircraft carriers, for example, has no implications for future operations and maintenance. Rather, the need to replace a weapons system often is generated not by its wearing out, but by its inability to cope with new offensive or defensive systems of a potential enemy or its being destroyed or damaged beyond recovery in a combat or training situation.

Furthermore, the federal government may undertake many nondefense capital expenditures more for macroeconomic policy reasons than for investment purposes. Because of the federal government's role in stimulating the economy, capital spending sometimes has the primary objective of assisting a state or local economy rather than providing a needed facility. Federal grants to state and local governments for nondefense physical capital exceeded $53 billion in 2001.[21] Unfortunately, this use of capital spending often leads to pork barrel decisions that place expensive projects in every congressional district.

There have been periodic calls for federal capital budgeting. At the time the unified budget was adopted at the recommendation of the 1967 President's Commission on Budget Concepts, a capital budget for the federal government was again rejected.[22] There was a resurgence of calls for capital budgeting at the federal level in the 1980s. In response to General Accounting Office (GAO) recommendations, the federal budget for fiscal year 1996 for the first time used as part of the *Analytical Perspectives* chapter on investment spending a capital budget presentation.[23] **Table 12–3** is the capital budget table from the fiscal year 2003 budget.

GAO and others argue that the federal government must adopt more contemporary financial management practices to improve the efficiency of government operations. Current federal management practices are inadequate for the task of achieving efficiency or effectiveness in government operations. This does not mean that GAO is in favor of a separate federal capital budget, but rather that much more systematic attention must be given to physical capital investments, to the value of those assets, and to their management.[24]

The second cause for renewed interest in federal capital budgeting is the concern that the nation is not investing sufficiently in basic infrastructure, to the long-run detriment of the economy. Legislation in 1984 established the National Council on Public Works Improvement and gave it the mandate to assess the state of the nation's capital infrastructure and make recommendations for improvement. The council's 1988 report concluded that infrastructure outlays should increase by 100 percent.[25] Further reports by associations of state and local governments, the Office of Technology Assessment, and researchers have continued to state the case that the nation's infrastructure base is eroding and the level of investment is woefully inadequate.[26] As cited earlier in this chapter, studies by the American Society of Civil Engineers continue to measure infrastructure deficits exceeding $1 trillion.

Many of those concerned that the level of investment in infrastructure is too low have argued that the federal budget is biased against such capital invest-

Table 12–3	Capital, Operating, and Unified Budget Concepts, United States Government, Fiscal Year 2003 (Billions of Dollars)

	$ billion
Operating Budget	
Receipts	2,048
Expenses	
Depreciation	82
Other	2,028
Subtotal, expenses	2,111
Surplus or deficit (-)	-63
Capital Budget	
Income: depreciation	82
Capital expenditures	100
Surplus or deficit (-)	-18
Unified Budget	
Receipts	2,048
Outlays	2,128
Surplus or deficit (-)	-80

Source: Office of Management and Budget, *Budget of the United States Government: Fiscal Year 2003, Analytical Perspectives* (Washington, DC: U.S. Government Printing Office, 2002), 148.

ments because it must show the full cost of the outlays in the construction years instead of showing only the annual depreciation of the investments over their long life.[27] A capital budgeting statement might show only one year's depreciation value in the current year budget, spreading the budget implications of such an investment over the expected years of benefits. This approach would more clearly isolate how much of the federal deficit is due to investments that will pay for themselves through future economic growth and might reduce some concern for the size of the deficit.

Developing a federal capital budget would not be a simple process. The sample capital and operating budget shown in **Table 12–3** was developed by the Office of Management and Budget (OMB) with considerable estimation required to determine depreciation values. In addition, what should count as investments in a capital statement is controversial, because as discussed previously, one can make a case for including many government expenditures for programs, such as education and health programs, that do not produce any physical asset but do produce future benefits. Naturally, all program advocates would want their programs included in the capital or investment budget, because only the annual amortized value of those programs would appear as an outlay in the operating budget, which typically gets more media attention. Carried to an extreme, the budget might shrink to a small proportion of its present size, covering only obviously current consumption expenditures. Yet the actual cash requirements of the federal government would not have changed.

For the most part, recent administrations have accepted the arguments and recommendations that federal budgeting must include more significant focus on capital spending. One section of the federal budget for fiscal year 2003 even used the (new) title *Federal Investment Spending and Capital Budgeting*. The 2003 budget also outlined legislation to be presented later that would create *Capital Acquisition Funds* and change the way agencies that acquire physical assets would show those acquisitions in the agency budget. Instead of the agency showing the full expenditure for the acquisition in the year acquired, the cost would be shown as the first year's depreciation, using straight-line depreciation. For example, if a physical asset had an expected life of 20 years, then 5 percent of the cost of that asset would show in the agency's budget, as if the agency were borrowing the full amount from the Treasury and repaying it at 5 percent per year for 20 years. The Treasury, however, would show the full outlay for the building, so the unified budget outlay total would not be affected by this presentation.[28]

The fiscal year 2003 budget discussed much of the argument and experience with capital budgeting in states, other developed countries, and some developing countries. But it is important to note that improved presentations of capital investments do not portend the adoption of capital budgeting at the federal level.

Outlays for acquisition of assets or construction of facilities are still recorded fully in the year acquired or constructed. In contrast, in state and local capital budgets, full investment cost is shown, albeit in connection with the method of financing. So when a state government borrows (typically issues bonds) to finance highways, the bond issuance and construction costs are fully disclosed, but the only budgetary impact of the project is the costs for debt service — principal and interest payments. Federal capital *budget* presentations are not linked to any specific method of financing, and they do record in the budget the full construction or acquisition cost incurred in that year. That is unlikely to change in the near future.

State and Local Bond Financing

State and local governments issue bonds to finance many types of public facilities and infrastructure. Commonly referred to as *municipal bonds,* bonds are issued by state and local general-purpose jurisdictions as well as many nonprofit public institutions, such as hospitals, and single-service authorities, such as school and water districts. The exemption from federal taxes of the interest earned from many of these bonds is a critical feature of their success and a controversial one.[29]

The two main categories of long-term bonds are *full faith* and *credit* bonds (or *general obligation* bonds) and *nonguaranteed* (or *revenue*) bonds. Full faith and credit debt is guaranteed by the general revenues of the issuing jurisdiction without regard to the purpose of the expenditures or the potential for direct cost recovery through user charges. Full faith and credit debt thus is considered guaranteed in that the full resources of the jurisdiction are pledged as security to potential investors. If a municipality offers the full faith and credit guarantee, it is obligated to raise taxes or reduce services to pay back the credit. What happens when a municipality refuses to raise taxes or cut services is covered later in the discussion of defaults. Nonguaranteed bonds do not have the full backing of the issuing jurisdiction's resources. Whatever security is offered, such as a pledge of the revenues from the services delivered by the new facility, no other resources are available to the creditor/investor. In that case, if the revenues fail to materialize, then the investor has no recourse to other sources of repayment.

Traditionally, municipalities and local utilities issued bonds in a fairly local market with the main purchasers being banks. Bonds issued were mostly plain vanilla. A general-purpose municipal government or school district almost always issued a general obligation bond, backed by the jurisdiction, mainly by property tax proceeds. The water and other utilities issued nonguaranteed revenue bonds backed by the future revenue streams from user charges. Local or nearby banks bought most of the issue. In recent times, these conditions have changed radically. The number of different instruments for debt, while still falling within the two general categories, has increased dramatically, and banks are no longer the largest holders of municipal debt.

For example, in 1996 the City of New York issued a $215 million bond backed solely by expected revenues from collection of delinquent taxes on commercial property. The city sold the property liens to a trustee, which in turn issued the bonds, contracted with private parties to collect the delinquent taxes, and returned to New York the difference between the amount required to pay off bondholders and the total collected. This bond issue was the first instance of a large tax lien-backed bond, and earned the bond issue *Governing* magazine's rating as one of the best municipal bond deals of the year.[30] Although the first major tax lien-backed bond, this issue is merely one example of the innovations in municipal bond finance. Numerous instruments are now on the market, as we discuss below.

Table 12–4 demonstrates the other major change in the municipal bond market — the shift from commercial banks to households as the predominant holders of municipal bonds. Although data on households' municipal debt holdings are incomplete for the earlier years, the reversal between commercial banks and households as the primary investors in municipal debt is striking. Property and casualty insurance companies also began to purchase more municipal bonds in the 1990s to diversify their investment portfolios. Mutual funds and money market funds are investing more heavily in municipal bonds too. In 2000, mutual funds and money market funds held approximately 15 percent and 16 percent, respectively, of the total outstanding municipal debt.[31]

Municipal bonds are debt instruments in that the issuer incurs an obligation to repay and the buyer becomes a lender with a claim on future repayments. The buyer, however, has no claim on the assets of the issuer. Equity ownership, such as is purchased with corporate stocks, is not a feature of municipal bonds. Private equity ownership is a feature of *build-operate-transfer* and *build-operate-own* forms of private financing of public infrastructure facilities (see Chapter 4), but the main form of state and local capital financing is likely to continue to be issuance of municipal bonds.

In most industrialized European economies, the banking sector is the primary source of finance to subnational governments. In some countries, such as the Netherlands, municipally owned banks, in addition to managing the accounts and financial transactions of owner municipalities, lend long-term to the municipalities. In other countries, commercial and investment banks are the primary lenders. In still other European countries, specialized financing institutions somewhat similar to U.S. state revolving loan funds, discussed below, have been established to provide credit to municipalities. In many developing countries, such as South Africa, Bulgaria, and Poland, municipalities are emerging as good credit risks and a variety of credit systems have developed or are developing, including bond markets, specialized financing institutions, and direct lending from commercial and investment banks.

Importance of Bond Financing for Infrastructure

Debt Financing Versus Pay-as-You-Go. State and local governments finance a major portion of their capital investment spending through long-term debt instruments. In 2000, state and local governments together issued $194 billion in new long-term debt; $65 billion was in the form of general obligation bonds and $129 billion took the form of revenue bonds.[32] Most state constitutions or statutes limit the issuance of long-term debt for both state and local governments to capital investment–type expenditures. Bond financing for infrastructure allows governments to build roads and bridges, schools, hospitals, water and wastewater systems, and numerous other major capital facilities before sufficient capital has been accumulated to pay for these facilities, in much the same way an ordinary consumer often borrows to finance the purchase of a home. The difference between bond financing and a consumer loan is that state and local governments issue debt instruments called bonds that are sold to various investors, giving the government issuing the bonds the cash to build the infrastructure facility and giving the bond purchaser a claim on that government for future repayment of both the borrowed amount and interest.

Some local governments try to avoid indebtedness as much as possible and work on a pay-as-you-go system. That means saving funds in advance until there is cash sufficient to build the infrastructure facility. These governments are like the car buyer who saves money until he or she has enough funds in the bank to purchase the car for cash. The motivations are similar: Both the government and the consumer avoid the interest costs for borrowing. If the jurisdiction can afford

Table 12–4 Holders of Municipal Debt, 1940–2000 (Billions of Dollars)

	1940	1950	1960	1970	1980	1985	1990	1995	2000
Commercial banks	3.6	7.4	16.8	61.2	148.8	231.7	117.4	93.4	114.0
Households	N.A.	N.A.	N.A.	N.A.	104.5	346.4	574.4	457.7	541.1
Property and casualty insurance	N.A.	N.A.	N.A.	N.A.	80.5	88.2	136.9	161.0	184.1

N.A. = Not available

Sources: 1940–1970, P.C. Wong, *Role of Private Financial Institutions in the Development of Local Infrastructure in Thailand* (Bangkok: U.S. Agency for International Development, 1995), 23; 1980–2000, *Bond Market Association, Trends in the Holdings of Municipal Securities: 1980–2001*, www.bondmarkets.com/Research/munios.shtml; accessed August 2002.

to wait for the facility or can plan far enough in advance to have the funds available when needed, then the prospect of financing without interest costs is attractive. Indeed, as the government is saving funds, it can invest them in interest-earning opportunities, which are becoming increasingly sophisticated for government investors.

Pay-as-you-go local governments tend to be smaller jurisdictions with relatively stable annual capital investment requirements. For example, if a small local government generally needs to spend about $500,000 per year on capital facilities and goods and that is a stable expenditure requirement, over time it will need to spend that same amount, plus interest, each year in debt repayment if it borrows for the capital facilities. So if the jurisdiction can plan far enough ahead or can afford to wait for the facility, by establishing a *capital investment sinking fund*, it can accumulate the funds necessary to meet the annual $500,000 per year capital spending requirement. This approach does not work as well for larger jurisdictions, which tend to have less predictable requirements, and it does not work well for lumpy investment patterns — that is, where large amounts are needed in some years for big construction projects and smaller amounts in other years. Some form of credit financing for most state and local jurisdictions is a necessity, and especially in rapidly growing areas where, regardless of size, pay-as-you-go financing cannot keep up with population growth and service demands.

Role of the Tax System and State and Local Bond Financing. A key reason for the attractiveness of bond financing for state and local government capital borrowing is that federal tax law exempts from the federal income tax interest earned by purchasers of many government bonds. In addition, most states with income taxes exempt interest earnings from state or local bonds for government entities within that state. Thus an individual who purchases state or municipal bonds retains the interest earnings tax-free in most cases. For individuals in the highest tax bracket, earning 6 percent interest on a municipal bond is equal to earning more than 9 percent taxable interest. Because the tax exemption for interest earnings attracts investors to the state and municipal bond market, a ready source of capital for infrastructure financing exists for government. The tax-exempt status of the earnings also enables jurisdictions to offer bonds at lower interest rates than they could get by borrowing from commercial lenders or issuing taxable debt securities. Tax exemption for the interest earnings on bonds, then, is the cornerstone of the U.S. system for financing public infrastructure for state and local governments.

The bonds' tax-exempt status is somewhat controversial, however. A wave of expansion in use of tax-exempt bonds to finance industrial development parks, incubator facilities to woo private developers to invest in local areas, and a wide variety of other essentially private endeavors led to significant curbs on state and local governments' authority to issue tax-exempt bonds in the Tax Reform Act of 1986 (TRA86) (private-purpose bonds are discussed in more detail in a following section). Other features of that tax reform also made municipal bonds a much less attractive investment for commercial banks, accounting in part for the trend noted in **Table 12–4**.[33] The securities industry clearly recognizes that there is a strong individual/household appetite for municipal bonds, as evidenced by the increasing availability of bonds as part of money market and mutual funds as well as the creation of tax-exempt bond funds. Concern for equity in taxation leads some to question whether interest on government and certain nonprofit bonds should be exempt. It is generally thought that mostly higher-income taxpayers benefit from this exemption, as they are the most likely purchasers of tax-exempt bonds and, therefore, that this exemption unfairly benefits those who can most afford to pay higher taxes. The growth of mutual funds in which middle-class individuals are making more investments is mitigating this equity argument.

Challenges to the general philosophy of granting tax-exempt status are unlikely to eliminate this fundamental feature of state and local finance in the United States.[34] At the same time, it is likely that the federal government will increase regulations regarding the issuance of tax-exempt bonds. The State of South Carolina challenged the constitutionality of any federal regulation of state governments' tax-exempt debt issuance in the 1988 *South Carolina v. Baker* case, questioning a law that denied tax-exempt status to bearer bonds (as opposed to registered bonds; see the discussion of bond features later in this chapter).[35] The Supreme Court ruled that the Tenth Amendment did not prohibit federal regulation of state and local governments and that there is no constitutional right to state and local immunity from federal tax provisions.[36]

Types of Bonds

General Obligation Bonds and Nonguaranteed Bonds. Since general obligation (full faith and credit) bonds typically are considered safer investments than nonguaranteed bonds because of the full backing of the jurisdiction's resources, these bonds typically carry lower interest rates than nonguaranteed bonds. The interest rate is critical in large bond issues, for which a difference of 0.1 percent can affect total interest payments by millions of dollars. However, revenue bonds from a well-managed special-purpose authority, such as a water district, with an excellent record of previous borrowing are likely to have a lower interest rate than a general obligation bond from a municipality with a declining property tax base and low personal income. For this reason, bonds not backed by the general revenue resources of a state or local government have become much more common. In addition, state limitations on general tax revenues, such as Proposition 13 in California, have forced state and local governments to favor revenue bonds over general obligation bonds.

Revenue bonds are politically easier to issue, for two reasons. First, voter approval is required in almost every instance of a full faith and credit bond, but is not required for revenue bond issues. Second, revenue bonds are repaid by the charges made to only those who consume or benefit from the services provided by the debt-financed facility or infrastructure, so taxpayers not using the service are not required to help pay off the debt. As noted above, revenue bonds have increased as voter approval has become more difficult to achieve.[37]

Nonguaranteed debt generally is restricted to the revenue earnings of the specific facility created by the investment. Many sources are used to repay these so-called nonguaranteed bonds. In the case of revenue bonds, the most common type, charges to users generate the funds necessary to repay the loans. Other sources include special assessments, in which the properties affected by an investment are assessed charges — for example, property owners might be assessed charges for sewer installations.

Revenue Bonds. Revenue bonds pledging the revenue from a specific tax or fee have the advantage of placing the burden for financing a facility on those who will use it. For example, using the parking fees from a parking garage to finance its construction places the burden on those who park in the garage. From an intergovernmental perspective, the revenue bond device forces nonresidents who use the parking garage or the highways to pay their fair share regardless of where they reside.

An invention in the last decade to finance airport facilities — the pledge of specific charges for use of the airport facility collected from the airlines through increments to the ticket price — is an example of the increasingly innovative ways to use revenue bonds to finance facilities. Airport operators (special authorities, municipalities that own the airport) apply to the Federal Aviation Administration to add a few dollars to the price of the tickets of passengers departing from or terminating their flights at the airport. Lansing, Michigan, and Little Rock, Arkansas, both financed major expansions and renovations through this device.[38] Broward County, Florida, added another wrinkle to the passenger facility charge instrument: It issued a 25-year bond to finance approximately $86 million in airport improvements. Repayment of these bonds will come solely from the FAA-approved passenger facility charge added to the price of tickets of passengers emplaning or deplaning at the airport. In 2012, however, the pledged security for the bonds will shift from the passenger facility charge to a lien on total airport system revenues until maturity in 2023. This so-called convertible lien bond device gives added security to the investors, thus presumably lowering the interest rate, and it may enable the airport to reduce the passenger facility charge later if the finances of the airport authority are sound.[39]

Tax Increment Financing Bonds. Tax increment bonds combine features of revenue bonds and general obligation bonds. They are used to finance local economic development by pledging future increases in property taxes of areas targeted for development or redevelopment. A city may decide to redevelop an area of the inner city through construction of housing or commercial facilities and may issue a bond to finance that redevelopment. Since the redevelopment will not directly generate revenues, it is not suitable for revenue bond financing. At the same time, the city may not wish to obligate its full resources to repay the bonds, may be at state debt-limit ceilings for full faith and credit bonds, or may wish to confine the repayment obligations to the direct beneficiaries of the redevelopment. A tax increment financing bond will back up the debt issue with the pledge of increased property tax revenue from the area being developed (the property taxes will rise because the property in the redevelopment area will become more valuable).[40]

Private-Purpose Bonds. Starting in the early 1980s, considerable use was made of state and local bonds to finance private construction and ownership of facilities that were then leased back to government entities. Similar use has been made of government bonds for lease and subsequent purchase of privately constructed facilities. In some cases, government bonds have been issued to finance a facility that then is leased to or purchased by the private sector. This last device often has been used to finance industrial development facilities, such as industrial parks and incubator facilities to help small businesses get started. State or local bonds issued for these largely private purposes were quite popular because the interest on the bonds was tax exempt. In 1985, more than half of a record volume in municipal debt issues involved these private-purpose activities.[41] This large volume was prompted by legislation under consideration to remove tax-exempt status from this type of bond.

TRA86 contained several provisions to limit tax exemptions. Interest earned on general-purpose bonds for construction of facilities or infrastructure to provide essential services remains tax exempt. Private activity bonds for construction of facilities such as airports, docks and wharves, hazardous waste treatment plants, and water supply facilities also retain their tax-exempt status, although interest is included in the alternative minimum tax base. The law removed the tax-exempt status of bonds for construction of industrial parks, parking garages, sports facilities, and convention or trade show facilities. In addition, each state and its local governments is limited in the amount of private-purpose bonds that can be issued in a year, and interest on any otherwise qualified bond issue is subject to tax if the bond issue exceeds the state cap. Since 1986, the issuance of private-purpose bonds has declined. Some states, however, continue to issue private-purpose bonds to finance facilities tied to economic development promotion, such as industrial parks; they consider the economic development benefit to be worth the higher-cost, taxable bond.

Municipal Minibonds. Most purchasers of municipal bonds are large purchase investors, including financial institutions that develop tax-exempt investment funds that then may be purchased by both large and small investors. Generally it is more difficult for all but higher-income individuals to get directly involved in purchasing bonds from their own jurisdiction because purchases often involve minimum amounts of $10,000 or more. Some cities, however, have begun issuing bonds in smaller denominations. Denver, Colorado, was one of the first issuers of minibonds, a $5.9 million issue in $1,000 denomination bonds in 1990.[42] The minibonds were issued directly by the city without an underwriter (see the discussion later on bond issuance), and purchase was possible only by Colorado residents. Almost 2,000 citizens purchased more than twice the amount initially expected. While not appropriate for large-scale bond issues because it becomes uneconomical to sell and track bonds in small denominations, minibonds have proved popular for financing smaller projects that especially interest local residents. They have not become a widespread instrument, however.

Certificates of Participation. One form of municipal debt issuance that is not legally classified as debt is the use of certificates of participation. Especially popular in California, which has placed severe restrictions on the ability of local governments to borrow, certificates of participation are municipal debt issues to construct facilities that will be operated by private contractors. The government leases the facility from the private operator and the lease payments are used to retire the debt (principal plus interest) from the debt issue. Certificates of participation can be risky investments. A school district in California (Richmond County Unified) and Brevard County, Florida, provide two examples in which the governmental entity was financially unable to make the lease payments (California) and unwilling to make payments (Florida), for a time, because of dissatisfaction with the facility.[43] Richmond County Unified School District subsequently defaulted on the lease payments due on the facility built via the certificates of participation debt issue.

Securitization and Tobacco Funds. Securitization of the future revenue stream from some activity or of a set of receivables was an innovation in the private sector in the 1980s. For example, credit card companies may issue a bond or borrow against the stream of receivables that will be flowing in from credit card users. This technique is called securitization because the credit card company issues a security — a bond — against the future payments that are already known because the credit card holders have already incurred the debt. On a larger scale, banks and housing finance companies may package a group of mortgages and issue a security — a bond — that is repaid by the known stream of revenues from those future mortgage payments. It is somewhat similar to a revenue bond, except that a revenue bond is issued against future revenues that are expected and estimated. Securitization involves a stream of payments that already are legal commitments — commitments by the credit card holder for charges already made on the card, or for mortgages already held by the institution securitizing that revenue stream.

New York City adapted this private market innovation by issuing a $709 million bond in 1999 that entitles the purchasers of the bond to the proceeds the city will receive under the tobacco litigation settlement funds (see the Chapter 4 discussion of the tobacco settlement).[44] That securitization of tobacco funds earned a *Governing* "deal of the year" award.[45] Virginia and other states have followed suit. The securitization of the settlement funds allows these governments to enjoy now the use of funds that they would otherwise have been receiving in the future — albeit at a discount.

E-trading Municipal Bonds. Just as on-line trading in the private sector has become the rage, so securities dealers now offer information about municipal bonds and offer the bonds themselves for sale on-line. Issuance costs have come down somewhat compared to trading through securities dealers; fully one-third of the muncipal bonds traded publicly on the market are now available on the Internet.[46] Of equal importance to on-line purchasing is greater access to information for individual investors about possible bond investments, which then are purchased through regular securities dealer channels, or sometimes directly from the underwriter.[47] Not just new issues, but the trading prices and detailed information on the issuers, is now regularly available on-line at sites maintained by regular securities dealers and specialized dealers in the fixed-income municipal securities market.

State Revolving Funds. Though they have been known for decades, state governments are now making increasing use of institutions created to assist local governments in obtaining better terms for debt financing. The most common form is the *revolving fund*; other forms include the state *bond bank*.

A revolving fund is created with some initial capitalization, often grants from the federal government plus state government bond issues, to lend to municipal borrowers. The premise is that the state government can get better credit ratings both because it has a better financial condition and because it can issue debt in larger amounts than individual small local governments. Repayments from the local governments that borrow from the fund keep the capitalization intact, allowing lending and borrowing to continue on a revolving basis. The original stimulus for many of these funds was federal environmental funding programs for water and sewerage systems. Massachusetts combined financing for programs related to the Clean Water Act of 1987 (reauthorization) to prevent water pollution and the Safe Drinking Water Act of 1974 as amended (1996) to sell $271 million in bonds to finance projects related to both acts, through the Massachusetts Water Pollution Abatement Trust.[48]

A bond bank is a variant on the same idea. The state bond bank may pool the borrowing needs of numerous, smaller municipal borrowers into a single state bond issue, and then finance the individual borrowers' requirements from the proceeds of the single state issue. Some state bond banks issue bonds to capitalize a fund for lending; then it is a form of revolving fund. Others accumulate individual municipalities' borrowing needs until a sufficiently large amount is reached and then issue a single bond to meet those specific needs.

Many of the state revolving funds and bond banks are used to finance federally mandated water and sewer system improvements. As of 2000, 22 states had issued debt through revolving funds or bond banks capitalized in part by Clean Water Act funds.[49] In 1995, federal legislation — the National Highway System Designation Act — created a pilot program to provide federal grant funding to capitalize state infrastructure banks to finance transportation projects. Initially, 10 pilot states were authorized, but the program was later extended to all states. However, uncertainty over the impact of regulatory requirements for second- and third-party borrowers under the program has largely killed the program, with only four states authorized to continue it.[50]

Overall, the use of bonds to finance state and local investments continues to increase as state and local financial conditions improve and federal transfers to assist state and local governments decrease. The distinction between general obligation bonds and limited revenue bonds is less important in practice than the financial condition of the borrowing entity. In fact, many water utilities and other users of more limited revenue bonds are in better financial shape than states and general-purpose local governments.

Bond Issuance Process

The process of issuing municipal bonds involves numerous steps, and the number of participants in these steps is quite large. **Table 12–5** lists the major participants, ignoring some of the minor players (for example, the role of bond printers). More detail on the main actors in the bond issuance process is included in the subsections on the major steps.

With so many steps and participants in the process, the costs to the issuing jurisdiction can be high. Numerous legal steps must be followed, numerous documents must be prepared, and numerous transactions with various financial and legal institutions must occur — transactions that require considerable personnel time or the purchase of consulting services. Total costs for these transactions vary widely, from less than 0.3 percent (District of Columbia) to as much as 1.3 percent

(Alaska); the average is just over 0.6 percent.[51] Costs vary by issue based on characteristics of the issue itself — size, complexity; the issuer — financial condition, experience with previous debt issues; market conditions; and general familiarity of investors with the issuer.[52] Variations by state are affected by state policies, the general economic climate, experience with defaults or other financial troubles, and, of course, market conditions. The underwriter's fee and/or the services of a financial advisor are the largest contributors to transaction costs. Issuers typically either secure the services of an underwriter to sell the issue or sell the bonds themselves while relying on a financial advisory service for assistance. Underwriting fees and financial advisory fees are about the same cost to the issuer, all other features of the bond and the issuer being similar. The cost of such services ranges from 0.4 to 0.5 percent added to the borrowing cost (usually referred to as 40 to 50 basis points; 100 basis points equal 1 percent). The percentages generally are higher for smaller issues, because some of the costs are rela-

Table 12–5 Participants in the Municipal Bond Market

Issuers

General-purpose municipalities, counties, and states; special-purpose governmental entities such as school districts and water authorities; and unique public service entities such as airports and transportation terminals

Financial Advisors

Finance specialists increasingly used by bond issuers to structure features of the issue to increase attractiveness to borrowers and/or to address a special need of the issuer — features such as issuer options to call the bond before maturity and structuring debt retirement to match the issuer's cash flow circumstances

Bond Counsel

Legal advisors to offer legal opinions on the legal authority of the issuer to borrow, on the tax-exempt status of the issue, and on the legal obligation of the issuer to repay

Dealers (Underwriters)

Investment firms, banks, and other financial institutions licensed to trade in municipal securities that sell the issuers' bonds

Trustee

Institution that serves mainly bondholders by securing from the issuers bond repayment cash flows and paying them out to bondholders when due

Investors

Individuals, investment banks, commercial banks, and other financial institutions

tively fixed. Issuance costs have been declining as the market grows and becomes more competitive.[53]

Voter Approval. In most states, a general obligation (full faith and credit) bond requires a referendum to secure voter approval. Revenue bonds and other forms of limited obligation financing generally do not require voter approval. In some cases, to avoid state limitations on general municipal borrowing, cities have established nonprofit building authorities to issue bonds and construct facilities. Such facilities are then rented to the municipality, and the rental payments secure the bond principal and interest. These special authorities, because they do not legally obligate in a direct way the general revenues of the municipality, can issue bonds without voter approval and without the debt counting as part of the municipality's overall debt. Of course, the source of funds used by the municipality to pay for renting the facility is, in fact, the general revenue fund.

Underwriting. Typically, the authority issuing a bond will secure the services of an underwriter, whose role is to arrange the actual sale of bonds to financial institutions. The underwriter for a small issue may well be a local bank or a major regional bank. Such firms as Goldman Sachs, Smith Barney Shearson, Merrill Lynch, A.I.G., Morgan Stanley Dean Witter, Citigroup, and other investment bankers and securities dealers typically handle major issues that are marketed nationally (and internationally). Individuals, banks, insurance companies, and mutual and money market funds invest in state and local bonds, as shown in **Table 12–4**. Legal counsel retained by the issuing authority provides a legal opinion on the status of the issue, the legal authority to issue the bond, and the tax-exempt status of the bond.

Public Sale Versus Negotiated Sale. Historically, bonds have been offered for public sale, with purchasers such as larger financial institutions, which might be purchasing for their own portfolio or for resale, effectively determining the interest rate by their offers. A public sale is initiated by a widely published official notice of sale. The notice of sale typically includes information such as the denomination of the bonds, bid conditions and requirements, and provisions for payment. More detailed information is provided in the *bond prospectus*. Sealed bids are submitted by interested institutional investors, brokerage firms, and even individuals, although individuals typically purchase through intermediaries. The issuing jurisdiction then is free to accept the lowest bid interest rate or to reject the bid according to the terms and conditions of sale. Jurisdictions with good ratings prefer this method, as they are likely to attract numerous bidders and thus be able to choose lower interest rates.[54]

Becoming increasingly common, however, is the negotiated sale. Negotiated sales are conducted between investment banks and the issuing government. The underwriter acts as a broker between the issuing jurisdiction and the investment community. If the issuer thinks the rates quoted by potential buyers are too high, the issuer is free to reject the bids, as in a public sale. A key advantage of a negotiated sale is that the bond issue can be spread over a period of time. If the interest rates in bids are high but the issuer cannot postpone the project, the issuer may sell only a portion of the total issue to start the project while the underwriter continues to seek additional bids. One disadvantage of negotiated sales is that some investors, including some pension funds, cannot purchase state or municipal securities except through public sale. Overall, negotiated sales seem to cost about 30 basis points more than competitive bids.[55]

Bond Features. Bonds differ from each other in a variety of ways.[56] *Term bonds* may be due and payable to the investors on a single date. *Serial bonds* are due according to a specific schedule of payments over a number of years. In recent years, serial bonds have largely replaced term bonds, in part because of statutory prohibitions against term bonds. Investors holding term bonds obviously must be concerned with whether a jurisdiction is annually setting aside sufficient funds to be able to repay its debt.

Another difference is between coupon and registered bonds. *Coupon bonds* have coupons attached indicating the bond's maturity date and the amount of payment. Whoever presents the mature coupons receives payment. *Registered bonds* require that the owner register with the government issuing the bonds. The advantage of a coupon bond is that it is easily transferred from one owner to another, whereas a registered bond offers protection against loss or destruction of the bond itself. States and municipalities prefer coupon bonds because the issuing jurisdiction is not responsible for keeping records of the purchasers. However, a provision of the Tax Equity and Fiscal Responsibility Act of 1982 requires that state and municipal bonds be registered to retain their tax-exempt status, and that requirement was upheld in *South Carolina v. Baker*. As a consequence, the use of coupon bonds has all but disappeared, although state and local governments continue to lobby for federal legislation that would permit issuing nonregistered bonds that are tax exempt.

Another feature of bond sales is *discounting*. A bond is discounted when it is sold at some fraction of its face value. For example, a $10,000 bond may be sold for $9,800. It is thus discounted below par (meaning below face value). When it matures and the principal is paid out, the investor will receive $10,000 in return for the $9,800 investment in addition to the interest payments the investor would have been receiving over the years. At times, a bond may actually be sold at a premium over its par value. This can happen when a bond whose fixed interest rate was set in a period of high interest rate becomes available for sale after interest rates have fallen. A potential new investor will be attracted to the higher interest rate bond, but the seller has less incentive to sell the bond because of the low return offered by other choices now available on the market. So the seller charges the new investor, say, $10,200 for a bond that will repay principal of only $10,000 at maturity. The bond investor must consider both the selling value — discounted, at par, or at a premium — as well as the interest rate in determining the return on investment. The secondary market, in which bonds already sold once are resold to other investors, rarely has bonds that are sold at their face value. Conditions now are almost always different from the time of issue, causing the bonds to be valued at either greater or lesser than their face value.

Bonds are becoming increasingly complex in the structure of their terms. Traditionally debt issuers were concerned primarily with the interest or coupon rate of the bond and the various costs of debt issuance. Today, however, issuers are incorporating detailed features, usually with the help of a financial advisory service, to vary the conditions of sale, the conditions under which the issuer may pay off the bond early, and variations in cash flows at different points in the life of the bond. Called *structured finance*, this approach of designing features into a bond issue unique to the cash flow characteristics of the borrower offers ways for issuers to tailor a bond issue to their specific situations.[57]

Zero Coupon Bonds. The typical municipal bond pays interest at specified points until the maturity date, when the principal is paid. Zero coupon bonds are growing in popularity, however. The coupon rate, in finance terminology, is the interest rate that the bond will pay. A zero coupon bond pays out no interest until maturity, when both the principal and the interest are paid at once. Attractive to the issuer because they have no annual cash flow requirements, zero coupon bonds naturally require some incentive to attract investors away from the more typical municipal bond, which pays in regular installments through the years until maturity. The usual means of attracting investors to zero coupon bonds is to sell the bonds for much less than their stated value — to discount the bond from face value. Zero coupon bonds typically call for the issuer to set aside funds with a trustee, on a regular basis, sufficient to pay off the debt at time of maturity.

Interest Rates. Interest rates, of course, are one of the most critical elements of bonds for both the issuer and potential buyers. As a hedge against changing interest rates or financial condition, the state or municipal authority may sometimes use a *call* feature. This means the authority may call or repay the bond in part or in full before the maturity date. The issuer can thus take advantage of falling interest rates by paying off all or part of the bond issue. Exercising this feature usually involves the payment of some premium. Callable bonds typically carry a higher rate of interest because investors would otherwise be less attracted to an investment that may be repaid sooner and therefore at a lower profit. A similar feature, which favors the bond buyer, is the *put* option. It allows the buyer, at specified intervals, to require paying off the bond. For this feature, the buyer agrees to specified discount rates at the different put options.

Variable interest rate municipal bonds have become common, just as variable rate financing has become standard in the financial industry. Many state and municipal issuers have taken advantage of variable rates both at the time of original issue and to refinance bond indebtedness.

The actual interest that the jurisdiction will have to pay on a bond issue depends on many factors related to the financial condition of the jurisdiction and the general market for other investments at the time of the issue. The tax-exempt status of the interest earned by state and local bonds means that the interest rate paid will be lower than comparably safe investments that do not enjoy tax-exempt status. If the jurisdiction has a good record of previous debt management, it will be perceived as a lower risk than one that has experienced trouble meeting its financial obligations. Likewise, if the jurisdiction is located in a good regional economy with low unemployment rates and a high tax base, it will be able to sell its bonds at lower interest rates. The issuing jurisdiction also will provide potential investors with information about other long-term obligations, including other debt and also unfunded pension liabilities (see Chapter 13). A reputation for good financial management is cited as evidence of creditworthiness.

Bond Ratings. Investors rely heavily on standard ratings provided by independent services, such as Fitch Investors Service L.P., Moody's Investor Service, and Standard & Poor's Corporation. Standard & Poor's uses nine ratings, ranging from AAA for the highest rating (best risk) to the lowest rating of D (worst risk).[58] Only bonds rated BBB- and above are considered investment-grade quality.[59] Moody's scale ranges from AAA to CA/C in a similar fashion.

The importance of bond ratings is illustrated by an upgrade in Allegheny County, Pennsylvania's rating by Moody's from A3 to A2. On a $50 million bond issue, the county estimated the savings due to the rating improvement would be about $50,000 in total bond insurance costs and $350,000 in total interest costs.[60] A downgrade in rating may come about because of the issuer's own investment practices, as in the case of the Orange County, California, bankruptcy (discussed later in this chapter). State and local governments that invest their own funds, such as pension funds and short-term deposit instruments, can have their borrower status downgraded if they invest too heavily in high-risk derivatives.

Credit Enhancement. One device that state and local governments use to control the costs of debt and debt issuance is insurance. About half of all new issues are insured by one of the four major bond insurers — Ambac Assurance Corporation, Financial Guaranty Insurance Company, Financial Security Assurance, and Municipal Bond Insurance Association. New York City's debt crisis in the 1970s and the Washington Public Power Supply System (WPPSS) default in 1983 were among the major contributors to the growth of municipal bond insurance. Bond insurance serves to earn the issuer a AAA rating. Usually through the payment of a one-time premium, the bond issuer purchases the guarantee that principal and interest payments will be made and will be made on time. The difference between the insurance cost and the interest costs of an A-rated bond versus a AAA-rated bond is in the issuer's favor. If the rating without insurance would be below A, the costs of insurance likely will exceed the interest savings as the risk to the insurer requires a high premium.

Another type of credit enhancement is a *bank-issued line of credit*. The line of credit assures the bond buyer that the issuer will not be delayed in meeting payments even if short-term fluctuations in cash flow cause a temporary problem. The line of credit can be accessed if necessary to meet the short-term cash flow problem.[61]

In some developing countries, central governments provide credit enhancements for local government borrowing through the use of an intercept mechanism. The central government agrees to intercept, if necessary, a stable source of revenues that otherwise would flow to the borrower, such as a portion of central revenue transfers to local government. This intercept is paid to the lender in the event of default or delayed payment by the local government. The municipal development finance agency of Colombia, *FINDETER*, relies heavily on the intercept of central government grants/transfers to municipal governments to collect on debt repayments. Some municipal borrowers/bond issuers, rather than repay loans, simply allow the intercept mechanism to make the payments.

Bond Trustee. A typical municipal bond issue will have a specified institution serve as the trustee to handle all transactions with the ultimate buyers. The trustee's function is to see that the contract between issuer and buyer is faithfully executed. The trustee ensures that all legal requirements are followed and acts as the holder of annual interest payments due and payable. If a feature of the bond requires the jurisdiction to make regular payments into a *capital accumulation fund* (or *sinking fund*) to be able to repay principal, the trustee sees that these payments are in fact made and secured.

Disclosure and Regulation

Municipal bond issuance is subject to the general regulatory functions of the Securities and Exchange Commission (SEC), as are all other public debt and equity issues in the U.S. financial markets. For decades, municipal debt instruments were specifically exempt from SEC regulation. Beginning in the 1970s, however, Congress began to increase the role of the SEC in regulating municipal bond issues. SEC regulations focus on the underwriter's role and set disclosure requirements that affect the type and quality of information that underwriters must provide to potential investors.[62] Significant new disclosure rules were adopted in 1990 (SEC Rule 15c-12) that pertain to the consistency and timeliness of an underwriter's release of information provided by the bond issuer. The quality of the information itself and all releases by the bond-issuing jurisdiction are still considered to be the jurisdiction's responsibility. The underwriter does not assume any liability properly borne by the issuer. Evidence suggests that disclosure improves the investors' ability to judge credit, and hence improves credit ratings for creditworthy municipalities.[63]

Amendments to the Securities Exchange Act created the Municipal Securities Rulemaking Board (MSRB) in 1975 in the wake of New York City's financial crisis and the revelation that some dealers in state and municipal securities were involved in unethical and "dangerous" conduct.[64] MSRB's authority extends only to dealers and others involved in municipal bond transactions, not to the actual issuing governments themselves. MSRB functions under the general authority of the SEC to ensure that the disclosure information is as accurate and timely as possible. It requires bond dealers to file repository copies of all official documentation on a municipal bond issue so as to make the information more widely available to all potential investors. Another step is to make bond pricing information more widely accessible, requiring dealers to report daily both interdealer transactions and retail transactions in municipal bonds.[65]

A large step in imposing public disclosure requirements on the issuing jurisdictions themselves has been the implementation of Nationally Recognized Municipal Securities Information Repositories; five exist, including such financial services organizations as Bloomberg Financial Markets, Moody's Investor Services, and Standard & Poor's. Municipal debt issuers must at least annually — and more often if conditions change — report on their financial condition. This reporting requirement extends for as long as the issuer has outstanding debt in the market, providing potentially valuable information to subsequent secondary market purchasers of municipal securities. Also, municipal debt issuers are required to maintain and report regularly on their overall financial condition, not just on the status of specific debt issues.

The additional disclosure requirements have caused considerable consternation among many of the participants in the municipal bond market.[66] One particular requirement that securities dealers feel is too vague is the requirement that brokers and dealers must judge whether a client is capable of understanding the risk involved in an investment before they issue a recommendation to the client. However, the Orange County, California, financial fiasco (see below and Chapter 10) has discouraged critics from attempting to reduce disclosure requirements of both issuers and dealers in the municipal securities market.

Debt Capacity and Management

Since the federal government borrows for purposes other than capital investment, we continue in this section to focus on state and local governments, reserving the topic of federal debt for Chapter 15. Media discussions of the federal debt and the size of the federal deficit raise citizens' consciousness of government debt, but locally people are asked officially to approve debt (bond issues) for financing everything from schools to new fire stations. More importantly, citizens are not given the opportunity to vote on an even larger component of state and local debt — debt that is issued by special authorities or that does not involve the pledge of full faith and credit of the jurisdiction. The questions to be addressed in this section involve how much debt can be managed safely and which debt management practices will ensure sound future financial condition.

Size of Debt

The size of debt can be assessed in several ways. The total amount of debt is probably the least meaningful measure. The fact that state and local governments' total outstanding debt at the end of 2001 was $1,688 billion, although this figure may sound staggering, is not really instructive.[67] Interest payments on general debt in 1998 amounted to $74.6 billion (on $1,284 billion in outstanding debt), or only 4.9 percent of total state and local expenditures, and interest payments have remained relatively constant over recent years at about 5 or less percent of total expenditures.[68] Individuals commonly devote more than 5 percent of their total expenditures on interest payments for home mortgages, car loans, and credit card debt.

Per Capita Debt. Per capita debt figures help put the total government debt in perspective. How much per capita do state and local governments owe? In 1998, they owed $4,750 per person. Is that too much, too little, or just about right? Is it growing, declining, or remaining more or less stable? The latter question is easier to answer than the former. **Figure 12–3** charts state and local per capita debt from 1970 through 1998. Per capita debt has risen at both the state and the local government levels, with local debt rising somewhat more rapidly than state debt. In addition, the amount of increase in the five-year period 1980–1985 was almost equal to the rate of increase for the preceding 10-year period (1970–1980), and the period 1985–1995 witnessed an even faster rate of growth. However, the recent trend is a slower rate of growth. Thus, state and local debt is rising faster than population, but is that cause for alarm?

Ratio of Debt to Personal Income. Relating debt to personal income instead of population makes the picture begin to clear. Calculating total debt outstanding per

$1,000 of personal income is one way of assessing whether debt is in danger of becoming an unreasonable economic burden. In 1992, state and local government debt per $1,000 in personal income was $184. These numbers are considerably less alarming. Over a 30-year period, combined state and local debt per $1,000 in personal income has remained very stable. **Figure 12–4** charts this historical trend. State and local debt per $1,000 of personal income in the 1990s, although showing a trend toward increase after a 10-year decline from the 1970s through 1982, was no higher than the previous high of $205 back in 1972 and has declined since that 1972 high.

Figure 12–3 State and Local Debt per Capita, 1970–1998.

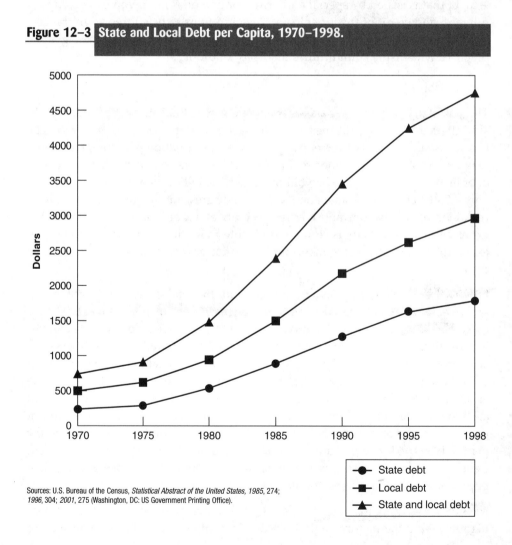

Sources: U.S. Bureau of the Census, *Statistical Abstract of the United States, 1985*, 274; *1996*, 304; *2001*, 275 (Washington, DC: US Government Printing Office).

Figure 12–4 State and Local Debt per $1,000 Personal income, 1962–1997

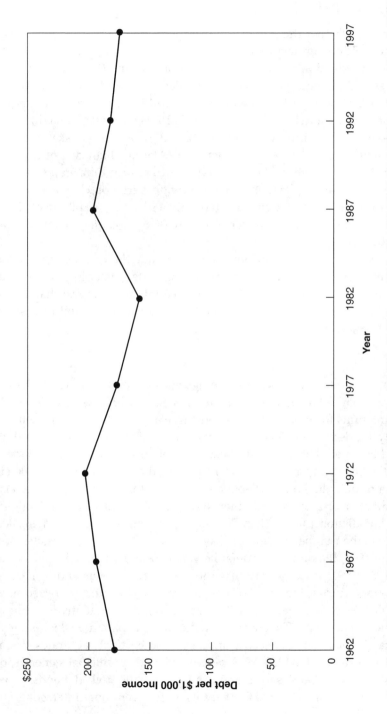

Sources: U.S. Bureau of the Census, *Historical Statistics on Governmental Finances and Employment* (Washington, DC: U.S. Government Printing Office, 1984), 113; U.S. Bureau of the Census, *Government Finances in 1985–86* (Washington, DC: U.S. Government Printing Office, 1998), 3; U.S. Advisory Commission on Intergovernmental Relations, *Significant Features of Fiscal Federalism, Volume 1: Revenues and Expenditures, 1992* (Washington, DC: U.S. government Printing Office), 245, 286; U.S. Bureau of the Census, *1992 Census of Governments. Volume 4, Government Finances: Number 5, Compendium of Government Finances* (Washington, DC: U.S. Government Printing Office, 1996, 152; U.S. Department of Commerce, *Statistical Abstract of the United States: 2001* (Washington, DC: U.S. Government Printing Office, 2001), 275, 424.

Distribution of Debt

Ultimately, whether the size of state and local debt is reasonable is a subjective judgment. The main factors used in making such an appraisal are the financial burden on individual taxpayers and the economy and the perceived value of the facilities and services purchased by the debt. Generally, debt varies somewhat with income and with the amount of state and local services. The state with the highest per capita debt in 1998, Alaska ($12,111), also was ranked fairly high — 16th — in personal income per capita ($27,835).[69] Hence, Alaska presumably has the income level to support a higher debt (Alaska's high cost of living tends to inflate all of its statistics, of course). New York ranked third in per capita income and third in per capita debt. There is wide variation, however. Connecticut ranked first in per capita income and only 48th in per capita debt; California's debt and income was closely correlated, with a per capita income ranking of 11 and a debt ranking of 16.

Indebtedness is not distributed evenly among the various types of local government. Local authorities and special districts, including water and sewer authorities, school districts, and the like, account for the largest share of local debt issues — 60 percent of new issues in 2000. Municipalities and townships are 29 percent of new issues, and counties are at 11 percent.[70]

Debt Default

It is important to remember that the figures on debt do not reflect the full scope of future financial obligations of governments. As will be seen in Chapter 13, pension programs for public workers constitute a form of debt and often are inadequately funded. Debt defaults are correlated with economic cycles, but it also should be noted that there have been few defaults on state or local indebtedness since the Great Depression of the 1930s.[71] In that decade, about 4,800 state and local units defaulted on their obligations. While that number may seem large, the total number of governments then was 150,000. Most of the defaults involved small jurisdictions; fewer than 50 had populations of more than 25,000.[72] Since that time, the number of defaults has been low. By number of issues, from 1940 through 1994, the number of defaults varied from less than 0.2 percent to 1 percent (1980–1994). As a proportion of the dollar value of outstanding indebtedness, the average during that period was less than 1 percent.[73] More recent research through 1999 shows that over a 20-year period, the cumulative default rate was less than 1.5 percent.[74] That average masks wide variation. Riskier issues, such as multifamily housing and electric utilities, experienced default rates ranging from 1 to 4 percent in the 1980–1999 period, whereas municipal general obligation bonds and water and sewer and similar revenue-backed bonds experienced default rates in the 0.01 to 0.04 percent range. Even more interesting is the fact that, since the Great Depression, no state has defaulted on a debt (even then, only Arkansas postponed payments). Astonishingly, of $300 billion in school district debt issued from 1979 through 1997, only two issues ($10 million) defaulted.[75]

Few public bond issuers have faced financial insolvency, although the exceptions have been noteworthy. In 1963, debt service payments on $100 million in revenue bonds for the Calumet Skyway in Chicago were interrupted.[76] In the mid-1970s, New York City came close to bankruptcy as a result of extensive borrowing to meet operating budget requirements and defaulting on some of its short-term debt. As a result, New York City was partially placed under the supervision of a financial control board (see Chapter 14). Only this intervention by the state government and the banking community prevented outright default on several bond issues. Also in the 1970s, Cleveland defaulted on just over $15 million in tax anticipation notes, largely because of poor financial management practices and inadequate accounting procedures.[77]

The largest failure has been the WPPSS. In 1983, after a more than decade-long program of construction of five nuclear power generating plants, WPPSS defaulted on more than $2 billion in revenue bonds. The revenue bonds were issued in anticipation of the sale of electricity. WPPSS got caught in the situation faced by the power industry in many parts of the country in the 1970s — a combination of slower rates of growth in electricity demand, rapid escalation in the costs of nuclear power plant construction, and rising interest rates.[78] In 1993, WPPSS successfully issued $800 million in bonds to refund the debt.[79]

In reality, defaults by state and local governments recently have been far exceeded by failures of banks and savings and loan institutions. Corporate bond defaults average closer to 2 percent.[80] However, periodic problems in the 1990s, headlined by the Orange County, California, financial collapse, keep the attention of both municipal bond market participants and the public. The financial collapses in both Bridgeport, Connecticut, and Cuyahoga County, Ohio, preceded Orange County. Bridgeport attempted to declare bankruptcy, although the bankruptcy was not permitted by the courts. Cuyahoga County perhaps lost its place in history to Orange County, although they share some similarities. Neither got into trouble as a result of overextending debt. Both counties became mired in financial difficulties as a result of their investment activities with their own pension funds and other sources of cash, plus those of numerous other local governments for which the counties acted as investment managers. Cuyahoga County lost $114 million on a $1.8 billion investment pool, but subsequently repaid most of the local government co-investors.[81]

Orange County, California, Bankruptcy. The bankruptcy of Orange County, California, set off shockwaves in the finance industry and in the press. Because it was so wealthy, no one imagined bankruptcy was even possible. The county was the investment manager for its own funds and almost 200 other local governmental units. At the high point, Orange County was investing more than $7 billion. A large proportion of the investments were in *derivatives*, a hybrid form of financial instrument that depends on changes in the value of other financial instruments. In this case, Orange County invested in instruments that depended for their value on the interest rates on other instruments. In effect, Orange County was betting on a certain directional movement in interest rates — upward — and when interest rates fell, Orange County did not have cash in the pool sufficient to cover the funds invested. The strategy had been successful in previous years; the pool earned rates of return ranging from 7 percent to 9 percent from 1991 to 1994.[82] In late 1994, the county petitioned for bankruptcy under Chapter 9 of the U.S. Bankruptcy Code. Subsequently, the county defaulted on various taxable pension fund and taxable arbitrage notes.[83] Orange County then filed suits of its own against its former auditor KPMG Peat Marwick and the investment firm that managed most of the derivative and other investments, Merrill Lynch. The aftershocks of the Orange County nightmare caused share prices of both insured and uninsured California bonds to drop dramatically, though insured funds rebounded quickly. Partly in continuation of trends toward increasing regulation of municipal debt and investment activities, and partly in response to Orange County's actions, the SEC has continued to increase its regulatory role in this area.

Debt Capacity

Measuring Debt Capacity. Measuring debt capacity is an art rather than a science. In recent years, the public finance and budgeting profession has paid considerably more attention to improving the level of the art. Three main factors influence debt capacity: expenditure pressures, resource availability, and the commitment of governmental officials to use resources to meet debt requirements.[84] Assessing resource availability involves analyzing all potential sources of revenue including own-source revenues; transfers from other levels of government; and types of self-financing including user charges, special assessments, impact fees, and a variety of other measures to collect fees or revenues sufficient to support the specific project or facility (see Chapter 4).

Expenditure analyses look at the present and potential future commitments of jurisdictions. Population growth, changing economic conditions, the state of the current capital facilities and infrastructure base, and the socioeconomic characteristics of the population are important influences on potential future expenditures. The willingness of lenders to purchase debt is reflected ultimately in the interest rate they will require to lend.

Revenue and expenditure analyses are used by state and local governments to support capital budgeting and debt management. Fiscal capacity analysis, focusing on the ability to generate revenues, and requirements analysis, focusing on expenditure needs, are used to determine present fiscal conditions and estimate future conditions. Against that backdrop, the financial requirements and budgetary impact of possible capital investments and debt financing alternatives can be assessed.

Debt Burden. The most common overall measure of debt burden is the ratio of debt to debt-carrying capacity, which reflects the extent to which revenues are sufficient to cover debt service, in addition to operating expenses.[85] The World Bank often looks at the ratio of debt service to current revenues, the ratio of capital expenditures to total expenditures, and the excess of current revenues over ordinary operating expenditures as indicators of the ability of a city to incur additional debt. More refined measures focus not on actual revenues but on the revenue base itself. U.S. local governments commonly use the ratio of debt to the assessed value of taxable property, because that assessed value reflects a local government's basic ability to generate revenues. These quick indicators are all useful, but ultimately they are interpretable only in the context of a jurisdiction's overall debt management strategy.

For enterprise-like operations, such as water authorities, conventional ratio measures of debt burden are in common use. The debt to equity ratio is a measure of the extent to which a utility is financing itself through debt relative to equity. The higher the ratio, the more risk there is in additional debt issues, as lenders want to see borrowers also making significant commitments of their own resources (equity). Another common ratio — interest share of operating income — measures the amount of debt, as a percentage, that operating income has to cover.[86]

Debt Management. In general, sound debt management at the state and local levels involves restricting debt primarily to financing long-term investments. A general rule is that borrowing should not be used to meet current operating expenses. The much-publicized financial crisis experienced by New York City involved short-term borrowing to finance current expenses. Occasionally, short-term borrowing is used to deal with emergencies but often is refinanced as part of a long-term debt issue. Moreover, the payout period of the debt should correspond to the useful life of the facility or infrastructure financed.[87]

The rule to restrict debt to long-term capital financing does not apply to financial emergencies resulting from major flooding or unusually heavy snows during the winter, for example. But this rule, along with the rule to match the payout period for the debt with the expected life of the facility, should generally be followed. Adherence to these two rules ensures that the jurisdiction will more or less match the benefit flows from capital facilities with the opportunity costs (see

Chapter 7 for a more detailed discussion of cost and benefit streams and the concept of opportunity costs).

One of the major positive results of the financial difficulties of cities such as New York and the major cutbacks in federal aid in the 1980s has been an increase in the sophistication of the tools used in analyzing the financial condition of governments. Furthermore, in the last two decades, state governments have become quite involved in regulating local government debt, not only by means of the more traditional statutory and constitutional provisions that govern the powers and authority of local governments but also by means of extensive state programs of technical assistance. Effective debt management requires the balancing of competing claims against the current annual budget and future annual budgets. As a consequence, state and local governments increasingly rely on methods to assess overall financial health and place potential bond issues in that context.[88]

Debt Refinancing. From time to time, substantial swings in market conditions bring interest rates down and spur a round of refinancing bonds. In 1998, of $279 billion in new debt issues, nearly $121 billion or 43 percent were refinancings. In 2000, less than 10 percent of $194 billion in new issues were for refinancing.[89] State and local governments also have become more sophisticated in their transactions in the financial markets. One strategy in use is to swap the interest owed on outstanding bonds for more attractive interest rates. A traditional method for accomplishing that is to call in bonds that have higher interest rates when the market changes and rates fall. That is possible, of course, only with bonds having call features. An alternative that does not require any actual transaction with outstanding bonds is an interest rate swap. In this type of transaction, the borrowing authority agrees to pay a third-party financial investor a variable rate of interest over a fixed period of time in exchange for payment of a fixed rate of interest by the third party. This is a synthetic variable rate financing deal in that the bonds themselves remain as they were, with the terms and conditions unchanged.

The interest rate swap works by introducing a third party into the transactions between issuers and investors. During a period of high interest rates, for example, bond issuers try several strategies to control the effects of high interest. One strategy is to issue serial bonds, breaking the total issue into several annual tranches. If interest rates do fall from the high at the time the choice is made to issue a bond over a series of years, then the later tranches carry lower rates. Another strategy is to issue variable interest rate bonds tied to some short-term rate index. The issuer then may enter into a contract with a third party in which, for a fee, the third party agrees to swap fixed rate payments for the variable rate payments. The issuer elects from time to time whether to take the swap. The issuer "bets" that the fee paid for the swap option over time will be less than what the issuer saves by exercising the swap option.

The Port Authority of New York and New Jersey, for example, in 1991 entered into an agreement with a third party for a 10-year period during which the third party agreed to pay the authority at a fixed rate of 6.5 percent on a $10 million value. In return, the Port Authority agreed to pay the third party an indexed variable rate. The Port Authority felt, and initial experience bore its expectations out, that the variable rate was likely to remain below the fixed 6.5 percent rate.[90] Subsequently, the Port Authority entered into a counter swap with the same third party, this time agreeing to pay the third party a fixed rate of 5.32 percent while receiving from the third party the indexed variable rate. What once had been $10 million in bonds outstanding at 6.5 percent was converted into the same value at 5.32 percent.

Wild speculation in interest rate swaps, of course, could put a state or local authority into a risky debt position. The Port Authority has a well-established debt management program with formally defined principles. The debt situation vis-à-vis the original bondholders remains unchanged in an interest rate swap. The state or local authority is simply trading in the financial market based on judgments about future interest rates. The original bond issue is not affected, in that investors will be paid according to the original terms. The borrowing authority, through a completely separate transaction, hedges against future interest rate changes and achieves, through a third party, a gain or a loss based on the marginal interest rate differences. The risk analysis focuses on whether the overall portfolio of the borrowing authority has been exposed to higher or lower future interest payments. Recent trends in lower interest rates make interest rate swaps an attractive possibility for borrowers who issued long-term debt a few years earlier when interest rates were higher. This is different from the Orange County, California, strategy for its investments. In the interest rate swap hedges, the party involved negotiates a known risk and return range, and it keeps its maximum risk exposure within bounds of good financial management practice. In the Orange County case, the county's investment manager was in effect borrowing to *bet* on interest rates rising. When they fell, the county could not pay off the borrowed money.

Summary

Every day we use physical facilities and infrastructure provided by state and local governments. Few of us stop to analyze how those facilities are paid for or what impact their construction has on state and local taxes — unless the extension of new water and sewer lines or a major street repaving project results in a hefty assessment on our own property. However, it is increasingly common for state and local governments to highlight capital facilities planning and budgeting and to involve citizens more directly in the planning process. Most of the government services and assets from which the ordinary citizen benefits, such as schools, roads, water, recreation facilities, libraries, and solid waste collection, require major investments. As a result, almost all state and larger local governments have identifiable capital planning and budgeting processes. Many of these are closely integrated with the annual current budget planning and decision-making process, and the trend is toward greater integration.

Because of the long life of capital facilities and infrastructure, extensive use is made of long-term financing in the form of various types of bond issues. Some local governments still consider it financially prudent to borrow little or not at all, but state governments and virtually all large cities are unable to provide the services demanded by citizens without resorting to some debt financing for capital investments. Although it is generally accepted that future generations should not be saddled with unreasonable debt burdens about which they have no say, most citizens recognize that capital facilities will be enjoyed by future generations. Debt financing provides a means for those future generations to share the costs as well as the benefits.

The municipal debt market has undergone remarkable changes in the last decade. Sophisticated structured financing tools developed for private debt and equity transactions are being applied to municipal debt issues. In addition, municipalities are using increasingly sophisticated money management techniques to minimize their cost of debt and to maximize the returns on their own investments. Occasionally these techniques result in major financial disasters. As a result, the SEC, which once took a hands-off attitude toward the municipal debt market, has adopted increasingly stringent disclosure requirements, and Congress has increased the SEC's regulatory role regarding municipal debt.

Effective debt management requires that the amount of debt incurred not impose infeasible burdens on future taxpayers and that it not force future cutbacks in operation and maintenance expenditures necessary to maintain capital facilities. State governments, through constitutional provisions and statutory requirements, regulate their own borrowing as well as that of local governments. These regulations mainly focus on the commitment of the "full faith and credit" of the jurisdiction. Partly because of the restrictions imposed on general obligation bonds and partly because of the efficiency of tying repayment of debt to specific revenues generated by the investment, there has been tremendous growth in the use of a wide variety of debt instruments. Overall, however, state and local debt has grown little over the past 30 years in relation to personal income. State and local governments also have become more sophisticated in their financial analysis of capital investments and debt financing.

Notes

1. Governmental Accounting Standards Board, *Statement of Governmental Accounting Standards No. 34, Basic Financial Statements — and Management's Discussion and Analysis — for State and Local Government* (Norwalk, CT: Governmental Accounting Standards Board, 1999), 11.

2. O. Kinnander, As Infrastructure Crumbles, Engineers Scream for Investment, *The Bond Buyer* 335 (March 9, 2001): 40.

3. U.S. Congressional Budget Office, *Future Investment in Drinking Water and Wastewater Infrastructure* (Washington, DC: U.S. Government Printing Office, 2002): 8.

4. T. Arrandale, Not Wet Enough, *Governing* 14 (2000): 42–46.

5. Drinking Water Bill, *Governing* 15 (December 2001): 49.

6. M.C.H. Kelly and M. Zieper, Financing for the Future: The Economic Benefits of Parks and Open Space, *Government Finance Review* 16 (December 2000): 23–28.

7. U.S. Bureau of the Census, *Statistical Abstract of the United States: 2000* (Washington, DC: U.S. Government Printing Office, 2000): 303.

8. *Capital Improvements Program for the Period 2000–2014 Including Five Year Capital Improvements Budget for the Period 2000–2004* (Carrboro, NC: Orange Water and Sewer Authority, 2001).

9. National Council on Public Works Improvement, *Fragile Foundations: A Report on America's Public Works* (Washington, DC: U.S. Government Printing Office, 1988).

10. Congressional Budget Office, *Trends in Public Infrastructure Outlays and the President's Proposals for Infrastructure Spending in 1993* (Washington, DC: U.S. Government Printing Office, 1992), 15.

11. U.S. Office of Management and Budget, *Budget of the United States Government: Fiscal Year 2003, Analytical Perspectives* (Washington, DC: U.S. Government Printing Office, 2002), 137.

12. D. Kittower, Making the Most of Public Assets, *Governing* 14 (January 2000): 58.

13. R.W. Johnson and C.C. Barnett, *Urban Services Delivery in CEE and the NIS*, prepared for U.S. Agency for International Development Zagreb Conference on Local Government (Research Triangle Park, NC: Research Triangle Institute, 1996).

14. S. Ammar, et al., Evaluating City Financial Management Using Fuzzy Rule-Based Systems, *Public Budgeting & Finance* 21 (Winter 2001): 70–90.

15. R. Berne and R. Schramm, *The Financial Analysis of Governments* (Englewood Cliffs, NJ: Prentice-Hall, 1986); S.M. Groves and M.G. Valente, *Evaluating Financial Condition: A Handbook for Local Government*, 3rd ed. (Washington, DC: International City/County Management Association, 1994).

16. B. Townsend, Development Impact Fees: A Fair Share Formula for Success, *Public Management* 78 (April 1996): 10–15.

17. Congressional Budget Office, *How Federal Spending for Infrastructure and Other Public Investments Affects the Economy* (Washington, DC: U.S. Government Printing Office, 1992), xv; C.L. Johnson, Alternative Debt Financing Mechanisms for Economic Development, *State and Local Government Review* 28 (1996): 78–89.

18. C.J. Germain, Balance Your Project, *Government Finance Review* 16 (August 2000): 15–20.

19. S. Ammar, et al., Evaluating Capital Management: A New Approach, *Public Budgeting & Finance* 21 (Winter 2001): 47–69.

20. R. Miranda and N. Hillman, Reengineering Capital Budgeting, *Public Budgeting and Financial Management* 8 (1996): 360–383.

21. U.S. Office of Management and Budget, *Budget of the United States Government: Fiscal Year 2003, Analytical Perspectives* (Washington, DC: U.S. Government Printing Office, 2002): 137.

22. *Report of the President's Commission on Budget Concepts* (Washington, DC: U.S. Government Printing Office, 1967), 34.

23. U.S. General Accounting Office, *Budget Issues: Incorporating an Investment Component in the Federal Budget* (Washington, DC: U.S. Government Printing Office, 1993); U.S. General Accounting Office, *Budget Issues: The Role of Depreciation in Budgeting for Certain Federal Investments* (Washington, DC: U.S. Government Printing Office, 1995).

24. U.S. General Accounting Office, *Budget Issues: Budgeting for Federal Capital* (Washington, DC: U.S. Government Printing Office, 1996).

25. National Council on Public Works Improvement, *Fragile Foundations*.

26. Several of these reports are summarized in U.S. Congress, Office of Technology Assessment, *Rebuilding the Foundations: State and Local Public Works Financing & Management* (Washington, DC: U.S. Government Printing Office, 1990).

27. U.S. General Accounting Office, *Budget Structure: Providing an Investment Focus in the Federal Budget* (Washington, DC: U.S. Government Printing Office, 1995).

28. U.S. Office of Management and Budget, *Budget of the United States Government: Fiscal Year 2003, Analytical Perspectives*, 12.

29. A. Kalotay and B. Tuckman, Subsidized Borrowing and the Discount Rate: The Case of Municipal Capital Budgeting and Financial Management, *Municipal Finance Journal* 19 (Winter 1999): 38–45.

30. D. Kittower, Municipal Bonds: The Deals of the Year, *Governing* 11 (March 1997): 56.

31. The Bond Market Association, Trends in the Holdings of Municipal Securities: 1980–2001, *www.bondmarkets.com/Research/munios.shtml*; accessed August 2002.

32. U.S. Bureau of the Census, *Statistical Abstract of the United States: 2001*, 275.

33. M.R. Marlin, Did Tax Reform Kill Segmentation in the Municipal Bond Market? *Public Administration Review* 54 (1994): 387–390.

34. M.A. Miller and M.A. Glick, The Resurgence of Federalism: The Case for Tax-Exempt Bonds, *Municipal Finance Journal* 19 (Winter 1999): 46–73.

35. *South Carolina v. Baker*, 485 U.S. 505 (1988).

36. For a discussion of the history of legal actions concerning state and local tax immunity, see M.T. Wrightson, The Road to South Carolina: Intergovernmental Tax Immunity and the Constitutional Status of Federalism, *Publius* 19 (Winter 1989): 39–55.

37. D. Kittower, A Muni Market Slowdown, *Governing* 14 (November 2000): 86.

38. C. Kyle, Airport Financing: Let the Passengers Pay, *Governing* 7 (March 1994): 18–19; P. Lemov, A Groundbreaking Bond Takes Off in Little Rock, *Governing* 10 (July 1996): 51.

39. P.C. Allen, Convertible Lien Bonds for Airport Expansion Program, *Municipal Finance Journal* 20 (Summer 1999): 109–112.

40. C.L. Johnson, Tax Increment Debt Finance: An Analysis of the Mainstreaming of a Fringe Sector, *Public Budgeting & Finance* 19 (Spring 1999): 47–62.

41. M. Kreps, Ups and Downs of Municipal Bonds' Volume and Yields in the Past Century, in *The Handbook of Municipal Bonds and Public Finance*, eds. R. Lamb, J. Leigland, and S. Rappaport (New York: New York Institute of Finance, 1993), 114.

42. L. Pohle, Marketing Mini-bonds: Lessons Learned from Denver's Successful First Issuance, *Government Finance Review* 7 (June 1991): 32–34.

43. C.L. Johnson and J. Mikesell, Certificates of Participation and Capital Markets: Lessons from Brevard County and Richmond Unified School District, *Public Budgeting & Finance* 14 (Fall 1994): 41–54.

44. P. Lemov, Tobacco Bonds Draw a Market, *Governing* 14 (January 2000): 54.

45. D. Kittower, Deals of the Year, *Governing* 14 (March 2000): 68–69.

46. J. E. Petersen, The Muni E-bond Revolution, *Governing* 14 (April 2000): 67.

47. R. Morgenstern, Electronic Bidding for Municipal Bonds: Technology Innovations for Competitive Bond Sales, *Government Finance Review* 16 (February 2000): 23–26.

48. D. Kittower, Deals of the Year, 73.

49. M. Francoeur, Current Issues in Municipal Finance, *Municipal Finance Journal* 20 (Winter 2000): 55–59.

50. D. Seltzer, Recent Federal Initiatives in Transportation Finance, *Municipal Finance Journal* 20 (Winter 2000): 44–49.

51. Bloomberg Financial, Municipal Bond Investors Pay Low Spreads in Nevada, cited in *Las Vegas Review Online Edition*, January 23, 2001, *www.lvrj.com/lvrj_home/2001/Jan–23–Tue–2001/business/15271455.html*; accessed August 2002.

52. M.D. Robbins, et al., Maturity Structure and Borrowing Costs: The Implications of Level Debt Service, *Municipal Finance Journal* 21 (Fall 2000): 40–64; K.A. Kriz, Do Municipal Bond Underwriting Choices Have Implications for Other Financial Certification Decisions? *Municipal Finance Journal* 21 (Fall 2000): 1–23.

53. P. Lemov, Muni Days Are Here Again, *Governing* 15 (May 2001): 62–66.

54. W. Simonsen and W.P. Kittredge, Competitive Versus Negotiated Municipal Bond Sales: Why Issuers Choose One Method Over the Other, *Municipal Finance Journal* 19 (Summer 1998): 1–29; G.L. Stevens and R.P. Wood, Comparative Financing Costs for Competitive and Negotiated Pennsylvania School District Bonds, *Journal of Public Budgeting, Accounting & Financial Management* 9 (1998): 529–551; P. Leonard, Competitive Bidding for Municipal Bonds: New Tests of the Underwriter Search Hypothesis, *Municipal Finance Journal* 19 (Winter 1999): 18–37.

55. W. Simonsen and M.D. Robbins, Does It Make Any Difference Anymore? Competitive Versus Negotiated Municipal Bond Issuance, *Public Administration Review* 56 (1996): 57–63.

56. J.C. Joseph, *Debt Issuance and Management: A Guide for Smaller Governments* (Chicago: Government Finance Officers Association, 1994).

57. L.H. Wadler, *The Art of Structured Finance* (Chestnut Ridge, NY: Linear Press, 1995).

58. Seattle-Northwest Securities Corp., How Safe Are Municipal Bonds?, *http://www.seattlenorthwest.com/munibonds/safe.htm*; accessed July 2002.

59. *Municipal Finance Criteria* (New York: Standard & Poor's, 2000).

60. T. McNulty and J. Cohan, City, County Get Better Bond Ratings, *Post Gazette.com:PG News*, November 28, 2000, *www.post-gazette.com/regionstate/20001128bond1.asp*; accessed August 2002.

61. P. Tigue, *Purchasing Credit Enhancement: How to Decide if Bond Insurance Makes Sense* (Chicago: Government Finance Officers Association, 1994).

62. P. Maco, Market Disclosure and Related SEC Enforcement Actions, *Municipal Finance Journal* 20 (Winter 2000): 3–6.

63. L.M. Fairchild, Are Federal Disclosure Requirements Beneficial for the Municipal Bond Market?, *Municipal Finance Journal* 21 (Fall 2000): 65–82.

64. R.W. Doty, The Role of the Municipal Securities Rulemaking Board and the Central Repository for Public Securities: Dealer Regulation or Market Regulation?, *Municipal Finance Journal* 11 (1990): 7–51.

65. S.C. Sollers, Introduction: Municipal Securities Rulemaking Board Forum on Disclosure, *Municipal Finance Journal* 20 (Summer 1999): 1–5.

66. P. Lemov, A New Investment Rule Requires "Suitable" Advice, *Governing* 10 (October 1996): 57.

67. The Bond Market Association, Outstanding Level of Public and Private Debt: 1985–2002, Q1, *www.bondmarkets.com/Research/osdebt.shtml*; accessed August 2002.

68. All remaining figures in this and the following paragraph are from U.S. Bureau of the Census, *Statistical Abstract of the United States: 2001*, 268, 274.

69. Per capita debt figures in this paragraph are from U.S. Bureau of the Census, *Statistical Abstract of the United States: 2001*, 274; personal income per capita figures are from *Statistical Abstract of the United States: 2000*, 460.

70. U.S. Bureau of the Census, *Statistical Abstract of the United States: 2001*, 275.

71. S. Dickson, Civil War, Railroads, and Road Bonds: Bond Repudiations in the Days of Yore, in *The Handbook of Municipal Bonds and Public Finance*, eds. Lamb, Leigland, and Rappaport, 166–173.

72. G.W. Mitchell, Statement before the Committee on Banking, Housing and Urban Affairs, *Federal Reserve Bulletin* 61 (1975): 729–730.

73. The Bond Market Association, Municipal Bond Defaults: 1940–1994, *http://www.bond-markets.com/Research/defaults.shtml*; accessed July 2002.

74. D. Litvack and F. Rizzo, Municipal Default Risk, *Municipal Finance Journal* 21 (Summer 2000): 25–42.

75. J. Petersen, All Hail the Dowager Queen, *Governing* 14 (December 2000): 74.

76. Dickson, Civil War, Railroads, and Road Bonds: Bond Repudiations in the Days of Yore, 172; R.W. Collin, What the Law Says about Orange County: Creditors' Rights and Remedies on Municipal Default, *Municipal Finance Journal* 16 (Summer 1995): 52–89.

77. N.R. Cohen, Municipal Default Patterns: An Historical Study, *Public Budgeting & Finance* 9 (Winter 1989): 62.

78. J. Leigland and R. Lamb, *WPP$$: Who Is to Blame for the WPPSS Disaster* (Cambridge, MA: Ballinger, 1986).

79. H.D. Sitzer, The Washington Public Power Supply System: Then and Now, *Municipal Finance Journal* 14 (Winter 1994): 59–78.

80. The Bond Market Association, *Municipal Bond Defaults: 1940–1994*.

81. P. Lemov, Two Down-and-Out Localities Are Back on the Fast Track, *Governing* 9 (December 1995): 49.

82. J.I. Chapman, The Challenge of Entrepreneurship, *Municipal Finance Journal* 17 (July 1996): 16–32.

83. D.V. Denison, Did Bond Fund Investors Anticipate the Financial Crisis of Orange County?, *Municipal Finance Journal* 21 (Fall 2000): 24–39.

84. R. Berne, Governmental Accounting and Financial Reporting and the Measurement of Financial Condition, in *The Handbook of Municipal Bonds and Public Finance*, eds. Lamb, Leigland, and Rappaport, 257–315.

85. J.R. Douglas, Best Practices in Debt Management, *Government Finance Review* 16 (April 2000): 23–27.

86. R.W. Johnson, *Capital Financing for Municipal Infrastructure: Choices as Viewed by the Enterprise and the Investor* (Research Triangle Park, NC: Research Triangle Institute, 1996).

87. D.M. Lawrence, *Financing Capital Projects in North Carolina*, 2nd ed. (Chapel Hill, NC: Institute of Government, University of North Carolina, 1994).

88. M.D. Robbins and C. Dungan, Debt Diligence: How States Manage the Borrowing Function, *Public Budgeting & Finance* 21 (Summer 2001): 88–105.

89. U.S. Bureau of the Census, *Statistical Abstract of the United States: 2001*, 275.

90. J. Haupert, Using Interest Rate Swaps as Part of an Overall Financing and Investment Strategy, *Government Finance Review* 8 (April 1992): 13–15.

Chapter 13

GOVERNMENT PERSONNEL AND PENSIONS

In his classic work on government budgeting, A. E. Buck wrote, "Personnel is the most important single factor in government both from the operating and the fiscal point of view."[1] Yet, despite the importance of personnel administration to budgeting, rarely has there been any attempt to integrate the two. The literature on budgeting has been almost silent on government personnel policies and procedures, and the literature on personnel or human resources administration has been similarly silent on budgeting.

Aspects of government personnel are reviewed here in two main sections. The first section reviews the effects of personnel decisions and expenditures on the budget and discusses the structure of personnel retirement systems. The second section suggests some reasons why budgeting and personnel administration have been separate activities and discusses budget staffs, including sizes, skill mixes, and training.

Personnel Impacts and Pension Plans

Personnel Considerations in Decision Making

Importance of Personnel Expenditures. The largest portion of any government's operating budget is typically devoted to personnel. In 1998–1999, salaries and wages on average accounted for 19 percent of total government expenditures. That percentage does not include costs for employee insurance and pension benefits. Local governments spent the highest proportion (40 percent) and the federal government the lowest (7 percent), with the states being near the average (15 percent). The federal percentage is low because entitlement costs, which involve transfer payments rather than the delivery of services, are part of total expenditures.[2] The percentage of the budget spent on direct personnel services for governments in the United States is low compared with the figure for most other countries, where 60 or even 80 percent is common. In many of these countries, privatization of services and budget deficit reductions leading to layoffs are dramatically lowering these numbers.

Pay rates vary from jurisdiction to jurisdiction, but all governments try to keep salaries and wages competitive with those in the private sector. However, making such needed adjustments is often a hot political topic, since a pay increase can have a major impact on the budget. In an attempt to avoid some of the political maneuverings within Congress (which sets pay rates) and maneuverings between Congress and the White House, Congress passed the Federal Employees Pay Comparability Act of 1990.[3] The law pegs pay increases to the Employment Cost Index, calculated yearly by the Bureau of Labor Statistics. In practice, this automatic mechanism has not been used, since double-digit pay increases would often be warranted. Instead, the president typically recommends a lower pay increase figure to the Congress, and a specific pay increase is enacted. In an effort to improve comparability given that pay rates vary across the country, the federal government has moved to locality-based pay for white-collar workers so that pay depends in part on the private sector salaries in any given geographic area of the country.

Public employment has been important for welfare purposes. Awarding government jobs to the economically needy and to the politically faithful has been a widespread practice. Patronage appointments have been common at all levels of government. In patronage systems, employees are hired, promoted, and fired based in part on their political affiliations. The Supreme Court, however, has ruled that such practices in state and local governments can be used only when there is a "vital government interest" at stake.[4] On the other hand, state and local governments sometimes have residency requirements for their workers. Such requirements are based on the premises that employees who are residents are likely to be more dedicated to serving the government than nonresidents and that employee-residents will spend their earnings in the place where they reside, giving an economic boost to the local economy.

Administrators have used personnel tactics to build empires. A large staff is often regarded as a sign of success for the administrator. Moreover, when staff increases, the administrator can make claims on other resources — namely, supplies, equipment, and the like. All administrators, of course, are not would-be kings. Many attempts to increase staff result in part from sincere convictions that the additional personnel will enhance effectiveness.

Controlling Personnel Costs. Since personnel expenditures constitute a large percentage of total budgets, controlling budgets in the short and long term necessarily depends on controlling personnel costs. Presidents have from time to time frozen scheduled federal employee pay increases as a means of curtailing growth in expenditures and dampening inflationary pressures on the economy. Actions such as these raise questions about whether public employees are unfairly denied pay increases that are due them and can lead to governments having difficulty attracting needed personnel because salary and wage levels are lower than those in the private sector. During budget execution, if revenues are lower than originally projected, hiring freezes and other personnel actions may be taken to reduce outlays. Hiring freezes are difficult to maintain, because employees are needed to make government run. As a consequence, some of the anticipated financial gains from these freezes are never realized.[5]

In the longer term, governments sometimes make concerted efforts to reduce their work forces on a permanent basis. In 1994 and again in 1996, Congress legislated *buyout* programs, which authorized agencies to grant incentives for their workers to retire early, as a means of reducing the size of the bureaucracy and cutting personnel costs.[6] In 2000, Congress provided a buyout program for the Treasury Department and explicitly stated that the positions vacated by employees would then be eliminated.[7] Periodic agency *reductions in force* have become more common in the federal government and in other governments, just as *downsizing* has become common in the private sector.

The Federal Activities and Inventory Reform (FAIR) Act of 1998 requires the executive to supply to Congress "annual lists of government activities not inherently governmental in nature."[8] An underlying assumption is that the activities and the related government jobs can be ousourced (see Chapter 10).

The events of September 11, 2001, greatly altered the dynamics of job-cutting in government. The terrorist attacks on the Pentagon and the World Trade Center made apparent the need for increased security in all aspects of government. A new Transportation Security Administration was created in the Transportation Department and then was moved to the new Homeland Security Department. Airport security jobs, which had been under private contract with the airlines, were converted to federal jobs. The situation created pressure against eliminating any jobs that were in the slightest way related to security and for establishing new security-related jobs, whether they be in law enforcement or in other areas, such as protecting the nation's water and food supplies.

Some personnel costs for state and local governments cannot be controlled because of stipulations of the Fair Labor Standards Act (FLSA), which was originally adopted in 1938 and in more recent times extended to state and local governments.[9] The law provides for minimum wage standards and overtime pay for more than 40 hours being worked in a week. Employees are exempt from these standards if they are salaried *and* their duties are of a nonproduction nature; conversely, employees are entitled to FLSA protection if either of these factors does not apply. During the 1990s, many court battles were fought by workers demanding backpay for overtime worked. The presumption had been that higher-paid workers were automatically excluded from FLSA protection, but through a variety of means, workers being paid even $100,000 have been able to gain coverage and win backpay awards.[10] One view is that the mandates in the FLSA impose unrealistic financial burdens on state and local governments (see the discussion of unfunded mandates in Chapter 14).

In the early 2000s, the applicability of the FLSA to state government was called into question. Namely, some wondered whether the Congress had the right to impose such legislation on the states. This issue is discussed below in regard to equal employment opportunity.

Budget Documents. Given the magnitude of personnel expenditures, the use of employment for patronage purposes, and tendencies toward empire building on the part of agencies, it becomes obvious why budgeting decisions often have focused on personnel practices. Budgets of many years ago indicated the names of individuals and their earnings. The purpose was to guarantee that individuals did not receive exorbitant salaries.

Today the practice of naming employees in the budget is far less common, although information on the wages and salaries of individual employees is available to the public for most government employees. Newspapers often report the salaries of the highest-paid state university employees, for example, and employees of nonprofit agencies sometimes receive the same attention. In contemporary budgets, salaries of heads of agencies are often reported in budgets, but itemized earnings of lower-ranked employees are not. Still, budgets usually at least report personnel expenditures by agency or bureau within them and may provide considerable detail, such as by class of worker (trades, clerical, administrative, professional, and technical) and type of pay (wages, salaries, holiday pay, overtime pay, shift differential pay, and callback pay).

Figure 13–1, drawn from the City of Los Angeles budget, illustrates one method for presenting personnel information. The number of positions in the police department, all other departments, and the total for the city are shown in graphic form for a multiyear period. Other governments report firefighter and police positions as distinguished from civilian personnel. Some governments, including the federal government, report *full-time equivalent* (FTE) personnel rather than simply the number of positions.

Figure 13–1 Authorized City Staff, City of Los Angeles, 1992–2003

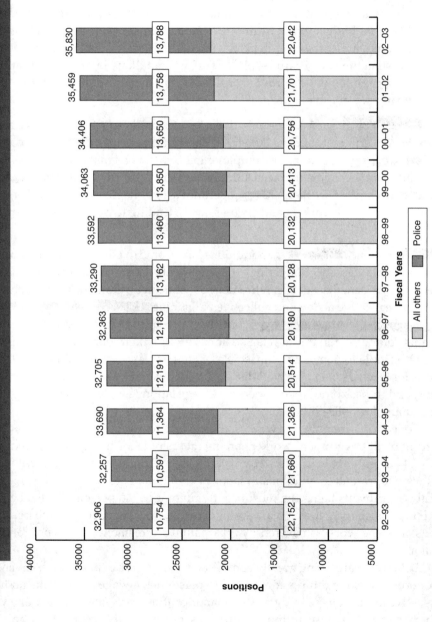

Source: City of Los Angeles, *Budget for Fiscal Year 2002–03* (City of Los Angeles, California, 2002).

Personnel Complement Control. Sometimes personnel tables are included in budgets only for informational purposes — that is, to provide the legislative body and the general public with information about the size of the personnel complement of agencies. In other cases, these displays exist for decision-making purposes. An agency may not be permitted to hire a new staff member, even though funds are available in its budget, without first receiving authorization for a new position. Budget offices and personnel departments often exercise such complement control, and sometimes legislatures place specific limitations in appropriation bills. Exercising complement control is considered one method of limiting growth in the bureaucracy and the budget.

Costs Created by Personnel. Not only does paying employees lead to considerable costs for government, but the actions of employees also can generate unwanted additional costs. Discriminatory employment practices by managers and coworkers can result in major financial burdens when a court awards compensatory damages to injured workers. Torts, especially acts of negligence by workers, can result in harm to coworkers and citizens, again leading to major financial awards (see Chapter 10).

Labor–Management Relations. Labor unions have come to play an important role in personnel matters and budgeting.[11] Governments set salary and wage levels as well as other benefits, such as retirement benefits, in a variety of ways, including through legislative action and collective bargaining. Unions obviously are deeply involved in collective bargaining, but they also influence the process of determining compensation through legislation. Through their lobbying efforts, unions have been able to persuade state legislators to pass laws setting minimum salary levels for teachers in local school districts, to impose standards for retirement systems, and to pass other related personnel legislation (e.g., laws mandating regular training for police officers).

Collective bargaining is well established in many governments. Nearly 40 percent of all government workers are members of labor unions, compared with only 14 percent in the private sector.[12] As of 2001, 42 percent of government workers were represented by unions in labor negotiations with their employers, with local governments being the most heavily unionized (48 percent).[13] Membership in unions is slightly lower than the number of workers covered by bargaining units, as some workers covered by a bargaining agreement choose not to join a union.

Collective bargaining greatly complicates the process of budgeting. Given the proportion of expenditures committed to personnel, a wage settlement can have a massive impact on the budget. Many labor contracts are valid for only one year, which means that year-round negotiations are likely to occur. This approach creates great uncertainty over what personnel costs will be for the budget that is being prepared.

Bargaining Units. The number of bargaining units and unions further complicates the situation. Employees bargain as a unit that is said to have a *community of interests*; one such unit might be clerical workers in a city government. Determination of the bargaining unit is made by an independent agency, such as a state labor relations board for both state and local governments within the state. In the case of the federal government, the Federal Labor Relations Authority makes this determination, except for postal workers, who are under the authority of the National Labor Relations Board. Those responsible for budgeting, then, have no control over the number of bargaining units and the number of unions that will be involved in negotiations. Thousands of bargaining units exist at all three levels of government, with some units having hundreds or thousands of workers and others only a handful.

Work stoppages or strikes have major budgetary implications as well as service implications. If workers go on strike, salary savings may occur, but backlogs in work may develop, later forcing payment of overtime. Federal workers are generally prohibited from striking, and the Federal Service Impasses Panel resolves impasses in negotiations between management and labor.[14] Where strikes do occur, the effects can be massive.

Bargaining's Impact on Personnel Costs. Although collective bargaining greatly influences the budgeting process, there is conflicting evidence on whether it leads to higher personnel costs and higher total spending. A major difference exists between labor relations at the federal level and at the state and local levels. Workers at the federal level may not bargain over salaries and wages, but those at the state and local levels may bargain over these critical aspects of employment. The economic "health" of a jurisdiction will affect its ability to grant wage and salary increases to workers, irrespective of whether the workers may bargain over these items. During recessions, wage increases at the state and local levels are routinely kept to a minimum largely because of tight budgets, regardless of worker unionization. However, political activity on the part of organized police officers, for instance, may protect jobs, result in hiring more police officers, and lead to gains in nonwage benefits (hours of work, uniform allowance, and the like), but may not necessarily result in higher pay than in locales without unions.

Further complicating matters are budget restrictions, such as tax and spending limitations, that prevent local governments from raising taxes (see Chapter 4). Unions often work actively to defeat such proposals on election ballots.

Another factor in wage determination is the spillover of decisions within a community and from one community to others. If unionized police in a city win wage increases, clerical workers in the same city are likely to benefit even if they are not unionized. Similarly, if a union is successful in bargaining for increases in compensation in one city, other cities may respond by granting increases to their workers so as to remain competitive in recruiting and retaining employees and in some cases possibly to avert unionization.

Labor Negotiations. To bargain for compensation increases, union leaders have had to learn about budgeting. Without a thorough understanding of a jurisdiction's budget, unions can be persuaded by management that funds simply do not exist to grant increases. The job of the union is to "find" budget surpluses that can be used to increase employee compensation. Some national unions help their state and local affiliates to analyze their governments' budgets.

Since the mid-1970s, important changes have occurred in the nature of bargaining between unions and management. In the early years of public sector collective bargaining, one of labor's main arguments was that salaries and wages in the public sector needed to be increased to match those in the private sector. While that argument is still used, negotiations have come to focus more on the productivity of workers. In some jurisdictions, wage increases have been dependent on measurable improvements in worker productivity. According to the concept of productivity bargaining, workers are entitled to benefit from the financial savings accruing from greater productivity.

Another change in bargaining has been management demands for concessions. As budgets have become tighter, some jurisdictions have demanded that workers take pay reductions. In other cases, agreements have been developed for hiring new workers at pay rates lower than current ones; this has occurred in the Postal Service, for example. Some negotiations have concentrated on job security — protecting workers from layoffs. While these types of negotiations are not nearly as common in government as in the private sector, the point is that collective negotiations in the public sector are no longer restricted to demands for greater pay and benefits.

Strong labor unions sometimes serve as the interpreters and enforcers of professional standards. In South Africa, the teachers' union has a powerful say in the policy process in reforming curricula, classroom instructional techniques, and classroom management practices.

The movement toward outsourcing of government services may have an unintended consequence in regard to labor relations. While many states have no policy on public sector labor relations, other than to ban strikes by public workers, most private sector workers may organize, bargain for wages, and strike. Shifts toward privatization, then, allow for more activity on the part of unions.

On the other hand, labor unions may oppose outsourcing, assuming that well-paying government jobs will be lost to lower-paying private sector companies that are non-unionized. The strength of labor unions may be great enough in some cases to prevent outsourcing of some services.

Future of the Labor Movement. What the future holds for public sector unionism, collective bargaining, and its impact on budgeting and finance is uncertain. On the one hand, unions usually win representational elections of workers; in other words, if unions are successful in having an election held, they usually win.[15] On the other hand, the labor movement may face an extremely hostile environment in many locales, a factor that can result in bargaining stalemates, strikes, and general unrest that contribute to an atmosphere of uncertainty in terms of budgeting. The George W. Bush administration, for example, has been seen as hostile to the labor movement. In the administration's first year, it scrapped labor–management partnerships created during the Clinton administration; urged Congress to enact Freedom to Manage legislation, which would give managers greater power in hiring and firing workers; and announced a goal of moving many jobs listed under FAIR from the public sector to the private sector.

Equal Employment Opportunity. A host of equal employment opportunity (EEO) laws apply to most employers — private and public — in the United States. The laws are too numerous to discuss in detail here but include protections from discrimination based on age, race, ethnicity, national origin, sex, and disability. Administrative regulations further back up protections for workers.[16] Despite these legal provisions, many of which have been on the books for decades, discrimination persists in some governmental agencies. Congress passed the Notification and Federal Employee Antidiscrimination and Retaliation Act of 2002, in response to a perceived need to thwart agencies in retaliating against workers who complained of discrimination and to make the agencies themselves pay for any financial settlements handed down by the courts.[17]

Equal employment opportunity is of importance to budgeting in at least two ways. One is the cost of defending the government in court when employees file suit and of paying any court settlements. The other is the uncertain status of this legislation as it pertains to state governments. The Eleventh Amendment to the Constitution says that state governments may not be sued in federal court, but the Fourteenth Amendment allows Congress to abrogate state government immunity in impementing laws that protect from states abridging the "privileges or immunities of citizens." Using this latter power, Congress has extended EEO laws to state governments.

The Supreme Court has reversed the Congress on two key laws, the Age Discrimination in Employment Act of 1967 and the Americans with Disabilities Act of 1990. The court has held that Congress did not have sufficient evidence that the states had discriminated against older workers and people with disabilities for the states' immunity to be erased.[18] The decisions have been viewed favorably by the states, because they now can handle these problems in state courts where financial settlements, if any, will be much smaller than in federal court. The decisions also left observers wondering whether the court will knock down other laws as they apply to the states. The assumption is that race discrimination will withstand any court test, but sex discrimination is another matter.[19] Also in question is the applicability of the Fair Labor Standards Act to the states.[20]

One other matter related to equal employment opportunity that causes considerable confusion in the personnel budgeting arena is the issue of *comparable worth* or *pay equity*. Simply stated, the concept of comparable worth maintains that workers should receive compensation according to their contribution to an organization. Where a problem arises is that many occupations in government that are held by women, although they require sophisticated skills, tend to be low-paying (clerical secretaries, librarians, nurses, and teachers). Demands are made that compensation levels be greatly increased for such occupations to avoid situations in which lawn maintenance personnel or garbage truck drivers receive substantially more than secretaries, who are expected to master sophisticated office equipment and a variety of computer software programs. Labor unions often are torn on this issue. On the one hand, they want to be strong advocates for comparable worth; on the other hand, they do not want to lose the support of workers in other occupations.[21]

Work Force Planning. Given the immense importance of personnel in the conduct of government's business and in the impact on the budget, work force planning seems like a natural activity to undertake. Such has not been the case, however. The General Accounting Office has said that agencies pay little attention to human capital management and has placed the topic on its list of high risks.[22] One of the chief concerns is preparing for massive retirements with the aging of the post–World War II baby boomers. This turnover may either pose a threat to managing the government or represent an opportunity to bring about needed restructuring.

In 2001, the Bush administration released *The President's Management Agenda*, in which five government-wide initiatives were identified.[23] One initiative was "strategic management of human capital." The report called for linking strategic work force planning with organizational missions. That same year, the Office of Management and Budget announced that agencies were to engage in work force planning with an eye toward restructuring. The administration wanted to "flatten" the bureaucracy by eliminating what was perceived as excessive layering of responsibilities.[24] The annual budget document, *Analytical Perspectives*, has shown the standards for success that agencies are expected to meet in improving their management of human capital.

Employee Benefits and Pension Plans

Both personnel administrators and budgeters view personnel expenses in terms of total compensation, which consists of salaries and wages plus employee benefits. Given scarce resources, increasing benefits in any given year may preclude raising wage and salary rates. Employee benefits include paid holidays, vacations, unemployment insurance, workers' compensation for injuries on the job, and Social Security retirement; they may also include child care, legal assistance, and employee assistance programs that deal with such problems as alcohol and drug addiction. Government contributions to Social Security and payments for laid-off workers have real price tags attached to them, but governments have come to recognize that other benefits such as paid holidays, vacations, and free parking are expensive, too.[25] Two benefits that are particularly expensive are health care and government-sponsored pension plans. Of concern to budgeters is the possibility that if the costs of these benefits are not controlled, the budget itself can get out of control. Decision makers may find themselves each year growing more concerned with how to cover the rising costs of employee benefits than with how to deal with policy issues. As of the early 2000s, federal benefits owed retirees and veterans were greater than the national debt.[26]

Health Care. No employer is immune from rapidly rising health care costs, including government employers, and as a result governments have sought alternative means of providing the health care that workers need at a cost that governments can afford.[27] Governments are turning to managed care programs, which provide employees with a package of health services at predetermined costs. *Health maintenance organizations* (HMOs) have become popular because they provide services to employees at a set fee. Some governments allow employees to choose among HMOs.

Governments to some extent have attempted to curtail their costs in this area by hiring temporary workers who are not entitled to health care benefits.[28] The practice, of course, is common in the private sector.

In an effort to curtail rising health care costs, some insurers are now offering *defined contribution plans* or *consumer-driven health benefits*. Under these plans, employees have some discretion in the health care they use up to some specified dollar amount. After that amount is reached, a more traditional form of insurance takes effect in which there is a deductible and then the insurance company pays most, but not all, of the health costs.

In other cases, experiments are under way with *medical savings accounts* (MSAs). These accounts, often compared with individual retirement accounts, become the repository of tax-free contributions by both employers and employees and are used to pay employee health care expenses. Unused monies are rolled forward from one year to the next. The merits of the MSAs are being hotly debated, especially regarding whether they should be made available to most workers. Proponents reason that the accounts are an effective means of reducing health care costs. Opponents contend that they are most likely to be used by better-paid employees, leaving lower-paid employees with insufficient funding for their health care needs.

More generally, employers are moving toward *cafeteria plans*, which allow employees to select the types of coverage they wish. Employees are given options and may choose to use some of their salaries and wages toward the purchase of additional benefits. For instance, federal tax laws permit the establishment of tax-free *dependent care accounts* and *medical expense reimbursement accounts*. In the latter case, an employee decides prior to the beginning of the calendar year how much to contribute each pay period to such an account and then the money can be used to pay medical expenses not covered by the employer's health plan. The monies in these accounts must be used during the year in which they are collected.

Structure of Retirement Systems. The most expensive part of an employee benefits package in a government consists of *public employee retirement systems* (PERSs). There are approximately 200 state-administered plans, some of which include local government employees as well as state employees, and about 2,000 locally administered plans.[29] In addition, there are thousands of other small plans involving annuity policies with private insurance carriers. The federal government has several plans, the main one being the Federal Employees Retirement System (FERS) for persons hired on or after January 1, 1984. Employees hired before that date may opt for FERS or remain in the Civil Service Retirement System (CSRS); most have chosen to continue with CSRS coverage.[30]

Retirement systems — both public sector and private sector — must comply with federal laws. The Employee Retirement Income Security Act (ERISA) of 1974 governs private sector plans.[31] Sections 415 and 457 of the Internal Revenue Code exert major controls over public retirement systems. In 1996, Congress amended these provisions to allow greater flexibility on the part of state and local systems in complying with federal law.[32]

Retirement systems generally are based on an assumption that a person will use a variety of measures to cover living expenses during retirement besides pension checks. First, living expenses may decline as the individual becomes less active and has fewer demands on income, such as support for dependents. Second, savings are used to cover expenses. Third, many government workers are covered by Old-Age and Survivors Insurance, disability insurance, and health insurance (Medicare) of the Social Security Administration. Members of FERS are required to participate in Social Security, while federal employees who belong to

CSRS do not participate. In FERS, workers may pay a percentage of their earnings into a tax-deferred plan, and the government matches part of the amount. These matching retirement accounts, 457 plans, are similar to private 401K plans, referring to that section of the Internal Revenue Code that covers employer–employee matching tax-deferred plans. Some state and local governments have initiated similar programs.

Contributions into Social Security constitute one area of government budgets that are uncontrollable. State and local governments once had the option of joining and withdrawing from Social Security; governments withdrew when their calculations indicated greater returns could be made on their own investments than Social Security paid in benefits. In the 1980s, however, Congress passed legislation barring withdrawal from Social Security, and the Supreme Court upheld the law.[33] About three-fourths of state and local employees participate in Social Security.[34] Additional legislation has required participation in Medicare, and when employees are not covered by an approved public retirement system, they must participate in Social Security. The result is that state and local governments must budget each year for increased Social Security and Medicare costs regardless of their budget situations. Monies paid on behalf of employees are known as Federal Insurance Contributions Act (FICA) taxes.[35]

Defined Benefit and Defined Contribution Plans. Pension systems in the public sector historically have used *defined benefit plans*, in which benefits normally are determined according to some combination of years of services, wages or salaries (for example, average salary of the last three years of service), and age at time of retirement. The longer one has worked for a government and the higher one's salary, the higher pension benefits will be. Most state and local government retirement systems use the defined benefit plan.

In addition to initial retirement benefits, *cost-of-living allowances* (COLAs) are usually assigned to pensioners, in some cases on an automatic basis according to an economic barometer, such as the consumer price index, and in other cases on an ad hoc basis. In the latter instance, a government might decide one year to increase retirement benefits by the same percentage as salary increases being awarded current employees. Other benefits are provided for disability retirement (for people who retire early because of poor health) and for survivors' benefits (covering family members who continue to live after the death of retirees). The vast majority of benefits paid each year go to elderly retirees, with the remainder divided between disability retirees and survivors.

Defined benefit plans coupled with cost-of-living allowances provide income security to employees and retirees and place investment risks on employers. Since benefits are determined in advance of retirement, employers must take steps necessary to ensure that sufficient funds will be available when employees retire. Cost accounting standards require that private sector companies "fund" the future liabilities created by these defined benefit programs. If projected earnings from investments of a company's pension fund are less than projected payouts, then the company must take an accounting adjustment, generally a writedown of profits, to cover the projected difference.

In an effort to curtail personnel costs, many governments periodically use incentive programs to persuade employees to retire early. The positions vacated may not be filled or can be filled with less experienced workers at lower salary and wage rates. The incentive offered in such programs is higher retirement benefits than otherwise would be provided. These incentive programs need to be structured carefully in defined benefit plans because they could result in a drain on the resources of the retirement fund.[36]

An alternative to defined benefits is the *defined contribution plan*. Under this plan, benefits are not defined in advance of retirement, but rather the employer commits to contributing regularly to an employee's retirement account (usually a percentage of compensation). The benefits received at the time of retirement are a function of the employer's and employee's contributions plus investment earnings on these contributions. While public employers use primarily defined benefit plans, most private employers use defined contribution plans. A key advantage of a defined contribution plan for an employer is its predictability; all that need be done each year is to set aside a percentage of salaries and wages for depositing into retirement accounts.

Funding. Pension plans are funded by a combination of contributions from government and employees and investment earnings on those contributions. In some cases, the retirement program is financed exclusively by government, but that practice is an exception to the rule. In 1999–2000, earnings constituted 78 percent of receipts for state and local retirement systems. Government contributions accounted for another 14 percent, and employee contributions accounted for the remaining 8 percent.[37] The federal government permits state and local employees to make some contributions to their retirement plans on a tax-deferred basis; individuals pay taxes on the income later when they receive pension checks and are presumably in a lower tax bracket.

There are basically two methods of financing retirement programs: *pay-as-you-go* and *advance funding*. With the pay-as-you-go method, all that is required in any one budget year is to raise sufficient revenue to cover retirement benefit checks. This method is generally discouraged because it allows for the accumulation of debt. Persons in the future will be owed benefits, and taxpayers at that time will be forced to meet those costs. Social Security operates on a pay-as-you-go basis.

The preferred method is advance funding, in which monies are accumulated for workers while they are working and those monies generate income through investments while workers are on the payroll and during retirement as well. If using this method, a retirement system must invest prudently but effectively to avoid any *unfunded actuarial accrued liability* so that the system is "actuarially sound." Advance funding uses the concept of *present value*. That is, future receipts, particularly contributions and investment earnings, are compared with anticipated costs (benefits) in terms of current dollars. The concept is analogous to the discount rate used in program analysis (see Chapter 7). Several methods are used in calculating actuarial assets and liabilities.

Investments. Since most of the money contributed to retirement funds will not be needed for years to come, the money is invested. State and local governments kept only 6 percent of their investment funds in cash, demand deposits, and short-term investments in 1999–2000. The rest of their monies were in longer-term investments. The largest single category was corporate stocks (36 percent), with corporate bonds also being important (16 percent). Some 12 percent of the funds were in U.S. Treasury and other federal securities. The remainder of the monies were invested in a variety of instruments.[38]

With so many of these funds being invested in corporate stocks, returns are dependent on the business cycle and the volatility of the stock market. One survey of retirement systems found that "the average annual rate of return fell from 15.04 percent in 1998 to 6.52 percent in 2000."[39] The precipitious decline was explained by the recession that began in 2000. This same survey noted a trend toward investing in international equities, resulting in the funds being more subject to international financial and other events than previously. The financial collapse of Enron in 2002 not only had a devastating effect on its workers' pensions since that fund was heavily committed to Enron stock but also had a negative effect on numerous private and public pension funds that had invested in the company.

Although retirement fund administrators have focused primarily on increasing the rate of return on investments while not becoming overly speculative, a new objective has emerged — to use pension funds to advance social and economic goals. For instance, a pension plan that invests in local economic development projects not only earns retirement benefits for employees but furthers the economic vitality of the community. However, a pension fund may be forced to choose between investing in a local project at one rate of return or investing in opportunities outside of the community at higher rates of return. Additionally, the local investment may entail greater risk than other opportunities, with the pensioners' future benefits possibly being put in jeopardy.

Clearly, a careful strategy for investment must be developed.[40] Priorities must be established in terms of what objectives are being sought. Some degree of balance must be achieved between risk-free investments, such as U.S. Treasury instruments, and higher-risk investments, such as corporate stocks. Investment advisers need to be chosen after thorough checks of their credentials, and fund managers need to have controls on them so that they do not make haphazard investment decisions or make personal gains through kickbacks on investments.

Liabilities. Until the 1970s, many public retirement systems were woefully underfunded. Over the years, governments had made pension plan commitments to employees but had failed to follow through by contributing sufficient funds to the plans. Today, most funds are actuarially sound.[41] For those governments that do have underfunded pension plans, serious problems loom. Meeting current operating needs and covering the costs of retiree benefits can easily put a budget out of balance and force a tax increase. Where jurisdictions are at their legal or political limits on tax rates, severe program cuts may be the only alternative. Pension fund liabilities can increase the cost of doing business, as interest rates may be higher for jurisdictions that have large outstanding pension debts.

Several options are available for improving the funding situation of retirement systems:

- An obvious option is to increase government and employee contributions.

- A jurisdiction can take advantage of economies of scale by combining systems; this technique may reduce administrative costs and make possible more lucrative investments.

- Retirement systems can pool their funds for investment purposes.

- A jurisdiction can make investments that are riskier but also have higher rates of return. The stock market crash of 1987 and the Orange County, California, bankruptcy of 1994 (see Chapters 10 and 12), however, are sobering reminders of the loss that can result from nonguaranteed investments. Models are available that suggest how to balance high returns with acceptable levels of risk.

- Some jurisdictions have sold bonds to obtain the funds needed to cover retirement liabilities.

- A pension system can have its creditworthiness rated in terms of the system's ability to meet its financial obligations. This rating then can be used to back other entities for fees, consequently increasing the revenue for the pension system.

Accounting and Reporting. Three statements and a technical bulletin issued by the Governmental Accounting Standards Board are the governing documents for accounting and reporting of public pension systems:

- Statement No. 25, Financial Reporting for Defined Benefit Pension Plans and Note Disclosures for Defined Contribution Plans
- Statement No. 26, Financial Reporting for Postemployment Healthcare Plans Administered by Defined Benefit Pension Plans
- Statement No. 27, Accounting for Pensions by State and Local Governmental Employers
- Technical Bulletin 96-1, Pension Disclosure Requirements for Employers

Overall, these documents require an annual reporting of assets, changes in assets from year to year, and actuarial information on the long-term prospects of pension funds. Statement No. 26 covers health care plans for retirees.

Personnel Operations

Personnel Administration and Budgeting

Because decisions related to personnel have major effects on budgeting, some linkage between budgeting and personnel administration is needed. However, just as constant tensions exist between budget offices and line agencies, so do tensions persist between the budget and personnel offices.

Historical Differences. A fundamental problem is that budgeting and personnel administration stem from different origins. As has been seen in earlier chapters, budgeting arose to provide information to executive and legislative decision makers. Central budget offices are intended to aid the chief executive, an elected politician. Budgeting is frankly political. Personnel administration, on the other hand, is a product of a reform movement designed to minimize political considerations and base personnel actions — appointments, promotions, and the like — on what employees know and do on the job rather than on whom they know. Personnel administration is expected to be apolitical. Some early reformists in budgeting may have sought to make budgeting less political but not to make it apolitical.

Not only do budgeting and personnel differ in their historical roots, but they also differ with regard to organizational structures. Since passage of the Pendleton Act of 1883, which established a merit system of employment in the federal government, the personnel function at all levels of government has tended to be organizationally beyond the control of political executives.[42] The justification for independent civil service commissions has been that they insulate personnel matters from the caprices of politics.[43]

A point of controversy is whether these independent commissions have outlived their usefulness and should be abandoned. Commissions are often seen as having negative influences and rarely as being innovative and supportive of improvements in managerial practices.

Reforms. At the federal level, reforms were instituted in 1978 with passage of the Civil Service Reform Act.[44] The Civil Service Commission was dissolved, and the Office of Personnel Management and the Merit Systems Protection Board took its place. The Office of Personnel Management, which reports directly to the president, is expected to take personnel actions conducive to implementing the policies of the political leadership. The Merit Systems Protection Board, in effect, is a watchdog guarding against political influences that might affect hiring, firing, and other personnel actions. State and local governments have shown reluctance to adopt the federal model, but some jurisdictions have created their own models of reform.[45] The Homeland Security Act of 2002 included important reforms that had been championed by President Bush.[46] The law instructed the new Homeland Security Department to develop a "flexible" and "contemporary" human resources management system but one that did not waive or modify such merit concepts as hiring, promoting, and firing people based on their competence and not their political connections or lack thereof.

The new law included within it the Chief Human Capital Officers Act of 2002 (Title XIII). That law required each federal agency to designate a human capital officer. The officers sit as a council chaired by the director of the Office of Personnel Management. Human capital strategic planning is required to be included in agency performance plans and program performance reports, thereby linking human capital with other critical resources (see Chapter 5). The law allows managers to use incentive schemes to encourage specific employees to retire or resign their jobs. This provision was justified as a means of eliminating dead wood but criticized as possibly opening the door to political influences on personnel decisions. The National Commission on the Public Service (Volcker Commission) recommended in 2003 that federal agencies develop "more flexible personnel management systems."[47]

Even when the central personnel agency reports to the chief executive, tensions persist between the agency and the budget office. The two may disagree on how to handle situations where their jurisdictions intersect. Budget and personnel offices are linked with each other on such matters as reclassification of jobs, complement control, collective bargaining, reductions in force (in which employees are laid off, usually for financial reasons), outsourcing, and efforts to "reinvent" government (see Chapter 5).

Personnel in Budgeting

It takes people to operate budgeting systems — people at the central location of a budget office, in line agencies, and in the legislative body. While only some personnel are assigned full time to budget matters, all personnel are inevitably involved with budgeting and budget decisions. In this section, we discuss the size and skill mix of budget staffs.

Census data provide some overall perspective on the number of government employees engaged in budgeting and finance. There were about 137,000 federal employees in financial administration in 2000, or 5 percent of total federal employment. State and local employment in financial administration was equal to about 372,000 full-time equivalent employees, or 2 percent of total employment.[48]

Federal Staff. At the federal level, both the executive and the legislative branches have sizable staffs. The Office of Management and Budget has a staff of about 490, and each department has personnel whose main function is budgeting. Congress has the Congressional Budget Office (230 employees), staffs for standing committees, staffs for each representative and senator, the General Accounting Office (3,100 employees), and the Library of Congress (4,300 employees, including the Congressional Research Service). Staffs exist for the House and Senate Budget Committees, the House Ways and Means Committee, the Senate Finance Committee, and the House and Senate Appropriations Committees. Not all of these staff members routinely work on budgeting, such as the staff of the Congressional Research Service, but these employees can be called upon as needed by congressional committees and individual members of Congress.

Altogether Congress has about 30,000 employees. Most of the people who work for Congress do not work on budgeting, such as employees of the U.S. Government Printing Office (3,000 employees) and the Architect of the Capitol, but many are assigned to work on budgeting and substantive matters with budgetary implications.[49]

State Staff. The sizes of state budget staffs vary greatly. New York has about 280 professional staff members, while California has about 130 and Virginia about 60. Other states with more than 40 professional budget office staff members include Georgia, Illinois, and New Jersey. On the other hand, many states have fewer than 10.[50] Professional fiscal staffs are to be found in virtually all state legislatures, but, as would be expected, there is great variation.

Detailed information is unavailable on the professional staffs working in municipal budget offices and for city councils and other local legislative bodies. Local staffs generally are small, and local legislative bodies — city councils, school boards, and the like — often have to rely mainly on executive branch staff for budget information and analysis.

The question of how many budget staff members are needed on either the executive or the legislative side of government depends on what the budget units are expected to do. Small staffs handling multimillion- or multibillion-dollar budgets obviously can be expected to do little more than superficially review materials prepared by agencies and perhaps devote in-depth effort to selected "hot" issues.

Skill Mix. Budget offices vary in the purposes that are pursued and the activities undertaken, both of which affect the mix of required skills. A budget office whose main purpose is to hold agencies accountable for spending in accordance with appropriations may prefer persons with business skills and accounting training. At the federal level and to a lesser extent at the state level, skills in public finance may be important for developing policies for economic growth. Still other skills may be sought by budget units engaged in policy and program analysis.

Budget office staffs at the state level have been increasing in their professionalism, especially in the last 10 to 20 years. Today, few offices hire people with less than a baccalaureate degree, except for clerical workers and technicians. Many state budget offices routinely hire persons with master's and doctoral degrees.

The typical state budget office staff now has a blend of educational backgrounds. Both business and the social sciences are represented along with other professional disciplines, including engineering, law, education, and labor relations. Indeed, categorization of staff has become difficult in that a staff member often has a baccalaureate degree in one field and one or two master's degrees in other fields.

A 2000 survey of state budget directors provided information about the people in these jobs. The mean age was 50 years, three-fourths were men, and almost all directors were white. All were college graduates, and more than half held a master's degree or a law degree. One-fourth reported holding one or more certifications. Half said they had held a political position prior to becoming budget director. The directors said that during the budget preparation period they spent 30 percent of their time with their staffs and 24 percent of their time with the governor and the governor's staff. During the legislative session, time spent with the budget staff dropped to 20 percent, time with the governor and staff was 21 percent, and time with the legislature rose from 4 percent during budget preparation to 19 percent during the legislative session. The directors were positive about their work, thought their prior education and work experience gave them the proper grounding for the job, and would choose to be director again if they had the chance to choose again.[51]

Whether the composition of the staff or the characteristics of the budget director have any bearing on the way a state budget system operates is unclear. Certainly, a staff cannot do something for which it is not trained and budget directors cannot use materials prepared by staffs for which the directors have not been trained. Only those trained in program analysis would be expected to be able to conduct such an analysis or understand the analysis prepared by the staff. On the other hand, it is possible that budget offices might recruit program analysts and not use their talents. The available evidence suggests that the use of effectiveness analysis in decision making is not significantly greater in social science–oriented budget units than in business-oriented units.[52]

Training. Aside from recruiting personnel with new talents, existing personnel can be upgraded through training programs. Budget offices routinely invest in training their staff either as a whole or selectively (e.g., by sending a few employees to special courses each year). The federal Chief Financial Officers Council has established a human capital committee, which is concerned with improving the recruitment, retention, and training of financial personnel. The committee has identified specific core competencies for several budget and finance jobs, including budget analysts, financial managers, accountants, and financial management for information technology personnel.[53]

Each year the Government Finance Officers Association (GFOA) and The National Association of State Budget Officers (NASBO) offer several training courses, and professional associations hold conferences and various meetings that can help budgeting and finance people keep abreast of changes. The Association for Budgeting and Financial Management, for example, holds an annual conference that covers both budgeting and financial management subjects and that gives attention to all levels of government plus the nonprofit sector. Financial management training is available through numerous private vendors as well. In addition to skills training, financial management employees need training in ethics, conflict-of-interest laws, and the like. With today's technology, some training is computer-based.[54]

Training often focuses on technical skills but other skills are important as well. For example, legislative staff not only need technical skills, but may also be called upon to make recommendations in budget hearings, be a facilitator for the committee chairs they serve, and work with the party caucus.[55]

The effectiveness of training depends in part on whether employees are given the opportunity to use their newly developed knowledge and skills. Training an employee in a budget technique that is not used by the jurisdiction has only a limited benefit. Conversely, training can be an effective way for a budget office to acquire the type of talent needed for its mission.

Certification. The budgeting and finance field has operated on a market basis, with each employer determining independently whether job candidates have the requisite skills, knowledge, and ability needed for any particular job. An emerging question is the extent to which certification programs should be used to help ensure that qualified individuals are hired. The Association of Government

Accountants has a system for issuing certificates in government financial management (CGFM), and the Government Finance Officers Association offers a Certified Public Finance Officer (CPFO) program. The latter consists of comprehensive examinations in five areas:

1. Governmental accounting, auditing, and financial reporting

2. Cash management and investments

3. Debt management

4. Operating and capital budgeting

5. Pension and benefits, risk management, and procurement[56]

The examinations are available only to Government Finance Officers Association members who have baccalaureate degrees from accredited institutions and have three years of government experience within the previous 10 years.

The Human Element. One should always be mindful that professionals in budgeting and finance are people and deserve to be treated accordingly. This book covers numerous changes under way that must be implemented by a relatively small cadre of professional workers. Changes in how work is performed and increases in the amount of work to be performed can have a telling effect on employees. For example, the Internal Revenue Service has encountered substantial problems in redeploying workers who have been displaced by redesigning of work, including the introduction of new technology. The agency's Ten Deadly Sins, while well intended, have had a down side to them. The sins provide for automatic termination of IRS employees for certain forms of conduct, such as recreational browsing through taxpayers' returns, but the list of sins has created morale problems among the agency's most ethical and responsible workers. Indeed, the IRS has recommended to Congress the elimination of the automatic termination provision.

Budgeting and finance personnel also need to know how to communicate and work effectively with line administrators. All too often, finance people are seen as roadblocks rather than facilitators in accomplishing the missions of agencies.

▮ Summary

The impact of personnel costs on any government budget is immense. Because labor costs represent a large segment of every operating budget, personnel may be the first to be cut during financially tight periods. Collective bargaining, while helping employees, has greatly complicated budgetary planning at the state and local levels; unresolved negotiations at budget time mean that personnel costs remain unknown.

Most retirement programs at the state and local levels are actuarially sound, but other programs face severe problems. In granting workers improvements in retirement benefits, government officials need to assess the current and projected impact on budgets. Advance funding is preferred over the pay-as-you-go method of financing retirement plans.

Despite the apparent linkages between the budget and personnel functions, the administration of these systems often has not been integrated. Tensions persist between the two, in part as a result of their differing histories. Budgeting is an openly political process, whereas personnel administration is intended to be basically apolitical.

Substantial budget staffs exist in the executive and legislative branches of government. Persons with social science training increasingly staff state budget offices, whereas business administration had previously been the most common background. Many local governments need more budget staff but do not have adequate resources for additional hiring. Training can be a useful method of acquiring needed talent.

Notes

1. A.E. Buck, *Public Budgeting* (New York: Harper and Brothers, 1919), 539.

2. U.S. Bureau of the Census, *Statistical Abstract of the United States 2001* (Washington, DC: U.S. Government Printing Office, 2001); U.S. Bureau of the Census, *Government Finances, 1998–99* (Washington, DC: U.S. Government Printing Office, 2001).

3. Federal Employees Pay Comparability Act, P.L. 101–509 (1990).

4. *Rutan v. Republican Party of Illinois*, 497 U.S. 62 (1990).

5. J. White, State Hiring Freezes Not So Tough, *Stateline.Org* (June 5, 2002), *http://www.stateline.org*.

6. Federal Workforce Restructuring Act, P.L. 103–226 (1994); Omnibus Consolidated Appropriations Act, P.L. 104–208, Sec. 663 (1996).

7. Treasury and General Government Appropriations Act for Fiscal Year 2000, P.L. 106–58 (2000).

8. Federal Activities and Inventory Reform Act, P.L. 105–270 (1998).

9. Fair Labor Standards Act, ch. 676 (1938).

10. C.M. Fagnoni for the U.S. General Accounting Office, *Fair Labor Standards Act: White Collar Exemptions Need Adjustments for Today's Work Place* (Washington, DC: U.S. Government Printing Office, 2000); M.A. Faillace, Automatic Exemption of Highly-Paid Employees and Other Proposed Amendments to the White-Collar Exemptions: Bringing the Fair Labor Standards Act into the Twenty-First Century, *Labor Lawyer* 15 (2000): 357–390.

11. J.M. Najita and J. L. Stern, eds., *Collective Bargaining in the Public Sector: The Experience of Eight States* (Armonk, NY: M.E. Sharpe, 2001); R.C. Kearney with D.G. Carnevale, *Labor Relations in the Public Sector* (New York: Marcel Dekker, 2001).

12. U.S. Bureau of Labor Statistics, Union Members Summary, 2002, *http://www.bls.gov/cps*; accessed June 2002.

13. U.S. Bureau of Labor Statistics, Union Affiliation of Employed Wage and Salary Workers by Occupation and Industry, 2002, *http:// www.bls.gov/cps*; accessed June 2002.

14. Federal Labor Relations Authority, *Guide to the Federal Service Labor-Management Relations Program* (Washington, DC: U.S. Government Printing Office, 2001).

15. Kearney and Carnevale, *Labor Relations in the Public Sector*.

16. C. Daniel, ed., Symposium on Keeping Selection Legal and Professional: Are the *Uniform Guidelines* Still Helpful?, *Review of Public Personnel Administration* 21 (2001): 175–247.

17. Notification and Federal Employee Antidiscrimination and Retaliation Act, P.L. 107–174 (2002).

18. *Kimel v. Florida Board of Regents*, 528 U.S.62 (2000); *Board of Trustees of Alabama v. Garrett*, 531 U.S. 356 (2001).

19. R.D. Lee, Jr., and P.S. Greenlaw, Employer Liability for Employee Sexual Harassment: A Judicial Policy-Making Study, *Public Administration Review* 60 (2000): 123–133; D. Burke and B. Little, New Twist in Sexual Harassment Cases: *Faragher* and *Ellerth*, *Journal of Individual Employment Rights* 9 (2000–2001): 95–108.

20. P. Clark, Do Federal Labor Laws Apply to State and Local Governments? Recent Court Decisions Make Enforcement of Federal Labor Laws Against States Impossible, *Government Union Review* 19 (2000): 1–34.

21. E.J. Arnault, et al., An Experimental Study of Job Evaluation and Comparable Worth, *Industrial and Labor Relations Review* 54 (2001): 806–815; G. Sulzner, A Pay Equity Saga: The Public Service Alliance of Canada vs. the Treasury Board of Canada Secretariat, *Journal of Collective Negotiations in the Public Sector* 29 (2000): 89–122.

22. U.S. General Accounting Office, *Managing for Results: Human Capital Management Discussions in Fiscal Year 2001 Performance Plans* (Washington, DC: U.S. Government Printing Office, 2001); U.S. General Accounting Office, *High-Risk Series: An Update* (Washington, DC: U.S. Government Printing Office, 2001); U.S. General Accounting Office, *Federal Employee Retirements: Expected Increase Over the Next 5 Years Illustrates Need for Workforce Planning* (Washington, DC: U.S. Government Printing Office, 2001).

23. U.S. Office of Management and Budget, *The President's Management Agenda* (Washington, DC: U.S. Government Printing Office, 2001).

24. U.S. Office of Management and Budget, Workforce Planning and Restructuring, Bulletin No. 01–07 (May 8, 2001). Also see P.C. Light, To Restore and Renew, *Government Executive Magazine* (November 2001), *http://www.govexec.com*; S.Z. Figura, The Human Touch, *Government Executive Magazine* (September 2000), *http://www.govexec.com*.

25. B.L. Ungar for U.S. General Accounting Office, *U.S. Postal Service: Workers' Compensation Benefits for Postal Employees* (Washington, DC: U.S. Government Printing Office, 2002).

26. J. Peckenpaugh, Future Federal Benefit Costs Exceed National Debt, *Government Executive* (March 29, 2002), *http://www.govexec.com*.

27. G.E. Roberts, An Examination of Employee Benefits Cost Control Strategies in New Jersey Local Governments, *Public Personnel Management* 30 (2001): 303–321.

28. U.S. General Accounting Office, *Federal Employees: OPM Data Do Not Identify If Temporary Employees Work for Extended Periods* (Washington, DC: U.S. Government Printing Office, 2002).

29. U.S. Bureau of the Census, *Public Employment Retirement System Survey, 2000, http:// www.census.gov*; accessed June 2002.

30. For details on federal systems, see *Federal Personnel Guide* (Washington, DC: Key Communications Group, published annually) and on-line at *http://www.fedguide.com*; accessed June 2002.

31. Employee Retirement Income Security Act, P.L. 93–406 (1974).

32. Small Business Job Protection Act, P.L. 104–188 (1996).

33. *Bowen v. Public Agencies Opposed to Social Security Entrapment*, 477 U.S. 41 (1986).

34. J.D. Harris, *2001 Survey of State and Local Government Employee Retirement Systems* (Chicago: Public Pension Coordinating Council, 2002), 4.

35. Federal Insurance Contributions Act, ch. 2 (1939).

36. N. Greifer, Best Practices in Pension Administration, *Government Finance Review* 16 (April 2000): 29–32.

37. U.S. Bureau of the Census, *State and Local Public Employee Retirement Systems, 2000* (Washington, DC: U.S. Government Printing Office, 2001).

38. U.S. Bureau of the Census, *State and Local Public Employee Retirement Systems, 2000.*

39. Harris, *2001 Survey of State and Local Government Employee Retirement Systems*, 7.

40. N. Greifer, Pension Investment Policies: The State of the Art, *Government Finance Review* 18 (February 2002): 36–40; M. Schneider and F. Damanpour, Determinants of Public Pension Plan Investment Return, *Public Management Review* 3 (2001): 551–573.

41. J. Dixon, Older and Wiser: The Economics of Public Pensions, *Journal of Policy Analysis and Management* 18 (1999): 527–528; Harris, *2001 Survey of State and Local Government Employee Retirement Systems*; N. Greifer and P. Zorn, Survey Indicates State and Local Retirement Plans in Great Shape, *Government Finance Review* 16 (August 2000): 7–9.

42. A Bill to Regulate and Improve the Civil Service of the United States (Pendleton Act), ch. 27, 22 Stat. 403 (1883).

43. D.D. Riley, *Public Personnel Administration*, 2nd ed. (New York: Longman, 2002); R.D. Sylvia and C.K. Meyer, *Public Personnel Administration*, 2nd ed. (Fort Worth, TX: Harcourt College Publishers, 2002).

44. Civil Service Reform Act, P.L. 95–454 (1978).

45. J.P. West, Symposium on Civil Service Reform in the State of Georgia, *Review of Public Personnel Administration* 22 (2002): 79–168; J. Lipiec, Human Resources Management Perspective at the Turn of the Century, *Public Personnel Management* 30 (2001): 137–146.

46. Homeland Security Act, P.L. 107–296 (2002).

47. National Commission on the Public Service, *Urgent Business for America: Revitalizing the Federal Government for the 21st Century* (Washington, DC: Brookings Institution, 2003).

48. U.S. Bureau of the Census, Federal Government Civilian Employment and Public Employment Data (State and Local Governments), April 2000, *http://www.census.gov/govs/apes*; accessed June 2002.

49. U.S. Office of Personnel Management, *Federal Civilian Workforce Statistics: Employment and Trends as of May 2001* (Washington, DC: U.S. Government Printing Office, 2001), Table 2.

50. R.D. Lee, Jr., and R.C. Burns, unpublished data from Survey of State Budget Offices (University Park, PA: The Pennsylvania State University, 2000).

51. R.D. Lee, Jr., and R.C. Burns, U.S. State Budget Directors: Characteristics, Experience and Attitudes, *Public Budgeting & Finance*, forthcoming.

52. R.D. Lee, Jr., Educational Characteristics of Budget Office Personnel and State Budgetary Processes, *Public Budgeting & Finance* 11 (Fall 1991): 69–79.

53. Chief Financial Officers Council, *http://www.cfoc.gov*; accessed June 2002.

54. C. Clifford, Computer-Based Training for Financial Management Systems: The City of Scottsdale Experience, *Government Finance Review* 16 (February 2000): 35–38.

55. D. Snow and K. Willoughby, Legislative Fiscal Staff Influence in Legislatures: A Model of Decision-Making, paper presented at the annual conference of the Association for Budgeting and Financial Management, Washington, D.C., 2002.

56. Government Finance Officers Association, *http://www.gfoa.org*; accessed June 2002.

Chapter 14

INTERGOVERNMENTAL
RELATIONS

Each level of government has discrete financial decision-making processes that determine matters of revenue and expenditure. Decisions about revenues and expenditures at different levels of government, however, are interdependent. Budgetary decisions made at one level are partially dependent on budgetary decisions made at other levels. Nonbudgetary decisions made at one level also may have dramatic impacts on budgets at another level.

This chapter examines the financial interdependencies among federal, state, and local governments.[1] The first section examines some of the basic economic and political problems that stem from having three major levels of government that provide various services and possess differing financial capabilities. The second section considers the patterns of interaction among the different levels, and the third section considers the main types of intergovernmental financial assistance programs. Devolution of responsibility from federal to state and local levels, especially welfare reform and health care for lower-income groups, are key topics. The chapter concludes with a discussion of current issues and alternatives for restructuring these patterns of financial interaction, including the controversial issue of unfunded mandates.

Structural and Fiscal Features of the Intergovernmental System

For convenience, we have commonly referred throughout this book to the three levels of governments, but at this point this simplification must be set aside. In this section, we consider the problems associated with having multiple levels and types of governments.

Areal and Functional Relations

Multiple Governments. In addition to the federal government and the 50 state governments, there are almost 88,000 local governments and the District of Columbia.[2] The local "level" is not a single level in that most states have county governments (more than 3,000 nationwide), and within their boundaries exist such general-purpose governments as municipalities and sometimes townships (more than 19,000 municipalities and 16,500 townships). Superimposed over these are numerous independent school districts and special-purpose districts such as irrigation and sewer districts. Special districts, of which there are more than 35,000, are the most numerous. There are more than 13,500 school districts.

These various local governments are not merely subunits of their state governments, nor are the states subunits of the national government. In a unitary system, policies are set by the national government, and their administration is delegated to lower levels of government, which are subunits of the central government. The United States and a few other large countries such as Australia, Canada, Germany, and India have federal systems.[3] In a federal system, each constitutionally spelled out level of government has substantial autonomous decision-making authority defined in the constitution.

Whether federal or unitary, many countries that heretofore have been characterized by high degrees of centralized governmental authority have implemented over the last two decades or are currently implementing policy, legal, and constitutional reforms to increase the autonomous authority of regional, provincial, or local-level governments, although that does not necessarily mean shifts from unitary to federal systems. India, for example, enacted in 1991 constitutional reforms to establish certain powers and responsibilities for local governments as a matter of national constitutional authority, effectively removing some aspects of state government control over local government. In the independent republics of the former Soviet Union, central authority over all governmental functions is gradually giving way to increased responsibility at the regional and city levels, but that authority is defined and delimited by the central government. In the United States, while the Constitution creates both the central and state governments, local governments are not constitutionally defined, but are instead subject to the discretion of their state governments.

Having myriad governments at different levels within a nation can be defended in several ways. By having multiple governments, an omnipotent, despotic type of government may be avoided. Another advantage is that the diversity of governments allows for differing responses according to the divergent needs of citizens in different locales. The Federalist framers and advocates for the U.S. Constitution defended a federal structure using three arguments:

1. It would promote a sense of community and affinity between citizens and the government.

2. It would promote efficiency by assigning functions that had mainly local importance to local governments and functions of national importance to the federal government.

3. It would promote liberty by avoiding concentration of power in the hands of a few.[4]

The existence of numerous units of government increases the probability that individuals will be able to find communities to live in that suit them. For example, people may locate in communities that offer desirable mixes of taxes and services. Of course, we do not suggest that such economic calculations are the sole criteria on which people base their location decisions, but the existence of multiple governments enhances that important aspect of quality of life.

Another advantage is that having multiple governments allows the achievement of economies of scale; functions may be performed by the size of government that is most efficient in carrying out the functions. Just as it may be advantageous from the standpoint of efficient resource use for private, profit-oriented organizations to grow to a large scale, so it also may be advantageous for one unit of government to conduct some government activities on a large scale.

On the other hand, to perform all government functions at the central level might result in inefficient conduct of some activities. Not only did the economic woes of the former Soviet Union demonstrate that overly centralized planning of the productive sector of the economy produced many inefficiencies, but the overly centralized administrative and fiscal systems also left a legacy of weak decision making not well adapted to provision of basic local public services.[5] Lessened flexibility of operations and other diseconomies suggest the need for some functions to be performed by units of government smaller than central government; geographically and economically smaller-scale activities are more efficient when carried out by smaller governments. Probably many services can be provided most efficiently at the local level.[6]

Of course, no government, no matter what the level, is free to do whatever it pleases. The Constitution provides for the federal government's powers (especially Article I, Section 8) and reserves all other powers to the states (Tenth Amendment). Each state constitution provides for the powers of that government. Local governments have fewer constitutional protections, because these governments have been created by their states. Within these constitutional and legal parameters, a higher-level government may impose standards upon lower levels.

Coordination Problems. The existence of thousands of governments results in coordination problems both geographically and functionally. Municipalities in a metropolitan area need some coordinative mechanisms. Road networks, for example, need to be planned in accordance with commuting patterns within a metropolitan area, and such plans should not be restricted to the geographical boundaries of each municipality. Before the federal government became involved in highway programs, many highways did not connect sensibly across state lines. Recreation and parks programs may be provided on a metropolitan or area basis and thereby achieve economies of scale. Numerous regional planning agencies, regional or metropolitan transportation planning groups, and regional economic development programs exist so as to consolidate an otherwise fragmented approach to interjurisdictional overlaps.

The need to avoid excessive fragmentation at the local level in a decentralized system has led some to argue for consolidation of the local governments in a metropolitan area, such as Miami–Dade County, Florida, and Nashville–Davidson County, Tennessee. However, some studies have shown that the savings expected from metropolitan consolidation have not been achieved. Rather, greater efficiencies seem to result from competition among the various local governments in a metropolitan area.[7] Where coordination is needed among the local governments of a metropolitan area, it seems achievable through cooperation and shared decision making rather than consolidation. However, there does seem to be evidence that consolidation has benefits in the case of very small local units of government.

Functional coordination among different levels is also necessary because the three main levels of government share responsibilities for some of the same functions. Criminal justice, for instance, is a shared function; some type of police, court, and prison system exists at each government level. The independent pursuit of similar objectives by different governments can result in wasted resources and ineffective services.

Multilevel overlapping and shared responsibility can make it difficult to design federal programs to achieve national objectives. A good federal assistance program for local governments in one state may be a poor fit in another state with a different allocation of responsibilities between state and local governments. Therefore, emphasis has been given to developing mechanisms for functional integration.[8] While program specialists stress functional integration, however, policy generalists may stress areal integration. This conflict has been popularized by Deil S. Wright as "picket fence federalism" — each picket represents a function, such as mental health or education, and all three levels of government make up part of each picket.[9] Another analogy used is that of silos.

A Case Example: Coordinating Air Emissions. Like watersheds, airsheds respect no political boundaries. Emissions from private vehicles, public facilities, and factories within the boundaries of one political jurisdiction effectively go where the winds blow. Unlike water, which has a stable pattern of flows, emissions into the air over time span the full 360 degrees of the map. In purely self-interested terms, it may not be rational for a local government with a strong "smokestack" industry that is employing a large percentage of the work force to regulate emissions from that industry, especially if the prevailing winds for the most part blow the polluted air away from the jurisdiction. For this reason, the federal government has for several decades played a significant role in setting limits on emissions. However, federally imposed limits rely on states and localities to develop policies and practices to meet the standards. Increasingly, states and the local jurisdictions within metropolitan areas realize that they cannot act unilaterally to solve the problems if their neighbors are not also taking care of the problems. They then act to create coordinated policies and programs to impose and enforce stronger controls.

One such example is a compact among New England and mid-Atlantic states to control ground-level ozone concentrations.[10] Members of this Ozone Transport Commission agreed on a budget, or a total amount of nitrous oxide emissions that would be allowed from sources within the states in the compact. States then allocate the allowable emissions among the major producers/sources, rewarding those that come in "below budget." Individual emitters and even states may trade in these permitted levels; those falling below the levels may trade for various compensations with those who cannot meet the allocated amount. Although substantial cutbacks in emissions have been achieved (more than a 50 percent reduction from 1990 to 1999), the scenario has not been all rosy. Midwestern states did not join the Commission, and prevailing winds bring large problems eastward, so the attorneys general of some states have sued coal-burning power plants in several Midwestern states.[11] While the legal steps may take several years to play out, the Ozone Transport Commission has achieved some significant progress on a common problem in intergovernmental relations.

While interstate compacts can be effective in addressing cross-jurisdictional issues, they are not easy to set up. Article I, Section 10 of the Constitution requires congressional approval of any interstate compact. Despite this step, this approach has proved a useful mechanism for creating interjurisdictional authority to address mutual interests.

Fiscal Considerations

Vertical Imbalance. The conflict between the organizing principles of geographic area and program function plays out within the context of need for services and the corresponding need for revenues, with differences in capabilities existing both within levels of government and among levels.[12] Vertical imbalance, or noncorrespondence, refers to the relative abilities of different levels of government to generate needed revenue and to produce specific public services. The intergovernmental fiscal problem is deciding upon assignment of expenditure responsibilities, and then designing an intergovernmental fiscal system of revenue authority, shared revenue sources, and transfers to match the expenditure assignments. Although one level of government may have a comparative advantage in providing a particular service efficiently, it may not have the same advantage in obtaining revenue. Conversely, another level of government may possess sufficient revenue capability but is not the most efficient unit to provide certain services. In the United States, it is typically the federal government that possesses the greatest revenue capacity but not the comparative advantage in providing many government services, while state and local governments have functional expenditure obligations that exceed their ability to raise revenue.

This disparity is due largely to the different revenue sources used by governments. The federal government, relying on personal and corporate income taxes, has a more elastic tax structure in which revenues increase with any increase in economic activity. While state and local revenue sources are relatively more inelastic, the demand for services provided by these governments is quite elastic. For example, the property tax does not change when the economy swings up and down. As discussed in Chapter 4, the property tax is based on the assessed value of the property. Assessments are expensive to carry out, so they are not changed frequently. Hence, we describe the property tax as inelastic with respect to changing economic conditions. When income falls, property taxes still must be paid, but the amount of tax paid on income drops. Of course, when property taxes increase or even remain stable but the economy takes a significant downturn, as happened in 2001–2003, property owners who have lost their jobs may experience extreme difficulty in making the property tax payments.

Superior fiscal capacity can be used by one level of government to entice or persuade another to provide a given service. For example, the federal government used its tremendous fiscal capacity to persuade the states to build an interstate network of highways. Had the federal government not been willing to pay 90 percent of the cost of the system, there would be far fewer highways today. Federal programs created by the Clean Water Act and the Safe Drinking Water Act, discussed in Chapter 12, initially provided grant funding for water and sewer systems, and then after some years of grant funding, provided capitalization funding for state revolving loan funds to lower the borrowing costs for water and sewer systems. Similar federal assistance to capitalize state education loan programs to induce more school construction have been proposed, but not implemented. States also induce local activities through grants and loans. Massachusetts has a loan fund to assist schools in meeting difficult problems associated with students with special education needs.[13]

Horizontal Fiscal Differences. Problems caused by differences in fiscal capacity also exist for governments at the same level. From state to state, there clearly are differences in income and wealth, which are the basic sources of government revenue. For example, U.S. per capita personal income in 2000 was $29,676, but Connecticut's was $40,640, or 137 percent of the national average, and Mississippi's was $20,993, or only 71 percent of the national average.[14] Differences in income and wealth lead to differences in revenue-generating abilities, tax burdens, and levels of public services, although no simple correlation exists between income on the one hand, and taxing and spending on the other hand.

There is disagreement over whether per capita income differences are a good measure, however, of the differing fiscal capacities of the states. Widely used since the 1930s as a measure to differentiate among the states' relative needs for federal assistance, per capita income does not fully capture ability to pay for services within a state. Other measures include retail sales and gross state product (the latter is a measure similar to the national gross domestic product, discussed in Chapter 15). Analysts often use full market property value to assess debt repayment capacity, but this measure reflects accumulated wealth and not necessarily the direct ability to generate revenues.

Another consideration is how diligently the state and its local governments are making the effort to tax the resources they have available. Before it was eliminated in federal budget cutting, the U.S. Advisory Commission on Intergovernmental Relations (ACIR) calculated a more complex measure that estimated the revenues a state would raise if it were to use the average tax system employed throughout the country. This *representative tax system* (RTS) measured tax capacity and, when divided by population, provided a gauge of a state's fiscal effort.[15] The ACIR subsequently added the concept of representative expenditures, including information about costs for public services, to help measure different states' financial abilities.[16]

There has been some reconstruction of the ACIR's work since its demise.[17] According to calculations from the Federal Reserve Bank of Boston, based on 1996 data, the District of Columbia had the highest measure on an *index of fiscal need*, suggesting that its expenditure requirements were 26 percent greater than the national index score (average) of 100. The measure of fiscal need is a comparison of what the states (and the District of Columbia) each would have to spend to achieve a basic standard of service, indexed against the actual national per capita spending. New Mexico, California, Mississippi, Louisiana, and Texas were all above or close to 110 on the index. Nebraska and Wisconsin were on the low end in expenditure requirements — 88 and 89, respectively.

The ability of a state to raise the revenue to meet spending requirements is called the *fiscal capacity* of the state. Two different indices of fiscal capacity, measuring the ability to raise the revenue needed to meet the expenditure requirements, were calculated by the Federal Reserve. One measure is the representative tax system developed originally by ACIR, discussed earlier. The other index is based on U.S. Department of the Treasury work. The Treasury calculates *total taxable resources* (TTR), which is an estimate of a state's gross state product, similar to the concept of gross domestic product calculated for a national economy (see Chapter 15). On either index, the District of Columbia scored well above the 100 mark — in fact, 158 on the RTS index. New Mexico, on the other hand, was well below on the RTS measure (88). Similarly, Mississippi and Louisiana were also well below; California was close to the average (103). Nebraska and Wisconsin were slightly below — 99 and 98, respectively. Overall, although there are plenty of arguments about the adequacy of any one or group of measures, the empirical research corresponds to common-sense expectations: Some poorer states in the country have greater needs for spending on services than they have the fiscal capacity to respond, and some richer states have greater fiscal capacity than their expenditure requirements.

Any comparisons among states or localities, whether based on income, wealth, or tax effort, cannot capture an essential feature determining levels of services and levels of taxation. Residents of each state do not make uniform demands for services. The index of fiscal need assumes that every state should be spending the national average. This does not take into account the fact that citizens may desire different levels of services. Even if the ability to tax or charge for services were distributed evenly across the country, expenditures would differ because citizens desire different levels of services. From a strict demand point of view, a state would provide only those services for which citizens are willing to pay. But willingness to pay for services, as measured by tax effort, still may not solve the problem. The need for many government services is greatest in those states where the fiscal capacity to meet those needs is lowest. Mississippi is a good example of a state that has high needs and, by various measures, makes a better-than-average effort to meet those needs, but still falls short. The problem is even more acute with respect to different local jurisdictions within the same state. Central city governments within large metropolitan areas face demands for services that increase at a faster rate than does the value of their revenue sources.

Fiscal Responsibilities. Another issue is the extent to which one government with greater revenue-generating capacity should be responsible for aiding other lower-level governments. The issue is whether and to what extent governments should redistribute resources among different segments of the population and geographic areas. Since the 1980s, there seemingly has been less support for redistributive activities, especially at the federal level, than in the decades beginning with the Johnson administration's War on Poverty. The two decades from 1960 through 1980 witnessed the largest effort ever by the federal government to redress disparities among the states and among regions within states. By 1979, questions had been raised about the ability of the federal government to sustain such a redistributive effort. In response, the New Federalism of President Reagan implemented significant reductions in federal programs to transfer funds to impoverished individuals and low-income states and localities. Balanced federal budgets in the 1990s came at the same time as economic prosperity produced state budget surpluses, so there was no great pressure to increase programs to equalize disparities among the states. The return to federal deficits after 2000 has discouraged such efforts, even in the face of severe state budget crises.

One governing principle is that a government should engage in such funding only when the problem addressed corresponds to its level of responsibility — that is, the federal government should deal with national problems and the states with state problems. That principle was articulated quite clearly by President Ronald Reagan's Executive Order 12612: "It is important to recognize the distinction between problems of national scope (which may justify Federal action) and problems that are merely common to the States (which will not justify Federal action because individual States, acting individually or together, can effectively deal with them)."[18] Though there have been differences in preference for various programs since then, both Democratic and Republican administrations since have tended toward devolution of responsibility.[19]

Disparities in fiscal capacity among governments at the same level lead directly to another problem, that of external costs and benefits of government functions. People of low income moving from states with low services to states with high services create new burdens on the high-service states. This occurred, for example, in the migration of the 1930s from impoverished areas to the West Coast and in later migrations from the rural South to cities in the North and West. Proportionately more people who move from lower-income to higher-income states receive welfare payments and generate greater demands on other public services than do those moving from states with similarly high levels of income and services. The flow of illegal immigrants into some states exacerbates those states' difficulties in financing social services and education.

Some of the costs of the failure to provide comparable levels of service across state lines are borne by those outside the low-service states. But the situation has positive aspects as well. Providing services at the most economical level may result in the benefits' spilling over into other areas. The most obvious example is education. Higher levels of education generally yield higher levels of income. Given the mobility of the population, the benefits produced by one local educational system may spread far beyond its geographic boundaries.

Economic Competition. Governments compete with each other in trying to attract businesses and industries.[20] Firms locate for a variety of reasons, such as access to markets, a good labor supply, and availability of other resources. Furthermore, they locate where there are clusters of related industries and suppliers. Because businesses seek to minimize production costs, the advantage lies with jurisdictions that have a high service level and low taxes on industry. Whether these are the main reasons businesses actually move or not is irrelevant. As long as governments compete on the basis of taxes and services, the fiscal effects are the same.

Competition for businesses among political jurisdictions can have important consequences, including distortions in revenue and expenditure patterns. When special concessions are granted to firms, needed revenues must be obtained elsewhere or the level of services must be reduced. Devoting resources to special facilities, such as industrial parks, which are frequently financed by long-term debt instruments, may affect a community's ability to finance other capital projects, such as a civic center or a new sewage treatment plant. The package of tax forgiveness and free services that Alabama gave Daimler Benz in return for locating its first U.S. manufacturing facility in the state was a gamble. So far the evidence has been discouraging. The cost to the state has been nearly $300 million, or $168,000 for every job created.[21] On the other hand, Daimler Benz has built additional factories in Alabama since the 1993 plant, and other automotive companies such as Honda have located facilities there. Each of these decisions has been accompanied by additional tax concessions — approximately $150 million in tax incentives for a $400 million Mercedes truck plant, or about $88,000 per job. The state also gave about $150 million in tax incentives for the $440 million Honda investment, or about $100,000 per job.[22]

Although intense competition among some states for industrial relocation does cause problems, there are important benefits from this competition. First, it serves as a market-like regulator, preventing state and local governments from overtaxation. Second, it increases the efficiency of the allocation of public sector resources. States and localities that offer uneconomical incentives to businesses ultimately cannot sustain those incentives. There is a tendency toward equilibrium in the balance of incentives and the taxes and other charges necessary to make services available to support industrial development. Some states have backed away from the use of high-cost incentives.

Overlapping Taxes. The taxes of jurisdictions overlap with each other, and ultimately the same people and firms must pay the various governments. Tax overlapping also occurs when all levels of government tax the same specific source, such as when federal, state, and local governments all tax income. Overlapping or multiple taxation in some sense is unavoidable and not necessarily undesirable. It causes serious problems only when a government at one level in effect preempts another government's ability to raise sufficient revenue. This can occur if the state sales tax rate is so high that it discourages local jurisdictions from levying such a tax. Indeed, states may preclude their local governments from having sales taxes but may provide them with alternative sources of revenue. The same kind of problem occurs as a result of heavy federal personal and corporate income taxes. State and local governments, while often criticized for failing to raise sufficient revenue to meet needs, may be largely preempted by the federal government from major reliance on income taxes. One proposal that has been dormant for years would cause a major reallocation of governmental responsibilities among federal, state, and local governments to address tax overlapping directly by introducing a new shared tax — a value-added tax (see Chapter 4) — and sharing corporate income and gasoline taxes. Differences in the latter two taxes among the states would be eliminated.[23] Shared taxes also would reduce tax competition among states. Shared taxes are common in developing countries, where decision makers typically revamp their countries' fiscal systems to support decentralization and devolution.

Patterns of Interaction Among Levels of Government

The structural and fiscal features of the U.S. intergovernmental system ensure that there will be numerous interactions among the differing levels of governments. Multiple governments within the same nation interact in numerous ways that directly involve budgetary and other financial decisions as well as each government's fiscal condition. Intergovernmental revenue transfers, such as grants, are a common form of interaction, but they are by no means the only important form. Federal direct expenditures and taxes that occur within a state or local jurisdiction are also important, as is the financial assistance that one level of government gives to another. Finally, regulations, statutes, and other actions that do not directly involve taxing and spending, but nevertheless affect taxing and spending, shape budgetary decisions.

Direct Expenditures and Taxes

Discussions of intergovernmental finance too often concentrate exclusively on financial assistance and neglect the importance of direct expenditures. How much the federal government spends in a state and, in turn, how much a state spends in specific local areas have large impacts. Direct federal expenditures have varying geographical impacts, and the same is true for state expenditures.

Nongrant Spending. Locating government-owned or -built facilities in a jurisdiction can substantially affect the jurisdiction's economy. Political considerations are crucial at the state level in regard to the location of highways, state hospitals, and parks. Local and state governments work actively to obtain federal projects in their jurisdictions as one means of guaranteeing future prosperity. At the federal level, military installations, the awarding of defense contracts to corporations (which, of course, are geographically based), and other civilian installations inspire intensive lobbying.

In an attempt to reduce the political bargaining over which military facilities to close during defense downsizing, Congress has several times — the last being in 1995 — created temporary commissions to make recommendations on base closings that then must be approved by the president and Congress. Since 1988, 95 military bases have been closed, for an estimated savings of $14 billion.[24] The George W. Bush administration took considerable heat from Congress for proposing to close more bases so as to fund additional weapons systems efforts.

Although some of the political bargaining was reduced in the past by the existence of these commissions, members of Congress still fight to save facilities in their home districts or states. The reality sometimes is that communities benefit more from the base closing than from the previous operations of the base. Facilities and space are turned over to the local community for economic development, and that new activity often proves more valuable. Portsmouth, New Hampshire, for example, turned the former Pease Air Force Base into an industrial park, and more than 10 times the number of people are employed in the industrial park than formerly worked at the Air Force base. Charleston, South Carolina's economy grew after a naval base closing, with new companies occupying old Navy sites.[25]

Beyond the physical items are various programs that disburse loans and grants to individuals and corporations. At the federal level, these programs include Social Security, Medicare, support to farmers, and small business loans. These direct and indirect payments to individuals account for more than 60 percent of federal grant spending distributed among the states.[26] States also distribute large welfare and other human services payments among local jurisdictions. Federal spending other than grants to individuals, organizations, and governments includes significant salaries and wages paid to federal employees and members of the military, most of whom live in one state or another. Defense payrolls in states ranged in 2000 from as low as $96 million in Vermont to as high as $11 billion in Virginia. Federal defense contracts with private firms and individuals in 1999 for work conducted within the United States totaled $116 billion.[27] These contracts, federal salaries, and miscellaneous other small programs are of greater economic significance than are actual federal grants given to state and local governments.

Tax Collections. In addition to spending, tax collections have varying effects on locales, and the resulting balance between federal tax collections and expenditures has significant effects upon jurisdictions. Generally, federal revenues raised in the Northeast and the Midwest have tended to be greater than the federal expenditures in these regions. The opposite pattern has existed in the South and the West, with the exception of Texas, California, Colorado, Nevada, and Oregon, where the federal tax burden also is greater than total federal expenditures.[28] **Table 14–1** indicates the states with the highest and lowest per capita federal expenditures minus per capita federal taxes in 1999. New Mexico topped the list; the federal government spent $3,944 per person more than all federal taxes collected per person in that state. Connecticut was at the other extreme, "losing" a net $2,840. Where the balance is less than even, federal finance has a negative impact on a state's economy. This has been the case in the Great Lakes states, which are part of the so-called Rust Belt. Federal tax collections from each of the following Northeastern and Midwestern states exceeded federal expenditures *in* these states in 1999: Illinois, Indiana, Michigan, Minnesota, New York, Ohio, and Wisconsin.

Table 14–1 **States with Greatest and Least Per Capita Federal Expenditures Less Federal Tax Burden, Fiscal 1999**

Greatest Net Per Capita Flow			Least Net Per Capita Flow		
Rank	State	Net Flow	Rank	State	Net Flow
1.	New Mexico	3,944	41.	New York	-890
2.	Montana	3,109	42.	Massachusetts	-895
3.	Virginia	3,069	43.	Delaware	-1,025
4.	North Dakota	3,043	44.	Michigan	-1,042
5.	West Virginia	2,808	45.	Minnesota	-1,294
6.	Alaska	2,777	46.	Nevada	-1,583
7.	Mississippi	2,684	47.	Illinois	-1,669
8.	South Dakota	2,327	48.	New Hampshire	-1,787
9.	Alabama	2,091	49.	New Jersey	-2,342
10.	Hawaii	1,982	50.	Connecticut	-2,840

Source: U.S. Bureau of the Census, *Statistical Abstract of the United States: 2001* (Washington, DC: U.S. Government Printing Office, 2001), 312.

Table 14–1 compares federal spending with federal taxing per person without regard to estimates of need or ability to pay. If one federal responsibility is to redistribute income from wealthier areas of the country to poorer areas, then it should not be surprising that some states send more taxes to Washington than the federal government spends in those states. **Figure 14–1** illustrates the relationship between the net revenue flow of federal expenditures and federal taxes, for all 50 states, and state per capita income. If this net federal flow is generally redistributive, then we would expect the pattern to be generally downward sloping to the right, which indeed is what **Figure 14–1** demonstrates. The lower the per capita income, the greater the net flow of federal funds to the state.

Figure 14–1 | Net Federal Flow to/from State as a Function of State Per Capita Income, 2000

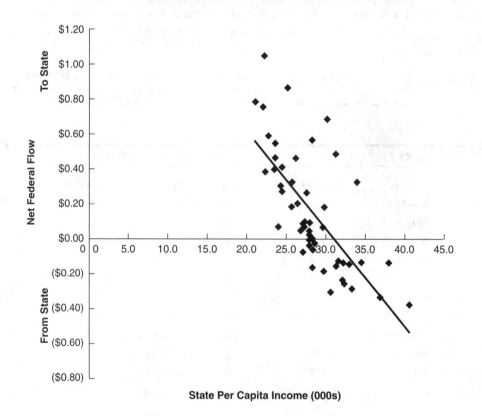

Source: Tax Foundation, *Tax and Spending Policies Benefit Some States, Leave Others Footing the Bill,* http://taxfoundation.org/pr-fedtaxspendingratio.html; accessed July 2002.

We inserted the overall, linear trend line in the figure; the correlation between net flow and per capita income is -70, which is consistent with the hypothesis that net federal revenue and expenditure actions are redistributive. Of course, numerous other factors are involved. **Figure 14–1** merely illustrates the general tendency of total federal activities in the states to be redistributive. As we noted previously, per capita income is not the only nor necessarily the best indicator to try to estimate the redistributive character of federal spending. **Figure 14–1** is important, however, because it includes not just federal grants, but all federal spending in states. It would appear that total federal spending is more redistributive than federal grants alone.

Intergovernmental Assistance

State Aid. The literature on intergovernmental relations tends to overemphasize federal aid to state and local governments and underemphasize state aid to local government. In 1998–1999, federal aid to states totaled $238.9 billion and to local governments was $31.6 billion.[29] State aid to local governments was $296.3 billion, about 13 percent more than what the federal government provided to state and local governments combined. State support of local governments for most states is the largest element in the state budget. Of course, state aid probably would be much smaller were states not receiving substantial federal support. As noted in Chapter 2, states receive slightly more than one-fifth of their revenue from the federal government. Local governments receive about 31 percent of their revenue from state governments and only 3 percent from the federal government; except for school districts, each type of local government obtains half or more of its revenue from its own sources. Differences in federal and state support exist among the types of local governments. **Figure 14–2** illustrates intergovernmental revenues provided to the different types of local government entities, as a proportion of those entities' total revenues. In the middle column, county revenues for 1996–1997 were 64.5 percent from their own sources. The remaining 35.5 percent came from intergovernmental transfers — 2.4 percent from federal, 31.6 percent from state, and 1.4 percent from other local entities. Similarly, one can see that school districts are the only local entity that receive more than half of their revenue from other governments — state governments provide a majority of the funds that school districts spend (55.3 percent).

Another way to look at intergovernmental aid is by considering where most of the federal intergovernmental transfers go, and similarly for state and local transfers. As of 1996–1997, nearly 40 percent of all federal aid to local governments went to cities, but these monies constituted less than 4 percent of city revenues. Special districts such as sewer and water districts are the most dependent on federal aid, which constitutes almost 12 percent of their budgets. Slightly more than half (53 percent) of state aid went to school districts, with these monies accounting for just over half of school district revenues (school districts are local governments that on average do not raise a majority of their revenues by themselves). Most of the other state aid was divided evenly between counties and cities.

These summary figures, of course, do not convey the great variety in patterns of state aid. Some states provide much greater assistance to local governments than other states; some states may provide a given service and thereby make direct expenditures, whereas other states may fund local governments to provide the service. New Hampshire, for example, provides only 12 percent of local government general revenues, much less than New Mexico, which provides 47 percent.[30] Several states provide more than $1,000 per capita to local governments — for example, Alaska and California. Others provide much smaller amounts — in

Figure 14–2 | **Intergovernmental Sources of General Revenues, 1996–1997**

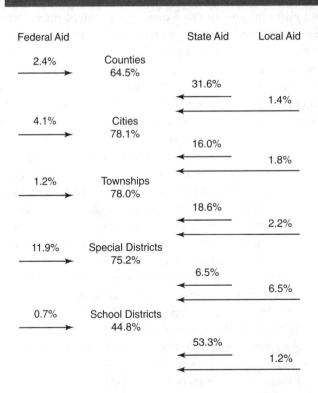

Source: U.S. Bureau of the Census, *Compendium of Government Finances: 1997 Census of Governments, Volume 4, Government Finances* (Washington, DC: U.S. Government Printing Office, 2000), 2.

addition to New Hampshire, the states providing the smallest amount of financial assistance to local governments are Hawaii, Rhode Island, South Dakota, and Tennessee.[31]

Aid to elementary and secondary education, as noted, constitutes the largest portion of state aid to local governments. Local school districts have not always depended as heavily on state and federal aid. **Figure 14–3** shows that local sources in the early part of the 20th century accounted for more than 80 percent of total funding, whereas it had declined to only 43 percent by 1980. Since then, local financing for education has varied, rising to 48 percent by the mid-1990s but then falling again to about 43 percent by 2000. Just as state aid to local governments in general varies considerably from state to state, so too does state aid to education, with New Hampshire again providing the lowest percentage of funding.

Because of the importance of external — mainly state — funding, the manner in which funds are distributed to local school districts is often a matter of some

Figure 14–3   **Federal, State, and Local Support for Elementary and Secondary Education, 1920–1994**

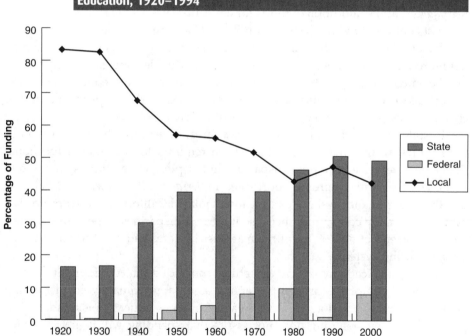

Sources: D.H. Monk, *Educational Finance: An Economic Approach* (New York: McGraw-Hill, 1990), 101; U.S. Bureau of the Census, *Government Finances: 1989–90* (Washington, DC: U.S. Government Printing Office, 1991), 7; 2000 data from U.S. Bureau of the Census, *Public Elementary-Secondary School System Finance Data*, http://www.census.gov/govs/school/00fullreport.pdf; accessed August 2002.

controversy. States use a formula for distributing these funds. Historically known as the *foundation plan*, such formulas are geared toward guaranteeing a minimum amount of educational expenditures either per pupil or per classroom. The word *foundation* connotes a definition of equality of educational opportunity, meaning that every student should have a minimum level of education — a foundation program. Formulas typically have been tied to real estate property assessments, with districts having low assessments per pupil receiving more aid than districts having high assessments. Although relatively rare, some state formulas even have recapture provisions in which state aid to wealthier districts can be negative, with the funds the state receives from wealthier districts being used to support the poorer districts. Separate formulas may be used for programs serving preschool, disadvantaged, and handicapped children as well as elementary-level children and secondary-level children.

These formulas were attacked in the courts starting in the 1970s as discriminatory; foundation plans were accused of failing to equalize educational opportunity among jurisdictions. While recognizing the great importance of education, in 1973 the Supreme Court decided in a Texas case, *San Antonio School District v. Rodriquez,* that the allocation of funds for education was a state responsibility and was not controlled by the Constitution.[32] The Court, in that case, was concerned that basing the formula on a macro measure such as the property tax base may not represent circumstances at the micro or individual level (e.g., extremely poor families might live in a wealthy district and not be receiving equal educational opportunity). Thus, the court ruled that the reliance on the property tax did not create any inequality challengeable on constitutional grounds.

Despite the Court's conclusion in *Rodriquez,* other cases have been won in state courts, so that many states have been required to alter their educational financing schemes to minimize disparities in per-pupil expenditures among districts. The California Supreme Court ruled in *Serrano v. Priest (Serrano II)* in 1976 that the state's finance system for education violated California's equal protection clause in the state constitution because it created disparities in per-pupil spending.[33] By the end of the 1990s, courts in at least 17 states had overturned state formula financing systems.[34]

A National Academy of Sciences study concluded that the foundation plan notion and its emphasis on equity defined as an approximately equal funding amount per pupil is no longer useful in assessing how education is financed and provided.[35] Equal spending does not assure that spending will be sufficient for each child to achieve desired outcomes. Adequacy is a more profound concept that links equity to educational achievement. The No Child Left Behind Act of 2001 reauthorizing the Elementary and Secondary Education Act expresses the philosophy that individuals should have equal chances to educational achievement and mandates individual testing to measure success.[36] That result would not necessarily be assured by some kind of equal funding. Some have argued that student performance is not correlated with funding amounts, calling into question both formula systems and states' attempts to equalize educational opportunity using various measures of equal spending.[37]

Other state aid programs are comparatively small. Education is followed in size by expenditures for welfare and highways. Aid for these programs is usually handed out based on some type of formula (welfare programs are often per-client reimbursement programs). Virtually all states have some form of motor fuels tax-sharing formula that benefits local governments as well as the states.[38] General local government support, as opposed to specific functional aid, is higher than support for any functions other than education and welfare.

Overall, state assistance has been more predictable than federal aid because of the extensive use of formulas. Formulas facilitate budget planning at the local level because jurisdictions from year to year have some knowledge of what state funds will be. The only major controversies have centered on the factors used in the formulas. Aid to local governments in many states rises and falls depending on the states' economic health. Local governments have shown resiliency in making up for state and federal decreases by drawing on their own resources and by placing greater reliance on user charges and other charges aimed at direct beneficiaries of programs (see Chapter 4). Local governments particularly were at the bottom end of the food chain in 2001–2002 when state budget deficits were redressed in most states at least in part by drastic cuts in aid to local governments. In some cases, states failed to live up to legislated formulas.[39]

Federal Aid. Federal grants have been aimed at inducing state and local governments to increase the level of services in specified areas and are not intended to replace state or local spending with federal revenues. The inducement effect is based on the theory that the more separation exists between taxing and spending, the more taxpayers will not perceive the full costs of local services. This is known as the *fiscal illusion hypothesis.* Matching provisions are usually required as a means of ensuring that grants will not merely result in a lessened tax effort by the recipients of the grants; without matching provisions, a $1 million federal grant could be offset by an equal reduction in local revenues supporting a program, thereby producing no increase in the level of services. However, substituting spending by a recipient government with a grant or transfer from another government may be the goal. States may want local governments to accept state aid and decrease reliance on the property tax. The reality is a mix of both. One study of state general grants to local education agencies found that grants do induce increased local spending for education, but not by as much as the amount of the grant funds.[40] The fiscal effect, inducing more local spending, is less when the grants are provided without any minimum requirements for tax effort or expenditure requirements. When there is no matching requirement, the greater effect may be on local tax relief — mainly property taxes in the case of education — rather than on increasing spending.

Where the objective is more clearly weighted toward redistributive effects, such as welfare assistance, there is the risk that states with less fiscal capacity may choose to spend less than nationally desirable. The various low-income assistance programs with which the federal government assists states and localities exhibit a range of federal involvement. Food stamps are fully federally funded — mainly federally funded in the case of the Supplemental Security Income (SSI) program for the low-income elderly and disabled — to fixed block amounts for Temporary Assistance to Needy Families (TANF).[41] State fiscal responses to this package of programs has been somewhat mixed, with apparent reduced efforts for cash assistance programs, but overall increased state and local spending for various welfare programs, especially Medicaid.

For grant programs aimed at inducing behavior changes and not necessarily fiscal responses, the task is more difficult. To accomplish changes in program emphasis at the state and local levels with grants, one has to believe that state and local preferences for service modes, such as transportation, are primarily driven by the cost and revenue availability. The Intermodal Surface Transportation Efficiency Act of 1991 (ISTEA) and the Transportation Enhancement Act of 1998 (TEA) were intended in part to encourage development and use of transportation modes other than cars on highways. In reality, states and localities are more likely to choose to repair and rehabilitate deteriorating highways and bridges than to fund mass transit and bridges.[42] The federal Children's Health Insurance Program (CHIP) was designed to induce states to implement programs to insure low-income children. It was designed with a punitive "use it or lose it" provision that gave states limited time to meet all the provisions; as a result, most states lost millions in unspent CHIP money — California in the first year forfeited nearly $600 million.[43]

During the 1960s, about 80 percent of all federal aid went for transportation and income security. As can be seen in **Table 14-2**, there have been substantial shifts since that time. Transportation, which accounted for more than 40 percent of the aid in the 1960s, declined at one point to less than 3 percent, but with new programs had increased again, to 11 percent by 2000, due to ISTEA and TEA. Aid for health programs rose to 44 percent. Income security accounted for about 24 percent of the aid. It has fluctuated widely — up in the 1960s, down to the current levels, then spiking in the late 1980s to 1990 and back down again, the last time in part due to welfare reforms limiting the number of years during which an individual can receive assistance (TANF program). Generally, the effects of rapidly rising health care costs and the number of individuals qualifying for income security programs explain most of the shifts that occurred between 1980 and 2000.

The amount of federal aid given to state and local governments varies among federal agencies. As can be seen in **Table 14–3**, the Department of Health and Human Services disburses the most aid by far, accounting for more than half of all federal grants. A different perspective, however, is gained by looking at the portion of an agency's budget committed to grants. While the Department of Health and Human Services spends about 43 percent of its funds on grants, the Department of Education spends over half (67 percent) and the Department of Transportation and the Department of Housing and Urban Development spend 67 percent and 77 percent on grants, respectively.

Regional Differences. Just as total federal outlays are not uniform from state to state, so too do grants vary. In 2000, the national average was $992 per capita in federal grants to state and local governments, up from $533 in 1990. The states

Table 14–2 **Percentage Function Distribution of Federal Grants-in-Aid, 1960–2000 (Percent)**

	1960	1970	1980	1990	2000
Administration of Justice	*	*	1	*	2
Agriculture	3	3	1	1	0
Community and Regional Development	2	7	7	4	3
Education, Employment, Training, and Social Services	7	27	24	19	13
General Government	2	2	9	2	1
Health	3	16	17	37	44
Income Security	38	24	20	30	24
Natural Resources and Environment	2	2	6	3	2
Transportation	43	19	14	3	11
Other	*	1	1	1	*
Total	**100**	**100**	**100**	**100**	**100**

Note: Includes grants-in-aid from federal funds accounts; does not include trust funds such as highway trust fund.
Totals may not equal 100 percent due to rounding.
* .5 percent or less
Source: Office of Management and Budget, *Budget of the United States Government: 2003, Special Analyses* (Washington, DC: U.S. Government Printing Office, 2002), 243.

receiving the highest per capita grants were Alaska ($2,225), Wyoming ($1,914), and North Dakota ($1,605). The group with the lowest per capita grants consisted of Arizona, Colorado, Florida, Georgia, Idaho, Illinois, Indiana, Kansas, Maryland, and Nevada, all with per capita amounts less than $850.[44]

These per capita grant figures must not be interpreted simply as revealing which areas are winners and losers in the federal aid game. As noted in the previous section, a state and its local governments might receive comparatively small amounts of grants but extensive economic support as a result of direct federal expenditures. Another consideration is what the corporations and individuals in a state pay in taxes. An apparent winner might turn out to be a loser when taxes paid are compared with federal dollars returned as direct expenditures or grants.

Assuming that the federal graduated income tax has the effect of drawing proportionately greater resources from wealthy states than from less wealthy

Table 14–3　Federal Agency Outlays and Grants to State and Local Governments, 2001 (Billions of Dollars)

Agency	Total Outlays	Grant Outlays	Grants as Percentage of Total
Agriculture	68.6	20.2	29.4
Commerce	5.1	0.4	7.8
Education	35.7	24.0	67.2
Energy	16.5	0.2	1.2
Health and Human Services	426.8	183.1	42.9
Housing and Urban Development	34.0	26.2	77.1
Interior	8.2	2.7	32.9
Justice	21.3	6.2	29.1
Labor	39.4	7.7	19.5
Transportation	54.8	36.7	67.0
Treasury	390.6	0.5	0.1
Environmental Protection	7.5	3.8	50.7
Emergency Management	4.4	3.2	72.7
Other	649.5	2.2	0.3
Total	**1,864.0**	**317.1**	**17.0**

Sources: Office of Management and Budget, *Budget of the United States Government: Analytical Perspectives, Fiscal Year 2003*, p. 237, and *Historical Tables*, p. 193 (Washington, DC: U.S. Government Printing Office, 1997).

states, federal aid could amplify or dampen this effect. For example, per capita federal aid to state and local governments might increase as per capita personal income declined, which would amplify the effect. This pattern, however, is not evident; the correlation between state per capita federal grants and transfers and state per capita income is negative, but is so small (-0.14) as to be meaningless. This indicates that federal grant amounts to state and local governments, at least in 2000, were distributed without apparent connection with per capita income. As already discussed, however, a strong relationship demonstrates redistributive effects when the total flows to states from all federal actions and flows of taxes from the states are compared to per capita income. Other factors explaining the distribution of federal grants include the number of Medicaid recipients and the amount of federal land in the state, which brings money from minerals, timber, and grazing rights. Again, caution is necessary when interpreting only one measure of federal economic impact on states. The lack of a clear pattern is explained by the numerous federal grant programs that tend to offset each other in benefiting particular types of states.

Studies that have compared federal aid and state aid to urban areas have concluded that, while both are responsive to need, state aid is more responsive. Cities with greater fiscal problems receive greater per capita state assistance. An important factor in this area is local initiative itself; some cities are much more aggressive and adept at securing federal and state aid, and this ability is not necessarily correlated with the extent of need.[45] In recent years, state governments have tried to offset some of the decline in federal aid to local governments, particularly by targeting their assistance to cities with the severest problems measured in terms of need, such as prevalence of poverty and low fiscal capacity. However, state budget crises beginning in 2001, as noted above, resulted in serious cutbacks in state assistance to all local governments, both rural and urban.

Within metropolitan areas, fiscal imbalances can cause problems in the pattern of services and the ability to pay for those services. Capital flight out of central cities in the form of wealthier households and businesses moving to the suburbs exacerbates differences, especially in the older cities of the Northeast and the Midwest, although cities in other parts of the country have experienced similar phenomena. One way that some metropolitan areas have combated this problem is to develop metropolitan area tax base sharing and other fiscal equalization strategies.[46] Although not a widespread practice, multiple municipal jurisdictions within the same metropolitan area have begun to see advantages in increased coordination as some city regions look to their potential fate in a global economy.[47]

Federal aid to local communities can be provided directly to these communities or indirectly through the states. In the latter case, state officials are allowed some discretion in distributing federal funds, although federal regulations may require that a given amount pass through to localities and that some of this money be distributed according to set criteria, such as population. State enabling legislation often is required before a local government may receive funds directly from the federal government.

Devolution and Future Trends. The dollar volume of federal grants-in-aid continues to climb each year, but federal aid as a percentage of state and local revenues reached a peak in 1980 and is not expected to grow again in the foreseeable future. The decline in federal assistance and the increasing responsibilities of state and local governments are changing the character of intergovernmental relations in the United States. As **Figure 14–4** indicates, federal aid in 1980 was approximately 28 percent of state and local revenues; since then, that percentage has been slipping. On various comparative measures, federal aid is expected to continue to decline. In 2000, it was about 15 percent of the federal budget, about the same as in preceding years. Federal aid hovered between 2 and 3 percent of gross domestic product throughout the period covered by **Figure 14–4**.[48]

Figure 14–4 also indicates the substantial change in character in federal aid to state and local governments. In the 1960s, federal aid focused significantly on physical capital investments; almost 50 percent of total grant outlays were for capital investment. By 2000, capital investment outlays had declined to only 17 percent. During the same period, payments to individuals went from 35 percent (1960) of total grants to 64 percent (2000). This shift toward payments to individuals has meant a change for state and local governments; rather than serving as active agents in implementing federally funded programs, they now play a role as conduits for channeling federal funds to individuals. During the 1960s, which saw extensive federal assistance to capital infrastructure programs, state governments mainly (but also local governments) were heavily involved in selection, design, and contracting for public works financed by federal dollars. Payments to individuals channeled by the states have meant hiring more staff to determine eligibility, to verify information, and to track benefits paid to recipients. Prior to welfare reform in the mid-1990s (discussed later in this chapter), the states were not extensively involved in program design.

Federal aid cutbacks in many states have created difficulties for many governments and have proved nearly devastating for others, especially when combined with reductions in revenue due to economic recessions and taxing limitations. The recessionary period of 1990–1992 caused enormous hardships for state and local governments; then, after almost a decade of prosperity, the recessionary period beginning in 2001 depleted state reserves and forced severe cutbacks. Prior to the 1960s, state and local governments had primary financing responsibility for domestic programs. Beginning with the 1960s and the antipoverty programs of

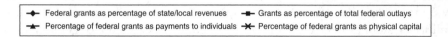

Figure 14-4 **Selected Characteristics of Federal Grants to State and Local Governments, 1960–2000**

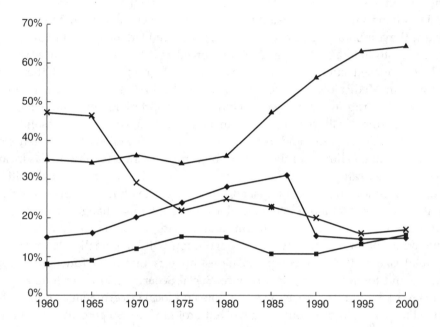

Sources: *Budget of the United States Government, Fiscal 1997* (Washington, DC: U.S. Government Printing Office, 1997), 194; *Budget of the United States Government: Historical Tables, Fiscal Year 2003*, 218; *Governing: State and Local Sourcebook*, 2002, 32.

the Johnson administration, the financial role of the federal government came to equal and, by the mid-1970s, even exceed the financial role of state and local governments. While state and local spending has not yet caught up with federal domestic spending despite the substantial shifts in spending patterns of the last decade, growth in state and local government spending has been more rapid than growth in federal spending. Not only have federal grants for capital declined, but state and local spending for capital investment as a percentage of gross domestic product has declined as well. Thus, states have been forced to scramble to keep services operating and in many situations have had little or no choice but to cut and sometimes eliminate programs.

The good news is that state and local governments have responded by improving management and efficiency, increasing their own-source revenue generation, and moving toward employment of user charges and other mechanisms that limit expenditures more to what people are actually willing to pay. This change is producing greater overall allocative efficiency in the economy. It signals a stronger role for state and local governments as determinants of domestic policy, and for many it represents a welcome shift back toward a more decentralized political system in which federal management expertise is no longer seen as significantly greater than that of state and local governments.

Devolving greater responsibility and control to state and local governments became the companion theme to achieving a balanced federal budget in the 1990s. The return to federal deficits in 2001 reinforced that trend. The fiscal year 2003 budget proposed cuts in formula-driven federal grant programs. Other than increases in Medicaid as a result of increased health care costs, federal aid to states would drop in other areas, including transportation, environmental, and energy programs.[49] As we will discuss in a later section, additional consolidation of federal grant programs and use of more block grants in lieu of more restricted programs is one hallmark of the devolution campaign. But devolution has meant not only a relaxation in federal requirements, but also a fundamental shift in responsibility for policy, programs, and financing. Devolution involves outright reductions in federal aid to state and local governments, changes in some programs from matching to nonmatching grants, and, of course, greater flexibility. Some critics point out, however, that devolution will have negligible impact on the total size of the public sector. One estimate is that if all functions except defense and foreign affairs, debt service, Social Security, and other federal payments to individuals were devolved to state and local governments, and if states proved to be able to carry out the devolved programs for 90 percent of the previous federal cost, the total cost of government would drop by less than half of 1 percent.[50] In response to the challenges, state and local governments have taken on much more activist roles in policy formulation, program design, and program implementation in assuming responsibilities that have been determined by federal policy and program design since their origins. States have become more activist in developing and implementing environmental programs, including some that exceed mandatory federal standards.[51] They have also taken the initiative in developing policies and programs in child health insurance, despite some of the disasters initially experienced as a result of rigid federal design, discussed earlier.[52]

September 11, 2001, brought an entirely new challenge to state and local governments, and one that possibly could have major effects on the pattern of intergovernmental relations. Although state national guard units under the authority of the governor have responded to natural disasters and occasionally social unrest, state and local governments are not accustomed to taking such a front-line role. But with terrorist threats having become a reality within the borders of the

United States, state and local governments are finding themselves at the forefront of a battle that is potentially more sophisticated in its demand for intelligence than state and local governments can achieve. The federal response, aside from defense spending for military buildup and conduct of actions outside the United States, was to create a new cabinet-level Department of Homeland Security to, among other functions, plan for significant grants to states to strengthen their health surveillance and public works protection programs.[53] These grant proposals include a block grant program exceeding $1 billion for bioterrorism threats and another $2 billion for training and communications, rescue equipment, and personnel. A major feature of the programs is to increase security around major public facilities such as bridges, dams, water sources, airports, public arenas, and other potentially threatened areas.

Welfare Reform as a Case Study in Devolution. The most prominent shift in devolving policy and program design in the last three decades has been reconfiguring the nation's welfare system. A number of changes in parts of the system took place over about a decade leading up to the Personal Responsibility and Work Opportunity Reconciliation Act (PRWORA) of 1996. Changes in the earned income tax credit increased disposable income among low-income, basically welfare-eligible households and individuals. Medicaid coverage expanded to include adults with dependent children, affecting mainly families with incomes putting them above welfare eligibility.

The big change in the intergovernmental system introduced by PRWORA was the shift of federal responsibility for setting welfare standards and the long-standing approach of federal matching grants to a fixed block grant program.[54] States have been given wide latitude in designing programs. From the point of view of welfare recipients, the major change was a maximum lifetime eligibility of five years for public financial assistance. This change involved the replacement of the Aid to Families with Dependent Children (AFDC) program with Temporary Assistance for Needy Families (TANF).

PRWORA was preceded by considerable relaxation in federal requirements through granting states waivers, thereby exempting them from many federal requirements, to develop their own policies and system designs.[55] Some states secured waivers to contract out to private organizations such previously state functions as eligibility determination, job counseling and training, and administration of the program.[56] Others consolidated numerous programs. States determine eligibility, set benefit levels, and design their own program administration. State programs are funded through a combination of federal funds (through the TANF block grant) and state funds. By 2002, states were required to have at least 20 percent reductions in the number of individuals receiving public assistance, as presumably some would have reached the end of their eligibility. Problems have, of course, cropped up, along with some fairly remarkable successes. Millions of individuals across the country have moved off of the welfare rolls and into paid employment. Innovative policy and program reforms in welfare-to-work transition, teen pregnancy reduction, health screening, and single-parent family issues have been developed as a result of the "experiments" conducted across the states. By the standard of intergovernmental reform and devolution, welfare reform has achieved large successes.[57]

Welfare recipients themselves have had varying experiences. Clearly, some have found productive employment and are unlikely to return to public assistance. Many have experienced frustrations at finding only minimum-wage jobs.[58] A study comparing former welfare recipients in terms of job retention with otherwise similar individuals not previously on welfare found that former welfare recipients are more likely to retain their jobs.[59] Some states have developed supplemental forms of assistance to address the group of individuals who are no longer on the welfare rolls, are working, but are earning wages that would otherwise qualify them for public assistance. Minnesota has implemented a state earned income tax credit and supplemental programs for child care subsidies and child care credits.[60] PRWORA was reauthorized in 2002, and though changes were necessary in some features and practices, this intergovernmental change is likely to be lasting.

Other Elements Affecting Intergovernmental Patterns

Direct expenditures and financial assistance provided by one level of government to another level are not the only factors in the U.S. system of intergovernmental relations that affect budgeting. In addition to restrictions and requirements built into most financial assistance, the programs financed by the assistance contain various requirements that influence how state and local governments plan and budget. Another element derives from the fact that state governments are the constitutional authorities for establishing local governments within their jurisdictions and thus have significant roles in determining which revenue sources local governments may use, which services local governments are responsible for providing, and under which circumstances local governments may enter into debt.

Features Associated with Financial Assistance. The preceding sections discussed the targeting aspects of grants provided by one level of government to another level. Additional controls often are built into the assistance arrangement. One of the fastest-growing budgetary components for all levels of government is the Medicaid program, which offers health assistance to the poor. Prior to 1991, some states adopted taxes on health providers as one means to raise the funds required by the state matching provision. In 1991, the Health Care Financing Administration (HCFA), now renamed Centers for Medicare and Medicaid

Services (CMS), prohibited the use of health provider taxes and prohibited counting private donations to health providers as part of the state match.[61] This particular regulation was aimed at increasing the likelihood that state matches would be additive, rather than federal funds substituting for state efforts.

Features Not Directly Associated with Financial Assistance. The federal government's authority under the Constitution has been used in other ways to preempt state authority, and state governments frequently preclude local action in various arenas. Since the late 1960s, coinciding with the development of many of the federal assistance programs, federal preemptions of state and local authority have increased at a rapid pace. From 1960 through 1995, more than 800 statutory actions were implemented preempting state policy or action in favor of federal policy or action.[62] Examples include the Clean Water Act amendments in 1987 and the Safe Drinking Water Act amendments of 1996. The former retained the regulatory requirements, but reduced federal financial assistance to state and local governments and shifted it to assisting states to set up revolving loan funds to finance systems. The 1996 amendments to the Safe Drinking Water Act strengthened the regulatory requirements to mandate stronger scientific studies of health risks. The result of those additional requirements has been increased costs to states.

Judicial strengthening of the federal government's preemptive right to regulate is often traced to the 1985 case of *Garcia v. San Antonio Metropolitan Transit Authority*.[63] The case focused on whether the federal Fair Labor Standards Act applied to a local government entity. The court ruled that since the transit authority had received considerable funding from federal programs (Urban Mass Transportation Act of 1965), it must adhere to fair labor standards requirements. In this case, the Court narrowly interpreted the extent to which the Constitution protects the powers and authority of the states.

Analysis of numerous other cases involving financial administration, personnel policies, and program management since *Garcia* suggests that there is no particular pattern of support either for a central government or a state government position. To the contrary, there has emerged some "resurgence of federalism" in Court decisions in recent years, although no dominant trend has been established one way or the other.[64] In *Printz v. United States*, the U.S. Supreme Court ruled that the provision of the Brady Handgun Violence Prevention Act requiring chief law enforcement officers of local jurisdictions to conduct background checks until a national system is in place was an unconstitutional requirement of state officials to enforce federal law.[65] This area of law is quite unsettled (see Chapter 13). The Age Discrimination in Employment Act and the Americans with Disabilities Act (ADA) have been held not to apply to the states, for example.[66]

State Control of Local Governments. These issues are not limited to federal effects on state and local governments. Since state governments have full constitutional authority over local governments, significant limitations on local authority may stem from state actions. Statutory debt limitations, usually expressed as a maximum debt to the property tax base ratio, are common, as are requirements that state legislatures approve through formal legislative enactment some local taxes, such as sales taxes.

A state also may assume direct control of a local government if it cannot exercise the capacity to govern itself. Instances of state takeover of municipal functions have been associated with some aspect or another of financial failure, but not usually bond debt failures. And it is not restricted to only cities of a certain size. In December 1996, the State of Florida appointed a State Control Board to supervise for a five-year period the City of Miami's budget and finances after the city was unable to balance its budget in two successive years, which is against state law. Although the city experienced considerable political turbulence, including a mayoral election that was invalidated several months after the mayor took office, by the end of the oversight board's commission, in 2002, the city had regained sound financial footing, and even was able to sell $32 million in bonds to refinance bonds sold previously at higher interest rates.[67]

In 1997, the State of North Carolina took over the small town of Princeville, under a previously never used state statute dating back to 1931. The state's Local Government Commission took over city finances and revenue collections, while the town commissioners continued to govern otherwise. Town officials had been unable, or unwilling, to collect taxes due, and the city sewer system was overflowing into the streets due to neglected maintenance.[68] Under the commission's financial oversight, Princeville began to restore its situation, but hurricanes Dennis and Floyd in 1999 severely flooded the town, overtaking the city's own fiscal crisis.

Philadelphia, New York, and East St. Louis are among other cities that have had state-appointed oversight or financial control boards. New York's board, appointed in 1975, will continue at least until 2008. Its Financial Control Board is under the supervision of the State Comptroller's office, which reviews rolling four-year financial plans prepared by the state-appointed control board.[69]

Somewhat analogous was the situation with the nation's capital, except that it is the federal government that statutorily controls the District of Columbia. Like cities in many states, the District operates under the auspices of a home rule charter that grants considerable autonomy to the District, albeit subject to change by the legislature. In 1995, a financial control board was appointed to supervise the finances of the District of Columbia, similar to one created by the New York legislature to supervise New York City's finances. As part of the 1997 Balanced Budget Agreement (see Chapters 9 and 15), Congress also developed a financial assistance package for the District of Columbia. The aid package focused on relieving the District of its unfunded pension liability, a tax credit package, Medicaid, and prison system financial relief. To end the oversight of the Financial Responsibility and Management Assistance Authority, the District had to become current with bond debt service, repay U.S. Treasury loans, restore access to short- and long-term credit, and achieve a balanced budget for four consecutive years. In 2001, the District of Columbia met all four conditions and the assistance authority ceased operations.[70]

State takeover of a general-purpose jurisdiction such as a city or town is not the only kind of state control over substate entities. After the Philadelphia school system finances spun out of control, Pennsylvania assumed control over the school system in 2001. Setting budget policy, managing the system's finances, and contracting out operation of about 40 percent of the schools in the system to three private companies were among the financial and operational controls imposed. Texas passed a law in 1995 that would allow the state to take over schools that failed to meet specified state standards. The law was challenged in the courts, but the Supreme Court determined that there was no need for a ruling at the time because no school takeover was impending.[71]

A state's assuming complete control over a city is a rare event, but it serves as a reminder that local governments are statutorily governed by state governments with nothing comparable to the federal Constitution's Tenth Amendment reserving a broad array of powers to state governments.

Types of Fiscal Assistance

Grant Characteristics

Of the numerous aspects of grants-in-aid, at least four are particularly important: (1) the purpose of the award, (2) the recipient, (3) the amount, and (4) the method of distribution. The purposes of awards will be discussed in some detail in the next subsection, but for the moment it should be noted that purposes range from narrowly defined functions to general support.

Recipients can be individuals or families who receive financial aid, as in the case of welfare payments or Medicaid payments to the poor and medically needy. When programs provide guarantees of aid to individuals and families, they are referred to as entitlements. Sometimes the term *entitlement* is used for programs providing funds to state and local governments, as in the instance of the community development block grant program (CDBG), in which entitlement communities receive funds on a formula basis — funds that are predictable by the cities in advance of their receipt.

The third aspect is the amount of aid that is made available. Some programs are open-ended in the sense that aid is provided to all persons who qualify. All persons meeting a needs test based on income, for instance, might qualify for aid; if the number of qualified applicants increases, then the amount of aid available must also increase. This type of grant, of course, complicates budgeting, because administrators do not know in advance the amount of funds that will be needed. An alternative is for the legislature to predetermine an amount that will be available regardless of the number of potential recipients. The Women, Infants, and Children (WIC) supplemental food program is an example of a program in which the amount that eligible families may receive is determined by a needs test, but funding may or may not be made available for everyone who is eligible. Once the funding limit in a particular state is reached, other eligible candidates are placed on a waiting list. For this program, the Food and Nutrition Service must annually estimate the number of eligible individuals so that appropriations can cover the number of people who are eligible. Some studies have shown that more people participate than are eligible, leading some in Congress to call for funding cuts, but other evidence indicates that there are more eligibles than actually participate.[72]

Fourth, different distribution methods are possible. In one method, would-be recipients compete for awards by submitting proposals to indicate how funds will be used. This tactic is common for demonstration grants available to private and nonprofit institutions and several categories of grants available to state and local governments. Another method is to use a formula that allocates funds among eligible recipients. Formulas can be used to help target money where it is needed most. Gaining agreement on specific provisions in a formula among legislators can be difficult; for example, members of Congress evaluate proposed provisions of a formula in terms of how their home districts or states will be affected. Sometimes the distribution is set by the legislative body, particularly in instances in which funds are provided for specified public works projects.

Categorical Aid

At the federal level, hundreds of grant programs exist. **Table 14–4** from the *Catalog of Federal Domestic Assistance* provides a count of various grant programs, by type of grant, with an illustrative and commonly known example of each. There are 1,499 federal domestic assistance programs in the catalog, of which only the grant programs (as opposed to loans and other programs) are listed in **Table 14–4**. A historically common designation, not used in the *Catalog*, are *categorical* grants. Rather, these grants are now separated into *formula* grants and *direct payments for specified use*. There are 311 of these programs identified in the *Catalog*, and summarized in **Table 14–4**.

Table 14–4 Federal Grant Programs by Type with Examples, 2002

	Number of Programs	Example
Formula grants	173	School Breakfast Program
Project grants	889	Small Business Innovation Research
Direct payments for specified use	138	Food Stamps
Direct payments with unrestricted use	38	Vocational Rehabilitation for Disabled Veterans
Sale, exchange, or donation of property and goods	23	Food Donation

Source: *Catalog of Domestic Federal Assistance* (Washington, DC: U.S. Government Printing Office, 2002); also available at www/cfda.gov/public/browse_by_typast.asp; accessed August 2002.

The number of federal categorical programs has fluctuated widely. In 1975, there were 422 categorical grant programs. That number fell to 392 by 1984, but reached nearly 600 by the mid-1990s, and, as noted, was back down to 311 in 2002.[73] The largest number of grant programs involved project grants, which may or may not be categorical. Typically, project grants are awarded on the basis of competitive or noncompetitive applications or proposals. Many project grants are appropriately considered categorical grants in that the program is created to fund applicants to meet a specific perceived national need, and specific funds are appropriated for grants and cooperative agreements to meet that need. The number of any of these types, of course, does not signify the amount of assistance available, but it does indicate the diversity of programs.

Categorical programs have a narrow focus and target aid to deal with perceived problems. If rat infestations are seen as a major problem in poor neighborhoods, an aid program can be established to support efforts to eliminate or control rat populations. Categorical programs presumably allow the federal government to target aid to deal with problems that are perceived to be national in scope and allow the state governments to do the same in regard to state problems. Many categorical programs were created during the War on Poverty initiated by President Johnson in the late 1960s. Part of the motivation for creating categorical programs was that state legislatures, then dominated in many states by politicians from rural areas, were unresponsive to urban needs, especially the problems of large center cities. Many categorical grant programs were intended to channel funds directly to cities, bypassing the state legislatures.[74] Another reason for creating categorical programs was to target and restrict assistance in various ways in an effort to control the recipients' behavior.[75] For example, assistance for community development projects required extensive community participation to ensure that low-income groups had an influence over program design.

Categorical grants typically require would-be recipients to apply for aid by preparing proposals. These proposals indicate how problems will be addressed and what the expected benefits will be. During the application process, applicants must engage in considerable preplanning, which is expected to help increase the chances that the money will be spent effectively. Funding agencies, by means of an application review process, presumably can weed out unsound projects.[76]

Criticisms of categorical aid programs abound. Grants may skew local priorities. A jurisdiction might apply for funds for one type of project even though some other project, for which no grant funding was available, would provide greater benefits to the jurisdiction.[77] Another criticism is that much time and energy are consumed in drafting grant proposals. Still another is that some jurisdictions do not obtain their "fair share" of federal dollars simply because they lack adequate staff for proposal writing; small jurisdictions, in particular, may have little "grantsmanship" capability. Categorical grants make budget planning difficult because proposals may be held pending for months. Another problem is that grants are not coordinated. Furthermore, state legislatures dislike being bypassed, and many grant recipients — whether governmental or private organizations — resent some of the restrictions that are attached to the use of funds.

One frequently made proposal is that the application process be simplified. Simplification includes reducing the amount of paperwork involved and standardizing some forms and procedures to make the process more comprehensible to applicants who may wish to seek funds from two or more agencies. OMB Circular A-102 and subsequent legislation reducing duplicative audit requirements have standardized some forms and procedures, but preparing individual grant applications is no less time-consuming. Some federal research agencies, such as the National Science Foundation, have automated the application process, making it possible for the entire process to be completed via a Web-based form. Of course, that step has not eliminated the actual proposal writing, but processing time has been reduced. The on-line application process is mainly limited to applications for research grants.

Revenue Sharing

General Revenue Sharing. A dramatic alternative to categorical grants is general revenue sharing (GRS), which at the federal level was created by the State and Local Fiscal Assistance Act of 1972. Under the original legislation, the federal government shared some of its revenue with states, counties, cities, and townships; in subsequent years, the states were dropped from the list of beneficiaries, in part because many had surpluses in their budgets and could hardly claim to be in need of general federal support.

Although general revenue sharing was allowed to expire in 1986, it is worthy to note in that it represents the opposite end of the spectrum from categorical grants. GRS also continues to be proposed from time to time, along with shared tax systems, as more radical overhauls to the intergovernmental fiscal system. The now-defunct program had three key characteristics:

- Preestablished amounts of aid
- Use of formulas for distributing the aid
- Considerable latitude to spend funds in terms of local priorities

When renewing the program, often for three years at a time, Congress set specific dollar amounts to be disbursed in given time periods. Such provisions allowed local governments to plan well in advance as to how GRS monies would be used; of course, the drawback from the point of view of the federal government was that this portion of the budget was relatively uncontrollable.

GRS allocations were made by a series of complex formulas. A ceiling was set to limit how much any jurisdiction would receive, as well as a floor to guarantee that most jurisdictions would receive some funds. A distinguishing feature of GRS was that jurisdictions received funds without having to make application for these monies.

GRS attempted to solve some of the problems associated with categorical grant programs. Jurisdictions had great freedom in deciding which functional areas would receive funds. Another benefit was that time and energy were not wasted in proposal writing. Jurisdictions that needed funds but lacked the staff capability to make application for categorical grants still received GRS funds.

On the other hand, there were many criticisms of GRS. The formula was said to provide unneeded monies to some jurisdictions. The floor provision may have propped up basically inefficient jurisdictions that might otherwise have been forced by economics to consolidate their services with those of other governments. The ceiling may have denied needed funds to many deserving jurisdictions, particularly center cities. Communities allegedly were allowed to squander their GRS funds, whereas categorical grants required more planning.

GRS expired because a compelling case could not be made for its continuation. As the federal government faced annual budget deficits in excess of $200 billion, federal officials could convincingly argue that there simply was no revenue to share with local governments. Additionally, proponents faced the difficult task of identifying a national purpose being served by GRS. In the short run, eliminating the program caused serious budgetary problems for municipalities with shrinking tax bases. In addition, many local governments shifted to user charges, which in some cases were regressive (user charges are typically based on the cost of the service rather than the ability to pay).

While revenue sharing is no longer in operation at the national level, it persists at the state level. States provide funds to local governments using formulas based on population and income. Fiscal pressures on state governments in the early 1990s caused many to reduce the amounts allocated to revenue sharing. Then, after almost a decade of surpluses, a return in 2001 to severe state budget pressures again caused states to drastically reduce funding.[78]

Block Grants

A form of compromise between GRS and categorical grants is special revenue sharing, or block grants. Under this system, a higher-level government shares part of its revenue with lower-level governments, but the use of funds is restricted to specified functions, such as law enforcement or social services. Sometimes a distinction is made between block grants and special revenue sharing, with the former requiring submission of an application and the latter not. More often, however, the terms are used interchangeably or the term *block grants* is used to cover both types of revenue sharing. State aid to education, using various formulas, is an example of a block grant, with the funds coming largely from state general revenue. State aid for local roads is another form of block grant, with monies coming from earmarked taxes on motor fuels. The Temporary Assistance to Needy Families program discussed earlier and the proposed block grant program for homeland defense are additional examples. The latter is likely to combine categorical or closely directed grants with a block grant program.

Block grants at the federal level have been used as a method for consolidating categorical grant programs. These categoricals are grouped together so that jurisdictions have greater flexibility within specified program areas. The application process is greatly reduced, because a jurisdiction applies for only one grant instead of several. Early block grant legislation included the Partnership for Health Act of 1966, the Law Enforcement Assistance Act of 1968, and the Comprehensive Employment and Training Act of 1973.

A landmark in block grant legislation was the Housing and Community Development Act of 1974.[79] This program provided entitlement funding to medium and large cities through the use of a formula and gave funds to states to award small cities on a discretionary basis. The law phased out programs for open space, public facility loans, water and sewer grants, urban renewal, model cities, and rehabilitation loans. Under the original legislation, entitlement cities were required to submit an application for funding; the process was considerably less detailed than had been required for the previous categorical programs. Later, the application process was dropped for the entitlement cities.

Various consolidations of categorical grants into block grants have taken place over the last two decades. The first wave started with the Omnibus Budget Reconciliation Act of 1981, which among other things consolidated many existing categorical grant programs and created nine new block grants, four in health-related services, to be administered by the states.[80] The most recent round of consolidation and relaxing federal control created the Temporary Assistance to Needy Families, the initial major reform of welfare assistance in an attempt to devolve responsibilities from the federal government to states, as discussed earlier.

The programmatic feature of federal block grants is that monies are granted in lump sums to states, which determine how the money is to be used and, when it involves local government assistance, how funds are to be divided among governments within each state. This approach has been championed as restoring power to the states. The fiscal feature of federal block grants, each time they are introduced, has been a substantial reduction in funds. These cuts are defended in part in the name of efficiency. Allowing states and localities to select the desired mix of activities and levels of quality and quantity, block grants reduce the costs of "one size fits all" categorical grants, which substitute federal judgments for those at the state and local levels. Further, since the block grants provide more flexibility to state and local governments, fewer federal officials are needed to administer the programs and fewer state officials are needed to oversee local government operations. Given that block grants almost always result in some degree of reduced federal financing because they are consolidating previous categorical programs, state and local governments have to achieve the supposed efficiencies, make up for the losses, or reduce quality or quantity of services.

Figure 14–5 illustrates that state and local governments have generally maintained their overall revenue growth since 1980, despite relative declines in federal grants — at least this was true prior to 2001. The economic downturn starting in 2000–2001 had major impacts on state and local revenues by 2002. In **Figure 14–5**, state and local total revenues are shown in billions of dollars on the left y-axis, and the percentage of state and local general revenues constituted by federal aid is shown on the right y-axis. State and local revenues as a whole have steadily increased, making up with their own sources for the drop in federal aid.

Figure 14-5 **Impact of Federal Aid Cuts on State and Local Revenues, 1952–1998**

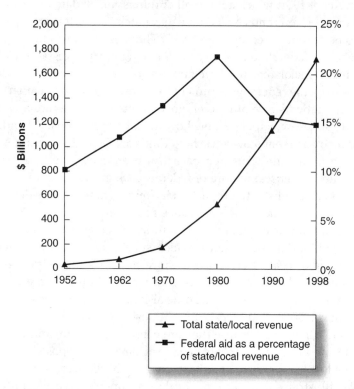

Sources: Tax Foundation, *Facts and Figures on Government Finance: 1992 and 1997* (Washington, DC), 230, 240, 289 from 1992 and 116 from 1997; 1998 data from U.S. Bureau of the Census, *Statistical Abstract of the United States: 2001*, (Washington, DC: U.S. Government Printing Office, 2001), 266.

Restructuring Patterns of Intergovernmental Relations

Tax Laws

Tax Deductions. A substantive change that could be made is to adjust taxes in ways that would reduce the need for financial assistance. By increasing the taxing powers of lower-level governments, the need for grants-in-aid may be reduced. For example, taxpayers currently may deduct many state and local taxes from gross income before computing federal tax liabilities. Included are state and local income taxes, property taxes, and some other lesser taxes. Excluded are state sales, gasoline, and similar consumption and excise taxes. The Tax Reform Act of 1986 (TRA86) is responsible for removing the deductibility of some state and local taxes, such as sales taxes. Federal tax law could be altered either to increase or decrease deductibility. Such tax policies affect disposable income, affect government revenue, and alter the distribution of taxing power among levels of government.

Economists have been particularly critical of deductions for property taxes in that this benefit is largely enjoyed by middle-income families. Lower-income families are less likely to own homes and therefore are unable to benefit from the deductibility, and higher-income families do not benefit appreciably from such deductions. The importance of the home building industry to the overall economy, however, has been used by lobbyists to argue in favor of property tax deductibility. TRA86 did limit mortgage interest deductions to only two homes, one of which must be a principal residence and the other a vacation or second home.

On the other side of the argument, tax deductions do provide some measure of latitude for state and local taxation. They reduce somewhat the differentials among states and among localities, and they mitigate some of the problems of tax overlapping. At least overlapping taxes may be held to a level that is not confiscatory. The strongest argument in favor of tax deductibility is that the practice is firmly entrenched and that any effort to eliminate deductibility for property taxes, for example, would be politically unacceptable without compensating tax relief.

Tax Credits. The institution of tax credits would be likely to cause a more substantial shift in revenue sources than would result from changes in tax deductibility. Tax credits would allow individual taxpayers to use taxes paid to one jurisdiction to reduce the tax liability owed to another jurisdiction. A tax credit reduces tax liability dollar for dollar, whereas a deduction of taxes paid to another jurisdiction from one's taxable income is worth only the marginal tax bracket percentage, the highest being 39 percent. One proposal sometimes made is to allow such credits for the federal income tax; the effect would be to redistribute revenue from the federal government to state and local governments. A tax credit on income taxes could encourage those states without income taxes to adopt them because the taxpayers would be less affected. However, if the tax credit is uniform regardless of income, it would benefit the wealthier states even more than the poorer ones.

Unemployment Insurance. The federal government has enticed or forced states to impose unemployment insurance taxes on employers by providing that most monies from such taxes may stay within each state; in the event that a state did not have an approved system, a tax presumably would be imposed by the federal government. Until TRA86, unemployment benefits were not treated as income under federal tax law, thereby providing an important benefit to individuals and creating a costly tax expenditure for the federal government. These benefits are now taxable. Inheritance taxes are practically forced on states by a federal tax provision deducting 80 percent of any state inheritance tax paid. Any state that did not adopt an inheritance tax would lose considerable appeal to retirees and other older citizens.

Taxes and Bonds. Another important benefit afforded state and local governments through federal tax law is the tax exemption on interest earned on bonds issued by these governments. Tax exemption has had the effect of allowing governments to pay lower interest rates to bondholders than if the bonds were taxable. An even more important impact of TRA86 on state and local revenues was the reduction in the types of municipal bonds that are eligible for tax-exempt status, particularly private-purpose activity bonds (see Chapter 12). Some have argued that TRA86 has farther-reaching implications because provisions relating to required registration of tax-exempt municipal bond buyers and state reporting on arbitrage gains from tax-exempt bond proceeds undermine the autonomy of state and local governments within the federal system. The Internal Revenue Service audits questionable tax-exempt bonds, suspecting that they may not meet the tax-exempt criteria. Some taxpayers have received unwelcome surprises when interest earned on what they thought were tax-exempt sources turned out upon later review by the IRS to be taxable interest.

Shared Taxes. Presently, the federal, state, and local governments in the United States have either exclusive or overlapping jurisdiction over various tax sources. Only the federal government may tax imports and exports. The federal government does not have a property tax or general sales tax. Federal, state, and local governments overlap in the use of personal and corporate income taxes. Some states benefit from linking their own personal income tax systems to the federal system. Individuals in North Carolina, for example, can file a state income tax form that bases taxes on the federal taxable income. This simplifies administration of the system and reduces state tax administration costs. When TRA86 expanded the federal tax base, it automatically expanded the base for most states, since their systems are tied in one form or another to the federal system. However, there is no shared link between the two — the federal Internal Revenue Service collects only federal income taxes, and state and local governments collect their own income taxes. State and local governments typically share a sales tax; it is collected by the state, but revenues are allocated to local governments that levy such taxes.

The Rivlin proposal calling for the adoption of a value-added tax included the idea that it would be shared among levels of government. This idea still has currency in intergovernmental fiscal reform discussions in that it would be a major rationalization of the tax system, rather than piecemeal reform.[81] Sharing the tax means that it would be a common tax, eliminating competition between states over the level of taxation. It would also mean shared administration, reducing the collection costs, and it would minimize the ability of one level of government to preempt other levels' use of a particular tax. State and local finance in the German federal system, for example, relies heavily on shared taxation. A national shared sales tax also would resolve the issues around states' inability to develop an effective way to tax e-commerce (see Chapter 4). Any major realignment of responsibilities among levels of government must include changes in revenue systems as well.

Grant Requirements

Mandates. Other proposals to improve intergovernmental fiscal relations pertain to mandates. For instance, when a state legislature passes a law requiring school districts to adopt certain procedures in dealing with gifted children or children with learning disabilities, a mandate has been established that has budgetary implications. Typically, federal mandates on state and local governments are tied to grants or other forms of federal assistance and contracts, making the stipulation that a government (or private party) must meet specified conditions to qualify for funds. Notable crosscutting mandates — requirements that apply to the work of most federal agencies and grant programs — require recipients to pay locally prevailing wages, meet Americans with Disabilities Act standards for removing architectural barriers for persons with disabilities, and prevent discrimination based on race, sex, and the like. These mandates are at a basic level unrelated to the purpose of the grant or contract or other funding. That is, a local government carrying out an activity funded under the Community Development Block Grant program related to building a community facility would be required to pay minimum wages and would be required to adhere to provisions of the Fair Labor Standards Act and the Davis-Bacon Act. The various requirements imposed have to do with federal policy as stated in legislation and regulation toward work and employment conditions including fair wages. These regulations would apply to the entire local government, not just the particular department involved with the facility. It is possible, however, that challenges in court to the applicability of these labor laws might be ruled in favor of state governments, but the courts generally have not exempted local governments.

Other mandates are directly related to the grant program objectives. As noted earlier, continued TANF funding to a state is contingent on its reducing the number of people on its welfare rolls. How the state accomplished that goal is open to wide latitude in this block grant program, but the state was required to achieve a 20 percent reduction by 2002 (the end of the first five years of the program). Medicaid is a categorical grant program that is always on the firing line because of the high and increasing costs of health care and because of the state funds that have to be committed along with the federal funds. Federal mandates limit state control of Medicaid by specifying in great detail who is eligible and what costs are reimbursable. As a result of these mandates, states have felt they are less able to make their own budgetary decisions.[82]

Unfunded Mandates. Another category for reform has been eliminating what many term "unfunded mandates." These are federal or state mandates that are not necessarily tied to particular financial assistance programs. For example, federal laws and court rulings have set standards for state prison systems that in many cases require additional prisons to be built — without federal assistance. These requirements are not associated with any program of financial assistance, and they are mandatory for all states (in the case of federal requirements) regardless of whether or not the state is a recipient of federal programs related to the justice system. They are a matter of a federal determination that it is in the national interest to require states to meet certain standards, but no help to do so is available from the federal government.

The Disabilities Education Act of 1975 and implementing regulations include detailed requirements for states to accommodate students with disabilites to enable successful educational outcomes. In the Disabilities Education Act, federal funding up to 40 percent of the amount states spend is promised to assist the states. In principle, one might call that a "funded mandate." However, appropriations have never come close in more than 25 years to meeting that 40 percent promise. Hence, the mandate is unfunded.[83] This is a common situation. Clean air and water standards have forced local governments to build new solid waste treatment facilities, substantially change wastewater treatment systems, and adopt numerous other practices. The City of Columbus, Ohio, estimated that 13 environmental regulations would cost the city as much as $1.6 billion between 1991 and 2000.[84] Of course, one cannot argue that local governments would otherwise spend nothing and attribute the total spending to federal, unfunded mandates.

State and local officials argue that these mandates should be accompanied by federal funding because they appear to be attempts to achieve goals previously set by the federal government through financial assistance programs and now, with federal aid being cut due to budgetary pressures, have become regulatory means to the same end. The contrary view argues that there are genuine national goals that relate to such public purposes as health and safety, environmental regulation, minimum living standards for every family, and so forth, and that these require federal action. Just because a national purpose exists, it does not necessarily mean there should be a matching federal payment to assist in achieving that purpose. The same line of reasoning is employed by states in their use of mandates for local governments.

The Clinton administration acted in 1993 through Executive Order 12875, Enhancing the Intergovernmental Partnership, to reduce unfunded mandates by requiring federal agencies either to provide funds necessary to comply with mandates or to show evidence of significant consultation with state and local governments before promulgating new regulations mandating state or local expenditures.[85] In 1995, Congress passed the Unfunded Mandates Reform Act, which requires any bill that would impose *new* unfunded costs greater than $50 million to be subject to a point of order in either chamber.[86] This procedural hurdle makes it much simpler for either the House or the Senate to kill the bill; a majority of members have to override the point of order.[87] Under the act, the Congressional Budget Office must estimate the costs of mandates in bills reported out of authorizing committees. Somewhat similar legislation in 1997 required the Congressional Budget Office to analyze the effects on the private sector of new mandates that may have compliance costs in excess of $100 million. From 1996 through 2000, CBO provided mandate cost statements on 3,000 intergovernmental mandates and nearly 3,000 private sector mandates. Of these, 32 intergovernmental mandates would have exceeded threshold costs of $50 million per year and 100 private sector mandates would have exceeded threshold costs of $100 million. Only two of the laws exceeding intergovernmental cost thresholds were enacted, and only 16 of the laws exceeding private sector cost thresholds were enacted. The CBO concluded that the analysis and information process substantially affected congressional decision making.[88]

The courts also have become somewhat involved in addressing federal mandates, although in cases not involving significant state and local financial issues. In 1995 in *U.S. v. Lopez*, the Supreme Court struck down a federal statute that regulated possessing a gun in a school zone; in 1997, it ruled that the provisions of the Brady Handgun Act requiring state and local law enforcement officers to conduct criminal background checks on persons applying to purchase guns were not enforceable.[89] Other court rulings noted earlier that, for example, exempted states from ADA requirements, suggest that the Supreme Court will not allow Congress to abrogate states' rights without documented evidence of a compelling need.

It is impossible to take any particular assistance program or any particular mandate and examine its effects in isolation. As shown throughout this chapter, some programs result in redistribution across states, other programs are intentionally targeted to the poorer states, and other programs are intended to affect classes of individuals wherever they might live. Intergovernmental questions are resolved not by considering one program at a time, but rather by considering the entire system of programs. Many argue that state and local governments have been strengthened in recent years by having to rely more on their own resources, not weakened by the combination of decreased federal financial aid and increased mandated requirements.

Civil Rights. One area of controversy concerns the extent to which a jurisdiction's operations must comply with civil rights stipulations. In *Grove City College v. Bell* (465 U.S. 555), the Supreme Court ruled that only that portion of an organization affected by federal dollars had to comply with standards protecting against discrimination based on race, sex, age, and handicapping condition. In that instance, the college's only federal support was for student-aid activities, so only those activities had to comply. In 1988, Congress reversed that decision by passing the Civil Rights Restoration Act, which provides that all operations of a recipient government must meet federal standards; the law was passed despite a veto by President Reagan.

Title IX of the Education Amendments of 1972 addressed the same issue — the applicability of the prohibitions against discrimination in educational institutions on the basis of gender to all activities of an institution, whether or not those activities received any federal funding. Title IX is applicable across the entire institution, without regard to specific links to federal funding. If a university, for example, participates in a federal student financial aid program or receives funding directly from the federal government or indirectly from state government agencies for construction of a library, then the university may not discriminate on the basis of gender in any program. Thus, women's sports programs have to be supported if men's sports programs are funded by the university. The Title IX impact on women's sports has received the most publicity, but it really was aimed at more fundamental equal opportunities for education, such as prohibitions on admission of married women.[90]

Streamlining and Paperwork Reduction. Related to mandates are various reporting requirements that create paperwork and thereby create costs. Reporting requirements may be associated with a single federally funded program, or often identical information is required for many programs funded by the same federal agency. States require local governments to submit numerous reports each year, and the federal government requires the same of state and local governments.

The Paperwork Reduction Act, a 1995 revision of the 1980 statute, regulates agency requests for information from state and local governments, and from private corporations and individuals (see the discussion in Chapter 10). Office of Management and Budget approval is required for any information form that is to be administered to 10 or more individuals or institutions. Agencies were to reduce the information collection burden they impose on others by between 5 and 10 percent per year through 2001. OMB is to report to Congress periodically on progress in meeting the targets (see Chapter 10).

The Regulatory Flexibility Act of 1980 and Executive Order 12291 of 1981 require agencies to conduct regulatory impact analyses to determine the effects of proposed rules or regulations, including the effects on state and local governments. Executive Order 12498 of 1985 further requires agencies to develop annual regulatory plans that must be submitted to OMB. While it may not legally "veto" agency plans to issue regulations, by using this review process OMB can stall, if not block, plans that would increase the paperwork burden on state and local governments. Executive Order 12866, issued in 1993, emphasized the role of comparing the costs of regulation (costs to society including costs to governmental institutions or private companies to comply) with the benefits of regulation (again to society); benefits must exceed costs for the regulation to be implemented.

A 1997 *Report to Congress on the Costs and Benefits of Federal Regulations* contains a good summary of the legislative and regulatory history of evaluating regulatory impact.[91] The George W. Bush administration has emphasized the importance of cost-benefit analysis in the regulatory process.

The Single Audit Act of 1984, amended in 1996, is an additional paperwork reduction device (see Chapter 11).[92] Implemented through OMB Circular A-133 (rescinding Circular A-128), the act allows a state or local government receiving funds through numerous different federal programs to comply with those programs' audit provisions by using a single financial compliance audit.[93]

The 1990 Cash Management Improvement Act introduced prompt payment provisions that require the federal government to pay interest to the recipient when a transfer is late. A related provision requires states withdrawing federal funds early to pay interest to the federal government. Streamlining cash flow has been achieved through the provisions of this act.

The Federal Financial Assistance Management Improvement Act of 1999, among other things, made changes in A-133 and other changes to "simplify federal financial assistance application and reporting requirements."[94] The act and its implementing regulations aim to create a standard format for applications for federal financial assistance. These are analagous to the National Science Foundation's and National Institutes of Health's on-line research grant applications. However, the Financial Assistance Management Improvement Act of 1999 would impose uniformity across all agencies.[95]

A further feature encouraged is the development of Web-based reporting systems that would enable recipients of federal financial assistance to file required reports and data on-line. These Web-based systems in many cases would make available information to the reporting entity on how that entity compares with other entities receiving financial assistance for the same or similar purposes. The new systems would not only be easier for many to use, but the feedback and comparative information would for the first time make the information collected useful to the entities who have to report. The George W. Bush administration made these implementing regulations a major feature of its attempts to reduce federal impositions on state, local, and private parties.

Besides the reduction of mandates, paperwork, and streamlining requirements, several other intergovernmental devices have been proposed and used. One concern is to ensure that jurisdictions have adequate information about grant programs. The General Services Administration, working with OMB, now publishes the *Catalog of Federal Domestic Assistance*; the *Catalog*, which gives capsule descriptions of grant programs, can help a local government determine whether it might be able to secure federal funding for a contemplated project. As noted earlier, the Financial Assistance Management Improvement Act would standardize application formats across programs and across agencies. These programs are covered in the *Catalog of Federal Domestic Assistance*. The on-line version of the *Catalog* allows searching and lists various federal domestic assistance programs by type of assistance, program title, functional area, agency, beneficiary, deadline for application, and several other categories. This improved access to information about federal grant programs enables potential applicants to more accurately identify programs suited to their needs.

Grant Coordination. Another concern is how to coordinate federal grants at regional and statewide levels. If a community is applying for a federal grant to assist elderly citizens, how would that grant complement other programs for the elderly in the region and how would it relate to state-level programs? In response to this type of question and as an outgrowth of the Intergovernmental Cooperation Act, the Bureau of the Budget (now OMB) in 1969 issued Circular A-95, which provided for the establishment of area-wide and state clearinghouses responsible for reviewing and commenting on proposed projects. The review and comment process offered the potential for eliminating waste in the use of federal funds. Jurisdictions applying for these funds were expected to respond to any objections made by the clearinghouses and, where appropriate, to modify the proposed projects. Circular A-95 was later rescinded and replaced by various executive orders. Ultimately, the state- and area-wide reviews proved slow and cumbersome. Fewer than one-third of the states and territories ever established a state-wide clearinghouse.

Federal–state, interstate, and interlocal arrangements have been developed for the provision of services (as distinguished from forums for discussion), including metropolitan councils of governments that involve officials from various communities in a region. One of the most successful interstate organizations is the New York Port Authority, established in 1921 by New York and New Jersey.[96] The authority operates terminals, bridges, and tunnels. It operated the World Trade Center until its destruction in 2001. Subsequently, the Port Authority and the Lower Manhattan Development Corporation approved plans for rebuilding on the site.

At the local level, numerous types of cooperative arrangements exist. Some counties provide services such as water and sewage treatment on a contract basis for municipalities within their jurisdiction. The choice of such an arrangement may be at the discretion of municipalities, as in the case of the Lakewood Plan, whereby communities can contract with Los Angeles County for virtually all city services, or at the insistence of state governments, which may require city–county cooperation for services such as police and fire protection.

Management Capacity. With the increasing emphasis on block grants, greater attention has been focused on the abilities of state and local governments to manage themselves. Devolving to these governments decision-making authority over the use of federal funds has been accompanied by a concern that they improve their management capabilities. There have been suggestions that the federal government assume responsibility for management capacity building, but the federal government has shown only a limited inclination to accept any such obligation. In fact, management improvements and other innovations at the state and local levels in recent years have led many to look to them as a source of management ideas for the federal government. The Clinton administration under the leadership of Vice President Gore undertook a major review of government performance and established a performance improvement reform program. As discussed in other chapters, Congress became engaged in the same effort with the Government Performance and Results Act. The George W. Bush administration's management agenda focused on five strategic initiatives: strategic management of human capital, competitive sourcing, e-government, financial management, and budget and performance integration, and created a new scorecard to measure performance.[97] Of course, Washington does not necessarily have superior management capabilities that, if only transferred to the state and local levels, would produce quick results.

Realigning Responsibilities. In the modern era, after the work of the Hoover Commission and other reform commissions of earlier decades (see Chapter 1), the Reagan administration proposed the first comprehensive strategy for relieving both states and localities of some of their financial burdens. This effort would involve reconfiguring responsibilities for major functions among the three levels of government. President Reagan in 1982 advocated two types of major revisions: swaps and turnbacks.[98] The *swap* proposal was for the states to accept financial responsibility for Aid to Families with Dependent Children (welfare) and food stamps and for the federal government in return to relieve the states of the financial burden of funding Medicaid. The *turnback* proposal was for the states to assume financial responsibility for 40 or more federal aid programs in social services, education, transportation, and community development. Neither the swap nor the turnback concept was well received by state and local governments. The administration's position called for a drastic cut in federal grants at a time when state and local governments were suffering through a major economic recession that had depleted their treasuries. The Reagan administration proposals were not enacted into law, but the idea of a major reorganization of government responsibilities remains an important proposal for improving how the overall government system meets the needs of citizens.[99]

Summary

Fundamental issues arise in regard to the question of how to structure intergovernmental relations. Functional integration results in picket fence arrangements that may deter geographic integration. Fiscal capacities differ among and within levels of government, so that the government that perhaps should provide services often lacks the necessary funding capability. Failure to provide services results in externality problems.

Both direct spending and grants-in-aid are important for intergovernmental relations. Decisions by federal and state agencies on the location and expansion of capital facilities affect the economic viability of local jurisdictions. Despite more extensive attention often being devoted to federal aid programs, state aid to local government is actually larger. Some states provide much of their local governments' revenue while others provide little, a point that should be stressed to avoid unwarranted generalizations. Aid to education constitutes the largest portion of state aid, with monies typically allocated on a formula basis. Federal aid is concentrated in the areas of education, income security, health, and transportation.

Major changes are occurring in the intergovernmental fiscal landscape, with substantial responsibilities for welfare reform already having been devolved to state governments, and numerous other proposals up for consideration. Furthermore, substantial concern has prompted legislative and executive action to mitigate the impacts of unfunded federal mandates. The fiscal impact of these changes is likely to be small, however, because they affect only newly proposed mandates.

Intergovernmental grants have at least four aspects: their purpose (narrow, broad, or general), the type of recipient, the amount, and the method of distribution. Categorical grants are criticized as deterring coordination, skewing local priorities, and needlessly wasting time in their proposal preparation. On the positive side, these grants are said to force planning in the preparation of their proposals and to allow for screening out poorly conceived projects. GRS supported local priorities and provided funds to jurisdictions that did not have staff available to apply for categorical grants. It was criticized as not targeting any national purpose and giving funds to many undeserving jurisdictions. Ultimately, the program was terminated at the federal level, but some states continue to engage in revenue sharing with their local governments. Block grants, a cross between categorical grants and GRS, have the advantages and disadvantages of both.

In addition to grant programs, numerous other intergovernmental devices are employed. They include provisions in federal tax law that benefit state and local governments and review and comment processes for grant proposals. Also, mechanisms have emerged for providing services on an intergovernmental basis, such as with the New York Port Authority and the Lakewood Plan in California. Proposals have been made for major reconfiguring of program responsibilities among the federal, state, and local governments. Since the 1980s, many state and local governments have shown a resurgence in this area, resulting in what many see as a healthy redress of balance between the federal level and the state and local levels.

Notes

1. R. Tannewald, Devolution: The New Federalism — An Overview, *New England Economic Review* (May/June 1998): 1–12; R.J. Dilger, The Study of American Federalism at the Turn of the Century, *State and Local Government Review* 32 (2000): 98–107.

2. U.S. Bureau of the Census, *Census of Governments: 2002, http://www.census/gov/govs/ cog/2002COGprelim_report.pdg*; accessed August 2002.

3. Organization for Economic Cooperation and Development, *Managing Across Levels of Government* (Paris: OECD, 1997).

4. D.B. Walker, *The Rebirth of Federalism: Slouching toward Washington* (Chatham, NJ: Chatham House, 1995).

5. T. Ter-Minassian, *Fiscal Federalism in Theory and Practice* (Washington, DC: International Monetary Fund, 1997).

6. C.M. Tiebout, A Pure Theory of Public Expenditures, *Journal of Political Economy* 44 (1956): 416–424; D. Epple, et al., *The Tiebout Hypothesis and Majority Rule: An Empirical Analysis* (New York: National Bureau of Economic Research, 1999), *http://papers.nber. org/papers/W6977*; accessed August 2002.

7. J.P. Conley and M.H. Wooders, Equivalence of the Core and Competitive Equilibrium in a Tiebout Economy with Crowding Types, *Journal of Urban Economics* 41 (1997): 421–440.

8. E.T. Jennings, Building Bridges in the Intergovernmental Arena: Coordinating Employment and Training Programs in the American States, *Public Administration Review* 54 (1994): 52–60; T. Arrandale, Four States Agree on the Basics of a Save-the-Salmon Strategy, *Governing* 14 (October 2000): 66.

9. D. Wright, *Understanding Intergovernmental Relations*, 3rd ed. (Pacific Grove, CA: Brooks/Cole, 1988), 83–86.

10. T. Arrandale, Balking on Air, *Governing* 14 (January 2000): 26–29.

11. T. Arrandale, Trading off Summer Smog, *Governing* 14 (June 2000): 52.

12. The discussion is based in part on B.P. Herber, *Modern Public Finance*, 5th ed. (Homewood, IL: Richard D. Irwin, 1983).

13. Commonwealth of Massachusetts, *School Finance: Special Education: FY 2001 Special Education Loan Fund, http://finance1.doe.mass.edu/seducation/spedloan01.html*; accessed August 2002.

14. U.S. Bureau of the Census, *Statistical Abstract of the United States: 2001* (Washington, DC: U.S. Government Printing Office, 2001), 426.

15. U.S. Advisory Commission on Intergovernmental Relations, *Significant Features of Fiscal Federalism, Vol. 2, Revenues and Expenditures: 1992* (Washington, DC: U.S. Government Printing Office, 1992).

16. U.S. Advisory Commission on Intergovernmental Relations, *Representative Expenditures: Addressing the Neglected Dimension of Fiscal Capacity* (Washington, DC: U.S. Government Printing Office, 1990).

17. Data in this paragraph are from R. Tannenwald, Fiscal Disparity Among the States Revisited, *New England Economic Review* (July/August 1999): 3–25.

18. Executive Order 12612, in *Federal Register* 52 (1987): 41686.

19. R. Tannewald, Come the Devolution, Will States Be Able to Respond? *New England Economic Review* (May/June 1998): 58–83; D.B. Walker, New Federalism. III. A Reformed System in the Making? *International Journal of Public Administration* 24 (2001): 51–75; Bush to Issue Order Shifting Power from Feds to States, *Government Executive* (February 2001), *http://www.govexec.com*; accessed July 2002.

20. M. Porter, Location, Competition and Economic Development: Local Clusters in a Global Economy, *Economic Development Quarterly* 14 (2000): 15–34.

21. A. Ehrenhalt, The Devil in Devolution, *Governing* 11 (May 1997): 7.

22. J. McCracken, Mercedes to Build 2nd Plant in Alabama, *Auto.com* (August 28 2000), *www.auto.com/industry/merc26_20000826.htm*; accessed August 2002.

23. A.M. Rivlin, *Reviving the American Dream: The Economy, the States and the Federal Government* (Washington, DC: Brookings Institution, 1992): 126–152.

24. J. Dao, As Defense Secretary Calls for Base Closings, Congress Circles the Wagons, *New York Times*, June 29, 2001, *www.nytimes.com/2001/06/29/politics/29MILI.html*; accessed August 2002.

25. The Real Math of Military Shutdowns, *Business Week Asian Edition* (April 5, 1999): 60–61.

26. U.S. Office of Management and Budget, *Budget of the United States Government FY 2003: Analytical Perspectives* (Washington, DC: U.S. Government Printing Office, 2002): 243.

27. U.S. Bureau of the Census, *Statistical Abstract of the United States: 2001*, 326.

28. Tax Foundation, *Tax and Spending Policies Benefit Some States, Leave Others Footing the Bill* (Washington, DC: Tax Foundation, 2001), *http://taxfoundation.org/ pr-fedtaxspendngratio.html*; accessed July 2002.

29. U.S. Bureau of the Census, *State and Local Government Finances by Level of Government: 1998–99*, *www.census.gov/govs/estimate/99stlss1.xls*; accessed August 2002.

30. U.S. Bureau of the Census, *State and Local Government Finances by Level of Government: 1998–99*.

31. U.S. Bureau of the Census, *Statistical Abstract of the United States: 2001*, 284, 21.

32. *San Antonio School District v. Rodriquez*, 411 U.S. 1 (1973).

33. *Serrano v. Priest (Serrano II)*, 557 P.2d 929 (Calif. 1976).

34. W.A. Fischel, School Finance Litigation and Property Tax Revolts: How Undermining Local Control Turns Voters Away from Public Education, *Developments in School Finance: Fiscal Proceedings from the Annual State Data Conference, July 1999 and July 2000* (Washington, DC: National Center for Education Statistics, 2002): 79–127.

35. H.F. Ladd and J.S. Hansen, eds., *Making Money Matter: Financing America's Schools* (Washington, DC: National Academy of Sciences, 1999); H.F. Ladd, et al., eds., *Equity and Adequacy in Education Finance: Issues and Perspectives* (Washington, DC: National Academy of Sciences, 1999).

36. No Child Left Behind Act, P.L. 107–110 (2001).

37. Erik Hanushek is an example, cited in *After the Bell: Education Solutions Outside the School*, New York University, *http://www.nyu.edu/fas/cassr/conf01.htm*; accessed August 2002.

38. See current issue of *Highway Statistics*, prepared annually by the Federal Highway Administration.

39. A. Greenblatt, Enemies of the State, *Governing* 16 (June 2002): 26–31.

40. R.C. Fisher and L.E. Papke, Local Government Responses to Education Grants, *National Tax Journal* 53 (2000): 153–168.

41. H. Chernick, Federal Grants and Social Welfare Spending: Do State Responses Matter?, *National Tax Journal* 53 (2000): 143–152.

42 J. Walters, The TEA Generation, *Governing* 16 (May 2002): 70–76.

43. J. Walters, CHIP on Their Shoulders, *Governing* 14 (November 2000): 12.

44. Federal Aid to States and Localities: 2000, *Governing: State and Local Source Book* (Washington, DC: Congressional Quarterly, 2002), 32.

45. M.J. Rich, Targeting Federal Grants: The Community Development Experience, 1950–1986, *Publius* 21 (Winter 1991): 29–49; D.J. Watson, Importance of Local Initiative in Targeting of Federal Aid: The Case of UDAGs, *Public Budgeting and Financial Management* 6 (1994): 201–215.

46. A.F. Haughwout, Regional Fiscal Cooperation in Metropolitan Areas: An Exploration, *Journal of Policy Analysis and Management* 18 (1999): 579–600; D. Miller, Fiscal Regionalism: Metropolitan Reform Without Boundary Changes, *Government Finance Review* 16 (December 2000): 7–12.

47. K. Ohmae, *The End of the Nation State: The Rise of Regional Economies* (New York: Free Press, 1995).

48. U.S. Office of Management and Budget, *Budget of the United States Government: Historical Tables, FY 2003* (Washington, DC: U.S. Government Printing Office, 2002), 218.

49. National Priorities Project, *Proposed FY 2003 Budget and Analysis: States and Local Governments to Lose Funding for Many Programs, www.nationalpriorities.org/budget/ FY03/index.html*; accessed July 2002.

50. J.D. Donahue, The Disunited States, *Atlantic Monthly* 279 (May 1997): 18–22.

51. T. Arrandale, The Pollution Puzzle, *Governing* 16 (August 2002): 22–26.

52. J. Buntin, The Increasingly Expansive Medicaid Machine, *Governing* 15 (October 2001): 30–32.

53. T.N. Ballard, Ridge Outlines Domestic Security Plan, Promises Mayors More Money, *Government Executive* (January 23, 2002), *www.govexec.com/dailyfed/0102/012302tl.htm*; accessed June 2002.

54. Personal Responsibility and Work Opportunity Reconciliation Act, P.L. 104–193 (1996).

55. B.D. Meyer and D.T. Rosenbaum, Making Single Mothers Work: Recent Tax and Welfare Policy and Its Effects, *National Tax Journal* 53 (2000): 1027–1061.

56. S. Arsnault, Welfare Policy Innovation and Diffusion: Section 1115 Waivers and the Federal System, *State and Local Government Review* 32 (Winter 2000): 49–60.

57. J. Walters, The Welfare Bonanza, *Governing* 14 (January 2000): 34–36.

58. J. Walters, The Flip Side of Welfare Reform, *Governing* 16 (March 2002): 17–20.

59. S.T. Gooden and M. Bailey, Welfare and Work: Job-Retention Outcomes of Federal Welfare-to-Work Employees, *Public Administration Review* 61 (2001): 83–91.

60. P. Wilson, Tax Implications of Welfare Reform: The Minnesota Experience, *National Tax Journal* 53 (2000): 417–437.

61. C.L. Eckl, et al., *State Budget and Tax Actions: 1991* (Washington, DC: National Conference of State Legislatures, 1991), 13.

62. D.B. Walker, The Advent of an Ambiguous Federalism and the Emergence of New Federalism III, *Public Administration Review* 56 (1996): 271–280.

63. *Garcia v. San Antonio Metropolitan Transit Authority*, 469 U.S. 528 (1985).

64. C. Wise and R. O'Leary, Intergovernmental Relations and Federalism in Environmental Management and Policy, *Public Administration Review* 57 (1997): 150–159.

65. *Printz v. United States*, 521 U.S. 98 (1997).

66. *Kimel v. Florida Board of Regents*, 528 U.S.62 (2000); *Board of Trustees of Alabama v. Garrett*, 531 U.S. 356 (2001).

67. M.J. Dluhy and H.A. Frank, Miami's Fiscal Crisis: Two Years Later, *Municipal Finance Journal* 20 (Spring 1999): 1–19; Once in Financial Straits, Miami Sells $32.5 Million in Bonds, *Naples Daily News*, March 28, 2002, *www.naplesnews.com/02/03/florida/ d755883a.htm*; accessed August 2002.

68. C. Kirkpatrick, State Seizes Town Drowning in Debts, Failed Infrastructure, *Durham Herald-Sun*, February 5, 1997, 1, 8.

69. Office of the State Comptroller, *Review of the Four Year Financial Plan for the City of New York*, July 2002, *www.osc.state.ny.us/osdc/rpt903/rpt903.pdf*; accessed August 2002.

70. *The District of Columbia Financial and Responsibility Management Assistance Authority Will Suspend Operations*, *www.cdfra.gov/*; accessed August 2002.

71. *Texas v. United States*, 523 U.S. 296 (1998).

72. M.VerPloeg and D.M. Betson, eds., *Estimating Eligibility and Participation for the WIC Program* (Washington, DC: National Academy Press, 2001).

73. U.S. Advisory Commission on Intergovernmental Relations, *Characteristics of Federal Grant-in-Aid Programs: Grants Funded in 1991* (Washington, DC: U.S. Government Printing Office, 1992); U.S. Advisory Commission on Intergovernmental Relations, *Federal Grant Programs in Fiscal Year 1992: Their Numbers, Sizes and Fragmentation Indexes in Historical Perspective* (Washington, DC: U.S. Government Printing Office, 1993).

74. B.D. McDowell, Grant Reform Reconsidered, *Intergovernmental Perspective* 17 (Summer 1991): 8–11.

75. M. Givel, *The War on Poverty Revisited: The Community Services Block Grant Program in the Reagan Years* (Lanham, MD: University Press of America, 1991).

76. U.S. Office of Management and Budget, *Grants and Cooperative Agreements with State and Local Governments*, Circular A-102 (1997), *www.whitehouse.gov/omb/circulars/ a102/a102.html*; accessed August 2002.

77. J.L. Mikesell, *Fiscal Administration: Analysis and Applications for the Public Sector*, 5th ed. (New York: Harcourt Brace Jovanovich, 1999).

78. A. Greenblatt, Enemies of the State, *Governing* 16 (June 2002): 26–31.

79. Housing and Community Development Act of 1974, P.L. 93–383 (1994).

80. U.S. General Accounting Office, *Block Grants: Lessons Learned* (Washington, DC: U.S. Government Printing Office, 1995).

81. R. Tannenwald, Come the Devolution, Will States Be Able to Respond?

82. D. Liska, *Medicaid: Overview of a Complex Program* (Washington, DC: Urban Institute, 2002), *http://newfederalism.urban.org/html/anf_a8.htm*; accessed August 2002.

83. J. Walters, States, Feds and Special Ed, *Governing* 14 (September 2000): 12.

84. R.C. Hicks, Environmental Legislation and the Costs of Compliance, *Government Finance Review* 8 (April 1992): 7–10.

85. W.J. Clinton, Enhancing the Intergovernmental Partnership, *Federal Register* 58 (1993): 58093–58094.

86. Unfunded Mandates Reform Act, P.L. 104–4 (1995).

87. Law Restricts Unfunded Mandates, *1995 CQ Almanac* (Washington, DC: Congressional Quarterly, 1996), 3.15–3.20.

88. Congressional Budget Office, *CBO's Activities Under the Unfunded Mandates Reform Act, 1996–2000* (Washington, DC: Congressional Budget Office, 2001), viii–ix.

89. *U.S. v. Lopez*, 514 U.S. 549 (1995); *Printz v. U.S.*, 521 U.S. 898 (1997).

90. U.S. Department of Education, *Title IX: 25 Years of Progress* (Washington, DC: U.S. Government Printing Office, 1997). Also available at *www.ed.gov/pubs/TitleIX/title.html*; accessed August 2002.

91. U.S. Office of Management and Budget, *Report to Congress on the Costs and Benefits of Federal Regulations* (Washington, DC: U.S. Government Printing Office, 1997). Also available at: *www.whitehouse.gov/omb/inforeg/congress.html*; accessed August 2002.

92. Single Audit Act, P.L. 98–502 (1984).

93. U.S. Office of Management and Budget, *Audits of States, Local Governments, and Non-Profit Organizations*, Circular A-133 (1997), *http://www.whitehouse.gov/omb/circulars/a133/a133.html*; accessed August 2002.

94. U.S. Office of Management and Budget, *Grants Streamlining Activities under P.L. 106–107, Federal Assistance Management Improvement Act of 1999, http://www.whitehouse.gov/omb/fedreg/preamble2.html*; accessed August 2002; and *http://www.whitehouse.gov/omb/fedreg/notice_announcement.html*; accessed August 2002.

95. Federal Financial Assistance Management Improvement Act, P.L. 106–107 (1999).

96. U.S. General Accounting Office, *Federal Interstate Compact Commissions: Useful Mechanisms for Planning and Managing River Basin Operations* (Washington, DC: U.S. Government Printing Office, 1981).

97. U.S. Office of Management and Budget, *Budget of the United States Government: Fiscal Year 2003*, 8.

98. T.J. Conlan and D.B. Walker, Reagan's New Federalism, *Intergovernmental Perspective* 8 (Winter 1983): 6–22.

99. R. Tannenwald, Come the Devolution, Will States Be Able to Respond?

Chapter 15

GOVERNMENT, THE ECONOMY, AND ECONOMIC DEVELOPMENT

The sheer size of the government sector in the U.S. economy guarantees that government action will have a major impact on overall economic performance; the total government share of gross domestic product (GDP) is more than 28 percent, and the federal share alone exceeds 18 percent.[1] Recognizing the importance of the federal government's role in economic affairs, the National Economic Council was created in 1993 to coordinate the numerous cabinet and Executive Office of the President agencies advising the president, including the Council of Economic Advisers (CEA), the Office of Management and Budget, and the Department of the Treasury.[2] The CEA is the primary economic advisory group to most presidents, although individuals outside the CEA are often more influential in a one-on-one sense with the president. The council's functions are to coordinate economic policy making and to ensure that any actions of the executive branch affecting the economy will be consistent with the president's economic policy. With the end of the Cold War, the government's economic policy apparatus was raised to a point of parity with the national security policy system.

This chapter focuses on the impact of government budgets — primarily the federal government's budget — on the overall economy. The first section considers the U.S. economy and its interdependence with the economies of other nations. Other governments and private individuals in other countries react to actions taken by the U.S. federal government, and these external reactions sometimes can cause economic changes within the United States. To understand government and the economy, one first has to understand the conditioning factors of the world economy.

The second section summarizes the major objectives sought by government economic policy. Included is a discussion of deficit control and management of the federal debt. In contrast to state and local borrowing, which is basically used as a means to finance capital investment, federal deficit spending and subsequent borrowing function more as macroeconomic policy tools.

The third section briefly discusses how governments and businesses attempt to forecast the economic future. The fourth section examines the principal tools used to influence the economy. For the federal government, these tools conventionally include fiscal and monetary policy; for state and local governments, they include infrastructure investments and taxing or spending decisions that are intended to affect the local and state business climate. The chapter concludes with a discussion of the distributional effects of overall economic policy. That final section focuses on the role of government in securing equity through influencing the distribution of income in society.

The United States and the World Economy

Cross-Border Economic Shocks

Most citizens once thought of the United States as not only the most significant contributor to, but also the controller of, the world economy. It took the shock of the Organization of Petroleum Exporting Countries' (OPEC's) curtailment of oil production in 1973 to 1974 to bring many to the realization that the world economy has significant controlling effects on the U.S. economy. Long gas lines and a doubling of gasoline prices caused many people to recognize that economic conditions are not completely in the United States' own hands. Once several nations, including Japan and Germany, surpassed the United States in some economic measures (though not in total production), most in the United States realized that our economy, although still a major component of the world economy, is merely one among several important national economies. Since that first OPEC production cut and the subsequent strengthening of other economies relative to our own, citizens have become more attuned to how much U.S. economic well-being depends on the economic behavior of billions of individuals around the world and on the economic policy decisions of dozens of other governments. The Asia financial crisis that started in 1997 caused economies first throughout Asia, then over the next two years in Latin America and Russia, to tumble. Investors rushed to sell off their Asian and other emerging-market portfolio investments, and many reinvested in the U.S. markets, contributing to soaring market values in the

United States. The value of international trade — exports plus imports — grew from 16 percent of U.S. GDP in 1975 to more than 26 percent in 2000.[3]

The notion that there is now a global economy, and that the United States is a part of that global economy but not the controlling agent, is accepted by most people, albeit for some quite uncomfortably. Of course, the United States is also vehemently criticized for its size and influence in some other countries.

The United States as a Debtor Nation

A second significant event, although less immediately apparent to many citizens, occurred in 1985. For the first time, the United States became a net debtor nation. Formally, that means that the value of foreign investments in the United States for the first time exceeded the value of U.S. investments abroad. In 2000, the value of foreign investments in the United States was approximately $9.3 trillion and U.S. investments abroad were valued at $7.2 trillion; both had nearly doubled since the mid-1990s. The net difference, about $2.1 trillion; did not grow quite as much as the two gross measures during the same period, indicating a combination of more U.S. investments abroad and some degree of selling off of some foreign holdings in U.S. securities. The latter trend accelerated as the U.S. stock market tumbled in 2001 and beyond.[4] In summary, the claims of foreign investors, both private and governmental, on assets in the United States exceed the claims of U.S. investors, private and governmental, on assets in other countries. Since 1985, the United States has remained a net debtor, with the cumulative value of foreign-owned assets in the United States exceeding the value of assets in other countries owned by U.S. investors.

Foreign assets in the United States are invested in descending order in three major categories: (1) debt and equity securities of U.S. companies; (2) U.S. government treasury securities (these two categories are termed portfolio investments); and (3) property, including buildings, factories, and even public utilities such as water companies. The inflow of foreign capital has helped keep U.S. interest rates low because it fills part of the demand for borrowing created by federal budget deficits. In addition, foreign investment produces jobs in the United States. On the other hand, when the net inflow of foreign capital replaces domestic investment, it has a potential long-run disadvantage. The U.S. savings rate may be too low to finance all the demand for investments, leaving the economy increasingly dependent on the confidence of foreign investors in the U.S. economy. Major threats to their confidence, such as the stock market drop beginning in 2000 and the disasters of September 11, 2001, have caused that source of external investment to diminish recently, prompting some foreign owners to dispose of a portion of their U.S. assets. If that tendency became a substantial trend, either less capital would be available for investment in the United States, or U.S. savings rates (postponing current consumption) would have to increase. That would likely mean an increase in interest rates, depending on monetary policy actions (discussed later in this chapter) taken by the Federal Reserve Board.

Value of the U.S. Dollar in the World Economy

The third phenomenon, noticed by many citizens beginning in the 1980s, relates to changes in the value of the *dollar* in the world economy. When not many citizens traveled abroad, relatively speaking, and trade accounted for less than 10 percent of the U.S. economy, most Americans never thought about the value of the dollar against foreign currencies. Early in the 1970s, the dollar purchased a lot of goods and services in or from other countries, as the dollar value was high relative to most major currencies.

By the 1980s, however, more Americans traveled abroad, and more enjoyed imported goods. Late in 1987, U.S. residents watched the flood of tourists reverse as European and Asian visitors came to the United States while prices for comparable trips for U.S. residents abroad climbed to new highs. Imported cars, stereos, and televisions that had been bargains a year before became unaffordable for many. This reversal occurred for two reasons. Per capita incomes grew faster in several other countries, which increased their purchasing power and drove up prices for goods produced in those economies. Also, deliberate action by the U.S. government to lower the value of the dollar relative to other currencies, in an effort to increase the foreign purchase of U.S. goods and services, made foreign goods and services relatively more expensive for U.S. consumers.

By the mid-1990s, the value of the dollar against other world currencies had stabilized, and then gained in value against other currencies, caused in part by the Asian and emerging-market financial crisis and struggling productivity levels in Western industrialized economies. Most recently, recession in the United States has caused the dollar to fall somewhat against other currencies, and the movement of most of Western Europe to a single currency, the *euro*, has begun to have a stabilizing effect, with the dollar and the euro varying within 10 percent of each other. We now understand that the value of the dollar fluctuates with changes both within the influence range of the U.S. private economy and government action and with changes in other economies. Since the mid-1980s, the dollar no longer dominates world currencies, but is merely one of several dominant currencies.

Competitiveness of the U.S. Economy

A fourth key economic phenomenon to note is the competitiveness of the U.S. economy relative to other emerging industrial powers. Ordinary Americans first took note of this competitiveness issue on a large scale in the 1980s. Although "cheap foreign labor" had been considered a threat by many traditional U.S. industries, such as textiles, for more than two decades, the 1980s saw problems in industries in which innovation and technology had constituted the U.S. competitive edge. For the first time, the United States encountered competitors in computer design, electronics, and other high-technology areas, which began to produce not only cheaper but, in the minds of many consumers, better products.[5]

A surge in the 1990s in U.S. productivity, led by significant private sector restructuring and manifested in part by downsizing of the work force in many industries, helped move the issue of government stimulation of U.S. competitiveness further off the national agenda. Aided by private sector restructuring and a balanced budget, by the middle of the 1990s the U.S. economy experienced both overall growth and strong competitiveness with other economies. A significant factor in the last three or four years of the decade was the massive investment in computer software and hardware to avoid some problems associated with old software that would not recognize dates beyond the year 1999 (the Y2K problem) and overall growth in the information and communications technology sector. Investment in new computer technology has slowed since that surge of investment, however. The *Economic Report of the President for 2002* noted that among all nations, only the United States had sustained productivity growth throughout the second half of the 1990s.[6] The major factors contributing to U.S. competitiveness and productivity levels are the openness of the economy to world trade, investment in education, health of the financial sector, infrastructure, and technological innovation.

The preceding phenomena indicate that the U.S. economy is so interdependent with those of other nations that no significant actions that the United States takes lack repercussions around the world. Likewise, no significant economic events in other major industrial nations or groups of developing nations fail to have repercussions in the United States. Understanding the role of the government in the U.S. economy thus means casting a wider net and considering also the actions and reactions of the country's major trading partners and major creditors.

Objectives of Economic Policy

The role of the federal government in the economy consists of several interrelated functions. First, the government provides the legal framework in which economic transactions take place. Second, it directly produces services and some goods, and it regulates private production. Also, it purchases significant quantities of goods and services and redistributes income among individuals and groups. Although the idea is not as widely accepted as these functions, some also argue that governments should promote their countries' economic competitiveness in the global marketplace.[7]

One goal of the government's regulation of economic transactions through setting the legal framework is sometimes described as maintenance of a "level playing field" — making sure that all economic actors play by the same rules and succeed or fail solely on the basis of their own strengths and weaknesses. The stock market scandals in which companies such as Enron and WorldCom apparently inflated earnings by using unacceptable accounting practices set off a flurry of speeches, proposed legislation, and stepped-up enforcement by the SEC and other regulators, in an attempt to "level the playing field." Setting the legal framework is the subject of texts on regulation, business, and constitutional law. This section and the following one focus on the government's effects on the economy's overall performance.

Although Franklin D. Roosevelt's 1932 election platform promised to involve the federal government in the solution to economic problems brought on by the Great Depression, it was not until after World War II that the overall role of the government in stimulating the economy became formalized through legislative enactment. The Employment Act of 1946, later amended by the Full Employment and Balanced Growth Act of 1978, set several macroeconomic policy objectives for the federal government.[8] Primary among these were full employment, price stability, and steady economic growth. To these have been added in practice, if not by formal legislation, equilibrium in the balance of transactions between the U.S. economy and other economies and debt management.[9] Most industrial nations share these objectives, whether they rely primarily on the private market, central planning, or a mix of central control and market activity to achieve them. Less industrial, developing, and emerging market countries also share these objectives, but the most prominent economic policy objective for these nations is the promotion of economic development. The success of Japan's economy through the 1980s and the apparent causal role played by the Japanese government's activist production and trade promotion policies intensified the debate in the United States and other industrial countries on the proper role of the government in promoting development, but the mood in most industrial economies has consistently favored a less activist role for government.[10] The U.S. economy's outstanding performance through 2000 without significant government stimulation quieted (at least in the United States) the call for government intervention to stimulate competitiveness, with key exceptions discussed below.

The first three objectives of the federal government are primarily domestic in nature. In many respects, they can be summarized in a single prescription: achieve a level of economic growth that produces full employment without unacceptable inflation. Economic growth is the engine that drives demand for employees. However, running that engine too fast or with too rich a fuel mixture may cause prices to rise unacceptably. The reformulation of these objectives into a single statement brings out the causal connection that exists between economic growth and employment. It also brings into the discussion two key value-laden terms: full employment and unacceptable inflation.

Full Employment

Definition of Full Employment. As a measure of economic performance, employment is the number of civilians over age 16 outside of institutions who are working in formal income-producing jobs. About 60,000 households, statistically representative of the country, are surveyed each month. The survey asks the respondent about his or her activities during the preceding week. If a person responds that he or she worked at a job for pay, or in a family enterprise without being paid, or was on vacation or some other similar situations, the individual is employed. If a person did not work in any of these situations or is not temporarily ill, on vacation, and so forth, and is looking for a job, he or she is unemployed. A person who has not sent out resumes, visited unemployment offices, called about employment, placed ads, or in some other way sought employment actively is not in the labor force.

The most commonly used measure of employment is the complement of employment — unemployment. The unemployment rate is the proportion of the work force not employed at a given time. To be considered unemployed, one must be seeking employment in the various ways described above. The definition of seeking employment was refined in 1994 to exclude individuals who reported they were discouraged by failure to find work but who had not looked for work in the last 12 months. Merely looking at want ads or on-line employment opportunities does not count. Individuals who have taken no active steps during the four weeks prior to the interview are not counted in the labor force.

There is no legislated definition of full employment, although an unemployment rate of 3 to 4 percent was often cited as the criterion of full employment after the 1946 Employment Act. Until the 1980s, the thinking was that about 3 to 4 percent of the work force at any given time will be between jobs or otherwise temporarily unemployed, and thus we can never achieve unemployment below that threshold. Some members of the work force are considered at least temporarily unemployable because of changes in the nature of jobs and skill requirements. Some economists do not count these "structurally" unemployed as part of the base for calculating full employment. Homemakers returning to the work force, young people switching jobs voluntarily, and fluctuations in demand in the global economy also make it difficult to achieve a 3 to 4 percent target.

The unemployment rate has been around 4 percent or below 12 times in the 55 years from 1948 to 2002, and it was not better than 4.9 percent since 1970 until 1998, when for four consecutive years the unemployment rate ranged from about 4 to 4.5 percent. Until that late-century boom period, most in the United States had come to accept an unemployment rate higher than 4 percent as consistent with the term "full employment." The economic downturn that caused unemployment to approach 6 percent by mid-2002 reinforced the old notion of 3 to 4 percent as unsustainable.

The adoption of a higher unemployment rate as the criterion of full employment is connected to the fact that the U.S. economy is much more susceptible to external events than it once was. As external economic shocks occur and consumer tastes change more rapidly, U.S. businesses simply cannot react as quickly as once they could, leading at times to downturns and unemployment. When unemployment dropped below 5 percent in 1997, coupled with low inflation rates and an unexpectedly high rate of growth in GDP, the U.S. economy had reached its strongest point in decades, and it was sustained for almost five years. During that period, debate centered on whether the United States had entered a new era of lower unemployment accompanied by low inflation, fueled by the greater value-added contribution of knowledge to production and a decline in the physical capital contribution to total production. It became clear that the paper wealth associated with the stock market boom, especially in Internet, telecommunications, and related industry stocks, was to some extent caused by a bubble economy. It also was apparent that at least some of the late 1990s spending on information technology was a concentrated spurt that would not be sustained annually. The conclusion to be drawn from this sequence of events is not entirely clear since it is possible that the economy was slowly recovering from the bubble collapse before September 11, 2001. Moving rapidly into government deficit spending, coupled with consumer confidence being already shaken by the stock market's reaction to the attacks, the economy did not rebound as quickly as at first seemed possible. It is unlikely that any real conclusion can be drawn about just how well the economy can function in terms of the combination of unemployment and inflation until the economic effects of terrorism are better understood, some stability is reached, and government spending is once more in line with taxes.

Political Acceptability of Unemployment. The political system has a varying capacity to accept unemployment. A nationwide unemployment rate of 9 or 10 percent, a rate reached in the early 1980s, is clearly unacceptable by current standards but is substantially lower than the peak of 24 percent unemployment during the Great Depression of the 1930s. As the rate declines toward 5 percent, acceptance increases. The extent to which society tolerates unemployment is partially dependent on who is unemployed. Although there may be a tendency to accept high unemployment among low-skilled, minority group, or younger workers, tolerance for unemployment quickly dissipates when it reaches middle-income, white-collar workers.

Politically, the unemployment rate is not the only important issue. Since the late 1980s, with the rate generally hovering around 5 percent, citizens have been more concerned with the types of new jobs that are being created. The concern is that many new jobs have been either service jobs that pay only the minimum wage or part-time jobs that pay few or no benefits. That certainly was a criticism of the 1990s boom, but the greater media attention paid to the number of instant millionaires generated as a result of one phenomenal new stock issue after another muted scrutiny of the types of jobs more ordinary people were obtaining. Another issue is the controversy over part-time work. Many people choose part-time work, but companies also have increased the number of workers they hire either as part-time workers or as temporary workers. As companies downsize their work forces during downturns, an increasing percentage of the national labor force has begun to work part-time and in temporary activity. Although their total employment often amounts to full 40-hour or more weeks, these workers lack the job security of regular employment and the benefits of health insurance and pension plans.

Controlling Inflation

Relationship between Unemployment and Inflation. The more the unemployment rate declines, the more difficult it becomes to find workers. As a result, wage rates may be bid up, creating inflationary pressures. Certainly through the mid-1960s the traditional assumption that rising employment leads to price increases and declining employment to price decreases seemed to hold up. However, the mid-1970s recession saw both rising unemployment and rising prices. At the peak, 1974 prices rose 11 percent over those of the year before, and 1975 prices rose another 9 percent. During that time, unemployment peaked at more than 8 percent. **Figure 15–1** illustrates this heretofore unconventional relationship. During the 1980s, the more conventional pattern held, with inflation and unemployment moving in opposite directions until the sustained growth period of the 1990s. By 2000, the economy was achieving both the lowest inflation rates in 40 years and low unemployment rates, as **Figure 15–1** illustrates.

The 1990s experience had economists reestimating the *natural rate of unemployment* and the *nonaccelerating inflation rate of unemployment* (NAIRU). The latter is the rate of unemployment below which excess demand for labor is thought to set off wage and price inflation. That rate was previously considered to be in the 5 to 6 percent range; unemployment below this range presumably would set off wage-led inflation. Milton Friedman in 1968 proposed to the American Economic Association that there is a natural rate of inflation on which the economy stabilizes for any given unemployment rate. At this natural rate, a rise in employment will set off no inflation, or a fall in employment will bring no price reductions.[11] The NAIRU concept particularly gained currency in the 1990s. **Figure 15–1** illustrates that a lower rate of unemployment (at or below 5 percent) did not result in wage-induced inflation between 1960 and 2000. If the natural rate or nonaccelerating inflation rate (they are different but related concepts) can be calculated accurately, then monetary policy actions to control inflation need be taken only when the actual unemployment rate falls below the NAIRU. There is no exact measure of NAIRU, and various methods yield ranges of plus or minus 1 to 2 percent.

The natural and noninflationary rates can change over time. Severe drought conditions can cause food prices to increase, contributing to overall higher consumer prices, unrelated to wage pressures. Increased worker productivity can increase output without setting off price deflationary pressures, and more workers can be hired as long as the productivity rate remains constant or increases without putting pressure on wages. This balance is one of the explanations for the recent ability of the U.S. economy to have low inflation and low unemployment. In addition, greater pressure on jobs from foreign competition holds wage rates down regardless of what is happening in the domestic economy. If wage

Figure 15–1   Inflation and Unemployment, 1960–2000

Sources: Executive Office of the President, *Economic Report of the President: 1997 and 2002* (Washington, DC: U.S. Government Printing Office, 1997, 2002), 370, 421 from 1997; 386 from 2002. 2002 unemployment: *Statistical Abstract of the United States: 2001* (Washington, DC: U.S. Government Printing Office, 2001), 386.

demands grow too high too rapidly, companies may intensify their search for foreign production sources.

Economic Growth

Economic Productivity. Unemployment is not the only — and perhaps not the best — measure of the economy's health. Even if the rate of unemployment and the rate of inflation are both at acceptable levels, the overall productivity of the economy could be seriously declining. The change in GDP is sometimes used as an indication of economic productivity. For the United States, the average annual growth rate in productivity (GDP) from 1965 through 1991 was 3 percent. For Japan, the comparable figures varied between 4 percent and 6 percent.[12] For the 1990–1999 period, the GDP growth rates for Japan and the United States were 1.4 and 3.4 percent, respectively.[13] Just as important, during that period the average annual rate of inflation in the United States varied between 4 percent and 6 percent, while for Japan inflation was less than 4 percent. Thus, during a 15-year period the productivity of the U.S. economy measured in terms of real output (adjusting for inflation) did not change. U.S. GDP actually dropped in 1991 (a recession year), but between 1992 and 1999 its growth rate exceeded 5 percent per year, in current dollars, with inflation in the 3 percent range — meaning real production gains. No other industrial economy matched that performance during the 1990s, as **Figure 15–2** illustrates.

Another important measure is GDP per capita. It paces GDP growth with population growth and is an important measure of wealth. From the 1960s through 1990, Japan led both the United States and the European industrialized countries in GDP per capita growth, achieving more than 7 percent growth in the 1960–1975 period compared to growth rates in the 2 to 3 percent range for the United States and Europe.[14] A major caveat to these comparisons, however, is that Japan's economy during that period was growing from a very low base. By the mid-1970s, Japan's was a mature industrial economy, and its stablized growth rates were more comparable to those of other mature industrial economies. Since 1990, U.S. growth in GDP per capita has outstripped that of Japan and the European Union, reaching an average of over 3 percent in the 1995–1999 period.

Beginning in 1996, the U.S. Commerce Department adopted a new method to calculate real GDP. Previously, real (inflation-adjusted) GDP was measured by comparing each year with the base year of 1987. Subsequent years' total production was adjusted for price changes using an index constructed on the base year, yielding real GDP growth rates. The problem with this methodology was that it implicitly assumed that all components of production changed prices by the same amount and in the same direction, although particularly since the 1970s that has not been the case. The new methodology computes price changes annually using a rolling average, called a *chain-weighted measurement*.[15] Historical series reported by the Commerce Department and used by other agencies have been revised to reflect the new methodology.

Impact of Government on Productivity. Most economists think that the primary impact of the government on economic productivity and long-term growth is due to influences on knowledge development and investment in productive capacity.[16] In addition to human capital investment, the government invests directly in research and development (R & D) to produce technological breakthroughs and indirectly supports private investment in R & D. One mechanism for encouraging private R & D has been to allow a tax credit for increases in such expenditures over prior-year levels. Congress considered a proposal in 2001 to make the R & D tax credit permanent, but the measure failed, although the tax credit was extended to 2004. President George W. Bush and President Clinton before him both emphasized the importance of government support for knowledge development. The impact of the direct and indirect actions of government on improving the productivity of the economy can be measured only in the long run. For example,

Figure 15-2 Growth of GDP Per Capita, United States, European Union, and Japan, 1960–1999

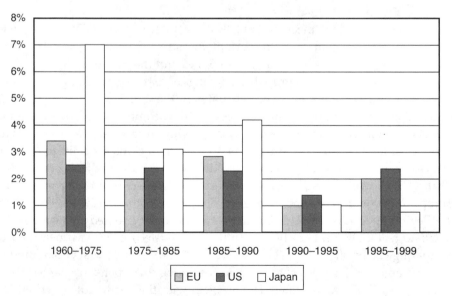

Source: Commission of European Communities, *European Competitiveness Report, 2002*, 6.

even if businesses substantially increase their expenditures for R & D as a result of government incentives, the payoff in productivity terms will show up only years into the future.

A Government Technology Policy. The question of whether the government should be more active in protecting and promoting critical high-technology industries first emerged in the late 1980s and persisted through the beginning of the current decade as a key policy issue when the U.S. economy began to lose ground in all areas, not just markets dominated by inexpensive labor. The George H. W. Bush administration was widely criticized for not protecting critical industries such as microelectronics, and President Clinton made stimulation of high-technology development an economic policy priority. The George W. Bush administration designated corporate tax reduction, repeal of taxes on dividends, and the R & D tax credits as the most important tools with which to support economic development.

The problem with providing more support to one segment of the economy than to another is that government rather than the marketplace "picks winners and losers," and there is little evidence that governments are good in that role. The decades of Japan's double-digit growth seemed to many sufficient evidence that government-led development was the proper path, but the last two decades have altered that view considerably. The federal government has difficulty determining which particular elements in a volatile industry such as electronics will be the most important determinants of U.S. global competitiveness in high-technology markets five or ten years from now.[17] The more widely accepted view is that government actions, rather than overtly promoting particular industries, should be directed toward improving the human and capital base, should encourage and certainly not discourage savings and investment, and should promote the international exchange of ideas, goods, and services.

Equilibrium in International Financial Flows

Important elements of government policy in this era of the global marketplace are actions designed to affect the balance of trade and other financial transactions between nations. Related to this balance is U.S. reliance on world capital markets to finance its domestic budget deficit. The U.S. financial position vis-à-vis the rest of the world is discussed in this section. A discussion of the overall deficit situation and debt management follows.

U.S. Transition from Creditor to Debtor. As noted earlier, in 1985 the United States became a net debtor nation. In the context of this chapter, being a net debtor means that there are more foreign demands on U.S. assets than there are U.S. claims on assets in other countries. It does not mean that the U.S. government is in debt to other countries, although institutions and individuals do purchase U.S.

Treasury securities. Rather, companies and individuals in the United States purchase more abroad than is sold to other countries (creating a trade imbalance). That is one contributing factor for the United States. The other major factor, as noted earlier, is the net balance of investments abroad and foreign investments in the United States.

Balance of Payments. Balance of payments refers to the value of goods and services and the financial assets and liabilities flowing between the United States and other countries. Historically, the balance of payments objective was to avoid a situation in which imported goods and services plus financial transactions created the potential for drawing down on the U.S. gold reserve. Today, with the rate of exchange between the U.S. dollar and other currencies freely set by the market and unrelated to gold reserves, the balance of payments objective is primarily a matter of maintaining equitable trade relationships between the United States and other countries. Trade negotiations between the United States and Japan, for example, are contentious because of the much larger value of goods that U.S. businesses and citizens purchase from Japan than Japanese customers purchase from the United States.

The balance of payments consists of several components or measures. The net balance of goods purchased abroad versus goods sold abroad is the *simple trade balance*. In 2000, for example, the current account deficit peaked at $450 billion.[18] To remedy an excess in net imports, either gross domestic product must rise faster than domestic demand, domestic demand must fall, or some combination of the two must occur. Although the U.S. economy was experiencing ideal conditions in terms of unemployment, production, and inflation, the International Monetary Fund warned that U.S. purchase of consumer goods from abroad coupled with a low domestic savings rate was likely to create future problems.

To the trade balance is added financial transactions. As noted earlier, the United States is a net borrower, which exacerbates the balance of payments problem. There is no universal agreement, however, on the extent to which a long-term current account deficit is a problem. On the down side, it can mean that consumer purchases of goods from abroad exceeds the ability of the economy to produce goods and services demanded abroad. That would indicate fewer funds available for investment in the U.S. economy for increased productivity. That, however, has not been the main issue for the United States. Overall, the consumption of foreign-produced goods has been a declining proportion of U.S. GDP since the early 1990s.[19] As noted earlier, the U.S. capital markets are attractive to foreign investors, and they were especially attractive after the Asian and emerging-market collapses of the late 1990s. Thus, the inflow of investments from abroad is a more important explanation for the current account deficit than is the purchase of goods from abroad.

The danger is that a major shock to the U.S. economy that causes investors from abroad to pull out large amounts of funds would both decrease the funds available for investment and decrease current consumption. The post–September 11 period suggests some of this withdrawal has happened, but actions by the Federal Reserve Board (discussed later in this chapter) to hold down interest rates and stable rather than falling consumer purchases have minimized its impact. As some foreign investments pulled out of the stock market and the decline in the value of the dollar against major foreign currencies decreased consumer purchases from abroad, the current account deficit shrunk marginally.

Financing the U.S. Economy. The flows of capital across international boundaries and the financing of investment will continue to be major focal points of both economists and governments. Globalization, while widely discussed, is still not entirely understood. Historically, investments made in other countries were substantial in productive capacity. When a company or an investment banking group invested in a factory abroad, the productive capacity in that country increased, and it is no easy matter for the investors to take their investment out quickly. Since the late 1980s, the growth of international transactions in financial instruments, such as stocks and bonds as opposed to physical capital, has substantially increased. One of the main reasons for the rapidity of the Asian and emerging-market collapses was the amount of foreign investment in tradable financial instruments, which allowed investors to pull their funds out quickly.[20]

The importance of these movements in the trade balance lies in their implications for how the economy is financed. From the mid-nineteenth century until the mid-1980s, the U.S. economy was financed domestically.[21] National saving was sufficient to provide funds for national investment, with the surplus national saving being invested abroad. However, the net national savings rate, which averaged just over 7 percent of GDP in the 1970s, declined to below 4 percent of GDP by 1980 and generally has remained around the 4 percent level.[22] One result has been that U.S. claims on foreign assets now are well below foreign claims on U.S. assets. Part of the U.S. economy has been financed not by domestic savings but rather by foreign investments in the United States. These foreign investments represent a future claim on U.S. assets that are not matched by equal U.S. claims on foreign assets.

Concern about this situation is not chiefly motivated by nationalistic pride. Foreign investments in the U.S. economy represent foreign confidence in the economy. Foreign investors have found U.S. Treasury notes an attractive investment because of the interest rates offered and because of their safety. Were the same foreign investments made in U.S. industry's stocks and bonds, financing would be available for economic expansion. To the extent that the investment in U.S. government debt does not produce expansion of domestic U.S. production capacity, the government's need for this investment competes with industry's need for financing. In macroeconomic terms, this external financing of the deficit creates a situation in which a greater quantity of U.S. goods and services has to be sold abroad in the long term to meet payments to foreign holders of U.S. debt. That quantity then is not available for U.S. consumption. Thus the trade balance, as well as the overall balance of payments disequilibrium, is intertwined with the domestic federal government budget deficit.

The late 1990s boom in the U.S. economy illustrates this point. The federal budget achieved balance in fiscal year 1998. Not only did the U.S. government not need to issue long-term securities to finance a deficit, but for three years the Treasury actually bought back higher-denominated debt with part of the budget surplus. By the end of the century, foreign borrowing to finance the deficit was becoming less of an issue.

The Decline in National Savings. A critical change in the U.S. economy relative to the economies of other nations up until the late 1990s was a decline in national savings. The balanced federal budget and increased investments by individuals in stocks and bonds reversed that trend. However, as the government entered into a deficit situation again in 2002, that problem will recur, unless a substantial change occurs in which consumers increase their individual savings rates. There has been no sign of that rebound so far, as investors have held off on the stock market.

National savings represent the source of funds for new investment in equipment, plants, and other physical facilities that allow total production to grow. **Figure 15–3** shows domestic savings for the United States relative to selected member countries of the Organization for Economic Cooperation and Development. The United States increased gross national savings from the roughly 13 percent level in the 1965–1969 period to 17 percent in 1999. This rate exceeded that for the United Kingdom, which experienced a somewhat smaller increase during that same period, but still fell below the rates for other countries. Economically strong countries in recent years, such as Japan and Germany, increased or maintained their high savings rates. Although not as high as some other countries, the growth in U.S. savings has financed increased investment and consequently brought an increase in the standard of living.

The data reported in **Figure 15–3** are *gross savings* as a percentage of GDP. Gross savings are adjusted by subtracting the consumption of fixed capital to arrive at net national savings. Consumption of fixed capital essentially means equipment and facilities that become old and useless and are not replaced. Thus gross savings could grow or remain constant while *net savings* actually falls because the rate of new investment is not sufficient to replace deteriorating production capacity. That is exactly what happened in the U.S. economy during the

Figure 15-3 U.S. Gross National Savings Compared with Savings Rates of Other Industrial Countries, 1965–1999

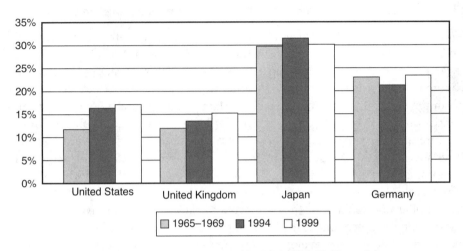

Sources: World Bank, *World Development Report, 1992 and 2000/2001* (New York: Oxford, 1992, 2001), 9, 298–299, respectively.

1970s and 1980s. Whereas gross savings in 1991 was 16 percent, net national savings was less than 2 percent, only one-fourth of the 8 percent rate of net national savings in the decade 1960–1969.[23] By 2000, however, net national savings had begun to increase again, to just over 5 percent.

The increase in U.S. net savings is attributable to two factors: substantial investments in stocks, bonds, and other savings instruments as the baby boom generation reached its peak earnings years, and the balanced federal budget. The stock market fall after 2000 and the return to federal budget deficits have both had some effect of reducing national savings, but investments through pension funds and individual investments have not declined to rates as low as those seen in the 1980s and 1990s.

Deficits and Debt Management

Chapter 12 described state and local debt primarily as long-term investment in physical infrastructure and other capital assets. It is therefore prudent for state and local governments to use short-term borrowing only for meeting the demands of short-term contingencies and to ensure that long-term borrowing is linked to the expected life of the investments financed. Federal debt policy, on the other hand, relates more to macroeconomic policy considerations than to capital investment requirements. Deficits in the federal budget accumulate as spending exceeds revenues, regardless of whether the spending finances investments in long-term growth, meets operating expenses, pays interest on previous debt, or provides transfer payments. While it is possible to make a numeric comparison between the investment levels in the federal budget and the size of the deficit, federal budget deficits have not been the result of conscious investment planning.

Developing-Country Debt Management. For developing countries, prudent debt management is more comparable to that of U.S. state and local governments. Developing countries as a rule have excess or idle labor capacity. The long-run economic strategy is to invest in education to improve the productivity of labor and in physical infrastructure to facilitate the production and flow of goods and services produced by the private sector. Typically, a shortage of physical infrastructure, such as transportation and communications facilities, retards the economic investment that would employ the excess labor capacity. Governments in developing countries borrow from donor agencies, such as the World Bank, and from banks in industrial countries to increase their physical infrastructure and other capital investments. If they are economically sound, the investments will produce long-run economic growth sufficient to repay the indebtedness. More often than not, however, developing countries encounter debt troubles when borrowing finances current consumption rather than investment and when physical infrastructure assets that have been built are not maintained. The economy then does not maintain a sufficient level of growth, revenues do not increase as expected, and debt exceeds capacity to repay.

U.S. Federal Use of Debt. In the post-Depression era, the federal budget deficit has been used as an overt tool to influence total demand in the economy and thus overall economic performance. According to the prevailing economic theory of that era, deficits should be managed to stimulate the economy without creating inflationary pressure. However, by the 1980s the size of the deficit had reached proportions that were out of step with economic policy objectives. Although there was general agreement on both sides of the political spectrum that deficit-reducing measures were necessary, it was not until 1997 that an overall agreement was reached between Congress and the president on specific tax and expenditure measures that promised a balanced budget by 2002. In actuality, the federal budget achieved a surplus in 1998, in part due to deliberate management, but largely due to tax receipts increasing with rapid economic growth. As already noted, 2002 marked a return to a federal deficit, but the unusual combination of an economic downturn and the September 11 events make interpretations of that deficit speculative at best (see Chapter 9).

Size of the U.S. Federal Debt. To understand the debate about government debt in recent years, it is first important to understand the relative size of the federal debt and then to consider its origins and implications. **Figure 15–4** shows the debt as a percentage of GDP, a useful measure for comparing the growth of the debt with the growth of the overall economy. Total federal indebtedness in 1950 equaled 94 percent of GDP, reflecting the financing of World War II. That figure steadily declined until it reached postwar lows around 35 percent between 1970 and 1980. Rapid increases after that brought federal debt up to 70 percent of GDP in 1995, the highest level since 1955.[24] From 1998 through 2001, federal debt as a percentage of GDP dropped again as GDP grew, and federal debt remained almost constant at around 60 percent of the GDP from 1999 through 2001.

Effects of Economic Performance on the Size of the Federal Debt. Two circumstances explain the rapid rise in the federal government's debt in the 1980s after a long period of decline. First, the federal budget, in terms of both revenues and expenditures, is affected by the overall performance of the economy. Oil price shocks and high inflation led to unbalanced federal budgets throughout the 1980s. Overall growth in the economy was virtually zero for the decade in real terms. This lack of growth created pressure on the budget because of automatic increases in expenditures for some social welfare programs that expand as unemployment goes up. It also caused a decline in federal revenues. The reverse occurred in the mid-1990s, as low unemployment and increased production combined to produce decreased demand for federal social welfare assistance and increased tax revenues.

Figure 15–4 Federal Debt as a Percentage of Gross Domestic Product, 1950–2003[*]

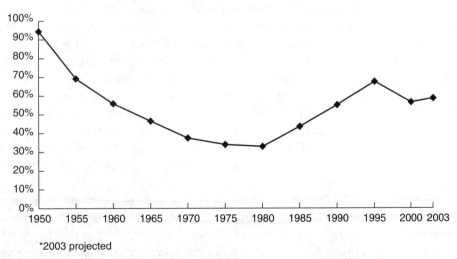

*2003 projected

Source: Executive Office of the President, *Economic Report of the President: 2002* (Washington, DC: U.S. Government Printing Office, 2002), 406.

Effects of Tax Cuts on the Size of the Federal Debt. The second circumstance affecting the deficit in the 1980s was a set of policy decisions. On taking office, President Reagan with approval by Congress initiated a sweeping set of economic reforms, including a major series of tax cuts beginning in 1981 and significant budget reductions in nondefense spending. However, as the program evolved, it proved politically impossible to reduce nondefense spending sufficiently to match increases in defense expenditures, and overall spending remained at prior levels or even went higher than before the tax cuts. The theory behind the tax cuts was that the funds not collected by the government would be better invested by the private sector, yielding a future revenue dividend in the form of increased tax yields from the heightened economic activity. In reality, the fiscal dividend never materialized. Federal revenue levels grew more slowly than at any time since the 1960s, while defense spending, entitlement program outlays, and interest on the debt soared to new heights. The tax cuts adopted in 1997, unlike those of 1981, were accompanied by offsetting expenditure reductions. The Economic Growth and Tax Relief Reconciliation Act of 2001 has made it more difficult to once again achieve a budget surplus. As noted earlier, however, it will take several years to sort out the net effects of the 2001 tax cuts, stock market problems, September 11, and the subsequent necessity for additional defense efforts.[25]

Anticipating Economic Conditions

Both the private and public sectors need tools to measure economic change and anticipate economic trends. If businesses are to make sound investment decisions (including the decision to hire new workers or build new plant capacity), they have to anticipate future economic developments. If interest rates are expected to fall, it is not the time to borrow to buy new production equipment. If a tax incentive that reduces overall tax liability when funds are invested in new productive capacity is about to expire, it is a good time to make new investments. Some of these events can be predicted with relative certainty. An investment tax credit may have a specific expiration date, and it may be easy to see that Congress is not likely to renew it. On the other hand, it may not be as easy to predict how much change will occur in interest rates. Forecasting tools are a vital ingredient in business economic planning.

If the federal government is to achieve its economic policy objectives, it also needs sensitive and valid measures with which to predict the direction of the economy. Likewise, it needs models of change that predict what will happen if specific policy changes, such as a change in the maximum corporate income tax rate, are enacted. Although forecasting techniques are beyond the scope of this text, some familiarity with the measures that are watched closely by business and government and with the analytical models used by forecasters is important for understanding government economic policy.

Business and government forecasters watch closely a number of individual economic indicators. Some indicators are related to the labor force, including unemployment, average weekly hours worked, and average hourly earnings. Other indicators reflect financial conditions, such as interest rates and new starts in home building. Businesses, forecasters, and public policy makers examine such indicators to understand current economic conditions and to predict turning points when the economy will begin to move up or down from its current state.

Of particular importance for anticipating economic turning points are *cyclical indicators*, also known as *leading*, *coincident*, and *lagging indicators*.[26] Leading indicators presumably show in advance what the economy will do, revealing the turning points, whereas lagging indicators report what already has occurred. Formerly, the Bureau of Economic Analysis of the U.S. Department of Commerce released the cyclical indicators monthly. Now the Conference Board, a private, not-for-profit economics research and business membership organization, maintains the *Business Cycles Indicators* database and has served as the official source since 1996 of the indices.

Coincident Indicators

Coincident indicators, those that report what the economy is doing now, are the ones that most commonly reach the public's attention. They include measures of industrial production, personal income, and manufacturing and trade sales.

Gross Domestic Product. GDP, one of the most important coincident indicators, is a measure of the total goods and services produced by the nation. GDP is the aggregate of personal consumption expenditures, gross private domestic investment, net exports of goods and services, and government purchases of goods and services.

An indicator similar to GDP, *gross national product* (GNP), previously was the common indicator of total production. In 1992, the federal government and most analysts switched to GDP for comparison purposes, since most other countries report production in terms of GDP. The main difference between the two is that GDP excludes the earnings of U.S. businesses and residents abroad, and excludes earnings of foreign workers in the United States that remitted abroad. Thus GDP reflects production within the U.S. economy as opposed to production by U.S. economic entities. Most commonly reported as an indicator is the rise or fall in GDP. For example, U.S. real (after adjusting for inflation) GDP grew 4.4 percent in 1999, but was negative in the third quarter of 2002.[27]

Net National Product and National Income. Two other coincident indicators, both derivatives of GDP, are net national product (NNP) and national income. GDP includes all capital investment, some of which does not produce new productive capacity but only replaces capacity that is being used up. NNP is the measure of investment after depreciation is removed. In 2000, the U.S. GDP was $9.9 trillion and the U.S. NNP was $8.6 trillion, meaning that approximately $1.3 trillion of GDP represented no new production. NNP thus tells what consumption and investment is net of capital stock replacement. National income is derived from NNP by eliminating indirect business taxes included in the price of goods sold and business transfer payments. **Table 15–1** summarizes the relationships among GDP, GNP, NNP, and national income from 1965 through 2000.

Prices. The four measures of national product and income indicate what is happening to the levels of production and income. Prices are another measure of what is happening. Wholesale prices may provide an earlier warning of potential problems than measures of national product because they indicate probable changes in prices about to be paid by consumers. The wholesale or producer price index covers about 2,800 commodities.

The *consumer price index* (CPI) is based on the cost of goods and services bought by urban wage and clerical workers. It is estimated from a periodic sample survey of about 5,000 households in urban areas around the country to determine buying habits, and monthly calls and visits to retail establishments and other vendors to collect price information on more than 80,000 items. The household sample includes two population groups — all urban consumers and urban wage earners and clerical workers.[28] Change in the CPI is widely cited as an indicator of inflation. One of its most important uses is to adjust various government benefit programs, most prominently Social Security, for the effects of inflation; Social Security payments are automatically increased based on changes in the CPI.

The methods used in constructing the CPI are controversial, largely because of the effect they have on the government budget and the deficit. The actual household survey of buying habits can take place as long as four or five years prior to the publication of the index. A one-point decrease in the CPI in 1997 would have reduced government expenditures by $6 billion.[29] While there is general agreement that the CPI overstates inflation, there has been no agreement on a fix. Problems in the methodology revolve around inadequacy in the way the index handles changes in the quality of goods and services and changes in consumer buying patterns.

Table 15-1 Relationships among Gross Domestic Product, Gross National Product, Net National Product, and National Income, 1965–2000 (Billions of Dollars)

Item	1965	1970	1975	1980	1985	1990	1995	2000
Gross domestic product	720.1	1,039.7	1,635.2	2,795.6	4,213.0	5,803.2	7,400.5	9,872.9
Plus:								
Receipts of factor income from the rest of the world	8.1	13.0	28.2	81.8	113.1	188.3	232.3	384.2
Less:								
Payments of factor income to the rest of the world	2.7	6.6	14.9	46.5	87.8	159.3	211.9	396.3
Equals:								
Gross national product	725.5	1,046.1	1,684.4	2,830.8	4,238.4	5,832.2	7,420.9	9,860.8
Less:								
Consumption of fixed capital	70.8	109.1	190.9	345.2	516.5	711.3	911.7	1,241.3
Equals:								
Net national product	654.7	937.0	1,457.5	2,485.6	3,721.9	5,120.9	6,509.1	8,619.5
Less:								
Indirect business tax and nontax liability	62.7	94.3	140.0	212.0	329.4	447.3	594.6	762.7
Business transfer payments	2.2	3.2	5.2	11.2	20.7	26.1	33.5	43.9
Statistical discrepancy	1.9	6.9	17.7	33.9	11.7	30.6	26.5	-130.4
Plus:								
Subsidies less current surplus of government enterprises	1.7	4.8	7.7	14.5	20.4	25.3	22.2	37.6
Equals:								
National income	589.6	837.5	1,302.2	2,243.0	3,380.4	4,642.1	5,876.7	7,980.9

Note: Totals may not match due to rounding.

Source: Reprinted from Executive Office of the President, *Economic Report of the President: 2002*, (Washington, DC: U.S. Government Printing Office, 2002), 343.

Unemployment. Two other measures provide good indications of the current state of the economy — unemployment and industrial production. Unemployment, a percentage measure of the people within the labor force who are not employed, is a common public policy target indicator. This measure is politically charged. A change in the unemployment rate of half a percent up or down is enough to send the president before the news media to announce significant economic progress or to have opposition leaders charge that the economy is failing. However, unemployment is subject to wide seasonal fluctuations, and the measurement of unemployment is subject to manipulation. Some job seekers may become discouraged and fall out of the count altogether. Women and members of ethnic minority groups may not be well represented in the count of job seekers because they may be convinced there are no jobs to seek or no jobs worth seeking. Therefore, unemployment data always have to be interpreted with some care.

Industrial Production. The industrial production index, prepared by the Federal Reserve System, is a measure of the manufacture of durable and nondurable goods. The durable portion of manufacturing is watched closely, particularly key industries such as steel. Steel sales reflect future intentions of manufacturing concerns. Rising sales may indicate the possibility of future investments in capital facilities. Falling sales may indicate lack of confidence in the economy and attempts by firms to keep inventories low. The value of this index has declined somewhat as the size of the manufacturing segment of the economy relative to the services segment has declined.

Leading Indicators

Although the coincident indicators are useful measures of the current or recent state of the economy, they often do not provide the lead time necessary to devise intervention strategies. The forecaster as a result turns to the leading indicators. Leading indicators include such items as average duration of unemployment, commercial and industrial loans, change in the consumer price index for services, and inventories to sales ratios in manufacturing and trade.

Employment-Related Indicators. A key leading indicator is the *average weekly hours in manufacturing.* Its usefulness is based on the practice of most manufacturers of cutting back on the length of the workweek rather than laying workers off if the demand for production starts to decline. A somewhat later indicator is the *average weekly initial claims for unemployment insurance.* This indicator provides evidence of the extent to which layoffs are increasing or decreasing. Both measures indicate employers' estimates of the direction of change in the economy.

Housing Starts. Private, nonfarm housing starts, measured by the *number of building permits issued for new private housing units*, provide a measure of the faith of builders and financial investors in the health of the economy. A decline in the number of starts can signal future economic decline. Housing is thought to be sensitive in that it reflects willingness to tie up investment dollars for several months to a year in an expensive commodity for which there may be no buyer at the time construction begins. However, housing starts are extremely sensitive to mortgage rates. During periods of extremely high rates, such as the early 1980s, many potential buyers were forced out of the market. In both the 1990s and again in 2001–2002, mortgage rates fell to their lowest points in nearly 40 years, and housing starts increased, even after September 11, 2001. A significant portion of 2001–2002 financing activity, however, was in refinancing existing mortgages as opposed to financing newly constructed homes. In recent years, housing starts have become a somewhat less reliable leading indicator. Growth in the use of adjustable rate mortgages allows home buyers to hedge against cyclical swings in interest rates, which in turn keeps demand for housing higher in the initial stages of rising interest rates.

Stock Markets. Stock markets are watched closely by the business community and government analysts, but their volatility makes them difficult to use as a leading indicator. The New York Stock Exchange (NYSE) historically was the market most carefully watched. The NASDAQ (National Association of Security Dealers Automated Quotation), where the large majority of technology stocks are traded, later became as important — and to some more important — due to the substantial increase in the information and communications technology sector's share of the economy. The Tokyo and London markets are watched as well. A substantial increase in investments in emerging markets and the swings in these markets have given prominence to several other markets, especially after the volatility of the late 1990s. The Hang Seng (Hong Kong) stock market index is reported daily, for example.

Several composite indexes of stock exchange transactions are used, the most notable being the Dow Jones Industrial and Standard and Poor's indexes. Changes are infrequent in the stocks listed in these indexes, although they became more frequent in the late 1990s as stock values for some of the companies included in these indices fell to near zero and some went out of business. For example, until a major change of dropping four stocks and adding four others occurred in 1997, the 30-stock Dow Jones Industrial index had remained largely intact since 1980. Enron, for example, was dropped after the scandal of its inflated and allegedly fraudulent earnings came to light.

Stock transactions are useful as leading indicators in that they reflect the faith of investors in the stocks traded on the open market and thus in the companies whose stocks are traded. As a barometer of investor confidence, stock transactions may be helpful. In principle, the value of a stock reflects the health of the firm. In reality, stocks may surge or decline wildly as a result of corporate takeover attempts and fights to prevent takeover or as a function of irrational investor behavior showing faith in unlimited growth potential in stock prices. Criticism of stock analysts recommendations abounded after the market crash started in 2000–2001. To the extent that stock prices reflect factors other than the economic health of the corporations, prices will be misleading as an economic indicator.

Composite Indexes. A variety of combined indexes are used to gauge economic changes and trends. As noted earlier, the private Conference Board took over the database and calculations of leading, lagging, and coincident indicators. The Conference Board's indicators and composites reflect the overall economy. Composite indices are published by the Board monthly, and combine several individual indices.

One type of composite is a *diffusion index*. It measures the proportion of individual components of the index that are moving in the same direction. The numerical value of a diffusion index is equal to the percentage of components of the index that are moving in the same direction. For example, the diffusion index of the leading composite index assigns values of 1, 0.5 or 0 to each component based on change of 5 percent or more, less than 5 percent, or no change or drop, respectively.[30] Stock analysts and trade publications also compute and publish indices of the major markets. The Dow Jones Publications group, for example, publishes a variety of indices including the Dow Jones Industrial Average, which includes 30 stocks such as Walt Disney Company and Exxon Mobil Corporation.

Forecasting

Despite the availability of a wide range of indicators and extensive historical series, forecasting remains a risky business. It is common to find two or more major federal organizations in substantial disagreement over expected economic trends. Rarely do the Office of Management and Budget (OMB) and the Congressional Budget Office (CBO) agree, for example, on the forecast of the federal deficit. However, the CBO calculated that the mean percentage error in forecasts of over a dozen economic indicators was rarely more than 1 percent for the CBO, administration forecasts, and private economic forecasters. CBO did observe that its estimates were (barely) more accurate than administration forecasts.[31]

To the extent that discrepancies arise, forecasts by the president's advisers, reflected in the annual budget, have tended to overestimate economic performance so that government receipts fall short of original estimates and expenditures tend to be higher due to programs such as unemployment benefits that kick in automatically. The CBO also has been overoptimistic but often is more accurate than OMB.[32]

Economic forecasts are based on informed judgment or a combination of judgment and sophisticated econometric models (see the discussion of forecasting revenues in Chapter 4). Several private organizations employ econometric models that include numerous variables — from around 100 to as many as 1,200. Among the more famous private models is DRI-WEFA (a merger of the former Wharton Econometric Forecasting Associates and Data Resources, Inc.). Several organizations, including the Institute for Survey Research, University of Michigan, conduct surveys of ordinary consumers and expert analysts to obtain estimates of economic trends. Judgment regularly is used to adjust the sophisticated mathematical models.

Not surprisingly, during major economic changes both business and government are sometimes criticized for not having anticipated the degree of change or sometimes even the direction of change. The recession year of 1982 had been predicted in 1981 to be a year of modest economic growth. The recovery in 1983 was predicted to be a period of slow growth, whereas actual growth in GDP turned out to be more than twice that forecast. The recession that plagued the last two years of the George H. W. Bush administration was reputed to be momentarily ending, but the Clinton campaign was able to make the case that recovery had not yet begun. Some economists, especially in Europe, forecast annually from 1995 through 2000 that the American economic bubble would burst.[33] Finally, in 2001, they were right. Models seem to fail when major structural changes are occurring, such as OPEC's gain of control over oil production in the early 1970s. When the economy is stable, various models are fairly successful, and popular opinion then generally agrees with the expert forecasts.

Given the conflicting interpretations possible even with sound information, economic forecasters as well as political leaders interpret the data from their own perspectives. The technical problems involved are great, but inevitably forecasting succumbs not to technical problems but to political resolutions. The president and his staff may attempt to focus attention on one indicator that shows signs of progress, while members of Congress from the opposing party may focus on another indicator. State and local political leaders are just as susceptible to coloring judgment with hope by trying to appear confident in the economic future while sometimes failing to address serious underlying economic and fiscal weaknesses. We return to the issues involved in conflicting theories of economic behavior and the implications for government economic policy in the next section.

Tools Available to Affect the Economy

Automatic Stabilizers

Government actions intended to achieve economic policy objectives can be either discretionary or automatic. In the case of discretionary actions, policy makers discuss alternatives and reach a decision as to how to intervene in specific circumstances. Automatic or built-in stabilizers, in contrast, do not require policy makers to take any special steps. Some government revenues and expenditures rise or fall automatically with changes in the economy. Revenues are especially sensitive to economic performance, with taxes falling due to falling incomes. **Figure 15–5** shows the relationship between the change in GDP and the change in federal revenues from 1981 through 2000. With few exceptions, GDP declines are matched by declines in revenues, and vice versa, though not always at the same rate. In most of the years illustrated in the series, the directional changes occur in the same year; there is little lag between a declining GDP and a decline in federal revenue since much of federal revenue derives from taxes on components of GDP (corporate and personal income). Government expenditures, at least at the federal level, do not automatically fall with declining economic performance; in fact, they tend to increase. The combined tax declines and expenditure increases have an automatic stimulative effect tending to encourage economic growth.

The progressivity of the tax structure is an example of a built-in or automatic stabilizer. As the economy declines, corporate profits decline and workers' salaries decrease. Both corporate and personal taxes thus go down, with the result that proportionately more funds are left available to the private sector for investment, stimulating demand. Similarly, tax revenues rise as the economy expands, providing some brake on growth so it does not lead to inflationary pressures. Unemployment insurance is another example of an automatic stabilizer.

Discretionary Policies

Nongovernmental stabilizers are also an inherent part of the economy and individual economic behavior. Recessions are resisted by individuals and corporations that use savings to maintain established levels of activities. Conversely, expansionary trends are resisted. As income rises, greater proportions of income are placed in savings rather than being used for consumption.

Discretionary interventions vary widely. They are based on economic theories of behavior, both micro- and macroeconomic, that anticipate the economy's responses to government actions involving taxing and spending and alterations in the flow of funds through the monetary system. The former actions are called fiscal policy; the latter are dubbed monetary policy. Fiscal policy and monetary policy are first reviewed separately, and then their integration into an overall strategy is discussed. A separate section is devoted to the public investment role of government — a role that is particularly important for developing countries and for U.S. state and local governments.

Fiscal Policy Instruments

The essential tools of fiscal policy are revenues, expenditures, and the implied surplus or deficit. Their use has evolved during the twentieth century, changing as different views of the role of government in the economy have held sway. The prevailing view early in the century was that little government intervention was necessary. If the economy seemed to be faltering, the government's role should be limited to an incremental increase in expenditures over revenues to "prime the pump." During the Great Depression of the 1930s, demand fell so rapidly and to such a depth, however, that small actions by the government had virtually no effect. It was only the extraordinary production demands of World War II that stimulated sufficient growth to pull the economy out of its freefall. The immediate postwar period rode on the demand for consumer goods that had been in short supply during the war, and there seemed to be little for the government to do for the economy one way or the other.

Figure 15–5 **Change in GDP Versus Change in Federal Revenue, 1981–2000**

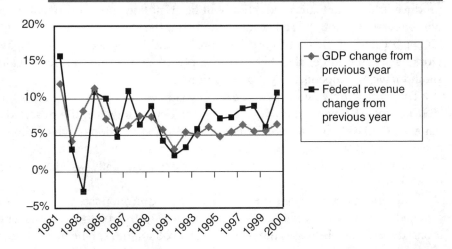

Source: Data from Executive Office of the President, *Economic Report of the President: 2002* (Washington, DC: U.S. Government Printing Office, 2002), 313, 406.

Keynesian Economics. Ideas about what the government should do in the event of a downturn have not stood still. John Maynard Keynes had argued in 1936 that the main cause of downturns was lack of demand.[34] According to this view, the government's aim should be to stimulate demand by spending, thereby ensuring that idle productive capacity is used. By 1946, the federal government assumed a formal role in the economy, and that role was guided by the prescriptions of Keynesian economics. Keynes focused on the problem of cuts in production in response to declining demand. Such cuts result in less purchasing power for consumers, which further reduces demand for goods and services. This still further decline in demand results in further reductions in production levels. The emphasis, according to Keynesians, should be on maintaining demand levels. The way to maintain demand levels, in their view, is to spend at a level higher than revenues — in other words, to incur a deficit whenever economic fluctuations threaten to reduce demand to levels that will generate unemployment and general economic decline.

Supply-Side Economics. Keynesian economics was widely accepted until the 1970s, when a contrasting view of the basic problem in a fluctuating demand cycle was given wide circulation. Some economists began to argue that the basic problem lay, not on the demand side, but on the supply side.[35] So-called supply-side economics became the dominant viewpoint of the Reagan and George H. W. Bush administrations. The supply-side view held that high tax burdens are the major contributor to reduced economic performance. The more taxes are collected, the less money is available for private investment and the less incentive there is to produce. If taxes are cut, production will be stimulated and additional workers will be hired. Although the tax rates are lower, the actual revenue yield will be higher because of increased corporate profits and increased take-home pay for workers. Furthermore, the increased supply of goods and services available should have a dampening effect on inflation.

The more extreme version of the supply-side view provided the basis for the 1981 tax cuts (Economic Recovery Tax Act of 1981). However, the expected revenue windfall did not materialize. The prevailing explanation of why it did not is consistent with the theory that tax cuts generally stimulate growth; the accepted view is merely that tax revenues from that growth are usually less than necessary to offset the government revenue loss.

The differences between the demand-oriented economists and the supply-oriented economists have moderated. The middle-of-the-road view is that specific and directed tax decreases or reductions in tax liabilities can be helpful, such as investment tax credits to encourage businesses to invest in capital facilities and an R & D tax credit to encourage private expenditures on research. A major multiplier effect, in which tax reductions yield tax revenue increases, is unlikely, however. Capital gains tax changes seem to produce the greatest level of response. Contemporary views tend to emphasize somewhat more the supply-side view than efforts to stimulate demand.

Contemporary Fiscal Policy. The contemporary view of fiscal policy is more pragmatic than theoretical. Budget deficits that overwhelmed incremental fiscal adjustments in the 1980s and early 1990s overshadowed debate among fiscal policy theorists. The current approach to fiscal policy calls for moderate fiscal efforts on the tax or expenditure side to counter trends rather than massive tax cuts or expenditure increases, although the George W. Bush administration pushed hard in 2001 for much larger tax cuts than Congress finally approved. Modest increases in government expenditures during periods of economic decline are expected to stimulate demand, which in turn will stimulate a higher level of production. Modest tax reductions, especially those designed to stimulate business investment, should have a similar stimulative effect on the supply of funds available to individuals. The balanced budget agreement of 1997 contained significant tax cuts, but only with accompanying expenditure reductions to ensure that the tax cut excess of the early 1980s without expenditure reductions was not repeated. As noted earlier, the effects of the Economic Growth and Tax Relief Reconciliation Act of 2001, the most recent example of supply-side stimulus, are sufficiently confounded with the effects of September 11, 2001, that it will be some years before the outcome of the tax cuts is, or is not, seen.

Multiplier Effects. Extracting taxes from the economy or adding expenditures will have not only immediate effects but also multiplier effects, as any transaction will generate several other transactions. For each government expenditure paid to industry or an individual, part is taxed while the remainder is divided between consumption and investment. The private citizen or firm spends, and in doing so places dollars in the hands of others. Some of those dollars will in turn be taxed and the rest spent or invested. Therefore, an increase of $100 in government expenditures will be multiplied in its effect on the economy.

Expenditures have a stimulative effect when they exceed revenues. An initial government expenditure financed by the deficit puts money in the hands of producers and consumers, who in turn pay a portion in taxes, save a portion, and spend a portion. An excess of revenues over expenditures has a dampening effect. An extremely large federal deficit, however, confounds the fiscal policy effects.

Response Lags in Fiscal Policy. One problem with implementing a modest fiscal policy is the gap between the time a revenue or expenditure response is necessary and the time it actually can occur. The lack of complete information about the economy produces a *perception lag*, the period of time that elapses between an event — such as the beginning of an inflationary period — and its recognition.

The perception lag contributes to a *reaction lag*, the time between recognition and the decision to act. Pluralistic or decentralized political systems are often unable to avoid substantial reaction lags. For example, in January 1967 President Johnson proposed a surtax on income to dampen the inflationary effects of Vietnam War spending. The proposed legislation was not introduced in Congress until August and, though finally approved, was not signed into law until July 1968. To close this gap, several presidents have attempted to gain congressional approval for moderate discretionary authority to raise or lower taxes. However, Congress has jealously guarded its prerogative to initiate and approve tax actions.

After the reaction lag is the *implementation lag*, the time required before the action taken actually affects the economy. Tax measures clearly are felt within a short period of time. The introduction of a new tax does require time to establish the specific regulations and mechanisms for collection. Once the tax is established, however, comparatively little time is required to make the necessary adjustments to the tax rate.

In contrast, extended implementation lags are likely when expenditures are adjusted for fiscal policy purposes. In the short term, the apportionment process that allocates funds to agencies may have some marginal influence on spending patterns during the various quarters of the fiscal year (see Chapter 10). Potentially more powerful tools include budget impoundments, which, within certain limits, allow the president to defer or rescind expenditures (see Chapter 9). Many expenditures, however, are basically uncontrollable in the immediate future because of previous commitments (for example, entitlement programs that provide assistance to the elderly and the poor). Furthermore, a large component of the federal budget is now devoted to meeting interest payments on the debt or to refinancing previous debt.

Capital construction has been suggested on occasion as one discretionary area where government expenditures could be used for fiscal policy purposes. The Clinton administration proposed grants to state and local governments for capital projects but failed to secure their passage in Congress. Construction would be initiated during slack periods and curtailed during periods of high employment. To some extent, public construction has been used for this purpose, particularly by the federal government during the Great Depression. The central government in a developing country, which typically has a much larger role in public infrastructure construction, is often in a better position to use this type of discretionary expenditure control. The short-term use of "stockpiled" capital projects that can be implemented when needed for their stimulative effects should not be confused with the role of government investment in long-term economic growth, discussed later.

Effects of Global Capital Flows. As noted at the outset of the chapter, in the United

States, changes in world markets were of little consequence for most of the twentieth century. Changes in the U.S. economy, such as the Great Depression and other serious recessions, rippled through other economies, but economic declines in other countries had less effect on the U.S. economy. We have already discussed the current interdependencies among the U.S. and other economies. The Asian and emerging-market financial crisis of the late 1990s has an additional demonstration value with respect to business cycles.

With hindsight, it is relatively easy to explain what happened in Asia. Indonesia and Thailand offer excellent illustrations. The Indonesian economy had been booming throughout the late 1980s and 1990s; towering buildings under construction dotted the Jakarta landscape, as was the case in Bangkok, Thailand. The values of the Indonesian rupiah and the Thai baht were both carefully controlled and pegged to the value of the U.S. dollar. Manufacturing and property investments were fueled by substantial lending from overseas investors, eager to participate in the Asian economic miracle. Portfolio investments in the Thai and Indonesian capital markets fueled the equity markets. Then in 1996–1997, vacancy rates in luxury hotels and office buildings began to climb. Lenders in turn began to reduce the volume of lending, putting pressure on the local currencies, which had to be converted to foreign currencies such as the Japanese yen and the dollar to pay for consumer goods imports and to pay debt service on some of the prior lending. The government of Thailand was unable to maintain the pegged value of the baht against the dollar, and ultimately devalued the baht. That meant that lenders who had lent yen or dollars and had *not* denominated the repayments in yen or dollars found their loans almost worthless. A majority of the loans extended by Japanese banks were denominated in local currencies rather than yen. Within weeks of the pressure in the Thai markets, Indonesian capital markets experienced the same pressures, and the value of the rupiah fell from around 3,500 to the dollar to nearly 20,000 to the dollar. Banks stopped lending and started calling in loans, investors rapidly sold their debt and equity holdings in Thai and Indonesian capital markets, and the bubble burst.

The economist Paul Krugman notes that it is too simplistic to describe the situation as purely a debt and equity market bubble. He has argued that the boom in Asian economies was mainly fueled by population growth and consumer demand as opposed to an especially productive set of proactive government economic policies. Once the pressure started on currencies, and Thailand and Indonesia were unable to defend those currencies, a vicious circle began consisting of loss of confidence in those economies, plummeting currency values along with rising interest rates, and financial problems for banks, households, and other institutions.[36] Neither fiscal nor monetary policy tools were sufficient to address the issues, and, at least in Indonesia, the political will to take the necessary steps was nonexistent. An important part of the problem for the world economy, and especially for Japan, was that there was no market information about the extent of exposure of foreign banks to losses due to lending in Thailand, Indonesia, and other emerging market countries in local currencies.[37]

Monetary Policy

Control Over the Money Supply. Both demand-side and supply-side economists focus on the role of taxing and spending in the economy. Although fiscal policy economists did not launch a major critique of demand-side theories until the late 1970s, other economists since the 1950s have argued that the government's main effect on the economy should not come through fiscal policy at all. Led by Milton Friedman, these economists argue that the main effects of government policy on the private sector should come through control over the money supply. In a simple economy, a government controls the money supply through its monopoly power over the printing of money. As the economy expands, the demand for money increases, and ultimately government meets this demand by printing more money. In a sense, the government literally can print currency and use that currency to meet its spending requirements. The increase in the money supply (over and above printing replacements for worn currency) is called *seignorage*. Clearly, if the government resorts to printing money without regard to demand, the value of the currency printed declines. U.S. news media in the early 1980s showed film footage of individuals in Bolivia actually pushing carts full of currency to pay for a few dollars worth of goods as the annual inflation rate reached several thousand percent. Inflation affected currencies so much in Russia and Poland shortly after the demise of the Soviet Union that the governments issued new currency, eliminating three zeros to ease the use of currency in ordinary transactions. Indonesia followed suit after the financial collapse in the 1990s.

In any complex economy, paper money and coinage in circulation are not the major component of the money supply. While the U.S. Treasury has created a small "profit" in the cost of the dollar coins it issues versus the denominated value, this increase is meaningless in terms of its revenue impact. In the United States, about 50 percent of the readily circulating money supply takes the form of paper money and coinage. The remaining 50 percent consists mainly of demand deposits in banking institutions. Together, currency, coinage, demand deposits such as checking accounts, travelers checks, and small time deposits constitute the principal money supply called M1. In 2001, M1 represented about 14 percent of the total money supply. Paper money and coins thus are about 7 percent of total money supply exclusive of debt. Before debt is counted, total money supply in 2001 was approximately $7.2 trillion.[38] Most ordinary financial transactions are conducted with checks, other paper documents, and by electronic means (ATM and debit card transactions) that transfer bank account balances from one individual or institution to another. The other main components of total money supply, exclusive of debt, are individual money market and mutual fund deposits, long-term deposits such as IRAs, and institutional mutual fund and longer-term deposits.

The banking deposit component of the money supply expands through credit or borrowing. When an individual borrows to purchase a new car, the bank increases the individual's bank balance, which allows a check to be written to the car dealer. In this case, the money supply grows by the amount of the loan. Similarly, banks can borrow from the Federal Reserve System, which also adds to the money supply. Deregulation of the banking industry and the growth of various stock and bond funds have further increased the number and types of negotiable instruments that constitute the money supply. Influencing the money supply thus grows ever more complicated. To complete the picture, debt, other than financial institutions debt to each other, equaled about $18.3 trillion in 2001.[39]

Role of the Federal Reserve System. In the United States, control over the money supply and interest rates, and hence monetary policy, is exercised by the Federal Reserve System, a quasi-public institution.[40] The system is headed by a board of governors consisting of seven members appointed by the president with the advice and consent of the Senate. The chairperson is designated by the president. The Federal Reserve Bank and its branches are augmented by all national banks and by state banks and trust companies that wish to join the system.

The Federal Reserve serves as a bank to the banking community. Financial transactions among banks and other financial institutions are cleared through the Federal Reserve. The system lends money to the member banks, which the banks can then relend to their customers. In setting its lending rates, the Federal Reserve influences the direction and magnitude of interest rates in the entire economy, in turn dampening or stimulating the credit system. The system also buys and sells government bonds ranging from short-term Treasury notes to long-term bonds (open market operations). In addition, the Federal Reserve controls the reserve requirements for member banks — the amount of money a bank must have available as a proportion of the total demand deposits of customers. Using these three tools — open market operations, lending, and control of reserve requirements — the Federal Reserve controls the money supply. In this way, it attempts to moderate demand that might lead to inflationary pressures by reducing the growth in the money supply, or to stimulate demand when the economy is faltering by allowing the money supply to grow.

Open Market Operations. Open market operations and setting of the discount rate are the most well-publicized operations because they occur daily. As the Federal Reserve purchases bonds, it increases the reserve holdings of the member institutions selling the bonds and hence increases the supply of money available to be lent. This increase in turn stimulates economic activity, because more investment funds are made available. As member banks buy bonds from the Federal Reserve, their cash reserves decrease, reducing the total supply of funds available to the economy.

Discount Rate. Frequently adjusted, the Federal Reserve's lending rate to member institutions, called the discount rate, has increased in prominence as a monetary tool. Banks borrow from the Federal Reserve to meet customers' demands for money. As the Federal Reserve increases the interest rate, the rate charged to final borrowers increases, which in turn decreases the demand for funds. Since the 1980s, these operations have become the main focus of Federal Reserve actions to control inflation in rapid-growth periods such as the late 1990s and to stimulate growth such as in 2001–2002.[41] In the boom of the 1990s, until the stock market decline of 2000–2001, the Federal Reserve was quite successful in using small adjustments in the discount rate to control inflation while not depressing the economy. As noted earlier, the increasing openness of the U.S. economy to world markets also has contributed to holding down inflation.

Reserve Requirement. Changing the reserve requirements of member institutions is done infrequently. For every dollar in customer deposits, member banks are required to retain a specific percentage. By increasing this percentage, the Federal Reserve can immediately curtail the amount of money available. Historically changed only every few years, the reserve requirement in the 1980s became a more prominent feature of monetary policy, with adjustments often occurring on an annual basis. The 1990s saw a return to infrequent changes in the reserve requirements.

Putting these monetary tools together, the government's monetary policy is described as *loose* or *tight* (or as *expansionary* or *contractionary*). Loose monetary policy usually involves lowering the prime rate, purchasing securities from member banks, and perhaps lowering reserve requirements. These actions increase the money supply, which permits banks to lend more to customers. As a result, private investment goes up and unemployment falls. The side effects are lower interest rates and higher prices.

A tight monetary policy entails the reverse — the prime rate increases, the Federal Reserve sells securities, and reserve requirements may increase. These actions reduce the ability of banks to lend. Tight monetary policy is pursued generally to dampen inflationary pressures and to slow down a speeding economy. In contrast, loose monetary policy is pursued to stimulate growth and reduce unemployment.

Role of the Chairperson of the Federal Reserve Board. It is highly likely that for much of the history of the Federal Reserve few Americans ever knew the name of an incumbent or former chair. While a majority no doubt still do not, it is reasonable to speculate that far more ordinary citizens now recognize his name. Alan Greenspan became almost a household name in the 1990s, at least to the millions of Americans who became first-time investors in the stock market or started paying attention for the first time to the value of their company pension fund investments in the market. As chair of the Federal Reserve, Greenspan appeared regularly on the news networks and was widely quoted in the press. When he described in 1996 investors' attitudes toward growth in the value of stocks as "irrational exuberance," prices plummeted the same and following days.[42] Subsequent tempering of his remarks over the next several years itself became newsworthy.

While the chair clearly is the spokesperson for the Federal Reserve, it is more likely that the news media and the investing public are now highly sensitive to actions by the Federal Reserve, and hence the chair is watched carefully for indications of where the Federal Reserve is going. Internally, the chair presides over a seven-member group and wields his or her influence through personality, force of argument, and relative prestige. The chair and the Federal Reserve are not synonymous.

Political Criticism of the Federal Reserve Board. Although the Federal Reserve Board is protected from direct coercion from the president because its members' terms are fixed without threat of removal, the board is periodically criticized for appearing to respond to political pressure. While there is little evidence of overt behavior in support of incumbent presidents, some evidence indicates that the Federal Reserve Board has done less than it could in some periods (for example, in the 1960s and 1970s) to offset cyclic movements in the money supply and that this lack of action coincided with the interests of incumbent administrations.[43] Until the stock market boom of the 1990s, the Federal Reserve was seen in a loose sense as somewhat more Republican Party–oriented mainly because of its role in managing monetary policy, with the association between monetarists such as Milton Friedman and more conservative public policies focusing on lower levels of federal spending, tax cuts, and balanced budgets. The achievement of a balanced budget during the Clinton administration, though obviously a cooperative result from both political parties, put the Democratic Party in the mainstream of monetary and fiscal policy, apparently diminishing some of the previous partisan differences over economic policy.

Combining Fiscal and Monetary Policy

Although economists differ on the emphasis given to fiscal versus monetary policy, the two sets of tools operate at the same time, whether deliberately or not. Sometimes they are complementary; at other times the effects of fiscal policy actions are offset by monetary policy actions. Many analysts are wary of advocating frequent changes in fiscal or monetary policy in response to changing economic conditions. The inability to predict economic change sufficiently far in advance and the slow response of governments suggests to many economists that fiscal policy should be oriented toward long-term economic objectives and that monetary policy should be used for effecting short-term adjustments. Although fiscal and monetary policy advocates disagree vigorously, most economists agree that the budget deficits of the 1980s and early 1990s were harmful.[44]

Public Investment Role of Government

Government Investment in Infrastructure. Fiscal policy and monetary policy are basically tools of central governments. State and local governments typically have balanced budget requirements, making it impossible to incur debt strictly for fiscal policy reasons, and neither type of government has a major influence on the overall money supply. However, state and local governments have significant impacts on regional economies, and increasingly state and local governments are adopting explicit economic development strategies. In this regard, state and local governments pursue strategies to create an effective economic climate to foster economic growth. Also, they inevitably change taxes and spending in response to general economic conditions, which, whether deliberate or not, has at least regional economic effects.

One of the major strategic elements available is public sector investment in the physical infrastructure necessary for business expansion. As discussed in Chapter 12, serious concern emerged in the United States during the early 1980s regarding the loss in economic productivity due to the deterioration in the infrastructure base of roads, bridges, streets, water and sewer systems, and other public facilities. According to some, fewer technological innovations, decreases in labor productivity, and inadequate capital investment in infrastructure were the major contributors to an overall worsening of the U.S. economy.[45] In developing countries, inadequate operation and maintenance of existing facilities has in many cases led to deterioration of physical facilities long before their expected depreciation. This deterioration has in turn created a decline in economic production.

State and Local Incentives for Private Sector Investment. Governments are a major source of total capital formation in many developing countries. Public sector investment in infrastructure including state-owned enterprises historically accounted for most of the capital formation in developing countries. With privatization of state enterprises and growth of the private sector, however, the public sector role in capital formation has diminished. Although state and local governments in the United States do not invest as high a proportion of their finances in infrastructure, their role in creating a favorable economic climate is important. Some state employee pension funds, for example, have been used as sources of venture capital and to capitalize industrial development funds to attract new business. Federal policies, such as giving municipal bonds tax-exempt status, also influence state and local investment spending (see Chapter 12).[46]

Similarly, even in the face of reduced federal financial assistance and difficult fiscal circumstances, state and local governments have over the last several decades increased both their relative share of infrastructure financing and the absolute amounts spent on public infrastructure. This stimulative effect, of course, required state and local tax increases.

State and local governments also actively compete with each other over the location of major industrial facilities.[47] However, to the extent that state and local governments offer special incentives, such as tax breaks and below-market-cost facilities for industrial expansion, little national economic growth is stimulated. Certainly it may be possible to induce a business to relocate or to locate a planned expansion by offering special incentives, but such a move represents for the national economy as a whole only a relocation of economic activity rather than net new economic growth. Of course, from a national point of view, attracting firms from other countries, such as the Daimler Benz plant in Alabama discussed in Chapter 14, results in net growth within the national economy, albeit at the potential expense of some other country. Matters are not really that simple; the Daimler Benz investment, for instance, was in new productive capacity, contributing to net growth in the world economy wherever that investment eventually turned out to be located.

Similarly, when public investment creates possibilities for new investment, not only the local economy but also the total economy expands. A joint public–private venture, for example, participated in the redevelopment of the Baltimore harbor area, which created conditions in which net new economic investment was attracted. Similar ventures have occurred in Portland, Oregon, and Seattle, Washington. Riverfront revitalization projects in San Antonio, Texas, stimulated downtown economic growth and have been emulated since.[48] The FedEx location of its worldwide central shipping point was a coup for the city of Memphis, Tennessee. Memphis offered many attractions related to such things as location, weather conditions, and volume of air traffic. The city also invested easily more than $100 million in airport runway and other facilities expansion. This was not a case of moving productive investment from one part of the country (or world) to another part with no net gain to the economy. Rather, FedEx was introducing a new business model of central hub air shipment, a major new investment in economic productivity that subsequently paid off handsomely for both the private and public sector investments.[49]

Link Between Public Infrastructure and Economic Growth. The causal link between public infrastructure investment and real economic growth depends on two conditions. The lack of facilities or infrastructure has to be a barrier to investment, and the costs of the investment have to be in principle recoverable through economic gains. For example, if poor road conditions slow the movement of goods and services, then the costs of those goods and services increase. In addition, firms may hold back on new investments because of the expected difficulty in transportation. Investment in road improvements under these conditions reduces transportation costs, which in turn either provides additional funds for investment or is passed on in savings to consumers, who can subsequently increase either savings or investment. If the economic returns on the road improvements exceed their costs, the result is a net economic gain to the economy. Conversely, if there are insufficient centers of production and consumption linked by those roads, then the volume of transportation will not be sufficient to yield sufficient economic gain, and the investment will not have been warranted.

Unfortunately, determining when an investment will yield a sufficient economic return is often difficult. Many local governments in the United States have invested in downtown revitalization, business incubator facilities, industrial parks, and other facilities without sufficient analysis of the local economy and have been disappointed with the returns.[50] Some investments that seem to have substantial benefits initially turn out later to be white elephants when the business some years later decides to relocate elsewhere.[51] Charlotte, North Carolina, lost its National Basketball Association team because it would not build a new stadium, though other factors such as less-than-full arenas after the early years of the team's history were cited by the owners. Similarly, in developing countries inadequate consideration of whether there are genuine economic opportunities to be stimulated by an infrastructure investment at times has led to indiscriminate construction of roads where there were no real market and production centers to link. One study of U.S. highway investments suggested that instead of significant new capital investment in highways, greater economic impact could occur from decreasing congestion and other planning improvements — for little more spending than current levels. Other studies have reached similar conclusions about a wide range of infrastructure investments.[52] Cities competing for the Olympics (and their national governments) gamble hundreds of millions in investments if selected against an uncertain return on that investment, though most observers agree that the competition is more about the symbolic recognition of the city and country that are expected to pay off forever than the more immediate returns from hosting an Olympics.[53]

Redistributional Effects of Economic Policy

Unintentional Redistributive Effects

To this point in the chapter, we have been concerned with the overall performance of the economy. Government involvement in the economy also has specific objectives focused on subsectors or individuals. Fiscal and monetary policy actions taken to control overall economic growth and price stability are not necessarily neutral in their effects on individuals and industries. If the government lowers corporate tax rates to stimulate business investment but increases other taxes to neutralize the effects on the budget balance, then those for whom taxes are raised are paying for the economic benefits whether they share in those benefits or not. Many developing country governments have attempted to address problems of the urban poor by imposing price controls on agricultural products. While the short-run effect may be to lower food prices in urban areas, the longer-run effect is to decrease agricultural production. In the short run, economic costs are imposed on one group, rural producers, for the benefit of another group, urban consumers. In the long run, overall economic performance declines. Developing country budgets, operating often in conditions of instability and uncertainty, frequently have difficulty achieving any specific policy objective, such as poverty alleviation, through the budgeting process.[54]

Economic policies aimed at stabilization also can have unintentional redistributive effects. Under inflationary conditions, persons on fixed or relatively fixed incomes lose purchasing power. This is especially true for retired persons living on pensions, but it is also true for workers who cannot command increases in wages. If the government takes no action to slow the rate of inflation, its inaction "redistributes" income from those on fixed incomes to those whose wages or other income rises with inflation. Higher interest rates favor income earnings from investments, usually held by upper-income families. Large federal deficits, which ultimately impose repayment costs on future generations, also may create intergenerational inequity (see Chapter 11).

Since the 1960s, the degree of inequality of income distribution in the United States has increased significantly. There was a sharp increase in inequality during the 1980s, attributed by many to a significant cut in federal corporate and personal income taxes, benefiting mainly the already wealthy, and cuts in programs of assistance to the poor.[55] The stock market boom of the 1990s substantially widened the gap between the top and the bottom, though the subsequent crash did convert many of the instant millionaires to ordinary income earners. Some economists, especially in Europe, who are critical of the "monetary policy only" view of the government's economic role, argue that the government should mitigate the negative distributional effects of economic growth that leaves only the middle- and upper-income classes better off. According to these economists, policies such as aggressive employment subsidies to reduce the number of unemployed should be implemented as direct measures to lower the nonaccelerating inflation rate of unemployment.[56]

Income Stabilization Policies

The most deliberate income stabilization policy would be to institute a *negative income tax*. This would involve determining an appropriate income guarantee, a benefit reduction rate, and a break-even income. The income guarantee is the amount of the transfer when the family income is zero, the benefit reduction rate is the rate at which the amount transferred is reduced as family income increases, and the break-even income is the point where family income reaches a level beyond which the family no longer qualifies for a transfer. The United States has no negative income tax, but its principles are incorporated to varying degrees in several income-related transfer programs.

Transfer Programs. Several transfer programs (food stamps; Supplemental Feeding Program for Women, Infants, and Children; Medicaid) provide a minimum or floor level of benefits comparable to the income guarantee. Major reforms in the welfare system, however, have severely curtailed the benefits by imposing lifetime limits on the amount individuals may receive and imposing strict work requirements (see Chapter 14).

Tax Policies. Expenditure programs are not the only form of income redistribution. As noted in Chapter 4, different taxes have different impacts on various groups. In addition, the overall structure of the entire tax system may operate to redistribute income among different groups. The Tax Reform Act of 1986 was in one basic aspect almost exclusively a redistributive act.[57] Throughout consideration of various possible changes, the basic principle followed was that the act had to be revenue neutral. In the face of huge budget deficits, neither political party was prepared to support a tax reform that reduced revenues, as the Economic Recovery Tax Act of 1981 had. As a consequence of the 1986 law, lower-income groups benefited from sharply reduced taxes, middle-income groups benefited from modest reductions, and upper-income individuals and corporations faced tax increases. In 1993, there were sharp increases in the top tax bracket. In 1997, tax decreases focused on both ends of the income bracket. The 2001 tax changes substantially benefited upper-income groups through the drop in capital gains rates and reduction of personal income tax rates.

Tax expenditures, discussed in Chapter 4, are often redistributive in effect. Not taxing interest on municipal bonds redistributes income toward the purchasers of municipal bonds, who tend to be retirees either directly or through pension fund investments. Allowing interest on mortgages, including second homes, to be deducted from taxable income has a redistributive effect toward middle- and upper-income individuals. The problem with the redistributive effects of tax expenditures is that they are much less transparent as a policy instrument. A tax expenditure does not appear plainly as an expenditure, nor does it appear directly as a tax reduction.[58]

While economic policy affects the distribution of income, it cannot be expected to address structural features of the labor market. For example, workers with minimal or obsolete skills will have difficulty finding employment even during periods of rapid growth. Economic policy also is of limited assistance in coping with readjustments in the economy, such as might occur with changes in defense — both homeland security and overseas military actions — as a result of the attacks on September 11, 2001. Other policies, of course, are designed to deal with more basic structural problems. Expenditures on education, both academic and vocational, are expected to increase the overall human resource base for the economy. Regulatory policies are expected to reduce private incentives to pollute the environment, a problem that imposes an eventual economic cost when the environmental damage is repaired.

No redistributive policy is neutral in its economic impact. Indeed, no economic act, no matter what its intended effects, is automatically neutral with regard to distribution of income. Designing redistributive policies should take into account the potential reduction in economic efficiency and try to mitigate any losses.[59] During a recessionary period, both the labor force and total plant capacity are underemployed, so that government action to stimulate the economy may do just that without causing significant unintended redistributive effects. But since recession is not the normal state of the economy, we have to assume for starters "that if the government expands its purchases of goods and services or provides additional benefits so that some group of private citizens can consume more goods and services, somewhere else in the economy purchases of goods and services for consumptionary investment, exports, or other government programs will have to be reduced."[60]

▉ Summary

Representing more than 28 percent of total economic activity in the United States, federal, state, and local government budgets have a tremendous combined effect on the economy. The federal government acts deliberately to intervene in the economy to achieve aggregate economic objectives. The major economic policy objectives of most central governments include economic growth, full employment, stable prices, and balance in the flow of funds into and out of the economy. Increasingly, as national economies become more interdependent, governments, including the U.S. federal government, are including specific competitiveness objectives as part of national economic policy. Because it has sometimes soared to unacceptable (politically and economically) heights, management of the federal budget deficit and the overall government debt also has been added as a major economic policy objective in the United States.

Fiscal policy and monetary policy are the main tools used to influence macroeconomic performance. Fiscal policy encompasses the use of the government's taxing and spending powers to stimulate or dampen economic activity. An excess of expenditures over revenues (a deficit) stimulates demand and thus employment. A possible consequence, however, may be inflation. An excess of revenues over expenditures (a surplus) has a dampening effect on the economy. Monetary policy affects economic activity through control over the money supply. By changing interest rates and reserve requirements and by buying or selling bonds, the Federal Reserve can speed up or slow down the pace of economic activity. In the latter half of the 1980s, debates over the theory and detail of fiscal and monetary policy were overshadowed by the huge federal budget deficit. Several years of balanced budgets, with a surplus for 1998 through 2001, have somewhat shifted the focus to delicate adjustments in interest rates to sustain economic growth.

Although state and local governments do not exercise fiscal and monetary control, their role in providing the basic infrastructure required for private sector business activity is important to regional economic performance. In this respect, state and local governments and developing country governments pursue similar ends. For developing country governments, their effective use of borrowed funds from donor agencies and commercial banks depends on putting the funds to use in increasing economic productive capacity.

Government policy interventions also have consequences for income redistribution. Changes in tax policy and increases or decreases in expenditures are almost never neutral as regards income distribution. In addition, there is general agreement that some level of redistribution of income is appropriate to address the problems of individuals with very low incomes. How extensive these programs should be, however, remains perennially controversial.

Notes

1. Executive Office of the President, *Economic Report of the President: 2002* (Washington, DC: U.S. Government Printing Office, 2002), 313, 410.

2. Executive Office of the President, Executive Order 12835 of January 25, 1983: Establishment of the National Economic Council, *Federal Register* 58 (1993): 6189–6190.

3. Executive Office of the President, *Economic Report of the President: 2002*, 247.

4. Executive Office of the President, *Economic Report of the President: 2002*, 264.

5. Executive Office of the President, *Technology for America's Economic Growth: A New Direction to Build Economic Strength* (Washington, DC: U.S. Government Printing Office, 1993).

6. Executive Office of the President, *Economic Report of the President: 2002*, 34.

7. Commission of the European Communities, *European Competitiveness Report 2002* (Brussels: Commission of European Communities, 2000), *http://europa.eu.int/comm/ enterprise/enterprise_policy/competitiveness/doc/compet_rep_2000/cr-2000_en.pdf*; accessed August 2002.

8. Employment Act, P.L. 79–304 (1946); Full Employment and Balanced Growth Act, P.L. 95–523 (1978).

9. R.A. Musgrave and P.B. Musgrave, *Public Finance in Theory and Practice*, 5th ed. (New York: McGraw-Hill, 1989).

10. O.L. Graham, Jr., *Losing Time: The Industrial Policy Debate* (Cambridge, MA: Harvard University Press, 1992).

11. FRBSF Economic Letter 98–28, *The Natural Rate, NAIRU, and Monetary Policy* (San Francisco: Federal Reserve Bank of San Francisco, 1998), *http://www.frbsf.org/econrsrch/ wklyltr/wklyltr98/el98–28.html*; accessed August 2002. Discussion and examples of NAIRU in this paragraph rely on this source.

12. World Bank, *World Development Report 1992* (New York: Oxford University Press, 1992), 241.

13. World Bank, *World Development Report 2000/2001* (New York: Oxford University Press, 2001), 294–295.

14. *European Competitiveness Report 2002*, 7.

15. Executive Office of the President, *Economic Report of the President: 1995* (Washington, DC: U.S. Government Printing Office, 1995). The 1995 report contains a detailed description of the methodology; data in all subsequent government economic series use the revised concept, and historical tables have been adjusted.

16. L.C. Thurow, *Building Wealth: The New Rules for Individuals, Companies, and Nations in a Knowledge-Based Economy* (New York: Harper-Collins, 1999).

17. G.M. Grossman and E. Helpman, *Innovation and Growth: Technological Competition in the Global Economy* (Cambridge, MA: MIT Press, 1992).

18. Executive Office of the President, *Economic Report of the President: 2002*, 33.

19. J.L. Hervey and L.S. Merkel, In Defense of the US Current-Account Deficit, *The McKinsey Quarterly* (2001): 166.

20. P. Krugman, *The Return to Depression Economics* (New York: W.W. Norton, 1999).

21. R. Chernow, *The House of Morgan: An American Banking Dynasty and the Rise of Modern Finance* (New York: Simon and Schuster, 1990).

22. Congressional Budget Office, *Assessing the Decline in the National Saving Rate* (Washington, DC: U.S. Government Printing Office, 1993), 2; Organization for Economic Cooperation and Development, *OECD Economic Surveys, United States: 1996* (Paris: Organization for Economic Cooperation and Development, 1996), 22; Executive Office of the President, *Economic Report of the President: 2002*, 6–8.

23. Congressional Budget Office, *Assessing the Decline in the National Savings Rate*, 2.

24. Executive Office of the President, *Economic Report of the President: 2002*, 406.

25. Economic Growth and Tax Relief Reconciliation Act, P.L. 107–16 (2001).

26. The Conference Board, *Business Cycles Indicators*, *http://www.tcb-indicators.org/methodology/di_computation.cfm*; accessed August 2002.

27. Executive Office of the President, *Economic Report of the President: 2002*, 22.

28. Bureau of Labor Statistics, *Understanding the Consumer Price Index: Answers to Some Questions* (Washington, DC: U.S. Government Printing Office, 2000).

29. J.L. Norwood, The Consumer Price Index, the Deficit, and Politics, *Government Finance Review* 13 (February 1997): 32–33.

30. The Conference Board, *Business Cycle Indicators*.

31. Congressional Budget Office, *CBO's Economic Forecasting Record: A Supplement to the Budget and Economic Outlook: 2003–2012*, *http://www.cbo.gov/showdoc.cfm?index=3285&sequence=0#table1*; accessed August 2002.

32. The CBO's annual analysis *The Economic and Budget Outlook: Fiscal Years [ten year period]* always contains a chapter explaining the differences between CBO and OMB estimates. A mid-year publication, *The Economic and Budget Outlook: Update*, reflects changes in the months since publication of the *Outlook*. Congressional Budget Office, *The Economic and Budget Outlook: Update* (Washington, DC: U.S. Government Printing Office, annually).

33. Trapped by the Bubble, *The Economist* 349 (September 23, 1999), *http://economist.com/displayStory.cfm?Story_ID=242025*; accessed August 2002.

34. J.M. Keynes, *The General Theory of Employment, Interest and Money* (New York: Harcourt Brace, 1936).

35. A.B. Laffer and J.P. Seymour, eds., *The Economics of the Tax Revolt: A Reader* (New York: Harcourt Brace Jovanovich, 1979).

36. P. Krugman, *The Return to Depression Economics*, 93–96.

37. J.C. Fuhrer and S. Schuh, Beyond Shocks: What Causes Business Cycles? An Overview, *New England Economic Review* (November/December 1998): 3–24.

38. Executive Office of the President, *Economic Report of the President: 2002*, 394–395.

39. Executive Office of the President, *Economic Report of the President: 2002*, 394–395.

40. L.E. Browne, The Evolution of Monetary Policy and the Federal Reserve System Over the Past Thirty Years: An Overview, *New England Economic Review* (January/February 2001): 3–11.

41. Browne, The Evolution of Monetary Policy and the Federal Reserve System, 5–6.

42. Greenspan Lets Things Simmer, *The Economist*, 346 (July 1, 1999), *http://economist.com/ displayStory.cfm?Story_ID=218974*; accessed August 2002.

43. N. Beck, The Fed and the Political Business Cycle, *Contemporary Policy Issues* 9 (1991): 25–38.

44. Federal Reserve Board Monetary Policy Report to Congress, *Federal Reserve Bulletin* (August 2000): 548–550.

45. O. Kinnander, As Infrastructure Crumbles, Engineers Scream for Investment, *The Bond Buyer* 335 (March 9, 2001): 40.

46. M.A. Miller and M.A. Glick, The Resurgence of Federalism: The Case for Tax-Exempt Bonds, *Municipal Finance Journal* 19 (1999): 46–73.

47. D.A. Rondinelli and W.J. Burpitt, Do Government Incentives Attract and Retain International Investment? A Study of Foreign-Owned Firms in North Carolina, *Policy Sciences* 33 (2000): 181–205; M. Porter, Location, Competition and Economic Development: Local Clusters in a Global Economy, *Economic Development Quarterly* 14 (2000): 15–34; S. Tuttle, Team NC, *North Carolina* 58 (September 2000): 14–29.

48. A. Jordan, River of Dreams, *Governing* 11 (August 1997): 26–30.

49. W. Fulton, The FedEx Story, *Governing* 14 (April 2000): 68.

50. D.M. Markley and K.T. McNamara, Local Economic and State Fiscal Impacts of Business Incubators, *State and Local Government Review* 28 (1996): 17–27.

51. C. Mahtesian, Throwaway Stadium, *Governing* 14 (January 2000): 41–42.

52. K.A. Small, et al., *Road Work* (Washington, DC: Brookings Institution, 1989); R. Krohl, The Role of Public Capital in the Economic Development Process, *International Journal of Public Administration* 24 (2001): 1041–1060.

53. Cities and the Olympics: Make or Break, *The Economist* 356 (September 16, 2000): 27–32.

54. R.D. Lee, Jr., Linkages among Poverty, Development and Budget Systems, *Public Budgeting & Finance* 12 (Spring 1992): 48–60.

55. C.J. Niggle, Monetary Policy and Changes in Income Distribution, *Journal of Economic Issues* 23 (1989): 809–822.

56. Up the NAIRU without a Paddle, *The Economist* 344 (March 8, 1997): 92.

57. J.H. Birnbaum and A.S. Murray, *Showdown at Gucci Gulch: Lawmakers, Lobbyists, and the Unlikely Triumph of Tax Reform* (New York: Vintage, 1988).

58. E.J. Toder, Tax Cuts or Spending — Does it Make a Difference?, *National Tax Journal* 53 (2000): 361–371.

59. E.K. Browning, The Marginal Cost of Redistribution, *Public Finance Quarterly* 21 (1993): 3–32.

60. C.L. Schutze, Paying the Bills, in *Setting Domestic Priorities: What Can Government Do?*, H.J. Aaron and C.L. Schutze, eds., (Washington, DC: Brookings Institution, 1992), 300.

Concluding Remarks

The field of public budgeting and finance in the coming years will be characterized by increased attention given to several areas:

- Integration of planning, budgeting, accounting, performance measurement, and evaluation systems
- Financial management
- Legislative–executive conflict over budgetary roles
- Achievement of an acceptable balance between the provision of public services and their financing within an intergovernmental framework
- Promotion of economic growth within an international context
- Preserving and enhancing the nation's security at home and abroad

A risk-free prediction is that budgetary decision systems will have increased capabilities to use program information. The steady development of systems oriented toward program information since the late 1950s shows no signs of abating. Whether the use of program information is desirable has been a moot question for years. The issue today is how to use program information, not whether to use it.

Advancements in computer technology — both hardware and software — will help strengthen the trend toward use of program data. Microcomputers make possible relatively sophisticated information systems for small governments and may even give them an advantage over many larger jurisdictions that still operate largely within a mainframe environment or some combination of mainframes, local area networks, and personal computers. Wider accessibility to computer technology also is spurring the rapid growth of tools that can help decision makers use the technology. Knowledge management systems and decision support systems will increase the capacities of decision makers to consider information, even under tight deadline pressures.

As planning, budgeting, accounting, performance measurement, and evaluation systems become increasingly sophisticated, the need for better integration increases. One of the essential emphases in program budgeting was, and is, to link budgetary, program, and accounting information into an integrated decision system. The trend toward integration, however, does not mean that political realities will be removed from budgetary decision making, as some critics have contended. Rather, a greater array of information will be more readily available than in the past, and decision makers will need to choose among that information in determining what positions to take on difficult problems.

Financial management has been of central concern since the 1980s and will continue to be so. In earlier times, unrepressed inflation and serious taxpayer recalcitrance forced government leaders to recognize that resources were limited and budget trimming was essential. Economic problems at the local, state, and federal levels have continued to make for "tight" budget situations that call for frugal measures. Only in the second half of the 1990s did a brief respite from this pressure occur. Budget execution, therefore, will receive greater attention in the future. Can savings be achieved through closer monitoring of program spending? Can improvements in accounting systems lead to savings? What alternative financial arrangements hold promise for reducing costs? To what extent should governments pursue contracting out of services, privatization, and leasing arrangements? Does the value that society receives from the public expenditure match or exceed the cost of the program or service? Growth in government programs will be accepted grudgingly, if at all, by taxpayers, who remain skeptical of the ability of governments to do many things well. Perhaps the one exception will be growth in security programs at home and abroad.

Executives and legislative bodies will continue their struggles with one another over their relative roles in budgetary decision making. The increased ability to collect, store, and manipulate data through computer technology makes possible far more detailed legislative involvement than was possible only ten years ago. Will that increased ability translate into greater legislative authority and control, and in what ways? Conversely, both executives and legislatures may be less than assertive in dealing with the most intractable problems. Gridlock existed largely from 1981 to 1993 when Republican Presidents Reagan and Bush controlled the White House and Democrats largely controlled Congress. A reverse form of gridlock developed in 1995 when the president was a Democrat, Bill Clinton, and Congress came under the control of Republicans. During the first part of the George W. Bush administration, the Republicans controlled the White House and the House of Representatives while the Democrats controlled the Senate. After September 11, 2001, Democrats and Republicans felt compelled to work together on security issues but still differed on many matters. Perhaps the most important issue that could not be resolved due to party conflicts was the thorny problem of restructuring programs such as Social Security and Medicare in light of the aging population.

If Congress is to play a bigger role in decision making, then one imperative is to realign powers and procedures within the two chambers. As noted earlier, legislative bodies have changed their operations, added staff, and more generally increased their ability to handle policy making. At the same time, Congress encompasses a complex maze of committees, processes, and political considerations that make difficult any coherent approach to policy making. Congressional leadership has been unwilling or unable to consider any thorough revamping of the organization and processes by which Congress operates. It did come to grips with security issues in 2002 by creating the Department of Homeland Security. The formation of the department involved transferring units out of existing departments into the new ones. This reorganization caused the realignment of powers among congressional committees, with many committees having reduced powers.

Governments will continue to be confronted with competing programmatic needs that must be met within a context of limited resources and intergovernmental relationships. Homeland security and the global fight against terrorism are likely to have the highest priority on limited resources for the foreseeable future. Small and larger scale wars also seem likely to continue putting pressure on the federal budget. Programs for the elderly (especially Social Security) and health care will continue to demand the attention of the federal government, while all levels of government will be called upon to deal with such intractable problems as HIV/AIDS and other infectious diseases, drug trafficking and drug abuse, and poverty and related conditions, such as homelessness. Whether addressed by the public sector or the private sector, the growth of the population aged 65 and older is inevitable, and health expenditures can be expected to account for an increasing proportion of gross domestic product. At the other end of the age spectrum, financing elementary and secondary education will require new approaches as traditional sources of finance decline or are limited by taxpayer resistance. Difficult choices must be made over how programs will operate and how they will be financed. Presidents, governors, and mayors may all lament the afflictions of AIDS and drug dependency, but where are funds to be obtained for dealing with these problems? Local governments may be willing to provide programs for the poor, but only if state and federal funds are available to support these efforts. The intergovernmental finance system will come under increasing scrutiny as the different levels of government vie for the same tax dollars.

The aftermath of the September 11, 2001, terrorist attacks posed a complex set of problems about program integration, appropriate funding, and government accountablity. The federal government wrestled with the age-old problem of how to provide coordinated policy in a decentralized environment. While a Homeland Security Department was formed to help integrate some agencies and functions, key agencies were not made part of the new department, including the Federal Bureau of Investigation, the Central Intelligence Agency, and the National Security Agency. Problems also existed within agencies, such as regional offices and headquarters of the FBI not suitably communicating with one another about potential terrorists.

Continued conflict among national, state, and local levels of government may be expected as new problems emerge that challenge existing intergovernmental divisions of authority and responsibility. Nowhere are the intergovernmental roles more complex than in attempting to ensure homeland security. How are security agencies at the federal level best able to relate to state and local agencies, especially given the long-standing tension that has existed among the levels of government? The budget systems of all governments allocate large sums of money to security efforts, but how are agencies to be held accountable for results when buck-passing for any failures can easily be done in such a decentralized environment? Other continuing intergovernmental concerns include preemptions of authority by the federal government over areas claimed by state and local governments, and mandates by the federal government to state and local governments and by states to local governments.

Promoting economic growth for the nation as a whole will continue to be a priority. In addition, Rust Belt states will continue their struggle to reorient their economies in search of new industrial niches. Other regions, such as those dependent on the price of petroleum, will continue through periods of boom and bust as petroleum supplies and prices fluctuate. The extent to which state and local governments can affect their economic futures will remain uncertain, since all governments are subject to the ups and downs of the business cycle.

One of the most important sources of the uncertainty in promoting economic growth by all levels of government is the rapid emergence of an international economy. What the U.S. economy makes and sells is intimately influenced by the economies of other nations. The industrial mix of the U.S. economy and its labor force will inevitably change. These changes will arise at a time when the U.S. labor force is growing older as a whole due to the aging of the baby boomers. How budget systems will be able to respond to these challenges is unknown.

These themes do not capture all that is likely to transpire over the coming years. Nevertheless, they do reflect many of the concerns of the future. One certainty is that budget systems will continue to undergo change as they are called upon to serve the needs of decision makers.

Bibliographic Note

This bibliographic note is intended to assist in finding materials for further reading on public budgeting systems. Because the preceding chapters have extensive endnotes, we make no attempt here to recapitulate everything cited earlier. Readers will find the index to be a handy guide to endnote references. This bibliographic note is meant as an aid in identifying general references as well as sources that have produced and can be expected to continue to produce literature on public budgeting.

Until the mid-1990s, any search for budget materials most likely began in a library. Today, however, the World Wide Web allows searches from wherever a computer is connected. Throughout this book we have cited various Web addresses in chapter endnotes, and in Chapter 11 we noted specific Web sites that can be of great use. Sites typically have links to other sites, allowing the user to click on an address in hypertext and move from site to site, literally traversing the globe in search of information.

Numerous periodicals provide information about the theory and practice of administration in general, and budgeting and finance in particular. Researchers frequently have a choice today of locating journal articles in print or on the Web. While many journals are available on-line, they are seldom free. Publishers commonly will provide only a free sample or abstact on-line, and then researchers must rely upon print or electronic subscriptions. On-line databases such as EBSCOhost or ProQuest Direct offer full-text access to collections of journals for subscribers. Researchers may want to check with their local libraries for access to these or other full-text databases, or for print copies of the journals described below.

Periodical indexes, once available in print and on CD-ROM (computer disk—read only memory), are now generally available on-line. Researchers may still need to rely on print indexes when searching for topics in older issues. As with the journals themselves, these on-line indexes are not free. Researchers should check with local libraries for access or may be able to pay a per-search fee individually for some databases. Periodical indexes include *Current Citations* (Ipswich, MA: EBSCO Publishing), *Current Contents* (Philadelphia: Institute for

Scientific Information), *Economic Literature* (Pittsburgh: American Economic Association), and *Public Affairs Information Service (PAIS) International* (New York: OCLC Public Affairs Information Service). *Current Citations* and *Current Contents* provide table of contents information for academic journals. *EconLit* is the American Economic Association's electronic bibliography of economics literature, containing abstracts, indexing, and links to full-text articles in economics journals. *PAIS*, as its title suggests, indexes journal articles in the field of public administration and public affairs.

Some of the most important journals that produce articles on budgeting and finance include the following. *Public Administration Review* (American Society for Public Administration) often publishes scholarly articles on budgeting. *Policy Studies Journal* and *Policy Studies Review* (Policy Studies Organization) include occasional articles related to budgeting in their regular issues and in special symposia issues. *State and Local Government Review* (University of Georgia) frequently includes budget-related articles that are particularly helpful to practitioners as well as scholars. *Public Budgeting & Finance* (Blackwell Association for Budgeting and Financial Management and American Association for Budget and Program Analysis), *Journal of Public Budgeting, Accounting, and Financial Management* (PrAcademics Press), *OECD Journal on Budgeting* (Organization for Economic Cooperation and Development), and *Public Finance and Management* (Southern Public Administration Education Foundation) focus especially on financial management and budgeting. *Government Finance Review* (Government Finance Officers Association) provides brief analytic pieces and news items on budgeting and finance.

Numerous journals cover the fields of public finance, policy analysis, and policy evaluation. Although occasional articles related specifically to budgeting systems appear in these journals, their usual focus is on specific budgetary subtopics. *National Tax Journal* (National Tax Association), *Public Finance Quarterly* (Sage), and *Public Finance Review* (Sage) publish empirical and theoretical analyses of economic policy concerns, including government growth and size, tax policy, and fiscal and monetary policy, as well as economic analysis. Numerous journals are devoted to policy analysis and policy evaluation. In addition to *Policy Studies Review* and *Policy Studies Journal*, the journals *Evaluation Review* (Sage), *Evaluation and Program Planning* (Pergamon), *Journal of Policy Analysis and Management* (Wiley Association for Public Policy Analysis and Management), and *Public Performance and Management Review* (Sage) all share that focus.

Besides the periodicals concentrating on budgeting or related topics, other professional journals publish occasional articles of relevance. These include *Administration and Society, Administrative Science Quarterly, American Economic Review, American Political Science Review, Journal of Public Administration Research and Theory, Management Science*, and *Public Management Review*. The Washington-based

National Journal and *Government Executive* provide news and analysis of the federal government, including budgetary events, and the *C. Q. Weekly Report* (Washington, DC: Congressional Quarterly) covers congressional actions in particular. Most of the journals listed have annual or occasional indices to facilitate general searches.

Another major source of up-to-date analysis and data consists of government publications. An excellent reference work that explains various types of documents and their sources is Joe Morehead's *Introduction to United States Government Information Sources*, sixth edition. (Englewood, CO: Libraries Unlimited, 1999). An annual index to many local, state, and federal documents is *Bibliographic Guide to Government Publications — U.S.* (Boston: Hall). Federal documents can be located through the Government Printing Office and its Government Information Locator Service's Web site (*http://www.access.gpo.gov*) and through the federal government's main Web portal, FirstGov (*http://www.firstgov.gov*). For statistical information, refer to the *American Statistics Index*, which indexes federal documents, and the *Statistical Reference Index*, which indexes state government publications. Both indexes are published by the Congressional Information Service (Washington, DC). Chapter 11 discusses Web sites that cover government publications and statistics.

Congressional documents can be identified and obtained through a variety of sources. A useful index is the *CIS Index to Publications of the United States Congress* (Washington, DC: Congressional Information Service). Many congressional documents are available through the U.S. Library of Congress's Web site (*http://www.loc.gov*). Congressional publications can be searched through *Congressional Masterfile*, and statistics can be located through *Statistical Masterfile*, both of which are available from the Congressional Information Service on CD-ROM. Information about legislation can be found through the Library of Congress's Web site (*http://www.loc.gov*). The General Accounting Office, which is an arm of Congress, has its reports available on-line as well (*http://www.gao.gov*).

There are numerous on-line subscription databases related to government. One of the most valuable is LEXIS/NEXIS (Reed Elsevier). Four major databases that are part of LEXIS/NEXIS are Congressional Universe, for information about Congress; Academic Universe, for legal research; State Capital Universe, for information about state governments; and Statistical Universe, for data searches. Westlaw (St. Paul, MN: West Publishing) is comparable to LEXIS/NEXIS Academic Universe.

Students of budgeting and finance will find themselves returning regularly to several key government sources. The Office of Management and Budget, Council of Economic Advisers, Treasury Department, Congressional Budget Office, and General Accounting Office produce publications of major import to the field. Reports from these agencies are available in print and on the Web (see Chapter 11).

Several annual volumes from various agencies contain basic data on revenues and expenditures for local, state, and federal levels and intergovernmental transfers among levels. Considerable care must be exercised when working from more than one source, as the figures do not always agree. The Census Bureau in the Department of Commerce publishes the *Statistical Abstract* and a host of materials on government finances. The Census of Governments is conducted every five years and contains not only financial data but also a wealth of organizational information. The Census Bureau is located on the Web at *http://www.census.gov*.

Besides the Census Bureau, other providers of statistical information are located on the Web. They include Statistical Resources on the Web, maintained by the University of Michigan (*http://www.lib.umich.edu/govdocs/stats.html*) and the Government Information Locator Service, maintained by the U.S. Government Printing Office (*http://www.access.gpo.gov/su_docs/gils/index.html*).

Analyses of federal budgeting and finance are published by private organizations such as the American Enterprise Institute (Washington, DC), the Committee on Economic Development (New York), the Heritage Foundation (Washington, DC), the National Bureau of Economic Research (New York), the National Industrial Conference Board (New York), and the Tax Foundation (New York). *The Guide to the Federal Budget* is an annual publication that critiques the president's budget (Washington, DC: Urban Institute Press). The Brookings Institution (Washington, DC) publishes numerous books on budgeting and taxation.

Books, of course, are an important source of information. Five of the classics in public budgeting, no longer subject to revision and updating, are William F. Willoughby's *The Problems of a National Budget* (New York: Appleton, 1918), A. E. Buck's *Public Budgeting* (New York: Harper and Brothers, 1919), Arthur Smithies' *The Budgetary Process in the United States* (New York: McGraw-Hill, 1955), Jesse Burkhead's *Government Budgeting* (New York: Wiley, 1956), and Aaron Wildavsky's *The Politics of the Budgetary Process* (Reading, MA: Addison-Wesley, 1984).

Histories of budgeting include Vincent J. Browne's *The Control of the Public Budget* (Washington, DC: Public Affairs Press, 1949), Bertram M. Gross's "The New Systems Budgeting" (*Public Administration Review* 29 [1969]: 113–137), C. W. Lewis's "History of Federal Budgeting and Financial Management from the Constitution to the Beginning of the Modern Era" (*Public Budgeting and Financial Management* 1 [1989]: 193–213), Irene S. Rubin's "Who Invented Budgeting in the United States?" (*Public Administration Review* 53 [1993]: 438–444), and Carolyn Webber and Aaron Wildavsky's *A History of Taxation and Expenditure in the Western World* (New York: Simon & Schuster, 1986).

Works on budgeting with a special focus, such as on the federal government, state governments, budget theory, and budget politics, include the following:

- Richard Allen and Daniel Tommasi's *Managing Public Expenditure: A Reference Book for Transition Countries* (Paris: Organisation for Economic Co-operation and Development, 2001)
- Robert L. Bland and Irene S. Rubin's *Budgeting: A Guide for Local Government* (Washington, DC: International City/County Management Association, 1997)
- Dall W. Forsythe's *Memos to the Governor: An Introduction to State Budgeting* (Washington, DC: Georgetown University Press, 1997)
- James L. Gosling's *Budgetary Politics in American Governments*, 3rd ed. (New York: Routledge, 2002)
- Jerry L. McCaffery and L. R. Jones' *Budgeting and Financial Management in the Federal Government* (Greenwich, CT: Information Age, 2001)
- R. Gregory Michel's *Organization and Design of an Effective Budget Function* (Chicago, IL: Government Finance Officers Association, 2002)
- John L. Mikesell's *Fiscal Administration*, 6th ed. (Belmont, CA: Wadsworth, 2002)
- David C. Nice's *Public Budgeting* (Belmont, CA: Wadsworth, 2002)
- B. J. Reed and John W. Swain's *Public Finance Administration*, 2nd ed. (Thousand Oaks, CA: Sage, 1996)
- Irene Rubin's *Balancing the Federal Budget* (New York: Chatham House, 2003)
- Irene Rubin's *The Politics of Public Budgeting: Getting and Spending, Borrowing and Balancing*, 4th ed. (New York: Seven Bridges, 2000)
- Allen Schick's *The Federal Budget: Politics, Policy, and Process*, rev. ed. (Washington, DC: Brookings Institution, 2000)
- Kurt M. Thurmaier and Katherine G. Willoughby's *Policy and Politics in State Budgeting* (Armonk, NY: M.E. Sharpe, 2001)
- Alan Walter Steiss and 'Emeka O. Cyprian Nwagwu's, *Financial Planning and Management in Public Organizations* (New York: Marcel Dekker, 2001)
- Aaron Wildavsky's *Budgeting and Governing*, edited by Brendon Swedlow (New Brunswick, NJ: Transaction, 2001)
- Aaron Wildavsky and Naomi Caiden's *The New Politics of the Budgetary Process*, 4th ed. (New York: Longman, 2001)

Edited volumes provide reprints of journal articles and originally prepared pieces. Among these are *Budgeting Formulation and Execution*, edited by Jack Rabin, W. Bartley Hildreth, and Gerald J. Miller (Athens, GA: Carl Vinson Institute of Government, University of Georgia, 1996); *Case Studies in Public Budgeting and Financial Management*, revised printing, edited by Aman Khan and W. Bartley Hildreth (Dubuque, IA: Kendall/Hunt, 1996); *Evolving Theories of Public Budgeting*, edited by John R. Bartle (New York: JAI, 2001); *Government Budgeting: Theory, Process, and Politics*, third edition, edited by Albert C. Hyde (Fort Worth, TX: Harcourt College Publishers, 2001); *Handbook of Government Budgeting*, edited by Roy T. Meyers (San Francisco: Jossey-Bass, 1999); *Management Policies in Local Government Finance*, second edition, edited by J. Richard Aronson and Eli Schwartz (Washington, DC: International City/County Management Association, 1996); *Managing Local Government Finance: Cases in Decision Making*, edited by James M. Banovetz (Washington, DC: International City/County Management Association, 1996); and *Public Budgeting and Finance*, fourth edition, edited by Robert T. Golembiewski and Jack Rabin (New York: Marcel Dekker, 1997).

A variety of simulations are available to assist students in appreciating the dynamics of decision making. Numerous simulations, directly or indirectly related to budgeting and finance, are listed on the Web site of the Association for Budgeting and Financial Management (*http://www.abfm.org*). The *Public Budgeting Laboratory* is a comprehensive set of materials prepared by Jack Rabin, W. Bartley Hildreth, and Gerald J. Miller. It consists of a book of readings, noted above, by Rabin, Hildreth, and Miller, plus a *Workbook*, *a Data Sourcebook*, and an *Instructor's Manual* (Athens, GA: Carl Vinson Institute of Government, University of Georgia, 1996).

For literature on decision making, program budgeting, zero-base budgeting, accounting, economic policy, personnel management, program evaluation, and the like, the reader is encouraged to turn to the endnotes for each chapter.

Happy reading.

INDEX